ALFRED HILLEBRANDT

ALFRED HILLEBRANDT

Vedic Mythology

Translated from the Original German by
SREERAMULA RAJESWARA SARMA

Volume One

MOTILAL BANARSIDASS PUBLISHERS
PRIVATE LIMITED • DELHI

3rd Reprint : Delhi, 2016
First English Language Edition: Delhi, 1980
Second Revised Edition, 2 Vols., Breslau, 1927, 1929
First Edition, 3 Vols., Breslau, 1891, 1899, 1902

ISBN : 978-81-208-0799-5 (Vol. I)
ISBN : 978-81-208-0800-3 (Vol. II)
ISBN : 978-81-208-0801-0 (Set)

Also available at :
MOTILAL BANARSIDASS
41 U.A. Bungalow Road, Jawahar Nagar, Delhi 110 007
8 Mahalaxmi Chamber, 22 Bhulabhai Desai Road, Mumbai 400 026
203 Royapettah High Road, Mylapore, Chennai 600 004
236, 9th Main III Block, Jayanagar, Bengaluru 560 011
8 Camac Street, Kolkata 700 017
Ashok Rajpath, Patna 800 004
Chowk, Varanasi 221 001

Printed in India

by RP Jain at NAB Printing Unit,
A-44, Naraina Industrial Area, Phase I, New Delhi–110028
and published by JP Jain for Motilal Banarsidass Publishers (P) Ltd,
41 U.A. Bungalow Road, Jawahar Nagar, Delhi-110007

ACKNOWLEDGEMENTS

It is a pleasant duty to record my gratitude to all who rendered assistance in translating Alfred Hillebrandt's *Vedische Mythologie*.

The German Academic Exchange Service of the Federal Republic of Germany enabled me through a grant to spend the summer of 1972 in Germany. There, at Marburg, Heidelberg and Berlin, I had the opportunity of consulting Hillebrandt's works and also other rare books and articles on Vedic mythology. I wish to thank the authorities of the German Academic Exchange Service.

I am greatly beholden to my revered teacher Professor Dr Wilhelm Rau, Professor of Sanskrit, Philipps University, Marburg, whose kindness and affection and whose interest in my work have always been a source of inspiration to me. Professor Rau offered me valuable suggestions and also translated a passage from Greek into English. Professor Ram Suresh Tripathi, Head of the Department of Sanskrit, Aligarh Muslim University, encouraged me in this work and lent me many a rare book from his personal library. I am highly thankful to him.

The German original contains many quotations from several European languages. I offer my sincere thanks to the following scholars who helped me in rendering these passages into English: Mrs K. Arhammer of Philipps University, Marburg, Dr Michel Arnaud, formerly of Aligarh Muslim University, Dr Bettina Bäumer of the University of Vienna and Dr Asko Parpola of the Scandinavian Institute of Asian Studies, Copenhagen. Thanks are due to Dr V. G. Paranjpe for his kind permission to quote from his translation of Abel Bergaigne's *Vedic Religion according to the Hymns of the Ṛgveda*. I am obliged to Dr Dieter Schrapel of Philipps University, Marburg, for making his unpublished bio-bibliography of Hillebrandt accessible to me. Mr N. P. Jain and Mr J. P. Jain of Messrs Motilal Banarsidass who commissioned this translation deserve my special thanks for all the consideration shown to me and for the efficient printing of this difficult text. Finally, a bouquet of thanks to my wife, Dr Renate Sarma, for her valuable help.

S R. SARMA

CONTENTS

ABBREVIATIONS

AĀr	*Aitareya Āraṇyaka*
ABr	*Aitareya Brāhmaṇa*
AF	*Arische Forschungen*
AIL	H. Zimmer, *Altindisches Leben*
AISAK	*Anzeiger für indogermanische Sprach- und Altertumskunde*
AJPh	*American Journal of Philology*
AKM	*Abhandlungen für die Kunde des Morgenlandes*
ĀpDS	*Āpastamba Dharma Sūtra*
ĀpGS	*Āpastamba Gṛhya Sūtra*
ĀpŚS	*Āpastamba Śrauta Sūtra*
ARW	*Archiv für Religionswissenschaft*
ĀśvGS	*Āśvalāyana Gṛhya Sūtra*
ĀśvŚS	*Āśvalāyana Śrauta Sūtra*
AV	*Atharvaveda*
BDS	*Baudhāyana Dharma Sūtra*
Bergaigne	Abel Bergaigne, *Vedic Religion according to the Hymns of the Ṛgveda.* Translated into English by V. G. Paranjpe. 4 vols. Poona 1969-73.
BGDSL	*Beiträge zur Geschichte der deutschen Sprache und Literatur*, herausgegeben von Paul und Braune
BhG	*Bhagavadgītā*
BI	Bibliotheca Indica
BKIS	*Beiträge zur Kunde der indogermanischen Sprachen*, herausgegeben von Bezzenberger
BKSWG	*Berichte der philologisch-historischen Klasse der Königlichen Sächsischen Gesellschaft für Wissenschaften*
BŚS	*Baudhāyana Śrauta Sūtra*
BSS	Bombay Sanskrit Series
comm.	commentary
DLZ	*Deutsche Literatur-Zeitung*
ed.	edition or edited
ERE	*Encyclopaedia of Religions and Ethics*, ed. by James Hastings

Frazer	Frazer, *The Golden Bough*
GBr	*Gopatha Brāhmaṇa*
GDS	*Gautama Dharma Sūtra*
GGA	*Göttingische Gelehrte Anzeigen*
GGS	*Gobhila Gṛhya Sūtra*
GIL	M. Winternitz, *Geschichte der indischen Litteratur*
Gr.	Greek
HGS	*Hiraṇyakeśīya Gṛhya Sūtra*
HŚS	*Hiraṇyakeśīya Śrauta Sūtra*
i.a.	*inter alia*, among other things
IA	*Indian Antiquary*
IAK	Lassen, *Indische Altertumskunde*
IF	*Indogermanische Forschungen*
ISt	*Indische Studien*, herausgegeben von. A. Weber
IStr	*Indische Streifen*, herausgegeben von A. Weber
JA	*Journal Asiatique*
JAOS	*Journal of the American Oriental Society*
JASB	*Journal of the Asiatic Society of Bengal*
JBr	*Jaiminīya Brāhmaṇa*
JPTS	*Journal of the Pali Text Society*
JRAS	*Journal of the Royal Asiatic Society*
JUBr	*Jaiminīya Upaniṣad Brāhmaṇa*
KBr	*Kauṣītaki Brāhmaṇa*
Keith	A. B. Keith, *Religion and Philosophy of the Veda and Upanishads*
Kleine Beiträge	Jarl Charpentier, *Kleine Beiträge zur indo-iranischen Mythologie*
KP	*Kātyāyana Paddhati*
KŚS	*Kātyāyana Śrauta Sūtra*
KUp	*Kauṣītaki Upaniṣad*
KZ	(Kuhns) *Zeitschrift für vergleichende Sprachforschung auf dem Gebiet der indogermanischen Sprachen*
Lāṭyāyana	*Lāṭyāyana Śrauta Sūtra*
LŚS	*Lāṭyāyana Śrauta Sūtra*
Ludwig	A. Ludwig, *Der Rigveda oder die heiligen Hymnen der Brāhmaṇa.* Zum ersten Male vollständig ins Deutsche übersetzt. Mit Commentar und Einleitung. Prag, Wien, Leipzig 1876-88
Macdonell	A. A. Macdonell, *Vedic Mythology*

Manu	*Manu Smṛti*
MBh	*Mahābhārata*
MBr	*Mantra Brāhmaṇa*
MGS	*Mānava Gṛhya Sūtra*
MS	*Maitrāyaṇī Saṃhitā*
MSL	*Mémoires de la Société de Linguistique*
MŚS	*Mānava Śrauta Sūtra*
MSt	A. Kuhn, *Mythologische Studien*
NGGW	*Nachrichten von der (Kgl) Gesellschaft der Wissenschaften zu Göttingen*
NN	*nomen nominandum*, used in the sense of : so-and-so
NSP	Nirṇaya Sāgara Press
NVO	A. Hillebrandt, *Das altindische Neu- und Vollmondsopfer*
Ormazd et Ahriman	J. Darmesteter, *Ormazd et Ahriman, leurs Origines et leur Histoire*
OST	*Original Sanskrit Texts on the Origin and History of the Peoples of India, their Religions and Institutions*, ed. by J. Muir. 5 vols.
PAOS	*Proceedings of the American Oriental Society*
PASB	*Proceedings of the Asiatic Society of Bengal*
PGS	*Pāraskara Gṛhya Sūtra*
PJAOS	*Proceedings and Journal of the American Oriental Society*
PJASB	*Proceedings and Journal of the Asiatic Society of Bengal*
PW	*Sanskrit Wörterbuch (Petersburger Wörterbuch)*, herausgegeben von O. Böhtlingk und R. Roth
RdV	H. Oldenberg, *Die Religion des Veda*
ṚV	*Ṛgveda*
SBBAW	*Sitzungsberichte der Berliner Akademie der Wissenschaften*
SBE	Sacred Books of the East, ed. by F. Max Müller
SBKBAW	*Sitzungsberichte der Königl. Bayerischen Akademie der Wissenschaften*
SBKPAW	*Sitzungsberichte der Königl. Preussischen Akademie der Wissenschaften*
SBKSGW	*Sitzungsberichte der Königl. Sächsischen Gesellschaft der Wissenschaften*

ŚBr	*Śatapatha Brāhmaṇa*
ŚGS	*Śāṅkhāyana Gṛhya Sūtra*
SII	*South Indian Inscriptions*, ed. and tr. by E. Hultzsch
ŚŚS	*Śāṅkhāyana Śrauta Sūtra*
SV	*Sāmaveda*
s.v.	*sub-voce*, see under the word
TĀr	*Taittirīya Āraṇyaka*
TBr	*Taittirīya Brāhmaṇa*
TMBr	*Tāṇḍya Mahābrāhmaṇa*
TS	*Taittirīya Saṃhitā*
v.	verse
Vāl.	Vālakhilya
v.l.	varia lectionis
VSt	Pischel und Geldner, *Vedische Studien*
VS	*Vājasaneyi Saṃhitā*
vv.	verses
VWB	A. Fick, *Vergleichendes Wörterbuch der indogermanischen Sprachen*
WB	Walter Neisser, *Zum Wörterbuch des Rigveda*
WZKM	*Wiener Zeitschrift für die Kunde des Morgenlandes*
Y	*Yasna*
Yājñavalkya	*Yājñavalkya Smṛti*
Yt	*Yašt*
YV	*Yajurveda*
ZB	*Zeitschrift für Buddhismus*
ZDA	*Zeitschrift für Deutsches Altertum*
ZDMG	*Zeitschrift der deutschen Morgenländischen Gesellschaft*
ZII	*Zeitschrift für Indologie und Iranistik*

Unspecified numbers, unless the immediate context states otherwise, refer to the *Ṛgveda*.

INTRODUCTION

"Nothing in all mythology is more difficult than the attempt to get a clear view of the gods of Vedic India."

Andrew Lang, *Myth, Ritual, and Religion*, Vol. II, p. 148.

My *Vedic Mythology* appears before the public for the second time after a thorough revision. The material has been rearranged, the interpretation has been modified in several cases, and some parts have been rewritten. Once again, I have adopted no other starting point than the Vedic texts themselves and followed no other principles than those of philological exegesis. However, I have not ignored the analogies or the warnings which ethnography offers to the student of mythology. The conclusions that I have arrived at by following the exclusively exegetical method differ often in fundamental questions from those of my predecessors. Although I have paid careful attention to the many publications and criticism which appeared during the long period since the first edition of this work came out, I have not been convinced that the interpretations of others are more correct than those of mine. This is particularly true of my interpretation of Soma. My critics, following their own methods, have come to see "puerile fancies" or a "formless confusion of images and mystic fantasies" in the 114 hymns of the ninth book with their different authors, supposed or real. But, in reality, the ancient Ṛṣis did not indulge in any hieratic game. On the contrary, they absorbed an old popular belief, which was lost later on; they preserved it and enlarged it into a ritual. I still adhere to my interpretation and do not see any reason to change anything basically. It appears that for many scholars of Vedic mythology cloud-castles and cloud-demons are still indispensable constituents of the Vedic landscape, although no passage speaks of cloud-castles; in their view the Paṇis are "misers" and remain so, although a thorough study of all the passages proves them to be a marauding tribe. Research is guided very much by the statements, or by the silence, of the Indian commentaries and does not take into account the historical development which took place during the millennium before and the one after Christ and which must have taken place in the natural course of events. This applies also to the interpretation of Indra-Vṛtra and Mitra-Varuṇa.

The method of interpreting mythology varies naturally from people to people; for the method is dependent upon the sources. The Sanskritists are not yet in a position to formulate problems and solve them as students of other mythologies do; but they have an advantage in another respect, viz. the rich collection of hymns used in worship and that of the ritual traditions. These allow a deeper probing into Vedic mythology than is possible with Classical and Germanic mythology. We do not find anywhere else such an abundance of literature, like a huge outer court leading to the sanctum of the gods, which teaches the cult of the gods in detail. The ritual literature in its extant version does not have a claim to great antiquity like the hymns of the *Ṛgveda*, but of all the aids to the interpretation of mythology it is the ritual literature that takes us nearest to the period when the collection of the hymns was made. No doubt, it does not cover all the rites anticipated in the *Ṛgveda*; it cannot answer some of our questions; still it remains the source in which the mythological tradition is preserved, relatively speaking, in its purest form. It is surprising, therefore, that works on mythology, while referring to tradition, look for it first of all in the later commentaries and not in the ritual texts or overlook these completely.

The sources from which myths are created are numerous. Whatever stirs the imagination, whatever induces fear or pleasure, or impresses the mind, dreaming or awake, becomes or can become the starting point of a divine being or of a demon. The myth-creating mind has always made use of all these sources; they converge in varying degrees of strength and create in their confluence the mythology of a people. Roscher is right in saying that all human experiences, those of external as well as those of inner life, can become myths when they are connected with a divine or a demoniac being, or when they are converted into such beings in poetry.[1] The character of a country, the psychological or cultural make-up of its inhabitants, influences the strength of individual sources and determines the traits of character of its pantheon. Mythology has a sister of kindred nature in poetry. The same power of fantasy which is active in the creation of the gods shows itself at work in poetry. Poetry also depends on the environment, on the phenomena of nature, on the climate and, of course, on spiritual factors, on the individuality of a people. The living conditions, climate, and vegetation differ from place to place. Consequently, there is also a difference in the pantheon and in the spirit of poetry.

As diverse as the powers which create the gods are those which change the gods already created. The process of myth-formation never comes to a rest; it discards outdated elements or moulds the traditional ones into new forms. This process is not governed by any teleological principle that leads to a specific goal but by the restlessness of the human mind, caused no less by psychological factors than by external conditions : migrations, contacts with other tribes, progress or decline in civilization, climate, acceptance of ideas by a new generation, creative power of individuals with far-reaching influence (like poets and priests) and the patterns of thought which emerge from unfathomable depths — these are the driving forces in mythology.

J. W. Hauer is of the same view when, quoting many examples, he says the following about the climate : "This influence of the climate and the surrounding nature on the development of religion should be studied much more systematically. The climate and the surroundings influence the entire mental and emotional experience of a race, and on this the new formation of a religion and its progress or decline depend."[2]

It is rarely that we know of the "becoming" or of the "beginning" of the gods; in most cases we comprehend only a short period of their "lives." The possibility is, indeed, rare of observing — as in the case of Indra and Vṛtra — the process of evolution in its different phases and of obtaining an insight, instructive from the point of view of methodology, into the historical changes. As in the case of Indra and Vṛtra, so also in the relationship between Indra and Viṣṇu we can see the secret of myth-formation which gradually subordinates the all-powerful Indra to the rising power of Viṣṇu, who was at first never mentioned at all, or was occasionally placed below the former, and who later rises high above him.

My interpretation has provoked the criticism that I am under the influence of the naturalistic school of interpretation, in spite of my assurances to the contrary. In any case, it has been far from my intention to turn this interpretation into a credo or an object of special worship. I have always adhered to the sources alone. The sun and the moon among other natural phenomena have greatly inspired the imagination of peoples of all times and races, and have given them an opportunity for a never-ending creation of myths.[3] It is but natural that they determined significant traits of Vedic poetry also. This being so, is it strange to conclude that in India a great number of the Vedic gods are to be traced back to local cults or clan cults of the sun and the moon, but not to many other natural phenomena? It is of course a fact that not only in Vedic mythology but in Indian mythology in general, so far only a few beings could be traced who were once human beings and then reached heaven directly without ever having mingled with real gods. On the other hand, it is also a fact that the Indians gave the discus to Viṣṇu, the half-moon to Śiva and that the worship of the sun has led to a *sūryasahasranāmāvali*. The *Saurapurāṇa*,[4] the *Sūryaśataka* and the entire literature give ample proof of the deification of the sun and of the moon as well. I wish to draw attention, inter alia, to MBh XIII.118.6 : *jīvan hi kurute pūjā viprāgryaḥ śaśisūryayoḥ*, to *Dīgha-Nikāya* I.240 (*Tevijja* 16ff.), to the many *Upasthāna*-s in the sacrifice, to the prayers to Sūrya in *Rāmāyaṇa* VI. 105.1ff., MBh III. 3.16ff., *Viṣṇupurāṇa* III. 5.15ff.,[5] to the existence of the solar and lunar dynasties and to the popularity of the sun and the moon in present-day India.[6] I do not understand how S. D. Barnett,[7] in spite of such evidences, could say : "I am a heretic in relation to both the Solar Theory and the Vegetation Theory, as everyone must be who takes the trouble to study Hindu nature without prejudice." The Hindus themselves do not agree with him, certainly not when he disapproves the solar theory.

If one were to follow the opinion current so far, then it would appear that in the Vedic period the cult of the sun was out of question except in a few instances, and that the cult of the moon was almost non-existent, while the lightning was a beloved appearance — not so much for the Hindus but for quite a few exegetical scholars. I do not subscribe to the interpretation of myths by Max Müller, but it appears to me that his views on the Vedic gods are still more valid than those of the recent interpreters, and that Sylvain Lévi's accusation against him that "the works which have been written in France and Germany during half a century have not supported his solar convictions"[8] is in fact a compliment. The opponents of Max Müller have recognized his weaknesses better than their own, and the works of "half a century" have failed to present enough evidence, although some of these works were inspiring to a certain extent. Many of their statements are no more logical than those of Max Müller; indeed they are more illogical. I think that, on the whole, ethnography would hardly oppose the tracing of many gods to natural phenomena; ethnographers raise their voices not against the tracing of many gods to natural phenomena, but only against the attempts to determine the character of the gods with the help of linguistic interpretation. Andrew Lang said, "No anthropologist, I hope, is denying that Nature-myths and Nature-gods exist." "We proclaim the abundance of poëtical Nature-myths, we 'disable' the hypothesis that they arise from a disease of language."[9]

The "lunar mythology" which, unlike the solar or the thunderstorm mythology, traces many phenomena to the moon has always been the object of a special ridicule; the former as well as the latter have often gone too far in their interpretations. I think the differentiation between the full moon and the new moon does not apply to Vedic mythology. But one should be grateful to those scholars — I mention especially Siecke — who recently defied current opinion and had the courage to draw our attention to a natural phenomenon which played, or should play, a greater role in the world of the primitives — not only in their lowest strata — than in the lives of the modern urban people.[10] The primitives needed the sun as well as the moon for their migrations, for their military campaigns, for the protection of their herds, for hunting, and for illuminating their paths from one village to another or from one camp to another; they saw that they and their food depended upon both these sources of light, and their imagination was caught by the remarkable changing phases of the moon. Why should all this not have occupied their minds and not have led to the worship of the sun and the moon ?

The ranks of thunderstorm mythology, solar mythology, lunar mythology, or soul mythology were joined recently by a new variety which I would like to call "Begriffsmythologie," since it regards abstract concepts or factors as the basis of the personification of the gods, or seeks the embodiments of abstract concepts directly in the gods of the Veda. The Vedic Indians liked to think in concrete terms, and the Ṛgvedic period was hardly favourable to philosophical contemplations. I do not completely deny the existence of gods based on concepts, but abstract concepts like Manyu, Kāma, Purandhi etc. are few in number. The word *ṛtá* alone has attained a special status, which, however, does not deny its abstract origin. The few philosophical hymns of the ṚV do not hide their naturalistic background. Even the Upaniṣads arrive at their philosophical observations primarily by reformulating or reinterpreting many things or events, as one can see from the beginning of the *Bṛhadāraṇyaka Upaniṣad*, the oldest of the Upaniṣads. Güntert's recent attempt[11] to see different aspects of gods of law in Mitra, Varuṇa and Aryaman seems to be a notion that attributes a more sophisticated legal sense to the semi-barbarous Indians of antiquity than is possible in view of their interest in conquests and booties, not to speak of the fact that this notion is devoid of any foundations in exegesis and ritual.

There is no denying the fact that the names of the gods are derived from appellatives, but they are merely "derived." The more frequently an appellative is applied to the same phenomenon, the more easily this appellative enters the realm of that phenomenon, becomes distinct from other vocabulary, ceases to be a commonly applicable name and becomes a proper name. In the present context it becomes an expression of divine personality, possessing nothing but the external phonetic form of the word which was once an appellative. The "Begriffsmythologie" makes no distinction between "once" and "now" and has not yet proved its worth. It cannot explain why and when so many naturalistic elements came to be associated with abstract concepts and why these took naturalistic forms after their semi-philosophical beginnings. Savitṛ, Dhātṛ etc. are to be considered new-comers, but Indra, Viṣṇu, Mitra and Varuṇa lost their appellative basis long ago, to such an extent that they cannot be recognized as appellatives any more, and appear in the Veda as firmly established personalities and complete gods. Even if we knew the correct etymology, it would not be of any profit to mythology; for the etymological meaning is too general to say anything significant about the individuality of a god. The students of mythology and those of etymology do not share common interests here; tracing the etymology can even lead to mistakes in mythology, as one can see from the old explanation of Vivasvat, and from Meillet's recent explanation of Mitra. If Varuṇa, Indra and Viṣṇu were once "Sondergötter" — it is useless to discuss this problem — then such a time falls considerably earlier than the Vedic period, earlier even than the conjectured Indo-Iranian period, and need not occupy our attention here any further.

I cannot agree with Oldenberg either when he, while discussing specific qualities that are considered special characteristics of one god or other, takes these qualities as the basis for his explanation and sees Pūṣan merely as "the god of the paths," or Viṣṇu as "the divine strider." This is not necessarily the basic idea of their original conception, but only a phase in their evolution. Why is Pūṣan called *ā́ghṛṇi* fifteen times, which is translated as "shining" or "glowing"?[12] In the absence of such an evidence, the prerequisite for us to accept this common view that Pūṣan is the lord of the paths also disappears.[13] We shall have to ask whether a "glowing" solar god who draws his paths through the heaven has better chances of developing into a "god and lord of the ways" than a lord of the paths into a "glowing" god. The decision does not appear difficult to me, particularly as in another hymn (II. 40) Pūṣan takes "his seat high in heaven" and remains there in dual association with Soma, the moon, while he should have taken his place more reasonably on the earth as "the lord of the paths." However, I am aware that there were attempts to show that Soma in the above-mentioned hymn was not the moon, but a drink or a plant. In such a case, I must leave it to others to make the meaning of the hymn clear to themselves.

We should not object to the fact that the ṚV gives preference to the gods of light. It is neither a book of folklore nor a primer composed with the intention of giving us an idea of the whole range of beliefs of that period. On the contrary, it owes its compilation to a particular tendency. No doubt, the tribes of the Vedic period had their rich share of demon-beliefs and spirit-cults. We find Piśācas, Yātudhānas and a great variety of magic in the ṚV also and a small Yamasaṃhitā in the book of additions. We encounter traces of the cult of the Manes which transports groups of ancestors to the world of heroes, of the worship of plants and trees, and of the deification of stones used for pressing the soma; but in general there is very little of this nature. Manes and Rākṣasas, witchcraft and exorcism of diseases play only a minor role in the ṚV. Among the gods of the ṚV we do not find the spirits of the deep and of the darkness, we find rarely personifications of the Manes and the demons, but predominantly personifications of the light and of its realm.[14] Why is this so? We must distinguish between the period of the gods and that of the Manes, between Devayāna and Pitṛyāṇa. The ṚV serves mainly the purpose of the Devayāna; its hymns, collected from various priestly families, serve only the higher gods; therefore so many other beings are excluded whom we encounter in the Gṛhyasūtras and in the AV, and whom we should find in the ṚV also, were it not compiled under one aspect, for one specific purpose only. Consequently, the great compilation of hymns contains only scanty references to the cults of the Manes, of the demons, of the "Sondergötter" and of the gods who are personifications of abstract concepts etc.[15] The ṚV does not intend to present a systematic arrangement of gods; it serves its own specific purpose, not our own. At the same time, it offers us an instruction worth remembering that the lower mythology is not a preliminary stage of the belief, but a different chapter altogether, even in the earliest period of Indian mythology and of the so-called Indo-Iranian mythology, that is to say, in times older than the sources of other mythologies.[16] The necessity to establish that the cult of the higher gods is as old as the worship of the Manes and demons does not exclude the possibility that occasionally gods turn into demons and demons into gods. The bridge between the two realms is crossed again and again, and one should determine in each case from which area a god or a demon originated.[17]

One special problem in Vedic mythology, which we hardly encounter elsewhere, is the fact that individual gods underwent a reinterpretation during the migrations of the Aryan tribes. Some Aryan tribes did not reach the tropics during their migrations. But those tribes who descended into the plains of India found there a contrast between the summer and the rainy season instead of the old change from summer to winter.

It is wrong to assume that Punjab is the home of Vedic mythology. Punjab is not the home of Vedic mythology just as it is not the home of Sanskrit. Some of the gods might have had their origin there, but not the others. The evolution of mythology does not follow simple rules; its life is no less complicated than that of a language, and it is the end-product of different external and internal laws which are not sufficiently known or appreciated. The people who moved into the land of the five rivers were not without religious notions just as they were not without a language. Their gods had their origin under a different sky and under different circumstances, and had to fade out or to pass through a reinterpretation under the impact of a totally different climate, as the example of Indra and Vṛtra shows. The hot season does not "fetter" any river, at the most it dries the river up. Even in India the rivers which, according to some students of mythology, are swallowed up in summer by a "demon of draught" have, at this time of the year, a significant increase in the water-level because of the thaw in the mountains. The fight between Indra and Vṛtra is the ancient glorification of the fight between the sun and winter which holds the rivers in its control. In fact the Vedic hymns do not refer to snow any more; they have lost the word for "to snow" completely. But the saga of that fight is preserved in these hymns; Indra still has the characteristics of a former sun god, but is already in the process of transformation into a rain god — a transformation that was completed in the post-Vedic period. Indra has still horses in the Veda; later the elephant also becomes his animal. This is a typical example of the transformation of a god and his adaptation to his new home. Uṣas is still glorified in the hymns of the ṚV as the bringer of light after darkness. The later poets of the tropical land with its shorter periods of twilight, with its insignificant amount of difference in the duration of day and night, had less reason to sing about the birth of light after darkness, and, as far as I know, did not do so. Uṣas did not originate in a tropical land; she is the daughter of other latitudes. The Vedic poets inherited her from a period which had greater reason to extol the New Year's Day, or Easter Day, as the return of light, although the celebrations of spring, the Vasantotsavas, were the favourite festivals of the people in later times just as in our days.

It is extremely difficult to trace the process by which myths take shape and to determine the different phases of such a process where psychological, climatic and other factors influence each other. Apart from those deities who are a legacy of the past and still continue to exercise their influence on the minds of the people, there are others who emerge from the soil of the new homeland and claim their share in the cults and the songs. Who can determine now whether Viṣṇu — to name only one of those whose home appears to be India itself — was a contribution of the neighbouring non-Ṛgvedic Aryan, or non-Aryan tribes to the ṚV, where he does not hold an important position, or whether the few hymns dedicated to him in the ṚV are the beginnings of his cult ?

Ethnography is an important aid to the student of Vedic mythology. It offers us a criterion by which we can, to a certain extent, judge our conclusions with regard to their probability; otherwise we might become victims of academic constructions. Ethnography enables us to appreciate some of these conclusions and prevents us from considering them eccentric. The brahmins incorporated many traits of folklore into mythology, as they did in the case of law and ritual; they stood above the Vedic tribes, but were not separated from them. The Vedic conception of the nature of the moon who feeds the gods with ambrosia, who is a lord of thunder and lightning and sends rain to the earth, can be understood easily and does not need analogies from ethnography. But other statements about the moon appear to us strange and eccentric. In the Veda the moon is considered a mighty warrior who has lightning as his weapon and thunder as his voice, and who "roars with vigour like a bull." Oldenberg objected to this, saying that this phenomenon, as far as he knew, was never observed in the case of the moon.[18] I have not observed it either. However, we are not primitives. They observed it, or believed that they did so. Tylor states that the Botocudos "assign the highest place among the heavenly bodies to the moon, as they believe that he releases thunder and lightning and causes bad harvests as well as fertility."[19] When the Vedic poets speak of the "roaring" of the moon, they are probably echoing a popular conception, just as their ritual is rich in ethnographic analogies enumerated by Oldenberg himself. We have, therefore, no right to correct this conception or to read our own sentimental lunar lyricism into the texts. The development of the moon into a pugnacious and fighting god also has its parallels; Mexican sources refer to lunar war-goddesses.[20]

But, apart from the ethnographic parallels, the Vedic tribes possess — as all other peoples do — a rich collection of unique concepts, based on their own circumstances and inclinations, to which ethnography cannot offer anything comparable. Thus the interpretations of the sun and the moon in India are limited through the masculine gender of both the words, with which the myths have to conform in so far as the two can appear only as father and son, as brothers, as male friends or as male enemies. Ethnography offers analogies even for these conceptions. But when the moon is called a Brahmacārin, a pupil, and the sun an Ācārya, a teacher, who carries the former for three days in his body, or when the relationship of teacher and pupil is represented by this comparison, then it is exclusively an Indo-Brahmanical mind which is speaking through this comparison, just as it speaks through the two new moon sagas of the *Śatapatha Brāhmaṇa*.[21]

Like ethnography, classical Sanskrit is also an aid, but it should be used carefully and to a limited extent only. I am inclined to see a greater difference between the Ṛgvedic and the classical Sanskrit than some scholars have done of late, thereby altering the historical limits. The difference is perhaps not so great as the difference in attitudes between the time of Wulfila and that of Schiller, but the difference is there, not only in the language but in the treatment of the subject as well. The antithesis between the Devas and Asuras was unknown to the ṚV except in a few cases and was perfected in the Brāhmaṇas for the first time. This antithesis divides the two periods almost in the same way as the demonization of the Devas separates the *Avesta* from the ṚV. There are evidences for the fundamental difference like the absence of any definite trace of the belief in the transmigration of souls,[22] the ancient custom of the burning of widows which is, however, unknown to the ṚV, the total absence of the cult of snakes — the word *sarpá* occurs only once in the ṚV — , the ignorance about the *dīkṣā*, the abundant use of the concept of *ṛtá*, which is closely connected with the *Avesta* and which is later replaced more and more by *dhárma*, not to speak of other phenomena like the Trimūrti and the linguistic evidences. We notice a considerable amount of difference even between the ṚV and the Brāhmaṇas, a fact which makes us doubt that the origin of the two is directly connected. I count among these differences the fact that the ṚV refers to many ritual customs, a real connection to which can be found in the verses only with difficulty or not at all, while on the other hand the Brāhmaṇas do not give information about the purpose and the position of many hymns in the ritual. It appears as if two different streams of tradition were flowing simultaneously side by side and came close to one another only at a later period. Much less can we expect that the post-Brāhmaṇa period can offer us an authoritative interpretation of the ṚV. Indian life also was subject to the law of evolution. This is seen already in the position of the Devas in Buddhism which, under the influence of religious movements, sees in the gods no more immortal beings who rule the world but, as Rhys Davids says, passable Buddhists, subject to the cycle of rebirth like human beings, mostly well-intentioned, but rather ignorant and foolish.[23] Śakra, an epithet of Indira in the ṚV, becomes his regular name in Pāli; the old name almost degenerates into a synonym for *rā́jan*:[24] *sakko* fights against the *"asurindo" vepacitti.*[25] Brahman has been replaced by a number of deities representing him.[26] If *gandhabba* and *gabbha* had really been used as synonyms in a Buddhist sermon, as some scholars believe, then this has nothing to do with a significant mythological statement. It would merely be a confusion between the two words in the mind of the Buddhist preacher and of his contemporaries.[27] It is too much to expect that the opponents of Brahmanism had a detailed knowledge of its mythology. Varuṇa becomes a Nāga king; the Asuras dwell in the great ocean.[28] We should not read the later developments into the ṚV now just as one did formerly look for Indo-European or even Christian ideas in the ṚV. As we have already emphasized, the ṚV is certainly not the epitomé of all the thoughts and beliefs of that age; there was also no dearth of undercurrents of all sorts which run through all times. But at the present stage we shall have to be content if we succeed in recognizing more clearly the main currents which, to judge from the compilation, were accepted as such by the brahmins.

Even if we erect boundaries between the classical literature and the Vedas, the former is nonetheless valuable for our purpose, because it preserves several legends, elaborates upon them or changes them, using old material in various ways. The classical literature is at its best in teaching us specific Indian attitudes, and it shows us the final stage in the evolution of the Vedic gods. Here Varuṇa is the god of the ocean and of the stationary waters, while the ṚV gives him a wider dominion. If he was exclusively a lord of the ocean in the oldest records available to us, how can one explain the other attributes ascribed to him in the ṚV which, otherwise, do not characterize the ocean? In the ṚV, but not in the later period, it is said of him that he scattered the attacks on him with his shining foot and ascended to the heaven, that he wanders in the midst of waters looking down contemptuously upon the laws and sins of men, and that he ascends the chariot *paramé vyòmani* along with Mitra. Thus, in the course of his evolution, Varuṇa must have lost those older traits of character which do not apply to the god of the ocean and was only gradually transformed into the lord of the ocean. With the help of classical Sanskrit we recognize what was probably the most recent trait in the evolution of Varuṇa, but nothing further. We must ask ourselves: where was the core centered in the oldest times which made this evolution possible — certainly not in his position as the god of law and of the court of law.

The ṚV is not the "Urmythologie," nor the beginning of Indian mythology, but only a chapter in the course of the mythological evolution, preserved by tradition only to that extent as it was compatible with the interests of individual families and schools. Which then is the oldest trait of character of each god in this average profile with its old and new accretions ? Oldenberg[29] wonders if I have never encountered a case where attributes were ascribed to a god sooner or later which were not connected with his original conception, but were transferred from other gods or borrowed from other tribes. He goes on to ask, "and is it not a fact that affinity towards light and enmity towards darkness is just the trait which the Vedic Indians could easily transfer to a god ?" One could answer this with a counter-question : is it not a fact that affinity towards light and enmity towards darkness can by itself easily create gods of light in conformity with the Vedic way of thinking and why should these attributes be transferred at all from other gods ?

No doubt, concepts of various kinds are not only lost in the course of time, but can also attach themselves to a given basic concept; to deny both these possibilities is to deny the law of evolution, which governs mythology no less than it governs language. The real difficulty, which is often underestimated, lies in comprehending the basic concept clearly and tracing the path through which this basic concept acquires new attributes or discards old ones. One could agree here in theory, but one could have a great divergence of opinion in its application.

We can obtain an important clue to the understanding of mythology by studying the various images and similes with which Indians refer to what are undoubtedly natural phenomena. We have hymns addressed to Sūrya, Agni and Dawn. Here one can still see pure nature-worship and the metaphorical description of natural events in all freshness. A study of this translation of the external world into the realm of human affairs is of great value to methodology. Uṣas, who is followed by the sun god, is regarded as his daughter, or his beloved, or his wife, or his mother etc. I would like to call all these images which are completely different from each other but can still be traced back to the same basic concept "mythological synonyms."[30] When the sun and the moon are called "the two calves of Virāj" in one passage, or "father and son" in another, then these are also "mythological synonyms." In many cases the study of purely poetic attitudes yields a clue and serves as an orientation into the sphere of images, out of which the gods could develop further. Since it cannot be shown from any concrete example that the sun was ever conceived as a feminine being in Sanskrit, we should desist from seeing a female sun god in Sūryā, whatever the Lettic myths might state. Linguistic usage tells us that in the Veda, Sūryā is nothing but a synonym for Uṣas and *sūryasya duhitṛ*. Furthermore, when Vivasvat has two wives, one of whom disappears and the other is "of the same colour," and when Sūrya similarly possesses two wives who are called at one place *uṣásā*, the day and the night, then we can conclude that Sūrya and Vivasvat are already identical in the ṚV. What the poet sees as images attains a concrete shape in mythology.

How does the ṚV arrive at different personifications for the same natural phenomenon ? The north-east wind has a different effect than the south-west wind or the whirlwind; the sun in spring is different from the sun in summer; the night can be a goddess adorned with stars, or the embodiment of darkness; the moon can be the controller of seasons, the container of ambrosia, or the lord of the waters. Imagination can take up any of these aspects of life and make it the starting point of a special deity. The very diversity in the names leads us to the assumption that the same natural phenomenon can be divided, to a certain extent, into the separate qualities inherent in it, depending upon the way one comprehends this natural phenomenon. Thus, Sūrya might have meant or may mean the shining sun god more than any other, Tvaṣṭṛ the creating sun god, and Savitṛ the regenerating sun god, for the sun shines, creates and regenerates; and all these three names could attain recognition as the names of separate beings. Therefore, the fact that the Sūrya-hymns deviate from the conception of the Savitṛ-hymns does not contradict the basic identity in nature of the two gods. Vāyu-Vāta, the Maruts and Mātariśvan are also different, yet the same power is manifest in them. This applies also to Mitra *vis-à-vis* Sūrya etc.

There is a diversity of names, but no diversity in meaning. Indra, Mitra and Pūṣan differed from each other not in their nature, but in their origin; they could have emerged from the cults of individual Gotras (or whatever one would like to call the individual centres of religious worship) as different aspects of the same phenomenon, and, with the progressive integration of the cults, they could have been woven into an external unity, just as the gods of Egypt emerged out of different local cults and different names of the same being.[31]

Even in the Vedic period the Indian branch of the Aryan peoples was not a closely-knit unit. The mere fact that in the cultural history of India the east plays a different role than the west, the fact that Vedic Sanskrit was not the mother of Pāli or of the MI languages, and that contacts with other dialects are traceable in Vedic Sanskrit[32] disprove the notion that there was a uniformity in beliefs, customs and memories of the tribes who were settling from the Arachosis and Kabul to the Sarasvatī and farther. It is difficult to adduce detailed evidence, but the premises for this supposition are available. In the ṚV we see not only different families of priests, but also different tribes often in feud with each other like the Bharatas, the Turvaśa-Yadus, the Pūrus, who are all called "*mṛdhrávāc*" etc.[33] The

Śatapatha Brāhmaṇa says that among the eastern people Śarva is the name for Rudra and that the Bāhlīkas call him Bhava. It would indeed be strange if from the beginning the many small tribes of the Vedic period had been connected by the same cult and by the same gods. It would also be strange if the words *ádeva, anindrá, ayajñá* did not have any background. Analogous processes, which led to a fusion of different gods and cults, are known abundantly among other peoples like the Romans, the Greeks and the Egyptians; the Vrātyastomas of the Indian ritual are the means employed in the later periods to admit the outsiders into the Brahmanical society. The difference between the Indians of the eastern regions and those of the western regions, which is clear from the evidence collected by Oldenberg, belongs to the Vedic period. We can speak of an antithesis between those tribes who were living in the Brahmanical way and those who were not, or we can place the Ṛgvedic tribes *vis-à-vis* other tribes, Aryan or non-Aryan. For instance, in the family books of the ṚV, which we should of course consider the basic stock of the entire collection, Tvaṣṭṛ is very rarely referred to; apart from the Tṛca VII. 34.20-22, the entire ṚV does not contain a single hymn addressed to him. But what the ṚV says about him are only the remnants of a cycle of myths. These myths are slightly touched upon by the literature of the ṚV, but they must have been fully developed by then. How does it happen that Tvaṣṭṛ, nevertheless, plays such a minor role in the ṚV ? I can think of only one answer : Tvaṣṭṛ did not stand — as Indra, Soma and Agni did — in the centre of the religious life of the Ṛgvedic people, but only on its periphery. In other words, we should assume that he was either antiquated or not yet fully recognized at the time of the ṚV. In their orthodox collection, the brahmins must have included all that appeared orthodox to them, but excluded, as far as possible, all that they considered foreign and not pertinent. The appearance of the AV, which was not recognized as canonical for a long time and the content of which is not younger than that of the ṚV in all cases, means in itself a great enlargement of the original area of belief. In their settlements and during their further incursions into the land, the Ṛgvedic tribes came into contact with an Aryan population which had migrated earlier. These contacts did not remain without influence upon their stock of ideas and upon their gods, just as the dialects did not remain without influence upon the language of the ṚV. In the absence of any information, this population of early immigrants is indistinguishable for us from the original inhabitants, and I call them "barbarians," or "followers of non-Brahmanical customs." Even at the time of the Jātakas there was a great difference between the brahmins of the east and those of the west.[34] It is even possible that the Soma sacrifice and other sacrifices were performed without the guidance of the brahmins. That it was possible can be seen in the example of the Iranians and their Haoma cult. Muir[35] finds it "remarkable that Mahādeva's worship should be ... described as performed without Brahmans."

I think the belief that the Vedic hymns originated in Punjab, or that the mythology reflects the circumstances of this region is a mistake, although Griswold[36] adduces arguments in support of such a belief. Apart from the rivers which are Indian to a large extent, I find very few statements which favour Punjab exclusively as the origin of the contents of the ṚV.[37] Here I may refer to Thibaut who says in a review of Volume III of the first edition of this work "that there is really no need for us to look for the natural antecedents of the oldest Indian myths exclusively in India itself or even of the Punjab only ... the fact of theI ranians and other northern nations having a Verethraghna and so on, renders the hypothesis of the Indra and Vṛtra story having originated in a more northern country distinctly probable."[38]

The cult-differences among the clans were obliterated to a large degree even at the time of the ṚV. Vedic mythology is not a system, but a conglomeration.[39] The confluence of different elements gives rise to a mixture of mythological language which obliterates all distinct lines and retains the differences only in faint outlines. However, they become visible if we look more closely, and I think that persistent scholarship would succeed in breaking up the syncretism into its constituents and in recognizing the share of ideas of each clan. The priests were diligently at work in bringing the different gods closer to each other. In some hymns and rituals, they join Indra and Pūṣan who were originally separate; they transform Indra into the defender of the laws of Mitra-Varuṇa; they place Viṣṇu, who was originally worshipped in quite different groups, next to Indra and secure for him part of the glory of Indra's fight against Vṛtra;

they make Sūrya the eye of Mitra-Varuṇa, or connect the Aśvins as well as Sūrya with Pūṣan, whose innate nature was totally different from all the three. These are the results of evolution, contaminations which do not emanate from of a naturalistic or other uniform source, but owe their existence to the priestly attempts at blurring the differences. The dual forms like Indra-Viṣṇu and Soma-Rudra also belong to this category. The trained eye can notice the imperfection of the theological work from the superficial connection and from the lack of vigour in the hymns. The mediators who made Kṛṣṇa an Avatāra of Viṣṇu at a later period have their predecessors even in the Vedic cult. But we need not always look for the hand of the priests. The process of myth-formation never comes to a stop; natural evolution takes its own course, weaving old elements into new images, transferring the qualities of one god to another or bequeathing on him the inheritance of a god who is sinking into oblivion.

It is a well-known fact of linguistics that words which were once independent become part of neologisms, or merely serve as emphatic particles, or fade into an existence of dependence, like *pumaṅs* in *puruṣa* or the suffixes in *Adl-er, atr-ox, super-bus* and so on. Similarly, in the evolution of myths it is possible that gods in course of time and in course of fading out pass through new mythological combinations with other gods, even with gods of the same origin.[40] Of course, the mind cannot operate with mythological material in the same way as language does with its material, but in mythology also it is possible that formations which are decaying or are deprived of their natural and original significance combine with other formations which can even be mythological synonyms.[41] When the Aśvins drive around the sun, this is an instance where their original nature is completely forgotten; they continue to live only in the general turns of expressions in the mind of the poet. We have a rare example in verses X. 17. 1-2 where a new mythology is formed out of old elements. A part of the glory of Mitra, who is fading out more and more, goes over to his old companion Varuṇa[42] (but not to Indra, who was never close to Mitra). Some attributes (weapons and thunder) of the Agni-form of the moon, which is fading out gradually, are transferred to Soma, the nectar-moon. If Bloomfield is right in his explanation of the Sārameya-dogs as "the sun and the moon" — an explanation which would agree with my interpretation of Saramā — then this would also be an instance where a piece of old mythology is incorporated into a new conception which makes them messengers of Yama.[43]

The Brāhmaṇa period inherited an abundance of names of gods which were derived from different sources and times. This period had the task of organizing these names into some kind of a system. The theologians assigned separate places to them and, at times, gave them attributes which were relics of past glory of their former mythology. The Samrājs of former ages became the Sāmantas. Thus we find in PGS I. 5.10 :

agnir bhūtānām adhipatiḥ sa māvatv indro jyeṣṭhānāṃ yamaḥ pṛthivyā vāyur antarikṣasya sūryo divaś candramā nakṣatrāṇāṃ bṛhaspatir brahmaṇo mitraḥ satyānāṃ varuṇo 'pāṃ samudraḥ srotyānām annaṃ sāmrājyānām ... soma oṣadhīnāṃ savitā prasavānāṃ rudraḥ paśūnāṃ tvaṣṭā rūpāṇāṃ viṣṇuḥ parvatānāṃ maruto gaṇānām adhipatayas te māvantu pitaraḥ pitāmahāḥ pare 'vare....[44]

This idea occurs not only in the later literature but also, at least in its beginnings, already in the ṚV; thus IX. 88.3 ff. : *vāyúr ná yó niyútvāṅ iṣṭáyāmā pūṣéva dhījávanaḥ* etc., and I. 89.6; more particularly in VIII. 29, the well known riddle-hymn which enumerates the gods according to specific prominent qualities only. This enumeration is a late and artificial piece of wisdom which attempts to make a theological distinction between the many inherited names according to certain signs, without, however, bothering about the origin of these names.[45]

One might think that I have treated some gods all too extensively and others too briefly. There is unevenness in the treatment, but it is not intentional. In this purely analytical treatment of the material, I have considered it more important to pause for a thorough investigation at such places where the situation was most difficult and where the opinions appeared least reasoned, in order to pass quickly over other areas which did not require a new investigation so urgently or about which there was hardly any dispute, such as Dyāvāpṛthivī or Sūrya etc. The most essential part of what I would have said in this context can be found in the works of my predecessors and partly in the smaller edition of my *Vedic Mythology* also, and does not need a fresh discussion at present. In some cases I did not achieve positive results; for instance, in the case of stellar constellations, the knowledge of which, though primitive, was nevertheless anticipated in the ṚV; however this possibility for the word *dhā́man* in some solitary verses does not seem to be ruled out; moreover, I think Brunnhofer's suggestion that *ajá* is to be interpreted as the Pole Star[46] is not appreciated sufficiently.

CHAPTER ONE

UṢAS

Let my exposition begin with Uṣas, the most graceful goddess adorning the Vedic heavens. The Indian poet's feeling for nature has opened up the most beautiful buds even during the early bloom of Indian literature. This feeling for nature, which is evident in their hymns dedicated to Uṣas, elevates some of these hymns to the best poetry of all times. It is not my object to evaluate these hymns from the point of view of a literary historian; the object of a mythologist is a more sober one. The hymns addressed to Uṣas offer us a methodologically important insight into the mode of observation of nature in ancient India and lead us into the workshops where myths take their shape. We shall see the process in which what was undoubtedly a natural phenomenon is transformed into a divine personality. Not always can we have such a clear insight into the workshop of myth-formation as here. Uṣas does not stand alone; she is associated with and made the sister of other gods like the night, the sun god and the moon, and this association produces an abundance of poetic and mythological images through which the poets speak. Uṣas becomes the sister or the enemy of the night; she is made the beloved of the sun god, who follows her as a gallant youth follows his girl; alone or along with her dark sister she becomes the wife, or even the mother, or the daughter of the sun god. The lessons which these images and thoughts impart to us are invaluable for the understanding of other gods whose concept dates back to older times and is in the process of disappearing under the thick fog of mythological fantasy which envelops it more and more. These lessons are the given and intelligible material from which we can step further into more obscure regions. For the sake of subsequent discussion it will be useful to give below once more the most important of these comparisons, even though all that is essential can be found in the works of Bergaigne and, more particularly, of Brandes.

A. UṢAS AND THE BEGINNING OF THE YEAR

It has always been taken for granted that only the dawn of each day is described in the Uṣas hymns; it is only in the work of Ludwig,[1] who follows Krichenbauer,[2] that I find a remark which has far-reaching implications, "that she is not merely the goddess of the morning of each day, but is primarily and originally the first dawn of the New Year."

The majority of the Uṣas hymns are employed at the Prātaranuvāka of the Soma sacrifice, called Agniṣṭoma, which is celebrated every year with great festivities. According to many texts, this celebration takes place in spring.[3] We may consider it a festival of spring. Its morning litany begins with Āgneya Kratu, the cycle of hymns for Agni; this is followed by the hymns to Uṣas, arranged according to the metre. The selection of the hymns is different in the two Sūtras available to us,[4] and they are followed by the hymns to the Aśvins. We come across such litanies already in the ṚV,[5] and we can conclude that a festival, similar in this regard to Agniṣṭoma, was known at the time of the ṚV.

From the fact that these hymns occur at the beginning of one of the greatest sacrifices, we may conclude that the ritual treats them as the New Year's hymns that hail the most important day. But one looks in vain for a clear reference to this in these hymns; however, the occasional reference to Uṣas as *prathamá*, first of the coming days, or expressions like *jānanty áhnaḥ prathamásya nā́ma* (I.123.9) could be cited in support of the above conclusion. Foy, Macdonell and others have argued against my view; but I cannot understand why the evidence of the Śrauta Sūtras, which assign a fixed position to the Uṣas hymns, should be ignored. A counter-evidence against these statements is not presented either. Should one believe that the Vedic Indians did not observe and celebrate the beginning of spring as much as they celebrated the dawn of every random day ? Here the Gṛhya ritual and some verses of other texts[6] come to our help. In the ritual of the domestic Sūtras the place of Uṣas is occupied by "Ekāṣṭakā," whose celebration, according to Hiraṇyakeśin, is observed from the seventh to the ninth day in the dark half of the month of Māgha, i.e., in winter. Other texts refer to several Aṣṭakās, all of which occur in the dark halves of the months in Hemanta and Śiśira (i.e., Mārgaśīrṣa to Phālguṇa), and are, as already noticed, associated with the passage of the year.[7] The *Taittirīya Saṃhitā* says in another context : "Those who consecrate themselves for an annual sacrifice (*sattra*) should do so on Ekāṣṭakā; *eṣā vai saṃvatsarasya patnī yad ekāṣṭakā*" (VII. 4.8.1). In the same text she is also referred to as *ahnāṃ vidhānī* (III.3.8.4).[8]

The verses recited during the festival of Ekāṣṭakā glorify Rātrī, the night of the New Year. The AV says in III.10.1: "First of all she arose and became the cow of Yama. Rich in milk, may she give us milk each coming year." 2 : "The night, whom the gods rejoice to meet as a cow coming unto them and who is the spouse of the year — may she be beneficial to us." 3 : "May you, whom we worship as the image of the year, unite for us long-living progeny with riches." 5 : "The Grāvans, originating from a tree, resounded while preparing the Havis for the completion of the year. O Ekāṣṭakā, may we have good progeny and sons and enjoy riches."[9] 8 : "The year, your spouse, came hither, O Ekāṣṭakā."[10]

In these verses, instead of Uṣas, we see her sister, the night. In the *Maitrāyaṇī Saṃhitā*, in a group of verses the last of which (II.13.10) is identical with AV III.10.1, Uṣas is addressed as *ṛtūnāṃ patnī, ahnām netrī* and so on[11] — expressions similar to those we know from the ṚV.[12]

The Śrauta ritual knows only one occasion for the recitation of these verses, namely the construction of the Citi with many iṣṭakā-bricks, which represent various natural phenomena and are called, in this case, vyuṣṭis, whereas the Gṛhya Sūtras still clearly show the original purpose of these verses. But the former has a substitute for these in the Uṣas hymns, the purpose of which is evident from the directions given for the Soma ritual.

These hymns of the ṚV which praise Dawn and which form part of the morning litany of the annual Agniṣṭoma sacrifice can certainly be regarded as the hymns of the New Year, as the hymns that praise the beginning of the most important day, the first day in the New Year, irrespective of the fact whether one places this day in winter or in spring.[13] The verses of the Vasiṣṭhas sound like a hymn to the New Year: "Facing Uṣas, the Vasiṣṭhas awoke with singing; at first the wise ones with hymns — facing her who separates the two united worlds from each other and makes all beings visible. Uṣas awoke, creating new life; she hid the darkness with her light. The maiden goes forward without any shyness. She made Sūrya, the Sacrifice and Agni recognizable" (VII.80.1,2).[14]

Thus we can establish a closer connection between the Ṛgvedic period and the Vasantotsava, the spring festival of India, which was celebrated on the day of the full moon in the month of Caitra, and now in the month of Phālguṇa, and which is identical with the Holi festival.[15] In fact we can establish a closer connection not only with the later period but also with the pre-Vedic period. Uṣas or *usrá* has been compared to the Germanic *austrō, ostara-eostre,* the Germanic goddess of light and spring. This has been upheld by Mogk and Kluge[16] as well as by L. von Schroeder[17] against various objections. The fact that Uṣas is compared to a dancer and that ṚV X.29.2 speaks of her dance was taken as a justification by L. von Schroeder to recall the "dancing places of Eos" and, in view of the close connection between the sun and Dawn, to connect this with the dances of the sun on Easter Day in Germanic and Slavonic mythology; he also gave an appropriate explanation for the Lettic refrain *lihgo.*

B. UṢAS AND THE MANES

The justification for associating Uṣas with the New Year will become clearer still through the connection between her and the Manes. It is well known that it is the Pitaraḥ and the Kavis of antiquity who find the hidden light and take part in the recovery of the cattle.[18] There was a period in the year during which the cult of the gods ceased. In ancient Rome the year of ten months was followed by an impure period which was dedicated to the Manes. The antithesis between the Devayāna and the Pitṛyāṇa,[19] between the Uttarāyaṇa and the Dakṣiṇāyana, has influenced the Indian sacrificial year also and has left its traces even in the ṚV.[20] On the basis of the Gṛhya literature we can be positive that the time for oblations to the Manes was especially at the end of the Dakṣiṇāyana; furthermore, the fact that some texts mention, besides the Pitaraḥ, Rātrī and the Ṛtus also among the beings who have a share in the Aṣṭakā celebrations is not without significance in our discussion. There is no doubt as to which night is meant here.[21] Ekāṣṭakā, the night of the New Year, is considered the festival of the Manes. "Ekāṣṭakā, the spouse of the year, who mortifies herself through penance, gives milk in abundance. May you, O Manes, live united from this milking."[22] From this we can draw a conclusion about the significance of Uṣas who is praised in the ṚV. The Manes found the light and released the cattle, i.e., out of the dark period of the year arises the new light, and Sūrya, Agni and the vanished sacrifice return again.[23]

In the place of the Manes, or "Pitaraḥ" as they are generally called, appear the ancestors of special clans like the Aṅgiras' and the Daśagvas, who, famous as singers, play a special role in the recovery of light with their hymns.[24] If I am not much mistaken, we are encountering here an old custom of the New Year. As I have shown earlier, metres and hymns are closely connected with the solstice festivals.[25] Sāmans are sung frequently at the Agnyādheya.[26] The statement of the *Chāndogya Upaniṣad* that a joyful exultation rose up behind the new-born sun, and that therefore joyful exultation rings out to meet the rise and the return of the sun,[27] is not without significance; it reminds us of ṚV V.45.10; VI.7.4; 10.88.10.[28] Thus we are induced to ask further and to enquire into the related customs of ancient peoples. Then we find that among the Germans almost everywhere songs are sung in praise of the New Year, that the poorer people come down from the hills to sing old songs in the villages below,[29] and that the Slavonic Kolenda is a festival in which song had a place since ancient times.[30] From this it is evident that the singing of hymns by the ancient Indian Kavis, Aṅgiras' and Navagvas—the singing which recovers the new light and blasts open the cow-shed — is closely related to the customs of other peoples of singing in praise of the New Year. I do not share the opinion of Foy that this custom was originally connected with a cosmological saga among the people of antiquity; on the contrary, I think that it was the reality of the image of the year which gave rise to this custom.

C. THE THREE UṢAS'

Uṣas is referred to in the singular at some places and at others in the plural. Among these some are of special interest where reference is made to three dawns.[31] According to Bergaigne,[32] they are probably "three forms of Dawn, corresponding to the three worlds," and according to Hopkins,[33] they are "the three dawn-lights, white, red and yellow." I connect these with the three seasons. Ludwig, Zimmer and others observed earlier that the Vedic year had three seasons. An allusion to the three seasons can be seen in the expression *trinábhi cakrám ajáram anarváṃ yátremā́ víśvā́ bhúvanā́dhi tasthúḥ* (ṚV I.164.2; AV IX. 9.2), while in other passages like I. 164.13 mention is made of *páñcāre cakré parivártamāne;* furthermore, the allusion occurs in the *tríṇi nábhyāni* I. 164.48, besides in the 12 rims of the wheel and the 360 spokes.[34] (Cf. also *tryudāyám* IV. 37.3).[35] The three seasons have been canonized in the Cāturmāsya or the tertiary ceremonies. There are still allusions to the character of the seasons in some of the mantras recited during the hair cutting, which is customary in the Cāturmāsya. During the first of these tertiary ceremonies the following words are spoken : *ṛtam eva parameṣṭy ṛtaṃ nātyeti kiṃcana / ṛte samudra āhita ṛte bhūmir iyaṃ śritā* (ĀpŚS VIII. 4.2); during the second: *yad gharmaḥ paryavartayad antān pṛthivyā divaḥ, agnir īśāna ojasā* etc. (VIII. 8.21); and during the third : *yo asyāḥ pṛthivyās tvaci nivartayaty oṣadhīḥ, agnir īśāna ojasā* etc. (VIII. 19.9). The ending is the same in all the three.[36] Accordingly, *ṛta*, although it appears in the refrain of all the mantras, is the characteristic word for the first season, *gharma* for the second and *oṣadhi* for the third. Of the later names for the seasons, the ṚV does not contain *varṣāḥ* for the rainy season; *grīṣma*, *vasanta* and *hemanta* occur rarely, and only *śarad* occurs frequently. In the Puruṣa Sūkta (X.90) spring, summer and autumn are mentioned, significantly enough, in connection with the sacrifice by the gods.[37]

This infrequent occurrence of names for the seasons in the ṚV is remarkable; it is to be assumed that other expressions were in use which we do not know. I count among them the triad *gāvaḥ, āpaḥ, svar*, which is repeated at two places in the ṚV.[38] *āpaḥ* could be the same as *varṣāḥ*; we may consider *svar* to be synonymous with *gharma* and "the cattle" perhaps with spring, which leads the cattle (of Uṣas) out of the cattle-shed; at two other places, however, Uṣas is mentioned separately from *gāvaḥ*.[39]

D. UṢAS AND THE CATTLE

Uṣas herself is referred to directly or metaphorically as a cow, occasionally as a mare; but more frequently she is the mother of the cattle, or she harnesses red cattle and horses to her chariot.[40]

I.30.21 : *áśve ná citre aruṣi ||*
92.1 : *etā́ u tyā́ uṣásaḥ ketúm akrata...|*
...práti gā́vó 'ruṣīr yanti mātáraḥ ||
2 : *úd apaptann aruṇā́ bhānávo vṛ́thā*
svāyújo áruṣīr gā́ ayukṣata |
12 : *paśū́n ná citrā́ subhágā prathānā́...*
15 : *yukṣvā́...áśvāṅ adyā́ruṇā́ṅ uṣaḥ |*
113.2 : *rúśadvatsā rúśatī śvetyā́gāt...*
14 : *prabodháyanty aruṇébhir áśvair óṣā́ yāti...*
124.5 : *gávāṃ jánitry*[41] *akṛta prá ketúm |*
11 : *yuṅkté gávām aruṇā́nām ánīkam |*
II.28.2 : *upā́yana uṣásāṃ gómatīnām...*
III.61.4 : *svásarasya pátnī |*
IV.14.3 : *āváhanty aruṇī́r jyótiṣā́gān*
mahī́ citrā́ raśmíbhiś cékitānā |
52.2 : *áśveva citrā́ruṣī mātā́ gávām*[41] *ṛtā́varī |*
5 : *práti bhadrā́ adṛkṣata gávāṃ sárgā ná raśmáyaḥ |*
V.1.1 : *ábodhy agníḥ...práti dhenúm ivāyatī́m uṣā́sam |*
45.2 : *órvā́d gávāṃ mātā́ jānatī́ gāt |*
64.7 : *ucchántyāṃ me yajatā́ devákṣatre rúśadgavi |*
75.9 : *ábhūd uṣā́ rúśatpaśuḥ*[42]*...*
80.3 : *eṣā́ góbhir aruṇébhir yujānā́...*
VI.64.3 : *váhanti sīm aruṇā́so rúśanto*
gā́vaḥ subhágām urviyā́ prathānā́m |
5 : *sā́ vaha yókṣábhir ávātā...*
65.2 : *ví tád yayur aruṇayúgbhir áśvaiś*
citráṃ bhānty uṣásaś candrárathāḥ |
VII.75.6 : *práti dyutānā́m aruṣā́so áśvāś*
citrā́ adṛśrann uṣásaṃ váhantaḥ |
79.1 : *susaṃdṛ́gbhir ukṣábhir bhānúm aśret...*
2 : *sáṃ te gā́vas táma ā́ vartayanti*[43]*...*

It can be seen from this compilation that there is no reference anywhere to "morning-clouds," but that the "cattle" and "horses" of Dawn[44] are only mythological synonyms for Dawn herself. The much-praised cloud-cows (rain-clouds) also can be erased from the mythological dictionary. Such a comparison is found very rarely.

There are frequent references to the driving away of the darkness by the light.[45] If the cattle of Uṣas return in the morning, where do they come from? In a hymn addressed to Indra-Agni, ṚV VI.60.2 speaks of *uṣása úḷhā́ḥ*, "the abducted Dawns." It is the darkness or "the shed of darkness" the "gates" of which are opened by the shining and purifying ones — IV.51.2 : *vy ù vrajásya támaso dvā́rocchántīr avrañ chúcayaḥ pāvakā́ḥ*. They open the shed themselves as cattle open their fence — I.92.4 : *gā́vo ná vrajáṃ vy ùṣā́ āvar támaḥ*.[46] Or, it is the other gods, Indra, Agni, Bṛhaspati and also the Manes who open with their magic the cow-shed, the rock in which the cows are shut in.[47]

When the first rays of the returning light redden the sky on the morning of any day, or of the New Year's Day, they appear like red cattle marching past in the east. Here also a memory of a past time and of an earlier home is woven into the fabric of the Vedic myth. In India the dawn lasts only for a short time.[48] In contrast to the ṚV, the AV already speaks of Uṣas relatively seldom; the ritual does not mention any special offerings to Dawn. The image of the rock, or of the cow-shed, out of which the Dawns are released could not have had its origin in the climate of India, but in a land where winter indeed banished the cattle into strong sheds, *paxrumaēšu nmānaēšu*, as *Vendidād* 2.24 says. Rock caves and rock sheds might have offered a more secure shelter than man-made sheds.

In a land where the shortest and the longest day differ only by about four hours,[49] there is less reason to celebrate the return of light. As far as I know, this theme does not play any role in the classical poetry. The Ṛgvedic poet still used the comparison between the rising of the year out of the night of winter and the releasing of cattle out of their winter shelters in spring — a comparison which had come down from old times, but had hardly any relevance in the Vedic period.

E. UṢAS AND THE SUN

Dawn is followed by the sun god. The Vedic hymns show how in the imagination of the poets this simple natural phenomenon is transformed into a living image and how the natural phenomena are replaced by personifications out of which fantasy creates the myths.

1. Uṣas leads Sūrya (the eye of the gods or the steed), creates a path for him; she is his mother etc. VII.77.3 : *devā́nāṃ cákṣuḥ subhágā váhantī śvetáṃ náyantī sudṛ́śīkam aśvám*, "the charming

one who bears the eye of the gods and who leads the white, beautiful steed." I.113.2 : *rúśadvatsā rúśatī śvety ā́gāt* (unless we consider *vatsa* here as a plural referring to her own rays). I.121.6 : *prá rocy asyā́ uṣáso na sū́raḥ.* I.113.16 : *ā́raik pánthāṃ yā́tave sū́ryāya.* I.136.3 : *ádarśi gātúr uráve várīyasī.* III.61.4 : *svàr jánantī.*[50] In another image the black one (the night) gives way to the red one (VII.71.1 : *riṇákti kṛṣṇī́r aruṣā́ya pánthām*), or she herself becomes the mother of the calf in AV XIII.3.26.[51]

2. Uṣas is the beloved or the wife of Sūrya or of Agni. VII.75.5 : *vājínīvatī sū́ryasya yóṣā ... uṣā́ ucchati.* I.115.2 : *sū́ryo devī́m uṣásam rócamānāṃ máryo ná yóṣām abhy èti paścā́t.*[52]

3. Uṣas is created by Sūrya and shines through his eye etc. VII.91.1 : *ávāsayann uṣásaṃ sū́ryeṇa.* VII.81.2 : *úd uśriyāḥ sṛjate sū́ryaḥ.* I.48.7 : *eṣā́yukta parāvátaḥ sū́ryasyodáyanād adhi.* I.92.11 : (see the previous note), 12 : *sū́ryasya ceti raśmíbhir dṛśānā́.*[53]

4. Particularly in the Aśvin hymns she appears as the daughter of Sūrya, and there the designations *sū́ro, sū́ryasya duhitṛ́, divó duhitṛ́* occur alternately with *uṣás* and *sūryā́.* E.g., VII. 69.4 : *yuvóḥ śríyaṃ pári yóṣāvṛṇīta sū́ro duhitā́ páritakmyāyām;* I.46.14 : *yuvór uṣā́ ánu śríyaṃ párijmanor upā́carat*; 116.17; 117.13; 118.5; 180.1; 183.2; IV.52.2; V.73.5: *ā́ yád vāṃ sūryā́ ráthaṃ tíṣṭhat*; VI.63.5; VIII.5.2; 22.1 etc.; AV VI.82.2.

F. SŪRYĀ

The complete synonymity between Uṣas and Sūryā implies that Sūryā is the same as Uṣas in the well known Sūryāsūkta also. Some scholars held the view that Sūryā in this hymn is the name of the solar woman,[54] and that the Sūryā hymn is a glorification of the marriage between the sun and Soma, the moon.[55] But this is totally against the Indian linguistic usage according to which the sun is always masculine.[56] As Sūryā and Uṣas are identical in all other passages, the marriage referred to in this hymn can only be between Uṣas and the moon; it should be the first full moon day in the New Year or in spring on which the marriage procession of Sūryā starts. As the daughter of the sun god, she is called *sāvitrī* in AV VI.82.2; XIV.2.30; *Aitareya Brāhmaṇa* IV.7.1.

There are references to the union of Uṣas (Sūryā) with the moon in other passages of the ṚV also, even though such references are of secondary importance. X.85.19 says that Candramas moves at the head of the Dawns, or in another passage it is said that Soma rules over the Dawns, or makes them shine.[57] Thus, on the one hand Uṣas is closely connected with the moon, on the other with the sun god, but never with the stars, be it the morning star or the evening star. In spite of all that was said elsewhere, we gain from this a clue to the original nature of the Aśvins, the two obscure deities, who are closely connected with Uṣas.

G. THE SUN DESTROYS UṢAS

V.79.9 : *vy ùcchā duhitar divo mā́ cirám̐ tanuthā ápaḥ /*
nét tvā stenám̐ yáthā ripúm̐ tápāti sū́ro arcíṣā /
sújāte áśvasūnṛte //

"Shine forth, O daughter of the heavens, do not delay the task, lest the sun should burn you with his ray like a hostile thief." Perhaps the following also could be added to this verse,

X.189.2 : *antáś carati rocanā́syá prāṇā́d apānatí /*
vy àkhyan mahiṣó dívam //

"[The mother of the coloured bull] moves between the luminous spaces, breathing her last before his breath; the bull surveyed the heavens." Howsoever one might interpret the second verse, the first verse leaves no room for doubt that there was the possibility of representing in poetry as well as in mythology the relationship between Dawn and the sun god not only as friendly but also as hostile. But this verse (V.79.9) has an additional significance, for it throws light on other verses in which Indra defeats Uṣas or destroys her chariot; these verses contain one more of the many images, or mythological synonyms, in which the poets or the people spoke of one and the same natural phenomenon; in this case, Uṣas is considered a wicked woman — a concept that has parallels outside India also.[58]

II.15.5 : *vájreṇā́na uṣásaḥ sám̐ pipeṣa /*
IV.30.8 : */stríyam̐ yád durhaṇāyúvam̐ vádhīr duhitáram̐ diváḥ//*
9 : *diváś cid ghā duhitáram̐ mahā́n mahīyámānām /*
uṣā́sam indra sám̐ pinak //[59]

X.73.6 : ...ávāhann índra uṣáso yáthānaḥ |
138.5 : índrasya vájrād abibhed abhiśnáthaḥ
prákrāmac chundyúr ájahād uṣā́ ánaḥ ||

Here, I think, we can see clearly how simple natural phenomena assume mythological garbs. In verse V.79.9 we find one of these solitary indications still available which lead us from the realm of inextricably mixed myths back to the solid ground of straightforward observation of nature, the ground in which the myths grew.

H. UṢAS AND THE NIGHT

The connection between the day, or the dawn, and the night also can show us the various images in which the same phenomenon is clothed by the imagination. Cited above (n. 45) are the passages that speak directly of the banishment of the darkness by the oncoming day. *Támas* and *rā́tri* are by no means identical; *támas* is more the enemy of Uṣas, *rā́tri* is always her sister. Where *támas* is chosen, it implies a somewhat different attitude: it is the antithesis between *andháṃ támas*, the real darkness, and *sujyótir aktú*, the bright night (cf. X.89.15), that finds its expression there; but the distinction is not always maintained; *támas svásuḥ* or similar expressions occur, which is but natural.

The day and the night—*uṣā́sānáktā*, *áhanī*, but rarely *dyā́vā*, or *uṣás* with *nimrúc* (TĀr II.5.11; AV XIII.3.21) — are "sisters" who move incessantly one after the other along the same path; they are the "daughters of heaven," the "mothers of the order," "celestial women," both adorned, both different; one dark, the other of light colour; one decorates herself with stars, or resembles a barren woman; the other shines with the splendour of the sun; one consents to give the other her own place, or is driven out by her. In III.55.12 they are called "mother-cow and daughter-cow."[60]

The verses which speak of Uṣāsānaktā and of the sun god are instructive from many points of view; it is the sun who creates the day and the night. It is said in ṚV I.50.7 :[61] "You stride through the sky, through the vast atmosphere, measuring the days with the nights." "When Sūrya unharnesses his horses, the night spreads her garment over everything."[62] "Everlasting is one, his shining light; the other, the black one, is rolled up by his horses."[63] Or the god goes forth, "spreading out the fabric with his fastest [horses] and withdrawing the black garment. Sūrya's rays hid the darkness like a hide in the waters, shaking it off thoroughly."[64] "One spreads light through the space, you, O Sūrya, rise with the other."[65] The image presents the day and the night as mothers,[66] also as the wives of Sūrya or of Agni who is of equal importance with Sūrya in many cases. Thus in I.95.1[67] it is two of different colours who suckle the infant alternately. In I.122.2 they are compared to "two wives," the night to a barren one and her sister to a woman adorned with gold;[68] in AV VIII. 9.12 they are described directly as wives of Sūrya.[69] This verse, which has parallels elsewhere,[70] has a special importance because it finally solves, I believe, the problem who Vivasvat is and who his two unequal wives are in the much-interpreted verses X.17.1,2. There can be no doubt that Uṣāsānaktā are meant by the two wives and that their suitor represents the sun god. Thus the sun god is certainly called Vivasvat already in the ṚV.

1. Saramā

Saramā, the much-disputed goddess, who goes to the Paṇis as Indra's messenger, is closely associated with the recovery of the cattle. The Paṇis were a tribe hostile to those Indians who pressed the Soma. It was the raids of these Paṇis in particular that the poets of the Bhāradvāja book had in mind. They are mentioned in the famous Saramā hymn of maṇḍala X — transformed into demons and elevated to the world of saga — and the poet looks for them in the far-off distance on the other side of the Rasā. Outside this hymn Saramā appears only in solitary instances; then she is no more the messenger of Indra, but appears always in connection with the cattle which she finds or helps to find.[71] Just as the recovery of the cattle is accompanied by the hymns of the singers (see p. 25 above), so is Saramā's task connected with them and is supported by Bṛhaspati and the Aṅgiras'. Who is Saramā ? In the ṚV she is not yet called a female dog as in the later period (Macdonell, p. 151).[72] The general character of the Saramā verses has an undeniable similarity with that of the Uṣas hymns. Exactly as Saramā moves *ṛtásya pathā́* in V.45.8 (*ṛtáṃ yatī́* 45.7), Uṣas moves along *ṛtásya panthā́m*, and accordingly the Dawns are called *ṛtásya devī́ḥ* (IV.51.8) and *ṛtájātasatyāḥ* (IV.51.7). The Soma stones resound *haviṣ kṛṇvantaḥ parivatsarīṇam* (see p. 23, n. 9 above). The Aṅgiras', the Daśagvas and Bṛhaspati take part in the opening of the cow-shed (p. 5 above). Likewise Bṛhaspati, Soma, the stones and the wise Ṛṣis[73] are closely connected in the Saramā hymn X.108.11, and "the stone flung by hand," the Navagvas and the Aṅgiras' in two other verses of Saramā (V.45.7,8). V.45.7 closes with the words *ṛtáṃ yatī́ sarámā gā́ avindad víśvāni satyā́ṅgirāś cakāra* and verse 8 begins with the hint *víśve asyā́ vyúṣi máhināyāḥ sám yád ... návanta*, which one can apply unhesitatingly to the above-mentioned Saramā.[74]

If at all we can draw a conclusion from this scanty material, we may regard Saramā as a synonym of Uṣas on the basis of these common traits. Then her character as the mother of the Sārameyas could be explained. Bloomfield interpreted the two Sārameyas as the sun and the moon.[75] If this is correct, then Saramā, the mother of the two Sārameyas, would be a mythological synonym for Uṣas, the mother of the sun and the moon. It is most likely that Saraṇyū, Vivasvat's wife, who abandons "the twins" and has the same colour as Uṣas is not different from Uṣas.[76] Then Saramā and Saraṇyū would be linguistic synonyms (provided the latter is not a mere adjective, which is not at all improbable), and the Aśvins and the Sārameyas, who faded out in Vedic mythology, would be mythological synonyms. However, there can be no certainty about this.

2. Virāj

Virāj is partly an adjective as in the combination which occurs thrice : *prajā́patiḥ parameṣṭhī́ virā́ṭ* (AV VIII.5.10; XI.5.7; XIII.3.5) or as in *vāc virāj* (AV IX.2.5), partly the name of a mystic Virāj. But there are other passages where neither of these meanings is sufficient; thus already AV VIII.8.23 : *saṃvatsaro rathaḥ, parivatsaro rathopasthaḥ, virāḍ īṣāgnī rathamukham*, shows that Virāj must somehow be connected with the year and the seasons. The indication that Virāj must be a natural phenomenon becomes much stronger in AV XIII.1.33.[77] In this verse, which occurs between Sūrya verses (32,35), mention is made of the calf of Virāj, which can only be the sun, while Virāj should refer to Uṣas — an assumption in which I agree with Bloomfield[78] almost completely. Another hymn of the AV

(VIII.9) — it refers to Uṣas frequently (vv. 11-13) — mentions in the first verse the "two calves of Virāj which emerge out of the ocean,"[79] i.e., as I and Henry[80] believe, the sun and the moon. Mention may be made here of verse 8 of the same, often very obscure, hymn. In this verse Virāj is clearly connected with the procedure of the sacrifices.[81] "When she moves forward, the sacrifices follow her; when she appears, the sacrifices go up to her.[82] It is Virāj in the highest heaven, O Ṛṣis, after whose ordinance and command the Yakṣa moves. Breathless herself, she moves through the breath of the breathing women. Virāj follows the Svarāj from behind."[83]

3. Uṣas and Prajāpati

Uṣas is mentioned several times as related to Prajāpati. KBr VI.1 says: "Prajāpati wanted progeny and did penance. Having done penance, he begot the five: Agni, Vāyu, Āditya, Candramas and, as the fifth, Uṣas. He said to them: 'do penance as well.' They were consecrated. When they were consecrated and had done penance, Uṣas, the daughter of Prajāpati, came to meet them in the east in the form of an Apsaras. Their senses were aroused by her. They let out their semen. They went and said to father Prajāpati: 'We let out our semen. This should not be lost to us.' Prajāpati made a golden vessel, an arrow high and wide, and poured the semen into this" and so on.[84] The story appears in another form also. Prajāpati himself has a sinful desire for his daughter and marries her. Here it can be clearly recognized that a natural phenomenon was given a mythological character.[85] The story goes on to say, "Prajāpati conceived a passion for his daughter, be it Dyaus, be it Uṣas.[86] Wishing, 'I would like to pair with her,' he united with her. To the gods it was a sin 'that he does this to his daughter, to our sister" (ŚBr I.7.4.1-2). Or, "on this [earth] as support, the beings and 'the lord of beings' consecrated themselves for the year; the lord of beings was the householder, Uṣas his wife. These beings are the seasons, the lord of beings is the year, and his wife, Uṣas, is the beginning of the day (*auṣasī*). These beings and the lord of beings, the year, poured their semen into Uṣas; then a boy was born within a year; he cried" (ŚBr VI.1.3.7-8). The legend, of which there are other versions, is well known to the Vedic poets also. In various passages this legend is alluded to, more or less in detail, as an incest between father and daughter, without, however, their names being mentioned. There is no doubt that like the Brāhmaṇas the Vedic poets also knew of the atonement for this violation by Rudra.[87]

CHAPTER TWO

THE AŚVINS

The Aśvin myths in the ṚV are the inheritance from an Aśvin cult which had obviously enjoyed a wide popularity at one time, but had already lost part of its innermost life, surviving in these remnants only. Celestial and terrestrial events might have been fused in these sagas which in most cases defy our interpretation.[1] Hymns like I.112 ff. (particularly 116) and X.39-40 which read like catalogues of such miraculous events show the richness of sagas once extant. A few of these reappear in different versions and are the evidence of a manifold narrative activity. We do not encounter in other gods the things that were reported about the Aśvins. Here also the distinguishing lines can be recognized very clearly; similarly, as far as I can see, the Vṛtra myths narrated by the worshippers of Indra are distinct from the sagas of the Aśvins. The idea of ever-returning spring is expressed in the former through the victory over Vṛtra, and here through the joint ride of the Aśvins with Uṣas.

It is not my intention to increase the number of interpretations of this mysterious pair of brothers who have kept scholars occupied since the beginning of our science. Like others, I am inclined to the view that they are old Aryan gods whom we encounter among the Greeks, the Germanic people[2] and the Letts, although the names do not have any similarity any more.[3]

It seems pointless to hold, or to defend, a specific opinion on gods like these who lost the lustre of their original nature as early as in the Vedic period and who illuminate only the horizon through their miracles. It is beyond our capacity to decide whether they were once different beings who formed mutually complementary opposites, or they were destined to become a pair of brothers through the similarity in appearance and in basic character. Even in classical Sanskrit they are regarded as youths with a radiant and glorious appearance. Just as "the two Aśvins, radiating with beauty, shining, and without blemish, follow Pitāmaha," so did Rāma and Lakṣmaṇa follow Viśvāmitra (*Rāmāyaṇa* I.22.8). That is why there was no dearth of interpretations and hypotheses of all kinds from Yāska to the recent times, and all these have shared the same fate of being considered irrelevant. According to some the Aśvins were supposed to represent the morning star and the evening star, according to others dawn and twilight; or they were explained as the sun and the moon, as Castor and Pollux, the twin stars in the sky, as two physicians famous for their healing powers, as rain-gods, as "the water-element and the fire-element joined with one another."[4] The "authentic tradition" of Yāska bequeathed to us four different interpretations simultaneously: *dyāvāpṛthivyāv ity eke 'horātrāv ity eke sūryacandramasāv ity eke rājānau puṇyakṛtāv ity aitihāsikāḥ.* Yāska could have added that they were also called "the two Adhvaryus of the gods" (TS VI. 3.6.3 etc.), or more often the "physicians" of the gods. In TS VI. 4.9.4 their graha denotes the "ear," just as the graha of Mitra-Varuṇa denotes the "eye." One can choose any of these interpretations as one likes, but one should not ignore the fact that each one of these theories is as unfounded as the next one. There has been an attempt to explain that these two gods are a phenomenon which spread from Babylonia towards the west and the east.[5] But we cannot accept this as long as neither the necessity for this hypothesis, nor the path through which this cult spread, is established.[6]

Without committing myself to one view or the other, I wish to examine the probability of individual opinions — recently postulated or repeated — successively and add some more material.

1. The Aśvins = Indian saints who help in distress (*Notheilige*). Geldner, *Vedische Studien* II.31: "We are not yet well informed about the nature of the Aśvins. Only through the better informed Aitihāsikas (Yāska XII.1.1) do we know that they were *rājānau puṇyakṛtau*, two kings who performed good deeds. Their good deeds consisted in cures and miracles. They are the Indian saints who help in distress (*Notheilige*). They do not represent any visible phenomenon of the sky. The saga of the Aśvins is truly an Indian heroic saga. Thrice at night and thrice in the day they ride out ... " Geldner does not tell us why he gives only one interpretation from Yāska, and why he gives greater credence to the Aitihāsikas than to others; for the

narrators and the creators of stories are not at all in the habit of preserving the tradition accurately. The stories change from generation to generation, if not from mouth to mouth. This we can see in the transformation to which the Vṛtra saga gradually became a victim. Geldner tempts us to believe that Yāska left only one interpretation instead of the four and leaves it to our discretion what to do with the other statements. There is also no explanation how then the chariot of the helpers in distress came to carry Uṣas, who has chosen the Aśvins for herself. But this is one of the Vedic conceptions stated very often.[7] This conception finds an expression in the ritual also in as much as the Āśvinakratu which precedes the morning oblation follows immediately after the Uṣasyakratu.[8] Had they been ancient heroes, we would have the least reason to expect them just here among the gods of the early morning rather than at the evening oblations. and in the vicinity of the Nārāśaṅsa fire. But even in the Āśvinakratu they receive an offering within the Soma sacrifice (during the Dvidevatyagrahas of the morning libation); the place assigned to them does not indicate their character of having been heroes once. Should then the tradition of the Vedic ritual be so bad and that of the Aitihāsikas so good that, although there is no trace of the earthly origins of the Aśvins in the Veda, we accept the statement of the Aitihāsikas who did not bear any sacred responsibility for what they narrated and for what they added out of their imagination? We would also like to know why at another place in the ritual the Aśvins were connected with the passage of the year. *Śāṅkhāyana Śrauta Sūtra* XIII. 10.11 states that in a particular context the number of verses or hymns belonging to the Aśvins is 360: *trīṇy āśvinaṃ ṣaṣṭi śatāni*.[9] The same is indicated at a still later period by a passage of the *Mahābhārata* which can be called a *khailikasūkta*.[10] We cannot separate this number 360 from the description of their chariot which has three wheels or is somehow or other connected with the number three. This number 360 can certainly be related to the passage of the year with its three great sub-divisions.[11] We also know that their chariot runs not only over streams and pastures but — like the chariot of Uṣas, or of the Ṛbhus, or of Sūrya — around the earth and the sky,[12] and we hear that they fasten one wheel of their chariot *aghnyásya mūrdháni* in order to drive around the sky with the other.[13] Already in the ṚV they are called *nárā diváḥ* VI.62.1, *divá ájātā divyá suparṇá* IV. 43.3; *śubhás pátī* VIII. 22.4. They are deified so completely in the ṚV that it is incomprehensible how the Aitihāsikas could still preserve authentic news of their human origins.

2. The Aśvins = the morning star and the evening star. This interpretation has found the greatest number of advocates,[14] but I cannot agree with the reasons given in support of this theory. A certain undeniable similarity with the two Lettic God's sons has led to inadmissible conclusions. Oldenberg[15] says: "The time of appearance, the lucid nature, the flying movement along a fixed path around the sky and around the sun, the return day after day like the sun and the dawn — all these characteristics apply to the morning star.[16] But of course not the dual nature of the Aśvins. However, is not the correctness of our interpretation confirmed by the fact that the strikingly appropriate meaning of this trait also can be brought out if only we assume that there occurred a shift in detail which is easily understandable? The concept of the morning star cannot be separated from that of the evening star; that is the second Aśvin. Thus what remains as a discrepancy between nature and myth is only (!) this: the morning star and the evening star are separated permanently, whereas the Aśvins are united as two beings of the morning. But is this shift in detail not understandable? It is said in an Aśvin hymn (V.77.2): 'Offer sacrifice in the morning and set the Aśvins in motion. In the evening, the sacrifice does not reach the gods; it is not welcome to them.' Because of this preference in the cult to the morning rather than to the evening, is it not possible that the conception of a pair of gods, one of the morning and the other of the evening, though otherwise unaltered, was changed to the conception of two morning gods?"

I cannot agree with any part of this reasoning. What Oldenberg pushes into the background with the word "only" is, in reality, the most valid objection against his arguments. Moreover, his reasoning cannot hide the fact that there is a fundamental difference between the morning star and the evening star on the one hand and the Aśvins on the other. The former are two phenomena, always separate, and the latter are two brothers, almost always united; of the former there is always only one at a time and of the latter there are always two. The morning star and the evening star are not merely separated by the night: when

Venus rises as the morning star, the evening star becomes invisible for months together, and when Venus rises in the west as the evening star during her eastern anomaly, the morning star disappears.[17] Can a pair of almost inseparable brothers emerge out of phenomena which exclude each other? I would like to have an example from the earlier or the later period of India, from astronomy or poetry, where these stars are regarded as a pair of brothers. One cannot bring the sun and the moon as comparison as Oldenberg does. After all, they appear every day and every night, with the exception of the short period of the new moon; they take turns, at times they are both visible in the sky simultaneously, at times separately; and thus they can easily be considered brothers because their relationship gives an occasion for all kinds of reflections even to the primitive observer. But the morning star and the evening star are always separate and relieve each other for long periods. One cannot refer to Sūryā either; for it was wrong and against all Indian conceptions that she was considered a feminine name for the sun, whereas in reality she is a synonym for Uṣas, the daughter of the sun. If the "two" who are supposed to accompany her are the morning star and the evening star, then there is, for months together, always only one, and for a long time she rises without any companion at all. It seems to me that in such a case the myth would have taken a different form. I am also against the reference to the two Lettic God's sons, who contribute a dubious factor to the argumentation and who could even have changed their own nature. After all, it has yet to be proved that the two Lettic God's sons are really the morning star and the evening star and have always been so. Indeed, when the Lettic myth mentions specific beings, it does not refer to the morning star and the evening star, but to the morning star, Perkúnas, and the moon.[18] If all the three groups, i.e., the Aśvins, the Dioscuri and the "God's sons" had been really identical with each other, and also with the "morning star" and the "evening star," then it would have given rise to a curious mythological phenomenon. Then the Aryans would not have preserved a memory of the sun and the moon, or of the seasons, or of any other stars, or of common ancestors and so on, but only of the morning star and the evening star, which should have made a greater impression upon them than any other celestial or terrestrial phenomenon, but which were much less important for their lives than anything else, in fact, were not important at all. Such a case is possible, but it would be an unusual and improbable whim of tradition. I think that we can set aside this interpretation also until better evidence is forthcoming.

3. The Aśvins = the constellation of Gemini.

As far as I know, it was Weber[19] who was the first to express this view, but he was under no illusions about the possible objections against such an interpretation. Considering their dual nature and their character as lucid spirits in the morning sky, one might very well think of directly recognizing in the Aśvins the double constellation belonging exactly to the northern hemisphere, the Dioscuri that often rose in the sky at the very break of dawn in the original home of the Indo-Europeans, and also in the old settlements of the Aryans in the northern Punjab. Weber realizes that the hymns of the ṚV do not offer any specific clue to such an interpretation and that certain objections could be raised against this theory even from the point of view of the Indology of his time. Weber (p. 266) cites a calculation by W. Förster according to which the twin stars could be regarded as the morning stars in the upper Punjab for four to six weeks from the end of April around 1200 B.C., and from the first one third of April around 2200 B.C. Weber seems to have overcome his doubts later; for he comes back to this in his *Vedische Beiträge* VII,[20] where he cites the calculation of Förster to the effect that the twin stars rose before the sun at the time of the vernal equinox in Armenia in the year 6000 B.C. Weber believes that with this a "suitable background" has been created for his hypothesis that the Aśvin-Dioscuri were the Gemini or had the characteristics of the morning star in the Indo-European period. Brunnhofer[21] follows Weber. Weber's hypothesis is one of those which can be neither proved nor disproved. The connection with Uṣas and the analogy with the Dioscuri of Greece speak in favour of this hypothesis. Yet it is curious that out of the entire Indo-European mythology nothing else should have been preserved among the Indians and the Greeks but this constellation which for a while (6000 B.C. !) proclaimed the coming of spring, and that other constellations which played the same role in later periods should not have been elevated to the same position in mythology. But the main argument against this is the silence of the ṚV, where there is nothing to warrant such a hypothesis. The ṚV offers such a big group of Aśvin sagas that it would indeed be surprising if the Aśvins originated from a single constellation. Miller[22] was right in saying that in such a case we would also have to believe that the entire cult of stars in which all outstanding stars were deified and worshipped existed in India. He is of the opinion that, like Mars among the Romans, Pūṣan and Bhaga among the Indians were connected with constellations. The Aśvins also could have been made the presiding deities of the Aśvayuj-nakṣatra at a later time only. There is also much else that remains unexplained, e.g., the number three connected with the chariot of the Aśvins which can hardly refer to something other than the three seasons, and which cannot be applied satisfactorily to this constellation. The statements *ihéha jātá* I. 181.4; *nắnā jātau* V. 73.4 would remain altogether unintelligible or would have to be later additions.

4. The Aśvins = rain gods.[23]

I have dealt with the most well known and most popular opinions at greater length and can forgo the task of discussing all the others except two which deserve some attention. One of these is the view of Vodskov that the Aśvins are rain gods. There are, of course, references to this quality, but this is by no means the sole quality of the Aśvins. Vodskov emphasizes that this is the oldest quality, without, however, giving any evidence for its antiquity. One could maintain the same view about Mitra-Varuṇa also with similar justification; for these "are among the gods most frequently thought of and prayed to as bestowers of rain."[24] I do not think that this quality of the Aśvins deserves precedence over the others, nor do I think that Vodskov has contributed anything substantial to show that the evolution of other qualities was possible from his standpoint, and particularly to explain their connection to Sūryā somewhat satisfactorily.[25] Only through far-fetched arguments the miraculous deeds of the Aśvins can be made compatible with their supposed nature as rain gods. Vodskov's argumentation becomes wholly implausible when he tries to show that the duality of the Aśvins is not their original quality, but is only caused by the union between the rain-bestowing power and the dew-bestowing power : "Originally there was only one Aśvin, a specially mild and beneficent rain god like Tvaṣṭṛ or Pūṣan. The function of bestowing dew was ascribed to him, and this doubled role doubled his nature, so that the god bestowing rain and dew became a god pair."[26] Of course, Vodskov himself admits that this is only one of the many possibilities, but an argumentation which violates one of the most positive aspects of the tradition can hardly be on the right path. What Vodskov offers is a mere academic construction. If one must hold fast to anything, it is to the dual nature of the Aśvins which may go back, as Vodskov himself considers still possible, to the pre-Aryan times, and every explanation which is not clearly compatible with this dual nature must be dismissed. Leaving aside the details, I would like to say only this much more against Vodskov's interpretation: it finds no support at all in the ritual, and it cannot explain the individual points that were raised against Geldner, e.g., the number three which is closely connected with the Aśvins etc. I think this interpretation can also be set aside.

5. The Aśvins = the sun and the moon.

This interpretation is one of the four given by Yāska and belongs to the same category as "*ahorātre*." As far as I know, only Miller and Ludwig have subscribed to it.[27] Quite justifiably Miller refutes the not very profound objections raised against this interpretation, viz., that the sun played a far more prominent role in Vedic mythology than one would find in these divine beings of the second order like the Aśvins, or that the moon played a far less prominent role. He argues that a myth makes room for another, disappearing itself,[28] or continues to live among other new myths which explain the natural phenomena differently. "The twins were no longer regarded as the sun god or the moon god; they were displaced by new types; but though robbed of their original significance, they continued to live in the folk-tradition. Therefore an attempt was made to assign them a place in the new pantheon and to determine their position in relation to the other gods. There were again different answers to these problems. Some look for the twins in the sky and point to the constellation of the Dioscuri, others look for them in the ocean"[29] etc. There is no doubt that this interpretation of Miller and Ludwig overcomes all the difficulties. There are several factors which speak in its favour: the close connection between the Aśvins and Uṣas, who is otherwise closely connected with the sun and the moon (p. 10 above); their threefold chariot or chariot-seat; their designation as *divó napā́tā* and as *divyā́ sūparṇā́*; their occasional separation in *ihéha jātā́* and *nā́nā jā́tau*[30] and yet the possibility of joining them in a dual form as in Agnīṣomau, Sūryacandramasau and Mitra-Varuṇa; furthermore, the number of hymns dedicated to them, i.e. 360, and their association with the passage of the year. The fact that the Aśvins do not enjoy a great importance in the Soma sacrifice and that they are distinguished everywhere clearly from Mitra-Varuṇa, Āditya and Sūrya could be explained by the fact that it was necessary to distribute the gods of the different tribes with reference to the Soma sacrifice, as far as possible, according to the tradition and to classify them with a certain amount of economy. As in the case of Mitra-Varuṇa etc., this must have been the tradition of one or several tribes and was incorporated into the collection of hymns and into the ritual. But the Vedic passages do not support the equation suggested by Miller and Ludwig just as they do not support the "Gemini" theory. The descent of the Aśvins from the sky and their humanization had advanced so far already that we cannot be certain of any interpretation. It is also risky to ask in very general terms, as Miller does, which of the natural phenomena are most likely to inspire the image of twin gods and which could lead to the creation of two bright youthful brothers and riders. The answer cannot but be subjective. Miller is right when he says: "In nature there is and was no other dual luminous phenomenon except the sun and the moon," but others could answer differently. Miller's explanation does not take into account the fact that the origin and the evolution of the Dioscuri myth might have been influenced by factors that are unknown to us. His view is contradicted also by the transformation into a constellation that takes place in the east as well as in the west in a remarkably parallel fashion. Although Miller's explanation would be objectively most appropriate and is intrinsically not so improbable as the theory of "the morning star and the evening star" or that of "the heroes," it is not fully convincing either.[31]

As far as the material is concerned, I cannot add anything substantial to the picture my predecessors have drawn of the Aśvins; the ritual also gives less information than on other gods. First of all, there is no doubt that the Aśvins received a share in the Soma drink also; this goes back to the time of the ṚV. We have the remnants of old litanies in individual hymns which belong to the Prātaranuvāka, e.g., I.22[32] and 92, and which praise the Aśvins. Similarly, there are other hymns which speak of the Soma offered to the Aśvins;[33] this is called *tiróahnya*[34] in I. 47.1; III. 58.7. They drink in the morning, at noon, and in the evening; their chariot is invoked in the morning and at night, and the glory of their deeds is proclaimed during the Savanas. In an Atri hymn, V. 77.1, they are assigned the place "before the miserly vulture," and this arrangement thus corresponds perhaps to that of the later ritual which enjoins that the Aśvin graha should be offered before the graha for Śaṇḍamarkau (see below). Besides the Soma drink, they receive gharma,[35] but preferably honey and surā as I shall show later.[36] I have no doubt that here we see the mutual impact of different forms of cult. According to the Brāhmaṇas, originally the Aśvins were even excluded from the sacrifice since they were considered impure.[37] If we make a close scrutiny of the maṇḍalas, as I have done repeatedly, with reference to the differences in cult still noticeable there, it would prove to be fruitful in the case of the Aśvins also. I shall restrict myself to the statement that book VI differs even with reference to the Aśvins from the others, particularly from books V and VII. Besides the two hymns addressed to them (VI.62 Aśvinau, 63 Nāsatyau), book VI refers to the Aśvins only once in a Viśvedevāḥ hymn (49.5).[38] Compared with this, book V has six Aśvin hymns (apart from the solitary passages) and book VII has eight Aśvin hymns (apart from the solitary passages which are not infrequent). This is a clear indication that the Aśvins were much more favoured by the Atris and the Vasiṣṭhas than by the Gṛtsamadas and the Bharadvājas and that in this point also the special family traditions might have been preserved. Later we shall see that the Vasiṣṭhas had their settlements in the interior of India, on the banks of the Sarasvatī. The data of book VII indicate that the Soma cult did not enjoy as high a prestige among the Vasiṣṭhas as among the other families. On the banks of the Sarasvatī, where the two *ándhas*' grew, the eastern Surāpāṇas must have come into contact with the Somapās who were moving forward from the north-west, and must have spread the Aśvin cult among these Somapās. When we recall the difference in the Aśvin cult between maṇḍala VI and maṇḍala VII, the different treatment of names like Paṇi, Śambara, Divodāsa, Dāsa, the almost complete disappearance of the Vṛtra saga and the fading out of the Indra cult in maṇḍala VII, we see clearly the outlines of cultural differences emerging out of what were once tribal differences.

When we now turn our attention to the position of the Aśvins in the actual ritual, we must mention, besides the invocation to them in the Prātaranuvāka (see pp. 22,38 above), their participation in the Dvidevatyagrahas, one of which belongs to them, as well as the accompanying Āśvinatṛca (of the Pra-ugaśastra) which prepares the "eye," as the Maitrāvaruṇatṛca prepares the "ear" (ABr III. 2.7). A greater importance than here is given to them in the Atirātra (and accordingly in the Aptoryāma based on the Atirātra), where a Stotra is sung in their honour and a Śastra that follows immediately is constructed in the form of one thousand Bṛhatī verses from the Prātaranuvāka with specific variations. The Hotṛ must recite it "in the position of a soaring bird" (p. 18, n. 9 above) — a clear indication, I think, that the ritual preserves the naturalistic character of the Aśvins. Since the ceremony is called *atirātrá*, the Aśvins receive here a cup of *tiróahnya sóma*; Puronuvākyā as well as Praiṣa repeat this word which characterizes the Soma of this ceremony. Besides their cup of Soma, the Aśvins receive one more Puroḍāśa in the Atirātra.[39] But in the ṚV it is honey in particular that is prescribed to them.[40] Of other offerings, I know only of the "red he-goat" *loho 'jaḥ* (ŚŚSXV. 15.2; KŚS XIX. 3.2) which is offered to them during the Sautrāmaṇī and which is used in the same context during the sacrifice for Indra Sutrāman (ŚŚS XIV. 13.1).[41] Furthermore, among the occasional offerings, mention must be made of a cow which should be one of twins if one desires prosperity (TS. II. 1.9.4), and which should be grey coloured with a white spot on the forehead[42] if an outcaste brahmin wishes to drink Soma (TS II. 1.10.1).[43] The association of the Aśvins with an outcaste brahmin is again characteristic; the Brāhmaṇa states explicitly as justification that earlier the Aśvins drank no Soma, and only later got a share in it. This by no means insignificant legend and many other circumstances (see below) indicate that they were gods of the lower, i.e., of the non-Brahmanical, strata of peoples. Moreover, we should mention that bricks are laid in their name in the Agniciti also. To sum up, besides the Prātaranuvāka of the Atirātra and the "Bṛhatīsahasra" that is recited there, the ritual does not offer much that could lead to a clear comprehension of the Aśvins. The ritual helps us to refute the fanciful notions of the Aitihāsikas that the Aśvins were once "beneficent kings," but it does not help us any more to recognize their real significance. Their true nature has faded out in the Indian cult also just as it had happened in the Vedic hymns.

Chapter Three

AGNI

The customs of the ancestors are kept alive in the cult. Indra is invoked to come and drink the Soma just as he drank it from Śāryāta; Atri is praised for his method of pressing the drink; likewise the Vedic clans kindle the fire of their altars according to the method of their ancestors. In III.17.1 a Viśvāmitra refers to *prathamá dhárma-s* as the precedent; a Kaṇva implores Agni not to neglect the friendship inherited from the ancestors. Or Praṣkaṇva wishes that Agni may listen to his call *priyamedhavát, atrivát, virūpavát, aṅgirasvát* (I.45.3); mention is made of an Agni of Divodāsa, of Vadhryaśva, of the Bharatas and of the Kauśikas. In I.31.17 we find the expressions *manuṣvát, aṅgirasvát, yayātivát*, and in VIII.43.13 *bhṛguvát, manuṣvát, aṅgirasvát*. The case is the same in the ritual as in the ṚV. Even in the simplest Śrauta ceremony the sacrificer associates himself with his ancestors with whom he is united through the common cult; the Hotṛpravara reads "may god Agni, the divine Hotṛ, abounding in knowledge and prudent, honour the gods as he did during the sacrifice of Manu, of Bharata, of NN, of the son of NN, just as he did during the sacrifice of Brahman, and lead the gods to the sacrifice." In the place of NN specific names are mentioned.[1] We see that before the names of the actual ancestors, Manu and Bharata are mentioned here as the mythical progenitors and likewise also during the first pravara, where the Hotṛ mentions the family names only after the invocation *agne mahāṅ asi brāhmaṇa bhārata* and before *deveddha manviddha*. However, Agni is not invoked *atrivát, bhṛguvát* or *aṅgirasvát* as in the ṚV, but only *manuṣvát* and *bharatavát*. At this place the ritual preserved only the names of Manu and Bharata instead of the multiplicity of earlier times.

The fire cult has maintained its position among the Hindus up to the present day. A basically uninterrupted tradition joins the oldest Vedic clans with the hereditary Agnihotrins among the "Pañca, Drāvira, or Dakṣiṇi Brāhmans" in present day India, about whom we find more detailed information in the writings of

Crooke.[2] Custom and law have surrounded the preservation of the cult with rules of all kinds. An *utsṛṣṭāgni*, i.e., one who gave up the fire cult, should not be invited to the feast in honour of the dead (GDS XV.16), and certain demands are made on him who has once installed the fires (cf. Manu III. 282; IV.27 ff.).

Like the divine drink, the fire is also a gift from heaven. Immortal himself, Agni has made his abode among the human beings and dwells among them as a guest. Just as in the Soma hymns the poets speak at times about the heavenly drink and at other times about the earthly drink, and just as their thoughts oscillate between the moon and his representative, the plant, so the fire burning in the sacrificial altars is considered an image of the heavenly fire in many verses, and the inner relationship between the two finds its expression in the hymns. Oldenberg is right when he says that, besides the regular maintenance and service that are anyway befitting the sacred fire, tending the fire and making offerings to it "are at the same time a magic directed towards the sun at least in older times. By kindling the fire one caused or promoted the sunrise."[3] It is also correct to say that Agni had "as good as no share, certainly none at the beginning" in the Soma sacrifice.[4]

Comprehending the nature of the Vedic fire god appears very simple, but a close study shows that it is one of the most difficult problems of Vedic mythology. Our sources do not, by any means, project the same picture everywhere. From the oldest parts of the ṚV to the mysticism of the Brāhmaṇa period with its fondness for fanciful interpretations various ages and attitudes have had their impact on this picture of Agni and left their confusing traces on it. There are two problems in particular the solution of which raises difficulties. Agni, it is said, had run away and hidden himself in water; his birth out of water is often recalled. Which Agni is meant by this? The majority of the Vedic scholars adheres to the view, prevalent since the beginning of the study of mythology, that the Agni born out of the waters is the lightning. This view is supported by the explanations of Indian commentaries, which occasionally see the lightning as a form of Agni.

Of course, Indians knew, as we do, that lightning was a form of fire. But those statements of the scholiasts do not prove that Agni in the form of lightning was really worshipped as a god, because not all manifestations of Agni — or of any other natural phenomenon — have been found suitable to be the objects of worship.

The gods kindle Agni as their sacrificial fire; their sacrificial fire is not the lightning, but the sun as can be seen in some passages without any ambiguity. When Agni flees from them, it is not the lightning, but the sun that disappears and hides behind the waters of the rainy season in the tropical climate at the time of the summer solstice. When, with the beginning of the Dakṣiṇāyana, the period of the gods comes to an end and that of the Manes begins, the fire "runs away" from them and hides "in the waters" or, according to the concept of the pre-Vedic period, dwells "in darkness."

But "Agni in the waters" is not always the sun god. We should not expect any logical consistency in mythology, whose garment is woven out of diverse kinds of threads. When ṚV X.45 states that the three places of origin of Agni are "in heaven," "in the waters" and among "us," this threefold division leads to a completely different point of view which clearly differentiates between the heaven and the "waters." The only positive point of reference for the explanation of these three places is supplied by the three fires of the sacrificial place; this threefold division is an ancient one, originating from the gods. The Āhavanīya in the east represents the heaven and the Gārhapatya the earth. The third of the old triad, the Dakṣiṇa fire, is assigned to the Manes and to the atmosphere.

Which of these fires can be considered typical of the atmosphere? All the doubts concerning this question and the apparent confusion caused by many statements are removed by the Śulva Sūtras, in the rules of which we may find the old traditions, because the Śulva Sūtras do not deal with interpretations, but with practical arrangements only. One of the rules enjoins that the hearth of the Dakṣiṇa fire should be constructed in the form of a half-moon. Here it is easy to recognize the old concept that the moon is the light of the Manes and to understand the use of this fire for magical purposes, for which the moon in his waning phase has always been a welcome ally. According to another text, the hearth of the southern fire has the form of a winnowing basket, which, as will be shown later, is the symbol of the wind. Thus we come to the second triad, "sun, vāyu,

Agni," which has an equal place in the tradition as the "sun, moon, Agni." This shows that two basically different concepts merged in the interpretation of the southern fire. One of these is based on the connection between the Manes and the moon, which was current in the later period also, while the second demonstrates the relation between the wind and the soul-cult in the ritual. This relation, though very ancient and certainly pre-Vedic, had receded into the background in the Veda. Both these concepts still continued in the thought patterns of the Brāhmaṇas, and by their merging contributed considerably to the fact that the confusion and ambiguity in the statements of the Yājñikas in the Brāhmaṇas appear greater than they are in reality. When reference is made to the threefold birth of Agni — in the heaven, on the earth, and in the "waters" — there should not be any doubt that the last-mentioned birth-place of Agni can only be the atmosphere and that Agni himself can only be the moon or the wind but not the lightning.

All scholars agree that the ṚV is familiar with the nature of the three hearths of the later ritual, but not with their names, except Gārhapatya. I have pointed elsewhere that the terminology of the ṚV was not always the same as that of the later period and that there was a difference between the two periods in the technical expressions as in other things. We may, therefore, ask whether in the place of Āhavanīya and Dakṣiṇa the ṚV uses other names which were replaced later, for reasons unknown to us, by the names current in the ritual. I think we can trace the older designations for the two in the ṚV, or at least show that they are probable; for it is evident from the ritual that Narāśaṅsa was once the name of the fire of the Manes and that Vaiśvānara was not only the name of the sun, but the name of the Āhavanīya also, which represents the sun. My view was opposed from different sides, among others by L. v. Schroeder,[5] who denies any connection between the three sacrificial fires and the threefold birth of Agni because, as he says, the birth of the lightning-fire, which he identifies with the third Agni, cannot be equated with the Dakṣiṇa, which suggests the moon or the wind. I do not deny the primitive view that the fire escapes into the water and hides there as an animal, or as a bird, or as a fish and so on, but I am basically opposed to the application of this view to the ṚV. When the gods seek Agni in the waters, it is not the lightning that they find there, but Agni Vaiśvānara, who is not the same as the lightning-fire. The lightning is only a weapon or an instrument and does not enjoy the same position as the three fires.[6] Macdonell[7] refers to the form of the Dakṣiṇa hearth which "must have been intended to represent the shape of the air as an arch, and not to symbolize the moon." Supposing that this is true, and that the shape of a semicircle or of a bow is given to the atmosphere,[8] whom should the fire that burns there represent ? Certainly one that corresponds to the atmosphere. We know that the hearth can have the form of a winnowing basket, which would correspond to Vāyu, to whom some ascribe the form of fire. Furthermore, Macdonell does not explain why the Manes receive food there and why magic is performed there. He seems to think of "Agni in the aerial waters," i.e. the lightning. I do not understand how the lightning could occupy the place of the Dakṣiṇa contrary to the very significance of the Dakṣiṇa. Besides the wind, only the moon can be regarded as its presiding deity. Considering how far-removed the Indian commentators were from the Vedic period, it is not surprising that they explain "Agni in the waters" as the lightning.

The Vedic poets were constantly striving to attribute new facets to the monotonous image of the blazing sacrificial fire. The narrower the range of ideas of the primitive people, the greater was often their ability to express subtle grammatical relationships and fine shades of views in language. Similarly, the singers of the Vedic hymns knew how to clothe the monotonous basic idea of the blazing sacrificial fire in manifold images. The soaring flames are compared with swift (birds) which fly upwards from a branch (V.1.1), with horses (VI.6.4; VIII. 43.16; X. 8.6; 79,7), chariots (X. 142.5), charioteers (X. 91.7), bulls (VI. 5.4), women (I. 140.4-8),[9] limbs (I. 141.8; III. 1.5), waves (I. 58.4; VI. 64.1). Or the flame is his tongue (VI. 6.5; 16.2); it resembles a knife (VI. 3.4; VIII. 19.23) or a missile of a warrior (VI. 6.5; VII. 3.4) and so on. He consumes wood like an animal grazing in the pasture (V. 9.4; VI. 2.9). When he is let free among twigs and wood, he fills his mouth with the food (X. 91.5); at the time of his birth he consumes his two mothers (X. 79.4). The laddle is his mouth (I. 12.6); full of oblations and butter, the laddle approaches him like a young woman — an image of the housewife who performs the Homa in the morning and in the evening (VII. 1.6). Emphasis is laid on Agni's "black path" and his "black rim of the wheel" and they are contrasted with his bright flame.[10] He awakens the songs — VII. 10.1 : *dhíyo hinvānā́ uṣatī́r ajīgaḥ*; VII. 9.4 : *práti gā́vaḥ*[11] *samidhānáṃ budhanta.* Just as the cows come to the shed for their calves, hymns come to him (VIII. 43.17); they follow him like horses (VII. 5.5), cover him like a garment (I.140.1). For him the thoughts drip down (*matáyaḥ pavante*) like dear Soma (VI. 8.1) or like clarified butter (VI. 10.2). Everywhere — in these examples and in the many collected by Bergaigne and Macdonell — we encounter expressions of a sensual and realistic mind, which is not at all looking for bodiless concepts. Just as primitive people offer their crude worship to the real flame, which appears to them agile, howling and rapacious like a live beast,[12] the Veda still shows a certain bluntness of expression which is not merely a relic of past times, but is the direct reflection of its religious thinking. Although the ṚV is not, as was supposed earlier, the product of poetic herdsmen or farmers, it is rooted in primitive conditions. The poets and singers, who undoubtedly used specific traditional art-forms and who might have been trained for their profession, stood above, but not outside the people. The view which regards the Vedic hymns in their entirety as the product of a considerably learned or sophisticated mind and which now appears to be replacing the earlier view is equally misleading as the earlier one; it only goes to the other extreme. Those who look for parallels in the songs of other tribes, like Brinton's *Ṛgveda Americanus* or other samples of religious poetry collected occasionally by ethnographers, will not fail to notice a certain amount of similarity. For instance, the Mangolian marriage song quoted by Bastian shows ideas related to the Vedic concepts.[13]

The manifestations of Agni are many; he lives not only in the sun, in the moon and in the fire of the hearth; he dwells also in all that shines and lives, in men as in animals, trees, waters and even in stones.[14] As fire-brand he burns the fortresses of the enemy,[15] as magical fire he destroys the demons and annihilates the army of the enemy.[16] The forest fire is his element; more than one passage describes how he runs amok over the earth, scorching and consuming.[17] Forest fire can be caused by a stroke of lightning, or in a tropical country by self-ignition,[18] or by human agency, be it that one wishes to make the land arable as we know from the well-known passage of the *Śatapatha Brāhmaṇa*, or that one wishes to drive out the enemies from all the hiding places and to destroy their strongholds.[19]

Among these different manifestations of the fire, we must make a distinction between those which were worshipped and those which did not find a special position in the cult or found it only occasionally. The devastating forest fire is the opposite of the tame domestic or sacrificial fire. The courtesans and others who did not lead virtuous lives are not burnt in the sacred fire, but in the forest fire.[20] The forest fire has its use in the Śrauta ritual also, but it is not invoked anywhere particularly. If one has behaved during a sacrifice "as though mixed" (i.e., partly good, partly bad), then, in order to undo it, he should sacrifice saktus with his own hand in a forest fire (*pradāvya*).[21] Here this fire is represented by the sacrificial straw set aflame on the Vedi[22] — an easily recognizable symbolism of *agnír ha dāti rómā pṛthivyā́ḥ*, the Vedi representing the earth. Other kinds of fire — some friendly to human beings and some hostile — are enumerated in PGS II. 6.10 with partly corrupted names (*gohya*, *upagohya*, *mayūkha* etc.). Whenever the sacrificial fires get mixed up with each other, or with an ordinary fire, or with a forest fire, or with a cremation fire, or when a lightning strikes them, offerings should be made respectively to Agni *vīti*, *vivici*, *saṃvarga*, *śuci* and *apsumat*;[23] at other occasions offerings are made to Agni *agnimat*, *pathikṛt*. TS II. 2.2 ff. enumerates Agni *pathikṛt*, *vratapati*, *rakṣohan*, *rudravat*, *surabhimat*, *kṣāmavat*, *kāma*, *yaviṣṭha*, *āyuṣmat*, *jātavedas*, *rukmat*, *tejasvat*, *sāhantya*, *annavat*, *annāda*, *annapati*, *pavamāna*, *pāvaka*, *śuci*, *putravat*, *rasavat*, *vasumat*, *vājasṛt*, *agnivat*, *jyotiṣmat* (MS II. 1.10 ff.) — almost all of them, as it were, gods of special occasions, who owe their existence to occasional wishes or specific needs and are derived from Agni, but not, to use the terminology of Usener, *Sondergötter* who would have merged together under the common concept of Agni afterwards. They do not even belong to the Vedic concepts, but are products of the later development in the ritual. The verses that serve as Yājyās and Puronuvākyās correspond to their purpose often in a very superficial way only and were obviously not composed for this sacrifice. This can be seen from the two verses — ṚV VIII. 75.11-12 — recited in the Saṃvarga sacrifice, in which no connection can be found either to the forest fire, or to the ordinary fire.[24] In our study we can, therefore, ignore these more or less ephemeral forms of the fire god in order to concentrate on those manifestations only which became objects of regular worship and which, as we may expect, give expression to the three most important forms of Agni in the ritual. In order to make our study comprehensive, we shall begin with a description of the production of the fire and related matters, although my predecessors have discussed all the important aspects.

A. THE PRODUCTION OF THE FIRE

1. The Two Araṇis

a. IN THE RITUAL

The method of lighting the fire differed much from people to people.[25] Of the five known methods[26] the ritual of the Sūtras is familiar with that of the fire-drill only. These manuals do not give any exact information about the nature of the implements for producing fire through friction, except to say that the Aśvattha out of which the araṇis are made should have grown on a Śamī tree.[27] For other details we must turn to the Pariśiṣṭas,[28] in which, we may rightly assume, old tradition is continued. The apparatus described in the Pariśiṣṭas is no more the simple "stick-and-groove" of Tylor, but the more complex "fire-drill," which can be called "the two araṇis" only in name since it is a small machine in reality.[29] However, the mantras which accompany the ceremony do not anticipate this somewhat complicated apparatus, but only the simple application of two sticks of wood; the two are the mystic womb out of which the fire is born and into which it is made to return symbolically on certain occasions.

As almost everywhere in the Indian ritual so also in the Agnyādheya there is no longer a larger community which congregates around a religious centre, but the festive act is carried out in each house individually. The central point of this act is the leaping up of the spark, for which the householder rewards the priest with a gift. The so-called Brāhmaudānika-fire is lit[30] and is maintained till the morning of the day on which the new fire is to be made. ĀpŚS V. 8.1 ff. says on this : "The sacrificer begins his vow and restrains his speech with the formula: 'I proceed from falsehood to truth, from the human to the divine. I hold back the divine voice.' 2 : During this night he is kept awake with the music of lute and flute. 3 : Or he remains neither awake nor silent. 4 : Sitting, he maintains the fire with chips of wood during this night and says: 'Maintaining the fire with chips, may I win both the worlds. Successful in both the worlds, I overcome death.'[31] 5 : In it he warms up the two araṇis at the break of day with the two mantras : (i) 'O Jātavedas, pour here the semen of the world, which will be born out of the heat; creating the fire from the Aśvattha that has grown on a Śamī, the fire which carries forth the sacrificial offerings and which creates joy' and (ii) 'this is your right womb born out of which you shine' etc.[32] 6 : The sacrificer consecrates (*abhi mantray*) the araṇis with the words : 'Agni wards off the Rakṣas', the brightly shining, the immortal, the pure, the purifying one, he that is worthy of invocation' and while they are offered to him, he looks at them with the formula:[33] 'you great mistresses at the seat of the right one, turn towards the place of riches; carrying the fruit in you, you beget Jātavedas, the one who must be begotten (*janyam*), the leader of the sacrifices.' 8 : The Yajamāna receives the araṇis saying : 'come into my ten fingers,[34] [and you] O Agni, [come] with righteousness, life and esteem so that I, living long, may perform the new moon and the full moon sacrifices each coming year,' and hereupon he recites the formula: 'you are ready to bear offspring; fire is your semen; you bear the embryo; in this condition I take you. It is true that you carry a man [in your womb] and that you will bring forth a man. Through me you will procreate in the morning. Having procreated, you will procreate me with progeny, cattle, theological dignity in the celestial world.' "

Like here the mystic significance of the fire-sticks is seen in the custom of the Samāropaṇa and Upāvarohaṇa also, i.e., when the fire is made to enter or leave the araṇis symbolically, this being the duty of the sacrificer at various occasions.[35] For instance, when he gives up his place of residence or goes on a journey for at least ten days, he either takes the fires with him on a cart[36] or makes the fires withdraw into himself or into the araṇis. ŚSS II. 17.1 ff. states thus : 1. "When he makes the fires withdraw into himself, he warms his hands at the Gārhapatya and touches the prāṇas (nose, mouth etc.) with the formula: 'come, enter my prāṇas.' 2: Each once with the mantra and twice silently. 3: Or he warms the araṇis with the verse, 'this is your womb' (ṚV III. 29.10). 4: Each once with the mantra and twice silently. 5: Similarly [he takes the fire] out of the Āhavanīya. 6: Out of a continuously maintained [Āhavanīya], however, into another [fire-drill].[37] 7 : The production of fire through friction takes place before sunset [and sunrise]. 8 : The production of fire through friction takes place after he has again caused the fire (i.e., his breath out of his nose) to flow (*upāvarohya*) into the two araṇis out of himself with the formula, 'enter there, O Jātavedas.' 9: Or into an ordinary fire [instead of drilling the fire anew]."[38]

b. IN THE ṚGVEDA

As in the ritual so also in the Vedic hymns the kindling of the flame is considered a solemn act. But, with the Sūtras themselves paying so little attention to the external form of the fire-sticks, there is less reason to expect an exact description in the hymns of the ṚV; these hint at the procedure in general terms only, but take pleasure in describing it in manifold images, just as in the case of the pressing of Soma. Through the use of the different tenses of the verb — at first imperative or the present and then the aorist — individual hymns indicate that they were meant to accompany the entire procedure. Thus in III. 29.5: *mánthatā naraḥ*; 12: *sunirmáthā nírmathitaḥ*; 13: *ájījanan*,[39] *jan*, *math* and *nirmath* are the terms used besides the general *idh* and *sam-idh*. The hand and the araṇis are mentioned in VII. 1.1 : *agníṃ náro dī́dhitibhir aráṇyor hástacyutī janayanta.* I. 68.2 speaks of the dry wood (*śúṣka*) out of which Agni is born; in I. 127.4 the araṇis are called *téjiṣṭha*; one rubs him with the "arms," according to III. 29.6 : *yádi mánthanti bāhúbhiḥ.* Human beings have taken hold of the immortal one.[40] Or like daring thieves the arms bind Agni with ten ropes (fingers).[41] In other passages the fingers are called "ten sisters" or "ten maidens"[42] just as in the Soma cult. Though not impregnated (*ápravītā*), the araṇi begets the fruit;[43] a barren woman, she gives birth as soon as she is "driven;"[44] on the other hand she is called "one who gives birth easily," *susū́r mātā.*[45] Or the production of the fire is considered an act of procreation,[46] a marriage procession in which the wife leads the husband.[47] But Agni as a god was born before the parents, the fire-sticks; he guards their birth.[48] Like here the fire-sticks are called "the parents" elsewhere also, but in each individual case one should judge carefully whether the "parents" denote the fire-sticks or heaven and earth;[49] the latter are likewise his parents. In the later literature the araṇis are called Purūravas and Urvaśī.[50]

In the ṚV there is no mention of the rope which the ritual employs in twirling the fire-sticks. The only passage that might refer to this is ṚV IV. 1.9 :

sá cetayan mánuṣo yajñábandhuḥ
prá táṃ mahyá̄ raśanáyā nayanti /

Here *raśanā* might, of course, refer to a real rope[51] (but not to the fingers as the plural does in X. 4.6), and might mean a rope with which the upper araṇi is twirled to and fro.[52]

Often there is a mention of the "two mothers" of Agni. He himself is called *dvimātṛ*.[53] The closest and most natural explanation is the connection of these two mothers with his twofold birth in heaven and on earth[54] since he is *dvijanman*.[55] But the Vedic poets are fond of representing the same thing in different images and, at the same time, of seeing different things in the same image. Thus Uṣāsānaktā who "suckle the infant,"[56] though not expressly called his mothers, are to be understood as such, and in view of the inclination of the poets towards paradoxical comparisons it is not surprising that in some passages his "two mothers" also mean fire-sticks.[57]

2. Other Methods of Producing the Fire

The ritual recognizes no other method of producing the fire than the one described above. Of course, the flint-stone was known; Vedic passages that speak of Agni "*aśmani*" and "*ádrau*" do not leave us in doubt about this; but there is nothing to indicate whether this was used for common or sacred purposes.[58] On the other hand, the lotus is associated with the sacred fire, first of all in the well-known verse of the ṚV, recited in the ritual of the piling up of the altar, according to which the Atharvan churns the fire out of the *puṣkara*.[59] Even otherwise a lotus leaf is mentioned in the ritual. ĀpŚS XVI. 3.3 states : "With the verse, 'you are the back of the waters,'[60] he fetches a lotus leaf, folds it[61] with the same verse, and spreads a black skin to the north of the pit, turning its neck towards the east and the hair upwards with the two verses, 'you two are a protection, an armour'; upon this he spreads the lotus leaf. 4 : Having recited over the mud pit the formula 'earthly are you, all-preserving,' he sprinkles [clay] on the skin and the lotus leaf with the four or three verses 'you (accusative), O Agni out of the *puṣkara*.'" The Brāhmaṇa (TS V. 1.4.2) comments on this as follows: "With the verse 'you are the back of the waters' he fetches a lotus leaf. The lotus leaf is the back (surface) of the water ... The lotus leaf is Agni's womb. He prepares Agni who is equipped with his womb."[62] And V.1.4.3: "Agni fled from the gods; Atharvan was on the look out for him; ... He found him leaning against a lotus leaf."[63] Furthermore, a lotus leaf is used in the piling up of the altar itself.[64] In the centre of the Citi a bundle of darbha is buried (ĀpŚS XVI. 17.7) and later a white horse is made to place its right forefoot upon it (ibid. 22.1).[65] Upon the imprint of the foot the lotus leaf that has been spread out is placed with the verses used before, "you are the back of the waters," and upon the leaf the golden disk is placed, its knobs pointing upwards, upon which the "golden man" comes to rest. Elsewhere (TBr I. 6.2.1) it is said that the Aṅgiras', when they went to heaven, placed *dīkṣā* and *tapas* in water and from both a *puṇḍarīka* arose.[66] Among the different inflammable materials made ready during the Ādheya there is also a lotus leaf. However, all these passages cannot prove that a lotus leaf was used for producing the fire; what is more, it appears that the lotus leaf was considered only a symbol of the water-womb out of which Agni is born; but the above-mentioned verse, ṚV VI. 16.13 (see p. 58, n. 58 above), gives such a positive evidence that we cannot completely rule out this possibility.[67]

Besides the use of the fire-drill, there is also the custom of fetching the fire from another hearth.[68] Not only the Gṛhya Sūtras, but the Śrauta Sūtras also know this custom of transplanting the flame from one hearth to the other, and it was probably the hope of a good omen that led to the injunction to choose the house of a pious or rich Aryan for taking out the fire.[69] ĀpŚS V. 14.1 ff. enjoins thus: "For one who desires prosperity he should fetch the fire from the house of a Brāhmaṇa or a Rājanya or a Vaiśya or a Śūdra[70] who is rich like an Asura, and install it. 2 : However, he should not eat in the house of that person from then on. 3: From a pan one who desires food; from the top of a burning tree one who desires theological reputation."

A third and unusual form is to let the fire arise through self-ignition in the vessel made during the Agniciti. The Agniciti is a cosmogony built in stone, which demonstrates even better than the texts how the world reflected itself in the eyes of that period.[71] *cayanena bhūmyutpattiprakāraṃ prapañcayate*, says the commentary on TS V. 227. Here Agni is the symbol of the celestial fire, the sun.[72] The Ukhā is brought to the Āhavanīya fire, and the flame arising in it by itself, called *svayaṃbhū*,[73] serves "a man of rank who desires welfare" (*bhūtikāma gataśrī*) as that fire which is to be carried for a year and then to be placed on the Uttaravedī of the altar; yet even here the other forms of producing the fire are not ruled out. A close relationship between this Agniciti and the Agnyādheya seems to be indicated by the fact that in the case of the Agniciti the fire in the vessel is to be carried for a year by the consecrated person,[74] and that similarly the Brāhmaudānika fire kindled before the Agnyādheya is to be maintained for a year;[75] in both cases rules for extenuating circumstances have been added.

B. THE TIME OF INSTALLING THE FIRE[76]

It is prescribed exactly when to install the fire according to the nakṣatra and the seasons. The individual statements of our texts are elaborated in the Brāhmaṇas with diverse tales. Not all of these are mere products of scholastic pedantry, but seem to be based on old legends.[77] But we need not discuss them here. ĀpŚS V. 3.3 ff. enjoins as follows: "A brahmin should install [the fire] in the Kṛttikāḥ; then he becomes the first theologian. 4 : In this case the fire endangers his house. If one installs the fire in Rohiṇī, he climbs all the heights (*rohas*). 6 : In Mṛgaśīrṣa one who desires theological reputation or sacrifice. 7: In Punarvasū one who has lived previously in happy circumstances and now got into evil times. 8: In Pūrve Phalgunī one who wishes, 'may my subordinates be charitable.' 9: In Uttare [Phalgunī] one who wishes to be respected (rich) and to become a lord."

These are followed by other statements that were probably

taken from old and, in particular, astrological sources. These need not detain us here any further. Furthermore, the Sūtras differentiated the three seasons according to caste, assigning spring to the Brāhmaṇa, summer to the Kṣatriya, autumn or winter to the Vaiśya, the rainy season to the "chariot-maker;"[78] but all castes can choose the Śiśira. It is quite likely that we have before us different beginnings for the year in the different periods assigned to each caste and that for each member of the class concerned the installation of the fire took place at the beginning of his year.

The sacrificer receives the araṇis with the words *jyog jīvanta uttarāmuttarāṃ samāṃ darśam ... yaja* (ĀpŚS V. 8.8) (See p. 56 above). The concept of the new fire that is to be produced year after year does not find expression, as far as I can see, in our texts, but various factors indicate that this concept was not unknown to ancient India. In this connection the interesting, but hardly noticed, statement of TS I. 5.7.3 is important, according to which the fire "becomes old" after the passage of a year and, in order to be renewed, must be worshipped with the Āgnipāvamānī verses.[79] We find similar instances in Germanic mythology, where the same attitude leads to the production of a new fire. Grimm states that "the fire which had been among the human beings for some time and had been transmitted from hearth to hearth was considered unsuitable for sacred purposes..."[80] Among Indians, where lighting the new fire was pushed into the background by the perpetual maintenance of the fire, the place of the former was taken by a symbolical renewal through the worship of the fire with twelve Vedic verses, the number of which is interpreted by the *Taittirīya Saṃhitā* in the sense of seasons and months.[81]

Perhaps no special significance ought to be attached to the fact that during the Agniṣṭoma, the spring sacrifice that occurs every year, a new fire is produced by friction and the new Āhavanīya is added to the old one,[82] because this process is repeated during other sacrifices like the Cāturmāsyas and Paśus also; but all the more important is the association of the Agnyādheya fire with the sun. A young steed, symbol of Agni or of the sun,[83] must be present at the ceremony and put its right forefoot on the hearth of the Āhavanīya; "out of the hoof of the steed Atharvan received the light at first." According to the

Vājasaneyins, instead of the steed a he-goat can be chosen, which is also a symbol of the fire like the horse.[84] This view is expressed at other contexts also. If an Āhitāgni cannot produce fire through friction and other fire is not within reach, he should place offerings "upon a goat" because the goat belongs to Agni. In the goat-fire the Agnihotra is offered to him.[85] *ajā hy agner ajaniṣṭa garbhāt sā vā apaśyaj janitāram agre*, says TS IV. 2.10. The Sāmavedins know the custom of producing the fire by friction upon the body of the Udgātṛ. The lower araṇi is placed cross-wise upon his right thigh and then as usual it is rubbed with the upper stick.[86] The Udgātṛ is regarded as connected with the sun; TMBr XVIII. 9.8 says: *srag udgātuḥ saurya udgātā* in the context of presenting a golden wreath to the Udgātṛ.[87]

There are still other factors which we can mention here. Thus, the Brahman drives a cart or a wheel three times around in the south of the sacrificial place[88] while the participants of the ceremony move behind the horse towards the Āhavanīyakhara. Furthermore, the number twelve is strikingly emphasized in many rites connected with the Agnyādheya although this number is substituted by a higher or a smaller number by other authorities. All this is very significant since this number twelve probably refers to the twelve nights. For twelve days the sacrificer himself must perform the Agnihotra with constantly burning fires, remain at home and wear new clothes.[89] Twelve is the basic number of the gifts to be given to the priests, which, however, can also be exceeded.[90] Twelve days (but also two or three or fourteen days, or a month, or a ṛtu, or a year) must elapse before the Tanūhavis are offered.[91] In this very context TBr I.1.6.7 speaks of the twelve nights as the image of the year, and further in the same Anuvāka[92] it speaks of Agni "as the beginning of the ṛtus."[93]

Let us now turn to the ṚV. If I have succeeded in establishing that Uṣas represents not merely the dawn of any random day, but the first day of the New Year also, irrespective of the fact whether the New Year commences at the winter solstice or at the vernal equinox, then we may at least anticipate that the Vedic poets and tribes were acquainted with the renewal of the fire at the beginning of the year. But there are still more positive reasons for this assumption. Among these I count the passages which speak of Agni's living in darkness. Of course, the sun wakes to life anew every day, and the glimmering fire is again fanned through the Prāduṣkaraṇa of the Agnihotrins; but this does not suffice to explain the diverse modes of expression concerning Agni's flight, his stay in darkness, his "long" dwelling in the dark and his release. Often I have drawn attention to the antithesis between Devayāna and Pitṛyāṇa, which influenced the Ṛgvedic world and thus permits me to understand these terms not in the special sense of the later period but in the sense of Uttarāyaṇa and Dakṣiṇāyana. With the end of the Devayāna the worship of the gods ceases and the period of the Manes, of the *pitáro devā́śatrāvaḥ* (ṚV VI. 59.1), begins. It is immaterial whether in the ritual the entire Pitṛyāṇa is assigned to the Manes or only a part of this period — perhaps the last months of the year — or whether there were different kinds of measurements current, one in the ṚV and another in the classical ritual, which prescribes the Vājapeya and other sacrifices in autumn. In southern regions the "dark" has less significance than in the north, and the whole attitude may be an inheritance from an earlier home at other latitudes; but one should not doubt the significance which the winter solstice had even during the Vedic period. With this period of Pitṛyāṇa, the period of the year that belongs to the Manes, I connect those statements which speak of Agni's dwelling in the darkness or similar matters. We should consider, e.g., ṚV III. 31.3 ff.; IV. 1.11 ff.; 2.17 ff. and ask if these passages with their allusions to the recovery of the cattle, to the opening of rock-sheds, and to light and darkness, were not based on the production of the new fire on the New Year's Day rather than on the Agnihotra of any random day;[94] X.35 reads — of course not comparable in other respects — like the *Carmen Saeculare* of Horace.

Probably the ṚV also knew the daily sacrifice of the Agnihotra. Therefore, it is difficult to determine in each case whether it is the performance of the Agnihotra or of the new fire to which an allusion is made because the passage of the day resembles the passage of the year in many respects. The Brāhmaṇas see a sun-magic even in the daily Agnihotra when they say that the sun would not rise without the morning offering;[95] but I would like to believe that greater units of time and solstices have had more influence on the first origins of such attitudes than the daily phenomena did.

C. THE MAINTENANCE OF THE FIRE

Here I shall add a few comments on the maintenance of the fire, more for the sake of completeness than with an intention of stating anything new; these comments contain little that has not been stated already by my predecessors. When fire is made by friction, a chip of wood and two blades of darbha grass[96] are placed under the araṇi; these were probably meant to catch the spark, just as in our country also wood-shavings were used with flint and steel up to the beginning of the nineteenth century.[97] According to the *Kātyāyana Paddhati*, the fire thus obtained is placed in a bowl with dry cow-dung and flour.[98] The sacrificer blows into the fresh flame, and when the flame leaps up he draws it in with his breath. To this act, which is of practical use, the accompanying mantras ascribe mystic meaning at the same time.[99] Then the fire is brought to the hearth that was prepared with special care. According to Āpastamba,[100] seven or five or more than seven different materials (saṃbhāras) are required for this: sand, saline soil, soil from a mole-hill, soil from an ant-hill, soil from a pond or lake which does not dry up,[101] soil that was dug up by a boar. Each of these substances, to which pebbles and gold are added, is fetched with mantras referring particularly to its origin and used in the construction of the hearth in the following way. Each substance is divided into two parts. One half is again divided into two, and each of these halves is placed upon the Gārhapatya hearth and the Dakṣiṇa hearth respectively. On the other hand, the other half of the original quantity is divided into three parts and these are brought to the places of the (three) fires in the front.[102] The hearth, thus constructed, is enclosed by stones and, according to some authorities like Āpastamba, is covered with a small sheet of gold.[103] Furthermore, wood of different trees, procured before the Agnyādheya, belongs to the Saṃbhāras. ĀpSS V. 2.4 enumerates *aśvattha, udumbara, parṇa, śamī, vikaṅkata*[104] and also wood from a tree destroyed by lightning — according to Baudhāyana, if such a tree is not available, also wood from a tree destroyed by cold or heat[105] — and a lotus leaf. It should be noted that the wood from a tree destroyed by lightning does not receive any preference over the other kinds of wood. Later, as soon as the fires are distributed on the hearths, three logs each of this wood are placed in each of the fires, or always three in the Āhavanīya only.[106] Of course, we should not expect to find in the ṚV something corresponding to these exact rules. Even if this process was followed in all its minute details at the time of the ṚV, there was no reason for the Vedic poets to describe this process. The hymns make only cursory allusions to solitary phases of the entire process, and such allusions are not many. Thus in some passages of the ṚV which speak of Agni *vātacodita*, or *vātajūto*[107] one could probably recognize the act of fanning the fire by the sacrificer. The kindled one is carried to his place like "a new-born child;"[108] *pra-bhṛ* is the term for the transportation to the hearth,[109] which must be situated on the Vedi according to the ṚV,[110] but contrary to the injunction of the ritual. The hearth is called Agni's womb (*yóni*) and also his house;[111] it longs for him as the wife longs for her husband (IV.3.2). It is called *ghṛtávat* and in VI. 15.16 *ūrṇāvat*, "equipped with wool," to be understood literally, I think, perhaps in the sense of tinder and not in the sense of barhis.[112] It is a good omen if the flame leaps high; it is customary to wish that the flame of the enemy may burn low.[113] One should offer fire-wood in honour of Agni — he is *drvànna* — and one has to strain one's head carrying it.[114] Besides the fire-wood, *óṣadhi* and *ghṛtá* are mentioned as concrete constituents of his worship,[115] and it seems that the verbs *vakṣ* and *vṛdh*[116] are used with *ośadhi* but not with *samidh*; consequently the *óṣadhis* are probably the twigs used for the first consumption of the fire.[117] The many offerings of butter that were made during the sacrifice must have served primarily the practical purpose of making the fire burn quickly. Butter, *ghṛtá* (called *tīvrá*, "piquant" in V. 5.1) and *sarpís* are therefore the favourite foods of Agni, apart from *óṣadhi* and *samidh*. In the ṚV he is called *ghṛtánirṇij*, *ghṛtaśrī́*, *ghṛtasnú*, *sarpírāsuti*[118] etc. The laddle (*sruc* and also *dárvi*) is the instrument for offering butter;[119] *údyatasruc* or *yátasruc* is one who performs this act . Of all the terms of the ṚV related to the cult of Agni, the word *mṛj* deserves our special attention. It is used in different meanings and occurs often in the Ṛgvedic Soma ritual. The "churning, tending" (*mṛj*) of Agni is done either with *ghṛtá* or with hymns.[120] Furthermore, it seems that in solitary instances *mṛj* could also refer to the daily *prāduṣkaraṇa*, the cleansing of the fire from ashes etc.

D. THE THREE FIRES IN THE RITUAL

The Āhitāgni, who builds three fires, is distinguished from the common householder, who lights his fire at the time of his marriage or at other important occasions of his life. Among these Āhitāgnis, the Nityadhṛt stands out, who must maintain the fire all his life. Not everybody can do this. It is the privilege of the dignitaries, i.e., learned brahmins, village chiefs, members of the warrior caste.[121] It seems that some maintain the fire of the household hearth as well,[122] but this is perhaps only a possibility and not an injunction, and nothing of this nature is reported about the still-existing Agnihotrins in India.[123]

All the Sūtras are unanimous in stating that the hearths are to be placed in the east, west and south respectively. The "householder's" fire, situated in the west, though not superior to the others in importance, has a right of priority because the other fires, or at least the Āhavanīya, are taken out of this. The Āhavanīya is lit with a fire-brand of Aśvattha wood, which is ignited in the Gārhapatya and is carried in a ceremonial way to the place determined for the Āhavanīya; our sources are at variance with regard to the other fires, which can include also the Sabhya and the Āvasathya apart from the Dakṣiṇa.[124] According to some texts, they are taken from the Āhavanīya; according to others, from the ordinary fire, or made afresh by friction. According to ĀśvŚS II. 2.2, one can fetch the fire-brand for the southern fire from the Agnihotra of the house of a Vaiśya or of a well-to-do person etc.; according to Śāṅkhāyana, the Āhavanīya and the Dakṣiṇa are taken out of the Gārhapatya and only the Gārhapatya is made by friction.[125] It is obvious that different customs were prevalent, and probably it would not be without interest to enquire further into the origin of these differences.

The order in which these individual fires are to be lit seems to be a subject of discussion in the ritual literature. TBr I.1.4.4-6 states expressly that at first the Gārhapatya must be installed, then the Anvāhāryapacana and then the Āhavanīya, because the Asuras who lit the Āhavanīya first, then the Gārhapatya and then the Anvāhāryapacana lost their luck, and the Devas who lit the Anvāhāryapacana at first did not obtain any progeny. But the purpose and the significance of the three fires interest us more than such points of controversy which, as far as we can judge today, were only of scholastic interest. It is known since long that the ṚV speaks of a threefold origin of the fire; Macdonell was right in stressing the fact that this origin, known to the ṚV already, must have an intrinsic relationship with the three forms of fire at the sacrificial place.[126] We can expect that the significance of these three fires of the ritual will enlighten us about the Ṛgvedic riddle also, i.e., about the significance of the three fires and their very controversial "place of birth" in the ṚV. Later texts, in spite of various occasional differences, show a great unanimity in the interpretation of the three fires, and their statements are corroborated absolutely by the ritual practice. There can be no doubt about the symbolism of the Āhavanīya, which is associated with the celestial world and is seen as the representative of the sun. It receives the sacrificial offerings for the gods. The Gārhapatya, with the exception of a few cases,[127] serves the practical purpose of baking and cooking the sacrificial food etc. The mantras uttered by the sacrificer while adding wood to this fire show clearly that the Gārhapatya is thought of as the fire of the house; the householder says: "may manifold progeny feel happy here, gathering around Agni, the lord of the house."[128] The third fire, the Dakṣiṇāgni situated in the south, belongs to the Manes, who are associated with the south already in the ṚV (X. 15.6; 17.9), and it serves for the oblations to be offered to the Manes;[129] a fire-brand is taken out of the southern fire for warding off the evil spirits during Piṇḍapitṛyajña;[130] in short, all that has to do with the Manes and evil spirits takes place as a rule at this fire or in its vicinity.[131] The arrangement of these three fires — the Āhavanīya higher up and the Dakṣiṇa in the middle — corresponds to the conditions in the Uttarāyaṇa, when the sun describes the highest circle and the moon the lower, the opposite being the case in the Dakṣiṇāyana.

The world is threefold like the fires and each of these three fires is assigned to one of the worlds; the Āhavanīya to the heaven, the Gārhapatya to the earth and the Dakṣiṇāgni to the atmosphere: *etad vai devānām āyatanam yad āhavanīyo 'ntarāgnī paśūnāṃ gārhapatyo manuṣyāṇāṃ*[132] *anvāhāryapacanaḥ pitṝṇām*, TS I. 6.7.1. Just as the heaven is considered the seat of the gods, and the earth the dwelling of the human beings, so is the atmosphere considered the place of the Manes: *divaṃ tṛtīyaṃ devān yajño 'gāt antarikṣaṃ tṛtīyaṃ pitṝn yajño 'gāt pṛthivīṃ tṛtīyaṃ manuṣyān yajño 'gāt*, ABr VII. 5.3. The Dakṣiṇāgni, therefore, is mentioned together with the atmosphere,[133] and further with Vāyu, the ruler of the atmosphere.[134] One might regard this association as the superficial outcome of the oft-mentioned triad of Agni, Vāyu and Sūrya[135] on the one hand, and that of Pṛthivī, Antarikṣa and Dyauḥ on the other, and suspect here also the influence of the fanciful interpretations of the scholiasts, who were fond of joining the ends of different threads. But I am convinced that this association of the fire of the Manes with Vāyu is not merely a fancy of the Yājñikas, but the continuation of an ancient concept, though it is unknown to the Brāhmaṇas: the connection between the dead and the wind. Of course, this concept receded into the background and was replaced by another that was current in the Vedic literature and also in the later period, viz., the concept which connects the moon with the world of the dead. The moon is the eye of the Manes just as the sun is the eye of the gods, or he is their light.[136] But a closer examination of the later literature might bring to light many vestiges of the earlier concept. An influence of this concept might be seen, e.g., in Manu III.189, where it is said that the Manes approach the twice-born who were invited, follow them "like the wind" and when the brahmins sit they sit with them.[137] It appears as though this concept still survives particularly in the above-mentioned connection between Vāyu and the fire of the Manes.[138]

The tradition of the Śulva Sūtras, as is well known, determines the form of the hearths also. While the hearth of the Āhavanīya is to be constructed in the form of a square[139] and that of the Gārhapatya in the form of a circle, two different sets of rules are given for the southern fire in the texts accessible to me; it should have either the form of a *śūrpa*, or that of an *ardhacandra* or *dhanus*. However, the first statement is not from a Sūtra; it occurs only in the modern *Śrautapadārthanirvacana*. But since this work follows Baudhāyana "in all the details"[140] we may assume that it is the view of the ancient Śrotriyas as well;[141] all the more so because the *śūrpa* form is not the usual form of this *khara*. The *śūrpa* is used for winnowing, and during this act which is performed even in the simple iṣṭis, the mantra, "*vāyur vo vivinaktu*" is recited.[142] Mahīdhara explains this as *vāyuḥ śūrpacālanotthaḥ*. The *śūrpa* form, therefore, is meant to represent the wind, thus reflecting the view of those people who connected the fire of the Manes with the concept of the wind as the ruler of the atmosphere and of the dead. We should not easily dismiss the repeated statements of the Brāhmaṇas that Vāyu is "Agni," reference to which will be made later on. As one can see from the *Śatapatha Brāhmaṇa*, Indian scholars disagreed even on the question whether one should worship the wind as fire or not, and thus obviously followed different traditions.[143]

The other tradition prescribes the form of a half-moon to the Dakṣiṇa fire.[144] This does not need any explanation. The old association between the moon and the Manes is well known to the Veda also, and is quite current in later times. According to MBh XIII. 1082 (XIII. 16.44-45), the sun is the gateway to the path which leads to the gods, and the moon is the gateway to the path which leads to the Manes.[145] The half-moon form for the Dakṣiṇa fire has probably had its origin in this idea.[146]

What can we infer from this ? With great unanimity our texts assign the Āhavanīya to the heaven, the Gārhapatya to the earth, and the southern fire to the Manes. Occasionally other views are stated, e.g. that "the son," who in fact performs the cult of the Manes, is equated with the Anvāhāryapacana;[147] but these do not have any special significance. Given the character of our sources, we must not take seriously the occasional fanciful interpretations and the flights of imagination which come and go[148] if we wish to find a clear path at all, and must adhere to the main evidence. So far as I know, a close relationship between even one of the three fires on the one hand and the lightning on the other cannot be found anywhere.[149] If the three fires are identical with the triad of the fires in the ṚV, and if this triad is to express the threefold origin of the fire in the heaven, in the waters and on the earth, then in the same context one cannot speak of the lightning as "Agni in the waters"; at least it is not one of the three forms of fire-worship which have become canonical, viz., the household fire, the sun-fire and the fire of the Manes; for these three represent Agni Gṛhapati, Agni Sūrya and, as the fire of the Manes, Agni Candramas or Agni Vāyu.

The Three Gharmas or Mahimans

We are now in a position to solve a difficulty that arose earlier (see Ch. I, n. 35) from the contradiction between a passage of the TMBr and an explanation by the commentary on TS. The commentary interprets the *trayo gharmāsaḥ* or *mahimānaḥ*, who follow Uṣas, as Agni, Candra and Āditya, whereas TMBr XX.15.2-3 states that Uṣas is followed by the three Gharmas, "Agni, Vāyu, Āditya." Now we can understand that these are not arbitrary arrangements, but two different traditions, one of which sees the moon and the other Vāyu as the second member of the series, i.e., the same traditions which associate the Dakṣiṇāgni with Candra, or with Vāyu respectively.

E. THE THREE FIRES IN THE ṚGVEDA

Like the ritual, the Vedic hymns also suggest that not all the fires are made with the araṇis; some are made from one that is already lit. I.12.6 has *agnínāgníḥ sám idhyate.*[150] He is taken first to the east and then back to the west when he is freed from the womb of the parents.[151] This, according to Sāyaṇa, is an allusion to the making of the Āhavanīya fire and the Gārhapatya fire. Often there is a mention of several fires: Indra-Agni should come *sámiddheṣv agníṣu,* says I.108.4. Particularly the number three is emphasized. "Sit down, O Hotṛ, on the three hearths," II. 36.4.[152] "Men have kindled Agni on the threefold seat."[153] Therefore, he is called *triṣadhasthá* in V. 4.8; VI. 8.7; 12.2 and *tripastyá* in VIII. 39.8. Thus the threefold division of the fire, which is traced back to the gods themselves,[154] is well known to the ṚV.[155] As I have said earlier, there is no reason either to make a distinction between the Vedic triad and that of the ritual from the point of view of their origin and significance, or to take other aspects into consideration for the kindling of the former than those which are prominent in the Śrauta Sūtras. This being so, it is all the more striking that we should not find also names for the individual fires in the ṚV and that only the Gārhapatya should be mentioned there.[156] But we must keep in mind that the names are not necessarily the same in the ṚV as they are in the later ritual and that often a change of terminology took place between the two,[157] a change based on a difference, not only of time, but also of tradition.

1. The Dakṣiṇa Fire in the Ṛgveda

a. NARĀŚAṄSA

The ṚV is primarily concerned with the worship of the gods. With the exception of a small group of hymns to the dead in book X, the ṚV does not speak of the Manes often. This might be due to the fact that the ṚV was compiled for purposes connected with the Devayāna; I use the word "Devayāna," as I already said, in its temporal sense and not in its usual meaning. If I consider Narāśaṅsa an old name for the fire of the Manes[158] and at the same time the designation of a god who is associated with this fire in the same way as Sūrya is connected with the Āhavanīya, then the basis for my view is, of course, not the ṚV, but the later, yet positive, tradition.

This name is of such an antiquity that it reaches into Indo-Iranian pre-history; an evidence for this antiquity is supplied even by an Armenian theophoric name like *Narses*.[159] Because of the antiquity of this phenomenon, the origins of which are lost in pre-history, it is difficult to identify its original meaning; but the evidence of the *Avesta* is of significance, the statements of which, though sparing, still supply what we primarily need, viz., the basic character of the Iranian god. The main passage, Y 17.11, mentions him in the midst of the names of the fire that are enumerated there.[160] This has led the Iranists to the almost unanimous view that he is a deity of the fire. Spiegel, *Eranische Altertumskunde* I. 434; II.45; Harlez, *l'Avesta traduit* I, v.264; Geiger (*Handbuch*, s.v.) "proper name of a fire-spirit, the messenger of Ahura Mazda"; Mills, SBE XXXI, p.258. According to Justi, *Preussische Jahrbücher* 88, p. 66, in Persia Nairyōsaŋha is that fire which is inherited in the royal household. (See also *Iranisches Namensbuch*, s.v.). It is also the view of Gray, ARW III, p. 47ff. etc. Nairyōsaŋha is mentioned here among other fires; the case is the same in the ṚV also. In some of the hymns of the ṚV he has a fixed place between verses which are all addressed to Agni. It follows from this that in these hymns Narāśaṅsa can hardly be regarded as an abstraction of the "hymn," but is to be considered a designation of the fire.[161] The situation would have been different if the verse to Narāśaṅsa had not been followed by any verse addressed to Agni, but stood immediately before the verse to Barhis. But here the verse stands in the midst of the verses addressed to Agni and is fully laden with predicates which otherwise apply to Agni. To this can be added the Āprī verse, AV V. 27.3 :

mádhvā yajñáṃ nakṣati praiṇānó nárāśáṅso agníḥ
sukṛd deváḥ savitá viśvávāraḥ //[162]

and the statement of an ancient exegete, Śākapūṇi, who says expressly about Narāśaṅsa: "*agnir iti*";[163] furthermore, ṚV III. 29.11,[164] which recognizes Narāśaṅsa as a form of Agni; X. 70.2, where Narāśaṅsa with his horses of all colours goes ahead of the gods and prepares their food; *Vendidād* 22.7, where Ahura Mazda gives him an order with the words: *para-āiδi, upa-vazaŋuha.* All this is incompatible with the abstraction of a "praise of men."[165] To a large extent, these verses are components of the Āprī hymns, i.e., old invocations to the gods, and are of interest to us only in so far as they suggest an ancient schism in the tradition,[166] but they are of no consequence for a more exact interpretation of Narāśaṅsa.[167]

But in the ritual there is a tradition which helps us to define this god more accurately. This tradition connects him closely with the Manes.

The Soma sacrifice has five Nārāśaṅsas, two in the morning, two at noon and one in the evening. This is the name given to certain Soma cups from which priests drink first, and which are then filled again and placed at the back under the southern Havirdhāna cart.[168] Since they have Narāśaṅsa as their deity, they are called Nārāśaṅsas (comm. on ĀpŚS XII.25.25). The connection between these Nārāśaṅsas and the Manes becomes more clear in ŚBr III.6.2.25: *yad dhavirdhānayor nārāśaṅsāḥ sīdanti tat pitṛṣu juhoti tasmāt pitaraḥ santi.* In the mantra which accompanies the drinking the key word is *narāśaṅsapītasya,*[169] which replaces other key words (like *indrapītasya* in the case of the Indragrahas), or according to a looser interpretation, may replace them. The close connection between the god Narāśaṅsa and the Manes can be seen still more clearly than in the previous case in the mantra which, according to Śāṅkhāyana,[170] accompanies this ceremony: *devo 'si narāśaṅso yat te medhaḥ svar jyotis tasya ta ūmaiḥ pitṛbhir bhakṣitasyopahūtasyopahūto bhakṣayāmi;* at noon *ūmaiḥ* is replaced by *ūrvaiḥ* and in the evening by *kāvyaiḥ.*[171] At noon when the

Nārāśaṅsas are put away, the dakṣiṇās are distributed among the priests;[172] in the evening a sacrifice to the Manes is closely connected with these Soma cups. In the evening when these cups are deposited in their places, each priest puts three small pieces of the remaining Puroḍāśa close behind his bowl for each of his ancestors and whispers: "this is for you, father NN, and for those who follow you," and then follow the Namaskāra formulas, "Respects to your semen, O Manes" etc.[173] Narāśaṅsa appears in the same close connection with the Manes in the Ṛgvedic verse X. 57.3 which, according to the statements of our texts,[174] is used during the sacrifice to the Manes:

máno nv ā́ huvāmahe nārāśaṅséna sómena |
pitṝṇā́ṃ ca mánmabhiḥ ||

The priest, according to Śāṅkhāyana, steps behind the Dakṣiṇāgni with vv. 3-5 of this very hymn. In view of the difficulty in obtaining information about the nature of Narāśaṅsa from the other statements of the ṚV, the wording of this verse, which agrees with the ritual practice, is of decisive significance.

It is well known that Narāśaṅsa also refers to certain texts. They are used in great number during the human sacrifice and there they alternate with the Ākhyānas, which are called Pāriplava and which glorify the historical and legendary prototypes of the king who is performing the sacrifice (ŚŚS XVI. 10.13).[175] They consist of the eulogy of the dakṣiṇās of liberal princes and their ancestors and of the recitation of different hymns connected with this, like e.g., the Śunaḥśepa hymns I. 24-25, or the hymn of the Manes X.62. Thus they are concerned essentially with the glorification of princes or prominent persons who are dead, i.e., with the cult of the Manes.[176] Apart from these Ākhyānas, single verses are also called by this name. In TĀr II.9 "Nārāśaṅsīs" are mentioned along with Itihāsas, Purāṇas, Kalpas, Gāthās (i.e., Yamagāthās according to the commentary).[177] They do not enjoy any special reputation. A statement at MS I.11.5 (167.8) censures these most sharply: *yo gāthānārāśaṅsībhyāṃ sanoti na tasya pratigṛhyaṃ / anṛtena hi sa tat sanoti.*[178] Not because they are "full of lies,"[179] but because they belong to the cult of the Manes, they are called *anṛta.* They are considered inferior to the praise of the gods just as Surā is denounced as "untruth, badness, darkness" *vis-à-vis* Soma. It would indeed be strange if one were to dismiss such verses simply as "lies."

The *Avesta* also shows a connection between Nairyōsaŋha and the spirits of the departed; particularly *Vendidād* 19.34, where righteous men gather in the house of Ahura Mazda and Nairyōsaŋha appears before them like a companion;[180] there is a faint suggestion of this relationship in Pahlavi literature where it is stated that "Ized Nēryōsang is the messenger of the gods, that is to say, he is sent with all the messages meant for the Kais and the heroes ... to give the help meant for the world."[181]

Since Narāśaṅsa is an ancient fire god and since the ritual still connects him with the cult of the Manes, I conclude that in the ṚV he represents the fire of the Manes, i.e., Dakṣiṇāgni. The argument that in the diagram of the sacrificial place given in the work of Caland-Henry, the Havirdhāna cart, under which the Nārāśaṅsa cups are placed, is situated too far from the fire of the Manes to make such an identification possible[182] does not disprove my conclusion. Firstly, it is doubtful whether the Ṛgvedic sacrificial place corresponded exactly to the scheme of the later sacrificial place with its *prācīnavaṃśa* and *mahāvedi*; secondly, this has nothing to do with a sacrifice but only with the storing away of the vessels until further use. We should consider if it is not a fact that in the enlarged sacrificial place of the later period the Mārjalīya hearth, situtated near the Havis cart, replaced the Nārāśaṅsa completely and the Dakṣiṇāgni partially and that the old name Narāśaṅsa is preserved only in the designation of the bowls and in the mantras. The Mārjalīya fire, burning in the south, is used not merely for purification but also for the sacrifice to the Manes and for the cult of the dead.[183]

Macdonell explains Narāśaṅsa as "'Praise of men' in the sense of 'he who is the object of praise.'"[184] Accordingly Narāśaṅsa should be a personification probably like the Avestan *mąθra*. In this case also experience shows that generally etymology does not bring us any nearer to the understanding of mythological beings. Till now it was presumed that *śáṅsa* is an action-noun; this is indicated by the accent also. But *híṅsa*, *yáva* and *úṣa*, though agent-nouns,[185] have the accent on the stem-syllable and suggest that for *śaṅsá* also there could be an agent-noun **śáṅsa* apart from the action-noun *śáṅsa*. The action-noun *śáṅsa* means "eulogy, praise" and also the opposite, "curse, malediction," as *aghásaṅsa* and *nṛ́śaṅsa* indicate.[186] Therefore, originally the word probably had a general meaning like "opinion, judgement, evaluation" as the Avestan *sah* and the Latin *censea, censor* also suggest. If we can assume that there was an agent-noun also, then it would roughly mean "judge, censor" (cf. Latin *dicere* in *vindex, judex*) and *nárāśaṅsa* would then mean a *hominum judex* or *censor*. For "praise of men" is a meaningless designation for a god of the dead or a god of the Manes,[187] even when we think of the festivals of the dead in which the ancestors are praised.[188] Thus the god is called Narāśaṅsa probably in the same way as in the later period Yama is called *prajāsaṃyamana, pitṝṇāṃ adhipa, śarīrāntakaro nṝṇām*. In MS IV.13.2 (200.4) Narāśaṅsa is called not only *nṛśasta* but *nṝṅṣpraṇetra* also.[189]

Of course, this is a weak hypothesis; but it is supported by the early pre-Indo-Iranian conception of our god, which has only a superficial connection with the frequent use of the word *śaṅsa* as an appellative in the sense of "praise" in the later period.

We should not ignore one characteristic of Narāśaṅsa mentioned in the Brāhmaṇa texts, viz., the designations *triśirṣan* and *ṣaḍakṣa*[190] in several passages of the black *Yajurveda*. I cannot imagine how the Brāhmaṇas could have mentioned these designations if a memory of Agni *triṣadhastha, tripastya, trimūrdhan, trikakudh* (MS IV.12.5). i.e., of Agni on the three hearths, did not play a role.

Narāśaṅsa has these epithets in common with Viśvarūpa, the son of Tvaṣṭṛ. Viśvarūpa is identical with Tvaṣṭṛ's son Agni, whom I interpreted as the moon. For reasons not known to us, Viśvarūpa, mentioned rarely in the ṚV, did not become the god of the fire of the Manes; but it is most likely that he is of the same origin as Bṛhaspati and Narāśaṅsa. Perhaps there is an allusion to the idea of the similarity in nature between the two when it is said that Narāśaṅsa as "*devatama*" prepares the sacrifice for the gods and goes ahead of them (X.70.2).[191] Thus he is characterized as the Purohita of the gods, and Viśvarūpa, who was killed by Indra, was also once the Purohita of the gods. A memory of this name is evoked by the statement of the above verse that Narāśaṅsa drives *viśvárūpebhir áśvaiḥ*, but our sources are too fragmentary to allow further comparison.[192]

b. KAVYAVĀHANA

In view of the fact that in the Vedic period Narāśaṅsa represents the fire of the Manes — I hope, I have established this convincingly — an evidence from the ṚV itself about the installation of the fire of the Manes will not be unwelcome.

Agni *kavyavāhana* is the opposite of Agni *havyavāhana* who brings food to the gods.[193] Agni Kavyavāhana replaces Agni Sviṣṭakṛt at the great sacrifice of the Manes during the last of the Cāturmāsyas.[194] On the afternoon of the new moon sacrifice he is invoked as *pitṛmat* along with Soma *pitṛmat* and Yama *aṅgirasvat*.[195] The name is translated by Eggeling as "the bearer of what is meet for the wise" (SBE XII, p. 430). The *Petersburger Wörterbuch*, which understands the word in the same way, states that it is formed in analogy to *havyavāhana*. Both are wrong.

In ṚV X.16.11 "*kravyavāhana*" stands for *kavyavāhana*, which Sāyaṇa interprets arbitrarily as *kavyasya haviṣo voḍhā*. That *kravya* here is the old form is shown by *kravyād* in vv. 9-10 of the same hymn. I think that *kavyavāhana* is a new formation of the older word, caused probably by a real change in sound or formed for euphemistic reasons.[196] It is clear that *kravyād* and *itaro jātavedas* form the opposites just as *kavyavāhana* and *havyavāhana* do in the ritual.

X.16.9 : *kravyā́dam agníṃ prá hiṇomi dūrám*
yamárājño gacchatu ripravāhā́ḥ /
ihaívā́yám ítaro jātávedā
devébhyo havyáṃ vahatu prajānán //[197]

Here the "meat-eating" fire which is sent far away to those "whose king is Yama" is distinguished from the "other" fire which is meant for the gods. Why is the former called "meat-eating" ? Because it originates from the cremation fire, which is kindled by fires that were maintained by the departed during their life time.[198] However, according to the ritual texts, the Aupāsana fire that is maintained in the house is to be extinguished completely or partially.[199] But vv. 10 and 12 show that the rite anticipated in this hymn does not agree with the Sūtra texts; for the verses speak of *kravyād* who has come into the house and who is now established as the fire of the Manes. Verse 12 cannot refer to anything but the installation of a fire — indeed, of the fire of the Manes:

12 : *uśántas tvā ní dhīmahi uśántaḥ sám idhīmahi* /
uśánn uśatá ā́ vaha pitṝ́n havíṣe áttave //

"May we instal you with desire, may we kindle you with desire, may you with desire lead the desiring Manes here to eat the Havis." Verse 10 informs us from where the fire for this is to be taken:

yó agníḥ kravyā́t pravivéśa vo gṛhám
imáṃ páśyann ítaraṃ jātávedasam |
táṃ harāmi pitṛyajñā́ya deváṃ[200]
sá gharmám invāt paramé sadhásthe ||

This verse anticipates that a fire-brand is brought from the cremation fire and used for making the fire of the Manes, which leads them here *háviṣe áttave*; this is contrary to the ritual practice. These verses can be seen in right perspective only when we interpret them in this sense.[201] Just as the deceased has gone from the world of the living to that of the dead, so the fire which belonged to him and devoured him does not serve the living any more but only the dead. The ritual texts speak of different occasions on which the domestic fire is lit: marriage, completion of the studies, and besides these, the death of the head of the family.[202] This last custom is anticipated in hymn X.16.

C. TANŪNAPĀT

We are at a disadvantage regarding this deity, whom the gods worship "three times a day."[203] There can be no doubt that the distinction between Tanūnapāt and Narāśaṅsa mentioned above (see p. 72, n. 166) is based on an old cult difference and that they are two different beings; for they change places only in the passages given earlier and do not take each other's place arbitrarily. Wherever the word *narāśaṅsa* or its derivative usually occurs, i.e., in Ākhyānas or in Camasas, Tanūnapāt cannot replace it.[204] But neither the ritual nor the ṚV gives more information about his nature. Usually the former speaks of him only in connection with the Tānūnaptra ceremony when the priests and the sacrificers swear an oath of allegiance to each other. The words uttered when the butter needed for this ceremony is taken out tell us little.[205] More important is the discussion in ŚBr III. 4.2.5, according to which the gods swear before the eyes of Prajāpati: "They said: 'he who transgresses our agreement shall be separated from us; he shall vanish.'[206] 'Who is the witness ?' 'Tanūnapāt, the mighty. He who blows yonder is Tanūnapāt, the mighty; he is the witness of living beings, entering them as the in-breathing and out-breathing.' " From this one could draw the conclusion that Tanūnapāt was a wind god, in this case a god of the Manes like Narāśaṅsa. But this is very doubtful because the ŚBr says at another place: *grīṣmo vai tanūnapāt grīṣmo hy āsāṃ prajānāṃ tanūs tapati* etc.,[207] thus declaring him to be a summer god or a sun god. The same seems to be the case in TBr II.6.7 where Tanūnapāt is identified with Indra in this Yājyā verse,[208] which, it must be admitted, is not authoritative. The MS,[209] which calls Tanūnapāt (similarly in a Yājyā) *aditer garbha, bhuvanasya gopā*, gives likewise no information. Hence we cannot establish anything with this material, and the same applies to the scanty information in the ṚV about Tanūnapāt. This is also true of hymn IX.5.2. Although it has the characteristics of an Āprī hymn, it is of no value, I believe, for the interpretation of mythology because of the obvious tendency of the poet to associate the individual Āprī gods with Soma Pavamāna. We must give up the effort to interpret Tanūnapāt more satisfactorily.[210]

2. The Āhavanīya Fire in the Ṛgveda

It was established long ago by other scholars[211] that in the Veda, Agni is a designation for the sun also[212] and that Agni Vaiśvānara in particular makes his appearance in this capacity. The small group of hymns ṚV VI.7-9, or the verses X.88.10-13 where Agni Vaiśvānara is only a synonym of Sūrya establish this beyond all doubt.

The identification of Vaiśvānara with Sūrya is continued in the ritual literature.[213] Although the lines of demarcation between the individual gods often shift, the main area of each individual god remains untouched — a fact which we should not ignore. This can be seen in the relation between Vaiśvānara and Narāśaṅsa. The former is never connected so directly with the Manes as Narāśaṅsa is. On the other hand, unlike Vaiśvānara Narāśaṅsa is never used as an expression for the "year." Offerings are made to Agni Vaiśvānara on various occasions; as a rule, they consist of Puroḍāśas which are made on twelve clay tablets. This is an easily intelligible allusion to the twelve months of the year, and often this is even stated expressly. Thus an *abhiśasyamāna* makes among others an offering of a cake called *dvādaśakapālā*, and the Brāhmaṇa comments on this: *yad vaiśvānaro dvādaśakapālo bhavati saṃvatsaro vā agnir vaiśvānaraḥ.*[214] Furthermore, the juxtaposition of Vaiśvānara and the Maruts as representatives of the ruler and of the subjects respectively is significant : *vaiśvānaraṃ dvādaśakapālaṃ nir vapen mārutaṃ saptakapālaṃ grāmakāmaḥ / āhavanīye vaiśvānaram adhi śrayati gārhapatye mārutam...*(TS II.2.5.6).[215] Considering the nature of Vaiśvānara, the association of this form of Agni with the Kṣatra can easily be understood; Kālidāsa calls the king *puruṣādhikāraṃ jyotiḥ.*[216] This association occurs at another place also. The son of a king must guard the Dhruvagraha, which belongs to Vaiśvānara and is placed on a sheet of gold during the Agniṣṭoma. A number of ceremonies associated with the removal of a usurper, the re-establishment of the rightful ruler etc., can be connected with this very cup.[217] Which then is the representative of the sun and of the sun-fire on the sacrificial place? The celestial fire and the fire of the sacrificial place are mentioned as closely connected :

I.59.2: *mūrdhā́ divó nā́bhir agníḥ pṛthivyā́ḥ*
áthābhavad aratí ródasyoḥ /
táṃ tvā devā́so 'janayanta devám
vaíśvānara jyótir íd ā́ryāya //

II.9.3: *vidhéma te paramé jánmann agne*
vidhéma stómair ávare sadhásthe /

Here we have one Agni as the head of heaven, one as the navel of the earth, or one "at the higher birth place" and one "at the lower seat;"[218] or

VI.9.3: *yá īṃ cíketad amṛ́tasya gopā́ḥ*
avā́ś cáran paró anyéna pā́śyan /

As in other passages, here also "below" and "above" refer to the god in heaven and the one on the earth, to the twice-born Hotṛ of the gods and of the men.[219] Agni is given the epithet Vaiśvānara in several of these verses (I.59.2; X.88.14; also VI.9.3 since the whole hymn deals with Vaiśvānara). Thus we have one Vaiśvānara in heaven and one on the earth. This explains the statement of *Nirukta* VII.23 that Vaiśvānara is the sun according to the Yājñikas but he is "this Agni" according to Śākapūṇi. Therefore in the ṚV we find occasionally Vaiśvānara as the designation of the sacrificial fire alone: e.g., when the *dhiṣáṇā*, the Vedi, is prepared for him in III.2.1,[220] or when

Mātariśvan brings him from afar in VI.8.4, or when he competes "with the sun" in another passage.[221] The fire which burns on the sacrificial hearth is the symbol of the celestial fire just as the sacrificial drink which men prepare is the image of that which the gods drink. Therefore, the thoughts go back and forth between Agni *pārthiva* and Agni *divya* in the same way as they do between the Soma-moon and the pressed drink; Agni Vaiśvānara on the earth corresponds to the Agni Vaiśvānara of the gods: *táva tridhấtu pṛthivī́ utá dyaúr vaiśvānara vratám agne sacanta* (VII.5.4).[222]

Now we have to decide whether Agni Vaiśvānara in the passages where he is not identical with the sun denotes the fire of the sacrificial hearth in general, or one of the three fires in particular. He is not connected with the Manes anywhere; this position, it was seen, belongs to Narāśaṅsa; therefore, the Gārhapatya fire or the Āhavanīya fire is left for Vaiśvānara. Which of the two fires we should choose is told by the ritual, which connects precisely the Āhavanīya with Vaiśvānara. One of the passages cited above (see p. 79), dealing with the Maruts and Vaiśvānara, assigns the Puroḍāśa for Vaiśvānara to this very fire. We encounter this association elsewhere also, viz., in an invocation to the same fire where it is expressly called *vaiśvānaraṃ jyotiḥ*. This invocation is used during the sacrifice of the new moon and of the full moon and is, consequently, repeated innumerable times with these ceremonies, giving expression to an obviously well-known association.[223] Furthermore, this interpretation is supported by the constant identification of the Āhavanīya with the sun or with the celestial world in the entire sacred literature. We can conclude that Vaiśvānara in the ṚV is not merely a name of the sun and of some sacrificial fire, but it is also the name, which we have missed so far, for the Āhavanīya, the third of the holy fires which represents the sun.

I think this interpretation is not contradicted by the fact that Vaiśvānara is designated as *triṣadhasthá* in one passage. Apart from him, among the specific forms of Agni, Bṛhaspati also carries this epithet. We do not know if in the Ṛgvedic period fire was distributed to the three hearths in the same way as it was done in the ritual, viz. from the Gārhapatya. The many differences which can be seen between these two periods lead us to the assumption stated earlier (p. 75, n. 192) that in this case also there might have been different customs: some started the distribution of the three fires from the Vaiśvānara-Āhavanīya,[224] the direct son of the sun, but others from the Narāśaṅsa-Dakṣiṇāgni; some divided the former into three, others the latter.

It will be the task of research to separate more precisely than has been done so far the areas of individual concepts which surround the individual gods even when they have their origin in the same natural phenomenon. It is true that these concepts have much in common but, on the other hand, they also have many independent traits. I have already mentioned the difference between Narāśaṅsa and Vaiśvānara from the point of view of the ritual. The difference between Sūrya and Vaiśvānara can be seen clearly in the hymns. For instance, it is not said of Vaiśvānara that he follows Uṣas like a suitor (as Sūrya or Agni alone does). On the other hand, as far as I know, the Veda does not associate Sūrya with the Maruts whereas Vaiśvānara is associated with the Maruts in the ṚV also. Even if he had his origin in the same phenomenon as the others, every Indian god is based on specific concepts and is by no means identical with his mythological brothers despite their common origin. More detailed studies might reveal if this differentiation is accompanied by a special mode of expression or terminology; thus, e.g., the verb *dīdi* is used for Agni, for Agni Vaiśvānara and even for Indra in solitary instances, but not for Sūrya (perhaps with the exception of one passage[225] which I myself interpret differently).

F. THE SABHYA FIRE AND THE ĀVASATHYA FIRE

The Pañcāgni enjoys an even greater reputation than the Vaitānika, who maintains the three fires. Like the Snātaka, the Mantravid and others, the Pañcāgni sanctifies an assembly by his mere presence.[226] In this case, the Āhavanīya, the Dakṣiṇa and the Gārhapatya are joined by a fourth and a fifth fire, i.e., the Sabhya and the Āvasathya.[227] Not everybody can install the Sabhya fire, which was mentioned as early as in the AV.[228] But according to the statements of several of our texts, only a Kṣatriya is entitled to do so; thus it appears to have been a prerogative of noble families,[229] if it was a custom at all. It is enjoined only by some teachers, others like Śālīki prohibit it and some others make it optional.[230] An important feature of the ceremony of lighting the Sabhya fire is the game of dice.[231] Kātyāyana has the following to say on this. KŚS IV.9.20: "[Thereupon] he makes through friction [in the manner of the Gārhapatya] the Sabhya fire [and places it in the Sabhā]. 21 : [The sacrificer] says [to the priests]: 'stake the cow.' 22: From then on [the Sabhya fire] is to be maintained [life long] and worshipped."

Āpastamba's statements on the next stage are, as usual, more detailed. ĀpŚS V.19.2: "... now in the middle of the Sabhā a dice board is drawn, water is sprinkled and dice are thrown on it. Gold is placed on the dice, they are thrown together, then they are pushed apart again, they are spread out,[232] and in the middle of the dice board an offering is made for the Rājanya with the verse, '*ni ṣasāda dhṛtavrataḥ*.'[233] 3: He places a piece of gold in the rest house (*āvasatha*) in the midst of the assembly [which is watching the *ādhāna*] and makes an offering on that with a verse containing the word '*mantra*': 'now Brahmaṇaspati proclaims the mantra from the Uktha, which pleased Indra, Varuṇa, Mitra, Aryaman and the gods.' 4: Thereupon he says: 'and may Ahi Budhnya, Aja Ekapāt, Pṛthivī, Samudra hear us; all the gods, the holy ones, invoked and praised; the mantras uttered by the Kavis may help us.'[234] Giving hundred dice to the sacrificer, he [the Adhvaryu] tells the players: 'stake the cow for rice;[235] divide the limbs without injuring.' 5: They act according to the instruction. 20.1: the Yajamāna wins with a throw called *kṛta* [which divides the 100 dice into four equal parts]. 2: They prepare all the food that they win for this cow and carry it [into the rest house] for the guests of the Sabhā. 3: It is eaten in the rest house."[236]

Sacra Publica

It is strange that in ancient India the *sacra publica* was pushed into the background by the *sacra privata*; we find only the Gṛhapati who maintains his household fire, the Agnihotrin and the Pañcāgni. But on closer scrutiny it appears as though there are still traces in the ṚV of an once-existing fire cult which was not only private but public as well. As I have shown earlier (p. 66), it is not incumbent upon common people to maintain the three fires continuously, but only upon dignitaries, learned brahmins, village chiefs, Rājanyas etc., that is to say, persons who are somehow or other prominent in their region. The fire of the hearth is common to both the dignitaries and other Hindus, although it can be separated into *aupāsana* and *gārhapatya.* The worship of the *dii manes* must have been cultivated in those families that were held in high esteem and were conscious of their tradition more than elsewhere. This explains the continuous maintenance of the Dakṣiṇāgni. I think that originally a special quality was inherent also in the third fire, the Āhavanīya. If my identification of the Āhavanīya with Vaiśvānara is correct, then the name Vaiśvānara itself, which can be translated as "*communis*," suggests that at one time the character of an *ignis publicus* might have been attributed to the Āhavanīya. It is immaterial whether it meant originally the fire of a region or of a community. It was at times the former and at others the latter according to the status of the *nityadhṛt.*[237]

I think that the institution of an *ignis publicus* can still be recognized in the ṚV; in several passages the Vaiśvānara fire has this character. The name does not occur in the second maṇḍala at all, in the eighth only once in a very general sense, which appears to rule out the possibility that this word was used as a proper name in this book.[238] But in other maṇḍalas Vaiśvānara is definitely a clan god, who leads victoriously the royal house and the clan of the Bharatas[239] in book VII, and the Pūrus in book I.[240] In VII.6 he is called the "breaker of fortresses"; he conquers the Paṇis who are without belief and sacrifice; he drives back the Dasyus who are unwilling to perform the sacrifice (vv. 2-3); he makes the Dawns the wives of the pious and forcibly induces the clans to pay tribute (v. 5). Here Vaiśvānara is not the god of the individual Gṛhapati but of the entire clan.[241] Likewise in I.59 Agni is not an enemy but the leader of the Pūrus.[242] He is called *nā́bhiḥ kṣitīnā́m* (v. 1) who supports men like a pillar, *mūrdhā́ divó nā́bhiḥ pṛthivyā́ḥ,* (v. 2) and *rā́jā kṛṣṭīnā́ṃ mā́nuṣīṇām* (v. 5). These statements also, I believe, imply the idea of a royal cult, of a Gr. *koinè estía* of the Pūrus.

As far as I know, the designation of Agni as *viśpati* was always considered to be a colourless epithet in the sense of "lord of men" or "lord of the house." We must examine more closely whether this view is justified. It can hardly be quite correct. Like the word *gṛhapati*, the word *viśpáti* or *viśā́m páti*, which corresponds to the Iranian *vīspaiti*, must have had a limited meaning originally.[243] The king is contrasted with the *viś*, the subjects.[244] When Agni is called the lord of the provinces or the lord of his subjects, this could mean that he is the lord of men in a general sense; but there are several verses which seem to contradict this view; thus e.g. V.1.6 : *dhartā́ kṛṣṭīnā́m utá madhya iddháḥ* and v. 10: *túbhyaṃ bharanti kṣitáyo yaviṣṭha balím agne ántita ótá dūrā́t*. It is obvious that one cannot speak in such terms of an ordinary sacrificial fire *dāśúṣo duroṇé*, but only of one which forms the centre of a larger community, be it the sacrificial fire of the king, or of the Samiti, or of the Sabhā. If the poet wanted to speak of a sacred object common to the whole clan, he could not have chosen any better words.[245]

If any cult of the later period can claim to be the continuation or a relic of the ancient fire of the province, it is the Sabhya fire which the king maintains. As the law books show, the ancient assemblies of people lost their importance in the later period.[246] The *parisā* or *palisā* of Pāli[247] cannot be regarded as a substitute for them. But the Vedic period is still familiar with these limitations to the royal power;[248] the change in the conditions between the Vedic period and the later period becomes evident here also. The men sitting in council in the Sabhā would not have been without the light of the sacred fire, which otherwise accompanied all the stages of human life. ṚV VII.1.4 speaks of the fires thus: *yátrā nárah samā́sate sujātā́ḥ*, "where the noble ones[249] meet"; VII.7.5 states that Agni sits down *nṛṣádane*. I do not think that here the poet is describing the cosy conditions of a domestic assembly but the sacrificial place or a Sabhā with its fire; *nṛṣádane*[250] is probably identical with the latter.[251]

Furthermore, Agni is installed *vára ā́ pṛthivyā́ ílāyās padé* in III.23.4;[252] this also does not indicate the hearth of an ordinary Gṛhapati or of an Agnihotrin but the centre of a large community or of a kingdom, i.e., the hearth of a ruler. The emphasis on the Sarasvatī, the Apayā and the Dṛṣadvatī in the same verse shows the extent and the location of his kingdom. This can be inferred more positively from the repetition of the same expression *várā ā́ pṛthivyā́ḥ* in III.53.11, a hymn dedicated to the horse sacrifice of the Kuśikas;[253] there can be no doubt that here the words refer to an established centre. It is the king who performs a sacrifice there after conquering his enemies in the south, west and north; the king is the "lord of the earth," *bhūpati, pṛthivīpati,* and his sacrificial place is, if the comparison is allowed, the *caeteris imparibus,* the Gr. *omphalós tēs gēs,* the *umbilicus urbis Romae.*

Besides the fire of the *nmānōpaiti* corresponding to the *gṛhapati,* the community hearth also was known to ancient Iran. According to Geiger and Spiegel, "it appears that a continuous fire was maintained in the hearth of the chief of each community and of the prince of each province. This was considered the centre of the community or of the province. It had the same role for this political unit as the fire of the domestic hearth had for the family."[254] After what has been said before, I do not doubt that the kings of the Vedic period also maintained not only fires serving their *sacris privatis* but those serving the *sacris publicis* also. But it is not possible to say if we must assume that, besides the domestic fire and the fire of the state, there was also a third fire which served the limited community of the village. Each fire that was meant for a community could certainly be called Vaiśvānara, and this word meant the one or the other according to the circumstances. Perhaps other scholars will be able to throw more light on this.

G. AGNI AND THE LIGHTNING

In the light of the above discussion, I maintain that the three or five hearths of the Vedic sacrifice were the most important ones of the Indian ritual and that these hearths represented those forms of the fire which were considered worthy of worship. The hearths of the individual priests, which are set up only during great sacrifices, are not nearly as important as these three fires, even if their symbolism was more distinct in some particulars. It was also shown that these fires represent the sun, the moon or the wind, and the domestic fire respectively but not the lightning. The lightning is never identified with any of these. Now we can make an attempt to determine the significance of the threefold birth of Agni, of which many verses speak and which was grossly misunderstood when interpretations were based on the later commentaries. Most important of these passages is X.45.1, which speaks of Agni's birth in the heaven, among us and in the waters.[255] There can be no doubt about two of these places of origin; *divás* (or *divijá* as the case may be) means the sun; the *asamád jātá* (or *sáhaṣkṛta*) is the fire made with fire sticks; *apsú* corresponds to the home of the fire embodied in the Dakṣiṇāgni, viz., the atmosphere, and denotes the moon or the wind according to the tradition concerned, but more often the moon. The case is somewhat different in I.95.3.[256] This verse also speaks of a manifold birth : *samudrá ékam divy ékam apsú*. However, we should not expect that the same views are repeated everywhere with the same degree of purity or that the poets expressed the same concepts consistently. The second verse,[257] which precedes the above-mentioned one, refers to the manifestation of Agni among the human beings; v. 3 mentions only the second and the third place of origin, and here *diví* is replaced by a more specific statement, *diví apsú*, i.e., "in the celestial waters," in which, according to one view, the sun also dwells; for the atmosphere (in the place of the earlier *apsú*) there is *samudré* — not a rare designation for the former. The *agní samudráyoni* of the present verse (as opposed to the *divyáyoni*) is identical with the *índu samudráyoni* of the TS.[258] Thus here also the ritual helps to solve one of the most difficult problems of Vedic mythology.

One might perhaps object to my view on the basis of the first verse of the riddle hymn I.164 in which, besides *vāmá palitá hótṛ*, *áśna* is mentioned as the second brother,[259] and where *áśna* is usually translated as lightning. But here also it should be clear that the three brothers cannot be different from the three Agnis of the sacrificial place and that, therefore, they are to be interpreted in this sense. There is one more point. It is not the lightning which is considered the "eater"; it is the sun who "consumes" or "devours".[260] On the other hand, if one were to dismiss this as an unusual view occurring in a few passages only, mention may be made of TS I.6.11.5-6; TBr III.4.1, where Agni is called the "consumer of the food" of the gods.[261] This can apply on the one hand to the Gārhapatya or to the Āhavanīya, and on the other to the celestial sacrificial fire (the sun), lit by the gods themselves, in which they make the offering of their havis (X.88.7). Then *palitá hótṛ* would mean the moon. Therefore, I think that *áśna* can easily refer to one of the fires, or we must join Sāyaṇa in supposing that Vāyu, the "*sarvatra vyāpta,*" is meant here, which does not seem to be logical.

The changeable nature of the lightning did not favour its evolution into a deity, instead it made the lightning a weapon or an instrument of a god like Indra or Thôr; on this point I agree with Hardy[262] and Oldenberg.[263] The notion that the lightning should be an independent deity does not seem plausible from a general point of view if we examine it in the light of ethnography or of the mythology of the European peoples; modern Indian sources do not support such a view either. I do not find any allusion to this either in Tylor's *Anfänge der Kultur* or in the works of Brinton,[264] Ehrenreich[265] or Lang.[266] Even Crooke, in whose *Popular Religion* above all one would expect to find such views, speaks in the section on "Thunder and Lightning" (2nd ed., vol. I, pp. 33-35) only of the evil omens caused by them and of the means to ward off the "lightning" or "thunder demon" but not of a deification of this phenomenon.[267] Even Germanic mythology, not to speak of others, does not seem to have created such a being.[268] Of course, we cannot draw any conclusions about the Vedic period from the silence of the anthropological or other sources, not even from the Buddhist sources which do not mention lightning among the gods worshipped by the brahmins.[269] On the other hand, we should not underestimate this silence either. Even the Vedic literature does not support the lightning-hypothesis. The evidences for this hypothesis are primarily the commentaries[270] and later sources, upon which Al-Berunī obviously relies.[271] Of course, there are other solitary statements in favour of this, for the Indians obviously observed the lightning and recognized its fire-like nature. However, the passages where the lightning is elevated to a deity are few in number and belong more to the Adbhuta ritual than to the regular cult. When the lightning strikes the fire of the sacrificial place, an offering must be made to Agni *apsumat*;[272] or the lightning is the cause of fever, headache etc.[273] Of course, among the types of wood used in the Agnyādhāna, there is also wood from a tree struck by lightning (see p. 64 above), but it is only one of the kinds of wood required there — by no means the only kind — and proves nothing in favour of the worship of the lightning-fire as "Agni in the waters." Generally speaking, we see the lightning as a weapon in the hand of Indra,[274] or of Soma, Bṛhaspati and others. It is forged by Tvaṣṭṛ for Indra, or Agni places the thunderbolt in the hands of Indra (X.52.5); elsewhere it is Soma who is to recover the lost "axe."[275] If we do not take mythological beings like Indra, Bṛhaspati etc. into account, and look at the transparent natural phenomena themselves, we can see that the lightning (*aśmán, vidyút*) is closely connected to the sun as his weapon:

AV XIII.1.32 : *udyáṅs tvám deva Sūrya... /*
ávainān áśmanā jahi... //
VIII.1.11 : *vaiśvānaró rakṣatu jātávedāḥ*
divyás tvā mā́ dhāg vidyútā sahá /
TĀr I.8.2 : *vidyút sū́rye*[276] *samā́hitā*
ṚV X.68.4 : *avaksipánn arká ulkā́m iva dyóḥ /*
TBr III.7.6.21[277] : *udyánn adyá mitramahaḥ sapátnān me anī-naśaḥ /*
dívainān vidyútā jahi //

According to TĀr I.10.5, out of the sky the *rātrī* is born, out of her *śveta āditya*,[278] out of him *vaidyuta* [*ātapa*], and out of it *nīhāra*.

Furthermore, the lightning is closely connected to the cloud and rain as is but natural.[279] Otherwise the lightning is symbolized variously,[280] but we never encounter statements like *agnir vai vajraḥ* (*vidyut*) or *devo vai vajraḥ*;[281] such passages could hardly have escaped my attention. In other words, the facts show that the lightning is never recognized as a deity; if at all, only in exceptional cases. I know only a few where it is worshipped: once in AV I.13, i.e., in a hymn which is preceded by a hymn (I.12) on exorcism of lightning and of its consequences like headache etc.;[282] furthermore, in ṚV VIII.100.9, where the thunderbolt, surrounded by water, rests in the ocean and receives tribute from those "who stream forward in concert." Thus it cannot be disputed that there are solitary statements of this nature. Their number could probably be raised by further research,[283] because in the range of the Vedic literature there is probably no view which is not represented. But such a small number of passages is not sufficient to prove that the lightning is the "Agni in the waters" or to attribute to this form of the fire characteristics of a deity,[284] thus giving it the same importance as the two other forms of the fire and making it the third manifestation.

Some might oppose this interpretation by referring to the oft-repeated legend of Agni who hid himself in the waters and whom the gods were eagerly looking for. Generally scholars have interpreted this Agni as the lightning. The two passages of the TBr which seem to support this view were given under n. 275; but they are isolated passages and are not compatible with the total view of the Veda, which I am attempting to present here.

H. THE GODS AND AGNI

1. The Gods install Agni

Oldenberg was right when he said that Agni holds a certain special position *vis-à-vis* the compact mass of the gods. Passages in which the gods are described as kindling the fire themselves are not isolated. There are also other images: Agni is the messenger, the leader of the sacrifice, the Hotṛ or the Purohita of the gods, their eye, their "animal,"[285] or their mouth. They create him not only for themselves, they also grant a share of him to men. Apart from Uśij, Aṅgiras and other ancient personages who have become more or less mythical, it is the gods who install the fire among the human clans. Only a few illustrations of this well-known concept will be cited here to show this in a proper perspective:

III.2.3: *krátvā dákṣasya táruṣo vídharmaṇi*
deváso agníṃ janayanta cíttibhiḥ /
8: *vícarṣaṇir agnír devắnām abhavat puróhitaḥ* /
9.9 (=X.52.6): *trī́ṇi śatá trī́ sahásrāṇy agním*
triṅśác ca devắ náva cāsaparyan /
aúkṣan ghṛtaír ástṛṇan barhír asmā
ắd íd dhótāraṃ ny àsādayanta //
29.9: *ayám agníḥ pṛtanāṣắṭ suvī́ro*
yéna deváso ásahanta dásyūn //[286]

2. The Gods and the Sun

Like the procedure of the Soma sacrifice, the procedure of the fire cult at the sacrificial place also is a reflection of the celestial world. Agni who is aflame in the hearth of the sacrificer is the earthly representative of that one whom the gods kindle. The foregoing analysis made it clear that none of the Vitāna fires corresponds to the lightning; our texts state expressly that it is Agni Vaiśvānara whom the gods create for the sacrifice.[287] However, as we have seen, Agni Vaiśvānara is the sun, and in hymn X.88, which deals with the sacrifice of the gods and which is significant from this point of view, it is expressly stated in v. 11 that *sū́rya āditeyá* is installed by them; hence Sūrya Āditeya and Agni Vaiśvānara are synonyms.[288] The present hymn says in the preceding verse that the gods created Agni in heaven with a stoma and that they divided him into three for the world.[289] Another hymn calls Sūrya explicitly "the Purohita of the gods."[290]

In many legends of the Brāhmaṇas, Sūrya plays an important role. The gods are afraid of him when he strides forth burning,[291] or he is the *yoddhṛ* whom the Rakṣas' themselves choose for a fight with the permission of Prajāpati (TĀr II. 2.1),[292] or the gods make him the goal (*kāṣṭhā*) in one of the races arranged by them (ABr IV.7.4; TMBr IX.1.35); in one of the sacrifices he becomes the "post" for the sacrificial animal (TBr II.1.5.2); they transform him into a white horse as the dakṣiṇā for Ayāsya (TMBr XVI.12.4). When Svarbhānu strikes Āditya with complete darkness, the gods rescue him with Svarasāmans. They brought him to the celestial world with the Svaras called Para (TMBr IV.5.2-3). Or they drive away the darkness with the Divākīrtyas (TMBr IV.6.13). Often it is said that the gods are worried that the sun might fall down from the sky or beyond the sky.[293] At the time of the solstice they support the tottering sun with metres and melodies. This can only be a reminiscence of the old solstice celebrations which were accompanied by the singing of hymns. Professional singers must have cultivated the art of heralding the New Year with songs (see p. 25 above), before this practice was incorporated into the ritual of the Brahmanical schools. The legend of the fire, kindled by the gods and installed for the sacrifice, with which we are concerned here is thus only one of the many myths connected with the sun. Like several other myths, it must have originated in folklore and must have been welcome to the ritualists who elaborated it to serve as an illustration or a starting point for their customs.

3. Agni's Flight

However, Agni does not always remain with the gods; the legend of his flight out of fear of serving in the sacrifice is known to the entire Vedic literature. TS II.6.6.1 narrates this legend as follows: "Agni had three elder brothers. These disappeared when they brought the sacrificial offerings to the gods. Agni got into a fright. He thought, 'similarly the one here (who brings the sacrificial offerings) will be a victim of bad luck,' and ran away; he went into the waters. The gods tried to get him out. A fish betrayed him. He cursed it ..." The same legend appears again in TS VI.2.8.4, differing from the one related above only in so far that here Agni does not enter into the waters, but into the plants and trees,[294] and is discovered by the gods without the help of the fish. It does not need any keen intellect to see that the three brothers of Agni who disappeared[295] are the three sacrificial fires which were extinguished and that the Agni searched for by the gods is the sacrificial fire which should serve them anew. I think that this has nothing to do with the performance of a single sacrifice but with the beginning of the ritual year, with the beginning of the Devayāna which follows the Pitṛyāṇa. The entire legend has too constant a character to have originated aetiologically from a single sacrifice ; Indian mythology has chosen the image of the "hidden" or lost fire which the gods or wise men search for,[296] in order to characterize the end of the Uttarāyaṇa.[297] We can see this from the ṚV itself. The ṚV says that Agni has gone away in anger; thus V.2.8 where it is said: "you have gone away from me in anger; the overlord of the gods told this to me; for Indra looked at you knowingly; instructed by him, Agni, I came here."[298] The three hymns X.51-53, which L. v. Schroeder interpreted as a "cult-drama," take us still closer to the actual beliefs.[299] In the first of these hymns we find a dialogue between Agni and the gods who look for him in the waters and plants and who induce him to return by promising him the Prayājas, the Anuyājas, a share of the Havis, "the butter of the waters," the pith of the herbs and a long life.

X.51.4: Agni: "O Varuṇa, I escaped for fear of the Hotṛ-duty, lest the gods harness me here. My bodies are hidden at many places. I, Agni, do not understand this object (the Hotṛ-duty)."

5: Varuṇa: "Come ! Man longs for the gods and desires to perform the sacrifice, being prepared for it. You live in darkness, Agni. Make the paths passable which serve the gods (*pathó devayā́nān*). Carry the oblations there with a kindly spirit."

6: Agni: "The elder brothers of Agni pursued this object (the Hotṛ-duty) with zeal, as a charioteer pursues his path; [and they perished]. Fearing this, Varuṇa, I went far away. I tremble like a buffalo in front of the bow-string of an archer."

It is obvious that it is not the lightning that is meant here, because it is not the lightning or the weapon of the gods which was extinguished, but it is their sacrificial fire; or to use another Vedic image, their Hotṛ fled and is recovered anew by them. The following hymn describes the installation of the Hotṛ.

X.52.4: Agni: "The gods have appointed me the bearer of the oblations, me who disappeared and encountered many dangers, [with the words :] 'Agni shall wisely prepare our sacrifice, the threefold and the sevenfold with its five courses.' "

5: "I wish to implore you for immortality[300] and progeny so that, O gods, I create wide space for you. I want to place the thunderbolt in the arms of Indra. Then he will win all the battles."

6: Poet: "Then 3339 gods worshipped Agni, they sprinkled him with butter, they strew Barhis on him. Then they installed him as their Hotṛ."

In v. 5 of the first hymn the *pathó devayā́nān*, which Agni should make ready, were mentioned as a contrast to the *támas* in which he dwells. Exactly the same contrast is made in X.124.1, where Agni is implored to come to the sacrifice and to be the bearer of the oblations and the leader; long indeed did he dwell in the deep darkness.[301] This can only mean a renewal of the sacrifice, which is opposed to *támas*, a dark period without the sacrificial fire. X.181.3, which speaks of the "scattered" or "lost" Yajus of the gods which the wise men found after zealous meditation is also to be understood in the same sense.[302]

The Manes are the opposite of the gods;[303] this opposition is seen everywhere in the ritual — in minor matters as well as in the major ones — with regard to the cardinal points, the position of the sacrificial thread etc. "When they go away after the sacrifice of the Manes and worship the sun in the east, [they do so because] the sun is the world of the gods, the Manes are the world of the ancestors; therefore, from the world of the Manes they come to the world of the gods."[304] In the world of the ancestors one should not see the sun.[305] It is said in the MŚS that "when the sun is still in the sky one should make a covering."[306] In TMBr VIII.7.6, in connection with the Yajñāyajñīya Sāman with its strange ritual which deserves further study, there is a peculiar compromise where the sun (here Agni Vaiśvānara) is contrasted with the Manes: "the Adhvaryu then brings the participants to Vaiśvānara, when he begins the Yajñāyajñīya Stotra. One should sing it after covering oneself so that one is not burnt by Vaiśvānara. But the Manes do not recognize one who is covered. During the Yajñāyajñīya Stotra the Manes wish to recognize their kin. One should cover oneself upto the ears only. That is covering as well as not covering. The Manes recognize and Vaiśvānara does not do any harm." The opposition between the gods and the Manes is expressed most significantly in the two periods of the year, the Devayāna and the Pitṛyāṇa, which were understood later in a purely spatial sense. The opposition is stressed in hymn X.2, cited in Ch. I, n. 20 ; it is specially emphasized in the hymn which deals with the installation of Sūrya as the sacrificial fire;[307] hymn X.52, which was the starting point of our present remarks, expresses this opposition in the words *támas* and *pánthāno devayā́nāḥ* (X.52.5). When Rudra shoots the sacrifice through the heart, the sacrificial fires are extinguished and the period of the Manes begins. Thus the designation of the *pitáraḥ* as *devá-śatru* in VI.59.1 becomes intelligible:

hatā́so vāṃ pitáraḥ deváśatravaḥ
índrāgnī jī́vatho yuvā́ṃ //

"Destroyed by the two of you are the Manes, the gods' enemies. Indrāgnī, you two survive," i.e., the Pitṛyāṇa came to an end and the Devayāna begins. Indrāgnī, whom I interpret on the basis of the ritual as the new moon just as I interpret Agnīṣomau as the full moon, seem to denote here the first new moon in the New Year.

4. Agni's Hiding Place

The two passages of the TS, cited earlier, do not mention the same place as the hiding place of Agni who ran away from the Hotṛ-duty; one mentions the waters the other various trees. Similar variance occurs in the ṚV, not only in different verses, but even within a single verse. Thus in VI.48.5 *ápo*, *ádrayo* and *vánā* are mentioned side by side.[308] On the other hand, there are also passages in the ṚV where only one facet of the theme is dealt with, sometimes the dwelling in the waters and sometimes the dwelling in vegetation, e.g.,

I.151.1: *mitrám ná yám śímyā góṣu gavyávaḥ*
svādhyò vidáthe apsú jījanan /

III.1.3: *ávindann u darśatám apsv àntár*
devā́so agnim apási svásṝṇām //

13: *apā́m gárbham darśatám óṣadhīnām*
vánā jajāna subhágā vírūpam /

9.2: *kā́yamāno vanā́ tvám yán mātṝ́r ájagann ápaḥ* /[309]

9.4: *ánv īm avindan nicirā́so adrúhah*
apsú siṁhám iva śritám / etc.[310]

a. IN THE WATERS

If we were to solve the question of this Agni in the waters without any reference to the context, then the sun, moon, lightning and other phenomena[311] would become the starting point for the creation of this myth. But when we examine the question more closely and notice that here it can only be the sacrificial fire of the gods or the Hotṛ of the gods and that there is neither an extrinsic nor an intrinsic reason to consider the lightning the one or the other, then the alternatives are narrowed down; then it becomes evident that only the sun and the moon could come into question. Both are closely connected with the waters — one should not confuse water with clouds, they are by no means identical in the Veda. The moon moves *apsv àntár ā́* (I.105.1); as Soma he is *apā́m gárbha* (IX.97.41); TĀr I.22.1 calls him *apā́m púṣpa.* The "hidden king in his hiding place on his glittering bed of straw" (I.23.14) whom Pūṣan finds is the moon. On the other hand, it is said of Sūrya that the gods brought out "the one who was hidden in the ocean" (X.72.7),[312] or that he "hides himself in the waters."[313] The sun and the moon together are called *apā́m vṛṣaṇvasū* (X.93.5),[314] and perhaps it is they who are meant in X.27.17 by the two who wander in the waters through the enormous surface.[315] Consequently, it is not easy to recognize whether it is the sun or the moon who is meant in a particular verse. It is likely that the poets, who saw clearly that the sun and the moon were only different manifestations of one and the same Agni, did not aim at a clear distinction. But we are in a position to determine who the Agni is who is fleeing into the waters, since there is a verse the statements of which are unambiguous. I do not take into account VII.49.4, because here Agni Vaiśvānara is mentioned with other gods only.[316] On the other hand, the following verse is important:

VI.8.4 : *apā́m upásthe mahiṣā́ agṛbhṇata*
víśo rā́jānam úpa tasthur ṛgmíyam |
ā dūtó agním abharad vivásvato
vaiśvānarám mātaríśvā parāvátaḥ ||

"The mighty [gods] seized him in the womb of the waters. The clans worshipped the king, who is worthy of praise. Mātariśvan brought Agni Vaiśvānara as a messenger of Vivasvat from afar." As I have shown, Agni Vaiśvānara is the sun, the sacrificial fire of the gods of which they gave men a share, and the Āhavanīya which represents the sun on the sacrificial place. Particularly hymns VI.7-9, which treat Agni Vaiśvānara as a synonym of Sūrya and in the midst of which our verse occurs, do not leave any room for doubt that it is the sun whom the gods seize in the womb of the waters.[317] In VI.9.7, i.e., again in the same small group, *támasi* stands for *apā́m upásthe*:

víśve devā́ anamasyam bhiyānā́ḥ tvā́m agne támasi tasthivā́ṅsam |
vaiśvānaró avatūtáye náḥ ámartyo avatūtáye naḥ ||

"All the gods bowed before you with fear when you, Agni, stood in the dark." Therefore, also in other passages where it is not so definite that Agni Vaiśvānara is being referred to, but where Agni who hides in the waters and whom the gods look for is mentioned in a general sense, we can assume that their sacrificial fire, their Hotṛ, i.e., the sun is meant by this.[318] It seems to me that all available facts speak against the view that Agni who has fled into the waters is the lightning.

In the above-mentioned verses *apā́m upásthe* and *támasi* replace each other like synonyms. The idea that the sun disappears into the waters is understandable only in a tropical country with its rainy season. There alone can the legend be conceived which we find in KBr XXV.1 : "that the waters practised *tapas* and, having practised *tapas*, they became pregnant. Out of these was born in the sixth month the sun (*āditya*) here..., 'out of the ocean emerged the sweet wave,' says the Ājyaśastra, because he arises 'out of the ocean,' (i.e.) out of the waters."

When *támasi* occurs besides this, then it can refer to the dark rainy season also,[319] but, as I have argued, it is more likely that in the case of *támas* a memory of older times under a different sky has been inherited and that originally the winter solstice was meant by it (see p. 63). But here the lines of demarcation are so vague that a clear distinction, I believe, is impossible; it is all the more likely that the views got mixed up because the rainy season occurs at the beginning of the Dakṣiṇāyana.

b. IN THE VEGETATION

Agni hides not only in the waters but in the plants also. Like the gods, the wise men find him in water and in vegetation. V.11.6 : *tvā́m agne áṅgiraso gúhā hitám ánv avindañ chiśriyāṇáṃ vánevane.*[320] As I have shown, water and plants are connected: "in the waters, O Agni, is your seat. You adhere to the plants."[321]

How does Agni come to the earth ? The lightning suggests itself as the bringer of the celestial fire, and this view finds support in the mention of a tree stuck by lightning which is used, besides other kinds of wood, for kindling the flame (see p. 64), as well as in the fact that the fire sticks are made out of the wood of an Aśvattha tree.[322] Not all trees are equally exposed to the lightning;[323] but the Aśvattha seems to have attracted the lightning and to have been easily inflammable. In the rules for the construction of a house (Gobhila IV.7), it is said that one should avoid the Aśvattha in the east because this tree, being dedicated to Āditya, brings with it the danger of fire. I cannot ascertain whether the same or another basic idea plays a role in the case of other kinds of wood chosen for preparing the fire. Apart from this transmission of fire from the lightning to the individual trees, there is another, I should say, peaceful transmission to which the verses above allude. Just as the Soma juice is obtained from certain plants containing milk, so is the fire obtained from certain plants and trees containing fire. The moon comes into this world at the time of the new moon, enters water and plants, and the sacrificer collects him out of the water and plants. Similarly the fire rises up in the plants when it is brought here from heaven "by the highest father."[324] It appears as though this mysterious transmission takes place in the form of rain.[325] Or there is still a third way for the descent of the fire: Mātariśvan brings the fire.

I. MĀTARIŚVAN[326]

The verses which speak of Mātariśvan as if he were the Prometheus of India are numerous enough to characterize him as the fire-bringer, but they do not explain the naturalistic beginnings of his character. Agni at first manifests himself to Mātariśvan (*āvir bhū* I.31.3; 143.2),[327] or Mātariśvan fetches him from heaven (*bhar, ā+nī*).[328] The root *math* is also used,[329] or *sam+idh* as in III.5.10 :

yádī bhṛ́gubhyaḥ pári mātaríśvā
gúhā sántaṃ havyavā́haṃ samīdhé //

In another passage it is said that he "creates" Agni along with other gods (*tatakṣur* X.46.9).[330]

In the later period Mātariśvan is always the wind. This meaning is not only found in classical Sanskrit, but goes back up to the portals of the ṚV; we find it in the YV,[331] and even in the AV — in the latter not only in isolated passages but in several passages where there can be no doubt about its meaning:

AV V.10.8 : *bṛhatā́ mána úpa hvaye mātaríśvanā prāṇāpānaú* /

VIII.1.5 : *túbhyaṃ vā́taḥ pavatām mātaríśvā*
túbhyaṃ varṣantv amṛ́tāny ā́paḥ //

X.7.2; 9.26 ; and

XII.1.51 : *yásyāṃ vā́to mātaríśvéyate*
rájāṅsi kṛṇváṅś cyāváyaṅś ca vṛkṣā́n /
vā́tasya pravā́m upavā́m ánu vāty arcíḥ //[332]

Since these passages speak of Vāyu Mātariśvan (YV) or of Vāta Mātariśvan, it is evident that Mātariśvan could not merely have been a synonym of Vāyu and Vāta, but a specific manifestation of the wind about which nothing more is said in detail. The verse cited from the AV, which describes how Mātariśvan raises clouds of dust and shakes the trees, recalls to mind the particularly intense storms, like dust storms, as they plague India;[333] but it is such an isolated verse that we cannot interpret Mātariśvan in this sense.[334] Suffice it to say that as early as in the AV, Mātariśvan was certainly a name of the wind.

Should we exclude the ṚV and limit the meaning "wind" exclusively to the later period from the AV onwards ? Recent research is in favour of this; according to Oldenberg, the meaning "wind" rests on "secondary speculations."[335] I do not think that this is correct.

In the ṚV, Mātariśvan brings the fire, makes it by friction and kindles it. If it is certain that Mātariśvan is a name of the wind in the AV, then it is possible that this word occurring in these passages of the ṚV also refers to the wind. The close relationship between wind and fire is indeed evident from the very nature of both these elements: *agner hi vāyuḥ kāraṇam vāyor agnir iti.*[336] MS III.1.10 (13.12)[337] says : "Agni follows Vāyu." When the fires go out and a new flame, produced quickly through friction, is brought towards the wind, an offering is made to Vāyu (KŚS XXV.10.20). In ṚV I.58.5; 141.7 Agni is styled as *vā́tacodita*; I.58.4 etc. *vā́tajūta*; X.91.7 *vā́topadhūta iṣitá.*[338] Consequently, it does not seem far-fetched, or difficult, to explain also the Ṛgvedic Mātariśvan who brings the fire from afar or kindles it as a wind god : "the production of fire by means of friction is a discovery which would naturally occur to jungle races, who must have constantly seen it occur by the ignition of the bamboo stalks rubbed together by the blasts of summer."[339] Other verses also fit into this explanation. ṚV IX.67.31: *sárvaṃ sá pūtám aśnāti svaditáṃ mātaríśvanā* can be compared with MS IV.5.8 (75.6) : *sa vāyur abravīd aham va etaṃ somaṃ svadayiṣyāmi*;[340] ŚBr IV.1.3.6 ff.

However, some other verses in which Mātariśvan is a direct name of Agni appear to raise difficulties. Among others, one such is the well known verse I.164.46, which is usually interpreted in a pantheistic sense (with a dubious justification), and according to which, "the wise call a being in many ways, they call it Agni, Yama and Mātariśvan"; furthermore I.96.4; III.26.2 and

III.5.9 : *mitró agnír ī́ḍyo mātaríśvā*
ā́ dūtó vakṣad yajáthāya devā́n ||

Another such verse is III.29.11, frequently cited above, which, whatever it might mean in detail, mentions Tanūnapāt, Narāśaṅsa and Mātariśvan as three forms of Agni. But all in all, the number of such verses is not big and the list given in the PW is, in any case, to be reduced considerably.[341]

Now there is the question whether we can explain the wind or a particular kind of wind as a form of Agni. The possibility does not seem to be ruled out, although, in view of the scanty material, only conjectures are possible. It was shown earlier (pp. 68-69) that in the Dakṣiṇāgni, whose hearth can have two shapes, two beings are fused together: Vāyu on the one hand and Candra on the other; we saw that the Indian scholars themselves differed on the question whether the wind can be regarded as Agni or not. The Maruts are compared to the fires. We also find isolated passages in the Brāhmaṇa literature, which directly or indirectly equate Vāyu with Agni. It is said of Vāyu in TS II.1.1 : *sainam (devatā) īśvarā pradaha iti*;[342] TBr III.10.11.7 : *sā vā eṣo 'gnir apakṣapuccho vāyur eva/ tasyāgnir mukham*; ABr II.34.3 : *agniḥ suṣamid iti śaṅsati vāyur vā agniḥ suṣamid vāyur hi svayam ātmānaṃ saminddhe svayam idaṃ sarvaṃ yad idaṃ kiṃca*; III. 4.3. : *sa yad agniḥ pravān iva dahati tad asya vāyavyaṃ rūpam*; ŚBr VIII.3.2.1: *atha viśvajyotiṣam upadadhāti / vāyur vai madhyamā viśvajyotir vāyur hy evāntarikṣaloke viśvam jyotiḥ*. I do not wish to attach any special significance to these passages; these may not be free from fanciful identifications and are not so authoritative as the passage cited under n. 143, according to which some worship Agni as Vāyu and others do not. Probably we may not be able to say much more than merely stating that there was a difference of opinion among the ancient scholars. If the evidence is not considered sufficient, we must leave aside the question whether in the ṚV also the wind under the name of Mātariśvan is a form of fire or not.[343] In this connection we should not forget either that the Maruts are *agnáyo ná śuśānāḥ* (II.34.1) and are called directly *agnáyaḥ* in III.26.4.[344]

Agni's relationship to Indra, to the Maruts and to some other gods still remains to be discussed, but it would be better to deal with it in Vol. II where Indra and others will be discussed. From the foregoing we can draw a conclusion which is important for the exegesis of the Agni hymns. The thoughts of the poets not only move from the celestial Agni to the earthly one, but they linger also on the three hearths and on his threefold birth. If this is kept in mind, it will be easy to follow the seemingly unconnected thoughts of the poets who describe, I think, sometimes one form and sometimes the other form of the fire or of its celestial representative according to the need of the cult.

J. BṚHASPATI

Another name of the fire is Bṛhaspati. Hardly any other Vedic god seems to have been accepted more positively and conceived more abstractly than this one whom Brahmanical theology declared to be its favourite and whom it made the Purohita of the gods and the prototype of all the priests. The PW says : "It is the name of a god in whom the activity of the pious towards the gods is personified. Bṛhaspati is the one who prays, the sacrificer, the priest, the one who intercedes with the gods on behalf of men, and their protector against the impious. Thus he appears as a prototype of the priest and of priestly dignity; he is also called the Purohita of the community of gods."

This definition, based on an article by Roth,[345] has been regarded as authoritative by some of the later interpreters and is preferred even today by Oldenberg and others. Obviously, it has also influenced Bergaigne when he says : "The idea of the necessary efficacity, of the characteristic power, of prayer stands out in a still stronger relief by the introduction into the Vedic pantheon of a divine being who symbolises precisely this somewhat magical influence of the sacred mantras and of whom the name, Brahmaṇaspati or Bṛhaspati, often invoked along with the names of the different deified elements of Vedic sacrifice, I.18.5; 40.3; X.36.5; 64.15; 100.5; 103.8, signifies 'the lord of prayer.' This word itself will be sufficient to indicate his nature."[346] Bergaigne does not stay with this view; he contradicts it partly when he says later : "The conception of a god who is an inspirer of priests and a priest himself is nevertheless not a mere abstraction in the Vedic mythology. We have already seen the same functions being attributed to divine beings of a naturalistic origin as well as of a liturgical one, viz. Agni and Soma. Brahmaṇaspati appears to have been sometimes identified with one or the other of these deities."[347]

It has been suggested earlier that Brahmaṇaspati and Agni are identical, but the suggestion did not attract any notice. Langlois[348] considers Bṛhaspati and Brahmaṇaspati the names of Agni; Wilson[349] appears to be undecided, for he says at one place that Brahmaṇaspati "seems to be identifiable with Agni, with the additional attribute of presiding over prayer," and at another place that Bṛhaspati is "identical with Indra, by his attributes of sending rain and wielding the thunderbolt." Max Müller[350] states: "Brahmaṇaspati and Bṛhaspati are both varieties of Agni, the priest and purohita of gods and men, and as such he is invoked together with the Maruts in other passages, I.40.1."[351]

I had stated my view in the first edition of this work and defended it against Otto Strauss in the smaller edition. Oldenberg has written against my view in great detail while Hertel, for other reasons, accepted it in its main points.[352]

The belief that Bṛhaspati is an abstract deity is shaken, if not altogether set aside, if we consider certain verses of the ṚV which stress his luminous character. In one passage he is unmistakably characterized as Agni:

V.43.12: *á vedhásaṃ nī́lapṛṣṭhaṃ bṛhántam*
bṛ́haspátiṃ sádane sādayadhvam /
sādádyoniṃ dáme ā dīdivā́ṃsam
híraṇyavarṇaṃ aruṣā́ṃ sapema //

This verse deals with the installation of a fire called Bṛhaspati in the hearth: "install in his seat the wise and lofty Bṛhaspati, whose back is dark; let us worship him who sits in the womb, who shines in the dwelling, the golden-coloured one, the luminous one." The wording refers to the fire cult so clearly that it can hardly mean anything other than the installation of a fire; neither in this verse nor in III.26.2 there is, as Oldenberg believes, a comparison or a similarity with Agni, but it is Agni himself who is conveyed to his seat. Here Bṛhaspati is called *nī́lapṛṣṭha*, which is a designation of Agni elsewhere. Like Agni he is *dáma ā dīdivát* and *híraṇyavarṇa*. There is no trace here of a human brahmin, identified with Agni and Bṛhaspati, as Oldenberg thinks. Of course, there are other passages inviting Brahmaṇaspati to take his seat, which need not necessarily refer to a priest. It is but natural that one wishes that the god who is invoked may take his seat. VII.97 deals with the god. v. 3: "Worship the best and gracious Brahmaṇaspati with obeisance and offerings; may the very divine verse (*śloka*) attach itself to Indra, the king of the magic (*bráhman*), created by the gods." 4: "May Bṛhaspati, the most excellent one, who holds all desires, take his seat (cf. v. 6 *yásya nī́lavat sadhástham*). May he fulfil the desire for riches and heroic strength and lead us safely through difficulties." 5: "This our hymn, which pleases you, the immortal one, was created long ago by the immortal ones for you. Let us invoke Bṛhaspati, the irresistible, who speaks benignly[353] and who is worshipped in the dwellings."

The hymn goes on to speak of the god whom powerful red horses draw, describing him as shining brightly, equipped with hundred wings and a golden sword. "With his salutary arrival[354] he brings happiness and to his friends the best occasion for pressing." I do not think that this is "the phraseology referring not so much to the fire, but rather to the conventional, stylized and mythologically formed fire"; on the contrary, the wording and the turns of expression (*śatápattra svāveśá āsutím káriṣṭha*) are original.

This hymn is so clear in its main points that we can, without going into such particular speculations, simply say that it is the description of a natural phenomenon the character of which is alluded to by these words. I cannot see why the designation *śatápattra* should be understood other than literally, nor do I agree with Oldenberg that it should merely serve the imagination of the poet "to describe the free and air-like agility of the god." From the mythological point of view this expression is similar to those like *jyótiṣmantaṃ rátham ṛtásya tiṣṭhasi* (II.23.3); *tám áśvā vahanti* (VII.97.6); *pári dīyā ráthena* (X.103.4).[355] The Vedic imagination was not at all extravagant; as the Agni hymns show, it was fond of characteristic comparisons, though sometimes they might appear strange to us. In the present case the images are not even far-fetched.[356]

We find passages scattered throughout the ṚV which praise Bṛhaspati as the enemy and subduer of the darkness. II.23.3;

II.24.3 : *úd gā́ ājad ábhinad bráhamaṇā valám*
ágūhat támo vy àcakṣayat svàḥ
VI.73.3 ; X.67.4,5,10; 68.5,9; 155.2;
IV.50.4 : *bṛhaspátiḥ prathamáṃ jā́yamāno*
mahó jyótiṣaḥ paramé vyòman /
saptā́syas tuvijātó rávena
ví saptáraśmir[357] *adhamat támāṅsi* //

These passages do not convey anything beyond what we know already from V.43.12 and VII. 97. They merely support the view that the Vedic period regarded Bṛhaspati as a god of light endowed with an abundance of cosmogonic power.[358] We can determine his nature more precisely from the fact that his traits agree in many respects with those of Soma. This fact suggests that the concept of Bṛhaspati, like that of Soma, had its origin in the moon, but with one difference, which is indeed substantial — namely that in Soma the ambrosia-nature of the moon predominates whereas in Bṛhaspati the Agni-nature of the moon is predominant.

It is certainly no accident that in the Soma book of the ṚV a Bṛhaspati hymn is included — a fact that testifies to the similarity between Bṛhaspati and Soma :

IX.83.3 : *árūrucad uṣásaḥ*[359] *pṛ́śnir*[360] *agriyáḥ*[361]
ukṣā́[362] *bibharti bhúvanāni*[363] *vājayúḥ* /
māyāvíno mamire asya māyáyā
nṛcákṣasaḥ pitáro gárbham ā dadhuḥ //[364]

Compare IX.83.1 : *pavítraṃ te vítatam brahmaṇas pate*
prabhúr gā́trāṇi páry eṣi viśvátaḥ /
with IX.97.55 : *sáṃ trī́ pavítrā vítatāny eṣi*
ánv ékaṃ dhāvasi pūyámānaḥ /
or IX.106.14 : *rébhan pavítraṃ pary eṣi viśvataḥ* //

Since Bṛhaspati is a form of Agni, IX.83.2 speaks of his *tápoṣ pavítram*; X.182.3 speaks of him as *tápurmūrdhan*; he has the lightning at his disposal and fights *agnitápobhir arkaíḥ.*[365]

An essential trait of character common to both, but not to other gods to the same extent, is that both are Kavis, that both are connected with mind, thought and song.

Bṛhaspati :

I.18.7 : *yásmād ṛté ná sídhyati yajñó vipaścítaś cana* /
sá dhīnā́ṃ yógam invati //
I.190.1 : *gāthānyàḥ surúco yásya devā́*
āśṛṇvánti návamānasya mártāḥ ;
II.1.3 : *tvám [agne] brahmā́*[366] *rayivid brahmaṇas pate*
II.23.1 : *...kavím kavīnā́m upamáśravastamam* /
jyeṣṭharā́jaṃ bráhmaṇāṃ brahmaṇas pate...
II.24.9 : *sá saṃnayáḥ sá vinayáḥ puróhitaḥ*[367]
IV.50.1; X.141.3 : *brahmā́ṇaṃ ca bṛ́haspátim* /

Soma :

IX.76.4 : *pitā́ matīnā́m...*
IX.96.6 : *brahmā́ devā́nāṃ padavī́ḥ kavīnā́m*
ṛ́ṣir víprāṇām...
IX.96.18 : *ṛ́ṣimanā yá ṛṣikṛt...*
sahásraṇīthaḥ padavī́ḥ kavīnā́m;
IX.11.8 ; 75.2; 86.19; 96.5; 97.32; 103.4;
VI.52.3 : *bráhmaṇo gopā́m.*

See also the section on Kavi Soma. (pp. 246-248).

Bṛhaspati :

II.23.2 : *devā́ś cit te asurya prácetaso*
bṛ́haspate yajñíyaṃ bhāgám anaśuḥ /
AV XIX.63.1 : *devā́n yajñéna bodhaya* /[368]
Candramas :
X.85.19 : *bhāgáṃ devébhyo ví dadhāti...*

There are also other gods like Indra who are called Kavi. But they are not connected with wisdom and sacrifice to the same extent like Soma and Bṛhaspati, who were elevated to the status of the Brahmán and the officiating priests of the sacrifice. The reason is clear : we know from the texts how closely the moon and mind are thought to be connected :

X.90.13 : *candrámā mánaso jātaḥ.*[369]

In the chapter on Soma, it will be shown that he is the "lord of speech." Bergaigne[370] says of him that "eloquence is attributed to him personally." Here also it is evident that Soma and Bṛhaspati are mythological synonyms. The passages dealing with Soma should be compared, among others, with I.190.4 : *asyá [bṛ́haspáteḥ] ślóko divī́yāte pṛthivyā́m.* Men and gods hear him when he speaks with the voice of thunder (I.190.1). As the priest of the gods, Bṛhaspati utters the mantra which pleases the gods.[371] In I. 190.1; IV.50.1 he is called *mandrajihvá*; VII.97.5 *śúcikranda*; MS II.6.6 (67.8) Vācaspati. ŚBr XIV. 4.1.23 says: *eṣa u eva brahmaṇaspatiḥ / vāg vai brahma / tasyā eṣa patiḥ / tasmād u ha brahmaṇas patiḥ.*[372] Therefore, he is closely connected with the *chandas* in MS I.9.2 (132.2); according to VS 9.32, the Gāyatrī metre is assigned to him; the Bṛhatī helped the voice of Bṛhaspati.[373] It should be remembered that Soma is not only called *vācás páti*, but that the ṚV often speaks of him also as thundering and roaring (*krand, dham, nad, mā, rū, vāś, stan*), which can hardly refer merely to the hissing and swishing sound of the Soma juice. According to the content of the individual verses it can also refer to the action of the celestial prototype who "created the gods with thunder." Thus IV.50 speaks also of the "roaring" of Bṛhaspati with which he forcibly lifted up the ends of the world, blew away the darkness and broke open the cave of Vala.[374] Just as IX.97.13 says about Soma : *vṛ́ṣā śóṇo abhikánikradad gā́ nadáyann eti pṛthivī́m uta dyām*, so does X.67.3 speak of Bṛhaspati : *bṛ́haspátir abhikánikradad gā́ḥ*; thunder and lightning appertain to him.

Oldenberg[376] reproached me, saying that I did not attempt to describe how Bṛhaspati "acted" as the lord of the Brahman and that I set aside this concept too quickly in order to turn my attention exclusively to what I considered to be the moon god. As a matter of fact, Bṛhaspati does not act at all or acts only in so far as he is the Kavi of all Kavis, creates or prompts the thoughts and hymns and inspires the "system of thoughts"; but he is not active himself and is no more identical with the sacrifice and its parts than Prajāpati with the beings. He is only the lord of the sacrifice just as in *Kumārasambhava* VIII.58 the moon is *yajvānāṃ patiḥ*. It is the sacrificial aspect of the moon as the lord of sacrifice and of magic that is expressed by this name Bṛhaspati..

Like Soma or Indra, Bṛhaspati is a powerful fighter[377] who opens up the mountain and breaks open the fortresses, conquers the enemies,[378] particularly Vala, and discovers the cows;[379] the drums help him to victory;[380] he opens the well covered with a stone.[381] Like Soma or Indu, he joins Indra to become his comrade in arms.[382] The alliance between the celestial king and the celestial brahmin — expressed not so clearly at first, but later distinctly — is the model for the alliance between the Indian king and the brahmin.[383]

Both Bṛhaspati and Soma — but more particularly Bṛhaspati — have comrades in arms; in IV.50.5 it is the "host endowed with verses" with whose help he breaks open the cave of Vala,[384] in X.67.3 it is the friends cackling animatedly like haṅsas, in v. 7 "his friends, loyal, shining and treasure-winning," in v. 8 "his comrades who protect each other from blame." Roth wished to interpret them as the Maruts. This is not improbable,[385] but is, after all, contradicted by I.62.3, where Bṛhaspati helps the Aṅgiras' and Indra.[386] Sāyaṇa cannot decide between the priests and the Maruts. But if we examine this in correct perspective, only the Aṅgiras', of whom Bṛhaspati himself is one, can be considered as his companions. Soma is also connected with the Aṅgiras' and the opening of the cowshed;[387] he is also an Aṅgiras himself (IX.107.6). But it seems to me that the comrades in arms of Soma are not mentioned as often as those of Bṛhaspati and that the connection of Bṛhaspati with the clan of the fire priests is an original and more natural connection.

While Soma is a *vīrudhām pátiḥ* and is often called their king,

Bṛhaspati is seldom connected with the plants; but such connections do occur. It is said in

X.97.19 : *yā́ óṣadhīḥ sómarājñīr víṣṭhitāḥ pṛthivī́m ánu |*
bṛ́haspátiprasūtā asyaí sáṃ dhatta vīryàm ||

Oldenberg and Strauss[388] are opposed to my view; the former says that the context of the hymn deals throughout with the magic in which plants are used. "For this magic they are made active by the brahmin whose magic spell they listen to...i.e., mythologically speaking, by Bṛhaspati." But in this verse the plants are described as *sómarājñīr* and *bṛ́haspátiprasūtāḥ*; what have these epithets to do directly with magic ? And should Bṛhaspati really stand for a brahmin here ? In TBr I.3.6.7 the gods organize a race to win the plants and it is Bṛhaspati who wins them;[389] it does seem that there was a tradition which assigned the plants to him. Finally there are three more parallels (leaving aside the others which are not equally important):

1) Soma is the father of the gods IX.86.10; 87.2; 109· 4; Bṛhaspati II.26.3. Further X.72.2 : *bráhmaṇas pátir etā́ [devā́nāṃ jánā] sáṃ karmára ivādhamat.*

2) Heaven and earth carry Soma as the mother carries the offspring III. 46.5; heaven and earth, who begot Bṛhaspati (*devásya jánitrī*), make him grow through their greatness VII.97.8.

3) Soma is the god of the Manes; Bṛhaspati is connected with them IX.83.3; X.68.11.

I believe that in view of the many common traits one can regard the same natural phenomenon to be the basis for the concept of both the gods with the difference that in one case the Agnirūpa-aspect and in the other the Amṛtarūpa-aspect of the moon predominates. Therefore, both the gods exist side by side and can be connected mythologically with one another, although there is no intrinsic objective reason. When e.g., it is said in ṚV X.109.5 (and also in AV V.17.5 in a different context) *bráhmacārī carati vévịṣad víśaḥ sá devā́nām bhavaty ékam àṅgam | téna jāyā́m ánv avindad bṛhaspátiḥ sómena nītām juhvàṃ ná devā́ḥ*, then a new formation was created from mythological fragments or atoms, which has no objective significance. Nor should we expect from one or the other name of the moon any hints concerning the concepts of the waxing or waning moon, of the moon's reign over the night, or over the months,[390] because each personification has been created with one specific thought in mind. Thus the sun can be divided into different aspects which are always governed by a specific area of views : Sūrya, Mitra, Viṣṇu, Savitṛ; the moon can be divided into Candramas, Soma, Bṛhaspati etc., and the wind into Vāyu, Mātariśvan, the Maruts, who are not arbitrarily interchangeable (Vāyu cannot stand for Mātariśvan, the Maruts for neither of the first two). These aspects, originating in different cults, merged in the ṚV and there they formed the basis and provided an occasion for new formations, which are mostly the signs of declining appreciation of the origin of one or the other of these deities.

Therefore, I would like to sum up by saying that Bṛhaspati or Brahmaṇaspati — the latter name should be regarded as a gloss to the former[391] — is no abstraction, but can be shown to be a form of the sacrificial fire on the basis of V.43.12, that the overwhelming majority of examples indicates a natural phenomenon which can be regarded as the eponym of that fire (just as Vaiśvānara is the eponym of the Āhavanīya), and that the many parallels with Soma, which cannot be ignored, indicate the moon god. It is not necessary to look for the Bṛhaspati fire among the three fires of the sacrificial place itself, although Bṛhaspati is also called *triṣadhasthá*. The connection of Bṛhaspati with the Aṅgiras', who are very closely connected with magic and exorcism,[392] and the fact that the adjectives *āṅgirasa* and *ābhicārika* are treated as synonyms in the ritual texts remind us of the exorcisms which one can perform not only at the Dakṣiṇa fire but at any magic fire, kindled in an unspecified manner. However, the lord of magic is the moon.[393] In TBr II.7.1.2 we find a strange injunction for the Hotṛ of the Bṛhaspatisava : he should wear his hair in the form of a wreath, have the colour of twilight (*aruṇa*), blink his eyes (*mirmira*) frequently and be an excellent scholar of the Veda. (Also *Kāṭhaka* 37.7).

In the later period Bṛhaspati became the planet Jupiter. This is an instructive example for the complete change of concepts of gods in course of the Vedic evolution. It has not been proved that the ṚV called the planets with names, and it is not likely that the ṚV conferred on one of them such a significant title as Bṛhaspati has and installed him on the altar as "fire." Like Roth, I cannot see a connection between the earlier and later positions of Bṛhaspati and I believe that his name was transferred to the planet only when his original character as a fire god and as the eponym of the fire god was forgotten.[394]

K. SOME CLANS BELONGING TO THE FIRE CULT

We have seen (p. 48) that two names are prominent in the Pravara : Manu[395] and Bharata. Bharata is the name of an ancient clan, and Agni is regarded as its progenitor. In the Adhvaryu ritual we encounter two more names : Bhṛgu and Aṅgiras. When the Puroḍāśa cakes have been placed on the hearth and covered with coals, one wishes that they should become glowing "through the *tapas* of the Bhṛgus and the Aṅgiras'."[396]

The same names appear in the Agnyādhāna. The glowing fire is placed *yatharṣi* into the newly constructed hearth and, according to ĀpŚS V.11.7, an Āṅgirasa puts it there *aṅgirasāṃ tvā devānāṃ vratena* and a Bhārgava[397] *bhṛgūṇāṃ tvā devānāṃ vratena.* In the case of those who do not belong to either of these two gotras, this place is taken by the Ādityas; a Rājan invokes Varuṇa and a Rājanya invokes Indra and so on.[398]

1. The Aṅgiras'

Who are the Aṅgiras' ? I think Ludwig was quite correct when he (III.138) "comes to the conclusion that they really formed a group, that the Āṅgirasas really existed" and that "it is obvious that we therefore do not necessarily have to believe in a personal Aṅgirāḥ who was supposed to be living at one time."[399]

Theoretically it would be possible that "Aṅgiras" was the name of those gods who were degraded to the level of heroes; on the other hand, it is also possible that these gods were elevated to heaven from among the Vedic families. In deciding this question one should not ignore the frequently mentioned gotra of the Aṅgiras'. We encounter members of this family or tribe among the poets of the ṚV: "Hiraṇyastūpa," "Savya," "Kutsa" etc. In all, the *Anukramaṇikā* shows about 45 different names of men who call themselves after this gotra.[400] Many of these names are fictitious or mythical, but it would not be correct to banish all of them into the realm of fantasy. We know that Vāmadeva, the Kaṇvas, the Pajras (cf. PW, s.v. Pajra) etc., and also the Maudgalyas[401] counted themselves among the

Aṅgiras'. We also know that Bergaigne speaks "of a primitive liturgy common to the whole family of the Aṅgiras'."[402] Aṅgiraso occurs together with Vessāmitto, Yamataggi, Bhāradvājo (*Vinaya Piṭaka*, vol. I, p. 245).[403] Buddha (as Gautama) is called an Aṅgiraso (ibid., vol. I, p.25).[404] Gṛtsamada Śaunaka was once an Āṅgirasa Śaunahotra and then became a Bhārgava Śaunaka;[405] that is to say, he changed his family just as Śunaḥśepa changed his from the clan of the Aṅgiras', to which the gruesome Ajīgarta Sauyavasi belonged, to the clan of Viśvāmitra Bhārata. Bṛhatsāman who was pierced by men was an Āṅgirasa (AV V.19.1). Saṃvarta Āṅgirasa consecrates Marutta Āvikṣita during the Rājasūya (ABr VIII.21.12). Following the example of Hiraṇyastūpa Āṅgirasa, the poet of X.149.5 invoked the god Savitṛ.

So far little attention was paid to the statements of the Brāhmaṇas about the contests between the Aṅgiras' and the Ādityas, between the Devas and the Asuras, and similar others. Although many of these statements might be worthless and aetiological, by studying them one would come to realise that certain characteristics and sagas were peculiar to the gotra of the Aṅgiras', which, it seems, other families did not know or, at least, did not cultivate. Thus, besides the Aṅgirasām Ayana, which was known even to the AV (XVIII. 4.8) and which will be discussed later, they performed a particular Dvirātra which consisted of a Jyotiṣṭoma, Agniṣṭoma and a Sarvastoma Atirātra with a specific arrangement of the Stomas.[406] It is different from the Dvirātra which the Kāpeya priests (the priests of the Kapi gotra) performed for King Citraratha; it also differs from a third variety by means of which Kāpivana Bhauvāyana got rid of his disease. Furthermore, during the construction of the Agniciti the twenty-one hiraṇyeṣṭakas[407] are piled with an express reference to the method of the Aṅgiras' with the formula : *tayā [prajāpati-] devatayāṅgirasavad dhruvāsīda.*[408] In other respects also, the ritual of the Agniciti has borrowed much from the custom of the Aṅgiras'. The spade with which the soil necessary for the ukhā is dug is taken *aṅgirasvat*; the clay is dug *aṅgirasvat* and carried in the same way (TS IV.1.2-3), and so on. Thus it seems that the Aṅgiras' had a considerable share in the development of these ceremonies.[409] The Aṅgiras' are known already to the ṚV as Sāma singers. According to X.108.8, they belong to the *ṛṣayaḥ sómaśitāḥ.* I.107.2 : *áṅgirasāṃ sā́mabhiḥ stūyámānāḥ*; X.78.5 : *viśvárūpā áṅgiraso ná sā́mabhiḥ.* Long ago they discovered the cattle with *āṅgūṣya sāman* I.62.2. They took part in breaking open the rock or cowshed and were Indra's assistants I.51.3; 62.3; 71.2; 132.4; II.11.20; 20.5; IV.2.15; 16.8; 51.4; V.45.8; VI.17.6; 18.5 etc.[410] While referring to them, Vedic terminology uses, apart from *sāman*, the nouns *ucátha* II.20.5; *gír* I.121.1; *arká, bráhman* VI.65.5;[411] *ráva* I.71.2; and the verbs *arc* I.62.2; II.17.1; III.31.7; *gṛ* I.62.5; II.15.8; IV.16.8 etc.; *nu* IV.3.11; V.45.8; *ribh* X.92.15; *vad* VI.18.5. The later tradition is in complete agreement with the ṚV. Like the Aṅgiras' of the past, their descendants also sing. A great number of Sāmans are traced back in the later literature to individual names of this clan; this is seen especially in the TMBr and, although a great number of the names listed there is fictitious, there is no reason even in this case to think that all of these are invented. I have collected the following from the TMBr and shall give below without, however, deciding the question as to which are invented and which are historical.[412]

In TMBr XIV.3.32, Ayāsya deprives the Ādityas of their food by eating it and saves himself with Sāmans; in XVI.12.4 as Udgātṛ he holds sway over the Ādityas and on the day of the Adyasutyā when he receives the white solar horse as remuneration for the sacrifice, he becomes weak and saves himself with specific Sāmans.[413] According to the *Anukramaṇī* also Ayāsya is considered the author of ṚV IX.44-46 and X.67-68. The last two hymns are dedicated to Bṛhaspati and at the same time praise the Aṅgiras' who assist Bṛhaspati. Ayāsya is mentioned in the ṚV itself : I.62.7 (?); X.67.1;[414] 108.8 (where he is mentioned with the Aṅgiras' and the Navagvas); he is one of the mythical progenitors of the Aṅgiras clan.

Other names mentioned in the TMBr are *Akūpāra* (*āṅgirasī*)[415] IX.2.13-14 and *Akūpāraḥ kaśyapagotra ṛṣiḥ* XV.5.30. Furthermore, *Uttāna* I.8.11 receives the inanimate as a gift.[416] *Karṇaśravas* XIII.11.14. *Kruñc, Kruñca*[417] XIII.9.10; 11.19-20; XIV. 11.29; TBr II.6.1.2 etc. *Go* XVI.7.7. *Ghora*[418] KBr XXX.6. *Tiryañc* XII.6.12 (wards off the Rakṣas' who follow the Aṅgiras' on the way to heaven just as Harivarṇa warded them off in VIII. 9.2). *Dāvasu* XV.5.14. *Nṛmedhas* VIII. 8.22 celebrates a Sattra and, while doing so, is chased by dogs and turns to Agni with

Sāmans. *Paṣṭavaḥ* XII.5.11. *Yuktāśva* XI.8.8. *Vyaśva* XIV. 10.9. *Śammad* XV.5.11. *Śiśu* (calls the Manes always *putraka*) XIII.3.24. *Śukti* XII.5.16. *Śnuṣṭi* XIII.11.21-22. *Haviṣkṛt* and *Haviṣmat*[419] XI.10.9-10; XX.11.3; TS VII.1.4.1.

It is clear that only a very small and indeterminable number of these names has any historical value; but it is also equally clear that the facts connected with some of the names anticipate a historical clan. It can be seen that these names and the events connected with them do not refer to the gods who punish and reward, or who prescribe laws, but to men to whom the invention of certain customs or sagas is attributed and who, however, stand firmly on this earth.

In the hymn to the dead, X.14, the ṚV mentions Yama and the Aṅgiras' together;[420] besides these, there are other names : Vairūpas, Kavyas, Navagvas, Atharvans, Bhṛgus, all of whom are beings who do not belong to the world of the gods. In the AV the "*áṅgirasaḥ sukṛtaḥ* follow the path of the *ṛtá*" XVIII. 4.13; like the sacrificer, they are called *sukṛt* in v.7 of the same hymn. In ṚV X.14.6 *ángiraso naḥ pitáraḥ*[421] are mentioned; AV XVIII.1.61 says of them that "they went to heaven."[422] ṚV X.62 praises them as Manes and as cosmogonic power. "Adorned" with sacrifice and dakṣiṇā, they attained the friendship of Indra and immortality; as ancestors they drove out the cattle from the hiding place; *parivatsare* they cleft Vala asunder through *ṛta*, made the sun rise and spread out the earth. In v. 4 they are addressed as *dévaputrā ṛṣayaḥ*. This shows that here we are dealing with the cult of the Manes. As the juxtaposition shows, the Aṅgiras' and the Pitaraḥ are not identical[423] — in TBr II.1.1.1 they are even antagonists — but they are Manes, not in a general sense, but as a particular group. They are the ancestors of a particular tribe or, at least, of a gotra. Probably a gotra is suggested also by ṚV I.121.3, which speaks of the *víśaḥ* of the Aṅgiras', but the interpretation of this verse is difficult.[424] The *pū́rvo áṅgirāḥ* in X.92.15 is not a real being but an abstract mythical progenitor like Manu.[425]

It seems that the cult of the Manes attained a special importance in the Āṅgirasa gotra. We are led to this conclusion by the close connection of their names with *abhicāra*, and also by the epithet *ghorá* given to them in X.108.10. In the Atharva texts the Atharvans and the Aṅgiras' are differentiated in such a way that *bhaiṣajya* and *śānta* fall to the share of the former and *abhicāra* to the latter.[426] In AV X.1.6 an *āṅgirasaḥ purohitaḥ* is the *adhyakṣa*, leader, during the exorcism. AV VIII.5.9 speaks of *āṅgirasī kṛtyā*. In *Kauśika Sūtra* XIV.30 etc. the magical fire is *āṅgirasa agni*.[427] In the magic directed against the army of the enemy in AV XI.10.10 ff. *Bṛhaspati āṅgirasa* and the *ṛṣayo brahmasaṃśitāḥ* are mentioned together. Neither the Bhṛgus nor the Atharvans are characterized in a similar way. It seems that among these the cult of the Manes did not attain equal prominence.

There are some other traits which seem to be particularly peculiar to the tradition of the Aṅgiras', though not exclusively so. A good example is the *tapas*. We have mentioned earlier the formula with which the Puroḍāśa cakes are placed : *bhṛgūṇām aṅgirasāṃ tapasā tapyadhvam*. It is said in the ṚV that they observe *tapas* and thus create the cattle.[428] TMBr XV.9.9 narrates that the Aṅgiras' get into heat through their penance and cause rain through a Sāman; according to TBr II.1.1.1 they create rain (by means of the Kārīrīṣṭi) and thus create the plants for their cow.[429] While explaining the sacrificial bath, TS VI.1.1.2 narrates that on their way to heaven the Aṅgiras' threw away *dīkṣā* and *tapas* into the water.[430] All these are family sagas starting from the same basic idea.

The "cow" which they own according to TBr II.1.1.1 is another motif from the treasure of their sagas. It is said in ṚV I.139.7 that the gods presented this cow to them.[431]

The girdle which the sacrificer puts on during the consecration for the Soma sacrifice is called *āṅgirasī* in the mantra which accompanies this act.[432]

A special saga, typical of the Aṅgiras', seems to have been connected with the Agniciti, which is closely linked with the Aṅgiras ritual. As an explanation why the tortoise is embedded in the altar, TS V.2.8.4 says : *aṅgirasaḥ suvargaṃ lokaṃ yataḥ puroḍāśaḥ kūrmo bhūtvānuprāsarpat*.[433]

In the legends of the Brāhmaṇas, the Aṅgiras' are often mentioned as connected with the Ādityas. As early as in the ṚV and AV they are mentioned together, though no reason for this is given there.[434] However, it is likely that even at the time of the ṚV similar legends existed as they were current in the prose literature. It is a special feature of the Aṅgiras tradition that it does not compare its progenitors to the gods (Devas) but to the Ādityas. The relation between the Ādityas and the Aṅgiras' corresponds to a certain extent to that between the Devas and the Asuras. Thus in TMBr XXIV.2 they celebrate together a Sattra of thirtythree days, where the Ādityas perform a sacrifice of twentyone days and the Aṅgiras' a sacrifice of twelve days and both attain success in this world and in the other. Or they build jointly the fire altar in TBr III.10.3.[435] As a rule, they are not as skilful as the Ādityas. They miss the right ceremony or the right moment and accomplish nothing at all or reach the goal only after the Ādityas have done so. Thus they organize a Sattra to attain heaven, but already on the second day they become confused, and find the sacrifice only with the help of a hymn suggested to them by Śāryāta Mānava (ABr IV.32.8). Or they become confused on the sixth day and receive a similar advice again from a Mānava, called Nābhānediṣṭha (ABr V. 14.3).[436] Elsewhere it is said that they reached heaven, but did not find the path of the gods.[437] According to AV IX.5.16, a "he-goat" shows them the way.[438] Or they reach there by themselves, but some of them remain behind; thus the above-mentioned Kalyāṇa, or Haviṣkṛt, and Haviṣmat,[439] who invent two Sāmans and incorporate them into the Dvirātra; or Cyavana in the well known legend of the Aśvins in ŚBr IV. 1.5.1, who remained behind when the Bhṛgus or the Aṅgiras' went to heaven. Often there is an antagonism or a rivalry between the Ādityas and the Aṅgiras'. While Āditya Bhṛgu and the Ādityas rise out of the flames of the semen of Prajāpati, the Aṅgiras' come out of the "coals" (probably a fanciful etymology based on the consonance between *aṅgiras* and *aṅgāra*) and out of the rekindled "coals" comes Bṛhaspati.[440] Besides the Gavām Ayana, there is the Ādityānām Ayana and the Aṅgirasām Ayana. While the Ayana of the Ādityas does not have any Pṛṣṭhyaṣaḍaha, that of the Aṅgiras' shows no Abhiplavaṣaḍaha.[441] The following legend seems to have had the widest circulation. ŚBr III. 5.1.13 ff.[442]: "There were two kinds of beings at the beginning, the Ādityas and the Aṅgiras'. Then the Aṅgiras' were the first to prepare a sacrifice. When they had prepared the sacrifice, they said to Agni : 'Announce to the Ādityas our Soma sacrifice for tomorrow. They should perform the sacrifice for us.' 14 : Then the Ādityas said : [We should] contrive that the Aṅgiras' perform the sacrifice for us and not we for them.' 15 : They spoke : 'There is no other way out of this except by a sacrifice. Let us perform another Soma sacrifice.' Thus they prepared a sacrifice. Having prepared it, they said : 'Agni, you announced to us a Soma sacrifice for tomorrow; now we announce to you and to the Aṅgiras' a Soma sacrifice for today. There you will be our Hotṛ., 16:...the Aṅgiras' ran after Agni and were angry at him [whom, as the ABr adds, they considered one of them].[443] 'Why did you not, as our messenger, think of us ?' 17 :...the Aṅgiras' performed the Sadyaḥkrī sacrifice for the Ādityas (as the hosts of the sacrifice); that is *sadyaḥkrī*.[444] 18 : These offered to them (the Aṅgiras) the Vāc as dakṣiṇā. This they did not accept...The performance of the sacrifice was not completed, for the sacrifice should have a dakṣiṇā. 19 : Then they brought them Sūrya as dakṣiṇā. Him they accepted. Therefore the Aṅgiras' say : 'We are worthy of the sacrificial office; we are also worthy to receive the dakṣiṇā. Even he that burns yonder has been received by us.' Therefore the dakṣiṇā for a Sadyaḥkrī sacrifice is a white horse." The saga of the Aṅgiras' receiving a horse as the sacrificial fee is narrated elsewhere too[445] and belongs to the most permanent family traditions of this clan. Legends connected with ritual should be used only with a great amount of caution; often they are purely aetiological and, as a rule, they cannot be used in interpreting mythology. But the motif of the "white horse" being transferred to the Aṅgiras' from the possession of the Ādityas cannot be ignored, particularly when we take into account a different version of this legend in the ABr. According to this text, the Aṅgiras' receive from the hosts of the sacrifice the earth full of dakṣiṇās before receiving the white horse.[446] "As the earth was received, she burnt them. They threw her away. Turning herself into a she-lion, she ran among men, opening her jaws wide. As a consequence of her heat, the crevices that were on her opened. Previously she was even..." The burning earth clearly indicates the summer season and the transfer of the white horse from the hands of the gods into those of the Aṅgiras' agrees with this. Whatever one might think of this legend otherwise, the two motifs which connect the Aṅgiras' with the declining time of the year are not without value and are quite compatible with the view which tries to prove that the Aṅgiras' were the ancestor-gods of a tribe. Other legends from the tradition of this clan may also be mentioned here; thus the saga which narrated that the Aṅgiras' get into heat through their penance and cause rain, or that by means of the Kārīriṣṭi they produce rain and through it herbs for their cow (see p. 112).

The Aṅgiras' reach heaven after the Ādityas and that too with the help of the Anukrī sacrifice. A further step on the euhemeristic path — if one may attempt to divide the statements about the Aṅgiras' into their individual phases — had led them to the side of the gods. Once it was believed that, like the Devas[447] or like the Ādityas,[448] they reached heaven,[449] then the last step could easily be added by tradition. Thus in TS VII.1.18 Vasus, Rudras, Ādityas, Viśve Devāḥ and Aṅgiras' stand on the same level : *aṅgirobhir devebhir devatayā...yunajmi.*[450] In ABr VIII. 12.4; 14.3 they follow the Vasus, the Rudras etc., and rule over the *ūrdhvā diś* along with the Maruts;[451] we find the same in the AV[452] and in the ṚV.[453]

To sum up, Aṅgiras is the name of an ancient family (clan) which had particular traditions in cult and in myth. Like the descendants, so also the ancestors, *pitaraḥ*, of this clan were called by their clan-name.

Furthermore, I shall attempt to show that the Paṇis were no traders or "misers," but a marauding tribe, which appears still in the sixth maṇḍala as an enemy of the Aryans, whereas in book X they appear in the form of demons hostile to Indra. It seems to me that the Aṅgiras' are an antithesis to them. Here we find a clan or a tribe — the lines of demarcation can hardly be drawn — which elevated its ancestors into gods or god-like beings who begin to enter the realm of mythology, and placed them in heaven. Here we encounter the impact of the cult of the Manes on Vedic mythology. The conclusion that they were messengers and travel between heaven and earth has no basis anywhere and was drawn only from a dubious etymology (Gr. *aggelos*). Nor can I find a connection between the Aṅgiras' and Iran.[454]

2. Bhṛgu[455]

The Bhṛgus cannot be separated from the Aṅgiras'.[456] But we should not treat them as identical, although they have several traits in common, and although in the later period there is a tendency to identify the two names. Even the compound *bhṛgvaṅgiras* would contradict such an identification.[457] By analysing the allusions to their nature in literature, howsoever scanty they might be, we can recognize the outlines of an independent group of sagas connected with the Bhṛgus. These sagas differ in many important aspects from those of the Aṅgiras', negatively as well as positively.

1. While the Aṅgiras' trace themselves back to Agni and treat Bṛhaspati as one of them, Bhṛgu, the progenitor of this clan, traces himself back to Varuṇa : the statement, *bhṛgur vai vāruṇih*, is well known to the Veda.[458]

2. While the Aṅgiras' open up the cowshed or assist Indra in this task with their singing (X.62), our sources are silent about this activity in the case of the Bhṛgus; instead, their service in installing or kindling the fire is emphasized. Of the 23 passages, 13 refer to this :

a) They search Agni or discover him in his hiding place X.46.2; they worship him at the seat of the waters II.4.2.

b) They produce him and install him.[459]

c) They kindle him with Stomas X.122.5; I.127.7.

d) Mātariśvan brings I.60.1, or kindles the hidden one for the Bhṛgus III.5.10.

In the case of the Aṅgiras' the ṚV touches upon this very motif of kindling the fire only slightly. Of course, Agni himself is often called Aṅgiras; in I.83.4 the Aṅgiras' are called *iddhágna-yaḥ*; Agni is invoked *manuṣvat*, *aṅgirasvat*, *yayātivat* to come near I.31.17, or he is invoked *aṅgirasvat*, *bhṛguvat*, *manuṣvat*.[460] It is said in V.11.6 that the Aṅgiras' found Agni in his hiding place; but, strictly speaking, they are not associated with the kindling of the fire so often as the Bhṛgus are. On the other hand, the Bhṛgus have almost no connection at all with the magic of the Aṅgiras'.[461]

Other Ṛgvedic passages that might be relevant here are VII. 18.6, where the Bhṛgus and the Druhyus are mentioned as the obedient clans,[462] and VIII.3.9; 6.18, where they, or their progenitor Bhṛgu, and the Yatis are closely connected, and mentioned as the worshippers of Indra.[463] It should follow, at least from the first passage, that the Bhṛgus are earth-born and not gods. The earlier attempts to connect them with Gr. *phlégyes* seem to be justified.

Otherwise the ṚV says very little about them. They defeat Makha (IX.101.13),[464] are called *dhī́ra* (X.46.2), *somyá* (X.14.6), and mentioned together with Apnavāna (IV.7.1), with the Aṅgiraḥ Pitaraḥ, Navagvas and Atharvaṇs (X.14.6) and parallel to different gods (VIII.35.3).[465]

We can obtain some characteristic details about the Bhṛgus from the ritual also.

a) They have the same position as the Aṅgiras' in the mantra *tapasā tapyadhvam* (see p. 108) and also in the formula for installation : *bhṛgūṇām* or *aṅgirasāṃ tvā vratenādadhe.*

b) They are seers of the Sāmans, but not so often as the Aṅgiras' (TMBr XIV.3.23; 9.39).[466] According to KBr XXII. 4, Gṛtsamada Bhārgava (*v. l.* Bābhrava) incorporates a Nivid in a certain Sūkta. Otherwise, of the names that are mentioned, we have only a Cyavana Bhārgava who consecrates Śāryāta Mānava (ABr VIII.21.4),[467] a "Bhṛgu" who is killed by the Sṛñjaya Vaitahavyas (AV V.19.1)[468] and Vidanvat (TMBr XIII.11.10).

c) They are mentioned as sacrificers or priests during the Agnisthāpana ceremony of the altar-construction in a verse (TS IV.6.5; AV IV.14.5) and also in a mantra (TS V.6.8.6; MS I.4.1)[469] although they do not play such an important role as the Aṅgiras' do in this ceremony.

d) They are to act as the Hotṛ in the Daśapeyakratu[470] — an allusion to the existence of a particular gotra.

e) When a Puroḍāśa is not a success and therefore "has Yama as the presiding deity," then an *odana catuḥśarāva* must be prepared after the sacrifice and served to four brahmins among whom there must be a Bhārgava (ĀpŚS IX.15.19).

f) They are *pañcāvattin* like the Jamadagnis and some others.[471]

g) The Aitaśāyana Ājāneyas are the offspring of Muni Etaśa and a curse was laid on them by their father. Therefore, they are regarded as the lowest among the Bhṛgus.[472]

h) Unlike the Aṅgiras' they have almost no share in the *abhicāra* (see pp. 111-112).

Although the references are meagre, I think that on the basis of these factors we can speak of a real historical gotra, which did not play any substantial role in the history of the Vedic tribes, and left behind only relics of its customs and sagas. Like the Aṅgiras' they were also elevated to the position of gods in worship; already the ṚV counts them among gods (p. 117). Of course, the compound *bhṛgvaṅgiras* indicates a close relationship, but on the basis of the above-mentioned facts we can still recognize sufficiently the difference in tradition and sagas between the two clans. The legend according to which the Bhṛgus and the Ādityas originate from the flames, whereas the Aṅgiras' from the coals of the semen of Prajāpati, insignificant in itself, still shows the difference between the Bhṛgus and the Aṅgiras'.[473] As far as I know, it is nowhere stated that the Bhṛgus compete with the Ādityas for heaven as the Aṅgiras' do, or that they lag behind them. This also can be regarded as a decisive factor in the tradition.

3. Atharvan

Besides the Bhṛgus and the Aṅgiras', the Atharvans are also mentioned in the hymn to the dead, ṚV. X.14.6.[474] But more often the word occurs with the Aṅgiras' only[475] and Atharvāṅgiras is a well-known compound like Bhṛgvaṅgiras.[476] The compound Bhṛgvaṅgiras or Atharvāṅgiras, important from the point of view of literary history, has, as far as I know, no counterpart like Bhṛgvatharvan. From this we may conclude that Bhṛgu and Atharvan are identical or at least closely connected. But of these two possibilities only the second can be correct. In the difficult task of finding the right answer we have to depend on the *Avesta* which knows Atharvan as an agent noun only, viz., as a designation of priests.[477] We can conclude from this that the word was once an appellative in the Veda also, and was, to a certain degree, the precursor of the later designation Agnihotrin. It occurs in the ṚV only 15 times[478] in 14 (13) hymns. It does not occur in books II-V, once each in books VIII and IX, four times in three hymns of book VI; the other references occur in books I and X. Atharvan as a proper noun in the singular is, as Ludwig (III.143) already remarked, "a mythical figure,"[479] which was derived from the appellative. In AV IV.1.7; VII.2.1 he is the *pitṛ devábandhu*, and the verses which speak of him have a mythical character, while the appellative meaning of the word comes out more clearly in the plural.

1. Atharvan and Fire. Only in one case the relationship has something characteristic, and does not occur often enough

so that we can ascribe a particularly prominent share in the fire cult to the Vedic Atharvans.

VI.16.13 : *tvám agne púṣkarād ádhi átharvā nír amanthata...*
14 : *tám u tvā dadhyáṅṅ ṛṣiḥ putrá īdhe átharvaṇaḥ* /[480]

The other passages are not significant. X.21.5 : *agnír jātó átharvaṇā*; VI.15.17 : *atharvavád agníṃ manthati.*[481]

2. In very general terms I.83.5; X.92.10; AV XIX.4.1 speak of Atharvan mythically as the first sacrificer. Cf. also I.80.16, where "Atharvan, Manuṣpitṛ, Dadhyañc" spread the *dhī*. In AV X.10.12, 17 Atharvan sits consecrated on a golden sacrificial bed of straw (cf. n. 486 below). AV X.2.26-27 is completely mystical.

3. Indra is his patron. *ahám índro ródho vákṣo átharvaṇaḥ* X.48.2; Bṛhaddiva Atharvan invokes Indra X.120.9; AV V.2.9.

4. His relationship to Varuṇa is rather more important. Varuṇa who presents "the cow" to Atharvan (AV VII.104; V.11.1) is also regarded as his father.

AV V.11.11 : *ájījano hí varuṇa svadhāvan*
átharvāṇaṃ pitáraṃ devábandhum /[482]

This statement is not unimportant, for it confers on the Atharvans the same progenitor as Bhṛgu has. Bhṛgu is also a son of Varuṇa (see p. 116 above). Thus the tradition joins them with a link, howsoever weak it may be; with this link they stand together *vis-à-vis* the Aṅgiras' who trace themselves back to Agni and regard Bṛhaspati as one of them, though he is not their progenitor. Bṛhaspati is not an Ātharvaṇa or a Bhārgava, but an Āṅgirasa. The poet of AV IV.1.7, by mentioning *atharvan pitṛ* and Bṛhaspati together,[483] refers to the progenitor of the Atharvans and the most typical god of the Aṅgiras'.[484]

We are on firmer ground when we discuss the use of the word Atharvan in the plural; the references may be few, but they deal with persons and not with abstract mythical beings.

1. The Atharvans use honey as a cult object. ṚV IX.11.2 : *abhí te mádhunā páyó 'tharvāṇo aśiśrayuḥ.* Dadhyañc who is a Ṛṣi and a son of Atharvan — one of the few names that occur[485] —informs the Aśvins where madhu may be found with Tvaṣṭṛ (ṚV I.117.22) etc.[486]; the later period has turned this into a Madhubrāhmaṇa.

2. Ātharvaṇa as singer and worshipper of Savitṛ. AV VI.1.1 : *doṣó gāya bṛhád gāya dyumád dhehy ātharvaṇa stuhí deváṃ savitáram.*[487]

3. The Atharvans receive chariots, horses and cattle as sacrificial gifts from Aśvatha (ṚV VI.47.24). There should not be any doubt that these are real sacrificial priests in this case as well as in paragraph 1. above.

4. In TBr III.4.1.11 an "*avatokā*" (who has had a miscarriage) is assigned to them. This probably indicates a dispicable position.

5. We learn nothing about their sacrificial requisites; but plants are connected with the Atharvans as they are with the Aṅgiras'. The Atharvans, Kaśyapa, Kaṇva etc., drive away the Rakṣas' with a plant (AV IV.37.1). The plants are *ātharvaṇīr āṅgirasīr daivīr manuṣyajā uta* (see n. 429 above).

This information is not enough to enable us to draw positive conclusions. But from the common progenitor Varuṇa and from the alternate inclusion of their names in the compounds *atharvāṅgiras* and *bhṛgvaṅgiras*, we can infer a close relationship between the Atharvans and the Bhṛgus. But this does not make the two words identical, for they are mentioned side by side in X.92.10 and in the hymn to the Manes, X.14.6. Like the Bhṛgus and the Aṅgiras', the Atharvans were also included among the ancestor gods and have their independent position. But if we adhere to the view that the word Atharvan is an appellative name of certain priests, then it would seem to follow that Bhṛgu is the name of the clan and Atharvan the designation of its priests. This is nothing but a hypothesis. But in *Māntrika Upaniṣad* 10 (ed. Bombay, p. 324b) there is a statement, to which I attach a slightly greater importance than Bloomfield[488] does : *paṭhanti bhárgavā hy ete hy atharvāṇo bhṛgūttamāḥ*; one could take this as a corroboration of my view. But I should not neglect to refer to *Gopatha Brāhmaṇa* I.2.22 which does not support my hypothesis.[489]

CHAPTER FOUR

SOMA

PART I

THE SOMA PLANT

The renowned Soma plant occupied such a prominent position in the cult of ancient India and of ancient Iran for thousands of years and occupies still that the question about its home and its original characteristics has attracted the attention of scholars even beyond the circle of Sanskritists, and has been the subject of much research.

It will be useful to make a brief survey of the present position of this problem, which appears to have become more difficult the more one attempted to solve it.

Anquetil Duperron[1] reports about a plant used in his time by the Parsees that it is a shrub which the Parsees regard as sacred and to which they ascribe the power to confer immortality. "They claim that there is nothing of this kind in India and add that this tree would never decay, that it does not bear fruit and that it resembles the vine. The *Farhang Jahangiri* mentions some characteristics which help us in recognizing the Hom. According to that work, Hom is a tree which grows in Persia; it resembles sweet heather, its knots are very close to each other and the leaves are like those of Jasmine. This description of the yellow and white Hom; the places where this tree grows, i.e., the mountains of Shirwan, Guillan, Mazendran and the neighbourhood of Yezd; the qualities which some books ascribe to it — all these details make me believe that Hom is the *amomos* of the Greeks and the *amomum* of the Latins..."

He goes on to say (p. 536) : "the Dasturs of India are in the habit of sending at the end of a certain season two Parsees to Kerman to search for the branches of Hom."

The plant used in recent times in India for extracting the juice is identified as *Sarcostemma viminale* by eye-witnesses and modern scholars : thus Stevenson[2] and also Windischmann.[3] The latter, like A. Kuhn,[4] calls the plant *Asclepias acida* or

Sarcostemma viminalis.[5] In his *Indische Altertumskunde* I, 2nd edn., p. 931, Lassen speaks of *Sarcostemma vim.*

The species used now is discussed in greater detail by Haug in *Göttingische Gelehrte Anzeigen* 1875, p. 568:[6] "The Soma plant is not a mere plant, but a creeping and somewhat twisting semi-shrub with a series of leafless shoots which contain an acidulous milky juice. Its present botanical name is *Sarcostemma intermedium* (de Candolle, *Prodromus*, p. 538). It grows everywhere in India. *Sarcostemma brevistigma* and *S. brunonianum* are closest to it (ibid). In *Icones plantarum Indiae orientalis*, vol. IV, No. 1281, R. Wight gives an illustration of it which should be compared with the text on p. 17."

All this, however, does not suffice to answer the question whether the Soma of the Vedic Indians and their ancestors is related at all to the present one and whether the Indians throughout their migrations in Punjab and in the Ganges valley did use, and could use, always the same plant as their ancestors and the ancient Iranians did. The enquiry into the nature of the plant used today is obviously quite different from that concerning the plant used in the ancient period. This is why Max Müller drew our attention years ago to a description of the Soma plant given in a book on medicine. Although this description does not inform us as to what kind of plant the Vedic Indians pressed, it nevertheless takes us back perhaps a thousand years or more:[7]

śyāmalāmlā ca niṣpattrā kṣīriṇī tvaci māṅsulā /
śleṣmalā vamanī vallī somākhyā chāgabhojanam //

i.e., the creeper called Soma is dark in colour, sour, leafless, milky, and fleshy on the surface. It causes phlegm and vomiting and is eaten by goats.

But this evidence, quite useful in itself, should not be overestimated. A passage which does not belong to the Veda proper can never be regarded as decisive for a period which is earlier by hundreds if not thousands of years — a period in which the Indians were settled in lands other than the one to which the above-mentioned text book of medicine supposedly owes its existence.

Alone the great distance which separated the Indians from their older home and which, at least, made the supply of the plant difficult makes it improbable that after their migration into the land of the five streams the Indians regularly used the same plant as their ancestors did.[8] On the contrary it is much more probable that a firm tradition developed with regard to the substitutes for the plant when migrations to other settlements made it necessary. This seems to be true also for certain parts of India, if not for all, in view of the fact that the description given by Haug agrees with the *śloka* cited by Max Müller. In the foreword to his *Elements of South Indian Palaeography*, p. 1, n. 1, Burnell informs us that in South India occasionally quite different plants are used; on the Coromandal coast *Asclepia acida*, but on the Malabar coast *Ceropegia decaisneana* or *Ceropegia elegans*, quite different in appearance from the former.

Therefore, an attempt should be made to collect from the oldest texts themselves whatever can be ascertained for the identification of the plant, which was the favourite of the Vedic Indians. In two excellent articles,[9] Roth has exposed the weak points in the prevailing notions and stated that *Sarcostemma acidum*[10] "has the best claim to be the Soma plant of today," "that the real Soma was likewise a *Sarcostemma*, or at least belonged to the family of *Asclepiadeas*, and that consequently the tradition in India was correct as far as it could be."

Both the articles were translated into English at the instance of the Government of India, Revenue and Agricultural Department (file 118), and caused some adverse remarks by Dr Watt; these remarks were appended to the translation and ended with the rebuke "that Dr Roth instead of propounding his own theory at such length and in attempting to confute arguments against it, did not rather publish briefly the leading passages from Sanskrit literature descriptive of the plant, which the Aryan poets found so pleasing a theme and simile of perfect happiness." Watt rejects the view that Soma must have been a plant full of sweet juice. He says that Roth has advanced no argument to support the view that Soma was a kind of *Sarcostemma* or any other *Asclepiadea*, and that nothing seems to speak against the supposition that the Soma juice was a decoction. On the other hand, he thinks, it is likely "that the oblong fruits of the Afghan grape (often not unlike in shape and size the joints of the human finger) were described as the joints of the stem of a succulent plant, and were thus refused the position of being regarded as fruits, and that these, imported into the plains, as they are at the present day, afforded the sweet and refreshing cup of which our Aryan ancestors became drunk while wrapt in the oblivion of religious enthusiasm." He believes that it could also have been one of the *Compositae* or *Umbelliferae* which supplied most of the precious produce of the Afghan-Persian region since time immemorial.

This publication was followed by an interesting exchange of letters between Max Müller, Roth, I. G. Baker, W. T. Thiselton Dyer, Charles G. Leland and A. Houtum-Schindler,[11] published in the weekly journal *The Academy* in 1884 and later reprinted by Max Müller in his *Biographies of Words*, p. 222 ff.

Max Müller opens the discussion with a renewed reference to that Āyurveda passage taken from a *ṭīkā*. Roth retorts that he cannot attach any value to a passage from a *ṭīkā*, i.e., a commentary on a commentary, and that these verses cannot serve as a guide to the botanist. He says further : "I am, indeed, still inclined to believe that the genuine original Soma, which will perhaps be discovered in the highlands beside the Oxus, will bear great resemblance to this (*Sarcostemma acidum*), its later substitute." Opposing Watt's theory, he adds : "I am sorry not to be able to conform my views to those of the distinguished botanist. The Aryans no more drank a decoction of the Soma plant than they drank tea or coffee. It would be, indeed, a disgrace to the interpreters of the Veda and Avesta if Dr Watt were right. Since this is not the place to enter into details, I will call attention to one place in the *Atharvaveda* V.29.12. The wish is there expressed to a convalescent, that all the flesh which his disease has stripped off, may be replaced on his body; 'that his limbs may increase in roundness; that he may grow plump like the shoot (*aṅśu*) of the Soma.'"

I. G. Baker takes up the argument from the point of view of a botanist. He is of the view that the description from a medical text cited by Max Müller appears to refer clearly to *Sarcostemma* because, as far as he knows, no other creeper existed in the old world with leafless and fleshy stems which supplied a sufficient quantity of milky juice. But in case this description is not sufficiently authenticated or old, then it is first of all necessary to collect the scattered authentic statements for further confirmation.

W. T. Thiselton Dyer, on the other hand, influenced by the negative attitude of Roth towards the *ṭīkā* passage, takes up again the idea of Watt that Soma could be the vine, because Roth looks for the genuine Soma in the highlands beside the Oxus and A. de Candolle, on the other hand, regards Bactria, Kashmir and Badakshan as part of the home of the vine.

Against this, Max Müller adheres to the importance of the Āyurveda passage, since this is the oldest available passage which gives an actual botanical report about Soma. It is the classical passage, he argues, and should be taken into account before we go further if only to determine what was understood by Soma. Moreover, he points to the fact that according to the statement of the hymns themselves the Soma juice was mixed with cereal (*yava*, probably barley) and milk, a fact which forces us to give up the idea of vine. He supposes that we could perhaps think of hops rather than of vine.

In continuation of this, Houtum-Schindler reports about a plant which was shown to him as the Hom plant during a journey between Bender Abbas and Kerman at a height of 7000 feet and which reminds us of the description by Anquetil, given above. "It was, as far as I could make out, a *Sarcostemma* or *Asclepias*, growing to a height of four feet, and having circular fleshy stalks of whitish colour, with light brown streaks;...the leaves had fallen off as well as the flowers which, I was informed, were small and white; some seeds adhered to the ends of some stalks...the juice was milky, of a greenish white colour, and had a sweetish taste. A Pârsī who was with me, as well as others in Kerman and Yezd, told me that the juice turns sour after being kept for a few days, and that the colour of the juice, as well as that of the stalks, turns to a yellowish brown. The plant I saw was not a creeper; but I was assured that when it grew near a tree it twined around it...The Hûm grows also in plains, but is then stunted and contains little juice..." Houtum-Schindler goes on to say that the botanical description cited by Max Müller agrees closely with that of the Persian Hom plant. But the description must have come from a person who had seen the plant not in its freshness, but only many days after it had been collected. Then the juice would have turned sour and the leaves fallen off etc.

Thiselton Dyer writes an epilogue to this exchange of letters, in which he weighs the different possibilities without, however, taking a decision himself. Of other theories, I came across only the following. The first is of Dr Aitchinson, who in a communication (not available to me) to the *Daily News* of March 13, 1885, has stated that Soma was probably the vine. The second is Dr Watt's *Second Note on the Soma plant*. This contains, i.a., a letter from Dr Rice, who considers the possibility that Soma could have been "sugarcane or some species of sorghum"; it also contains a letter from Rajendra Lal Mitra to the Government of India, where he says:

"In the later Vedas, the juice of the plant appears to have been used, like hops in Europe, as an ingredient in the preparation of a kind of beer and not as a beverage by itself. In poetry of course they talk of drinking the Soma juice, but this, in the Brāhmaṇa period of the Vedas, is looked upon as a figure of speech. The rituals nowhere enjoin the use of the juice by itself as a meet of offering. If we may rely on this interpretation of the Brāhmaṇas and the rituals as the right one, it would be in vain to search for a plant with profuse sweet juice, for the Soma. The word 'sweet' which so much puzzled the learned Professor von Roth, may be safely, nay appropriately, used in a poem in praise of bitter beer."

To this highly dubious statement, the improbability of which will be shown in my exposition, Watt adds the following : "This exceedingly valuable contribution gives a completely new phase to the enquiry, rendering the idea of a 'sweet sap' no more a necessary quality of the Soma of the ancients. If this be accepted, the *Homa* may after all prove to be the *Soma*, the dry and bitter twigs having, as at the present day with the Homa, been simply used to flavour some other beverages, much in the same way as *Acacia* bark is used throughout India. This completely removes all necessity for searching for a succulent plant and renders *Sarcostemma* the least likely of all the plants which have been mentioned as the possible Soma of the Vedas." Watt then suggests *Periploca aphylla*.

Long before this time Lagarde, in his *Gesammelte Abhandlungen*, pp. 172-176, made a distinction between the Soma of the Indians and that of the Iranians; he saw in the oldest Soma plant a kind of rue, in fact that which is called *sahásrapājas* in the ṚV. It corresponds, he said, to *peganon* of the Greeks, called *moly* in Cappadocia; it was described by Homer as a plant with black roots and milk-white blossom, "difficult for the mortals to dig."

Brunnhofer took up the idea of Lagarde and saw an important clue in the mention of Cappadocia by Dioscorides. He wishes to take ṚV IV.3.4 also into account, an obscure passage as he himself admits, where he interprets *kṛṣṇā́ satī́ páyasā pīpāya*, "although it is black, it is full of white nourishment," as the Soma plant, the mountain-rue. These views of Brunnhofer and Lagarde take us across too many shaky bridges and should be regarded as mere hypotheses.[12]

Recently Havell[13] and Bhraja Lal Mukerjee[14] joined the discussion. Havell thinks that Soma is *Eleusine coracana* or *rāgi*. Mukherjee opposes this identification and gives much data, the usefulness of which is, however, doubtful. But he is right when he rejects an identification of Soma with *Canabis* (bhāng).[15]

In view of this great divergence of opinion, we cannot claim that the joint efforts of philologists and naturalists have led to positive results. It appears to me that Vedic philology has certainly not responded sufficiently to the oft-repeated wish for a collation of all passages in the Veda about the Soma plant, and the little it could offer has not been well authenticated. Watt's rebuke towards Roth is not without foundation, and he is not wrong when he says : "that the exceedingly desirable enquiry would be best conducted by placing in the hands of the naturalist to the Commission a brief abstract from the Sanskrit authors, and thus leave his mind unbiased by theories."

However, the nature of our sources makes it more difficult than one who is unaquainted with Vedic philology could imagine to fulfil the demand for a "brief abstract from the Sanskrit authors"; because the oldest sources, to which we turn at first, do not contain a single exact description of the plant, the juice of which the singers do not grow tired of praising. I have examined the question as thoroughly as possible, and present here for further examination the material collected by me, without attempting at a botanical identification — unfortunately not with the desired brevity, since it is impossible not to devote more space to the exegesis than would appear necessary to the non-Sanskritist.

It can be shown with great certainty, I hope, that the ingredient used for the beverage was not a blossom and that the hypothesis, postulated at first by Max Müller, that it could be hops which was added to a beverage does not find any support in the Vedic sources. Furthermore, it will become evident that, besides water, cow milk was one of the most important things to which the Soma juice was added, or more correctly, which were added to the Soma juice — cow milk in different forms, sour or sweet — and also barley flour. But the latter is by no means more important than the admixture of milk, since it is used generally on two occasions only. Finally there is a rarely done mixture with a drink called Surā, as well as an admixture of honey, which is hardly extant in the ritual any more, but can still be deduced from the Vedic hymns. It will also be shown that the Soma juice was offered in sacrifices without any admixture also and that it cannot be regarded as a mere admixture to other drinks in view of the quantity which had to be produced with the help of stones or mortar.[16] I have not come across any positive evidence that Soma was extracted from grapes. Everywhere it is the juicy "shoots" of light colour with joints, perhaps also with edges, called occasionally "fingers," "reeds," once or twice directly "branches," that are mentioned in the hymns, but not the berries. The view entertained by Thiselton Dyer that the designation *aṅśu* dates from a period which did not know the morphological difference between shoot and fruit as clearly as we do today, and that *aṅśu* in the passage from the AV, cited by Roth, could probably refer to the plump berries of the vine also, does not find any support in any passage of the ṚV.[17]

I do not have the impression that the plant, regarded as the most excellent one by the ancestors of the Vedic Indians, must necessarily have been the same as the one used by their descendants in India for obtaining the divine drink. Even the statements of the Vedic texts seem to contradict each other; this is not at all surprising because the Vedic texts were composed in various periods and in various places. But this contradiction, if it exists at all, would always be with regard to the plant as such; all the passages agree that it is the "shoots" or "stalks" which supply the drink. The ṚV states repeatedly that these are bright-coloured; with a rare degree of unanimity all the text books of the ritual stipulate that the plant should possess this quality; therefore, this must be based on the oldest tradition. The Vedic Indians had a naturalistic reason for this. The Soma plant is a lunar plant. Stevenson called it the "moon plant."[18]

A bird brought it from heaven and its bright stalk is a bright "moon beam." Of course, there is the heresy of an emancipated person who proclaims : "One thinks that one is drinking Soma when one crushes the plant; but none enjoys drinking that which the brahmins know as Soma." But it is partly because of the above reason that we have a series of expressions which designate the moon in the same way as they designate the plant and which reach even up to the ṚV. The moon and the plant are called Soma, *aṅśu* is his ray as well as its shoot, *āpyāyana* his waxing and its swelling with juice. The plant is the highest in vegetation and the moon is the lord of vegetation. This parallelism is enlarged further and is transferred to the simple rites at the sacrificial place, which were generally considered the imitations of the celestial events. The *pavitra*, the strainer through which Soma flows, is like the *pavitra* in the heavens, the colour of the drops is golden like the lustre of the moon, the drops flowing through the strainer are like rain.

Let us, however, discuss the plant first.

A. CHARACTERISTICS OF THE SOMA PLANT

1. Soma has hanging Branches

In the ṚV there is a verse, III.53.14, which, because of wrong interpretation, has not been used so far in the enquiry into the external appearance of the plant :

kím te kṛṇvanti kī́kaṭeṣu gā́vo
nā́śiraṃ duhré ná tapanti gharmám /
ā́ no bhara prámagandasya védo
naicāśā́khā̃ṃ maghavan randhayā naḥ //

In the *Festgruss für Böhtlingk*, p. 43, I have ventured a hypothesis, based on the 11th verse of the above hymn, that this hymn belonged to the ritual of the Aśvamedha, a sacrifice which kings performed in order to ensure victory and booty for themselves and their tribe. The verse cited above refers comtemptuously to the Kīkaṭas and their chief Pramaganda as the enemies of that king whom the singer served. The translation of the first two pādas is not difficult. It follows from these two pādas that the antipathy towards the Kīkaṭas was based not merely on the racial differences, but more so on the differences in cult, which are indicated by the use of words, *āśír* and *gharmá*; these words are normally used in the ritual. *Āśir* is the term, known even to the ṚV, for the milk added to Soma; *gharmá* is the word for the vessel used in the Pravargya ceremony, which is likewise, as Garbe has shown, not unknown to the Vedic hymns. As against this, the rest of the verse, which was interpreted variously, presents more difficulties.

Here we are concerned with the question whether it is correct to render *naicāśākhá* as "inferior tribe" or as "riff-raff" as some people have translated. Although Sāyaṇa and even Böhtlingk-Roth share this view, it can be shown that this is not correct, because neither in the RV nor in the AV nor in the YV the simple word *śākhā* had the secondary meaning, "stock of a tribe or people," but merely that of "bough, branch" of a tree or of a plant. Still less can this meaning be anticipated in a compound; *daśaśākhá*, "with ten fingers," is no proof against this. Accordingly, *naicāśākhá* can only mean "that which belongs to one which has low branches." It is formed like *naiyagrodha* from *nyagrodha*; one can regard it as a substantive or add *védas* to it.[19] Hence, the verse should be translated as follows :

"Of what use are the cows among the Kīkaṭas to you, Indra ? They do not milk for you, nor do they cook gharma. Bring here to us the possessions of Pramaganda. Hand over to us whatever they have of the one with low branches."

The tree or shrub "with low branches" which appears so desirable to the Viśvāmitras could hardly have been anything but the Soma shrub that supplied the most delicious of the drinks. Thus quite significantly a third member joins the ranks of *āśir* and *gharmá* : Of what use are to you the cows of the Kīkaṭas, who neither prepare any milk-drink for you nor perform the Pravargya ? Better give them to us. Give us also their possession of the Soma plants, "because," we should add, "they do not press the Soma plants for you."

Unfortunately the meaning of Pramaganda is not certain. Yāska IV.33 says that *maganda*=*kusīdin*, i.e., usurer. Pramaganda would then mean "arch-usurer," and we would have to look for tradesmen in the tribe of the Kīkaṭas. But the association of the Kīkaṭas with Pramaganda indicates that it is more likely that Pramaganda is the name of the king of this tribe, which in all probability was non-Aryan. We do not know where this tribe lived. Zimmer, AIL, p. 31, places it in the region south of the Yamunā and the Gaṅgā, which is cut across by the lower Śoṇa and the smaller parallel rivers in the east. But this view is based merely on the unauthenticated statements of two later lexicographers, viz., the author of *Trikāṇḍaśeṣa* II.11 and Hemacandra IV.26, who equate Magadha with Kīkaṭa. Therefore I share the doubts which Oldenberg[20] had towards this identification. I also think that, even if this identification is correct, the possibility is not ruled out that the name was transferred in the later period.

The statement of the Viśvāmitra hymn that the Soma has hanging branches is based probably on an old tradition. For my interpretation is supported by an epithet of Haoma, which occurs once in the *Avesta — Yasna* 9.16 : *nąmyąsuš*, which, when interpreted correctly, proves to be almost synonymous with *naicāśākhá*. Ever since Justi rendered the Avestan word as "with soft and moist stalks," most of the German translators[21] have understood it in the same way. In this process Neriosengh's *mṛdupallava* as well as the Persian word *nam*, "moist,"[22] played a greater role than is admissible. For to connect *nąmyąsuš* with *nabh* and related words, on which this interpretation is based, is more than questionable from the linguistic point of view. Therefore Mills is more correct when he renders its a "with bending sprouts."[23] We should compare the first part of this doubtful word, *nąmi*, with another expression in *Yasna* 36.2 : *nąmištahyā nəmaŋhā*.[24]

There is no reason to treat *nąmišta* as quite different from the present *nąmin* (*namra*); it is the most obvious superlative for the latter. Thus *nąmyąsuš* means "with bending and low-hanging branches" and agrees with *naicāśākhá* completely.

The same expression *śākhā* referring to the Soma branches meant for pressing is found in another verse. This takes us a step further.

2. Soma has bright-coloured Branches

a. *aruṇá*, BRIGHT-RED, BRIGHT-COLOURED

The verse occurs in hymn X.92, addressed to the Soma stones. The name of the author of this hymn, Arbuda Kādraveya Sarpa, is apocryphal. The third verse of this hymn reads as follows :

eté vadanty ávidann aná mádhu
ny ūṅkhayante ádhi pakvá ámiṣi[25] /

vṛkṣásya śā́khām aruṇásya bápsataḥ
te sū́bharvā vṛṣabhā́ḥ prém arāviṣuḥ //

"These speak. They found honey there. They hum over the ripe flesh. Chewing the branch of the reddish tree, the bulls roared."[26]

It follows from this that at the time when this hymn was composed and in the ritual of its author the fleshy ripe branch of a reddish tree or tree-like shrub was used for the extraction of the Soma juice. This fact is after all of some importance; for, although this hymn belongs to the later part of the collection of the hymns, it still belongs to the ṚV, that is to say, it belongs to the oldest evidence we possess.

There is no doubt about the meaning of *aruṇá*, "reddish." In the ṚV it is a frequent epithet for Dawn, for the sun, his rays, or "cattle." Also the steeds of Vāyu and of the Maruts, the adornment of lightning in which they clothe themselves, and the wolf are "*aruṇá*."

There is one more passage which can be cited as evidence. VII.98.1 : *ádhvaryavo aruṇáṃ dugdhám aṅśúm*
juhótana vṛṣabhā́ya kṣitīnā́m /

"Adhvaryus, make an offering of the reddish shoot which was milked to the lord of the people."

A third passage, X.144.5, is rather doubtful :

yám te śyenā́ś cā́rum avṛkám padā́bharad
aruṇám mānám ándhasaḥ /
enā́ váyo ví tāry ā́yur jīváse enā́ jāgāra bandhútā //

The word *māná*, with its divergent accentuation, creates great difficulty and prevents us from making any use of this verse.[27]

The fact, attested by two passages of the ṚV, that the Soma stalk has a reddish colour is not to be underestimated. For the rule that the Soma plant or its substitute should be "aruṇa-coloured" or of similar hue extends through the later literature of the Brāhmaṇas and Sūtras in so far as any colour is mentioned there. Apparently Roth did not attach any value to this point. Nevertheless, I do not hold this point to be so insignificant that it should remain unstated. Adalbert Kuhn[28] has rightly paid greater attention to the statements of the Brāhmaṇas. It is said in ŚBr IV.5.10.1 ff.[29]

"If one wants to carry off Soma, one should say : 'run and search.' If they find it, then there are no consequences. But if they do not find it, then atonement is made. 2 : There are two kinds of Phālguna plants, some with red blossom and others with reddish blossom. He should press those which have reddish blossom. For these with reddish blossom are akin to Soma. Therefore he should press these which have reddish blossom. 3 : If one cannot find (Phālgunas) with reddish blossom, then one should press the Śyenahṛta plant. For when Gāyatrī flew in search of Soma, a Soma shoot fell down from her while she was bringing it, and became the Śyenahṛta plant. Therefore he should press the Śyenahṛta plant. 4 : Should he not find the Śyenahṛta plant, he should press the Ādāras. Because when the head of the sacrificial victim was cut off, the Ādāras took shape from the juice squirting forth from it. Therefore he should press the Ādāras. 5 : If one does not find the Ādāras, he should press the reddish Dūrvā plants. For the reddish Dūrvā plants are akin to Soma. Therefore he should press the reddish Dūrvās. 6: If one does not find the reddish Dūrvās, then he can also press any gold-coloured grasses."

Although the colour is not specifically mentioned in the case of many plants enumerated here, still from these rules the preference for the aruṇa-coloured plants as the substitute for the lost Soma can be recognized. We see that of the two kinds of Phālgunas, those with reddish blossom and those with blood-red blossom, only the former can be chosen as the substitute, and when such a one is not available, not the other type but a completely different plant should be used as a substitute, about the colour of which nothing further is said. Also of the Dūrvās only the reddish variety is mentioned, and even the Kuśas, permitted as a last resort, should at least fulfil the condition of being *harita*, "yellow."[30] These rules should not be completely ignored simply because it is possible to suppose that the choice of a substitute was narrowed down to such plants which corresponded to Soma in juiciness as well as in appearance, particularly with regard to the colour of the stalks, and in this choice it is certain that the taste of the juice was sacrificed to the external appearance. With regard to such substitutions we find two criteria mentioned by Śāṅkhāyana III.20.9ff., which have too much of inner probability not to have been in currency for a long time. 9 : "Should this [enjoined] material be not available, he should substitute it with that which he regards as most similar.

10 : That is the custom during the substitutions.[31] 11 : A change in the wording [of the mantras, verses etc.] does not take place."

Thus when Soma was not available it was not any random milky plant that was chosen as the substitute but, from time immemorial, only such plants which showed also the most of the external similarities. I do not share the view of Roth that it was a mere theory of the priests when they applied the rule of the substitute material to the case when Soma was stolen. For even in a land where the plant grew in abundance there must have been miscreants who grudged others the pleasure, or who secretly took away the herb which had been freshly brought from the mountains or collected in the valleys from the pious men who were getting ready to offer it in sacrifice, whether to sell it again or to enjoy it themselves. For it is not likely that Soma grew on the roadside within easy reach of everybody. One had, at least, to fetch it from the mountains or collect it in the valleys, either oneself or make others to collect it, and even from this fact it follows that the plant had a certain commercial value in the ancient period.

b. *babhrú*, RED-BROWN, BROWN

babhrú is a colour, though not exactly identical,[32] still close to *aruṇá*. The word appears as the designation of the steed, of the cow, of Rudra (who is also called *aruṣá*, "reddish," and in the later period *tāmrá*, *aruṇá*, *lóhita* etc.),[33] of Agni, of the dice, of a vulture (AV V.23.4) and of some plants not identified further.[34] However, nowhere was it used for the colour of the Soma plant but only for the drops and for the god Soma himself. If I mention it all the same, I do so because of a rule in *Tāṇḍya Brāhmaṇa* IX.5.3, which prescribes substitutes of this very colour.[35] Considering the close affinity between the expressions *aruṇá* and *babhrú*, this close agreement between the statements of this Brāhmaṇa and those of the ŚBr is not insignificant. It will be seen, moreover, that as in the case of *aruṇá* so also in the case of *babhrú* there is a complete agreement between the colour of the plant or of its substitute and that of god Soma, which is explained in the commentary of the TS in the following words : *candramaṇḍalasya suvarṇatvād babhrutvaṃ somasya rūpam*,[36] i.e., *babhrú* is the colour of Soma because the disc of the moon is golden. It will be shown later that this explanation, which appears at first sight to be of no great value and of later origin, has a material background.

c. *hári*, GOLDEN

The epithet *hári*, which is almost synonymous with *aruṇá* and *babhrú*, is not used often for the Soma plant; only in one passage it is positively connected with Soma, namely in IX.92.1 :

pári suvānó hárir aṅśúḥ pavítre
rátho ná sarji sanáye hiyānáḥ |

"the golden shoot was pressed and hurled on the strainer like a chariot despatched for profit."

This designation with *hári* has a special significance; for it is well known that the Avestan texts speak repeatedly of *zairi*, *zairigaonō haomō*,[37] without however informing us whether this refers to the stalk, or leaves, or fruits.[38] Thus it is quite probable that as early as in the Indo-Iranian period the same colour was regarded as the characteristic of the genuine Soma plant.

Like *aruṇá* and *babhrú*, the epithet *hári* is also used to designate the Soma drops and the god Soma.

Moreover, the bright-coloured exterior of the plant is evident from a comparison in ṚV I.137.3 :

tā́ṃ vāṃ dhenúṃ ná vāsarī́m aṅśúṃ duhanty ádribhih |

"They milk for you the shoot, which is like a bright-coloured cow, with stones." The usual rendering of *vāsarī́* as "of morning" is hardly correct. Ludwig translates it as "leuchtend" (shining) and means probably the same as I do. *vāsará* as a substantive means, as is well known, "day" and not "morning." In any of the three passages where the word is used as an adjective it is neither necessary nor admissible to interpret the word *vāsará* as anything but "bright." In ṚV VIII.48.7, *áhāni vāsarā́ṇi* are bright days. And in our passage Soma is compared to a bright-coloured cow precisely because of its colour.[39]

d. THE COLOUR OF THE SOMA COW

In connection with the preceding I would like to discuss one more point from the ritual literature, which shows unmistakably how much significance was attached to the golden-yellow or bright colour of the Soma plant in the later period. Even

Ludwig[40] refers to the colour of the cow which serves as the price for Soma.

It is an easily understandable feature of the ritual that the animals which were consecrated to the gods must have the same colour that was ascribed to the life-element or the form of manifestation of the god concerned.[41] The choice of colour therefore plays a great role in all ritual injunctions. It will be seen now that in the choice of a Soma cow precisely the two colours are considered which are regarded as the distinguishing marks of the Soma plant. For instance, it is said in ŚBr III.3.1.14 ff.[42] : "the red-brown one with reddish-brown eyes is the Soma cow. The red one is the property of the Vṛtra-killer, which the king takes over here after he has won the battle. The red one with white eyes,[43] this one belongs to the Manes, which they slaughter for the Manes. 15 : The red-brown one with reddish-brown eyes, that is the Soma cow. If he does not find such a one, it should be a bright-coloured one.[44] If he does not find a bright-coloured one, it should be a red one that belongs to the Vṛtra-killer. But he should never think of a red one with white eyes." The passage that follows this is less interesting since it contains the obvious rule that the Soma cow should be without any blemishes, i.e., not horn-less or tail-less etc., and also not with calf.

We learn from this extract that the colour of the Soma cow must be "red-brown" or "bright-coloured" (reddish) as the case may be. All the texts of the Vedic literature that I have gone through are agreed on this condition. It is said, e.g., in TS VI.1.6.7 : *aruṇáyā piṅgākṣyā́ krīṇāti | etád vái sómasya rūpaṃ sváyaivaínaṃ devatáyā krīṇāti*, "he buys for a bright-coloured, yellow-eyed cow. That is Soma's colour. For its own deity he buys it."[45] Similarly VII.1.6.2 : *tásmād róhiṇyā piṅgaláyaíkahāyanyā sómam krīṇīyāt*, "therefore he should buy Soma for a red, yellow-eyed, one-year-old cow." Furthermore, MS III.7.4.1 : *yā́ruṇā́ bábhrulomnī śvetópakāśā śucyadakṣī́ tát somakráyaṇyā rūpáṃ svénaivá rūpéṇa krīyate*,[46] "a bright-coloured, red-brown-haired one with white spots and bright eyes; that is the form of the Soma cow. He buys it for its own form." TMBr XXI.1.3 : *sā babhruḥ piṅgākṣy ekavarṣā.* Likewise the Sūtras are unanimous in emphasizing this colour.[47]

It is far from my intention to overestimate the importance of this injunction; on the other hand, one should also not disregard the fact that the regular recurrence of this injunction guarantees a certain antiquity and that it forms one more link in the chain of evidence which from the *Avesta* and the ṚV onwards up to the later literature testifies to the fact that the colour of Soma, of the god as well of the plant, is given as golden, bright red, or something similar to that. To this should be added that almost everywhere where a sacrificial animal is prescribed for Soma the colour of this animal is given as *babhrú*.[48]

3. Other Statements about the Soma Plant

Two passages from the ṚV were cited earlier which show that the "branches" themselves were used for the extraction of the juice, but not the fruits. This is stated in ṚV X.85.3 also :

sómaṃ manyate papivā́n yát sampiṅṣánty óṣadhim

"he thinks that he has drunk Soma when they trample the herb"; also the use of some other words like *párvan, aṅśú* etc. appears to establish positively that it is only the stalks, the cylindrical parts of the plant, which supplied the juice.

a. *párvan, párus*, JOINT, STALK

párvan, like its synonym *párus*, means originally "joint, node,"[49] and then through an easily understandable transfer of sense "that which lies between two joints," limb or stalk. Thus it is said of Bṛhaspati in ṚV X.68.9 that he drew the marrow out of Vala as out of the stalk of a plant. AV IX.8.19 says :

yā́ majjñó nirdháyanti párūṅṣi virujánti ca

"they suck the marrow out and break the limbs." Therefore there can be no doubt about what should be understood by *párus* or *párvan* when they refer to the Soma plant. They occur in TBr III.7.13 (*Vaitāna Sūtra* 24.1) : —

yát te grā́vṇā cicchidúḥ soma rājan
priyā́ṇy áṅgāni svádhitā párūṅṣi |
tát saṃdhatsvā́jyenotá vardhayasva
anāgáso sádam ít sáṃkṣiyema ||

"O King Soma, that part of you which they broke to pieces with the stone, your lovely limbs,[50] your sweet joints,[51] you cure that again and let it grow with butter. May we live together without guilt." Furthermore it is said in *Vaitāna Sūtra* 24f. :

abhikṣáranti juhvò ghṛténa
áṅgā párūṅṣi tava vardhayanti

"the ladles pour butter over you and strengthen your limbs and joints." Finally, a third instance occurs in a mantra of the VS, which I shall quote under *aṅśú.* The *párvans* of the Soma plant occur in a passage of the ṚV also, viz., in I.9.1, which was explained by Roth and others in a completely different way :

indréhi mátsy ándhaso víśvebhih somapárvabhih |
mahā́ṅ abhiṣṭír ójasā ||

In both his dictionaries Roth explains *somapárvan* with the words : "probably the period of the Soma festival." Ludwig (no. 448) surmises a pun and translates it as "in all the limbs of the Soma stalk and at all the Soma festivals."[52] It is, however, not likely that *somapárvan* means the festival of Soma; for, although *párvan* can actually mean the festival period in one or two passages of the ṚV, viz., in I.94.4 and X.53.1, and although it has this meaning in X.53.1 ("Knotentag," the day of the joints), still it is those verses where the word has its original meaning that predominate. The two examples cited above which speak indeed of the *párūṅṣi* of Soma make it likely that our verse has this meaning. Therefore I translate as follows : "Come, Indra, rejoice in the drink, [rejoice] in all the shoots of Soma, mighty and benevolent through your strength."[53]

b. *aṅśú*, SHOOT, STALK

aṅśú belongs to the Avestan as well as to the Vedic literature and is employed in both cases for the Soma plant. Besides in the passage *Yasna* 9.16 (*nąmyąsuš*) mentioned on p. 111, it occurs in *Yasna* 10.2, a passage which gives no precise information about the meaning :

fratarəmčiṭ tē havanəm
vaca upastaomi huxratvō
yō ąsuš hangə̄urvayete

"one who collects your shoots." It also occurs in one more equally insignificant passage of the *Nīrangistān*, which Bezzenberger has discussed.[54]

In Sanskrit, *aṅśú* means "ray," besides the parts of a plant. In AV XIII.2.7 the sun-chariot is called *aṅśúmát*, "endowed with rays." Alone from this metaphorical meaning it appears likely that the usual translation as "shoot" is correct. This can be established from another example. In VS XX.27, which deals with the mixing of the Surā and Soma, the Surā, or the plant supplying the Surā as the case may be, is addressed thus :

aṅśúnā te aṅśúḥ pṛcyatāṃ párusā páruḥ |
gandhás te sómam avatu mádāya ráso ácyutaḥ ||[55]

"may your *aṅśú* mix with *aṅśú*, *párus* with *párus*."

If we examine the words that are usually connected with *párus* as *anśú* is here, we find repeatedly *áṅga* and also *kāṇḍá* occupying the place of *aṅśú*.[56] One can see from this that *aṅśú*, as well as the above words, must mean "limb, limb between two joints," and thus further "sprout, shoot." The commentary on the TS explains *aṅśú* quite correctly as *sūkṣmo 'vayavaḥ*, "slender sprout," and *párus* as *párva* (I.347).[57] In the magic formula AV V.29.12-13, where the wish is expressed to a convalescent that his limbs may gain in weight, that he may swell up *aṅśúr iva*, the word *aṅśú* requires the meaning of "shoot, sprout of a plant." The patient should swell up again like the juicy shoot of a plant.[58] It is therefore unlikely that this comparison could refer to "the swelling berries of the vine" as Thiselton Dyer believes[59] because, according to him, the morphological difference between a young shoot and fruit was not understood as clearly in that period as it is today. If we examine all the passages where *aṅśú* occurs, and for the time being leave those aside which refer to the god Soma and have a mythological content (e.g., IX.15.5; 67.28; 86.46; I.46.10), in no passage is it possible to speak of fruits or berries that could have been used for pressing.

It was shown above that these shoots must be of bright colour. Another characteristic of these shoots is the abundance of juice.

VIII.919 : *yád ápītāso aṅśávo gávo na duhra ūdhabhiḥ |*

"when these swelling shoots gave milk like cows with udder."

The Soma plants are called *tṛptáṅśu* in I.168.3 :

sómāso ná yé sutás tṛptáṅśavo
hṛtsú pītáso duváso násate

"[The Maruts] are like the pressed Somas with juicy stalks, which rest in the inside [of the body] like friends, after one has drunk them."

IX.74.5 : *árāvīd aṅśúḥ sácamāna ūrmíṇā*
devāvyàm mánuṣe pinvate tvácam |

"United with the wave, the shoot 'roared.' He makes his skin, which delights the gods, swell for man."[60]

Therefore it is said of Soma in VIII.12.5 : *samudrá iva pinvate*, "he swells like an ocean"; similarly IX.64.8; also IX.107.12 :

síndhur ná pipye árṇasā, "like a stream he was full of juice"; VI.44.21 : *vṛ̥ṣṇe ta índur pīpāya* etc.

The juice of the *aṅśú* is called *pīyū́ṣa*, derived from this very root *pī*, *pyā*.

III.48.2 : *yáj jā́yathās tád áhar asya kā́me*
aṅśóh pīyū́ṣam apibo giriṣṭhā́m /

"On the day of your birth you drank, full of longing, the juice of the shoot — the juice which descended from the hills." Likewise II.13.1; X.94.8. The milk of the shoot (*aṅśóh páyas*) is mentioned in IX.107.12,[61] and the wave of the shoot (*aṅśór ūrmíḥ*) in IX.96.8.

This juice is extracted by "pressing" the shoot; this is called *su*; *asāvi* IX.62.4; *sūvanó* IX.92.1; *sutá* I.125.3. More often, however, mention is made of the milking of the shoot : *duh* I.137.3; III.36.6-7; V.36.1; IX.72.6; 95.4; X.94.9. The choice of this expression also, which brings to mind the teats of the cow-udder and which indeed ought do so,[62] makes us assume that it was not the fruits which were used for extracting the Soma; they must have been at least longish and unlike berries.

The shoot is called "intoxicating," "inebriating," "sweet" : *madirá* VI.17.11; 20.6; *matsará* I.125.3; *mádhumat* IV.97.14. More important is the epithet *sugábhasti* in V.43.4 :

dáśa kṣípo yuñjate bāhū́ ádrim
sómasya yā́ śámitā́ra suhástā /
mádhvo rásaṃ sugábhastir giriṣṭhā́m
cániścadad duduhe śukrám aṅśuḥ //

The subject of the second half of this verse is, as can easily be recognized, *aṅśú*, and *sugábhastir* is an adjective to it. Ludwig has correctly understood this, but not the PW. Elsewhere *sugábhasti* is employed for those who press the Soma and for Tvaṣṭṛ.[63] There it means "dexterous" like the epithet *suhásta*, frequently used for the Adhvaryus. Of course, this meaning does not apply to the Soma shoot. With reference to a plant the epithet "with beautiful hands" can only mean a number of beautiful sprouts growing closely together. Ludwig translates the word as "thickly branched."[64] The translation is supported by a passage — to be discussed soon — where the "fingers" of Soma are spoken of, and also by the expression *bahulā́nta* in X.42.8 :

prá yám antár vṛṣasaváso ágman
tīvrā́h sómā bahulā́ntāsa índram /

So far this word has been interpreted variously. The PW renders the word, which occurs in this passage only, as "having a thick end (deposit)" and Grassmann shares this view. Ludwig translates it as "having a vast girth." I see no reason at all for the first of the two explanations. Even Sāyaṇa's explanation, *bahulam annādikam ante yebhyas te*, which even Ludwig considers "quite possible," seems to be closer to the correct meaning. As early as in the ṚV, *bahulá* means "much," besides "thick." Consequently *bahulā́nta* can very well mean "with numerous ends or stolons." *tīvrá* means "pointed"[65] and *sóma* stands for *somāṅśu*. Thus the verse should be translated as follows : "into whom the pointed Soma shoots with multiple branches entered in powerful pressings."

Consequently ṚV V.43.4 is to be translated thus : "The ten fingers and the two arms, the skilful slaughterers of Soma, harness the stone. The shoot with a beautiful stem milked its glimmering bright juice."[66]

Another passage in which probably the "hands" of the Soma plant are referred to is IX.110.5, to be cited below under *śárya*; however, its interpretation is not quite certain.

The expression *aṅśú* receives one more characteristic through the adjective *tigmá* in VIII.72.2 :

ní tigmám abhy àṅśúm sīdad dhótā manā́v ádhi
juṣāṇó asya sakhyám //

tigmá means "sharp, pointed," and is used in the ṚV for axe, thunderbolt and radiance; in one instance also for Soma itself, where it could only mean "tasting strong and pungent," III.48.3:

upasthā́ya mātáram ánnam aiṭṭa
tigmám apaśyad abhí sómam ū́dhar /

"He approached the mother and asked for food. He looked at the pungent Soma in the udder" (Geldner : "he looked at the hot Soma as the udder").

It cannot be decided whether in our first passage *tigmá* means "pointed" (with reference to the plant) or "pungent" (with reference to the juice); both would be materially correct.

It is said often that the shoot roars, thunders, hisses.[67] It is quite possible that during the crushing with stones the bursting shoots or the drops gushing out made a loud noise, or that the juice, streaming out of the shoot, made a hissing sound when it was mixed with milk.[68] That is not much relevant here since we are concerned only with the characteristics of the Soma plant. The emphasis given to these qualities will be understood only when it is presumed that the activities on the sacrificial place are imitations of those in heaven, and that the quality of the thundering and roaring bull is derived from the god Soma, who, as the favourite of Vāyu, accompanied by the Maruts, under thunder and lightning, shares with Indra the task of recovering the celestial cows. Soma is merely the terrestrial representative of the god of the same name. Expressions of his might are easily transferred to his representative. Unless we keep this in mind, we cannot understand several expressions. Thus it is said, e.g., in IX.68.6 that the *aṅśú* moves around;[69] in 74.2 that the support of heaven, the well-fitted container, the filled *aṅśú* moves around from all sides;[70] 71.9 : "like a bull which circles around the herd, [Soma] roared; he assumed the radiance of the sun";[71] 84.4 : "he excites the oceans with the winds."[72] Hence it would be better to interpret the words *dhámat* and *stanáyat* in the mythological part of this chapter.

c. *kṣip*, FINGER [73]

This word, used elsewhere only in the concrete sense of "finger," is the term for the shoots of Soma in IX.79.4, which speaks of their celestial origin :

diví te nā́bhā paramó yá ādadé
pṛthivyā́s te ruruhuḥ sā́navi kṣípah |
ádrayas tvā bapsati gór ádhi tvací
apsú tvā hástair duduhur manīṣíṇah ||

The second pāda is not a sort of gloss to the first, but one of the four independent feet which describe successively Soma's origin in heaven, his growth on the earth, the pressing and the admixture of water. The idea expressed in the first half of the verse occurs again in another version in IX.61.10 (VS XXVI.16) :

uccā́ te jātám ándhaso diví ṣád bhūmy ā́ dade |
ugrá̄ṃ śárma máhi śrávaḥ ||

"the origin of your herb is in the heights. The earth has received from heaven [that which was situated in heaven]..."

Soma descends to the earth from heaven. This is proved, apart from the many other verses which emphasize the celestial origin of the herb, by the parallel passage just cited above, IX.79.4 : "the place of your birth is in heaven[74]..., your 'fingers' grew on the back of the earth. The stones chew you on the hide of the cow, with their hands the wise milked you into the waters." Whichever version one might prefer, there can be no doubt about the translation of the second pāda, which is important here; and this states that the "fingers" of Soma grow on the back of the earth. Thus this word also seems to lead us to the fact that the young shoots of Soma must have been finger-like longish parts.

The same is shown by the expression, *vakṣáṇā*, which occurs once.

d. *vakṣáṇā*, TUBE

VIII.1.17 : *sótā hí sómam ádribhir ém enam apsu dhā́vata |*
gavyā́ vástreva vāsáyanta in náraḥ nír dhukṣan vakṣáṇābhyaḥ ||

As Pischel has shown in VSt I.178 ff., *vakṣáṇāḥ* here must mean the stalk as the hollow place (the tube) which contains the juice. "Press out the Soma with stones; wash it in the waters. May men milk it from the stalks by dressing it as it were in the robes of milk." The verb *duh* occurs here also as it does often with *aṅśú*,[75] and *vakṣáṇā* is used repeatedly for the udder or for the teats of the cow.

e. *vāṇá*, REED, CANE

vāṇá can also be shown as an expression for the Soma shoot. Two passages come into question; firstly the following verse, which is interesting not only from this point of view, viz., IV.24.9 :

bhū́yasā vasnám acarat kánīyo
ávikrīto akāniṣam púnar yán |
sá bhū́yasā kánīyo nā́rirecīt
dīnā́ dákṣā ví duhanti prá vāṇám ||

This verse, like the two which follow it, is an addition to the hymn at the end of which they occur. Oldenberg (*Hymnen des Ṛgveda*, I, p. 153) has convincingly explained that the tenth verse is, so to say, the query of a sinner who offers his Indra for sale. But it is not probable, as Oldenberg supposes, that there is more than a superficial connection between the verses 9 and 10. Common to both the verses is merely the idea of the offer for sale and this superficial connecting link was probably the reason why these two verses were put together here. The use of the neuter *kánīyas* and above all the *ví duhanti prá vāṇám* in the last pāda speak against the view that the ninth verse refers to Indra. Ludwig's translation[76] does not hit the right mark either, because it is not quite possible to connect *vasnám* with *kánīyas*. *kánīyas* is the subject in pāda *a* as it is the object in pāda *c* and governs *vasnám acarat* which is comparable to Latin *veneo*. Therefore I translate as follows : "too little came for sale [or for trading] at too high a price." This is a rebuke coming from the mouth of one who is fond of buying and is addressed to a miserly trader. The pronoun *sa* in the third pāda refers to this trader : "he did not let go even the too little for too high a price [now]." About the wording of pāda *b* inbetween : *ávikrīto akāniṣam púnar yán*, we can say the following : the speaker, as is seen from *a* and *c*, is not the seller but the buyer. But it is difficult to explain *ávikrīta* correctly. All the translators passed over the difficulty in explaining the passive sense of this participle, "unsold"; but "without having sold" would certainly be *avikrīya*. Therefore I think it is more appropriate to see a Bahuvrīhi in it, "one to whom nothing was sold," just as *áhuta* in AV VII.97.7 is one "for whom no sacrifice was performed."[77] This usage is also somewhat rare, but it can be grammatically explained and the meaning fits into the rest of the content of the verse.

The fourth pāda of the verse informs us what the object of the sale was : *vāṇá*, the "reed," the Soma shoot. Therefore I propose the following translation for the verse :

"Too little came for sale at too high a price. When he did not sell to me, I wanted, coming again, to be satisfied with that. Then he (the trader) did not [any more] let the too little go to me for too high a price. Now feeble minds are milking the reed to pieces."[79] It should be noted that, instead of the usual *duh*, *vi-pra-duh* is used here which I attempted to render as "to milk to pieces."

The poet speaks contemptuously of the miserable seller in whose hands the reed remained and will be used for the drink : "Miserable ones use it for their own benefit." As we have seen earlier, another singer voiced his resentment quite similarly against the Kīkaṭas and their possessing the "low branches."

There Soma was in the hands of a hostile tribe and here it remains the property of a trader.

This verse offers us a picture of the bargaining for the Soma plant and is all the more valuable since otherwise there is no mention of this in the hymns of the ṚV for reasons that will be discussed later.

f. *upārúh*, YOUNG SHOOT

This expression occurs in IX.68.2 :

sá róruvad abhí pū́rvā acikradat
upārúhaḥ śratháyan svādate hárih /
tiráḥ pavítraṃ pariyánn urú jráyo
ní śáryāṇi dadhate devá ā́ váram //

This word does not occur anywhere else; hence we are left with surmises about the exact meaning and cannot deduce from this passage anything characteristic of the Soma plant. Sāyaṇa interprets the word as referring to plants that break through the ground, *ūrdhvaṃ prādurbhavanaśīlā oṣadhayaḥ*; the PW says "shoot;" Ludwig translates *pū́rvā upārúhaḥ* as "tips of the branches." The three Avestan names for the parts of the Haoma plant in *Yasna* 10.5, *varšaǰiš fraspara*γ*ə fravāxsə*[80] are obscure. Only this much can be ascertained from these, if we take at least the native tradition and Neriosengh into account, that here also there is no mention of the fruits of Haoma.

g. *ándhas*, PLANT, DRINK

A study of the word *ándhas*, used so frequently for the Soma, leads to the least significant results. According to the testimony of the PW, the word belongs almost exclusively to the ṚV, does not occur at all in the *Avesta*, only twice in the AV, and very seldom in the rest of literature; it appears to have become extinct quite early. Nevertheless, it is old because its relation to the Greek *anthos* is clear as the day. Haug explains *ándhas* as the Soma branch in bloom.[81] It is likely that this was the meaning of this word once; but the passages in the ṚV where this word occurs do not permit us to apply this meaning to the ṚV.

A number of passages are eliminated at the very outset because *ándhas* occurs there in associations which have become formalized already and do not yield any information.[82] From the rest of the passages it can be seen, first of all, that the eagle collects and brings it,[83] that it originates in heaven,[84] that it is called *sómasya ándhas* or *somyám ándhas*,[85] and that it occurs in X.94.8 together with *aṅśú* and seems to be the more general expression.[86] In all these cases *ándhas* is simply the Soma plant.

Of the adjectives that are connected with *ándhas*, I have noticed the following : *śukrá* IV.27.5; *śubhrá* IX.62.5; more often *mádhu* I.135.4; III.40.1; V.34.2 etc.; *mádya* VII.92.1; *góṛjīka* VII.21.1; *vivákṣaṇa* VIII.1.25; *manīṣín* II.19.1; *sudákṣa* IV. 16.1; *sudákṣa, prahoṣín* VIII.92.4. All these do not mean much; later I shall discuss the slightly more significant *pṛṣṭhyà* IV.20.4.

Somewhat more important are, however, the substantives and verbs which occur with *ándhas*; they show that in the ṚV this word means, besides the Soma plant, Soma juice also. In this connection it should be noted that the verb *duh*, used often with *aṅśú* etc., never occurs, if I am right, with *ándhas*. Also this fact, like the verse X.94.8 mentioned above, indicates that *ándhas* is the general expression; on the other hand, that from which the juice is actually extracted is the *aṅśú*.

1. *ándhas* means the "Soma plant."[87]
su : III.48.1; *tásmā íd ándhaḥ suṣumā sudakṣam* IV.16.1; V.30.6; 51.5; VII.21.1; 90.1; VIII.2.1; IX.58.1; 62.5 (?); 101.13; X.76.6; *ándhasaḥ sutám* VI.42.4. *baps* (*bhas*) : I.28.7. *kṛ* : *ákāryándhaso várīman* VI.63.3. *pí* : IV.27.5.

2. *ándhas* means the "Soma drink" or "Soma juice."
arṣ ándhasā IX.1.4; 86.44 (nominative). *dhanv ándhasā* IX.67.2. *vas apó ándhasā* IX.16.2. *sru+pári ándhasā* IX.55.1. *dhārā ándhasaḥ* IX.58.1. *indavo ándhasaḥ* AV VI.2.2. *pū* IV.1.19; IX.55.3; 61.19. *siñc* with or without *pári* II.14.1; IV.1.19; VI.68.11; VIII.24.16; X.116.4; AV VII.58.2. *und+vi* V.54.8, *mádhvo ándhasā*. *yam* VII.92.1. *hu* II.14.5. *bhṛ+pra* V.41.3. (see, however, *ándhasaḥ prá bharā sutám* VI.42.4). *aś+vi* IX.51.3. *úc+sam* VII.20.4. *pā* I.135.4; II.19.1; 35.1 etc. (for other examples see n. 82); *yātánándhāṅsi pītáye* VII.59.5. *mad* IX.107.2. *mand* (see n. 82). *járhṛṣāṇo* and *dhṛṣámāṇo ándhasā* I.52.2, 5. *pápri* I.52.3. *vṛṣ+ā* VIII.50.3. *avitá* VIII.13.15. *bhárad vájam no ándhasā* IX.52.1. *budh* X.32.1. *á ándhāṅsi madiráṇy...agaman* VI.69.7; similarly VII.68.2; 73.4.

One may think that some of the examples in the first group should rightly belong to the second or vice versa. The interpretation of some others like VIII.67.1; IX.101.1; X.144.5 is quite uncertain. But this would not alter our conclusion that at no place *ándhas* means the blossom of the Soma plant as one would expect from the testimony of the Greek *anthos*, but merely the plant (i.e., Soma plant) and the Soma drink. In order to present my conclusion with the greatest certainty, I have given my collection of passages more exhaustively than it would otherwise be necessary. It can be seen that the statements of the commentaries that *ándhas* is synonymous with *anna* is not without justification because the Soma drink is indeed a "food" by itself; it is even designated as such in ṚV VIII.4.12 :

svayáṃ cit sá manyate dā́śurir jáno yátrā sómasya tṛmpási /
idám te ánnaṃ yújyaṃ sámukṣitaṃ tásyéhi prá dravā píba //

A third meaning akin to the first, viz., the exterior of the plant, bark, which occurs only once, will be discussed under section h. below (p. 149 f.).

In two passages the god Indu is clearly distinguished from his representative, the *ándhas*.

IX.51.3 : *táva tyá indo ándhaso devā́ mádhor vy àśnate /*
pávamānasya marútaḥ //

"Indu, the gods enjoy your sweet *ándhas*, the Maruts [enjoy] the one who purifies himself."

X.115.3 : *táṃ vo víṃ ná druṣádaṃ devám ándhasaḥ /*
índuṃ próthantaṃ pravápantam arṇavám //

"This your god (accusative) of *ándhas*, who nests like a bird, the Indu, the snorting one, the one who shakes the waves (?)."[88]

There is one more verse worth discussing, in which the Vedic interpreters customarily attributed to our word a meaning quite different from the usual, viz. VII.96.2 :

ubhé yát te mahinā́ śubhre ándhasī adhikṣiyánti pūrávaḥ /
sā́ no bodhy avitrī́ marútsakhā coda rā́dho maghónām //

Considering the abundance of evidence for the usual meaning of *ándhas*, the only meaning *ándhasī* could have is "the two plants" or "the two juices." As a matter of fact, the commentary on the ŚBr says "*anne*." The question is if something specific is referred to by this.

In his commentary, Ludwig has referred to ŚBr V.1.2.10 where it is said : *prajāpater vā ete andhasī yat somaś ca surā ca / tataḥ satyaṃ śrīr jyotih somo 'nṛtam pāpmā tamaḥ surā / ete evaitad ubhe andhasī ujjayati*, "both these drinks, Soma and Surā, belong to Prajāpati. Therefore Soma is truth, prosperity, light. But Surā is untruth, baseness, darkness. He gains both these drinks." There is also another passage in the ŚBr, viz., XII.7.3.4 : *ta etad andhasor vipānam apaśyan*, "they saw the drinking off of both the drinks." Here also the Soma and Surā are meant. Soma and Surā, as will be discussed later, are used together in the Sautrāmaṇī ceremony, in which the plant used for preparing the Surā is purchased in the same way as the Soma herb. KŚS XIX.1.18 prescribes for this *śaṣpakraya*, the "purchasing of *śaṣpa*," and the commentary explains *śaṣpa* as germinated rice; others think that it is only a kind of grass.

Besides Indra Sutrāman, only the Aśvins and Sarasvatī are mentioned as the gods to whom offerings are made during the Sautrāmaṇī. The reference to the last one in this very context appears to me to be significant; for the deity, who is addressed as *śubhra* in our Ṛgvedic verse, is precisely the Sarasvatī on whose banks the Pūrus were settled. In Indian tradition the Sarasvatī is regarded as the stream on whose banks the gods sowed barley mixed with sweets. At least, in a magic formula of the AV (VI.30.1) it is said :

devā́ imā́ṃ mádhunā sáṃyutaṃ yávam
sárasvatyām ádhi maṇā́v acarkṛṣuḥ /
índra āsīt sī́rapatiḥ śatákratuḥ
kīnā́śā āsan marútaḥ sudā́navaḥ //

"The gods sowed at the Sarasvatī barley mixed with honey over an amulet. Indra Śatakratu was the lord of the plough, the abundantly bestowing Maruts were the drivers."

Here the stream is closely associated with the Maruts, and this is exactly the case in the Ṛgvedic verse. In the latter verse the reference is to the celestial Sarasvatī and in the former to her terrestrial sister. Just as the divine one is rich in *aṅśús* or *párus*', so is probably her earthly counterpart, and *ándhasī* are the two plants which supply the most delicious of drinks, Soma and Surā. *adhikṣiyánti*, "to spread out over," means just as much as *ujjayati* in the passage from the ŚBr cited above.[89] Therefore I translate VII.96.2 as follows : "When the Pūrus seize both the *ándhas* [on your banks] by force, then, you radiant one, be merciful to us as the friend of the Maruts and direct the favour of the mighty ones towards us."

h. THE BARK OF THE SOMA PLANT

When the stalk is crushed by stones[90] and the juice flows out, what is left behind is the bark. This bark is called *ándhas* in one passage, IX.88.44 *bc* :

mahī́ ná dhā́rā áty ándho arṣati |
áhir ná jūrnā́m áti sarpati tvácam

"like a great stream he flows over the bark (the herb). Like a snake he crawls over the old skin." Besides this, there are the following designations :

vavrí IX.69.9 :

sutā́ḥ pavítram áti yanti ávyam
hitvī́ vavríṃ haríto vṛṣṭím áccha |

"Having been pressed, the golden ones pass over the sheep's wool strainer, leaving the covering, and become rain."[91]

tvác, apart from ṚV IX.86.44, also in TBr III.7.13.1 :

yát te tvácam bibhidúr yác ca yónim

"when the stones tore your skin and your womb."[92]

śárīra TBr III.7.13.2 :

áhāc chárīraṃ páyasā samétya
anyònyo bhavati várṇo asya |

"He left his body. During the union with milk the colour of the one becomes the colour of the other." (Milk and Soma exchange, as it were, their colour.) Synonymous with *śárīra* is *śáryāṇi tánvā* in ṚV IX.14.4 :

niriṇānó ví dhāvati jáhac cháryāṇi tánvā |
átra sáṃ jighnate yujā́ ||

"stripping off [his covering], he flows down, leaving aside the torn limbs of his body,[93] and joins his comrade."

śárya IX.68.2 :

tiráḥ pavítraṃ pariyánn urú jráyo[94]
ní śáryāṇi dadhate devá ā́ váram |

"hurrying over the strainer into freedom, the god lays aside, according to desire (?), the residue."[95]

tánva IX.78,1 :

gṛbhṇā́ti ripráṃ ávir asya tā́nvā
uśddhó devā́nām úpa yāti niṣkṛtám ||

"the strainer takes upon itself his impurity, the remnants of his body. Purified, he goes to the festival of gods," i.e., the strainer catches the dirt and residue.

The PW understands *śárya* as the reed-mesh of the Soma strainer; but neither in the ṚV nor in the later literature the strainer is a "reed-mesh." The expressions *áti sarpati tvácam, hitvī́ vavrím* and *áhāc chárīram* enable us to understand also *jáhac cháryāṇi tánvā* correctly. These *śáryas* are the scraps of the stalk, the body of the Soma, torn asunder by the stones. *Śárya* is derived from *śara*, "reed," and brings to mind *vāṇá*, "reed," which we encountered under section e. above as the designation of the Somastalk. It also follows from this that we have to relate *tánva* to *tanu*, "body," as Ludwig does, and not to the root *tan* in the sense of "plaited, woven" as the PW does.

Besides *śárya*, there is a feminine form *śáryā*, which occurs twice in plural; in IX.110.5 :

> *abhyàbhi hí śrávasā tatárditha*
> *útsam ná kaṃ cij janapā́nam ákṣitam |*
> *śáryābhir ná bháramāṇo gábhastyoḥ ||*

and in the obscure verse X.61.3, where the commentators explain the word as *aṅgulī*, "finger." In fact, in *Nighaṇṭu* 2.5 *śáryā*, like *śākhā* etc., is mentioned as *aṅgulināman*. But since the word cannot be separated from *śárya*, its original meaning must have been "reed." The neuter form has come to have a special meaning in the sense of "remnants of the reed" or "residue"; perhaps the choice of a feminine form indicates a differentiation that *śáryāḥ* are really the reed-stalks. I propose a probable translation as follows : "Through your fame you have indeed opened for us an inexhaustible well, as it were, for men to drink from; carried in the hand (?), as it were, by the reeds."[96] Compare this with *aṅśú sugábhasti* discussed above.

i. DOES THE SOMA STALK HAVE EDGES ?

The material that can help us in answering this question is scanty and does not permit any conclusion. There is a mythological element here also, and it must be excluded if we want purely factual results. The word *pṛṣṭhyà* is of importance, which is an epithet of the Soma and of the juice. IV.20.4 :

> *pā́ indra prátibhṛtasya mádhvah*
> *sám ándhasā mamadaḥ pṛṣṭhyèna*

The PW says under this word : "belonging to height, coming from the heights." I doubt if this explanation is correct, although in the ṚV the mountains are considered to be the home of this plant. Roth's translation cannot be accepted because *pṛṣṭhá* alone does not mean "mountain," but simply "back." At least, in the two Ṛgvedic passages cited for this word by the PW, *párvatasya* occurs with *pṛṣṭhyà*.[79] Therefore *ándhaḥ pṛṣṭhyàm* would probably be the juice coming out of the *pṛṣṭhá* of the plant, and not that which comes from the mountains. Likewise IV.3.10 : *pumā́ṅ agníh páyasā pṛṣṭhèyena* means "the male Agni is anointed with the milk of the *pṛṣṭhás*."[98] What this means is indicated by IX.14.7, which speaks of the "*pṛṣṭhá-s* of the strong one" :

> *abhí kṣípaḥ sám agmata márjayantīr iṣás pátim |*
> *pṛṣṭhā́ gṛbhṇata vājínaḥ ||*

"the fingers joined together to cleanse the lord of food; they grasped the back of the strong one." The connection between these three passages makes us surmise that the young shoots were not completely round, but had edges. But I am not able to present more arguments than this.[99]

j. SOME STATEMENTS OF THE BRĀHMAṆAS

In ABr II.20.15 a Nigada reads as follows : *adhvaryo indrāya somaṃ sotā madhumantaṃ vṛṣṭivaniṃ tīvrāntaṃ bahuramadhyaṃ vasumate rudravate...*, "O Adhvaryus, press the Soma, rich in honey, *vṛṣṭivani*, sharp-ended, thick in the middle,[100] for Indra, whom the Vasus, the Rudras etc. accompany." ŚŚS VI.7,10 adds more adjectives : *ūrjasvat, payasvat*, "rich in nourishment, rich in milk."[101]

vṛṣṭivani means "rain-loving." According to Pāṇini III.2.27, *vani* forms an agent noun. In TS II.4.10.3 it is said of the *varṣāhvá* or *varṣābhū*, a plant that appears in the rainy season : *eṣā́ vā́ óṣadhīnāṃ vṛṣṭivánis táyaivá vṛ́ṣṭim ā́ cyāvayati*, "this among the plants loves rain; through it he brings the rain down." Thus according to the ABr this is also a characteristic of the Soma plant. When we consider the fact that the drink prepared from it rightfully belongs particularly to Indra and Vāyu, and also to the Maruts, that is to say, above all to those gods whose reign heralds the rainy season, then it is not unlikely that the Soma drink was prepared from a plant that was full of juice exactly at this time of the year. What the ṚV offers us in corroboration of this is not much; however, attention may be drawn to this little. :

II.13.1: *ṛtur jánitrī tásyā apás pári*
makṣū́ jātá ā́viśad yā́su várdhate /
tád āhanā́ abhavat pipyúṣī páyaḥ
aṅśóḥ pīyū́ṣaṃ prathamáṃ tád ukthyàm //

"The season is the mother. Born of her, he soon entered the waters in which he thrives. Then she became puffed up and swollen with milk. The first juice of the stalk is to be praised." There can be no doubt as to which season was meant. *pipyúṣī páyas* refers to the *jánitrī* in pāda *a*. The mother becomes rich in milk after the delivery. Swollen with milk and abundant is, however, only the rainy season. Therefore, the Indian commentary says : *ṛtur varṣākhyaḥ kālah somasya jananī bhavati.* Her son, the subject of *jātáḥ várdhate*, is the juicy *aṅśú*, who thrives in her. *āhanás*, "puffed up," also an epithet of the Soma itself elsewhere (IX.75.5; X.125.2), refers here to the mother. This word has been related to the Greek *aphenos*.[102] This evidence of the ṚV is not without significance because in the *Avesta* also (*Yasna* 10.3) cloud and water are praised, which cause the body of Haoma to grow on the heights of the mountains.[103]

Besides the above passage from the ṚV, we should also consider IX.82.3 :

parjányaḥ pitā́ mahiṣásya párṇino
nā́bhā pṛthivyā́ giríṣu kṣáyaṃ dadhe /
svásāra ā́po abhí gā́ utā́saran
sáṃ grā́vabhir nasate vīté adhvaré //

"Parjanya is the father of the mighty bird.[104] This one took his seat on the mountains in the middle of the earth. The sisterly waters streamed to the milk-drinks. When the sacrifice is desired, he unites himself with the stones."

I shall cite a third instance which closely touches upon the ideas expressed in II.13.1 and IX.82.3, viz., IX.113.3 :

parjányavṛddhaṃ mahiṣáṃ táṃ sū́ryasya duhitā́bharat /
táṃ gandharvā́ḥ práty agṛbhṇan táṃ sóme rásam ā́dadhur
índrāyendo pári srava //

"Sūrya's daughter brought the mighty one who was made strong by Parjanya. The Gandharvas seized him and laid the juice in the Soma. For Indra's sake, Indu, flow on."

Here Sūrya's daughter is not Sūryā, but the *ṛtur janitrī*, the rainy season.[105] Just as it was said above that he thrives in the waters and that Parjanya is his father, so this verse describes him as "made strong by Parjanya."

ṚV V.83 leaves no room for doubt as to when Parjanya begins his reign : in the rainy season. Similarly with regard to the time of the Soma plant the parallelism between the god and the plant remains valid. Just as the former enters into a special relationship with the rainy season,[106] the latter also might be full of juice exactly at this time.

Besides *vṛṣṭivani*, the ABr contains other epithets for the Soma plant : *tīvrānta* and *bahuramadhya*. The first epithet is explained in the PW as "probably becoming hot or strong at the end (through fermentation)," and in the smaller edition as "roughly having a strong effect." I do not understand at all the explanation of the second epithet in the PW; but later the smaller edition gives the only correct explanation, "thick in the middle." The contrast between *tīvrānta* and *bahuramadhya* indicates that *tīvrānta* should be regarded as the characteristic of the Soma plant, and not of the Soma juice. The original meaning of *tīvra* was "pointed, sharp"[107] like that of *tigma* and *tīkṣṇa*, which go back to the same root : "pointed at the ends and thick in the middle." The Soma stalks are called "pointed" in X.42.8 also. The other expressions (*bahulānta* in X.42.8 and *bahuramadhya*) are not identical, nor do they contradict each other, because *bahura* and *bahula* are not synonymous.[108]

The fact that Soma is also called *madhumat* in the ABr and *ūrjasvat* and *payasvat* in the ŚSS does not add anything new to what we know already. Abundance of juice was too necessary a pre-requisite not to be emphasized everywhere, in the ṚV as well as in the Brāhmaṇas. Even when substitutes represent the genuine Soma, the richness of milk of the substitute material is an obvious condition emphasized by the authors of the Sūtras (see p. 132, n. 29). In the ŚBr in the section dealing with the purchase of Soma (III.3.3.18) it is stated : "when he buys it near water — water is juice — then he buys it rich in juice; since there is gold, he buys it bright-coloured; since there is cloth, he buys it with the bark; since there is a goat, he buys it full of fire; since there is a milch-cow, he buys it with the admixtures of milk; since there is a pair, he buys it with a mate."[109] Thus the qualities of the plant and of the juice stressed by this Brāhmaṇa are *rasa*, *śukra*, *tvac*, *tapas*, i.e., juice, bright colour, bark and fire.[110]

One more passage from the ŚBr may be cited here. It contains a name that does not occur anywhere else for the plant that supplies the Soma, III.4.3.13 (=IV.2.5.15): *devo vai somo divi hi somo vṛtro vai soma āsīt / tasyaitac charīraṃ yad girayo yad aśmānas tad eṣośānā nāmauṣadhir jāyata iti ha smāha śvetaketur auddālakis tām etad āhṛtyābhiṣunvanti,* "Soma is a god. Soma is indeed in heaven. Soma was Vṛtra. The mountains and stones are his body. There grows a plant, *uśānā* by name. Thus speaks Śvetaketu Auddālaki. They bring it hither and press it."

4. The Plant grows on Mountains

Here it is not necessary to discuss all the passages which speak of the mountain-origin of Soma since several of these deal with the god Soma and not with the plant. For the plant the following verses are of interest.

V.85.2 : *vā́jam árvatsu páya usríyāsu /*
hṛtsú krátuṃ váruṇo apsv àgním
diví sū́ryam adadhāt sóman ádrau //

I.93.6 : *ámathnād anyáṃ pári śyenó ádreḥ /*

"[Mātariśvan brought the one from heaven]; the eagle seized the other from the mountain."

V.43.4 : *mádhvo rásaṃ sugábhastir giriṣṭhā́m*
cániścadad duduhe śukrám aṅśúḥ /

"the shining stalk with a beautiful stem milked its mountain-grown, bright honey-juice."

IX.62.1 : *ásāvy aṅśúr mádāya apsú dákṣo giriṣṭhā́ḥ /*
śyenó ná yóniṃ ā́sadat //

III.48.2 : *yáj jā́yathās tád áhar asya kā́me*
aṅśóḥ pīyū́ṣam apibo giriṣṭhā́m /

Furthermore IX.18.1; 82.3 (the latter cited on p. 152 above) together with IX.79.4 and 61.10 (both cited on p. 129 above). Worth discussing here is also V.36.2 :

ā́ te hánū harívaḥ śūra śípre[111]
rúhat sómo ná párvatasya pṛṣṭhé /

"May Soma, the hero, the lord of bay horses, climb into your cheeks, your jaws, like on to the back of a mountain." Therefore, Soma is called *parvatāvṛ́dh,* "mountain-grown," in IX.46.1 and in the obscure verse IX.71.4. In AV III.21.10 the mountains are styled *sómapṛṣṭha,* "carrying Soma on their back."[112]

If from this we can conclude with some certainty that mountains are the home of Soma, then we obtain a result which is established for the Indo-Iranian period also by similar statements of the *Avesta*. For these texts speak more than once of the mountains that bear Soma. From the tenth chapter of *Yasna* (referred to on p. 152 above) I cite some more passages below.

Y10.3 : *staomi garayō bərəzantō yaϑra haoma urūruδišа...*[113]
4 : *staomi zəmō yaϑa raoδahe hubaoiδiš aurvōčarānəm...*
haoma raose gara paiti uta frāδaēša višpaϑa[114]
haiϑīm ča ašahe xå ahi /
11 : *mərəγa vīžvanča vībarən...aoi paurāna višpaϑa*
aoi spitagaona gairi /
12 : *āaṭ āhva paurvatāhva pourusarəδō vīraoδahe*
haomō gaoma zairigaonō

"The birds carry you to all sides, to the heights, through air, to the mountains shimmering in white. On these mountains you grow, O Haoma, rich in milk, golden in colour, in many heaps."[115]

17 : *vīspe haoma upastaomi*
yaṭčiṭ barəšaušva gairinąm
yatčit jąfnušva raonąm
yaēciṭ ązahu dərətåŋho
jaininąm upadarəzāhu

"I praise all the Haoma plants, as many as there are on the high plateaus of the mountains, as many as there are in the depths of the valleys, as many as there are in the gorges, which are tied into the bundles of women."

From this it follows that the Haoma grows in fact in the hills, more exactly perhaps in the mountains (or mountain ranges); more so on plateaus, it seems, rather than in valleys, but valleys are also mentioned. It grows in abundance and is distinguished by its fragrance.[116] As far as I can see, the ṚV mentions mountains only, but not valleys, unless of course the passage with deals with the two *ándhas'* of the Sarasvatī is to be understood in this sense.

Can it be ascertained where the mountains were situated whose slopes bore our plant ? III.53.14 which speaks contemptuously of the Kīkaṭas does not give us any information on this, because it does not tell us anything about the settlements of these aliens, and it probably refers to the Nyagrodha tree. Only in one other passage of the ṚV a name occurs, mentioned rather in passing, in a verse which praises the dice and compares them to the Soma Maujavata in order to describe their charm, X.34.1 :

sómasyeva maujavatásya bhakṣó
vibhī́dako jā́gṛvir máhyam achān /

Nirukta IX.8 says that this Mūjavat is a mountain : *maujavato mūjavati jāto mūjavān parvato* / *muñjavān*...Sāyaṇa comments on ṚV I.161.8 thus : *muñjavān nāma parvataḥ somotpatti-sthānam.*[117] Tradition must have attributed special excellence to the Soma that grew in this place. This is proved, besides by the Ṛgvedic verse above, by the question which the Adhvaryu puts to the seller in the Baudhāyana ritual[118]: *mūjavatāḥ?*, "is this from the Mujavat ?" and the latter replies : *mūjavato hi* (*mūjavat-parvatād*[119] *āhṛta iti dhyāyet*). This is indeed significant, since from this question and answer it follows that other Soma plants also came into the market and that in the ritual tradition those from the Mūjavat were still considered to be particularly valuable.[120]

The above-mentioned verse from the ṚV praises the Soma from the Mūjavat in the form of a comparison only. For the Vedic Indians this Mūjavat was situated already at a great distance. At least, in the texts of the YV this name means the end of the civilized world, as it were. For instance, at the end of MS I.160 the sacrificial offerings for Rudra are placed in a basket and hung from a tree with the words : "this is your portion, O Rudra. With this food pass by beyond the Mūjavat(s)."[121] This name occurs repeatedly in a hymn, AV V.22,[122] discussed in detail by Zimmer in his *Altindisches Leben*, p. 380 ff. We can infer from this hymn also that the Mūjavats were a tribe, hostile to Indians, and lived far away.

Unfortunately we know as little about the settlements of the Mūjavats as we do about those of the Kīkaṭas. Zimmer has collected all the material that has a bearing upon this question. According to him and Grill,[123] they were settled near the Gandhāris, and these Gandhāris lived on the south bank of the Kubhā up to the Indus and also on the eastern bank of this stream. The Balhikas must have been their neighbours on the other side. But with the hypothesis that the Mūjavat was a mountain in the western Himalayas, "probably one of the less high mountains which stretch around the famous Kaśmīra valley on the south-west," Zimmer goes beyond what we know for certain. It cannot even be ascertained definitely that Mūjavat was a mountain; at least, we have no evidence for this other than the Indian interpreters, Yāska being the foremost of these.

5. Soma's supposed Relationship with other Plants

To the preceding we should add some more vague statements from the Vedic literature; although these do not have any positive value for our enquiry, these cannot be passed over in this context, because they set Soma in a certain relationship to other plants. One of these plants is *kúṣṭha*, identified mostly as *Costus speciosus* or *arabicus*, and according to *Materia Medica* 180, *Saussurea auriculata*. About this plant it is said in AV V.4.7 :

devébhyo ádhi jātó 'si sómasyāsi sákhā hitáḥ |

"From the gods you are born; you are appointed as friend of Soma." Quite similarly AV XIX.39.5 and 8 :

sá kúṣṭho viśvábheṣajaḥ sākáṃ sómena tiṣṭhati |

"this all-healing Kuṣṭha stands along with Soma." Like Soma, Kuṣṭha grows on mountains and is the strongest among plants; it wards off fever and evil spirits. It is said further about this plant :

AV V.4.2: *suparṇasúvane giraú jātám himávatas pári* |
dhánair abhí śrutvā́ yanti vidúr hi takmanā́śanam ||
3: *aśvatthó devasádanas tṛtī́yasyām itó diví* |
tatrā́mṛtasya cákṣaṇaṃ devā́ḥ kúṣṭham avanvata ||

"On the mountain where the eagles nest, is its origin from the Himavat. One hears about it and attains it through gold, because it is known as the destroyer of fever. A fig tree, on which the gods reside, stands in the third heaven from here. There the gods obtained the sight of the *amṛta*, the Kuṣṭha."

8 : *údaṅ jātó himávataḥ sá prācyā́m nīyase jánam* |
tátra kúṣṭhasya nā́māni uttamā́ni ví bhéjire ||

"Born from the Himavat in the north, you are conducted to men in the east. There they divided the best varieties of the Kuṣṭha among themselves."

Thus we find several common points between Soma and Kuṣṭha. The latter is collected in the north and brought to the east. Both are purchased for gold. Not insignificant is the connection between the Kuṣṭha and the Aśvattha tree. Although the Aśvattha tree is purely mythical here, it still recalls the connection between the Soma and the fig tree, emphasized earlier by A. Kuhn in *Mythologische Studien*, I.173 ff. KŚS X.9.30 enjoins the priests not to give the genuine Soma to a Rājanya or to a Vaiśya, even when it is available, but instead one should give them the juice of Nyagrodha fruit, squashed in milk.[124] Among the Kṣatriyas and Vaiśyas the juice of Nyagrodha must have pushed the Soma more and more into the background, either because the original plant became rarer and rarer, or because its enjoyment became more and more the privilege of the brahmins.[124] The Nyagrodha tree was regarded by the Kṣatriyas as the symbol of kingship. ABr VII.31.2 ff. : *parokṣam iva ha vā eṣa somo rājā yan nyagrodhaḥ*...3 : *kṣatraṃ vā etad vanaspatīnāṃ yan nyagrodhaḥ, kṣatraṃ rājanyaḥ*...VIII.16.2 : *tad yat kṣatriyo yajamāno nyagrodhasyāvarodhāṅś ca phalāni ca bhakṣayaty ātmany eva tat kṣatram vanaspatīṇāṃ pratiṣṭhāpayati kṣatra ātmānam.*

The above-mentioned rule is not an isolated one. Kuhn refers to the Ilpa or Ilya which, according to KBrUp I.3, stands in the world surrounded by the ocean Ara, on the other side of the ageless stream. The commentary on this says that the tree is otherwise called *aśvattha somasavana.* This view is shared not only by the commentaries. It is said in the *Chāndogya Upaniṣad*, VIII.5.3 : *araś ca ha vai nyaś cārṇavau brahmaloke tṛtīyasyām ito divi / tad airammadīyaṃ saraḥ / tad aśvatthaḥ somasavanaḥ*, "Ara and Nya (araṇya !) are two oceans in the world of Brahman, in the third heaven from here. This is the Airammadīya lake; this the 'Soma-bestowing' fig tree." The other passages, *Kāṭhaka Up*. VI.1 and BhG XVI. 1, have already been discussed by Kuhn. It should not be overlooked that in the magic formulas also the name of this tree is mentioned among Indra's assistants in overpowering his enemies.[126] Almost everywhere this tree is seen against a mythological background. The only exceptions are Kātyāyana and ṚV I.135.8, a verse in which it cannot be decided whether *aśvattha* is to be understood as a vessel or as a drink.

In his *Herabkunft des Feuers*, A. Kuhn has shown that the myth of the fig tree from which honey drips down is a continuation of the Aryan conceptions. This idea was still alive in India and is seen in the use of Nyagrodha as the substitute for the Soma drink, which was more and more reserved for the brahmins. It seems to me that the word *naicāśākhá*, discussed above, is a synonym for the similarly constructed *naiyagrodha*, and that as early as in the ṚV it denotes the possession of Nyagrodha trees and their produce. But it is doubtful whether *naicāśākhá* and *nąmyąsuṣ̌* can refer to the same object; the only common features are the "hanging branches."

Another plant that is equated with Soma is *parṇa* or *palāśa*. We find this identification repeatedly in the Brāhmaṇas. For instance, KBr II.2 says : *somo vai palāśaḥ sā prathamā somāhutiḥ* etc. ŚBr VI.5.1.1 : *parṇakaṣāyaniṣpakvā etā āpo bhavanti sthemne nv eva yad v eva parṇakaṣāyeṇa somo vai parṇas* etc. VI.6.3.7 : *somo vai palāśaḥ*. TBr I.2.1.6.

I cannot say how this identification took place. This seems to be entirely based on mythological factors, viz., on the oft-narrated legend of Gāyatrī who transformed herself into an eagle and brought the Soma; from this eagle's feather (*parṇa*) which was shot down the Parṇa tree sprang up.

With this all the material that I can offer about the external appearance of Soma is exhausted. This is not much, but it is more than what has been so far ascertained from the ṚV for the determination of the external characteristics of Soma. I cannot judge whether this will be sufficient to identify the plant botanically. It seems me that several statements of the ṚV hardly agree with each other and give occasion to the supposition that different plants were in use even at the time of the ṚV. Deceit is also not ruled out; X.89.5 says : *sómo víśvāny atasā́ vánāni nā́rvā́g índraṃ pratimā́nāni debhuḥ*.

B. THE BUYING OF SOMA

One had to buy Soma before one could press it. This procedure of buying is so well known to all the texts of the Yajus literature and is taught with such a great unanimity in all the Sūtras that it must be regarded as an old constituent of the ritual, reaching back to the earliest times. The fact that there is no information about this in the ṚV except in the one passage discussed above, which happened to be preserved by accident, does not detract from our thesis. In order to understand the silence of the ṚV, we must keep in mind that a considerable majority of its hymns were composed for sacred purposes and that on such occasions there was no opportunity or possibility to think of the mundane trader from whom the plant was obtained after much bargaining. For the poet the plant was nothing but the representative of the god Soma on the earth, that is to say, a sacred plant, irrespective of the fact where it came from and whether it was the genuine Soma or a substitute. To make all the necessary preparations was the duty of the Adhvaryu by virtue of his office and was far removed from the mental horizon of the Hotṛ. Soma, however, must always have been bought. If we assume that it did not grow on the roadside, freely available to all, and if we believe the quite plausible statement of our sources that mountains were its home, then acquiring it, as has been said above, was not an easy task. There must have been no scarcity of people who made profit out of collecting and selling the plant; not all the sacrificers or priests must have been capable or willing at all times to collect Soma themselves even when it grew in their own region. There is also the following to consider. If Soma was really a precious possession, as the singers praise it, then it was hardly likely that it was a *publici juris*, and its habitats must have had their rightful or pretended owner who guarded his property. No matter whether the owner was an Aryan or not, whether it was a mountain chief who ruled over the peaks and valleys where the Soma grew particularly well, or it was a tribe, traders must have, in any case, taken off from there in order to offer the precious produce of their homeland to their neighbours for sale.

However, this would not suffice to answer the question why then this trade, with all its details, found a place in the ritual of the Adhvaryu. Its inclusion there has a deeper symbolic meaning.

I will describe the ritual procedure, first of all as enjoined by Āpastamba, leaving out those rules which are not important for our purpose. The statements of the *Śatapatha Brāhmaṇa*[127] and of Kātyāyana[198] wherever they differ from Āpastamba will be discussed in the notes occasionally. The fact that in some details the sequence of the rules is different in other sources is not relevant here.

ĀpŚS X.20.12 : "He should buy king Soma from the son of a Kutsa or from any other brahmin. Also from a non-brahmin.[129]

13 : "In the area of the Uttaravedi or of the Uparava he

spreads out the red skin of a draught-ox in such a way that the neck points to the east and the hair is outside (cf. KŚS VII.6.1). He throws 'the king' on the southern part of the skin and the seller of Soma sits on the northern part.

14 : "After he has made a shed around the three, i.e., the water pot,[130] king Soma and the seller of Soma [which are prescribed], and has made a door in the north,[131] then follows what is said [in the Brāhmaṇa] during the deliberation whether Soma is to be sorted out or not.[132]

15 : " 'Soma seller, cleanse the Soma,' he says and turns away.[133]

16 : "He should not step near it, watching partially. The sacrificer should not cleanse Soma.

17 : "Neither his servant, nor the Adhvaryu, nor a servant of the Adhvaryu should watch this."

Then follows the description of some offerings like Prayāṇīyā-iṣṭi, which can be passed over here since they are not important.

Further it is said in X.22.2 : "the cow — one-year-old, or two-years-old, or older — meant as the price for Soma stands from east to west."

3-6 : Here follows the description of the cow in the same way as was given on p. 136 above.

9 : "It should be neither held by the ear nor bound by the feet.

10 : "He looks at its right fore-foot with the words : 'May Mitra bind you by the feet,' and when it goes forward he says to it : 'May Pūṣan protect you from the path' etc.

11 : "With his right foot the Adhvaryu follows the six foot-prints [which the cow makes with its right fore-foot] and utters the six mantras one after the other : 'you are a Vasvī; you are a Rudrā; you are Aditi' etc.

12 : "The sacrificer follows the seven steps of the cow with the seven mantras : 'May Viṣṇu follow you one step for food, two for *ūrj*' etc.

23.1 : "During the seventh step he whispers : 'We became friends through the seven steps. I may gain your friendship' etc.[134]

2 : "With the words, 'may Bṛhaspati please you with favour,' the Adhvaryu puts his hands around the seventh footprint, places a piece of gold on it, and makes an offering on this with

the words : 'on the head of the earth (on the sacrificial place etc.) I besprinkle you.' Then he takes away the gold and catches hold of the *sphya* (wooden sword) with the words : 'by the order of the god Savitṛ' etc. He draws a circle three times around the footprint from left to right as far as the butter has spread and utters : 'The evil spirit is enclosed in a circle, enclosed are the *arātis*.'[135]

3 : "With the horn of a black antelope he traces gently over the circle, digs out the soil as far as the butter has spread, and puts it in a pot[136] with the words : 'wealth is with us.' Then he gives the pot to the sacrificer with the words : 'wealth is with you.'

4 : "Then he gives it to the wife of the sacrificer with the words : 'yours is the wealth.'

6 : "He makes the Soma cow look at the wife, during which he utters : 'look at yourself with the divine Urvaśī.'[137]

9-10 : "At the place where the footprint is dug out he washes his hands,[138] which hold the gold, and pours the water with the mantra : 'Tear up the soil and split the celestial cloud. Give us from the celestial water. Being the lord, open up the tube.'[139] He breaks the [soil of the] footprint into three parts, scatters one part to the north of the Gārhapatya, another part to the north of the Āhavanīya into the cold ashes,[140] and gives the third part to the wife who places it in her dwelling.

24.2 : "[Adhvaryu, Brahman and the sacrificer] go with a cart which is curtained off all around,[141] covered on the top and from which the front plank is removed, towards the east to Soma. During which they utter the mantra : 'we walked on this path which leads to happiness' etc. (ṚV VI.51.16).

3 : "If the place is on a mountain, then they carry Soma on the head after purchasing it. [Thus they do not need a cart].[142]

4 : "To the west or north of king Soma the cart is placed with its pole to the east or north in such a way that the cart rests on the ground with its front part; there its yokes are tied firmly to the end of the pole.

5 : "The sacrificer says to king Soma : "May your young shoot unite with the young shoot' etc.

7: "The Adhvaryu places upon the skin a linen garment, folded twice or thrice, with its seam directed towards the east, or upward, or towards the north.[143]

8 : "On this he holds the *aṁśus* with his fingers — with the gold in the fingers and without bending the thumb and the little finger — and measures with the Aticchandas verse : 'I praise the god Savitṛ, the wise' etc.[144]

9 : "In the same way he measures, each time with the [next] finger, leaving [the previous one].[145]

10 : "In all [measurements] he uses the thumb."

This is followed by different rules about measuring Soma, which are not relevant here.

This done, he steps forward to buy Soma.

25.1 : " 'God Sūrya, we want to buy Soma. We proclaim him to you; you [proclaim] him to all gods. Prepare the sacrifices,[146] prepare the remunerations for the sacrifice according to the season and deity.' With this he worships the sun, gives king Soma [which is tied] to the Soma seller and bargains.

2 : " 'Soma seller, will you sell king Soma ?'

3 : "The latter replies : 'I will sell it.'

4 : "After having said : 'from you I buy Soma, juicy and rich in milk,'[147] he tells him : 'I want to buy it from you for one-sixteenth [of the cow].'

5 : "The Soma seller replies at each bargain till the end: 'King Soma is worth more than that.'[148]

6 : "At the second time he says : 'I want to buy it from you for a *kuṣṭhā*'; at the third time : 'I want to buy it from you for the hoof (1/8)'; and at the fourth time: 'I want to buy it from you for the foot (1/4).'[149]

7 : "This is repeated thrice.

8 : "Or each of these thrice.

9 : "At the end he says : 'I want to buy it from you for the cow.'[150]

10 : "Or, he should not say 'for the cow.' Pointing to it with the word 'this one,' he whispers : 'it has its soul, its beauty, its progeny, its milk, its relatives.'

11 : "Having whispered : 'I buy your lustre with lustre' etc., he buys for gold.

12 : "Having whispered : 'you are a body of heat' etc., he buys for a goat.[151]

"[He buys] once for each of the rest.[152]

14 : "Should he want to buy for a bull, he would buy for

Prajāpati. His place is taken by a male calf, already weaned and uncastrated.

15 : " 'A pair,' that is a male calf and a female calf, already weaned.

16 : "Ḥaving bought with these two at the same time, he closes the bargain with a garment.

26.10 : "With the words : 'let the gold be with us,' he takes away the gold from the Soma seller.[153]

11 : "He gives a bundle of white wool to the sacrificer with the words : 'let the light be among us.' This he makes into the *nābhī* of the woollen strainer at his own time.

12 : "The white woollen strainer is woven at home with the threads from the wool of a white sheep.

14 : "He moistens a bundle of black wool with water, twists it with the words : 'here I twist the necks of the biting snakes,' and throws it at the Soma seller, saying : 'may darkness dwell in the Soma seller.'[154]

15 : " 'O Svāna ! Bhrāja ! (?) Aṅghāri ! Bambhāri ! Hasta ! Suhasta ! Kṛśanu ! These are the prices for you. Guard them. May you not be cheated.'[155] With this he points to the prices and takes away the king Soma from the Soma seller with the mantra : 'You are created from your own self. You exist through your own self. You are created for this task. I take you according to merit. You protect me according to merit.'

16 : "Should the Soma seller give trouble, then he should snatch Soma from him.

27.1 : "The sacrificer uncovers [the shoulder and head][156] with the verse : 'feathered birds' etc. (ṚV X.73.11).

2 : "He gives the staff used during the consecration of Soma to the Maitrāvaruṇa.

3 : "The sacrificer takes Soma with the mantra : 'Mitra, come to us'; he places it on his right thigh, saying : 'enter Indra's thigh,' and presses it down constantly with the hands.[157]

5 : "With the words : 'Rudra, turn towards us,' he drives the Soma cow around from left to right, and, having bought it off with another, he lets it into the shed of the sacrificer.

6 : "Should the Soma seller object, then one should strike him with a spotted[158] leather strap and drive him away.

7 : "Some hold that he should be beaten with a log of wood.

8 : "Some hold that beating must take place."

Thus ends the buying of Soma, the procedure of which is wonderful enough to deserve an analysis here. Roth[159] says that this is a fiction of the ritual or at best a farce. Eggeling[160] states more clearly that "the whole transaction was evidently a feigned purchase, symbolising acquisition of the Soma by the gods from the Gandharvas. The real bargain was probably concluded before the sacrificial performance." Thus he comes quite close to the correct interpretation, but we should go some more steps further. Let us visualise the situation.

A Śūdra is assumed to be the Soma seller. The mantra addressed to him, *svāna, bhrāja* etc., shows that he is thought of as one of the hostile guards who deprive the plant or the god, as the case may be, of the rightful destination. Also the mantras like "let the brightness remain with us" allude to the fact that the symbolic significance of a fight between quite different higher powers is ascribed to the fight between the Ārya and the Śūdra. Similarly, it follows from the mantras addressed to the Somakrayaṇī cow that it is not an ordinary cow that is offered to the owner of Soma but the replica of a celestial cow. In the words *vāg vā eṣā nidānena yat somakrayaṇī*,[161] the ŚBr informs us as to who is represented by this cow. According to the unanimous statement of the different sources, Vāc was the price for which the gods bought Soma from the Gandharvas. "Soma was in heaven," says ŚBr III.2.4.1 ff.,[162] "and the gods were on the earth; then the gods wished : 'may Soma come to us. When it has come, let us offer it in sacrifice.' They created the two Māyās — Suparṇī and Kadrū. In the Brāhmaṇa which deals with the Dhiṣṇya it is narrated how the story of Suparṇī and Kadrū runs. 2 : For them Gāyatrī flew to Soma. While she was bringing it, Gandharva Viśvāvasu robbed her of it. The gods knew : 'Soma is removed from there; but it does not come to us, because the Gandharvas stole it.' 3 : They said : 'The Gandharvas lust for women; let us send Vāc. This one will come to us with Soma.' They sent Vāc to them. She returned to them with Soma. 4 : The Gandharvas followed her and said : 'Let Soma be yours and Vāc ours.' 'Yes,' said the gods in reply, 'but since this one came to us once, do not take her away, so to say, by force. We shall call her from both the sides.' They called her. 5 : The Gandharvas recited the Vedas for her and called: 'such things we can do ! such things we can do !' 6 : But the gods created the lute and sat singing and playing. 'Thus we will sing to you, thus we will please you,' they called. She turned to the gods, and it was not wise of her that she turned away from those engaged in reciting and praying in favour of dance and song."

This legend shows the great vividness with which the old saga of the acquisition of the divine drink was depicted. This saga appears to have been current in more than one version, and the dialogue between Kadrū and Suparṇī, handed down to us by our texts, can be regarded as one more example of the dramatization of a theme.[163] Obviously, it is the old popular motifs which are presented to us here — motifs which have been the object of popular belief and thinking to a greater degree than one would suppose from the evidence of the ṚV. In the entire range of the Vedic hymns, I know only one verse from which one could infer a similar competition — note the choice of the verb *vihve* — between the singer and the Asuras for Soma, viz., I.108.6 : *yád ábravaṃ prathamáṃ vāṃ vṛṇānó*
ayáṃ sómo ásurair no vihávyaḥ /[164]
But life in India as such was richer in content than is shown by the collection of hymns made for specific purposes. I have shown elsewhere how at the time of the solstice, contests or competitions between "Āryas" and "Sūdras" followed the performance of sacrifices. Like here, there also a, Śūdra is beaten and driven away during the buying of Soma.[165] Actually, he must not have been beaten any more severely than was necessary for the purpose of such ceremonies, in the same way as the *Bösewicht* is beaten in our folk dramas. I think that the buying of Soma included in the Soma sacrifice is to be understood exactly in the same way. The Śūdra is not merely a trader; he acts the role of the Gandharva. In other words, here we have the first authentic beginnings of the dramatic art in ancient India. The buying of Soma is nothing but a scene from the folk drama which deals with the acquisition of Soma from the Gandharvas, and the Śūdra, duped and sent home with beatings, is the foolish devil of our own literature.[166]

Through its injunction that the Soma seller must be a Śūdra, the ritual alludes to his origin from foreign tribes or demons. A foreign tribe which possessed Soma without pressing it was probably the Kīkaṭas, mentioned on p. 129 (provided the passage does not refer to the possession of *ficus indica*). Perhaps it was not the only tribe of its kind which was hostile to the Vedic Indians. But it would be superfluous here to look for specific names and peoples. Perhaps the ritual procedure was merely a religious act.

C. THE SOMA DRINK

From the plant a drink is extracted which is designated, like the plant, by the word Soma. Besides the general expressions like *mádhu, rása* etc., I have come across only one different name, *pitú,* in the Agastya hymn I.187, which probably meant "food" in the general sense only.

The praise of the Soma drink resounds in the hymns of the Veda as in the *Avesta*, and the art of preparing it goes back to the darkest antiquity. It will be shown below in the chapter on Paṇis that the antithesis between the *sunvát* and *ásunvat* represents the difference in belief that separates the worshipper of Indra from his national and religious opponents. The importance of pressing Soma and the high esteem the Soma presser enjoys among the gods and men is the favourite theme of the Vedic singers. Further material can easily be added to what has already been said on this subject.

1. The Antithesis between the Soma Pressers and the Asunvats

VIII.2.18 : *icchánti devā́ḥ sunvántaṃ ná svápnāya spṛhayanti*
"The gods like him who presses Soma; they do not desire drowsiness."

VIII.62.12 : *mahā́ṅ ásunvato vadhó bhū́ri jyótīṅṣi sunváto*
bhadrā́ índrasya rātáyaḥ ||

"Severe is his death who does not press Soma; numerous are the days of the presser, and the gifts of Indra are auspicious to him."

I.110.7 : *abhí tiṣṭhema pṛtsutī́r ásunvantām*
"May we win in fights over those who do not press."

II.30.7 : *ná mā taman ná śraman nótá tandran*
ná vocāma mā́ sunotéti sómam |
yó me pṛṇā́d yó dádad yó nibódhāt
yó mā sunvántam úpa góbhir ā́yat ||

"May it not make me exhausted, nor tired, nor indolent. May we not say : do not press Soma for him who makes me rich, bestows gifts on me, protects me and comes with cattle to me when I press."

V.34.3 : *yó asmai ghraṅsá uta vā yá ū́dhani*
sómaṃ sunóti bhávati dyumāṅ aha

"He who presses Soma for him, in hot season as well as in the wet season, remains in high esteem."

V.34.5 : *nā́sunvatā sacate púṣyatā caná*

"He does not enter into an alliance with one who, though thriving, does not press."

VIII.14.15 : *asunvā́m indra saṃsádaṃ viṣūcīṃ vy ànāśayaḥ* /
somapā́ úttaro bhávan //

"You scattered the settlement[167] of the non-pressers, maintaining your upper hand as the Soma drinker."

Also IV.17.17; 25.6-7; V.37.3; VI.41.4; VII.26.1; X.42.4; 160.4; MS II.90.15 etc.

However, it is not sufficient to press occasionally.

VIII.32.21 : *átīhi manyuṣā́viṇam suṣuvā́ṅsam upā́raṇe* /
imā́ṃ rātā́ṃ sutàṃ piba //

"Go past him, [O Indra], who presses only out of anger and who has pressed improperly."

Of all the gods of the Vedic Olympus, Indra is the one god to whom the drink is due; only Vāyu, his companion, enjoys a position next to him. To win Indra's favour is the endeavour of every sacrificer.

2. Saṃsava, the Competition among the Sacrificers

There is an antithesis not only between the *sunvát-s* and the *ásunvat-s;* the pride in the excellence of one's own preparation and in one's own manner of offering it to the gods leads to a kind of competition which is called *saṃsava* in the ritual and for which the ritual prescribes certain rules of behaviour. The commentary on the ABr[168] says that a Soma sacrifice, performed at the same time by two Yajamānas who were not separated either by a hill or by a river, is a severe offence, but it does not affect the one who was consecrated first. Several texts give detailed rules on how to get the better of the rival.[169] The beginnings of this practice can be traced back to the ṚV; for we find there unmistakable traces of such pious rivalry, which must have had its natural starting point in the feuds with other tribes who were also devoted to the Soma cult.

II.18.3 : *mó ṣu tvā́m átra bahávo hí víprāḥ*
ní rāraman yájamānāso anyé|

"Let not the other sacrificers hold you up here;[170] many indeed are the wise."

VIII.33.14 : *váhantu tvāratheṣṭhā́m ā́ hárayo rathayújaḥ |*
tirā́ś cid aryā́ṃ[171] sávanāni vṛtahan anyéṣāṃ
yā́ śatakrato ||

"May the harnessed horses bring you, the fighter on the chariot, here; away from the pressings of the enemies and others, O killer of Vṛtra, O Śatakratu."

VIII.66.12 : *pūrvī́ś cid dhí tvé tuvikūrmin*
āśáso hávanta indrotáyaḥ |
tirā́ś cid aryáḥ sávanā́ vaso gahi[172]
śáviṣṭha śrudhí me hávam ||

"Many hopes and assurances of favour are calling after you, Indra, the mighty one. Come away from the pressings of the enemies, O good one, and hear my call, O most powerful one." In VII.32.2 the Vasiṣṭhas boast of their Soma drink which Indra preferred to that of Pāśadyumna Vāyata :

dūrā́d índram anayann ā́ suténa
tiró vaiśantám áti pā́ntam ugrám |
pā́śadyumnasya vāyatásya sómāt
sutā́d índro avṛṇīta vásiṣṭhān ||

"From afar they led the mighty Indra hither with their pressed Soma, away from the drink as big as a pond. Indra preferred the Vasiṣṭhas to the Soma pressed by Pāśadyumna Vāyata." Perhaps the somewhat difficult verse, VIII.4.17, can also be cited here :

vémi tvā pūṣann ṛñjáse vémi stótava āghṛṇe |
ná tásya vemi áraṇam hí tád vaso stuṣé pajrā́ya sā́mne ||

"I long for gaining you, Pūṣan, I long for praising, O glowing one. I do not long for singing the Pajra Sāman, for that is a strange one."

In LŚS VII.3.3.4 the Pajra Sāman is mentioned along with the Tauraśravasa Sāman. According to *Tāṇḍya Brāhmaṇa* IX.4.10 these two Sāmans were conceived by Tauraśravas, with which he conquered the Pārāvatas in a *saṃsava*.[173] It seems that the Pajras have invented a special form of sacrifice; they have earned much praise and much censure.[174] The desire to win over the gods exclusively for oneself as far as possible was probably the reason for the invention of new customs and various differentiations in the ritual,[175] some of which can be traced back to the time of the ṚV itself. But these customs were not studied seriously so far. Some of these will be discussed later in this work.

3. Was Soma still a popular Drink at the Time of the Ṛgveda ?

Among the innumerable hymns which invite the gods to the Soma drink, there are very few which have a popular character. In the great mass of hymns it is only the metre which still alludes — through the light-footed Gāyatrī or the Anuṣṭubh — to celebrations that were merrier than the common Vedic sacrifices. What I have as evidence of popular character is limited to that short hymn VIII.69, which is used during the Ṣoḍaśin according to ĀŚvŚS VI.2.9, and to some solitary verses.

VIII.69.8 : *árcata prā́rcata*
príyamedhāso árcata |
árcantu putrakā́ utá
púraṃ ná dhṛṣṇv àrcata ||
9 : *áva svarāti gárgaro*
godhā́ pári saniṣvanat |
píṅgā pári caniṣkadad
índrāya bráhmódyatam ||
10 : *ā́ yát pátanty enyàḥ*
sudúghā ánapasphuraḥ |
apasphúraṃ gṛbhāyata
sómam índrāya pā́tave ||

"O sing, O laud !
Sing Priyamedhas !
Let the young boys speak !
Praise him ardently who resembles a fortress !
"Let the Gargara resound !
Let the Godhā ring high and clear !
Let the Piṅgā[176] swing fast !
The Brahman rose up for Indra.
"When the colourful ones approach,
milking easily and willingly,
then take Soma, the turbulent one (?)
for Indra as a drink."

There is no mistaking the fact that these verses differ considerably from the others in content. Music and song join together in honour of the great god, and children have their share in the joyous festival. These verses recall to mind the songs of maidens[177] who dance around the fire during the Mahāvrata and appear to be more popular in character than the other Vedic hymns.

With this solitary example, however, all that is available of continuous passages of this kind in the ṚV is exhausted. Occasional outbursts of joy may owe their origin to the priests who were stimulated by the draught of Soma. The hymn VIII.91, which is a Soma charm and which a maiden chants in order to become beautiful, has probably had a less liturgical character.[178] Otherwise there are only isolated verses like VIII.31.5 where the married couple who press and wash the Soma with one mind is praised;[179] furthermore I.28.5, which will occupy our attention later also :

yác cid dhí tvám̥ gṛhégṛhe úlūkhalaka yujyásé |
ihá dyumáttamam̥ vada jáyatām iva dundubhiḥ ||

"When you, Ulūkhala, are set in motion in house after house, then resound here quite loudly like the drum of the conquerors."[180]

In general, however, the ṚV does not reflect any more such simple and natural state of affairs. That the Vedic sacrifices had become rather expensive affairs already at the time of the ṚV is proved not only by the three groups of priests who divide the ritual activities among themselves and by the multitude of Hotṛs and Adhvaryus, but to a greater degree by the Dānastutis, the songs in praise of the distribution of rich sacrificial remunerations to priests as a reward for their efforts. The ṚV already anticipates the injunctions of the law-books according to which only those who possess provisions for three or more years are entitled to drink Soma.[181] Again and again the ṚV speaks of the Maghavans whose hearts Indra or other gods should move to generosity. Vedic singers lived at the courts of princes or noble patrons; it seems that they also offered their services from place to place as travelling priests. Oldenberg has explained ṚV IV.24.10[182] as the words of a poet who recommends himself as an agent of divine favour, " as one who offers the god on hire." We encounter the picture of a vagrant priest still more clearly in hymn I.25, which transports us into the midst of a group of travelling singers and shows us the picture of a priest who travels around, calling upon the people to give sacrificial offerings to Indra. Whosoever receives him amiably long life is guaranteed to him; his progeny will flourish; horses, cattle and gold will be his reward.[183]

4. Prototypes of the Sacrificer and the Evolution of a Soma-Aristocracy

Ancient Soma pressers are mentioned often in the ṚV; they are praised as models for successful sacrificers. Atri's way of preparing the drink is praised in V.51.8; 72.1; VIII.42.5; Śāryāta's method in I.51.12; III.51.7; VS VII.35; TS I.4.18[a]; *Vālakhilya* V.4 states that the Soma made by the Śiṣṭas is particularly sweet, and so on.[184]

Gods themselves were witnesses when Indu purified himself for Indra; IX.101.5 : *índur índrāya pavata íti devā́so abruvan.* In *Vālakhilya* IV.1, Manu Vivasvat and Trita are mentioned among the sacrificers whose Soma pleased Indra once.[185] Although this statement occurs only in the *Vālakhilya* text, it still deserves our attention because it agrees with the content of the *Homa Yašt*, which mentions Vīvahvat, Āθwya and θrita as the first Soma pressers. In both cases the beginnings of the Soma cult are lost in the darkness of the remote antiquity when the gods themselves pressed Soma, and the agreement between these names shows that the association of these two gods with the Soma must have been based on an ancient pre-historic tradition.

A part of the glory of such high ancestors reflects on the man who presses Soma. "A *somayājin* is a *bahuyājin*," thus runs an ancient statement quoted in the ĀpŚS :[186] he who has performed a Soma sacrifice has, in effect, performed many sacrifices.

The author of III.43.5 poses the following question :

kuvín mā gopā́ṃ kárase jánasya
kuvíd rā́jānaṃ maghavann ṛjīṣin |
kuvín ma ṛ́ṣiṃ papivā́ṅsaṃ sutásya
kuvín me vásvo amṛ́tasya śíkṣāḥ ||

"Will you not make me the protector of people, make me the king, O Soma-drinking lord, make me the Ṛṣi, after I have drunk of Soma ? Will you not give me of the excellent Amṛta ?" (Ludwig).[187] To have Soma drinkers among one's ancestors is a matter of great glory in the earlier as well as in the later period.

In the prologue to his *Mālatīmādhava*,[188] Bhavabhūti boasts with pride that his ancestors were Soma drinkers. Similarly, the Vedic singers also recall fondly the association of their ancestors with Soma. A *homo novus* praises a new hymn.

VIII.38.9 (=42.6) : *evā́ vām ahva ūtáye yáthā́huvanta médhirāḥ* //

VIII.76.7 : *índraṃ pratnéna mánmanā* [189] *marútvantaṃ havāmahe* /
asyá sómasya pītáye //

IX.96.11 : *tváyā hí naḥ pitáraḥ soma pū́rve*
kármāṇi cakrúḥ pavamāna dhī́rāḥ /

"With you, O Soma, our wise Manes conducted their affairs, O Pavamāna."

X.15.8 : *yé naḥ pū́rve pitáraḥ somyā́saḥ*
anūhiré somapīthám vásiṣṭhāḥ /[190]

"our Soma-loving Manes, the most excellent ones, who came for the Soma drink."

Tradition plays nowhere a greater role than in the Vedic sacrifice. The Pravara requires that at the time of installing the sacred fire the sacrificer should associate himself with his ancestors by mentioning several of his progenitors by name. Likewise, the person who is consecrated for the Soma sacrifice must mention, besides his own name, the gotra of his father, of his grandfather, of his great-grandfather, or, if he is not a brahmin, he should make use of the gotra of his priest.[191] Atonement must be made for an interruption in tradition. The TS states that an ox must be sacrificed to Indra-Agni, if one did not drink any Soma since three generations. "For the Soma drink is broken away from him who, being a brahmin, did not drink Soma since three generations. He approaches Indra-Agni with their own share for help. These grant him the Soma drink. The Soma drink falls to his share" etc.[192]

A clear distinction developed in the literature between *somapa* and *asomapa*. This distinction can be seen, among others, in the fact that the law-books place an *asomapa* almost on the same level as an *anāhitāgni* and a Śūdra.[193] One who he has been consecrated for the Soma sacrifice belongs, even before he has bought Soma, to those persons who are to be honoured with a greeting.[194] ĀpŚS I.9.24.24 discusses the punishment for killing a brahmin, to be awarded to a person who has studied the Veda and completed the ceremonies of the Soma sacrifice. It seems that the character of a genuine Aryan is determined by his being a *somapa* and an *āhitāgni*.

Soma sacrifice is not open to every one; one has to be invited to it, and Indra himself forfeits the claim to Soma because he takes it by force.[195] The character of an aristocratic exclusiveness finds expression in the so-called Daśapeya, a sacrifice that can be regarded as the joint celebration of a Soma nobility because the organisers of this sacrifice must belong to an uninterrupted line of ten Soma-drinking ancestors. KŚS IX.8.16 states the following on this : *pitāmahadaśagaṇaṃ somapānāṃ saṃkhyāya sarpaṇam*, "after they have enumerated a line of ten Soma-drinking ancestors, they crawl."[196] ŚŚS XV.14.8 speaks not of *puruṣas* but of *śrotriyas*;[197] thus it lays down the condition that only the priest should have ten such ancestors, and that too ten each on the father's side and on the mother's side. But this deviation betrays clearly its late origin. Just as in the Pravara a non-brahmin makes use of the gotra of the priest, so also here the line of the *śrotriya* was probably made use of when a *homo novus* desired admission into the exclusive circle of ancient families of the Soma sacrificers, or when his admission was considered desirable for some reason or other.[198] However, we can draw an important conclusion from this fact. The Soma drink lost its popularity and has become the prerogative of aristocratic circles. The understanding of its original significance began to be lost, and by the time of the commentaries it was no more recognizable to them. Therefore, if we wish to understand the earliest significance of the Soma hymns, we should not take recourse to these late writers. During the intervening millennia the original views underwent a change.

5. Ancient Settlements of the Soma Pressers

It is obvious that the spread of the Soma cult must coincide geographically with the expansion of the Aryan tribes. It is not my intention here to enter into a discussion on the settlements of the Vedic tribes, although most of the views held so far require certain modifications if my own studies on the Paṇis are correct. Here I am only interested in analysing some passages which enrich our knowledge considerably about the expansion of the Vedic settlements.

VIII.64.11 : *ayám te śaryaṇā́vati suṣómāyām ádhi priyáḥ* /
ārjīkī́ye madíntamaḥ //

"This Soma is dear to you at the Śaryaṇāvat, at the Suṣomā, but it is the sweetest in the Ārjīkīya." If, for the time being, we disregard the meaning of the individual words, we can see that in the parts of this verse there is an unmistakable gradation indicated by *priyá* and *madíntama*. The Soma is sweeter *ārjīkī́ye* than *śaryaṇā́vati* and *suṣómāyām*. The person who speaks thus is a Pūru-son, as is evident from the tenth verse.[199]

If we closely examine this passage, which forms our starting point, we can see that in this contrast between Suṣomā and Ārjīkīya the latter as well as the former can only be geographical names. This is all the more probable since both the names occur not only here, but also in VIII.7.29 and in the catalogue of rivers X.75.5, only with this difference that in the last two cases the two names are masculine while they are feminine in VIII.64.11. There is no reason whatsoever not to regard all these verses as closely related. VIII.7.29 reads as follows :

suṣóme śaryaṇā́vati ārjīké pastyā̀vati /
yayúr nícakrayā náraḥ //

30 : *kadā́ gacchātha marutaḥ itthā́ vípraṃ hávamānam...*

In v.19 of this hymn a Kaṇva is mentioned as the singer.

X.75.5 : *imáṃ me gaṅge yamune sarasvati*
śútudri stómaṃ sacatā páruṣṇy ā /
asiknyā́ marudvṛdhe vitástayā
ā́rjīkīye śṛṇuhy ā suṣómayā //

6 : *tṛṣṭā́mayā prathamáṃ yā́tave sajū́ḥ*
sasártvā rasáyā śvetyā́ tyā́ /
tváṃ sindho kúbhayā gomatī́ṃ hrúmum
mehatnvā́ sarā́thaṃ yā́bhir ī́yase //

I consider the last passage important enough to make it the starting point for further discussion, for the repeated association of the two names in the ṚV cannot be accidental but only the result of an actual geographical association, precisely to which our verse leads. Zimmer states that the catalogue of rivers is unreliable from the Ārjīkīyā onwards, while the first part is reliable. I do not share his suspicion, or I do so only to a small degree, because, although these verses make many streams into the tributaries of the Indus, which in fact they were not, still the names mentioned at the end, viz., Kubhā (Gr. *Kōphēn*), Gomatī

(Gomal) and Krumu (Kurum), rest, except for their sequence, on an equally solid ground as the first ones so that we could assume that the names in between are similarly not fictitious. In fact, Vivien de S. Martin also looked for Suṣoma in Gr. *Sóanos*, the modern Suwan, and saw in Ārjīkīya the name of the land through which the upper course of *Sóanos* flows. Since then Stein has proved the reliability of the hymn.[200]

If we accept what the catalogue of rivers states, then we are led to Kashmir or the adjoining lands in the south-west through which the Ārjīkīyā must have flowed. There are other arguments in favour of this.

With Ārjīka a second name, *śaryaṇávat*, is associated. Besides the two passages cited above, I refer to IX.65.22 ff. and IX.113.1-2. In these verses as well as in VIII.7.29 we see these expressions juxtaposed almost like in a formula.

The first of these passages runs as follows :

IX.65.22 : *yé sómāsaḥ parāváti yé arvāváti sunviré* /
yé vādáḥ śaryaṇávati //
23 : *yá ārjīkéṣu kṛ́tvasu yé mádhye pastyānā́m* /
yé vā jáneṣu pañcásu //
24 : *té no vṛṣṭíṃ divás pári pavantām á suvī́ryam* /
suvānā́ devā́sa índavaḥ //

Verse 25 states that the singer is a Jamadagni.

In v. 22 we find a threefold division of *parāvát* "distance," *arvāvát* "proximity" and *śaryaṇávant*. This is quite similar to that found in VIII.13.15 except that in the latter the third unit is *samudré* in stead of *śaryaṇávati*.[201] Corresponding to this threefold division in v. 22, we find again three units in v. 23 : 1. *ārjīkéṣu*, 2. *mádhye pastyānā́m*, 3. *jáneṣu pañcásu*, so that we come to the conclusion that the second verse is only an elaboration of the first, that is to say, that *parāváti, arvāváti, śaryaṇávati* correspond to *ārjīkéṣu, mádhye pastyānā́m, jáneṣu pañcásu* respectively. The fact that in both verses the three units are connected syntactically in almost the same way supports the impression that both these verses are closely related.

The case is the same with the following two verses.

IX.113.1 : *śaryaṇávati sómam índraḥ pibatu vṛtrahā́* /
bálaṃ dádhāna ātmáni...
2 : *ā pavasvā diśāṃ pate ārjīkā́t soma mīḍhvaḥ* /
ṛtavākéna satyéna śraddháyā tápasā sutáḥ //

"May Indra, the killer of Vṛtra, drink the Soma at Śaryaṇāvat, acquiring strength thereby... 2 : Come here, O lord of the celestial regions, from Ārjīka, O merciful Soma." If we compare this passage with VIII.64.11 cited on p. 175 above, we notice a slight difference. There it is said : the Soma at Śaryaṇāvat is dear to Indra, but the one at Ārjīkīya is the sweetest of all; here Soma is implored to come away from Ārjīka; but Indra, however, should drink at Śaryaṇāvat. Thus we find a pious rivalry of the sort described above between the singers of the two hymns, on the one hand a Pūru and on the other the author of X.113 whom the *Anukramaṇī* describes as a Kaśyapa, which is, however, very doubtful. Everywhere we are led to see this as a proper noun.

When we turn to the native interpreters, then it is striking that Sāyaṇa explains, with a logical consequence otherwise unusual for him, *ārjīká* as the name of a land; hence there can be no doubt about the reliability of the sources availabe to him.[203] I do not see any reason why these statements should not be trusted completely when an examination of the sources leads us also to the same conclusion and when there are additional factors in its favour.

The fact that *ārjīkī́ya* is mentioned always in combination with the other two words, or at least with one of them, makes it probable that all the three places or regions stood in close relation to each other. It also appears as though they were the sacred places of the Soma cult, at least in the mind of the poets in whose hymns these place-names occur. Of course, the three forms *ārjīká*, *ārjīkī́ya*, *ārjīkī́yā* must be related; *ārjīká* seems to be the name of a tribe or of a land, the adjective derived from it denotes that which belongs to this tribe or the inhabitants of this land, and the feminine form of the adjective denotes its river.[204] It is immaterial whether the name *ārjīká* itself is derived from the name of a hill *ṛjīka*.[205] More important is the fact that in a passage Sāyaṇa refers to this land as situated far off; for this statement is in complete agreement with the fact that in the two parallel verses IX.65.22 and 23, *ārjīkéṣu* of the latter corresponds to ***parāváti*** of the former, and thus Ārjīka must have been a distant and strange land for the singer of this hymn also.

The author of VIII.64.11, cited on p. 175, was, as the immediately preceding verse shows, a Pūru-son. He boasts that in Ārjīkīya, Soma is the sweetest for Indra. Therefore, we must expect that he belonged to this land, that he lived in Ārjīkiya.

When Alexander of Macedonia invaded India, the kingdom of Poros, who resisted him, extended from the Vitastā up to the Asiknī. "The Greeks borrowed the name Poros from the dynasty; the *Mahābhārata* mentions a kingdom of the Pauravas or Pauras near Kaśmīra. The territory of Poros stretched up to the Asiknī in the east. Spittakes, a nephew of Poros, ruled over a small territory on the west bank of the Vitastā; a cousin of Poros governed in the east between the Asiknī and the Irāvatī. The territory of Poros was separated in the north from that of the king of Kaśmīra by some small tribes only."[206]

This is to say that in historical times the Pūrus lived in that place where, following the statements of the catalogue of rivers, we must look for the Ārjīkīyā and the land of the Ārjīkas. This is in conformity with what is said in the hymn of the Pūrus, VIII.64.11, viz., that Indra finds Soma the sweetest in Ārjīka.

At the time of the ṚV we find the Pūrus on the banks of the eastern Sarasvatī, i.e., beyond the domiciles which they had during the historical times. Therefore, it is probable that their settlements extended further towards the west, and we must expect to find their traces in this direction, irrespective of the fact whether they advanced from the north-west towards Kashmir, or from the west through Takṣaśilā. The sixth maṇḍala even reports of an enmity between a Pūru and the Paṇis; thus, it is very likely that they must have settled across the Indus in the west — an assumption which would not give rise to any objection in view of the great difference in time which we must assume between the core (not the final shape) of the sixth maṇḍala and that of the seventh maṇḍala.

Because of the scanty material at our disposal, it is not possible to decide whether the Pūrus were identical with the Ārjīkas. I do not think that it is likely, because more than one tribe must have lived under the mighty sceptre of the Pūru dynasty.

In the first edition of this work I have stated the hypothesis that Ārjīka is identical with the territory of the Arsas, but this hypothesis is proved to be untenable in the light of the evidence presented by Aurel Stein, who says that "by Gr. *Arsákēs* is meant the chief of Uraśā or Hasāra, the name of whose territory figures as *Arsa* or *Onarsa* in Ptolemy's *Geography*."[207] Whether the Ārjīkīyā was one of the rivers of the mountain region itself, which was full of streams, or whether the Indus itself bore this name in its upper course, or it was the upper Vitastā, or, to follow the statements of Sāyaṇa, it was a part of the Vipāś — these are questions which I am not in a position to decide. Only this much seems to be certain : Ārjīka was in fact the name of a territory or of its inhabitants; this territory was situated between the Indus and the Vitastā, approximately on latitude 32°N. From what we know about the settlements of the Pūrus in historical times, it is likely that a Pūru lived in the territory of the Ārjīkas and boasted that the Soma there was the sweetest.

By placing the Ārjīkas in Kashmir or in its neighbouring regions, we add only one more link to the chain of evidence which shows the importance of this mountain region for the oldest cultural history of the Indian peoples. In his *Der Atharvaveda in Kaschmir*, p. 27, Roth says : "It is not only the native tradition according to which Kashmir has a very ancient Hindu population, but the assumption becomes self-evident that the Indian tribes in those days when they were settled at the upper Indus and in the land of the five streams, or to put it briefly, in the Vedic period, were also in possession of the territory on the upper course of the Vitastā, i.e. the valley of Kashmir. ... At the time of Alexander, Indian tribes were settled in all parts of that area, including the mountain region. It was only very gradually that these tribes entered into a loose association with the main tribe, after the centres of brahmanical learning had expanded more and more southwards into the Peninsula." Both Zimmer[208] and Ludwig[209] have adduced various evidences in favour of this view.

In one of the verses cited above, i.e., in IX.65.23 (p. 176) the Ārjīkas, who lived far away according to the singer of the hymn, are called *kṛtvan*. This adjective means "active," which makes no sense in this context. It also means "magical;"[210] *kṛtyā́* is a common word for magic. If we saw in one passage that a Pūru found Soma the sweetest in Ārjīka, then some one other than a Pūru could very well have been of a different opinion. The Pūrus were not popular everywhere. They were called *mṛdhrávāc*, "barbarians," in the seventh maṇḍala (18.13). The author of IX.113.2 also does not appear to be favourably inclined towards the Ārjīkas, for he wishes that the Soma should come away from there to him. Therefore *kṛtvan* in our passage also should be more of a censure rather than a praise.[211] Remarkably enough, a statement of Hsuan Tsang confirms this. Cunningham[212] says : "Hwen Thsang states that the neighbouring kings held the base Kashmiris in such scorn that they refused all alliance with them, and gave them the name of ki-lo-to or Krityas... The term which I have heard used is Kīr-Mlechchas or 'the Barbarian Kīras' and Wilson gives Kīra as a name of the valley of Kashmir, and Kīrāh as the name of the people."[213]

In fact, Sāyaṇa has almost hit the right mark when he says in his commentary on IX.65.22 that *kṛtvan* is a *deśābhidhāna*.

From what has been said it follows immediately that *saryaṇávat* is not a "Soma vessel" but a geographical name. The contrast between *ārjīkīya* (or *ārjīká*) and *śaryaṇávat* in the verses cited earlier is sufficient to prove this.

While explaining the word *ārjīká* we have shown that the statements of Sāyaṇa lead us to the right path. In several passages he explains *śaryaṇávat* so consistently as a "lake" situated in the hinterland of Kurukṣetra that we have no reason to trust him less in this case.[214] Another point, though not very cogent, indicates that the evidence of Sāyaṇa is roughly correct. The two verses IX.65.22 and VIII.13.15 correspond in the first two pādas, where the words *parāváti arvāváti* occur, so completely that we can assume that the corresponding words of the third pāda also, i.e., *adáḥ śaryaṇávati* and *samudré*, may refer to the same thing and that *śaryaṇávat* may be the name of a lake.

Already in I.84.14 *śaryaṇávat* has a mythical character :

icchánn áśvasya yác chiraḥ párvateṣv ápaśritam |
tád vidac charyaṇávati ||

"He looked for the head of the horse which was hidden in the mountains and found it in *śaryaṇávat*." This probably refers to the head of Dadhyañc. Here *śaryaṇávati* is, whatever its etymology may be, contrasted with *párvateṣu* and can therefore be only a "valley" or "lake."[215] The statement of Sāyaṇa makes it clear as to which of the two is more probable. We should perhaps compare this verse with VIII.100.9 :

samudré antáḥ śayata udná vájro abhīvṛtaḥ.

There is a second passage where our word is mentioned along with *párvata*, viz., X.35.2 :

divásprthivyór áva á vrṇīmahe
mātṝn síndhūn párvatāñ charyaṇávataḥ /
anāgāstvám̐ sūryam uṣásam īmahe
bhadrám̐ sómaḥ suvānó adyá kṛṇotu naḥ //

"We implore heaven and earth for help; we ask the motherly streams, the mountains and their lakes, the sun and Dawn for sinlessness ..."

Here *śaryaṇávataḥ* belongs, if one looks at *mātṝn síndhūn* next to it, clearly to *párvatān*, and Sāyaṇa renders it with *sarasaḥ sambandhinaḥ parvatān.* The company of Uṣas, Sūrya, Mātaraḥ Sindhavaḥ, Parvatāḥ makes us look for something divine in that also which was enclosed by these Parvatas. Sacred hills have their sacred lakes. The Seven Ṛṣis pluck lotus flowers from the lakes on the peaks of the Himavat;[216] Kailāsa is the seat of gods, and the two lakes situated nearby, Mānasa and Rāvaṇahrada, are regarded as famous places of pilgrimage.[217] Obviously the heart of the Vedic Indian was touched by the quietude of the solitary mountain lakes, and he conceived them as the favourite abodes of the gods. There can be no doubt, therefore, in the translation of this verse. In both the cases the PW has given the correct meaning of the word.

There is no reason to separate the two passages from the rest. As in I.84.14 and X.35.2 so also elsewhere *śaryaṇávat* means "lake," and the frequent parallelism with *ārjīká* proves that it is also the name of a specific lake. However, I have not been able to ascertain its location.[218] Ludwig's view that it is the eastern Sarasvatī[219] has not convinced me, because Śaryaṇāvat has to be a lake and not a river, and it is not likely that a stream which does not flow into the sea but disappears into the desert is called a lake because of this; nor do I think that the Sarasvatī was ever called a *hrada* or something similar in the later period. Brunnhofer[220] follows Ludwig's hypothesis, but he tries to see in *śaryaṇávat* the western, i.e., the Iranian Sarasvatī. The arguments against Ludwig's view apply to a still greater degree to Brunnhofer's view. Moreover, the distance at which the Sarasvatī would then be situated from the genuine Ārjīka and the etymological reasoning of Brunnhofer go against his view. In *śaryaṇā* he sees "a derivation of *darya*, 'ocean, river,' preserved still in modern Persian with an initial *d* in stead of *z*, a variation of which, preserved in the Zend *zrayaṅh*, forms the basis of Sanskrit *śaryā, śaryaṇāvā*." I doubt this very much. Only this much is certain : the repeated juxtaposition of *śarya-ṇávat*, *ārjīká*, *suṣóma* and *pastyávat* indicates that here we are dealing with a specific region, a territory which has certain common features. This becomes all the more likely because this juxtaposition is limited exclusively to the eighth (three passages) and ninth maṇḍalas (not counting the catalogue of rivers, which does not mention *śaryaṇávat* at all).

The author of VIII.6.39, a Kaṇva, Vatsa by name, lives at the Śaryaṇāvat :

> *mándasvā sú svàrṇara uténdra śaryaṇávati* /
> *mátsvā vívasvato matí* //[221]

and also the author of IX.113.1-2,[222] who desires the Soma from Ārjīka. The situation is different in two further cases. Hymn VIII.64, which states in v. 11 that the Soma at *śaryaṇávat* is of course dear to Indra but the one at the *ārjīkīya* is the sweetest, must have had its origin, as we saw, among the Pūrus. Its author must have lived not very far from but also not very close to the *śaryaṇávat*, to which he makes a friendly reference.

This is not the case in the next hymn, IX.65. Its author is, (to conclude from v. 25), a Jamadagni. In the light of the earlier discussion (p. 176) if it is permitted to regard vv. 22 and 23 as two verses which complement one another in such a way that the second one is a kind of elaboration of the first, then this poet lives *mádhye pastyānám*, which corresponds to *arvāváti* of v. 22, but at a distance from *śaryaṇávat*, which for him is *adás*, "there." The third pāda of v. 23 shows, if we follow the parallelism further, that this "there" is situated in the land of the *pañcá jánāḥ*.

Thus we may assume that the *śaryaṇávat* is situated in the land of the *pañcá jánāḥ*, that the Pūrus were settled in Ārjīka not far from it, and that a Jamadagni lived quite far from it.[223]

Sāyaṇa states that the lake is situated in the hinterland of Kurukṣetra. If Ārjīka borders on to Kashmir, or extends up to the mountain valleys, and if Śaryaṇāvat is situated nearby, then we may consider a further possibility. The earlier settlements of the Kurus were situated, as Zimmer has shown, near Kamboja in the territory of Kashmir.[224] Should it not be the case that an old name from those settlements is preserved in the word *śaryaṇåvat*, which, limited only to a few passages, occurs in formula-like associations only, and which has already assumed a mythical character in another passage (I.84.14) ? If that were the case, *śaryaṇåvat* would then be the name of one of the lakes of this land, perhaps the name of the biggest among them, of the Walar. Then Ārjīka belongs to the southern part of Kashmir and Śaryaṇāvat to the middle part. Here I cannot go beyond a mere conjecture.[225]

6. The Effect of the Drink

Soma was poured into the fire as an offering to the gods,[226] or was drunk by the priests. The Hotṛ drinks it at first.

I have nothing to add to what was said about Soma and the drink in this connection by Zimmer, Kaegi, Spiegel, Bergaigne etc. The Soma drink inspires and stimulates one to compose hymns.[227] The significant position which the sacred drink occupied in the belief of the Vedic Indian is expressed at its best in hymn VIII.48.

One should not translate the last pāda[228] of the eleventh verse as Zimmer has done : "we have reached that stage of intoxication where one forgets worry and disease, where one drinks forth merrily, without caring about the time." Soma bestows not only long life but also immortality. It bestows on him who drinks it the hope of being there where his ancestors are.[229] This is the only idea that the eleventh as well as the third verse, which agrees with the former completely, are to express; it is this idea that gives the Soma cult its deeper significance.

Just as in his battles against Vṛtra, Indra himself acquires the strength through Soma,[230] so does the prince, to whose Soma sacrifice Indra comes, gain the power to strike his enemies. The drink removes the sin from the heart and takes away the disease from the weak, for it is medicine for the infirm. Soma bestows the rain of heaven, the wealth of the earth, reputation and fame,[231] protection against human wickedness, also against bad omens;[232] it encourages truth and destroys untruth; it does not let the bad ones go free and also not the Kṣatriya who assumes false dignity. In the Brāhmaṇa period it is even said that the brahmins who drink Soma can kill with their glances.[233]

For the Soma sacrificer the metres lose their power for one year.[234] In the law books Soma is regarded as a purificatory drink.[235]

The great importance ascribed to Soma is a legacy from the past, for the *Avesta* praises its divine power no less than the Vedas. Haoma has given the possession of heroic sons as a reward to Vīvahvat and Yima, who were the first to press the Haoma. It bestows upon its worshippers the best of the worlds, namely the celestial world. It is medicine and confers health and longevity, victory over the attacks of the enemies; it elevates the hearts of the poor as well as of the rich (*Yasna* IX-X).

Spiegel is not wrong when he maintains (*Arische Periode*, p. 177) that there was little mention of the intoxication of the singers and priests. It is enough, as I see it, that it is mentioned at all,[236] because these hymns, after all, occupy themselves more with gods than with men. We also know that now and then the sacrificial drink did not agree with its worshippers, because either one drank it without any admixture, or the substitute plants did not serve their purpose well, or excess led to ruinous consequences. The non-Ṛgvedic texts often discuss the possibility of spitting the Soma. The drink was sacred, and one who vomits it commits naturally a sin.[237] But Indra, the great model for all Soma drinkers, led the way here also. He drank pure Soma which pressed forward again through all the openings of his body so that the gods had to cure him by means of the Sautrāmaṇī ceremony which was intended for this very purpose by the Brāhmaṇas.[238] Zimmer has already discussed this, as well as the disease called Viṣūcikā, caused by the partaking of Soma.[239]

PART II

KING SOMA

Soma is not merely a plant but also a god. Like the other inhabitants of heaven, he is invited to sacrifices and requested under the name of Soma or Indu to sit upon the sacrificial bed of straw and receive the offerings.[1]

"This Soma is identical with the moon in the later hymns of the ṚV only" — no other view appeared to be as firmly established as this one. Barth,[2] Bergaigne,[3] Darmesteter,[4] Eggeling,[5] Kaegi,[6] Lassen,[7] Max Müller,[8] Muir[9], Roth,[10] Zimmer,[11] von Schroeder[12], Whitney[13] etc. were unanimous in the view that it is only a deification of the Soma drink which was glorified in the Vedic hymns. This view was shared by the majority of the scholars and is not given up even today. In reality no other view was less substantiated.

Bergaigne[14] has made a most thorough and penetrating study of the god Soma and stated views that differ considerably from those of all other Vedic scholars. It is in keeping with the high esteem in which this scholar is held that I quote his conclusions in his own words, although I do no agree with him.

He admits that in some passages of the ṚV, Soma denotes the moon, but he does not think that it is his usual name there. "While contesting the view that the word Soma is in the ṚV itself a commonly accepted word for the moon, I am not inclined to deny that Soma has been sometimes identified in the ṚV itself with the moon" (I, p. 159). "The specific and definite identification of Soma with the moon belongs in my opinion to a secondary mythological formation, very nearly as in the case of the stellar myths" (I, p. 161). Furthermore :

"Soma, as a matter of fact, has been identified in the mythology of the Brāhmaṇas with a heavenly body which has ever since received its name from it; but this heavenly body is the moon of which the phases have been spoken of as forming the food of the gods and the pitṛs, which successively reduces its substance, viz. the ambrosia, originally identical with the celestial Soma. We shall see in what immediately follows that the germs of the myth are to be found in the ṚV itself. Nevertheless the identification of Soma with the moon does not exclude its identification with the sun and this latter has a very special importance in the general system of the Vedic mythology. The moon as well as the stars as a matter of fact play a very limited role there, at least, if we have to judge it, as we necessarily have to do, by the texts where these heavenly bodies figure in their current names" (pp. 156-57).

We see that Bergaigne looks for the real meaning of Soma somewhere else than where one did so far. According to him, Soma is of course the moon occasionally, but after all "the intoxicating liquor which men drink and offer to gods in sacrifice is only one of the forms of Soma. Like Agni he has celestial forms. On this point everybody is agreed. I have to add that his principal forms in heaven, like those of Agni, are the sun and lightning" (I, p. 155). Nor can I share the view of Hertel (*Die Arische Feuer-Lehre*)[15] who sees in Soma, as in milk, blood etc., a "liquid manifestation of the celestial fire."

Here I must avoid discussing the views of Bergaigne in detail, because the following exposition of my own views would constitute at the same a critique of Bergaigne's views. Nevertheless I cannot abstain from pointing out already at this stage the improbability of Bergaigne's thesis that a single name of a god has so many meanings. Bergaigne has frequently gone past the truth so closely that it appears almost accidental that he did not arrive at the correct understanding. In order to prove his thesis that Soma was often identical with the sun, he uses, *inter alia*, such comparisons which, as he says, "one is tempted to interpret as an identification," e.g., IX.54.2 :

ayáṃ sū́rya ivopadṛ́g ayáṃ sárāṅsi dhāvati |
saptá praváta ā dívam ||

"In appearance like the sun, he runs through the lakes, the seven streams and heaven."

3 : *ayáṃ víśvāni tiṣṭhati punānó bhúvanopári |*
sómo devó ná sū́ryaḥ ||

"Soma stands, purifying himself, above all the worlds like the god Sūrya." Bergaigne finds ṚV IX.71.8 f. particularly important, which he renders as follows : "His colour becomes brilliant...9 : He bellows like a bull while going around a herd of cattle, is *clad in the lustre of the sun*; the divine bird looks from high on the earth. Soma surveys the races with intelligence."[16]

If one were to encounter these verses without knowing that they are from the ṚV and read them therefore uninfluenced by the established view that Soma generally did not yet denote the moon in the ṚV, then, I think, one would not doubt even for a moment that the god who runs through the "lakes" like the sun, who rules over all the world like the god Sūrya, who clothes himself in the lustre of the sun is none other than the moon god.

There are many other verses which read quite similarly. In all these cases the question would arise whether one would ever have connected these verses with something other than the moon if there was not always the idea behind that the ṚV knew no moon cult and that in the ṚV, Soma was not yet a commonly used name for the moon god. The true understanding is made difficult by the difference between what we think about the moon on the one hand and the conceptions of the Vedic period on the other. Our own views of the moon have been transposed to the ṚV and conclusions have been drawn which surpass the imagination of the Vedic singers. For it is much more difficult to believe that the Soma drink represents the cosmic power which creates and upholds the heaven and earth and that Soma moves at the head of the Dawns, than to believe that Soma is the moon who, endowed with the highest virtues, becomes in the eyes of the Vedic poets the creator and lord of the heaven and earth. Here we are dealing with one of those views which, expressed prematurely by important scholars, became on their authority scientific dogmas and were accepted by scholar after scholar as self-evident truth. Even the native commentaries, unlike the conceptions of the Brāhmaṇas and the ritual, were not aware of the true significance of Soma any more. By their time the Soma-moon cult lost its popularity and the significance of *somaṃ candramasaṃ bhakṣayāmi* disappeared completely; on the other hand, what remained and spread further was the concept of the nectar-containing moon. Only one different view is known to me, viz., that of Gubarnatis, who says in his *Mythologie des Plantes* (II.351) : "the terrestrial Soma is nothing but the symbol of the celestial Soma." However, he does not explain there whether by this he means the Soma of the Brāhmaṇa period or that of the Vedic period. But in his *Lettura sopra*

Mitologia Vedica he makes it clear that he does not differentiate between the two. There he says on p. 106 : "In the Vedic Soma we find expressed sometimes the nectar which can reside in several things, and sometimes the moon which contains, carries and protects this nectar and administers it to the gods who, while drinking it, become immortal, strong and victorious in their heavenly battles against the demons. Soma is not only nectar, but also the water of youth, the water of health and of strength, and he himself is represented as ever-victorious warrior. The rain is Soma, the dew of the dawn is Soma, but more often still Soma is the lunar plant, the juice of the moon, the luminous and celestial herb; it is the moon itself. Together with Soma the god Indra drives away the demons from heaven. The moon increases in as much as the gods drink from it, or rather, because the moon generates the gods, it increases in as much as the luminous gods approach it."[16a]

Not all that Gubarnatis says is correct but, all in all, nothing more correct was ever said about the Vedic Soma. However, Gubarnatis has not proved his thesis; he did not follow the nature of the Vedic god through the oldest texts, nor did he attempt to resolve the difficulties which one encounters while elucidating this mythological figure from all sides; therefore his views did not receive any attention. In my studies, which I began under the influence of older and more current views, I have come almost to the same conclusions as he did. In the entire ṚV — in its earliest as well as the latest portions — Soma has only this meaning : Soma plant or drink, and the moon. The latter meaning is not limited to isolated and late hymns of the tenth book only, it occurs everywhere; the whole of the ninth maṇḍala is devoted to the glorification of the great moon god, to whom almost all the hymns of this book refer; it is a book of hymns to the moon; the drink which men prepare is a part of the divine ambrosia which the moon contains. While the immortals revel in his drink, man partakes of the juice of the plant brought from heaven, which is not only a symbol of the god Soma, but a real part of him; man presses the plant for the gods. Thus Indra enjoys twofold Soma.

X.116.3 : *mamáttu tvā divyáḥ sóma indra*
mamáttu yáḥ sūyáte pártthiveṣu /

"Let the celestial Soma intoxicate you, Indra, let that

intoxicate you which men press." The Brāhmaṇas state clearly that one partakes of the moon himself when one drinks the juice of the plant. On the sacrificial place Soma is received ceremoniously as a king and this symbolism pervades the entire ṚV; god Indu himself enters the strainer.

For the Vedic Indian, or for his ancestors who gave shape to their gods, the moon is not merely the quiet ruler of the night. This is only one facet of his manifold character, but not the most important one. Much more important is the following aspect : the moon contains the drink of the gods; he swells up to become their food; he is a drop, a wave, a well, and also an ocean full of delicious food for the gods, just as he is called "a ball of fresh butter" in the common speech of the later period.

It is the Veda that attributes to the moon many of his qualities which owe their existence to the inventive faculty of the popular conceptions and which make him, for instance, a warrior god by placing weapons like lightning in his hand. We learn from ethnography that such concepts were widespread; on Indian soil these concepts are seen on the coins of the Indo-Scythian kings, where the moon is depicted with bow and arrow. We judge the moon according to the sentiments of lyric poetry; the Vedic Indian did not do so. The most natural enemy of Soma is the darkness of the night; he fights like Indra, and also with Indra, against enemies of all kinds and helps his friends in battle. Soma has inherited these characteristics from Moon-Agni who was in the process of fading out. Agni dwells in everything that shines and gives warmth. Agni is the flame of the hearth and of the sacrificial fire; he is the sun and, in one aspect, the moon also.[17] Some verses indicate that there is still a Moon-Agni in the ṚV, but in general he has receded into the background behind the representative of the divine drink, not without bequeathing some of his own characteristics to him, such as the trait of the warrior god, just as Mitra had transferred some of his characteristics to his old companion Varuṇa.

candrámā apsv àntar, "the moon moves in the waters," is a remark in the ṚV (I.105.1). This simple idea, which is quite current in the later mythology, has been embellished in manifold ways by the fantasy of the Vedic period. It makes him the lord and friend of the waters, compares him with a bull which stands in the midst of cows; it also sees him as the young of the cow, as its offspring.

Moreover, the moon is the abode of the departed souls. Soma is called *pitṛbhiḥ sáṃvidānaḥ*. "united with the Manes." His drink promises immortality to the living also. Thus he comes close to Yama.

Not the least of all, he is a lord of the seasons. He controls the course of the months and regulates the festivals of the gods. He knows all the secrets and is rich in hidden wisdom. The Veda praises him as Brahman among the gods, as the one who leads the way among the poets, as Ṛṣi among the wise. That is to say, he has the same character as Bṛhaspati.

Not all these characteristics, which can easily be ascribed to the nature of the moon, are developed in the Veda in connection with the name Soma, because this name signifies, above all, just his nectar-aspect. However, the beginnings of all these characteristics can be seen in this name also. The further development of these characteristics was hindered because of the existence of other older deities who are to be seen, with greater or lesser probability, as the personifications of this very moon god from different aspects. He had already acquired a pre-Indian personification as the "son of the waters" in Apāṃ napāt and as the god of the Manes in Yama.

With regard to the names of the gods like these two which were already part of mythology in the Ṛgvedic period, evidence cannot be adduced beyond a certain degree of probability, because the remote antiquity when they were created does not speak to us any more in the voice of the Vedic singers. Nevertheless it can be shown that this explanation is basically more probable than the earlier ones and that it is basically in agreement with all that is said in the Veda or in the *Avesta*.

There are still other names which have to be explained in the same way; it is no more surprising that there should be different moon gods at the same time, not all of whom are still seen as such, than to have Viṣṇu besides Sūrya, Savitṛ or Pūṣan.

A. CELESTIAL ORIGIN OF THE SOMA PLANT

It is an ancient belief that plants and water bestow health and immortality. In his *Haurvatāṭ et Ameretāṭ*, Darmesteter has traced this belief to the Aryan period. Closely related to this is the myth of the celestial origin of the plants in the Indo-Iranian circle of ideas. Like Haoma, Soma is the king of herbs. Its juice is called "that which was brought from heaven,"[18] and is regarded as the milk of heaven.[19] The belief in the celestial origin of Soma is expressed most often in the saga according to which the eagle brings Soma. This saga is so well known that it appears superfluous to discuss it by giving examples; I may, however, be forgiven if I repeat the well known facts in order to make this study comprehensive.

I.80.2 : *sá tvāmadad vṛṣá mádaḥ sómaḥ śyenábhṛtaḥ sutáḥ/*
I.93.6 : see Ch. III, n. 328.
III.43.7 : *índra píba vṛ̥́ṣadhūtasya vṛṣṇaḥ*
á yám te śyená uśaté jabhára /
IV.18.13 : *ápaśyam jāyám ámahīyamānām*
ádhā me śyenó mádhv á jabhāra /

"I saw the woman in distress; then the eagle brought me the Madhu," (says Indra).

V.45.9 : *raghúḥ śyenáḥ patayad ándho ácchā*
yúvā kavír dīdayad góṣu gácchan /

"the swift eagle flew after the Soma plant; the youthful Kavi shone, walking among the cattle."

VI.20.6 : *prá śyenó ná madirám aṅśúm asmai*
śíro dāsásya námucer mathāyán /

"while [Indra] severed the head of the Dāsa Namuci, just as the falcon [severed] the sweet shoot for him."

VIII.82.9 : *yám te śyenáḥ padábharat tiró rájāṅsy áspṛtam /*
píbéd asya tvám īśiṣe //

"that one which the falcon brought for you [O Indra] with its foot through the atmosphere, without its being snatched away, drink of it; you are its lord."

VIII.100.8 : *mánojavā áyamanaḥ āyasī́m atarat púram /*
dívaṃ suparṇó gatváya sómaṃ vajríṇa ábharat //

The bronze fortress is conceived as the fortification of heaven, as the outer fortification after conquering which he can hasten to heaven.

IX.68.6 : *mandrásya rūpáṃ vividur manīṣíṇaḥ*
śyenó yád ándho ábharat parāvátaḥ /
táṃ marjayanta suvṛ́dhaṃ nadī́ṣv áṅ
uśántam aṅśúṃ pariyántam ṛgmíyam //

"The wise knew the form of the lovely one when the eagle brought the plant from afar. They adorned him who thrives in the waters, the shoot (ray) that is desiring, going all around, and laudable."[20]

IX.77.2 : *sá pūrvyáḥ pavate yáṃ divás pári*
śyenó mathāyád iṣitás tiró rájaḥ /
sá mádhva á yuvate vévijāna it
kṛśánor ástur mánasáha bibhyúṣā //

"The ancient one purified himself, the one whom the eagle swiftly tore away from heaven through the atmosphere. He partakes of the Madhu, trembling and with frightened heart before the archer Kṛśānu."

IX.86.24 : *tváṃ suparṇá ábharad divás pári*
índo víśvābhir matibhiḥ páriṣkṛtam /
X.11.4 : *adhá tyáṃ drapsáṃ vibhvàṃ vicakṣaṇám*
vír ábharad iṣitáḥ śyenó adhvaré /[21]
X.144.4 : *yáṃ suparṇáḥ parāvátaḥ śyenásya putrá ábharat* /
"whom a bird, son of an eagle, brought from afar."[22]

In hymns IV.26 and 27 the saga of the Soma bird is elaborated in much greater detail than in these verses cited above; these two hymns have become the object of much discussion.[23] Jarl Charpentier has done a laudable study of these two hymns as well as the entire Suparṇa myth, but did not set at rest the objections against seeing the eagle as the subject of IV.27.1-2.[24] It is not the eagle who "knows already in its mother's womb" all the clans of the gods, but it is Soma according to the evidence of verses IX.81.2; 95.2; 97.7, 41; 108.3, which will be cited later. It is not the eagle that is detained in hundred fortresses but Soma whom the eagle decides to fetch. Therefore we should read with Roth *nír adīyat*[25] in IV.27.1. The next verse, IV.27.2, reads *ápa-jabhāra*, i.e., "took," "carried away," and not *abhí babhūva* or something similar. The one who is carried away by the eagle is Soma. This task is not made easy for the eagle — he does not carry the Soma away "*jóṣam*" — because the fortresses are naturally defended. I do not understand how Indra, for whom the Soma is brought, could be considered an enemy here on the authority of texts which date much later, or how an enmity between him and the eagle could be read into the ṚV. Nothing of this sort is stated in the two hymns;[26] on the contrary, the eagle is praised in IV.26 and the drink is offered to Indra in IV.27.5. Responsible for this misconception is the unfortunate reading in IV.27.4 : *índrāvato ná bhujyúm* where *índrāvato*, which belongs to *ná bhújyum* and refers to the Aśvin-miracle, wrongly stands for *údrāvato*,[27] which was either misread or misheard in transmission. This mistake caused a great and unnecessary headache in the exegesis. I do not understand why Soma should claim to be stronger than the eagle in vigour and virility. In that case he could have resisted the eagle if he did not want to be abducted; therefore *āsa* in IV.27.2 has to be third person singular. The eagle fought with the guards of the fortress (like Kṛśānu) and overpowered them with his strength. It is not likely that this Soma-eagle is identical with Viṣṇu's bird or with Viṣṇu.[28] They belong to another group of sagas and have nothing to do with the former, at least not in their origins.[29] I cannot say that I agree with Sieg's interpretation of this passage either.[30]

The saga which has come down to us in the ṚV about the robbing of Soma by an eagle or falcon is not the only one known to the Vedic antiquity.[31] There are a number of myths which describe the same event. But most of them are outside the ṚV. It is difficult to say whether these should, therefore, be regarded as later ones, for some of them might belong to areas different from those where the hymns of the ṚV had their origin. Therefore, I limit my task to a general outline of the different view-points.

Closest to the saga current in the ṚV is the statement of the Yajussaṃhitās and of the Brāhmaṇas that Gāyatrī brings Soma. "Soma was in the third heaven," narrates MS IV.1.1, "Gāyatrī turned herself into an eagle and brought him. A feather was severed from her; from this the Parṇa tree grew. Therefore the Palāśa tree is called Parṇa."[32] ŚBr I.7.1.1 goes into more details : "When Gāyatrī flew to Soma and brought him, a footless archer (?) took aim at her and shot down a feather (leaf) of Gāyatrī or of king Soma. This fell down and became a Palāśa tree." With slight variations the same legend occurs again at III.2.4.1, which has been cited on p. 165.

In the dialogue between Kadrū and Suparṇī, to which a reference is made there, it is said (III.6.2.2)[33]: "Suparṇī was the speech, Kadrū the earth. They (the gods) caused a dispute between them. 3 : They argued among themselves and said : 'which of us can see farthest shall win the person of the other.' 'So be it,' said Kadrū, 'you look thither.' " (After this follows the contest and Kadrū wins). 8 : "Then Kadrū said : 'I have won your person. Soma is there in heaven; fetch him for the gods. With that redeem yourself from the gods.' 'So be it.' She created the metres, and Gāyatrī fetched Soma from heaven."[34]

It is only Gāyatrī who is certainly in the position to bring Soma. MS III.7.3 (77.10) narrates how Jagatī and Triṣṭubh flew out on the same errand, and how one returned with *paśus* and *dīkṣā* and the other with *dakṣiṇā* and *tapas*, but neither with Soma. Only Gāyatrī was successful.[35] Or, if the other metres succeed in bringing Soma, they do so only with the help of Gāyatrī. In the same book of the MS (III.7.7) it is said : "When the metres fetched Soma from there, they did not find their way because of darkness. Then Gāyatrī flew with a she-goat upwards. She created light for them. Only after this they brought Soma."

It is hazardous to propound theories explaining why Gāyatrī alone should have the inherent capability to bring Soma. But we can safely assume that the choice of this metre is based on the same attitude which makes Soma the friend of Vāyu and of the storm-gods. Soma himself is a lord of Vāc. Vāc, on the other hand, is called Somakrayaṇī. Thus Gāyatrī, the "metre of song," is probably the favourite metre of the god who loves the song of the Maruts.

We learn from the ŚBr where the abode of Soma is : in the moon. For only the moon could be meant by the two golden bowls about which it is said in III.6.2.9 : *hiraṇmayyor ha kuśyor antar avahita āsa / te ha sma kṣurapavī nimeṣaṃnimeṣaṃ abhisaṃdhattaḥ / dīkṣātapasau haiva te āsatuḥ / tam ete gandharvāḥ somarakṣā jugupuḥ*, "he was enclosed between two golden bowls (?). At every twinkling of the eye they closed shut with sharp edges. These were *dīkṣā* and *tapas*.[36] The Soma-guarding Gandharvas watched over him."

Another series of myths narrate that Indra drinks Soma in the house of Tvaṣṭṛ and robs him, or kills Tvaṣṭṛ's son Viśvarūpa whose blood Soma is. Besides this, there are other demons like Namuci[37] who is closely associated with Indra and the Aśvins, and who might originally have been the devil of the tribe which worshipped the Aśvins as the most noble gods.

It is evident from these different sagas how many variations this theme has undergone. In the same way, Soma attains a mythological character through his manifold associations with other gods like Vivasvat, Tvaṣṭṛ etc.

We gain a greater certainty with regard to the ṚV when we ask the question : what was the home of the divine drink according to the conceptions of the later period ? If we trace these conceptions backwards up to the portals of the ṚV, if it is established that the view current in the Purāṇas and other branches of literature is also the view of the Brāhmaṇas and that the view of the Brāhmaṇas indisputably extends into the ṚV itself, then such a continuity of development justifies the further question : should we not regard this view as applicable to the entire treasure of hymns ? This question can be answered in the affirmative, and this can be done with such completeness of material and with such positive evidence that few other aspects of Vedic mythology enjoy. It would be sufficient to arrange the texts correctly and let them speak for themselves.

B. THE MOON AND THE DRINK OF THE GODS IN THE LATER LITERATURE

It is well known that the classical Sanskrit literature exhibits a great number of names for the moon, all of which are based on his nectar-aspect : *amṛtadīdhti*, *amṛtadyuti*, *amṛtaraśmi*, *amṛtasū*, *amṛtāṅśu*, *sudhāṅśu*, *sudhākara*, *sudhāṅga*, *sudhādīdhiti*, *sudhānidhi*, *sudhābhṛti*, *sudhāmaya*, *sudhāyoni*, *sudhāraśmi*, *sudhāvāsa*, *sudhāsū*, *sudhāsūti* etc. This richness in formations, which indicates a popular (and not a priestly) origin, corresponds to the innumerable evidences from all branches of literature that the moon is the drink of the gods. There is an abundance of such evidence, particularly in Indian poetry from which I shall emphasize some examples that I collected occasionally.

Vikramorvaśīya (ed. Bollensen) p. 9 : *amadaṃ khu de vaaṇam adhavā candādo amadaṃ*; p. 41 : *amiyagabbhā candabālā*; p. 39, v. 49 on the moon :

> *rucim āvahate satāṃ kriyāyai*
> *sudhayā tarpayate pitṝn surāñś ca* |
> *tamasāṃ niśi mūrchatāṃ nihantre*
> *haracūḍānihitātmane namas te* ||

Kumārasaṃbhava V.22 : *rasātmaka uḍupati*

Śiśupālavadha IX.36 :

amṛtadravair vidadhad abjadṛśām
apamārgam oṣadhipatiḥ sma karair /

Bhojaprabandha (Kālidāsa) :

jyotsnāpīyūṣavāpī, "the pond of moon-nectar."[38]

Viṣṇupurāṇa II.12 : "The chariot of the moon has three wheels. Ten white steeds are harnessed in front of it on the left and on the right. On this chariot, which hangs from the Pole Star and glides swiftly along, he drives to the constellations that lie on his path. Like the rays of the sun, his rays also wax and wane alternately. As in the case of the sun, these horses which originated from the womb of the waters pull, once they are harnessed, for an aeon. After having been drunk by the gods, when the moon wanes and consists of a single *kalā* only, the sun fills him with a single ray. The sun, the thief of the waters, fills the moon day by day in the same order as the gods have drunk him up. The nectar-consuming gods drink the *amṛta* in the moon which has been collected for half a month; therefore, they are immortal...When only two *kalās* are left in him, he enters the disc of the sun. Since he dwells in the ray called Arkā, this is called the Amāvāsyā night. For a day and night the moon dwells first in the waters, then in the plants,[39] and then enters into the disc of the sun. Whosoever cuts the plants while the moon dwells in them, or even causes a leaf to fall down, becomes guilty of brahmin-slaughter. When there is still something left of the rest — the rest that is one-fifteenth consisting of one *kalā* — the Manes approach the last *kalā* in the afternoon. The Manes drink the *kalā* which is left [by the gods] and which consists of nectar and is sacred. On the night of the new moon the nectar is exhausted in the rays. Having attained full contentment for one month, the Manes are happy...Thus [he pleases] the gods in the bright half, the Manes in the dark half, and the plants with his cool nectar-rays consisting of atoms of water."

Vāyupurāṇa 52.50 ff.[40] says almost the same : "Know this, the chariot of the moon stands with both sides on three wheels. The chariot, equipped with horses and charioteer, originates from the womb of the waters. It has three wheels with hundred spokes and is harnessed with ten best slender celestial horses which do not need reins and have the speed of the mind. Once this chariot is harnessed, they pull it till the end of the aeon...

Surrounded by the gods and the Manes, he goes forth amiably... Thus the body of the moon is filled through the power of the sun. On the night of the full moon one sees him shining brightly with a full disc. Then from the second day onwards for fourteen days of the dark half, the gods drink of the pleasant sweet draught consisting of water and nectar of the moon, who is formed out of the quintessence of water and who consists only of *rasa*. For half a month the nectar is collected through the light of the sun. On the night of the full moon they approach the lovely Amṛta to enjoy it...At the beginning of the dark half, when the moon turns towards the sun, his interior vanishes; the *kalās*, being drunk one by one, disappear in the dark half and become full in the bright half. After the sequence of days is over, the gods, having thus drunk the moon for half a month, go away and the Manes approach the moon on the night of the new moon" etc.

When we turn from the Purāṇas to the period represented by the Upaniṣads, we should mention, first of all, the famous passage of the *Chāndogya Upaniṣad* (V.10.1 ff.) according to which "those who, living in villages, see the gift in the sacrifices and pious deeds, go to smoke, from smoke to night, from night to the dark fortnight, from the dark fortnight to those six months during which the sun travels southward. They do not reach the year. From those six months they go to the abode of the fathers, from the abode of the fathers to the void, from the void to the moon. That is king Soma and he is the food of the gods. This the gods enjoy."

More important than this is the evidence of the Brāhmaṇas since they are relatively closest to the ṚV.

ŚBr 1.6.4.5 narrates thus : "The gods said : 'nothing but Soma will satiate Indra. Let us prepare Soma for him.'...This king Soma, the food of the gods, is the moon.[41] During this night [of the new moon] when he is visible neither in the east nor in the west, he comes into this world, enters into the waters and plants.[42] He is the wealth of the gods, for he is their food. Since he dwells here during this night, it is called Amāvāsyā. 6 : They prepared it, after having it collected by the cows : from the plants when the cows ate the herbs, from the waters when they drank the water.[43] Thus they prepared it and let it curdle; they made it pungent and offered it to him."

The same passage occurs again at I.6.4.15 with a variation at the end:[44] "The moon enters into the waters and plants, and he (the performer of the Sāṃnāyya-sacrifice), having collected him (Soma) from the waters and plants, recreates him out of libations. Recreated out of libations, he appears in the west."[45]

II.4.2.2 : "Then the Manes approached Prajāpati, wearing the sacrificial thread on the right shoulder and bending their left knee. He said to them : 'your eating shall be monthly, your nourishment, the swiftness of your thought; and the moon your light.'

II.4.2.7 : "When the moon is seen neither in the east nor in the west, he makes offerings to them, for the moon is king Soma, the food of the gods. He disappears during this night. When he has disappeared, he makes offerings to them. If he were to make offerings as long as he has not disappeared, he would sow discord between the gods and the Manes. Therefore, he makes offerings to them when he is seen neither in the east nor in the west.

II.4.2.12 : "He makes offerings to Agni and Soma. He makes offerings to Agni, because Agni has a share everywhere, to Soma because Soma is the deity of the Manes.[46]

II.4.4.15 : "The moon is king Soma, the food of the gods.[47] When they want to eat him early, they press him the day before. When he wanes, then they eat him.

IV.6.7.12 : "Now here on the Havirdhāna cart Soma as the husband approaches the waters as his wives; from this union the moon is born, from the food the food, namely, from water and Soma the moon. For the moon is the food of him that burns there (Sūrya).

VI.1.2.4 : "Prajāpati...entered into union as Soma with the sky. From this an egg was born. He touched it with the words 'bring the seed.' From this the moon was born, because he is seed. But all the tears which had flowed out became the Nakṣatras."

ABr VII.11 : *etad vai devasomaṃ yac candramās.*

TBr I.4.10.7 : *somo vai candramāḥ / eṣa ha vai sākṣāt somaṃ bhakṣayati ya evem vidvān sākamedhair yajate* etc.

One can see that the concept of the moon containing the food of the gods and of the Manes is current here also. Similarly, the Soma who is brought to the sacrificial place ceremoniously in the shape of the plant and is used for preparing the drink is regarded as the moon god himself. KBr VII.10 : *asau vai somo rājā vicakṣaṇaś candramāḥ / sa imaṃ krītam eva praviśati / tad yat somaṃ rājānaṃ krīṇāty asau vai somo rājā vicakṣaṇaś candramā abhiṣuto 'sad iti tasmai krītāya navānvāha,* "This omniscient moon is that king Soma. He enters into that which was bought. Therefore, when he buys king Soma, he does so thinking : 'this omniscient moon is king Soma. May he be pressed.' He recites nine [verses] for this which was bought."

VI.4 : *somaṃ rājānaṃ candramasaṃ bhakṣayāmīti manasā dhyāyann aśnīyāt*[48] *tad asau vai somo rājā vicakṣaṇaś candramās / tam etam aparapakṣaṃ devā abhiṣuṇvanti / tad yad aparapakṣaṃ dākṣāyaṇayajñasya vratāni carati devānām api somapītho 'sānīti.* "He should eat thinking, 'I eat king Soma, the moon.'[49] The omniscient moon is king Soma. The gods press this one in the dark fortnight. When he takes the vows of the Dākṣāyaṇa sacrifice in the dark fortnight, he does so thinking, 'I shall partake of the Soma drink with the gods.' "[50]

These statements are not based on occasional mystic impulses or on fanciful interpretations. The reception of king Soma, described in the ABr and elsewhere, as soon as he is brought, after the buying, to the sacrificial place on the Havirdhāna cart, and the mantras used in this connection, though originally belonging to another context, make it abundantly clear that this Brāhmaṇa also sees in the plant the representative of the moon god or the moon himself, in whose honour the festive ceremony is performed. Thus the Brāhamaṇa states on the buying of Soma:[51] *prācyāṃ vai diśi devāḥ somaṃ rājānam akrīṇaṅs tasmāt prācyāṃ diśi krīyate / taṃ trayodaśān māsād akrīṇan / tasmāt trayodaśo māso nānuvidyate / na vai somavikrayy anuvidyate / pāpo hi somavikrayī / tasya krītasya manuṣyān abhy upāvartamānasya diśo vīryāṇīndriyāṇi vyudasīdan...*

When Soma is carried on the cart, the Hotṛ says : "May he go from the good to the better," and the Brāhmaṇa explains : "good is this world, better than this is the other world. He causes the sacrificer to go to the celestial world. All rejoice at the radiance[52] that has come. Radiance is king Soma; everyone is glad when he is bought : he who is to get something from the sacrifice as well as he who is to get nothing."

The attitude of the Brāhmaṇa is expressed clearly in the

employment of the Ṛgvedic verse IV.53.7 on the same occasion. (This verse actually refers to Savitṛ, but is chosen here because of certain characteristic words.) *ágann devá ṛtúbhir várdhatu kṣáyaṃ dádhātu naḥ savitā́ saprajā́m íṣam*, "the god approached along with the seasons. May he make the house prosperous. May Savitṛ give abundant progeny and food," on which the Brāhmaṇa comments : *ṛtavo vai somasya rājño rājabhrātaro yathā manuṣyasya, tair evainaṃ tat sahāgamayati.*

The same result is obtained by an examination of the individual mantras of the YV which accompany the rites connected with the bringing of Soma. As soon as the cart, laden with Soma, starts moving, the Adhvaryu says to Soma:[53] "Go forward, O lord of the earth, towards all dwellings. May no thieves, no bandits, no wicked wolves find you; may Gandharva Viśvāvasu not attack you. Turning into a bird, fly to the festive place in the house of our sacrificer for being pressed for the gods."[54] The arrival at the sacrificial place is followed by the Ātithyeṣṭi, the offerings of welcome in honour of the high guest who approaches the house of the sacrificer.[55]

He is taken down from the cart. The mantra then runs as follows : "With uninjured wing, descend to men, longingly to the longing ones, friendly to the friendly ones. King Soma, descend fully to men, all men descend to you." He steps forward with the words, "stride through the atmosphere."[56]

Soma is placed on a throne and is addressed as king Varuṇa. Everywhere he should approach king Soma with the words : "Worship the great Varuṇa. Worship the wise guardian of the *amṛta*. May this one grant us threefold protection."[57]

Soma is worshipped throughout as god, and is enveloped in a veil of symbolism which would have remained unintelligible had we not considered the Soma here in the ritual as god, as the moon god, who approaches the hut of the sacrificer.[58]

C. THE MOON AND THE DRINK OF THE GODS IN THE ṚGVEDA

The passages cited from the Brāhmaṇas have taken us up to the portals of the ṚV. It is well known that Soma denotes the moon in several passages of the AV. Should we then assume that this concept which is found in the entire later literature from the period of the Brāhmaṇas onward and represents one of the most popular traits of this literature was accepted only after the period of the ṚV, or that it was an outcome of popular concepts to which the priestly ritual gave a place and elaborated upon ?

In the first edition of this work, I have advocated the second view. I shall do so here afresh.

Of those who opposed my view, A. B. Keith was the last to voice his objections. In his *Religion and Philosophy of the Veda* he says : "The most serious objection to this view is the fact that, while in the later literature...the nature of Soma as the moon is apparent on every hand, in the Rigveda it can only be restored by conjecture, and there is a definite assertion in one hymn that the conception of Soma as the moon is mythic and known to the Brahmans only. Again, in the vast majority of passages, it is perfectly plain that the Soma plant and its qualities are referred to. If we could show *ab extra* that the plant is also the moon, this would not be a fatal objection to the theory of Hillebrandt, but, as this cannot be done, and as the ordinary view that the plant is deified and made into a great god is adequate to account for the facts, it is an offence against sound principles of method to adopt any other theory." (p.171).

Let us examine the outcome of these "sound principles," proclaimed so proudly. I held the same view as Keith does so long as I followed the beaten track and looked at the hymns of the ninth book superficially and did not take any offence at the inconsistencies which became evident while doing so. By a close study, however, the picture changed completely. Keith attaches great importance to X.85.3-4 where "a distinction is drawn between the Soma which the priests know and that which they crush. That the identification was priestly and late is here asserted as clearly as anything of the sort can be expected to be asserted" (p. 170). Keith has misunderstood the passage. It contains merely a refutation of the popular belief that one drinks "the moon" when one crushes the plant; it is the statement of a brahmin who fights against the popular belief, viz., *somaṃ rājānaṃ candramasaṃ bhakṣayāmi*, and nothing more. Keith cites the authority of the commentaries. But these commentaries are, to a large extent, responsible for the confusion in Vedic mythology and, by their silence, only prove that in their period the popularity of the Soma sacrifice and the knowledge of its significance had disappeared.[59] It is still kept alive in the Śrauta ritual, but, as the Daśapeya suggests it is more and more restricted to small circles even there. What remained in the later period was the belief — it must be said, in its entirety — that the moon contained the ambrosia for the gods. The mystery has disappeared.

However, Keith himself is not unaware of the inconsistencies connected with his view, for he says : "In the chaos of ideas of the ninth book of the ṚV there are passages which may be referred to Soma as the moon" (p. 171). Earlier he states : "As a thunderer and a loud-sounding god, Soma is a bull and the waters are his cows : he fertilizes the waters. He is a sharp-horned bull. But he is also for his swift flow a steed or bird, and again he is identified for his bright colour with the sun, and made to dispel the darkness and defeat it. In all this there is clearly evident the fact that Soma is no mere plant on earth, but is in addition a great celestial deity" (p. 168). But Keith does not discuss the significance of statements like the following : Soma shines with the sun (*sáṃ sū́ryeṇa rocate* IX.2.6); purifying himself, he runs with the sun in the sky (*eṣó sū́ryeṇa hāsate ádhi dyávi* IX.27.5)[60]; he ascends the chariot of the mighty sun (*á sū́ryasya bṛható...ádhi rátham...aruhat* IX.75.1); he sits in the lap of the sun or of the old father; he becomes the "king of the streams," the "support" or the "head" of the sky.

What then is the outcome of these "sound principles of method" ? Keith sums it up in the following words : "The monotony of the ninth book is only equalled by its obscurity in detail, and, it must be admitted, much of the obscurity hides no real depth of thought but merely puerile fancies" (p. 167); that is to say in plain language, the ninth book contains mere nonsense; this is an accusation not only against certain hymns, but against the entire book with its more than hundred hymns, not only against one or two poets, but against several poets from ancient Vedic families, against a book which the compilers had included in the great collection of which it forms more than a tenth part ! I would like to save the ancient Ṛṣis from this outcome of "sound principles."

Therefore, I repeat what I have said in my *Vedische Mythologie*, (smaller edition) p. 73 : "The hymns lose all their oddity and stiltedness when we identify Soma with the moon and consider the pressing of the [terrestrial] plant merely as a symbol of the celestial process. Then we understand completely why Soma ascends the sky 'as a bull,' why his light rises with bright radiance and illuminates the sky and the earth, why he is called the 'one who arranges the days,' and why he clothes himself in a garment which touches the sky and fills the space, why he is called thousand-eyed and thousand-rayed, why he dispels the darkness and travels with the sun in the sky. He is called *ukṣán*, *vṛṣabhá*, *paśu*, celestial bird" etc. We do not need any "conjectures" when the text itself speaks so clearly, nor do we need the evidence of late commentaries; the logical meaning speaks for itself. Thus the "riddles" posed by the ninth book dedicated to the cult of the moon are solved; thus "the formless confusion of images and mystic fantasies which," according to Oldenberg, "these hymns abound in," vanishes; thus "the atmosphere of the priestly art of sacrifice which pervaded already in the Indo-Iranian period,"[61] i.e., the absurd state of affairs for which fortunately so far no one has employed the ready-made word "mystic," gives way to a clear and simple conception with which we alone are unfamiliar and the supposedly priestly traits of which are basically in conformity with those of an ancient belief. The only riddle that remains unsolved is how long one could follow the former view. Eggeling, August Barth, Max Müller, von Schroeder, Windisch, Winternitz etc. have joined my view. I mention this because I heard it occasionally said that I encountered opposition "from all sides." I would like to quote the following from Barth's review : "The basic proposition of the book of Mr. Hillebrandt has been presented with such an abundance of evidence so patiently pursued in all its consequences and in all the minute details that it must be accepted, in our view, as one of the most solid contributions to Vedic philology."[62]

The concept of the nectar that flows in the moon for the gods and the Manes is represented on the sacrificial place by the reddish, or bright yellow, shoots of a milky plant the intoxicating juice of which is extracted through a careful and complicated pressing and is mixed with milk and water.

X.116.3 : *mamáttu tvā divyáḥ sóma indra*
mamáttu yáḥ sūyáte párthiveṣu |

Only when we see the cult of the plant *sub specie lunae*, we arrive at the correct understanding of this great cult and its symbolism, which is alluded to in the hymns of the first and tenth books also, where even the earlier Vedic scholars recognize the identity of Soma and the moon.[63] The line of demarcation between these two books and the ninth is drawn only by the interpreters.

From hymn X.85, in which even according to views of the sceptics the identification of Soma with the moon must have been completed, I shall cite v. 19; it speaks of Candramas and contains parallels to the Soma verses of the ninth and other books, which will be cited soon.

X.85.19 : *návonavo bhavati jā́yamāno*
áhnām ketúr uṣásām ety ágram /
bhāgáṃ devébhyo vi dadhāty āyán
prá candrámās tirate dīrghám ā́yuḥ //

Exactly in the same way the following verses speak of Indu who is identical with Soma.

VI.39.3 : *imáṃ ketúm adadhur nū́ cid áhnām*
śúcijanmana uṣásaś cakāra //
4 : *ayám rocayad arúco rucānó*
ayáṃ vāsayad vy ṛténa purvīḥ //

(IX.86.45 : *vimā́no áhnām*). Just as it is said of Candramas that he precedes the Dawns, of Indu that he created them or made them shine, so is it said in IX.83.3; 86.21[64] that Soma makes them shine (*vi+ruc*); in 71.7; 75.3 that he rules over them (*vi+rāj, adhi+rāj*); or that he is the promoter (*pratarītṛ*) of the day, of Dawn and of the sky (86.19). Here Candramas, Indu and Soma are synonyms. In X.85.5 it is said of Soma that the gods drink him and then he becomes full again. The same is said also in

IX.67.28 : *prá pyāyasva prá syandasva sóma víśvebhir aṅśúbhiḥ*
devébhya uttamáṃ havíḥ // and

I.91.17 : *ā́ pyāyasva madintama sóma víśvebhir aṅśúbhiḥ*
bhávā naḥ suśrávastamaḥ sákhā vṛdhé //
18 : *sáṃ te páyāṅsi sám u yantu vā́jāḥ* / . . .
āpyā́yamāno amṛ́tāya soma
diví śrávāṅsy uttamāni dhiṣva //

It is certain that here *aṅśú* is to be translated as "ray." I.91.1, 3-4, 19, 22 clearly refer to the moon. One can in fact speak of the "shoots" also. The expressions *aṅśú, sóma, pū, pyā* apply, in view of the parallelism between the plant and the moon, to both of them and are intended to have a double meaning.[65] Soma's rays, called sometimes *raśmi* and sometimes *ketú*, are mentioned in several passages.

IX.86.5 : *víśvā dhā́māni...*
prabhós te satáḥ pári yanti ketávaḥ |
vyānaśíḥ pavase soma dhármabhiḥ
pátir víśvasya bhúvanasya rājasi ||
6 : *ubhayátaḥ pávamānasya raśmáyo*
dhruvásya satáḥ pári yanti ketávaḥ ||

This is said of Soma who purifies himself, i.e., also of the flowing Soma. The same verb *pári-eti*, which makes good sense when it refers to the ray of light but not when it refers to a mere stalk of a plant (unless of course it refers to a stalk which is passed from hand to hand) occurs again in 74.2 in association with *aṅśú* :

IX.74.2 : *divó yáḥ skambhó dhárunaḥ svātataḥ |*
ā́pūrṇo aṅsúḥ pary éti viśvátaḥ ||

Similarly in IX.68.6 : *uśántam aṅśum pariyántam ṛgmíyam.*
Or IX.15.5 : *eṣá rukmíbhir īyate*
vājī́ śubhrébhir aṅśúbhiḥ and
IX.100.8 : *pávamāna máhi śrávas*
citrébhir yāsi raśmíbhiḥ,

where *raśmíbhiḥ* and *aṅśúbhiḥ* cannot be distinguished from one another. I would not know how the "strong" (steed) who hurries forth with his bright and radiant *aṅśús* can be anyone other than the moon god.

How easily the poet's mind jumps from the plant and drink to the moon, or *vice versa*, is shown by hymn I.91 where v. 21 speaks of the drink (*tvā́m ánu madema soma*) and v. 22 of the moon :

tvám ā́ tatanthorv àntárikṣam
tvám jyótiṣā ví támo vavartha;

VI.47.3-4; IX.86.1-4 refer to the drink and the above-mentioned IX.15.5 to the moon.[66] From IX.86 where the first verses and several others speak of the drink, I shall cite the following :

IX.86.14 : *drāpím vásāno yajató divispṛ́śam*
antarikṣaprā́ bhúvaneṣv árpitaḥ |
svàr jajñānó nábhasābhy àkramīt
pratnám asya pitáram ā́ vivāsati ||

We should not lose sight of the fact that he who fills the space, is installed in the worlds, and wears a garment which sweeps the sky cannot be merely the drink or the plant but only the moon. *antarikṣaprá* is an epithet of gods (Savitṛ, Indra and also Urvaśī) but not of the sacrificial offerings. *nábhasā* does not refer to the "admixture of water," but to the path *antárikṣeṇa* taken by the heaven-born one,[67] from where the bird brought him *divás pari, tiró rájāṅsi.* The garment is mentioned in

IX.100.9 : *tvám̐ dyám̐ ca mahivrata pṛthivím̐ cáti jabhṛṣe /*
práti drāpím amuñcathāḥ...[68]

This verse, preceded by the words *citrébhir yāsi raśmíbhiḥ... támāṅsi jighnase*, is easily intelligible in connection with the moon but meaningless with reference to the drink.

Furthermore, we have

IX.86.40 : *ún mádhva ūrmír vanánā atiṣṭhipat*
apó vásāno mahiṣó ví gāhate /
rájā pavítraratho vájam áruhat
sahásrabhṛṣṭir jayati śrávo bṛhát //

Above *mádhva ūrmíḥ* and below *ápo ví gāhate.* Like Agni or Bṛhaspati (IX.67.23-24; 83.2), Soma has his Pavitra;[69] certainly *sahásrabhṛṣṭi* refers neither to the plant nor to the drink.

42 : *só ágre áhnām̐ hárir háryato mádaḥ*
prá cétasā cetayate ánu dyúbhiḥ /[70]
dvá jánā yātáyann antár īyate
nárā ca śáṅsam̐ daívyam̐ ca dhartári //

Compare *ágre áhnām* here with X.85.19 (p. 204) or with

VI.39.3 : *imám̐ ketúm adadhur nū́ cid áhnām*...(see p. 204)

IX.86.45 : *agregó rájápyas taviṣyate*
vimáno áhnām̐ bhuvaneṣv árpitaḥ /
hárir ghṛtásnuḥ sudṛ́śīko arṇaváḥ
jyotīrathaḥ pavate rāyá okyàḥ //

"Walking in the forefront, the king of the waters becomes strong; as the one who regulates the days, he is installed in the worlds. Golden, butter-backed, beautiful to look at, billowing, riding on a chariot of light,[71] the friend of the house purifies himself to become the wealth for us."

The case is the same in the entire ninth book as in these solitary verses. Sometimes the plant is meant, sometimes the moon or the drink which symbolizes his nectar. However, there are passages which distinguish between the two. Some of these are already discussed on p. 147.

IX.12.5 : *yáḥ sómaḥ kaláśeṣv ā́ñ antáḥ pavítra ā́hitaḥ /*
tám índuḥ pári saṣvaje //

"The Soma who is inside the jars and the strainer — him the moon held in embrace."

IX.38.5 : *eṣá syá mádyo ráso áva caṣṭe divā́ḥ śíśuḥ /*
yá índur vā́ram āviśat //

51.3 : *táva tyá indo ándhaso devā́ mádhor vy àśnate /*
pávamānasya marútaḥ //

However, these verses show the close association between the celestial and the terrestrial drink. Seen from this point of view, viz., that the Soma drink pressed on the sacrificial place symbolizes the nectar contained in the moon, the ninth book makes sense. Vedic poets and priests were neither the followers of Shamanism nor performers of orgies, but, following a popular belief and not — I emphasize once again — a priestly belief, they saw in the moon the container of ambrosia which flows in him for the gods and the Manes; in ambrosia they saw the sacred drink which they prepared, in imitation of the celestial procedure, on the sacrificial place from the reddish shoots of a plant, for the gods and the Manes and consumed it in the company of those two. In their eyes the moon becomes a mighty god who dispels darkness, causes the sun and the stars to shine and, elevated to a cosmic power, has become the creator and the regent of the world.

At first I shall cite some more passages.

1. Soma and Light

IX.9.3 : *sá sūnúr mātárā śúcir jātó jāté arocayat /*[72]

9.8; 49.5 : *pratnavád rocayā rúcaḥ //*

15.5 : *eṣá rukmíbhir īyate vājī́ śubhrébhir aṅśúbhiḥ /*

17.5 : *áti trī́ sóma rocanā́ róhan ná bhrājase dívam /*[73]

35.1 : *ā́ naḥ pavasva dhā́rayā.../*
yáyā jyótir vidā́si naḥ //

41.5 : *...ā́ mahī́ ródasī pṛṇa /*
uṣā́ḥ sū́rya ná raśmíbhiḥ //

59.4 : *pávamāno svàr vido jā́yamāno 'bhavo mahā́n /*

66.24 : *pávamāno ṛtáṃ bṛhác chukráṃ jyótir ajījanat /*
kṛṣṇā́ támāṅsi jáṅghanat /

86.6 : *ubhayátaḥ pávamānasya raśmáyo*
dhruvásya satáḥ pári yanti ketávaḥ /[74]
100.8 : *pávamāna máhi śrávaś citrébhir yāsi raśmibhiḥ* /
śárdhan támāṅsi jighnase víśvāni dāśúṣo gṛhé //[75]
108.12 : *vṛ́ṣā vi jajñe janáyann ámartyaḥ*
pratápañ jyótiṣā támaḥ /
furthermore, 68.3; 85.12; 88.5; 107.26 etc.[76]

2. Soma and Dawn

see pp. 29-30 above.

3. Soma causes the Sun to shine

IX.28.5 : *eṣá sū́ryam arocayat pávamāno vícarṣaniḥ*
víśvā dhā́māni viśvavít //
37.4 : *sá tritásyā́dhi sā́navi pávamāno arocayat*
jāmíbhiḥ sū́ryaṃ sáha //
61.16 : *pávamāno ajījanat...jyótir vaiśvānaráṃ bṛhát* /
23.2; 42.1 ; 63.7; 86.22, 29, *rocay* is almost a synonym of *ārohay* in 86.22; 107.7 or of *janay*.

4. Constellations and Luminous Spaces

IX.36.3 : *sá no jyótīṅṣi pūrvya pávamāna ví rócaya* /
86.29 : *táva jyótīṅṣi pávamāna sū́ryaḥ* //
42.1 : *janáyann rocanā́ divó* (celestial spaces) *janáyann apsú sū́ryam* /
85.9 : *arūrucad ví divó rocanā́ kavíḥ* /
Moreover, 66.2-3 where, in my view, *dhā́man* means the "lunar mansion" (see IF 44, p. 143 ff.).

5. Soma as Bird

IX.71.9 : *divyáḥ suparṇó 'va cakṣata kṣā́ṃ*
sómaḥ pári krátunā paśyate jā́ḥ //
97.33 : *divyáḥ suparṇó 'va cakṣi soma...*
85.11 : *nā́ke suparṇáṃ upapaptivā́ṅsam...*

6. Soma as Child

V.45.9; IX.9.5; *diváḥ śíśuḥ* 33.5; 38.5; son of the waters (see below) etc.

7. Soma as the Support of the Sky

IX.72.7 : *dharuṇo mahó diváḥ*
74.2 : *divó yáḥ skambhó dharúṇaḥ svā̀tataḥ*
ápūrṇo aṅśúḥ paryéti viśvátaḥ |
76.1; 86.8, 35, 46; 89.6; 101.15; 108.16 : *divó viṣṭambhá uttamáḥ*; 109.6 etc.

Thus we see that he becomes a demiurge whose power of creation is excellently described in VI.44.21 ff. where, as also in other passages, he appears as a loyal comrade in arms of Indra.

The majority of the miracles praised by the singers here is the work of Soma-Indu alone.[77] He creates the husband of the Dawns, supports the sky and the earth, places light in the sun, and holds the well in the sky. If we see in this Indu only the drops of Soma flowing out of the strainer, we would then overestimate the imagination of the Vedic singers. In the statement that "he harnessed the seven-reined chariot" (VI.44.24) there is a reference to the moon who, like the sun, rides on a chariot of light (see pp. 202, 206 above).

The poor quality and the deficiency of the transmitted tradition in Germanic mythology as well as in the mythologies of other Indo-European peoples might very well be the reason why the concept found in the ṚV and in the ritual literature of a mighty moon who creates the worlds, and who is the abode of the Manes or the destroyer of enemies, encountered an opposition in our country and was rejected for the Vedic hymns, to be replaced by a vague concept of a plant moving in the sky, or supporting it, or of a drink of similar nature prepared from that plant. The purely lyrical role which our poetry customarily ascribes to the "good old moon" might have contributed to the fact that we ignore the necessity of the above concept at all. Indians thought differently, and in this concept they inherited a treasure of pre-historic attitudes.[78] However, on Indo-Scythian and Bactrian coins we can still see the moon as a warrior god with a sword in the girdle. Above all, ethnographic data shows that these concepts are not unique, but have analogies among quite different cultures and that we are on a firm foundation of ethnology.[79]

8. Soma as King

IX.35.5 : *jánasya gópatim* ||

45.4 : *índur devéṣu patyate* ||
48.3 : ...*rā́jānaṃ sukrato diváḥ*
suparṇó avyathír bharat ||
83.5 : *rā́jā pavítrarathaḥ...*
85.3 : *abhí svaranti bahávo manīṣíṇo*
rā́jānam asyá bhúvanasya niṅsate ||
86.5 : *pátir víśvasya bhúvanasya rājasi* ||
33 : *rā́jā síndhūnāṃ pavate pátir diváḥ* |
96.10 : *bhúvanasya rā́jā...*
97.24 : *pavítrebhiḥ pávamāno nṛcákṣā*
rā́jā devā́nām utá mártyānām |
56 : *eṣá viśvavít pavate manīṣī́*
sómo víśvasya bhúvanasya rā́jā |
113.2 : *diśaṃ pate...*etc.[80]

Hence, he is called *suvratá* IX.20.5; *puruvratá* 3.10; *vṛ́ṣavrata* 62.11; 64.1; *mahā́mahivrata* 48.2; *vratéṣu jāgṛhi* 61.24; *dhármāṇi dadhṛṣe* 35.6 etc.

The concept of his being a king is in complete accord with the ritual practice of receiving him with festive ceremonies and keeping the royal throne ready for him.

The Soma cult is based on symbolism. The procedure in which the gods and the Manes partake of the nectar of the moon in heaven is imitated by the rites on the sacrificial place. This symbolism does not originate in the ritual. As I have already stated, the ritual only takes up the old concept of the nectar-containing moon and presents it in the form of a cult through the bright-coloured plant. The concept of nectar in the moon does not date from the Indo-Iranian period only; it goes back, as Roscher has shown conclusively, to the Aryan period. Indian ritual has preserved an ancient tradition; the rare phenomenon that a concept of the early Aryan period continues almost without any change up to the classical writings of India can be observed here; the only difference is that in the Vedic period one believed that one drank "the nectar of the moon" itself when one had pressed Soma.

V. Henry's explanation that "Soma [is] the rain-magic" (*l'Agniṣṭoma*, p. 486; de la Vallée-Poussin, *Indo-Eropéens*, 1924, p. 72)is too one-sided to answer all the questions connected with Soma and its cult; it is not capable of explaining the ritual either.

As far as symbolism in India is concerned, we are not without analogies. The Mahāvīra vessel which forms the central point of the Pravargya ceremony is to be regarded as the symbol of the sun (*Rituallliteratur*, p. 136). It is placed on a throne which should be, "according to some," bigger than the Rājāsandī for Soma; sun and moon find symbolic representation here, not as a later addition, but in the direct context of the entire ceremony. The two Rauhiṇa cakes of the same ceremony are dedicated to the "night and day." Probably they also symbolize the "night and day." As in other cases like the Ukhyāgni rites, we are dealing here not with poetic concepts, but with symbolic representations which alone necessitate the rites and which border on mimicry. Brinton says : "...in truly primitive condition the rite is constantly a mimicry of the supposed doings of the god...the mimicry or imitative origin of rites is well illustrated in that in use for 'rain-making,' one of the commonest of all."[81] Frazer states that "the event which it (sympathetic magic) is desired about is represented dramatically, and the very representation is believed to effect, or at least to contribute to, the production of the desired event." At another place he adds : "by imitating the desired result you actually produce it; by counterfeiting the sun's progress through the heavens you really help the luminary to pursue his celestial journey with punctuality and despatch."[82]

Indian ceremonial is rich in mimicry. The ritual is governed by the maxim *similia similibus*, which is in operation in minor as well as in major sacrifices.[83] Like the majority of the customs of the solstice festival, so also the cult of Soma which radiates from the moon-hymns of the ninth book falls into the area of "symbolic magic." The Agniṣṭoma, the basic form of all Soma sacrifices, is performed in spring. Soma is recovered from the clutches of winter for the sake of the gods, and now he roars for them during the festive sacrifice which, repeated in innumerable variations at different occasions, has become the most sacred of all celebrations.

D. INDU AND OTHER RELATED DESIGNATIONS FOR THE MOON IN THE ṚGVEDA

The moon is a drop in the sky, a drop of golden Soma; therefore one of his names is *indu*. As the PW noticed long ago, this view is already current in the ṚV and is evidenced by VI.39;

VI.44.21 ff. This view has led to other images also, which should find a place here because these also support the view that the moon contains the drink of the gods.

1. *drapsá*

IX.78.4 : *gojín naḥ sómo rathajíd...pavate... /*
yáṃ devā́saś cakriré pītáye mádaṃ
svā́diṣṭhaṃ drapsám aruṇáṃ mayobhúvam //

This victorious drop which the gods there prepare into an intoxicating drink for themselves is the moon. Therefore the adjective *viśvárūpa*, which suits the moon particularly and which has become the name of the son of Tvaṣṭṛ, is attributed to him in

VI.41.3 : *eṣá drapsó vṛṣabhó viśvárūpaḥ*
índrāya vṝṣṇe sám akāri sómaḥ /

The word *drapsá* occurs also in

VIII.17.14 : *drapsó bhettā́ purā́ṃ śā́śvatīnām índro múnīnām sákhā //*

IX.89.2 : *rā́jā síndhūnām avasiṣṭa vā́saḥ...*
apsú drapsó[84] *vāvṛdhé śyenájūto...*

X.123.8 : *drapsáḥ samudrám abhí yáj jígāti*
paśyán gṝdhrasya cákṣasā vídharman /

The PW and Grassmann have already noted that it is the moon who is meant here.[85]

2. *ūrmí*

The drops of Soma streaming forth from the press are compared to the waves in water : *síndhor ivormíḥ pávamāno arṣasi*, "during your purification you stream like the wave of a river" IX.80.5; similarly 33.1; 108.5 etc. The drop is also called directly a "wave," or a "wave of honey."[86]

Just as the lower speech of the later period refers to the moon as *heaṅgavīṇapiṇḍo*, "a ball of fresh butter,"[87] so do the Vedic singers call him a "wave of sweetness."

ún mádhva ūrmír vanánā atiṣṭhipat
apó vásāno mahiṣó ví gāhate //

Thus reads verse IX.86.40, which we have cited earlier also.[88] It is in this way that the designation *ūrmí* for the Soma drop in the jar is explained. This would remain unintelligible if this drop was not the replica of the celestial Soma in IX.78.2 :

indrā́ya soma pári ṣicyase nṛ́bhiḥ
nṛcákṣā ūrmíḥ kavír ajyase váne /

Here *nṛcákṛas* and *kaví* are epithets transferred from the moon to the drop, and for the same reason the self-purifying Soma is called *svādúr ūrmír vājasánir varivovíd vayodhā́ḥ* in IX.110.11.

In these verses the moon himself is *ūrmí*. Occasionally, however, the moon god is distinguished from the *ūrmí*.

IX.107.15 : *tárat samudrám̐ pávamāna ūrmíṇā*
rā́jā devá ṛtám̐ bṛhát /

"Pavamāna, the king, the god, crossed the ocean [of heaven], the great Ṛta, with his wave." Or

X.123.2 : *samudrā́d ūrmím úd iyarti venó*
nabhojā́ḥ pṛṣṭhám̐ haryatásya darśi /

"The seer (moon), born from the waters, raises his wave from the ocean. The back of the beautiful one became visible."

3. *útsa*

The ṚV speaks often of a "golden well" in the skies. From some of these passages we learn that it is Soma. Thus

IX.107.4 : *punānā́ḥ soma dhā́rayā apó vásāno arṣasi* /
ā́ ratnadhā́ yónim ṛtásya sīdasi útso deva hiraṇyáyaḥ //

89.6 : *viṣṭambhó divó dharúṇaḥ pṛthivyā́ḥ*
víśvā utá kṣitáyo háste asya /
ásat ta útso gṛṇaté niyutvān
mádhvo aṅśúḥ pavata indriyā́ya //[89]

I do not think that it is right to dismiss these verses with the assumption that here we are not dealing with a direct meaning, but with a metaphorical meaning since the other passages refer to a well full of Vasu.[90] There are of course many verses which refer quite concretely to a well in the skies, and there the well does not always denote Soma as such. Thus I.154.5 : *víṣṇoḥ padé paramé mádhva útsaḥ*;[91] V.45.8 : *útsa āsām* [*gavā́m*] *paramé sadhásthe*; VS XVII.87 : *útsam juṣasva mádhumantam arvan*; X.30.9 (Apāṃnapāt hymn) : *madacyútam auśānám̐ nabhojā́m̐ pári tritántum̐ vicárantam útsam*, (the wandering well of Uśanas ?). Apart from these, there are also similar images[92] and others listed elsewhere,[92a] which belong particularly to the cycle of the Marut hymns. A remarkable variation on this theme which does not fit easily into our concept is offered by the verses that speak of milking the "old Ṛṣi," e.g,. IX.54.1: *śukrám̐ duduhre áhrayaḥ / páyaḥ sahasrasā́m ṛ́ṣim //* "they milk the Ṛṣi, who bestows thousandfold, for his bright semen."[93] It is difficult to determine whether in all these cases the comparisons denote the moon-well which moves in the skies; but it is certainly so in some cases.[94]

4. *samudrá*[95]

The designation of Soma as *samudrá* is on the same lines as *útsa* and *ūrmí* — not as ocean in the figurative sense that he is the bestower of infinite riches, but in the concrete sense that he contains the Amṛta and the celestial liquid which is synonymous with the former in mythology.

V.47.3 : *ukṣā́ samudró aruṣáḥ suparṇáḥ*
pū́rvasya yónim̐ pitúr ā́ viveśa /

"He, a bull, an ocean, a reddish bird, entered the womb of the ancient father (the sun)."

IX.64.8 : *ketúm̐ kṛṇván divás pári víśvā rūpā́bhy àrṣasi /*
samudráḥ soma pinvase //

"Making a sign from the skies, you stream forth to all the forms; Soma, you swell up to be an ocean."

97.40 : *ákrān samudráḥ prathamé vídharman*
janáyan prajā́ bhúvanasya rā́jā /

"The Samudra, the king of the world, roared in the first realm, producing the creatures."

86.29 : *tvám̐ samudró asi viśvavít kave*
távemā́ḥ páñca pradíśo vídharmaṇi /
tvám̐ dyā́m̐ ca pṛthivī́m̐ cā́ti jabhriṣe
táva jyótīm̐ṣi pávamāna sū́ryaḥ //

30 : *tvám̐ pavítre rájaso vídharmaṇi*
devébhyaḥ soma pavamāna pūyase /

"You are an ocean, omniscient, O Kavi. The five cardinal points are in your realm. You reach beyond the earth and the sky. The sun and the stars are yours, O Pavamāna. You purify yourself for the gods, O Pavamāna, on the strainer in the realm of the atmosphere." Furthermore IX.2.5; 101.6; 109.4. Perhaps VIII.41.8 also.[96]

5. *máda*

IX.86.42 has been cited on p. 206; v. 46 of the same hymn reads as follows :

ásarji skambhó divá údyato mádaḥ
pári tridhátur bhúvanāny arṣati ...
IX.27.5 : *eṣá sū́ryeṇa hāsate pávamāno ádhi dyávi /*
pavítre matsaró mádaḥ //

"Pavamāna runs with the sun in the sky, the intoxicating drink on the [celestial] Pavitra."

Or IX.38.5 : *eṣá syá mádyo ráso áva caṣṭe diváḥ śíśuḥ /* etc. Assuming that *máda* denotes the moon, or the ambrosia contained therein, we can explain why IX.6.3 can speak of *pūrvyá máda*, and 109.6 can refer to *śukráḥ pīyū́ṣaḥ* as *divó dhartá* and similarly 76.1 *kṛ́tvyo rásaḥ* as *dhartá diváḥ.*[97]

6. *ūrjā́ṃ pati, svadhā́vat* etc.

There are other attributes, related to those discussed above, which describe him as the lord of nourishment,[98] as *ghṛtásnu,*[99] *mádhupṛṣṭha,*[100] or *svadhā́vat.* I.95.1, where the moon is called *háriḥ svadhā́vān* will be discussed on p. 216 below. If we were to render *svadhā́vat* there with "independent, authoritarian," then the effect is diminished because the contrast with the sun mentioned in the next pāda would not attain its full expression. The food of the gods is in the moon; he is called *āpyā́yamāno amṛ́tāya* in I.91.18. Therefore the epithet in our verse should mean "rich in nourishment" and would have the same meaning as *ūrjā́ṃ páti.* Similar is the case with

I.95.4 : *ká imáṃ vo niṇyám á ciketa*
vatsó mātṝ́r janayata svadhā́bhiḥ /
bahvī́nāṃ gárbho apásām upásthāt
mahā́n kavír níś carati svadhā́vān //

"Which of you has recognized the hidden one ? The child produced the mothers through his nourishments. From the womb of the many industrious ones comes out the offspring, the mighty Kavi, endowed with *svadhá.*" To this may be added one or two verses of the riddle hymn, I.164, the interpretation of which creates difficulties.[101]

7. *kóśa*

The concept expressed in the epithets like *drapsá, ūrmí, samudrá* is closely related to another concept which, however occurs rarely and which designates the moon as a "vessel." If the interpretation of Eggeling that *kuśī* is the same as *kośī*[102] is correct, then ŚBr III.6.2.9 would mean that Soma was enclosed between two golden bowls. The Ṛgvedic verses V.53.6; VIII. 72.8; IX.83.3, and some others to be quoted below, belong to the same category.[103] In AV IX.4.3 — a difficult but important hymn from the point of view of mythology — an old virile man, rich in seed, carries a bowl full of wealth (*vasóḥ kábandha*); v. 6 informs us that this old man is called Tvaṣṭṛ and that he holds a cup full of Soma (*sómena pūrṇáṃ kaláśam*). The celestial vessel that stands in the fortress of gods, surrounded by radiance, denotes the moon.[104]

E. AGNI SOMAGOPĀ

The moon is a drop of the golden Soma in heaven, or a bowl containing the drink of gods. This concept is original to this name Soma, while several other forms of manifestation and activity of the moon inspired the imagination in other directions and created new personifications. The occasional appearance of the moon in the Veda in the form of Agni creates special difficulties in interpretation. It is a variation on the theme, well known to ethnography, but which occurs rarely in the ṚV. However, this concept is noticeable in the Soma hymns, and we have to treat Soma and Agni as synonyms in some isolated passages like IX.83 (see p. 103).

In those Ṛgvedic verses which speak of the sun and the moon as two forms of Agni we have the evidence that Agni can be a form of the moon. One such verse is

I.95.1 : *dvé vírūpe carataḥ svárthe*
anyányā vatsám úpa dhāpayete /
hárir anyásyāṃ bhávati svadhávān
śukró anyásyāṃ dadṛśe suvárcāḥ //

"Two women of different colours go forth, pursuing the same goal. They suckle the calf alternately. While with one it is golden and endowed with *svadhá*, with the other it appears shining brightly and full of beautiful radiance."

There can be no doubt that the two women are the day and the night, and that Agni is their "calf" which appears with one as the sun and with the other as the moon. The same idea is expressed by I.96.5;[105] IX.97.9;[106] and X.88.6.[107] (Of these the second, IX.97.9, corresponds to verse I.95.1 cited above). The ritual texts see the altar fire in the nocturnal Agni; there has been no lack of people who interpret the "fire" into which the sun dissolves himself in the evenings as the sunset sky.[108] Both these views are wrong. The sunset sky did not develop into an important factor in Vedic mythology. Secondly, the interpretation as the altar fire by the ritual texts contradicts the above-mentioned verses I.96.5; IX.97.9; X.88.6 and AV XIII.3.13. At the time of the composition of these verses the concept of the Agni-form of the moon was still current. However, it was gradually forgotten and needed a reinterpretation.

In my first treatment of the material I was induced, by some passages where the moon and the drink were regarded as different, to see a form of this Moon-Agni in Agni *sómagopā* X.45.5-6. That this view is wrong is shown by v.12 of the same hymn, which refers to *vaiśvānará* as *sómagopā*, and thus calls the sun god the guardian of Soma. Sūrya and Soma are conceived, even if we disregard the scanty astronomical information in the ṚV for the time being, in the closest innate association, which found expression in the ritual also. Thus in ĀpŚS X.25.1 the priest says to Āditya : *deva sūrya, somaṃ kreṣyāmas taṃ te prabrūmas, taṃ tvaṃ viśvebhyo devebhyaḥ kratūn kalpaya.* In ĀpŚS X.27.10 a black skin is hung as a protection against the evil spirits in front of the cart in which Soma is carried, while a verse addressed to Sūrya (ṚV I.50.1) is recited. For the same ceremony the white YV selects the verse at VS IV.32 (cf. KŚS VII.9.9) for recitation; and on this ŚBr III.3.4.8 makes the following remark: *sūryam evaitat purastāt karoti sūryaḥ purastān nāṣṭrā rakṣāṅsy apaghnann ety athābhayenānāṣṭreṇa parivahanti.* Even elsewhere Soma is left in the custody of the sun. In ĀpŚS XI.18.1 he is given over to the sun and the gods for protection with the words, *eṣa vo deva savitaḥ somaḥ.* Thus it is not at all against all expectations if at other places also a verse addressed to Sūrya is inserted during the forward movement of the cart.

ĀpŚS X.29.4 : *ajenāgnīṣomīyeṇa karṇagṛhītena yajamāno rājānam ohyamānaṃ pratīkṣate namo mitrasyeti.* 5 : *lohas tūparo bhavati*... It would indeed be strange if here Soma were to be addressed as Sūrya, or interpreted as such, which does not happen elsewhere. The commentary on the ĀpŚS does not help us here. The commentary on TS I.2.9.1, which borrows from Baudhāyana (*ohyamānaṃ rājānaṃ pratimantrayate*), says of course that *asmin mantre sūryarūpeṇa somaḥ stūyate*; but that is a mistake. For the TS itself says at VI.1.11.6: *varuṇo vā eṣa yajamānam abhyaiti yat krītaḥ soma upanaddhaḥ | namo mitrasya varuṇasya cakṣasa ity āha śāntyā | ā somaṃ vahanty agninā prati tiṣṭhate | tau saṃbhavantau yajamānam abhi sam bhavataḥ.* Thus this verse is thought of as a charm of exorcism against Soma who is approaching here as Varuṇa. The BŚS reads *pratimantray* and not *ā, abhi,* while the TS has *agninā prati tiṣṭhate.* Hence the mantra should refer to the goat that was held by the ear, rather than to Soma. In this interpretation I am supported by the KŚS also. VII.9.21 : *pratiprasthātāgnīṣomīyaṃ paśum ādāya tiṣṭhati kṛṣṇasāraṅgam*... 22 : *namo mitrasyety enam ālambya vācayati.* That is to say that the priest causes the sacrificer to recite the mantra clearly as referring to the goat at the same occasion. Accordingly, here the goat is the representative of Agni (i.e., Sūrya), "the eye of Mitrāvaruṇa." Besides the horse, the goat usually appears as his symbol, not only here but elsewhere also.

F. MORE ON SOMA

1. Soma Tigmaśṛṅga

The ṚV speaks often of the horns of Soma. We may assume that the expression *tigmáśṛṅga* refers to the thorns on the stalks, or to the tips; in some cases it might mean the rays and in others the horns — it cannot be determined always which the correct connotation is. We know from VII.55.5 that the moon was regarded as a bull with thousand horns (or rays).[109]

A survey of the beings to whom this or a similar epithet is attributed shows that this word is not applied to the Soma plant. Agni is called *tigmájambha* and *tigmábhṛṣṭi,* the Dityus are called *tigmámūrdhan,* Agni and Soma-Rudra *tigmáheti,* the son of Tvaṣṭṛ *tigmánīka.* Indra, Rudra, Soma and Soma-Rudra are called *tigmáyudha.* The *nárāḥ agnirūpāḥ* are *tigméṣu.* Apart from Soma, Rohita also is called *tigmáśṛṅga* in AV XIII. 1.25; moreover, it is applied twice in comparisons (*vṛṣabhó ná tigmáśṛṅgo*) to Indra[110] and Agni.[110a] In the ṚV, *tīkṣṇáśṛṅga* is an epithet of Brahmaṇaspati; in the AV it is used twice for animals and only once for plants.[111] Thus we can see that the probability is not too great to speak rightly of the "horns" of the Soma plant. An analysis of the passages in which Soma is mentioned leads also to the same result. Besides IX.97.9, we should also discuss X.48.10[112] in this connection. The view that this verse refers to the moon was stated long ago by Ludwig (V, p. 477), who rightly connects *asthā́* with *asthán*, "bone." The PW (smaller edition) is wrong in rendering *asthā́* with "forthwith," because it is accusative plural[113] and is an alternative form of *asthīni* just as *akṣāṇi* is that of *akṣīṇi*. I translate this verse (X.48.10) as follows : "In one half Soma is visible in him (the drink in the moon), while during the other the herdsman [of the constellations] shows his bones. He who wants to fight the sharp-horned bull gets stuck in the thicket of evil."

Westergaard quotes Durgādāsa s.v. *kṛś* to the effect that the dark half of the month makes the moon "become lean."[114] In AV XII.3.16[115] the animal which is bright-coloured and becomes lean might similarly be the moon. For Soma is often called *ukṣán*, *vṛ́ṣan*, *vṛṣabhá*, and in ṚV IX.86.43 a *paśu*.[116] In I.164.4[117] also it is the moon who is meant by *asthanvát* whom the *anasthā́* carries.[118]

Besides these verses, there are others which state that he "whets his horns," and which deserve our attention. Thus it is said in

IX.15.4 : *eṣá śṛ́ṅgāṇi dódhuvac śiśīte yūthyò vṛ́ṣā /*
nṛmṇā́ dádhāna ójasā //

"Shaking, the bull of the herd whets his horns through his might, full of heroic deeds." It is indisputable that the plant or the juice could not have been meant by this. It becomes all the more improbable if we consider the following verse which certainly refers to Soma.

IX.15.5 : *eṣá rukmíbhir īyate vājī́ śubhrébhir aṅśúbhiḥ /*

"The steed hurries forth with his bright and radiant rays"[119] (p. 205 above). In IX.5.2 the same is said of Agni Tanūnapāt, who is identified there with Soma :

tánūnápāt pávamānaḥ śṛ́ṅge śíśāno arṣati /
antárikṣeṇa rā́rajat //

"Tanūnapāt flows, purifying himself, sharpening his horns,[120] radiating through the atmosphere" (see p. 78 above).

Primarily it might indeed be his rays that are meant here. But the concept of the horns of the moon is as popular in India as among us, and is likewise employed in poetry.[121] For example, Cārudatta in the *Mṛcchakaṭika*[122] says : "The moon makes way to the darkness and goes down with uplifted horns. Only the sharp tips of his tusks remain visible like those of an elephant which is immersed in water." In *Kumārasaṃbhava* II.26 there is a mention of the heads of the Rudras, from the braids of which the horns of the moon hang down. In the *Śakuntalā*[123] the king speaks of the lotus-bracelet around Śakuntalā's arm thus : "In the form of a lotus the young moon leans against your hand, joining his horns together" etc. It is not necessary to give more examples. If we consider Soma as the moon everywhere in the ṚV, then all difficulties in interpretation disappear.

2. The Weapons of Soma

Not to be confused with the above aspect of Soma is his other aspect : that he wields weapons. Thus it is said in

IX.61.30 : *yā́ te bhīmā́ny ā́yudhā tigmā́ni santi dhū́rvaṇe |*
rā́kṣā samasya no nidā́ḥ ||

"Protect us from every enemy with your terrible weapons which are sharp enough to injure." Soma is called in IX.90.3 : *śū́ragrāmaḥ ... jétā ... tigmā́yudhaḥ kṣiprádhanvā samátsu,*[124] in IX.31.6 and 87.2 *svāyudhá* etc. Thus he is a warrior god. Here also ethnography teaches us that this concept, though not current among us, is nevertheless possible (see pp. 189, 209 above). By his very nature he is first of all a fighter against darkness.[125] From this stage he develops into a subduer of his enemies and those of his worshippers. He is called e.g., *rakṣohā́* IX.1.2; 37.3; *vṛtrahā́* IX.25.3; *vṛtrahántama* 24.6; *aghaśaṅsahā́* 28.6 etc.[126] He is stronger than the strong, more heroic than the heroes.[127] He wins horses and cattle in battle, but above all he wins the Svar.[128] He creates light and causes the sun and the stars to shine.

The natural weapons of the moon are his rays; with them he subdues darkness like any other light-god. But this is not enough for us. It is said in VI.52.3 that he throws his "burning missile" against the enemy of the Brahman.[129] IX.91.4 reads thus :

rujā́ dṛḍhā́ cid rakṣásaḥ sádāṅsi
punānā́ inda ūrṇuhi ví vā́jān |
vṛścópáriṣṭāt tujatā́ vadhéna
yé ánti dūrā́d upanāyám eṣām ||

"Smash the strong seats of the Rakṣas. Purifying yourself, O Indu, open up the foods. With the swift weapon tear off from above the leader of those who are near or distant."

This allusion is strengthened by VI.44.42, according to which Indu, in league with Indra, steals the weapons of his father. The poet of VII.104 praises the burning hot weapons of Indra-Soma with which the two drive away the enemies from heaven.

VII.104.4 : *índrāsomā vartáyataṃ divó vadhám*
sáṃ pṛthivyā́ aghā́śaṅsāya tárhaṇam /...
5 : *índrāsomā vartáyataṃ divás pári*
agnitaptébhir yuvám áśmahanmabhiḥ /
tápurvadhebhir ajárebhir atríṇo
ní párśāne vidhyataṃ yántu nisvarám //

"Indra-Soma, hurl from heaven and from the earth the crushing weapon upon the wicked...Indra-Soma, hurl from heaven the weapons of stone, made hot in the fire, the burning missiles that do not grow old, upon the Atrins. Push them into the abyss. Let them go there without a sound." The weapon of Indra is the thunderbolt. Therefore Soma must also carry it in the fight against his enemies.[130] There are several verses which associate the thunderbolt closely with the purification of Soma.

IX.41.3 : *śṛṇvé vṛṣṭér iva svanáḥ pávamānasya śuṣmíṇaḥ* /
cáranti vidyúto divi //

"The hissing of the strong Pavamāna is heard like [the pattering] of rain. The lightnings are flashing in the sky." This association would have been meaningless if the purification of the celestial Soma was not accompanied by lightning.

IX.84.3 : *ā́ yó góbhiḥ sṛjyáta óṣadhīṣv ā́*
devā́nāṃ sumná iṣáyann úpāvasuḥ /
ā́ vidyútā pavate dhā́rayā sutáḥ
índraṃ sómo mādáyan daívyaṃ jánam //
4 : *eṣá syá sómaḥ pavate sahasrajít*
hinvānó vā́cam iṣirā́m uṣarbúdham /
índuḥ samudrám úd iyarti vāyúbhiḥ
éndrasya hā́rdi kaláśeṣu sīdati //

"He who unites himself with the cows among the plants, bestowing wealth by growing stronger in the gods' favour; accompanied by lightning, the pressed Soma flows in a stream, gladdening Indra and the god-folk. Soma purifies himself, conquering the thousandfold, inspiring the diligent speech that wakens with dawn. Indu excites the ocean with the winds. He sits in Indra's body, in the jars." Both these verses show the origin of the concept that is connected with the Soma juice. That "Soma excites the ocean with the winds" would be intelligible only when it is assumed that the procedure on the sacrificial place was seen as a symbol. In reality, the gale is assigned to our god like the lightning. The expression, transferred to the terrestrial representative, becomes an image, a symbolic statement.[131]

IX.80.1 : *sómasya dhárā pavate nṛcákṣasaḥ*
ṛténa devā́n havate divás pári |
bṛ́haspáte ravátheṇā ví didyute
samudrā́so na sávanāni vivyacuḥ ||

"The stream of Soma, who beholds mankind, purifies itself. By the divine law he calls the gods from heaven. There is lightning accompanied by the roaring of Bṛhaspati. The oceans were not able to contain the pressings." There is one more verse which speaks of the moon and immediately thereafter of the lightning, suggesting thus that the lightning and the moon were closely associated in the mind of the poet.

I.105.1 : *candrámā apsv àntar ā́ suparṇó dhāvate diví |*
ná vo hiraṇamayaḥ padáṃ vindanti vidyutaḥ...||[132]

"The moon runs in the waters, a bird in heaven. One does not find your place, O lightnings with golden rims."[133]

The passages that can be cited are not many. This concept did not develop further, probably because the form of the thunderbolt-bearer had already been assigned to Indra. But the available passages cannot be explained away.[134] I agree, therefore, with Bergaigne in so far as he maintains that "the manifestation of Soma evidently takes place here in the phenomenon of a storm," but not when he says that "it is the flashes of lightning which are intended to represent it."[135]

It has been stated on p. 141 above that the ṚV speaks often of the "roaring, thundering and hissing" of the Soma stalk. It is evident that these cannot be the natural characteristics of the Soma plant, but like *svāyudhá* etc. are attributes that were symbolically transferred from the lord of the plant, from the god Soma, to the plant.

3. Soma Stanayat and Related Expressions

There is no doubt about the meaning of the words *krand*, *ru*, *vāś*, *stan*, "to roar, to thunder." It is likely that when the plant is crushed it splits with a loud noise, or that the juice makes a hissing sound when it is mixed with milk; but certainly this could not be the reason for the employment of such typical verbs. It is precisely the activities in heaven that were regarded as the prototypes for the plant and its juice. The following examples will illustrate my point.

krand

IX.97.33 : *divyáḥ suparṇó 'va cakṣi soma...* /
éndo viśa kalaśaṃ somadhā́nam
krándann ihi sū́yasyópa raśmim //

"O Soma, the celestial bird, you look down...Indu, enter into the Soma-jar. Go thundering to the ray of the sun. (?)"

IX.97.40 : *ákrān samudráḥ*[136] *prathamé vídharman*
janáyan prajā́ bhúvanasya rā́jā / See p. 214 above.

64.9 : *hinvānó vā́cam iṣyasi pávamāna vídharmaṇi* /
ákrānt devó ná sū́ryaḥ //[137]

Often this concept of thundering is transferred to the self-purifying juice, which roars towards the cows, or streams into the vessels. In the above-cited passages also the poet moves from Soma directly to the drink. IX.42.4 shows once again how both the god and the drink are interchangeable.

duhānáḥ pratnám ít páyaḥ pavítre pári ṣicyate /
krándann devā́n ajījanat //

"Milked for the ancient milk, he is poured on the Pavitra. Thundering, he caused the gods to be born."

dham

VIII.96.14; IX.73.1 : *srákve drapsásya dhámataḥ sam asvaran* /[138]

nad

IX.70.6 : *sá mātárā nā dádṛśāna usriyo*
nā́nadad eti marútām iva svanáḥ /

"As though he has seen the parents, the reddish one goes forth roaring aloud, like the sound of the Maruts."

mā

IX.69.4 : *ukṣā́ mimāti práti yanti dhenávaḥ*
devásya devī́r úpa yanti niṣkṛtám /

"The bull roars. The cows go towards him, the goddesses to the abode of the god."

rū

IX.70.7 : *ruváti bhīmó vṛṣabhás taviṣyáyā*
śṛ́ṅge śiśāno háriṇī vicakṣaṇáḥ |

"The terrible bull roars violently, sharpening his golden yellow horns, the all-knowing one."[139]

IX.71.9 : *ukṣéva yūthā́ pariyánn arāvīt*
ádhi tvíṣīr adhita sū́ryasya |

"He roared like a bull pacing around the herd; he assumed the lustre of the sun."

IX.85.9 : *ádhi dyā́m asthād vṛṣabhó vicakṣaṇáḥ*
árūrucad ví divó rocanā́ kavíḥ |
rā́jā pavítram áty eti róruvat
diváḥ pīyū́ṣaṃ duhate nṛcákṣasaḥ ||[140]

"The all-knowing[141] bull ascended to heaven. The Kavi caused the spaces of heaven to shine. The king passes through the Pavitra with a roar. They milk the juice of heaven which beholds the mankind." From god Soma this word is transferred to the plant or to the juice : IX.65.19; 68.2; 74.5; 86.7; 91.3 etc.

vāś

IX.95.4 : *aṅśúṃ duhanty ukṣáṇaṃ giriṣṭhā́m* |
táṃ vāvaśānáṃ matáyaḥ sacante[142]

"They milk the shoot, the bull who dwells on mountains. The hymns follow the one who roars aloud."

stan

IX.86.9 : *divó ná sā́nu stanáyann acikradat*
dyaúś ca yásya pṛthivī́ ca dhármabhiḥ |

"With his roaring he made the back of the sky resound as it were, he by whose laws the heaven and earth exist."

IX.72.6 : *aṅśúṃ duhanti stanáyantam*[143] *ákṣitam* |
kavíṃ kaváyo ...

Since the entire cult of Soma is a symbolic act based on popular concepts where the offering of the celestial drink is represented with the help of the shoot of a reddish plant, the poets who speak of the roaring of the moon have preserved once again what was probably another popular concept which we should not dismiss in all our wisdom. People who were closer to nature believed that they had noticed such a phenomenon. We should not underestimate their help where we have ethnographic parallels.[144]

4. Vācaspati

Soma is a "lord of speech,"[145] i.e., the lord of thunder as well as of the voices and songs of the celestial and terrestrial singers who were inspired by his drink. Bergaigne[146] is right when he says that "eloquence is attributed to him personally, VI.39.1, and this he communicates to those who drink him. He is compared to a singer, IX.71.7, or is directly called a singer, IX.7.6; 66.9."

IX.68.8 : *yó dhā́rayā mádhumāñ ūrmíṇā diváḥ*
íyarti vā́cam rayiṣā́d ámartyaḥ //

IX.95.4; 84.1 :
kṛdhī́ no adyá várivaḥ svastimát
urukṣitaú gṛṇīhi daívyam jánam //

"Create space and glory for us today. Sing in praise of the godfolk in the wide realm."[147] He inspires the voice of the singers as the Upavaktṛ inspires that of the Hotṛ (IX.95.5), or he drives the voices as the oarsman drives his ship (95.2); he is called *vācamīṅkhayá* 35.5; 101.6; *hinvānó vā́cam iṣirā́m uṣarbúdham* 84.4;[148] hence he is *vācó agriyá* or *ágre vācáḥ* IX.7.3; 62.25; 86.12; 106.10. Perhaps it is this effect of Soma on the singers that is primarily meant here. But the fact that Soma himself raises his voice shows that it would be a mistake to think, on the basis of a single verse like VI.47.3,[149] that the close association between Vācaspati and the voices of his laudators rests merely on the effect of the intoxicating drink. There is also a mythological factor at play here. The lord of speech rules over the speech even at the sacrificial place. The mythological relation between Soma and Vāc is evident from the sagas of the Brāhmaṇas, cited on p. 165f. above, according to which Vāc was the price paid by the gods for Soma.[150]

5. Soma Marutvat

Soma is not only the drink of Indra but also his comrade with equal rank during his heroic deeds (see p. 221 above).

Soma is associated with the wind-gods almost so closely as Indra is : *túbhyam vā́tā abhipríyas túbhyam arṣanti síndhavaḥ* IX.31.3.[151] This friendship is expressed mythologically in IX.84.4,

"Soma excites the ocean with the winds." On the other hand Vāyu is called the guardian of Soma in X.85.5. He drinks mostly the pure Soma and has the first share in sacrifice. Soma's friendship with the Maruts is stated very clearly. The "daring ones" who milk the semen of the Ṛṣis, those who behold mankind and milk "the bull of heaven" (i.e., Soma) are the Maruts in both the cases. To these verses, IX.54.1 and 108.11, (see p. 214 above), we may add

IX.96.17 : *śiśuṃ jajñānáṃ haryatáṃ mṛjanti*
śumbhánti váhniṃ marúto gaṇéna |
kavír gīrbhíḥ kā́vyenā kavíḥ sán
sómaḥ pavítram áty eti rébhan ||

"The Maruts along with their hosts wash the lovely infant that is just born and adorn the leader. Soma, a seer through his songs, a seer through his power of seeing, passes through the Pavitra with a murmur."[152] Here the "infant" is Soma. The concept expressed in these passages is not based on occasional flights of fancy — the association between Soma and the Maruts is too firmly established for that — but is based on old popular belief. He is called *marútvat* VI.47.5, *marúdgaṇa* IX.66.26.[153] Occasionally Soma is mentioned together with Rudra also. For instance, ṚV VI.74 is addressed to Soma-Rudra. AV XIX.17.3 reads *sómo mā́ rudraír dákṣiṇāyā diśáḥ pātu*; 18.3 : *sómo rudrávān.* MS II.9.7 (126.1) : *namaḥ somāya ca rudrāya ca*; III.7.10 (90.1) : *agnir vasubhiḥ somo rudrair indro marudbhiḥ*; IV.12.2 (180.1); TS II.1.11[1k]; ŚBr V.3.2.1-2; ŚŚS III.6.2 etc.

These Maruts are the Venas about whom Indra speaks as follows in

VIII.100.5 : *ā́ yán mā́ venā́ áruhann ṛtasyaṅ*
ékam ā́sīnaṃ harayatásya pṛṣṭhé |
mánaś cin me hṛdā́ ā́ práti avocat
ácikrandañ chíśumantaḥ sákhāyaḥ ||

"When the seers[154] of the Ṛta climbed up to me while I was seated alone on the beautiful back [of the sky], then my mind spoke to my heart : it is the friends with the infant who roared." These Venas are not, as one might suppose, mere spirits who guard Soma in the atmosphere and in the sky, nor are they, as Oldenberg[155] thinks, demons; but they are the Maruts. It is not the demons whom Indra refers to as his Venas — after all he fights the demons — but it is the Maruts,, or the gods of storm, who accompany the moon god. Just as they are called *śiśumat* — Oldenberg notices correctly that the *śíśu* is Soma — so is the moon often called *diváḥ śíśu* or *yúvan* (see p. 208 above). The following verses support our point.

IX.64.21 : *abhí venā́ anūṣata íyakṣanti prácetasaḥ |*
májjanty ávicetasaḥ ||

"The seers sing to him. The wise hurry to perform the sacrifice. The unwise sink."

IX.85.10 : *divó nā́ke mádhujihvā asaścáto*
venā́ duhanty ukṣáṇaṃ giriṣṭhā́m |
apsú drapsáṃ vāvṛdhānáṃ samudrá ā́
síndhor ūrmā́ mádhumantam pavítra ā́ ||
11 : *nā́ke suparṇám upapaptivā́ṅsam*
gíro venā́nām akṛpanta pūrvī́ḥ |

Just as the terrestrial Soma has its prototype in the moon, the strainer in the Pavitra and the hissing of the Soma stalk in thunder, so do the hymns of the priests correspond to the hymns of the Maruts. The Maruts are called *kaví* in I.87.5 and elsewhere *ṛkvan*; they are the laudators in heaven. Therefore it is not always possible to determine whether it is the celestial singers or those on the earth that are meant. Probably the poets themselves did not intend to differentiate between the two,[156] because the rites on the sacrificial place were regarded as the replica of those in heaven.

Parjanya is also associated with Soma. In IX.82.3 (see p. 152 above) he is called the "father of the mighty bird," and this bird is the moon as in 97.33; 85.11 (see p. 208 above) etc. In IX.113.3 (see p. 152 above) Soma is called *parjányavṛddha.*

G. SOMA AND THE WATERS[157]

It is an ancient belief — not only in India — that the moon is the lord of the waters.[158] The Purāṇas state that the chariot of the moon consists of water. ABr VIII.28.15 says that "the rain comes from the moon" (*candramaso vai vṛṣṭir jāyate*); TĀr I.22.1 : *candramā vo apāṃ puṣpam*; ṚV I.105.1 : *candrámā apsv àntar ā́.* The ninth maṇḍala is full of verses which pursue this idea, employing manifold turns of expression and images, mainly in order to emphasize again and again the idea that the terrestrial Soma is a replica of the celestial one and that like the latter the former also rests in the womb of the waters.[159]

IX.31.3 : *túbhyaṃ vā́tā abhipríyas túbhyam arṣanti síndhavaḥ|*

IX.15.5 : *eṣá rukmíbhir īyate vājī́ śubhébhir aṅśubhiḥ|*
pátiḥ síndhūnāṃ bhávan ||

70.2 : *ubhé dyā́vā kā́vyenā ví śaśrathe |*
téjiṣṭhā apó maṅhánā pári vyata...

82.5 : *táva vratám ánv ā́paḥ sacante ||*

86.12 : *ágre síndhūnā́ṃ pávamāno arṣati*
ágre vācó agriyó góṣu gacchati |

33 : *rā́jā sindhūnāṃ pavate pátir diváḥ*
ṛtásya yāti pathíbhiḥ kánikradat |
sahásradhāraḥ pári ṣicyate háriḥ...

45 : see p. 206 above.

8 : *rā́jā samudrám nadyó ví gāhate*
apā́m ūrmíṃ sacate síndhuṣu śritaḥ |

89.2 : *rā́jā síndhūnām avasiṣṭa vā́saḥ*
ṛtásya nā́vam ā́ruhad rájiṣṭhām |

107.15 : *tárat samudráṃ pávamāna ūrmíṇā...*

16 : *rā́jā deváḥ samudríyaḥ...*

X.61.16 also belongs here although the moon is not expressly mentioned there : "the wise one crosses the waters on his own bridge." The view expressed in these passages occurs often in a different image also and it makes him a "bull" and the waters the "cows." Like a bull he moves in the middle of the herd. For instance,

IX.16.6 : *śū́ro ná góṣu tiṣṭhati ||*

72.4 : *pátir gávāṃ pradíva índur ṛtvíyaḥ*[160]

967 : *antáḥ páśyan vṛjánemā́varāṇi...*[161]
ā́ tiṣṭhati vṛṣabhó góṣu jānán |

69.4 : *ukṣā́ mimāti práti yanti dhenávaḥ...*

71.7 : *...aruṣo diváḥ kavír*
vṛṣā tripṛṣṭhó anaviṣṭa gā́ abhí |

9 : *ukṣéva yūthā́ pariyánn arāvīt*

110.9 : *yūthé ná niṣṭhā́ vṛṣabhó ví tiṣṭhase;*

32.5; 34.6; 89.3 etc.[162] We should take note also of VI.44.21 : "you are the bull of heaven, the bull of the earth, the bull of the streams."[163]

He is called *apā́ṃ péru*, an "impregnator of the waters," in IX.36.8; *apā́ṃ gandharvá* in IX.86.36. In IX.19.5 the author asks : "Has he not, during his purification, impregnated those who were longing for the bull and who give white milk ?"[161] Therefore in the ṚV, and more particularly in the YV, the moon is called *retodhá*. ṚV IX.86.39 : *retodhá indo bhúvaneṣv árpitaḥ*, "O moon, you are placed in the worlds as the semen-bearer." MS I.6.9 (100.18) : *rohiṇyāṃ paśukāmasyādadhyāt / somasya vā etan nakṣatraṃ yad rohiṇī / somo retodhā / reto 'smin dadhāti* /[165] 10.8 (149.11) : *vanaspatiṃ yajati / somo vai vanaspatiḥ / saumīr imāḥ prajāḥ / prajāsv eva rasaṃ dadhāti*; II.2.4 (18.7) : *somo vai retodhāḥ pūṣā paśūnāṃ prajanayitā / soma evāsmai reto dadhāti*; TS I.7.4.5 : *somāsyāhaṃ devayajyayā suretāḥ reto dhiṣīyety āha / somo vai retodhās tenaiva reta ātman dhatte;* VI.5.8.3 : *reto vā induḥ* etc. ŚBr VI.1.3.16 : *prajāpatir vai candramāḥ* etc.

The view that Soma confers fertility, expressed in these Yajus-texts, is shared by the ṚV also as IX.86.39; 60.4 etc. show. "Bring us the semen which produces progeny" (*prajávad réta á bhara*) says IX.60.4; furthermore

IX.74.5 : *dádhāti gárbham áditer upástha á*
yéna tokáṃ ca tanayáṃ ca dhámahe //
86.28 : *távemáḥ prajá divyásya rétasaḥ* /[166]

It is evident that between these verses of the Veda and the remarkable statement of the Upaṇiṣads that the moon "rains down" to men, there is a connecting link provided by the Brāhmaṇas. The new-comer, asked about the moon, says : "O you Ṛtus, the semen comes from the radiant one (the moon), who has fifteen parts, who is created [by the sacrifice] and is inhabited by the Manes.[167] Therefore put me into a begetter, and through the begetter pour me into the mother."[168] Here also we are dealing with concepts that have their origins in folklore.

The lord of the celestial waters rules naturally over the rain.

IX.74.3 : *máhi psáraḥ súkṛtaṃ somyáṃ mádhu*
urvī́ gávyūtir áditer ṛtáṃ yaté /
ī́śe yó vṛṣṭér itá usríyo vṛ́ṣā
ápaṃ netá yá itáūtir ṛgmíyaḥ //
I.91.22 : *tváṃ apó ajanayas tváṃ gáḥ* /
IX.8.8 : *vṛṣṭíṃ diváḥ pári srava dyumnáṃ pṛthivyá ádhi* /
18.5 : *yá imé ródasī mahī́ sáṃ mātáreva dóhate*
49.1 : *pávasva vṛṣṭím á sú no 'páṃ ūrmíṃ divás pari* /

"Through your purification create rain for us, from the sky the wave of the waters."

86.21 : *ayáṃ síndhubhyo abhavad u lokakṛt*[169]
96.3 : *kṛṇvánn apó varṣáyan dyā́m utémā́m*[170]
Compare also v. 14.
97.17 : *vṛṣṭíṃ no arṣa divyā́m...*
108.9 : *ví kośáṃ madhyamáṃ yuva* //
10 : *vṛṣṭíṃ diváḥ pavasva rītím apā́ṃ jinva*[171]...
106.9 : *ā́ naḥ sutāsa indavaḥ punānā́ dhāvatā rayím* /
vṛṣṭídyāvo rītyāpaḥ svarvídaḥ //

"O pressed drops, wash forth riches to us, purifying yourself. Let the sky rain, let the waters flow. You find the light." The drops flowing through the strainer are compared here with the rain drops. The words *vṛṣṭídyāvo rītyāpaḥ* become intelligible only when it is assumed that the flowing juice of Soma is meant to be an imitation of the rain gushing down. Hence in IX.63.27 the rain drops are directly called *pávamānāḥ* :

pávamānā divás pári antárikṣād asṛkṣata /
pṛthivyā́ ádhi sā́navi //

Therefore comparisons of the drops flowing through the strainer with the rain drops are not rare.[172]

IX.41.3 (see p. 221 above) :
śṛṇvé vṛṣṭér iva svanáḥ pávamānasya śuṣmíṇaḥ /
89.1 : *divó ná vṛṣṭíḥ pávamāno akṣā́ḥ*; 69.9 etc.

Bergaigne (I.166) is right in distinguishing between the rain-waters and the celestial Soma. This distinction, however, is not maintained always (cf IX.63.27 cited above), because the images change, and because the rain also appears as the semen or urine of the celestial Soma-bull, of the Ṛṣi whom the Maruts milk; IX.85.9-10; 54.1; 108.11.[173]

Because Soma, as *retodhā́*, grants fertility and because he also rules over the rain, he confers all the riches of heaven and earth, nourishment, food, cattle, horses etc. e.g., IX.45.3; 49.4; 52.1; 57.4; 61.3; 69.8.

Soma is called not only the king of the waters, he is also the one who impregnates them, their bull. Another image, already mentioned earlier, speaks of the drop which grew in the waters.

IX.85.10 : *apsú drapsáṃ vāvṛdhānáṃ samudrá ā́* /
89.2 : *apsú drapsó vāvṛdhe śyenájūto* /

It is the young waxing moon that is meant here.[174] Moreover he is called the son, the offspring, of the waters, the infant who walks forth among the cows.

IX.61.7 : *etám u tyáṃ dáśa kṣipo mṛjánti síndhumātaram* /
"The ten fingers decorate him, the son of the streams."
IX.97.41 : *mahát tát sómo mahiṣáś cakāra*
apā́ṃ yád gárbho avṛṇīta devā́n /
V.45.9 : *raghúḥ śyenáḥ patayad ándho ácchā*
yúvā kavír dīdayad góṣu gácchan /[175]

ŚBr IV.4.5.21 : *devīr āpa eṣa vo garbha ity apāṃ hy eṣa garbhaḥ / taṃ suprītaṃ subhṛtaṃ bibhṛteti / tad enam adbhyaḥ paridadāti guptyai / deva somaiṣa te loka ity āpo hy etasya lokas* etc., " 'Divine waters, this is your offspring,'[176] [he says] because [Soma] is the offspring of the waters. 'Carry him well-fostered and well-fed,' with these words he gives him away to the waters for protection. 'God Soma, this is your world.' The waters are his world." Furthermore

ṚV IX.31.5 : *túbhyaṃ gā́vo ghṛtáṃ páyo bábhro duduhré ákṣitam* /
várṣiṣṭhe ádhi sā́navi //
9.5 : *tā́ abhí sántam ástṛtam*
mahé yúvānam ā́ daduḥ / índum...
"They (the rivers) have brought the surpassing, invincible, youthful moon to power."
70.1 : *trír asmai saptá dhenávo duduhre*
satyā́m āśíraṃ pūrvyé vyòmani /
78.3 : *samudríyā apsaráso manīṣíṇam...abhí sómam akṣaran* /
86.36 : *saptá svásāro abhí mātáraḥ śíśum*
návaṃ jajñānáṃ jényaṃ vipaścítam /
X.13.5 : *saptá kṣaranti śíśave marútvate*
pitré putrā́so ápy avīvatann ṛtám /
The fifth verse of hymn X.123 belongs here :
apsarā́ jārám upasiṣmiyāṇā́
yóṣa bibharti paramé vyòman /
cárat priyásya yóniṣu priyáḥ sán
sī́dat pakṣé hiraṇyáye sá venáḥ //
"The Apsaras, the woman, smiling at the lover, carries him in the highest heaven. Befriended, he walks in the dwellings of the friend. The seer sat on the golden wing."

1. Apāṃ Napāt

Here we have a god whose pre-Indian origin is not in doubt. There is an excellent work on him by Windischmann, posthumously published in the *Zoroastrische Studien*,[177] edited by Spiegel. There Windischmann comes to the conclusion that the Veda and the *Avesta* are in agreement not only with regard to the name but also about the nature of this god. This is one of the most well-founded conclusions of our science, and remains so in spite of the objections of Gruppe.[178] Probably the name Apāṃ napāt is contained in the following words, *Napas ē khrēnē epi ton oron tēs Persidos istoreitai ē pherousa ta aphode*, of the gloss to the *Hesych* to which Paul de Lagarde makes a reference.[179] If that is so then this evidence also suggests that the concept of this god belongs to the Indo-Iranian period. Because of its origin in such an early period of mythology,[180] it is difficult to determine the starting point of this concept. Therefore the views on this concept varied until the most recent times. Windischmann holds that the Vedic god is the impregnating heat in the waters of the rivers, of the ocean and clouds, and that the Vedic conception places the igneous nature of this god in the foreground while the *Avesta* lays greater emphasis on his aqueous nature. Max Müller[181] understands the sun by Apāṃ napāt. In his commentary on ṚV II.35, Ludwig[182] says that "*apāṃ vatsa* is the name of a star in the Constellation Virgo, either δ or θ." The majority of scholars considers Apāṃ napāt to be the lightning. Thus e.g., the PW (and following it Grassmann also) states s.v. *ap*, in fact on the authority of Sāyaṇa : "Agni is called *apāṃ napāt* or *apāṃ garbhaḥ*, son of the waters, because he is born as the lightning from the waters of the atmosphere." In the same vein Darmesteter[183] declares that "the sky is not at all the sole origin of the lightning. It is born in the sky, but it is born in the waters of the thunderstorm also. It is Apāṃ napāt, the son of the waters." Spiegel[184] sees "in Apāṃ napāt a rather vaguely held superintendent of the celestial waters who lives in a far-off dwelling and from there looks after their distribution," and so on. The view held by Bergaigne follows a different course. "...Apāṃ napāt, the son of the waters, identified in turns with Agni and Soma. We shall see also that this son of the waters may represent not only the sun, in whom we have already recognized a form common to Agni and Soma, but that he represents especially lightning, whose identity with Agni has not been contested by any one" (I, p. 168). "The idea that the fire is born from the waters of the clouds has as a matter of fact been rendered concrete in the term Apāṃ napāt, 'the son of the waters,' which has become a recognized name of Agni and, what is more, it is possible for us to say that he has become a god whom the poets identify, not only with Agni himself, but, as we shall see, with the liquid fire, that is to say, with Soma, and also with god Savitṛ" (II, p. 17). "In this context I would like to remind the reader that Savitṛ is also called Apāṃ napāt, 'son of the waters,' and that this word denotes the celestial fire chiefly under its form of lightning" (III, p. 47).[185]

Bergaigne draws our attention repeatedly to the identity of Soma with Apāṃ napāt (II, pp. 36-37). He would certainly have found a more uniform explanation for Apāṃ napāt had not his own view of Soma as "liquid fire" or as "the sun" stood in his way. Since then Gray, Magoun, Oldenberg[186] and others have come out with their own views on this subject. Gray considers Apāṃ napāt a water-god; so does Oldenberg as far as the origin of Apāṃ napāt is concerned, but he adds that the original form has become obscure through contamination with the concepts of the water-born Agni. I cannot share these interpretations. If at all, I would rather agree with Oldenberg who takes the two aspects of Apāṃ napāt's conception into account more than any one else does; but he makes far-fetched surmises on the basis of the material offered by the ṚV and does not give due credit to the points of agreement between Apāṃ napāt and Soma. Magoun's explanation contradicts the images of the ṚV which would have been wrongly chosen if Apāṃ napāt were the lightning; for one can hardly call the lightning which is the very image of mobility *avyathyá*, "unshakable," or *asmín padé paramé tasthivā́ṅsam* (II.35.14).[187] ṚV V.10.5 speaks of lightning as *párijmāno* (*párijmāno na vidyútaḥ*), and the latter period makes lightning a symbol of fickleness,[188] or it becomes a weapon or a tool in the hands of a god like Indra, Bṛhaspati or Thôr. But it is very rarely personified.[189]

Apāṃ napāt has nothing to do with rain. He does not bestow rain, nor does he live in it. *apsú* refers to the celestial ocean.

In the first edition of this work I have explained Apāṃ napāt as a form of the moon; I still believe that I have taken all the difficulties into account, although I must concede that this interpretation is uncertain. But I think that just as Soma is called an *apā́ṃ gárbha*, a *śíśu*, to whom the cows in the highest heaven give milk and butter, so was this particular form of the moon embodied in Apāṃ napāt. In the hymns there are so many common points between the two that we are justified in seeing a mythological twin. We should, for instance, compare IX.33.5 (Soma) with II.35.4 (Apāṃ napāt).

IX.33.5 : *abhí bráhmīr anūṣata yahvī́r ṛtásya mātáraḥ*
marmṛjyánte diváḥ śíśum // (and also IX.9.5; 78.3)

II.35.4 : *tám ásmerā yuvatáyo yúvānam*
marmṛjyámānāḥ pári yanty ā́paḥ /
sá śukrébhiḥ śíkvabhī[190] *revád asmé*
dīdā́yānidhmó[191] *ghṛtánirṇig*[192] *apsú* //

In one case it is the mothers who decorate the offspring of the ocean (i.e., Soma) (or the Apsaras of the ocean who run towards him) and in the other it is the virginal waters which move around, decorating Apāṃ napāt.

Therefore we can assume that Soma and Apāṃ napāt derive a part of their characteristics from the same source, without thereby mixing up their separate identities. This view becomes more convincing when we study other verses like II.35.7 along with their parallels from the Soma hymns.

II.35.7 : *svá ā́ dáme sudúghā yásya dhenúḥ*
svadhā́ṃ pīpāya subhv ánnam atti /
só apā́ṃ nápād ūrjáyann apsv àntár
vasudéyāya vidhaté vibhāti //[193]

"He, in whose house the good milch-cow is, swells in nourishment and eats excellent food. Apāṃ napāt, swelling up with food in the waters, shines forth for the good fortune of the pious."

II.35.9 : *apā́ṃ nápād ā́ hy ásthād upástham*
jihmā́nām ūrdhvó vidyútaṃ vásānaḥ /
tásya jyéṣṭhaṃ mahimā́naṃ váhantīr
híraṇyavarṇāḥ pári yanti yahvī́ḥ //

"The son of the waters climbed to the bosom of those who were lying athwart, rising up among them and clothed in lightning. Carrying his highest glory, the youthful ones, gold-coloured, move around him." *vidyútaṃ vásāṇaḥ* does not prove the identity of Apāṃ napāt with the lightning — lightning is merely his garment — but it makes the close relationship between Soma, Candramas and the lightning obvious. IX.80.1 : *bṛhaspáte ravā́thenā ví didyute* is also worth mentioning in this context. Finally, for the individual parts of the wording we should compare.

I.95.5 : *āvíṣṭyo vardhate cárur āsu*
jihmā́nām ūrdhváḥ sváyaśā upásthe /

"Visible, the lovely one grows in them (in the waters), rising up full of splendour in the womb of the lying ones." The moon grows in the waters (IX.85.10; 89.2), he is the offspring of the waters. In the same way the following verse can be explained:

II.35.11 : *tád asyā́nīkam utá cā́ru nā́ma*
apīcyàṃ vardhate náptur apā́m /
yám indháte yuvatáyaḥ sám itthā́
híraṇyavarṇaṃ ghṛtám ánnam asya //

"The visage and the dear secret name of the child of the waters grow, the child whom the maidens kindle together. Gold-coloured butter is his food." Compare II.35.9 : *tásya jyeṣṭhám mahimā́nam* with VS VIII.30 : *purudasmó viṣurūpā índur antár mahimā́nam ānañja dhī́raḥ*, and II.35.9 : *híraṇyavarṇāḥ* (*yuvatá-yaḥ*) with IX.70.2c : *tájiṣṭhā apáḥ*, with which Soma is clothed (see p. 228 above).

In conformity with II.35.8[194] it is said of Soma that the human beings are produced from his divine semen (IX.75.5; 86.28; see p. 229 above). Thus in the ṚV there is an agreement with regard to Soma and Apāṃ napāt in so many points that it would not be rash for us to conclude that the two are personifications of the moon god.[195] Of course, I do not mean that Soma and Apāṃ napāt are identical, but that they are different aspects of the same natural phenomenon which can be comprehended in various ways. However, for this reason we should not equate the two as little as one would equate Sūrya, Viṣṇu, Mitra and Vivasvat, each of whom is surrounded by a special aura of individual peculiarity. The hypothesis of a complete identity is ruled out by verse II.35.12, which deals with the fire cult :

asmaí bahūnā́m avamā́ya sákhye
yajñaír vidhema námasā havírbhiḥ /
sáṃ sā́nu mā́rjmi dídhiṣāmi bílmaiḥ
dádhāmy ánnaiḥ pári vanda ṛgbhíḥ //

"May we worship him, the nearest friend among the many [gods], with sacrifices, obeisance and havis. I clean his back, try to gain him with chips, equip him with food and do homage with verses."

It would follow from this that Apāṃ napāt, unlike Soma, is worshipped in the form of fire.[196] This is supported by II.35.11 : *yám indháte yuvatáyaḥ*, by the epithet *dīdivā́ṅsam* in vv. 3 and 14, *dīdā́yānidhmó* in v. 4, *ví bhāti* in v. 7, as well as by the employment of hymn X.30 in the ritual while fetching the Vasatīvarī waters. This is one of the few occasions in the ritual when Apāṃ napāt makes an appearance. The special feature of the drawing of these waters — and this seems to contain an allusion to Agni *anidhmá* — is that this must take place in a shadow, or if the sun were to set before these waters are fetched, a fire-brand must be held above the drawing vessel, or a piece of gold dropped into it.[197]

Therefore, I consider the Apāṃ napāt hymns to be the expression, and the relics, of a special cult of water connected with the moon. This cult was incorporated at an appropriate place into the Vedic ritual, which itself is an amalgam of several cults. The special position of one of these hymns, viz., X.30, becomes evident when we consider the saga that this hymn was composed by Kavaṣa Ailūṣa after he was expelled as *dāsyāḥ putra, kitava* and *abrāhmaṇa* from the circle of the performers of the Soma sacrifice.[198]

The information which the *Avesta* yields is not much. Its statements are not decisive and speak in support of a water-demon, although here also the association with "radiance" is plain to see. In the *Avesta* also Apąm napå̊ appears, as his name denotes, as the son of the waters, and is often invoked along with the waters.[199] Windischmann[200] and Geldner[201] hold the view that in one passage, Yt 5.72, the name denotes a locality, which is not probable either by itself or in the light of other statements of the *Avesta*. For the epithets which are applicable to Apąm napå̊, as Geldner himself emphasizes, fit neither in the context nor in the metre. We may conclude from this that in the above passage there is an interpolation which begins with the words *bərəzantəm ahurəm* and which includes also the words *apąm napātəm*, and that the original text ends incompletely either before or after *upa*. More important are the following portions. Yt 8.4 : *tištrīm....yazamaide...apąm nafəδraṭ hača čiθrəm.* 34 : *apąm napå̊sə tå̊ āpō spitama aŋuhe astvaite šōiθrōbaxtå̊ vībaxšaiti vātasča yō daršiš awz [mazda] dātəm ča xvarənō ašaonąm ča fravašayō* /[202]

"O Spitama, Apąm napå distributes the waters among the countries for the material world [and the mighty wind with the waters and the radiance created by Mazda and the Fravasis of the righteous]".

Yt 19.51 : "This glory rolled up to the lake Vourukaša. There Apąm napå, the swift-horsed, seized it at once. [For] Apąm napå wishes thus : I want to seize this glory that cannot be seized (?) at the bottom of the deep lake, at the bottom of the deep abyss. We worship the great lord, the ruler,[203] the radiant (*xšaētəm*) Apąm napå with swift horses, the strong one, who helps one at his appeal, who created men and gave shape to them, the god who dwells in the waters, and who is the first to hear when he is worshipped."

Windischmann has already remarked that the creation of men attributed to Apąm napå, a subordinate Yazata, is in conflict with the usual theory of creation prevalent in Iran and that it is incorporated into the Zarathustran belief as a piece of ancient Aryan mythology.[204] This shows that Apąm napå could not always have occupied this modest position. (In the *Avesta* the moon, *māh*, is also called *gaočiθra*, one who contains the semen of a bull;[205] his light causes, according to Yt 7, the plants to grow; he bestows wealth and welfare). When Apąm napå is called the creator of men here, this accords well with the words of the ṚV, *bhúvanā jajāna*, and also with what the ṚV says about Soma. The epithet *aurvaṭaspa* attributed to him in the *Avesta* is not without significance. In the ṚV he is called *āśuhéman*.[206] ṚV I.186.5 states that bulls, swift like the mind, pull him. *aurvaṭaspa* is an epithet for the sun and Apąm napå only. This also speaks in favour of the view, without however being a decisive factor, that he is a moon god because after the sun the moon is the first god to whom swift horses are assigned.

Thus we find a number of indications which suggest that Apāṃ napāt is the moon god and which, I believe, support the view that the Indo-Iranian god Apāṃ napāt is a form of the moon god, of *candrámā apsú*.

2. Sarasvat

Just as Apāṃ napāt is closely associated with the waters, so is Sarasvat with the celestial Sarasvatī. About this word the PW states that it is the name of one of the guardians of the celestial waters, who was counted among the gods of the higher region and who bestows fertility through rain and rivulets. Bergaigne says : "The bird-Agni may sometimes be the sun, sometimes lightning. Under the name Sarasvat, as we shall see, it is Agni who is called in I.164.52 the divine bird" (I, p. 146). "The heavenly bird who is at the same time the foetus of the waters and of the plants and who consequently can only be Agni or Soma is called in I.164.52 Sarasvat, the corresponding feminine form Sarasvatī being the name of the celestial river *par excellence*" (II, p. 48).

I think that after my exposition the nature of the god can be delineated more sharply and that Sarasvat can be identified directly with Apāṃ napāt or with Soma. The important verse I.164.52 shows that all the basic qualities attributed to Sarasvat in this verse agree with those which are regarded as the characteristics of the moon god.

I.164.52 : *divyáṃ suparṇáṃ vāyaśaṃ*[207] *bṛhántam*
apā́ṃ gárbhaṃ darśátam[208] *óṣadhīnām* /
abhīpató vṛṣṭibhis[209] *tarpáyantam*
sárasvantam ávase johavīmi[210] //

Besides being the "son of the waters" — a characteristic common to all the three — Apāṃ napāt is also called [*divyá*] *suparṇá* in X.30.2. Soma is called the same in IX.71.9; 85.11; 97.33. Soma rules over rain. In X.30.4 Apāṃ napāt is called upon to confer the sweet waters.[211] According to the *Avesta*, he distributes waters to the countries. Sarasvat refreshes men with rain. I need not stress the point that the words *dárśatam* (or *vṛṣabhám*) *óṣadhīnām* indicate a god identical with Soma.

We should not ignore the fact that the verse discussed here is included in the TS (III.1.11) also and that there it is followed by two verses addressed to Sinīvālī, i.e., to one of the phases of the moon. There is a further point of agreement in the fact that it is said in *Tāṇḍya Mahābrāhmaṇa* XVI.5.15 that Sarasvat is *svargo lokaḥ*. On this the commentary cites the following words from another Brāhmaṇa : *amāvāsyā vai sarasvatī paurṇamāsaḥ sarasvān*. (TS III.5.1.4).[212] The god endowed with *saras*, water, recalls the qualities of Soma mentioned earlier : *ghṛtásnu, svadhā́vant, ūrjā́m pátiḥ*. This fact explains the reason why ṚV VII.96.6 could speak of Sarasvat in the following words :

pīpivā́ṅsaṃ sárasvataḥ stánaṃ yó viśvádarśataḥ |
bhakṣīmahi prajā́m íṣam ||

"May we enjoy the swelling breast of Sarasvat who is visible to all; may we enjoy progeny and food." The "swelling breast of Sarasvat" is to be compared with the "*payas* of the Ṛṣi," with the milking of the bull which lets out a thousandfold stream, and with similar other mythological expressions that have been discussed earlier.[213] Similarly the words *sá vāvṛdhe náryo yóṣaṇāsu vṛ́ṣā śíśur vṛṣabhó yajñíyāsu,* VII.95.3, (which should refer to Sarasvat because of the association with Sarasvatī) make sense when we see the moon god in Sarasvat. Sāyaṇa is wrong in speaking of Vāyu in this connection.

Sarasvatī is closely associated with Sarasvat (VII.95,96). In these two hymns Sarasvatī is called "the divine one among the streams," and obviously denotes not only one of the terrestrial streams — the sacred stream of the middle country — but also a spirit of this river, i.e., its prototype in the sky. Thus I have no doubt that Sarasvatī cannot signify a phase of the moon as the above-mentioned commentary says, but only the celestial stream, befriended by the Maruts,[214] which pours out its waters in the rainy season, that is to say, the milky way.[215]

H. WHY IS THE MOON CALLED PAVAMĀNA ?

It will be shown later that the Soma juice passing through the strainer is called "Pavamāna." Here we are interested in the meaning of this epithet when it is applied to the god Soma. The god Soma Pavamāna is the friend of Indra, of Vāyu and of the Maruts. He is the lord of the waters and confers rain. Therefore, Soma Pavamāna's efficacy would come into full force in the very season to which the above-mentioned gods predominantly belong. The king who purifies himself is the moon god who causes his rain waters to flow through the celestial strainer.

The rainy season is followed by autumn. There is a marked contrast between the long nights of the rainy season and autumn with its moonlight and the glimmering stars. The autumnal season with its moonlight and the clear starry nights is the favourite theme of Indian singers. The *Sāhityadarpaṇa*, I, describes Sarasvatī as *śaradindusundararucis...sā me girāṃ devī*, "she whose radiance is lovely like that of the autumnal moon." In the same work the autumn which has driven away the rainy season and is now resplendent in the moonlight is compared to Rāma who has vanquished the ten-headed monster.[216] MBh III.182.11-12 (Bombay ed.) speaks of the autumnal nights, bright with the moon, as follows :

vimalākāśanakṣatrā śarat teṣāṃ śivābhavat...
dṛśyante śāntarajasaḥ kṣapo jaladaśītalāḥ
grahanakṣatrasaṅghaiś ca somena ca virājitāḥ ||

Kumārasaṃbhava VII.26 : *paryāptacandreva śarattriyāmā.* *Raghuvaṃśa* XV.54 : *mahaujasā saṃyuyuje śaratkāla ivendunā* [*agastyena*]. *Ṛtusaṃhāra* III. 7, 21, 22. The *Brahmavaivartapurāṇa*[217] describes Kṛṣṇa's face thus : *śaratpārvaṇacandrābhaṃ sudhāpūrṇānanaṃ.* In the beautiful description of autumn in the *Viṣṇupurāṇa*, V.10.7 reads as follows :

tārakāvimale vyomni rarājākhaṇḍamaṇḍalaḥ /
candraś caramadehātmā yogī sādhukule yathā ||

"In the clear starry sky the moon is shining with his full disc like a yogi with his last body and spirit in the company of the good."[218]

This contrast between the rainy season and autumn which appeared significant enough to the poetic imagination of the later period must certainly have made its impact on the minds of the Vedic times as well. I think we find the expression of these feelings in the Pavamāna hymns of the ninth maṇḍala. They deal with the purification of the divine moon who is shining again in his fullest splendour after the rainy season. His rise after a long darkness indicates the end of the rains. We may look at these Pavamāna hymns as a collection of hymns connected with the moon festival. These hymns belong to poets of different times and clans, and they indicate by their number the popularity of the festival or festivals dedicated to the moon as the god of the waters and also as the vanquisher of darkness. As a comparison we may think of the Viṣṇuprabodha festival which was celebrated in later times on October 26 (i.e., on the eleventh day of the bright half of Kārttika) in honour of Viṣṇu who rises from his bed after a sleep of four months. This or one of these moon festivals must have had a similar significance, but differing according to the various aspects of the moon god.

The MBh narrates that during the churning of the ocean with the Mandara by the gods and the Asuras a fire broke out, which

Indra extinguished with water from the clouds. When all the juice of the mighty trees and plants flowed into the ocean, and after renewed efforts of the gods, there arose from the waters of the ocean — the waters that were mixed with the most exquisite juices and were curdling into butter — the god Soma (the moon), shining hundred-thousand-fold and cool, and after him Śrī with a beautiful garment. With this description of the succession of Grīṣma, Varṣāḥ and autumn the later period has indeed perfected the concepts of the ṚV from a poetic point of view, but otherwise preserved them without any basic change.

I. SOMA GIRIṢṬHĀ

In the first part of this chapter on Soma (p. 154) we have seen that not all passages which speak of Soma as mountain-dweller denote the plant through this epithet. Because of the fundamental parallelism between the god and the plant, it is difficult to decide in each case which of the two is meant. IX.85.10 (see p. 227 above) refers in my view to the god Soma : "In the vault of heaven the sweet-tongued seers (the Maruts) are milking continuously the bull which dwells in [or on] the mountains." The same perhaps is the case with

IX.95.4 : *táṃ marmṛjānáṃ mahiṣáṃ ná sā́nau*
aṅśúṃ duhanty ukṣáṇaṃ giriṣṭhā́m /

"They milk the stalk, the bull, who dwells in [or on] the mountains and who is being combed on the back like a buffalo." But no particular value should be attached to this verse, which may also refer to the plant.

At the beginning of the fourth Act of the *Śakuntalā*[219] it is said that the moon sets his foot on the top of the Sumeru which bears the earth. About Sūrya, ṚV I.191.9 states : *údapatat... párvatebhyaḥ*. Viṣṇu is called *giriṣṭhā́* and *girikṣít* in I.154.2-3. It would not be surprising if in the ṚV not only the plant but the moon god also is occasionally designated as *giriṣṭhā́*.

J. SOMA OṢADHIPATI

The parallelism between the god and the plant goes still further. The moon is the lord of all growth. Thus he is the lord of the herbs also while the Soma plant is the most distinguished of its kind.[220] In the *Viṣṇupurāṇa*, for instance, it is said at I.22.2 that the Brahman installed the moon (Soma) as the lord over the stars, planets, brahmins, plants, sacrifices and penances.[221] *Vāyupurāṇa* XXVII.37 says that Soma is the moon, and his breath the multitude of plants.[222] In *Kumārasaṃbhava* VII.1 he is called *oṣadhīnām adhipa*. Raghunandana's *Smṛtitattva* has a description of the gods in ch. XII. There I notice a mention of a *gauravarṇaḥ pumān saumyaḥ sarvauṣadhisamanvitaḥ nakṣatrādhipatiḥ saumyaḥ*.

This concept, quite popular in the later period,[223] is shared by the Brāhmaṇas also. Thus ŚBr XII.1.1.2 : *candramā vai brahmā somo vai candramāḥ saumyā oṣadhayaḥ*. Passages which speak merely of *oṣadhayaḥ saumyāḥ*,[224] without identifying this Soma as Candramas, are more numerous. But since the Brāhmaṇas always stress the identity between Soma and the moon, there should not be any difficulty in interpreting these modes of expression. Furthermore, we should remember the passage discussed on p. 197 above, according to which, during the time of the new moon, the moon dwells in the herbs (and in the waters). A comparison with ṚV IX.84.3 etc. shows that this concept is known to the Vedic period also. The belief that the moon exercises an influence on the growth of plants is so widespread — one need only to think about the beliefs prevalent now — that in India also this view, which found expression in the later literature, must have had its beginnings in the popular beliefs.[225] There is no reason to assume that this Soma who is called the lord of the herbs is not identical with the moon in the ṚV also, as he is in the later period. In hymn I.91, which even according to the PW refers to the moon, v. 22 reads as follows:

tvám imā́ óṣadhīḥ soma víśvās ... ajanayaḥ and

IX.114.2 : *sómaṃ namasya rā́jānaṃ yó jajñé vīrúdhāṃ pátiḥ* /

Thus there is a complete agreement between the Veda and the later literature. This unanimity becomes very clear from

IX.12.7 : *nítyastotro vánaspatir dhīnā́m antáḥ sabardúghaḥ* /
hinvānó mā́nuṣā́ yugā́ //

"The lord of the plants, who possesses his own Stotras,[226] who causes the thoughts to flow abundantly through [our] mind (?) and who dispatches the families of men." Therefore I think that in X.97.18, 19, 22 also we should understand the moon under Soma, the king of the plants. Since he has a representative on earth in the Soma plant, this plant holds the foremost place among all terrestrial plants by virtue of its origin. The Soma plant also is the overlord of all the other plants.

K. SOMA TRIPṚṢṬHA

I have not been able to determine the meaning of this word when it refers to Soma. This epithet is attributed to the god in several passages, and to the juice in one passage.[227] Sāyaṇa explains it in the last passage as *kṣīradadhisaktumiśra*. But it is improbable that the three *āśirs* were called the "three backs." One should rather think of the expression *triparvāṇaḥ somāṅśavaḥ* (cited in Part I, n. 53 above), i.e., the young shoots of Soma that consist of three parvans or limbs, or of what has been said about Soma's "back" on p. 151. Then Soma *tripṛṣṭhá* would denote a Soma stalk with three edges. But none of these views can really be upheld.

The same is true of the passages which refer to the god Soma. There are four verses that are worth considering.

IX.71.7 : *párā vyàkto aruṣó diváḥ kavíḥ*
vṛ́ṣā tripṛṣṭhó anaviṣṭa gā́ abhí ||
75.3 : *abhī́m ṛtásya dohánā anūṣata*
ádhi tripṛṣṭhá uṣáso ví rājati ||
90.2 : *abhí tripṛṣṭhaṃ vṛ́ṣaṇaṃ vayodhā́m*
āṅgūṣā́ṇām avāvaśanta vā́ṇīḥ |
106.11 : *abhí tripṛṣṭháṃ matáyaḥ sám asvaran* |

One who has "three backs" would also have three heads. IX.73.1 speaks of three heads; but this verse is too obscure to be of any help.[228]

L. SOMA AND THE MANES

It is well known that the moon is associated very closely with the Manes in the later literature.[229] The assumption is well-founded that in the few passages of the ṚV where the god Soma is associated with the Manes the former is similarly identical with the moon god. Thus a continuity in tradition is established for the Indian context also, and thus some light is shed on all verses that belong here. This idea is widespread outside India also — among the Greeks as among primitive tribes. Particularly valuable to us is the statement of Plutarch that "the souls of the good, after their sojourn in the place between the earth and the moon, reach heaven, released from the remnants of their gross bodies," or that "the moon, the soul and the sun confer the intellect."[230]

VIII.48.15, the most important passage of the ṚV in this context, reads as follows :

tvám soma pitṛbhiḥ saṃvidānáḥ
ánu dyā́vāpṛthivī́ ā́ tatantha /
tásmai te indo havíṣā vidhema
vayáṃ syāma pátayo rayīṇā́m //

"In concert with the Manes, O moon, you have spread out the heaven and earth. May we worship you, O Indu, with Havis. May we be lords of wealth." This Soma is the same as the *sóma pitṛ́mat* of AV XVIII. 4.72 and of the Brāhmaṇa texts which mention him often with this or similar epithets.[231] The Manes are called *somyá* in ṚV X.14.6; 15.1 ff.; AV II.12.5, and also *sómajāmayaḥ* in ṚV X.92.10 (see Bergaigne I, p. 185). In hymn X.57, several verses (3-5) of which are employed during the sacrifices to the Manes, Soma Nārāśaṅsa and the Pitaraḥ are mentioned together in v. 3.[232]

Soma confers longevity not only in this world[233] but also in heaven. He has called the gods to immortality.[234] The drink of his plants confers also upon man the hope of being there where his ancestors are. This is stated at several places including in hymn IX.113.7-11 *yatrá jyótir ájasraṃ yásmin loké... ákṣite* (see Part I, n. 229).

One does not speak of the plant in these terms, but only of the moon god. This becomes sufficiently clear from v. 2 where Soma is addressed as *diśāṃ pate*.

In one passage creative activity is attributed to the Manes which they accomplish with the help of Soma.

IX.97.39 : *sómo mīḍhvā́n abhí no jyótiṣāvīt* /
yénā naḥ pū́rve pitáraḥ padajñā́ḥ
svarvído abhí gā́ ádrim uṣṇán //

"Soma helped us graciously with his light, with which our Manes of yore, who knew the place, found the light and stole the cows from the mountain" (Ludwig).[235]

This enables us to answer the question why the *Sāmaveda* is assigned to the Manes. As is well known, the *Sāmaveda* is primarily an extract from the ninth maṇḍala and consists exclusively of Soma verses.[236] It has been shown that Soma is the moon and that the hymns of the ninth maṇḍala are the songs of the moon festival. Thus it is obvious that the *Sāmaveda* is assigned to the Manes since it is these who are closely associated with the moon.[237]

This is all that the ṚV has to offer on Soma and the Manes. This aspect of Soma has not been developed further in the ṚV because the office of the god of the dead was already connected firmly, according to the old tradition, with Yama, the son of Vivasvat.[238]

This is not to say that the moon is always considered the abode of the Manes. The ŚBr states in a passage (VI.5.4.8) : *nakṣatrāṇi vai janayo ye hi janāḥ puṇyakṛtaḥ svargaṃ lokaṃ yanti teṣām etāni jyotīṅṣi,* "the stars are women. These stars belong to those men who reach the celestial world virtuously." Kaegi (*Ṛgveda* 286a) has drawn our attention to this passage and emphasized that this view is akin to the Iranian belief.[239] In the ṚV also there are two verses which see the stars in close association with the Manes.

X.68.11 : *abhí śyāvám ná kṛśanebhir áśvaṃ*
nákṣatrebhiḥ pitáro dyā́m apiṅśan |
rā́tryāṃ támo ádadhur jyótir áhan
bṛ́haspátir bhinád ádriṃ vidád gā́ḥ ||

"The Manes have decorated the sky with stars like a dark horse with pearls. They gave darkness to the night and light to the day. Bṛhaspati split the rock and found the cattle." Commenting on this, Ludwig (No. 927) has stated that the stars obviously mean the Manes themselves. In IX.69.8 those who were meant by "the heads of heaven" are certainly the Manes :

yūyáṃ hí soma pitáro máma sthána
divó mūrdhā́naḥ prásthitā vayaskṛ́taḥ ||

"because you Manes are indeed appointed, O Soma, as the heads of heaven, conferring strength."[240]

Besides the concept that the Manes dwell in the realm of the moon, or that they are the stars, there is another — as far as the naturalistic point of view is concerned — which associates them with the rays of the sun.

Weber,[241] Muir,[242] Kaegi,[243] Ehni,[244] and also Bergaigne[245] and Oldenberg[246] have discussed this concept, which we shall not take up here. It is based on passages like ṚV I.109.7; X.107.2; 154.5. The Upaniṣads have attempted a synthesis between these two concepts.

M. KAVI SOMA

Grassmann's *Wörterbuch zum Rigveda* shows the high frequency with which Soma is designated as Kavi in the ṚV. Besides this, there are other attributes like *kavīyát* (in one passage), *kavíkratu, kratuvíd, dhī́ra, manīṣín, médhira, vípra, viśvavíd* etc., which express the same idea; Bergaigne has listed most of such attributes. The evolution of Soma into the god of wisdom is based on his character as the moon god. For the moon god is the lord of the seasons. He knows them and regulates their course. He lengthens the life of men.[247] In the Veda he is the soul of the sacrifice and in the later period he is the lord of the sacrificers.[248] He assigns to the gods their share in sacrifice.[249] In X.90.13 the moon occupies the foremost position among the gods; he is born from the mind of the Brahman :

candrámā mánaso jātáḥ cákṣoḥ sūryó ajāyata /
múkhād índraś cāgníś ca prāṇā́d vāyúr ajāyata //[250]

IX.6.8 : *ātmá yajñásya*[251] *ráṅhyā suṣvāṇáḥ pavate sutáḥ /*
pratnáṃ ní pāti kā́vyam //

87.2c : *pitā́ devā́nāṃ janitā́ sudakṣo...*

3 : *ṛ́ṣir vípraḥ puraetā́ jánānām*
ṛbhúr dhī́ra uśánā kā́vyena /
sá cid viveda níhitaṃ yád āsām
apīcyàṃ gúhyaṃ nā́ma gónām //

"A father of the gods, their strong begetter...a Ṛṣi, a wise one, a leader of men, a steadfast Ṛbhu, an Uśanas in wisdom, he found what was hidden of that, the concealed secret name of the cows."

96.6 : *brahmā́ devā́nāṃ padavī́ḥ karvīnā́m*
ṛ́ṣir viprāṇāṃ mahiṣó mṛgā́ṇām /
śyenó gṛ́dhrāṇām...

18 : *ṛ́ṣimanā yá ṛṣikṛ́t svarṣā́ḥ*
sahásranīthaḥ padavī́ḥ kavīnā́m /

"He who has the mind of the Ṛṣis, creates the Ṛṣis, recovers the light, knows thousand wise men and is the forerunner among the Kavis."

97.2 : *mahā́n kavír nivácanāni śaṅsan /*

By virtue of his much emphasized wisdom[252] he knows and proclaims the names and the families of the gods. Even as an embryo he knew them already.[253] As in IX.87.2, he is called *pitā́ devā́nām* in 86.10; 109.4.

As the treasure-house of all wisdom, he is the source of all thoughts and songs. He is described as *pitā matīnā́m ásamaṣṭa-kāvyaḥ* IX.76.4; *vṛ́ṣā matīnā́ṃ pavate* 86.19; *janitā́ matīnā́m* 96.5; *netā́ matīnā́m* 103.4; *hinvānó vā́caṃ matibhiḥ kavīnā́m* 97.32 and so on.[254] The means through which he becomes effective is the drink; through it he bestows inspiration and thoughts. Hence he is called *pátir dhiyás, mánasas páti* IX.75.2 99.6; 11.8; 28.1 etc.[255]

He is a *puraetā́ jánānām* IX.87.3 (see p. 246); *purogā* ŚBr XI.5.9.10; *gātuvíd* IX.92.3; *gātuvíttama* as in

IX.107.7 : *sómo mīḍhvā́n pavate gātuvíttamaḥ*
ṛ́ṣir vípro vicakṣaṇáḥ /
tváṃ kavír abhavo devavī́tamaḥ
ā́ sū́ryaṃ rohayo diví //

"Soma, the merciful, purifies himself; the best one in finding the way,[256] the Ṛṣi, the wise one, the all-knowing. You have become the Kavi who is dearest to the gods. You caused the sun to climb to heaven."

IX.96.10 : *abhiśastipā́ bhúvanasya rā́jā*
vidád gātúṃ bráhmaṇe pūyámānaḥ /

"The king of the world protects from curse. May he, purifying himself, find a way for the Brahman." He is the Brahman himself among the gods IX.96.6 (see p. 246 above), a guardian of the Brahman.

VI.52.3 : *kím aṅgá tvā bráhmaṇaḥ soma gopā́m*
kím aṅgá tvāhur abhiśastipā́ṃ naḥ //

"Why then, O Soma, do they call you the guardian of the Brahman ? Why then do they call you the one who protects us from curse?

Thus Soma is called the king of the brahmins[257] TS I.8.10d; VS IX.40; TBr I.7.4.2; MS II.6.9 (69.7); ŚBr V.3.3.12; IX.4.3.16; *saumyo vai brāhmaṇo devatayā* MS II.1.4 (6.8); AV V.18.6 and

14 : *sómo hy asya [brāhmaṇasya] dāyādáḥ*
índro asyābhiśastipáḥ

ŚBr XII.1.1.2 : *atha brahmāṇaṃ dīkṣayati candramā vai brahmā somo vai candramāḥ*; ABr II.41.6 : *candramā vai brahmā.* During the selection of the Brahman it is said : *candramā me daivo brahmā* ŚŚS V.1.3 etc. The moon as a representative of the Brahman is contrasted with the sun, the Kṣatriya — no matter whether the sun is called Indra or Āditya. To v. 387 of the *Dhammapada* where both are juxtaposed (*divā tapati ādicco, rattim ābhāti candimā; sannaddho khattiyo tapati, jhāyī tapati brāhmaṇo / atha sabbam ahorattiṃ buddho tapati tejasā*) we may add *Raghuvaṃśa* XI.64 where Daśaratha, who received from his father the sacrificial thread and from the mother a bow as an inheritance, is called *sasoma iva gharmadīdhiti.*[258]

We see that Soma in this aspect as the god of wisdom is a rival to that form of manifestation among the Vedic gods in which the essence of the priestly wisdom has attained the most perfect expression — namely, Bṛhaspati, whom we have discussed earlier.

N. SOMA AND GANDHARVA

If I take up at this stage the much-discussed figures of Vedic mythology, viz., the Gandharvas, I do so neither to enlarge the material offered in the works of A. Kuhn,[259] E. H. Meyer,[260] L. v. Schroeder[261] and others, nor to raise once again the question of their relationship with the Centaurs, but only to re-examine the Vedic sources in accordance with my intention of making exegesis useful for Vedic mythology and to sketch the picture of the Indian Gandharvas exclusively after these sources. This picture will differ from its predecessors in some points. But in general it is considerably closer to the view of Meyer and Schroeder than to the view, stated by Pischel in the *Vedische Studien* I.77 and modified by others, that *gandharva* and *garbha* are one and the same concept.

In the majority of the Buddhist texts also the evolution of this word follows the same lines as indicated by the oldest Vedic texts. The interpretation as "embryo" is ruled out in this context. Such an interpretation is the product of the ignorance of the later Indian authors, or of their misunderstanding, or at best the result of a later shift in meaning. But such a meaning is alien to the Veda.[262]

So far Vedic mythology has not been studied from the point of view of the Buddhist texts. It does not, however, appear advisable to make use of their statements for the interpretation of the former. In the Buddhist texts Varuṇa becomes a Nāgarāja[263]; the Asuras are represented in *Cullavagga* IX.1.3 ff. "as being fond of sojourning in the great ocean as often as they observe it for the sake of its foremost miraculous and amazing quality."[264] This does not tempt us to make use of such material.

The word *gandharvá* occurs twenty times in the ṚV and seventeen of these occurrences are in the singular.[265] The ratio changes in the AV; for sixteen singular forms there are the same number of plural forms. Thus it appears as if the evolution into a class of gods took place very gradually, beginning in the ṚV; for the *Avesta* knows the word only in the singular as *gandarəwa*.

The passages of the ṚV do not support the usual view that this word is used there throughout as a proper name, because it is not used for one god only and because it is mostly an appellative. This is shown by ṚV IX.86.36 when it refers to Soma as *apā́ṃ gandharváṃ divyáṃ nṛcákṣasam.* We arrive at the right meaning if we follow the clue given in the above usage further, keeping in mind that Soma is not only an "offspring of the waters" but also their husband, king, "bull." Which of these designations must have been intended by *apā́ṃ gandharvá* becomes clear from the contrast between *gandharvá* and *apsarás* — a contrast that is emphasized in the ṚV[266] and is quite familiar to the later period. *apsarás* is to be derived, with the Indian commentators and E. H. Meyer and Pischel,[267] from *ap-saras* and denotes water-spirits, aqueous women, celestial nymphs. If this interpretation is correct, then the Gandharvas are their masculine counterparts, the "celestial men." *apā́ṃ gandharvá* should therefore mean as much as the "husband of the waters," i.e., it is synonymous with *pátiḥ síndhūnām* IX.15.5; *pátir jánīnām* 86.32; *pátir gavā́m* 72.4; *vṛṣabhó góṣu* 96.7; *vṛṣabhá, vṛ́ṣan*. All these are designations used in the ṚV for Soma (who is also called *retodhā́*). Soma represents the masculine principle as opposed to the feminine element of the waters. *vṛṣabhó góṣu* and *apā́ṃ gandharvá* are mythological synonyms, and I prefer the words "giant," "husband" as the correct translation for *gandharvá*.

From the use of the word *gandharvá* in IX.86.36 it follows 1) that it can be an appellative of Soma in other passages also and 2) that it is not necessarily the name of a wind god but is an appellative to other gods also (of course, with a limited usage). This is seen also in the linguistic usage of the Yajus texts, e.g.,

VS XVIII.39 ff.; ŚBr IX.4.1.9; MS II.12.2 (145.3) : *saṃhito viśvasāmā sūryo gandharvas tasya marīcayo 'psarasa āyuvo nāma* /[268] *suṣumṇaḥ sūryaraśmiś candramā gandharvas tasya nakṣatrāṇy apsaraso*[269] *bekurayo nāma* / *iṣiro viśvavyacā vāto gandharvas tasyāpo 'psarasā ūrjo nāma*[270] etc.[271] Here *gandharva* is used in the same sense as *vṛṣabhá*, *vṛ́ṣan* or *páti*, that is to say just as in IX.86.36.

The Ṛgvedic passage mentioned above is not the only one where the moon is called a Gandharva. In the same ninth maṇḍala we encounter v. 85.12, in which Bergaigne (I, p. 178) has already seen a reference to the moon :

IX.85.12 : *ūrdhvó gandharvó ádhi nā́ke asthāt*
víśvā rūpā́ praticákṣāṇo asya /
bhānúḥ śukréṇa śocíṣā vy àdyaut
prā́rūrucad ródasī mātárā śúciḥ //

"The giant climbed high to the vault of heaven, looking at all his forms. The light shone with bright splendour. Radiant, he caused the earth and heaven, and the parents to shine."[272] Compare this with :

9 : *ádhi dyā́m asthād vṛṣabhó vicakṣaṇó*
árūrucad ví divó rocanā́ kavíḥ /

"The all-knowing bull ascended to heaven. The Kavi caused the spaces of heaven to shine." In the same way as in these two verses Sòma is called a *gandharva* in one more hymn. X.123,[273] in the first verse of which Roth[274] and afterwards E. H. Meyer[275] saw a reference to the rainbow.

Leaving aside a few insignificant exceptions, the ideas in these verses do not differ from those of the Soma hymns. In these verses Gandharva means the moon-giant. Similarly we can easily recognize with PW the moon god in the bird which carries the speech in its mind and as Gandharva pronounces it in the womb of the mother (X.177.2); for the Vedic singers have made the bird a Vācaspati and said that it knows and proclaims the nature of the gods already in the womb of its mother.

In this context we should refer to the Atharva verses II.2.1 ff.[276] because after what has been said above it is not improbable that the Gandharva who knows the Amṛta, who, shining like the sun, has his seat in heaven, and who is led by the Apsarases (like Soma or Apāṃ napāt) is a designation of this god Soma. In one of these verses the Gandharva has the epithet *viśvā́vasu*.

Assuming that the hymn forms a whole, *viśvávasu* in this case must be, like *gandharvá* itself, a designation of the moon. The fact that in another passage this word is applied to another god does not contradict this view, for this usage shows only that, like *gandharvá*, *viśvávasu* also has not lost its original sense of an appellative. Whom else, apart from the moon, we should understand under the expression *gandharvá viśvávasu* becomes indeed clear from TS VI.1.6.5 : "As Soma was brought, Gandharva Viśvāvasu stole it. It remained stolen for three nights. Therefore Soma remains bought for three nights."[277] The mention of the "three nights" gives us a clue to the nature of this thievish Gandharva. For as long as the moon is not visible at the time of the new moon, he dwells in the sun who, as already the ṚV believes, swallows him. Therefore, in this case Gandharva Viśvāvasu must be the sun.

This expression does not have any specific association in ṚV X.85.21,22 and in the corresponding verses AV XIV.2.33, 35, where Viśvāvasu appears only as a demon who is asked to give up his claim to the bride and to go to his Apsarases. Apparently here the word is limited to the sense of a spirit of fertility.

Besides the marriage hymn, there is one more passage in the ṚV where Gandharva Viśvāvasu appears : X.139.4.[278] This passage creates some difficulties in interpretation. It is clear that Gandharva Viśvāvasu is not conceived as a hostile spirit here. Although according to this verse waters flow apart at his sight, IV.22.6 shows that we should not overestimate this expression because in this latter verse from an Indra hymn it is said that the waters run forward in haste "out of fear of Indra." Moreover, the wording of vv. 5 and 6 of X.139 excludes the possibility of a hostile Gandharva — 5 : "May Viśvāvasu grant us this; the celestial Gandharva who measures heaven," and 6 : "The Gandharva proclaims the *amṛtāni* of the [rivers]; Indra tested the strength of the dragons." The Gandharva is thought of as an ally of Indra for whom he proclaims the immortal names of the streams. But there is not enough material to enable us to make a choice between all the gods who could have been meant here.

On the other hand, in two passages of the eighth maṇḍala he plays the role of a hostile demon whom Indra conquers.

VIII.1.11 : *yád tudát sū́ra étaśaṃ vaṅkū́ vā́tasya parṇínā |*
vā́hat kútsam ārjuṇeyā́ṃ śatákratus tsárad
gandharvā́m ástṛtam ||

"As he drove the sun's horse with the winged whip of the wind (?),[279] it led away Kutsa Ārjuṇeya. The versatile one outwitted the invincible Gandharva."

VIII.77.5 : *abhí gandharvā́m atṛṇad abudhnéṣu rájaḥsv ā́ |*
índro brahmábhya íd vṛdhé ||

"To the delight of the brahmins, Indra pierced the Gandharva in the infinite spaces." E. H. Meyer has remarked that with this point of view the eighth maṇḍala differs from all the other books of the ṚV. Here we encounter a new cycle of myths, the saga of the gods of another tribe. This is not at all surprising since there are many differences in the ritual (see Appendix I) which characterize this very group of hymns. Besides these material differences, there are differences in language[280] which attest to the special position of the Kaṇvas in ritual and mythology. We should not overlook the fact that a Kutsa is mentioned here. Kutsa belongs to those names in the ṚV which were the objects of respect as well as hatred. He is regarded as the enemy of Indra in I.53.10; II.14.7; IV.26.1 (?); *Vālakhilya* 5.2. On the other hand, the dual form *indrākutsā́* V.31.9 indicates their close friendship.[281] The name plays a role in the ritual also in so far as the Soma seller ought to be a Kautsa or a Śūdra (see p. 160 above). Since the Soma seller represents the Gandharva, this name in the ritual is closely connected with our Ṛgvedic passage.

As E. H. Meyer emphasizes,[282] the world Gandharva, with the sole exception of III.38.6, does not occur in any of the family books II-VII, and only as a hostile name in the last family book, i.e., the eighth. It follows from this that this word must have had its origin outside the strictly Brahmanical circles. It is also not ruled out that the names of other tribes were treated as the names of their gods. We should note that in VS XXX.8, a Vrātya, i.e., a man living outside the Brahmanical order, is assigned to the Gandharva-Asparas.[283] It is perhaps not without significance that in the Brāhmaṇas the Gandharvas are occasionally placed, like the Asuras, against the gods as combatants of equal rank. In the passage of the ŚBr, cited on pp. 165-166 above, it is narrated how the Gandharvas recited the Vedas in order to win Vāc, while the gods created the lute and settled down to playing and singing. "The Vāc turned to the gods, and it was not wise of her that she turned away from those engaged in reciting and praying in favour of dance and song." This rebuke does not give the impression as if it has come from a Brahmanical speaker. In another passage it is stated that the Gandharvas approached the Ṛṣis who were performing a sacrifice and told them what they had done insufficiently and what they had done superfluously.[284] When they grant a wish to Purūravas and he requests them to let him become one of the Gandharvas, they reply to him thus : "men do not possess the form of fire suitable for the sacrifice, sacrificing with which one could become one of us."[285] Such passages do not reflect the hostile attitude of the eighth maṇḍala, nor are they compatible with the demonization which is attested by the magic formulas of the AV.[286] E. H. Meyer[287] is of the view that an older popular belief, originated in a stratum of a very low culture, is reflected in the AV and that a liberal priesthood has drawn this belief "into the sanctity of the ṚV" and "surrounded it with a new holy aura." It does not look improbable to me either that the Gandharva belief has had its origin outside the actual circle of the Brahmins in so far as it is reflected in the family books. But beyond this, all that is said by E. H. Meyer is pure hypothesis. What is more, the difference between the eighth book and the others leads to the assumption that the complete demonization was the obvious outcome of the differences in cult and tribe as indicated above and took place in those circles to which the authors of ṚV VIII.1 and 77, who were hostile to the Gandharvas, belonged.

The plural of the word *gandharva* occurs only three times in the ṚV : III.38.6; IX.113.3; X.136.6. The first passage — it does not matter whether the hymn itself is old or a later one — states clearly through the epithet *vāyúkeśa* attributed to the Gandharvas that it understands them to be wind-giants.

III.38.6 : *trī́ṇi rājānā vidáthe purū́ṇi*
pári víśvāni bhūṣathaḥ sádāṅsi |
ápaśyam átra mánasā jaganvā́n
vraté gandharvā́ṅ ápi vāyúkeśān ||

"You two kings adorn the seats at the sacrifice, the three, the many, indeed all. I went there in my mind and saw the 'wind-haired' Gandharvas also at their work."[288] Thus the concept of the Gandharvas as the wind gods, prevalent outside the ṚV in the Brāhmaṇas and the Purāṇas, has its beginnings in the ṚV. The Gandharvas, the "giants," are the spirits of fertility, and already in the ṚV the winds, usually called Maruts, are regarded as the husbands of heaven : *nárah̤, vṛ̥ṣaṇah̤* or (*máruto*) *vṛ̥ṣā gaṇáh̤*. They impregnate the earth as the husband impregnates his wife.[289] Thus it is obvious that the name "giants" is applied primarily to them. According to IX.113.3,[290] the Gandharvas seize Soma and place the semen in him, i.e., they bestow his manliness on him.[291] The Gandharvas of this verse are akin to Uśij in IX. 86.30[292] and to the Venas or the Maruts who escort the *śíśu* and are called *śíśumat* (see p. 226 f. above) just as Vāyu is called *sómasya rakṣitá*. It is only a continuation of these Ṛgvedic concepts when it is said in the Brāhmaṇas (e.g., ABr I.27) that Soma was once with the Gandharvas. Furthermore, when the Gandharva is called *śikhaṇḍín*, this recalls to mind the joy of the peacocks at the approaching rainy season.[293] Just as the winds are fragrant and Vāyu the lord of the fragrances,[294] so is "fragrance" one of the characteristics attributed to the Gandharvas.[295]

In the Brāhmaṇas the name "giant" is applied to the wind gods most frequently. Ultimately the plural form of this word has become completely a synonym for the wind gods; according to the *Viṣṇupurāṇa* the king of the Gandharvas is Vāyu. Like Vāyu or the Maruts, the Gandharvas are no more the hostile guards. The thievish Gandharva Viśvāvasu has only the name in common with them. The "giants" guard the Soma for the gods, but allow it to be robbed from them and are excluded from the Soma drink as a punishment for their carelessness.[296] A legend narrates about their request to the gods not to exclude them from the sacrifice. " 'Just as we were his guards in heaven, so would we like to be his guards here also.' The gods agreed. With the mantra, 'this is your reward; protect him; may you not be cheated,' he points out to them the prices for Soma. Then the gods said to the Gandharvas : 'at the third pressing a libation of Ghṛta shall fall to your share, but not of Soma. The Soma drink is taken away from you. Therefore you do not deserve the Soma libation.' " Remarkably enough the dhiṣṇyas, the fire hearths of the priests, are regarded as the representatives of the Gandharvas;[297] each one of them is called after the name of a Gandharva and butter is poured over it during the evening sacrifice.[298] When the Adhvaryu carries Soma, he should not pass close to them[299] "because they wait with open mouths for Soma and it would fall into their open mouths." I cannot say how much of this myth is transmitted tradition and how much of it should be ascribed to the ritualistic urge for interpretation. While deciding these questions we should not overlook one legend connected with Acchāvāka, one of the priests originally excluded from the Soma drink.[300] According to ŚBr III.6.2.12 he is held responsible for the fact that he allowed Gāyatrī to steal Soma which was under his care, and therefore the share in the Soma drink was denied to him.[301] The remarkable coincidence that we see here in the treatment of the Gandharva and in that of Acchāvāka leads us to the assumption that the connection between these two must be similar to the one that can be shown to exist between Neṣṭṛ and Tvaṣṭṛ, between Praśāstṛ and Mitra-Varuṇa etc This agreement also recalls to mind the contradictions that exist between the individual passages in the ṚV with regard to the conception of the Gandharvas.

The Apsarases are closely connected with the Gandharvas — in one passage as early as in the ṚV and later on more regularly. This connection is a mythological expression of the close relationship that exists between the wind and water. "Wheresoever the wind goes there follows the rain," says ŚBr VIII.2.3.5 in plain language.[302] The connection between the Gandharvas and the Apsarases has been discussed by others at such a length that I have nothing of importance to add.[303]

The plural form of Gandharva has, of course, established itself primarily as a name of the storm gods, yet there are traces in Vedic literature where the plural form is used in a freer sense. In VS IX.7 twentyseven Gandharvas are mentioned who "harnessed the horse and gave him speed."[304] Because of the characteristic number it is not the winds but the constellations that have to be the giants here. Though normally the Nakṣatras are considered to be the wives of the moon,[305] we need not take it for granted that Indian poetry has employed only this single image. For after all the stars are called e.g. *pitaraḥ*. The wise, especially the seven Ṛṣis along with Agastya, are placed among the stars.[306] Even among the Nakṣatras there are some with masculine names like Tiṣya, Hasta, Śravaṇa.[307] Therefore, the idea that the constellations are the "giants" is not beyond the realm of poetic possibilities and is required here by the characteristic number twentyseven. Hence the explanation of Mahīdhara that the Gandharvas are the Nakṣatras is quite correct.[308]

In the light of the above discussion Gandharva has the following meanings :

1. Giant (in the friendly as well as in the hostile sense)
2. The "wind-giants" especially in the plural — in solitary instances in the ṚV and very common in the later literature. I do not find any reference to the souls of the dead.

The *Avesta* does not contribute much in the way of explanation. As has been stated already, there *gandarəwa* occurs in the singular only and that too in three passages which do not yield enough information to determine the nature of the Iranian Gandarəwa. As Spiegel has already stated in the *Arische Periode*, p. 215, Gandarəwa is not associated in any way with the Haoma. But he is clearly a demon as in the eighth maṇḍala of the ṚV. Darmesteter[309] has compared the words *abhí gandharvám atṛṇad abudhnéṣu rájaḥsv á* (ṚV VIII.77.5, see p. 252 above) with the Avestan passages. But the latter are of no help in answering the question whether we are to understand under this Gandharva — as we may indeed suppose — the thievish Gandharva Viśvāvasu, the sun god. In the above-mentioned work, Spiegel has stated the view that the expression *zairipāšan* (Yt 5.38) refers to the Gandarəwa (who lives at the lake Vourukaša) as a god of light. But as far as I can see, it is not possible to go beyond this hypothesis.[310]

A spirit akin to this Gandharva in character and who was even called a Gandharva in the Yajus literature[311] is the celestial archer Kṛśānu[312] who shoots the Soma bird[313] and oppresses the human beings,[314] but who, on the other hand, appears also as a protégé of the Aśvins[315] and is invoked as Rudra and Tiṣya.[316] Thus exactly like the Gandharva he appears in friendly as well as in unfavourable light. Here one more point might deserve attention. It has been shown earlier that it is likely that Gandharva Viśvāvasu who steals Soma and through whose fault Soma remains "stolen for three nights" might be the sun god because of this last statement. In view of the multiplicity of the spirits that are called Gandharva, the possibility does not seem to be ruled out that Kṛśānu is a personification of the sun god himself. That he is a "demon of the rainbow" is an improbable idea based on a wrong interpretation of X.123.[317]

Kṛśānu has been identified long ago with the Avestan Kərəsāni. In spite of the objections by Harlez,[318] I accept this identification, suggested at first by A. Weber[319] and later taken up by Kuhn[320] etc., and also by Darmesteter.[321] In doing so I am supported by the connection between Kṛśānu and Soma, and between Kərəsāni and Haoma.[322]

It seems that in the *Avesta* also Gandarəwa does not denote a hostile demon throughout. At least this is obvious from a passage pointed out by Spiegel — Yt 13.123 : *paršintahe gandərəwahe ašaonō fravašīm yazamaide.* Bartholomae, however, does not think that this passage belongs in this context. The first word of this passage (for which the MSS read also *pərəs°* or *pariš°*) remains obscure. Howsoever one might decide this case, from no passage of the *Avesta* could an objection be raised against what I consider to be the most important aspect of this study, viz., that *gandharva* is merely an appellative with the basic meaning "giant."

O. HAOMA IN THE AVESTA

The *Avesta* also distinguishes between the god and the drink and envelops Haoma in a completely mythological garb by associating him with Vīvaṅhvaṭ, Kərəsāni etc. Soma is *vṛtrahan* and possesses sharp weapons; Haoma is *vərəθrağan* and hurls his *vadarə* (*Yasna* IX.30 ff.). A bird brings Soma from heaven; sacred birds carry Hoama to the mountains. Just as Soma grows in the celestial waters, Ḥaoma grows in those of Ardvī Sūra.[323] Like Soma, Haoma confers "the best world of the pious, the luminous world." There is every justification to transfer the information obtained from the Veda to the *Avesta* and to explain — in view of the many points of agreement stressed often between the Iranian and the Indian god — the former also as the moon god. This interpretation not only fills a lacuna in the Iranian Pantheon, it also proves its correctness by immediately solving a number of difficulties. *Yasna* X.10 reads thus:

aurvantəm θwā dāmidātəm
baγō tatasaṭ hvāpå
aurvantəm θwā dāmidātəm

baγō nidaθaṭ hvāpå
haraiθyō paiti barəzayå

"The skilful god has formed you who are swift and created by the creator; the skilful god has placed you who are swift...on the high Haraiti." Mills translates *aurvaṭ* as "swift" and explains it very laboriously as "having immediate effect." Geldner, posing the question, "What should the Haoma plant do on the Alburz as a horse or as a rider ?"[324] suggests that this word should be translated as "ruler, lord, master." This expedient will become superfluous if we regard Haoma, who is a *giriṣṭhā* like Soma and who, as we have seen in the case of Apāṃ napāt, drives with swift horses, as the moon god. The words *bərəzaṭ*, *srīra*, *xšaθrya*, *zairidōiθra*, "golden-eyed,"[325] also become easily intelligible if they are applied to the moon god. Two passages in particular seem to come under this aspect. *Yasna* IX.26 :

frā ča tē mazdå baraṭ
paurvanīm aiwyåṅhanəm
stəhrpaēsaŋhəṃ mainyutāštəm
[*vaŋuhīm daēnąm māzdayasnīm*]

The last three words seem to be a gloss — called forth by passages like *Vendidād* XVIII.2 (*anaiwyāstō daēnąm*) — with which a scholiast explained to himself the girdle of Haoma from a theological point of view.[326] The vault of heaven in the midst of which the moon shines or — more correctly — his celestial path is denoted by this girdle which is "embroidered with stars." Then the "obscure" word *paurvānīm* becomes clear. For it is to be derived from *paurvan* (Skt. *parvan*) and means "knotted," and refers to the periods of the new moon and full moon.[327] Therefore, I translate the verse thus : "Mazda has brought for you a knotted girdle, embroidered with stars and created by God."

The other passage, interpreted correctly by Geldner,[328] occurs in *Yašt* VIII.33 : *yąn paθō āiti haomō*. "The paths which Haoma traverses" are the paths of the moon. My view is corroborated by Louis H. Gray (*Spiegel Memorial Volume*, 1908, p. 160 ff.) who shows in his article on *måṅha gaočiθra* that this one corresponds to the semen-containing Soma (Indu) *retodhá* and that *måṅha gaociθra* is identical with the white Hom which grows in the depths of the lake Vourukaša and which bestows immortality upon men in concert with the bull Haθayoš. Gray compares with ṚV I.84.15. which speaks of the "name of the cow" in the house of the moon, the legend of the *Bundahiš* according to which the arch-bull was "white, brilliant as the moon" and "even in the domoniac age Gōṣūrūn receives the seed of the animals from the sphere of the moon and makes it circulate in the world to aid Rām the good."

PART III

SOMA AND THE SUN

A. COMPARISONS

Because of his radiance the moon is often compared to the sun. It is hardly necessary to prove this obvious idea for the Veda through quotations. The following verses may be added to those already mentioned on p. 186 above. IX.63.13 : *sómo devó ná sū́ryo ádribhiḥ pavate sutáḥ*; 64.30 : *pávasva sū́ryo dṛśé* (54.2 : *sū́rya ivopadṛ́k*); 66.22 : *sū́ro ná viśvádarśataḥ*; 64.7; 69.6; 94.1; 97.9 : *sá raṅhata urugāyásya* [*viṣṇor*] *jūtím*; 98.8; 110.6; 2.6 : *mahā́n mitró ná darśatáḥ* etc.[1]

B. ASTRONOMICAL RELATIONSHIP

The position occupied by the moon in the ṚV justifies the question whether no attention was paid to the phenomena of the new moon and the full moon, and whether no explanation — even a primitive one — was attempted.[2] We shall find an answer to this if we start, as we did on an earlier occasion, with the later literature and approach the ṚV from there.

1. New Moon

On p. 196 a passage from the *Viṣṇupurāṇa* has been cited, according to which the moon enters the sun on the night of the new moon. In a similar way the *Skānda Nāgarakhaṇḍa*[3] states the following :

> *amā nāma rave raśmiḥ sahasrapramukhaḥ sthitaḥ |*
> *yasyāsya tejasā sūryaḥ proktas trailokyadīpakaḥ ||*
> *tasmin viśati yenendur amāvāsyā tataḥ smṛtā |*

"Amā is the name of a ray of the sun, which is the foremost among thousands and with the light of which the sun illuminates the three worlds. Because the moon enters it, this night is called the Amāvāsyā night."[4] On p. 198 we have come across a passage of the ŚBr which says that the moon is "the food of him that burns there."[5] I.6.4.18 states this fact in even clearer terms : "the one that burns there, (the sun) that is Indra and the moon is Vṛtra. By his very nature the latter is hostile to the former. Therefore, even though the latter had risen [the night] before at a great distance [from the sun], yet he swims during this night towards him and falls into his (the sun's) open mouth. 19 : Having swallowed him, he (the sun) rises. And one sees him (the moon) neither in the west nor in the east...20 : Having sucked him empty, he (the sun) throws him out. The latter, having been sucked empty, appears in the west and becomes full again. He becomes full again in order to serve the sun as his food." X.6.2.3 : "the sun is the one who consumes. The moon is his food ('offering'). They place the moon in the sun (like the Āhutis in Agni)."[6] XI.1.6.19 : "of these two (Agni-Soma), one became the food and the other the eater — Agni the eater, Soma the food."[7] Similarly XIV.4.2.13. In the Yajus texts this is described through another image, viz., Gandharva Viśvāvasu stole Soma, and Soma remains hidden for three nights.[8] From the mention of these three nights, it is clear that the Gandharva in this passage means the sun.

This concept, stated in the ŚBr and other texts,[9] that at the time of the new moon the moon enters the sun, or is the food of the sun, occurs in the ṚV also. Its poets employ different turns of expressions to state this. Thus it is said by way of comparison in X.138.4 that Indra has seized the wealth hidden in the forts of his enemies, just as the sun has seized that of the moon (or the moon himself) :

māséva sū́ryo vásu púryam ā́ dade
gṛṇānáḥ śátrūn̐r aśṛṇād virúkmatā //[10]

More important are the following verses :

X.55.5 : *vidhúṃ dadrāṇáṃ sámane bahūnā́m*
yúvānaṃ sántaṃ palitó jagāra /
devásya paśya kā́vyaṃ mahitvā́
adyā́ mamā́ra sá hyáḥ sám āna //

"The old one has devoured the youth, the moon who ran in the company of many. Behold the wisdom of the god in its greatness : yesterday he died and today he lives forth."[11]

IX.25.6 : *ā́ pavasva madintama pavítraṃ dhā́rayā kave* /
arkásya yónim āsádam //

"Purify yourself, O most intoxicating one, over the Pavitra in a stream in order to place yourself in the womb of the sun."

V.47.3 : *ukṣá samudró aruṣáḥ suparṇáḥ*
pū́rvasya yónim pitúr á́ viveśa / (see p. 214 above).

Here the "father" is the sun and not the sacrificial fire. Accordingly, IX.71.2 speaks of the young moon who becomes visible again after the night of the new moon :

jáhāti vavrím pitúr eti niṣkṛtám

"He throws off the covering and goes to the festive place of his father."

IX.75.1 : *á́ sū́ryasya bṛható bṛhánn ádhi rátham* /
víṣvañcam aruhad vicakṣaṇáḥ //

"The mighty and omniscient one climbed the mighty sun's chariot which turns to all."[12]

Later on I shall attempt to show that Vivasvat means the "sun" already in the ṚV as in the later period. If this is correct, the following verses are worth mentioning here. VIII.72.8 and

IX.26.4 : *tám ahyan bhuríjor dhiyá́*
saṃvásānaṃ vivásvataḥ /

"With the dexterity of the arms they sent the fellow-resident of Vivasvat."

2. Full Moon

Now comes the question whether the Vedic singers knew that the moon receives light from the sun. The possibility that they might have known was at first suggested to me by a verse of the *Sāmaveda*, which I cannot explain in any other way.

SV II.9.2.12.1 : *abhí vājī́ viśvárūpo janítram*
hiraṇyáyaṃ bíbhrad átkaṃ suparṇáḥ /
sū́ryasya bhānúm ṛtuthá́ vásānaḥ
parí svayáṃ médham ṛjró jajāna //[13]

"The strong one who has many forms [went] to his birth place — the bird in the golden garment. Wearing the ray of the sun according to the season, he, the brownish one, himself created the sacrifice." Other Ṛgvedic passages follow this verse — above all IX.71.9 which we have cited earlier quite frequently :[14] "he roared like a bull pacing around the herd; he assumed the lustre of the sun."

76.4 : *yáḥ sū́ryasyá́sireṇa mṛjyáte*
pitá́ matīnā́m ásamaṣṭakāvyaḥ //

"[He] who is adorned with the ray of the sun, the father of hymns he of unattainable wisdom."

86.32 : *sá sūryasya raśmíbhiḥ pári vyata*
tántuṃ tanvānás trivṛtaṃ yáthā vidé |

"He clothed himself with the rays of the sun, knowingly spreading a threefold fabric."[15]

C. ĀCĀRYA AND BRAHMACĀRIN

In AV XI.5 the imagination of the Vedic singers found pleasure in describing the relationship between the sun and the moon through the image of an Ācārya and a Brahmacārin. I do not claim to be able to explain all the ideas of this obscure hymn. But some of its verses can be understood from this point of view without any difficulty. The verse that offers the most positive clue is the third. It states that during the initiation the Ācārya takes the pupil into himself as *garbha* and that he carries the latter in his body for three nights.[16] We have seen above that the sun swallows the moon at the time of the new moon, or steals him as Gandharva Viśvāvasu and holds him hidden for three nights. The Ācārya who carries the pupil in his body for three days, the old father into whose womb Soma enters, the old man who eats the youth, Gandharva Viśvāvasu who steals Soma, the sun who "swallows the moon" — all these are images through which the Vedic poets described the conjunction of the sun and the moon in the same constellation at the time of the new moon.

Some more verses of this hymn can be explained under the assumption that Brahmacārin means the moon.

AV XI.5.1 : *brahmacārīṣnáṅś carati ródasī ubhé*
tásmin devā́ḥ sáṃmanaso bhavanti |
sá dādhāra pṛthivī́ṃ dívaṃ ca
sá ācāryáṃ tápasā piparti ||
2 : *brahmacāríṇaṃ pitáro devajanā́ḥ*
pṛ́thag devā́ anusáṃyanti sárve |
gandharvā́ enam ánvāyan tráyastriṅśat triṅśatā́ḥ etc.

"The Brahmacārin goes forth, setting heaven and earth in motion; in him the gods are of one mind. He holds earth and heaven. He fills the Ācārya with his *tapas*. The Manes, the god-folk, all the gods individually, follow the Brahmacārin; the Gandharvas follow him..."

6 : *brahmacāry èti samídhā sámiddhaḥ*
kā́rṣṇaṃ vásāno dīkṣitó dīrghásmaśruḥ |
sá sadyá eti pū́rvasmād úttaraṃ samudrám
lokā́n saṃgṛ́bhya múhur ācárikrat ||

"The Brahmacārin goes forth, kindled by firewood, clad in the skin of a black antelope,[17] consecrated, with a long beard;[18] he goes at once from the eastern to the western (rear) ocean, embracing the worlds and drawing them repeatedly towards him. (?)"

D. SOMA AND THE DAUGHTER OF SŪRYA

There is nothing else of significance to add about this relationship between Soma and Sūrya. However, there is one point that defies explanation, viz., the oft-mentioned relationship of Soma to the daughter of Sūrya. This is described in three passages, the first and last of which have been discussed above.

IX.1.6 : *punā́ti te parisrútaṃ sómam sū́ryasya duhitā́ /*
vā́reṇa śáśvatā tanā́ //
72.3 : *áramamāṇo áty eti gā́ abhí*
sū́ryasya priyā́ṃ duhitús tiró rávam /
113.3 : *parjányavṛddhaṃ mahiṣā́ṃ*
tā́ṃ sū́ryasya duhitā́bharat /

Here we can only attempt at conjectures. There is an echo of fairy tale motifs like those found in Mannhardt's Lettic songs that are far removed from real mythology. If we venture to give an explanation at all, then we should at first distinguish clearly between the daughter of Sūrya who stands in a motherly relation to Soma on the one hand and Sūryā whom he married on the other, and explain the former — on the authority of II.13.1 (see p. 152 above) — as the season, more precisely as the rainy season because Parjanya is mentioned along with her; for it is in the waters of this rainy season that the Soma plant grows.[19] There is a second possibility to overcome the difficulties. In IX.113.3 the daughter of Sūrya is mentioned along with Parjanya; the two clearly make a pair. We know from AV X.10.6 that the wife of Parjanya is Vaśā. Vaśā means the same as Pṛśni, the wife of Rudra and the mother of the Maruts.[20] The latter is identical with the *apsarā́ yóṣā* who, according to X.123.5 (see p. 231 above), carries (*bibharti*) Soma "in the highest heaven" — that is to say, exactly as the *sū́ryasya duhitā́* does in our verse. In other words, *pṛ́śni, vaśā́, apsarā́ yóṣā* are mythological synonyms for *ghṛtáṃ dúhānā áditiḥ paramé vyòman*. We may conclude from this that the "daughter of the sun" who is mentioned along with Parjanya in IX.113.3 is the *vaśā́* or *pṛ́śni* or *apsarás*, i.e., the same *yóṣā* who, according to another version of the myth in III.48.2,[21] as the mother of Indra, pours for him the Soma in her father's (i.e., the sun's) house.

This interpretation is not substantially different from the first. The effectiveness of Pṛśni or Vaśā coincides, as her relationship to Vāyu, Parjanya, Rudra and the Maruts indicates, with the rainy season.

This daughter of the sun god to whom the rainy season belongs should be carefully distinguished from Uṣas whose bridegroom Soma becomes in the well known marriage hymn ṚV X.85.

Sūryā, "the shining one," cannot be identical with Pṛśni, the other daughter of Sūrya. It is obvious that the shining one is a counterpart of Pṛśni who rules over the rainy season, and thus denotes the bright season, i.e., autumn or spring. Just as the day and night are his wives, so are the two halves of the year like his unequal daughters.

E. AGNI-SOMA

Sūryasiddhānta XII.24 speaks of Agni-Soma as the sun and the moon. The statements of the Yajus texts should be understood in a like manner. ŚBr I.6.3.23 ff. states this quite explicitly : "What is dry belongs to Agni, what is wet belongs to Soma... 24 : The sun belongs to Agni, the moon belongs to Soma; the day belongs to Agni and the night to Soma; the half month which increases belongs to Agni, that which decreases to Soma. 25 : He attains the sun and the moon through two offerings of butter [for Agni-Soma] and the day and the night through Upāṅśuyāja."[22] The same is implied when another passage of the ŚBr states that Agni-Soma are *bhrātarau*,[23] or when MS III.7.1 (75.12) speaks of them as the "two eyes."[24] In a different context the MS narrates how the gods Agni, Soma and Indra organized a Sattra in Kurukṣetra and said to each other : 'To whomsoever among us the splendour [of victory] reaches first to him should come what belongs to us.' It reached Soma among them. They came together to him. Therefore they come to Soma, because he is the most splendid. After that, however, Soma desired that. He went on to the mountain. Agni followed him. Both — Agni and Soma — became one on the mountain. Therefore Agni burns always on the mountain, Soma [burns] on the mountain."[25] The last words leave no room for doubt that they refer to the sun and the moon. For the mountain on which Agni or Soma burns is the eastern mountain behind which the sun and the moon are supposed to rise. The frequent appearance of this pair of gods in the sacred literature[26] indicates a popularity which is alien even to the Vedic hymns. There is only one complete hymn (I.93) in the Vedas dedicated to Agni-Soma and two isolated verses without much substance.[27] In I.93 we are primarily interested in vv. 4-6 which state that Agni-Soma together stole the cows from the Paṇi, set up lights in heaven and freed the rivers, and that Mātariśvan brought the one (the sun) from heaven [as fire] and an eagle tore off the other (the moon) from the mountain [as the Soma plant]. Here Agni-Soma are the divine beings as well as their earthly representatives, viz., fire and the Soma plant. The former had its origin in the sun and from him came to the earth through lightning. When it is often stated that Soma also carries fervid weapons, the Vedic imagination has attempted to remove the inconsistency by explaining that Indu (the moon) stole the weapons of his father (the sun),[28] or that Tvaṣṭṛ (the sun) sharpens the axe for Bṛhaspati (the moon), whereas in reality this is only a transference of the qualities of Moon-Agni to Indu or Soma.

It is not possible to explain why Agni-Soma, who were so familiar to the later literature, play an insignificant role in the ṚV. Oldenberg[29] thought that this was a sign of their late origin. Elsewhere[30] I have refuted this view because this does not take into account the possibility that a non-Ṛgvedic tribe (or Gotra) might have contributed this pair of gods to the pantheon of the later period. The special position the two gods enjoy in the ritual is quite clear to see. As far as I can see, they never receive a Graha, a share in the Soma sacrifice, but only cake offering[31] or animal offering;[32] the later in such a form that the *agnīṣomīya paśu* has become the model for all the other animal sacrifices.[33] Therefore, it appears as though the Agni-Soma cult might have originated in a tribe (or Gotra) which introduced the animal sacrifice into the ritual. It is, however, not possible to explore these circumstances more deeply.[34]

APPENDIX I

THE PREPARATION OF THE SOMA DRINK AND ITS OFFERING

The plant was conveyed to the sacrificial place in a cart; sometimes it was also carried on the head. These Havirdhāna carts are known to the ṚV; for of the verses of hymn X.13 that are recited while these carts are being driven, the second verse is so appropriate to the occasion that we cannot doubt the congruence between the content of the verse and the custom.

The Soma drink was prepared in two ways — with the Soma stones or with the mortar. The former was the more common method. At first I shall give the rules of a Śrauta Sūtra in order to use them as the basis for the information that can be gleaned from the ṚV. I give below the rules of Kātyāyana,[1] omitting certain details.

A. APPARATUS FOR PRESSING

1. In the Ritual

KŚS VIII.4.28 : "He digs the resonance holes (*uparava*)[2] under the shaft of the cart standing in the south.

5.2 : "He draws their outlines — four in number — diagonally as in sprinkling butter.

3 : "Or at first in the north-west [and then in the south-east, south-west and north-east].

4 : "Or in a continuous order [SE, SW, NW, NE].

5 : "[In any case] he ends with the north-east.

6 : "He makes them one span wide and separated from each other by one span.[3]

7 : "In the same order as he has drawn these outlines, he digs the resonance holes uttering the mantra, 'mighty are you with a mighty sound. Utter mighty speech for Indra.'

8 : "In the same order as he has dug, he throws the earth out of the holes uttering the mantras:[4] 'Here I dig out the magic which a stranger or a servant has buried.'

10 : "He digs them one arm deep.

11 : "He should connect them diagonally[5] [with an underground channel].

12 : "If this is not possible, then in a continuous order.

13 : "In the same order as they have been dug, [the Adhvaryu] makes [the sacrificer] flatten the resonance holes with the mantras : 'Self-ruling are you, killing the rivals' etc.

14 : "The Adhvaryu and the sacrificer touch each other [through the connecting channels in the following way].

15 : "The Adhvaryu [streches his hand] into the hole in the south-east and the sacrificer into that in the north-west.

16 : "The Adhvaryu asks [immediately after touching] : 'O sacrificer, what is here ?'

17 : "The latter replies : 'It is prosperity.'

18 : "The Adhvaryu whispers : 'This is common to us both.'

19 : "Once again the Adhvaryu at the south-western [resonance hole] and the sacrificer at the north-eastern one.

20 : "[After they have given each other their hands through the opening below], the sacrificer asks : 'O Adhvaryu, what is here ?'

21 : "Upon being told 'prosperity,' the sacrificer says : 'this is for me.'

22 : "He besprinkles these holes with the words : 'I besprinkle you, you who kill the Rakṣas, you who kill the magic, you who belong to Viṣṇu.'

24 : "He pours [the rest of the water into the holes] with the words : 'I pour upon you, you who kill the Rakṣas' etc., and covers them with Darbha grass etc.

25 : "Having placed thin blades of kuśa grass over the resonance holes, he puts over them two boards[6] on which the Soma is to be pressed. They are [made of Varaṇa wood and one span wide] separated from each other by two fingers width, ends pointing to the east, cleansed, one arm in length and joined to each other or not joined.[7] He heaps [earth][8] around them so that they remain steady and do not move during the pressing.

26 : "On these two boards he places a red skin[9] cut equally all around [with the fur upwards and the neck towards the east], saying 'you belong to Viṣṇu.'

27 : "Upon this the five stones : 'You all belong to Viṣṇu.'

28 : "To the east of this he raises a square mound[10] with sand [for the Soma vessels] on a place marked and besprinkled earlier."

Āpastamba describes these five stones thus :

ĀpŚS XII.2.15 :[11] "They are one span wide with a high back and are suitable for hitting. He places the biggest one, the Upara, in the middle as the fifth.[12]

16 : "The others are pointed towards this one.

3.1 : "The hitting surfaces are rather wide.[13]

2 : "He addresses them with the mantra : 'You the abodes of the waters, offsprings of the Ṛta, guardians of the world, eagles, guests, peaks of mountains...invoke Indra with your sound, chase the enemies away with your thunder. You have been harnessed. Drive on ! Drive the sacrificer to the celestial world !' "

2. In the Ṛgveda

a. THE STONES

In the ṚV they are not only called "men" repeatedly (X.76.6 ff.), but they are also equal to the gods and are mentioned as such.[14] They prove their magical power in chasing away the evil spirits. This is stated in the mantras addressed to them in the ritual as well as in many Ṛgvedic verses. These include, besides the verses of the three hymns dedicated to the "stones" (X.76, 94, 175)[15], where they are treated quite like high personages, also other passages like the following.

V.31.5 : *grā́vāṇo...anaśvā́so yé paváyo 'rathā́ḥ*
índreṣitā abhy ávartanta dásyūn ||

VII.104.17 : *grā́vāṇo ghnantu rakṣása upabdáiḥ* ||

X.36.4 : *grā́vā vádann ápa rákṣāṅsi sedhatu*
duṣvápnyaṃ nírṛtiṃ víśvam atríṇam |[16]

X.100.8 : *ápā́mīvāṃ savitā́ sāviṣan nyàg*
várīya íd ápa sedhantv ádrayaḥ |
grā́vā yátra madhuṣúd ucyáte bṛhad...||

The name for the press stone is *ádri* or *grávan* (Iranian *bro*, millstone); in one passage each also *aśna* VIII.2.2; *bharíta* III. 36.7; *párvata* III.35.8; *párvatā ádrayaḥ* X.94.1.

The first two words are usually regarded as complete synonyms; nevertheless we should keep in mind that a difference between the two is indicated by the linguistic usage. It is indeed striking that the root *su* is connected more often with *ádri* while the root *vad* and related words are used with *grā́van*.[17] This becomes obvious from the collation of such citations given below in the footnote. From this classification of the verbs we see that *grā́van* is more personally conceived than *ádri*.[18]

Since I wrote this, S. G. Oliphant has investigated the relationship between *grā́van* and *ádri* and has arrived at conclusions which go far beyond what had been suggested by me.[19] The difference can be seen not only in the case of *vad* and *su*, but in so many other aspects that on the basis of a careful statistical analysis Oliphant comes to the conclusion "that in the Vedas we have two types of press, and only two, one the mortar and pestle, and possibly derivative forms of the same, the other a press of the type described by Āpastamba,[20] with possible variations also; and that in the Vedas *grā́van* regularly refers to the former and *ádri* to the latter."

grā́van and *ádri* occur rarely in the dual, almost always in the singular or in the plural. In the ṚV the former occurs in the dual only once — in II.39.1. But in this hymn *grā́van* is among many other words like *nāvā́*, *śvā́nā* etc. that are used in the dual simply because of the two Aśvins who are compared to the two *grā́vans*; hence this occurrence is without significance.

ádri occurs only three times in the dual in the ṚV : I.109.3; VII.39.1; 42.1, that is to say, very rarely indeed as compared to the great number of the singular and plural forms.[21] It follows from this that just as in the later ritual, so also in the ṚV more than two stones were used for the extraction of the Soma juice. How the stones were arranged is not stated in any passage. On the other hand, it is evident from X.94.5 that one stone served as the base :

suparṇā́ vā́cam akratópa dyávi
ākharé kṛ́ṣṇā iṣirā́ anartiṣuḥ /
nyàṅ ní yanty úparasya niṣkṛtám
purū́ réto dadhire sūryaśvítaḥ //

"The birds (stones) raised their voice to heaven. The nimble black ones hopped on the hollow. They go down to the abode of the Upara. From it, which is bright like the sun, they receive much juice." We can see that *úpara* here, as in the Sūtras, is a sort of technical term, the name of the stone which served as the base during the pressing, or more correctly the pounding, of the Soma plant.[22]

Placing the Soma stones in position is called *yuj*, "to harness."[23] They are also compared to horses. In X.175.1 they are told :

dhūrṣú yujyadhvam. Cf. X.94.6 also. Or the stones were held in the hands. AV XI.1.10 : *gṛhāṇá grávāṇau sukṛ́tau vīra háste.*

Furthermore ṚV VII.22.1 :

yáṃ té suṣáva haryaśvádriḥ
sotúr bāhúbhyāṃ súyato nárvā /

"O [Haryaśva, let the Soma exhilarate you], which the stone, directed by the presser's arms, like a well-guided charger, has pressed for you."

V.43.4 : *dáśa kṣípo yuñjate bāhū́ ádrim*
sómasya yā́ śamitā́rā suhástā /

"The ten fingers and the two arms, which are the skilful slaughterers of Soma, harness the stone."

Therefore they are called *hástacyuta* IX.11.5; *hástayata* V.45.7; X.76.2; *dáśayantra* X.94.8. One who holds them in his hands is *grávahasta* I.15.7, *grāvagrābhá* I.162.5.[24]

The priests who held these stones in their hands and did the pressing were the Adhvaryus. This is stated not only in the ritual, but quite clearly in the ṚV itself, e.g. in

VIII.4.11 : *ádhvaryo drāváyā tváṃ sómam índraḥ pipāsati* /
13 : *ratheṣṭhā́yādhvaryavaḥ sómam índrāya sotana* /[25]

When it is occasionally said that the Brahman harnesses the sacrificial stones, we should not conclude from this that the priest called Brahman does this, here Brahman is merely the generic term meaning the brahmin or priest, whereas Adhvaryu is the more precise word.

It cannot be discerned whether occasionally holes were made in the stones in order to tie them to straps and thus to hold them better. The only expression which can throw light on this — X.94.11 *tṛdilá átṛdilāsaḥ* — is too obscure to prove this point. The smaller PW translates these words as "with holes" and "without holes" respectively.[26]

It was, of course, important that the stones did not break. This was regarded as a bad omen in the later period. The texts give rules as to how the inauspicious consequences of such a mishap should be averted. *Tāṇḍya Mahā Brāhmaṇa* IX.9.13 prescribes a special Sāman because the sacrificer would lose his cattle if a stone were to break.[27] That is why, when the stone is raised for hitting, the priest says : *mā bher mā saṃvikthāḥ.*[28]

I find nothing in the ṚV on this point; but it is only natural that the breaking of sacred tools must have been an undesirable event, and it might have been so even in the Vedic times. Likewise the base must not shift from its position. In ṚV X.94.12 the stones are reminded of the exemplary conduct of their fathers who remained always firm, who loved rest and who did not "move" from their seat.[29] In order to keep the stones steady the above-discussed *adhiṣavaṇas* or *adhiṣavaṇaphalakas* were used in the ritual, which have been mistaken for boards that were used for the actual pressing. These are not mentioned in the ṚV.

The ṚV does not know the resonance holes either, which have to be dug in accordance with the rules of the ritual. Ludwig believes that *ākhará* in ṚV X.94.5 is a name for these. Whatever the case may be, the many allusions to the loud sound of the stones give rise to the assumption that even at the time of the ṚV some simple means were used in order to amplify the resonance of the stones, which drives away the Rakṣas.

According to the ṚV the stones rest at first on the skin and then on the vedi; the custom is different in the later period. Thus it is said in

V.31.12 : *vádan grā́vā́va védiṃ bhriyāte*
yásya jīrám adhvaryávaś cáranti ||

"The speaking stone should be placed on the vedi, the stone for whose quick movement the Adhvaryus approach." Other examples shall follow later.

b. THE MORTAR

Besides the usual method of pressing by means of the stone press, there is a second method, namely by means of the mortar. This is rarely mentioned and appears to have been pushed into the background by the former. We have only one indisputable evidence for this in hymn I.28, which speaks of the Soma as *ulū́khalasuta*. Ulūkhala, as we know, is the mortar; *ulū́khala* and *músala*, the mortar and pestle, are mentioned in the technical literature on the sacrifices, and even in the AV, as the tools for husking the grain. Probably Soma also must have been treated thus with mortar and pestle. This mode of extraction is very old and was probably in use as long as Soma served not only as the sacrificial drink but as a household drink as well. I think that is what is suggested by vv. 3 and 5 of our hymn.

I.28.3 : *yátra nā́ry apacyavám upacyavám̐ ca śíkṣate |*
ulū́khalasutānām ávéd v indra jalgulaḥ ||
5 : *yác cid dhí tvaṃ gṛhégṛhe ulūkhalaka yujyáse |*
ihá dyumáttamaṃ vada jáyatām iva dundubhíḥ ||

"There where a woman is busy pushing backwards and forwards, O Indra, drink eagerly of the ulūkhala-pressed [drops].

"When you, Ulūkhala, are set in motion in house after house, then resound here quite loudly like the drum of the conquerors."

A woman who sets the mortar in motion has no place in the ritual of the ceremonial Soma sacrifice at which, as we have seen, it was the duty of the Adhvaryu to press Soma even in the ṚV. Her place is at the more simple events of the domestic worship of gods. That with this interpretation we are on the right track is shown by v. 5 above which speaks of the ulūkhala used in every house. Moreover, this hymn is not recited during the Grāvastotra of the great Soma sacrifice, but only during the *añjaḥsava*, the "quick pressing," as it was undertaken by Sunaḥśepa under extraordinary and urgent circumstances. It also follows from this that the most natural method of pressing was with the mortar and pestle.[30] Another fact which speaks in favour of the antiquity of this method of pressing is the custom of the Pārsi ritual in which likewise a mortar is used in the place of the stones.[31]

It is necessary to discuss this hymn in further detail. It consists of two parts distinguished by the metre — vv. 1-6 and 7-9 — of which the latter, however, does not refer to the ulūkhala any more. But as the parts are included together in the Śunaḥśepa Ākhyāna, they must have been regarded as belonging together already at the time of the *Aitareya Brāhmaṇa* and even earlier.[32] Let us examine at first the remaining verses of the first part.

I.28.1 : *yátra grā́vā pṛthúbudhnaḥ ūrdhvó bhávati sótave |*
ulū́khalasutānām...
2 : *yátra dvā́v iva jaghánā adhiṣavaṇyā̀ kṛtā́ | ulū́khala°...*
4 : *yátra mánthāṃ vibadhnáte raśmī́n yámitavā́ iva |*
ulū́khala°...
6 : *utá sma té vanaspate vā́to ví vāty ágram it |*
átho índrāya pā́tave sunú sómam ulūkhala ||

In the fourth verse there is the mention of a *mánthā* and of "binding" the same. This is followed by the refrain : "drink eagerly of the ulūkhala-pressed [drops]." No other conclusion can be drawn than the following, viz., that here it is to do with a *mánthana*, a pounding of Soma, and that the *mánthā* is a part of the ulūkhala and most probably the pestle itself.[33] The procedure must have been similar to the Agnimanthana, the production of fire. This is suggested by the words *apacyavám* and *upacyavám* in the third verse and by the mention of the *raśmi*, the reins, in the fourth : "where they bind the churning staff as with the reins to guide [a horse]."

The churning motion of a wooden stick occurs, besides in the Agnimanthana, in butter-making. TS II.2.10.2 : *dugdhaṃ mathitam ājyaṃ bhavati.* Wilson[34] describes this as follows : "In churning, in India, the stick is moved by a rope passed round the handle of it, and round a post planted in the ground as a pivot; the ends of the rope being drawn backwards and forwards[35] by the hands of the churner, gives the stick a rotatory motion amidst the milk, and thus produces the separation of its component parts."

Grierson[36] enumerates the names for the individual parts of this apparatus. Even now in some parts of India this churning staff is called *mahannī, mahān, mahonni.*[37]

The first part of our hymn suggests that a similar apparatus, a form of manual grinder, was used for crushing Soma. Apart from *mánthā*, we have *ulū́khala* into which the *mánthā* is inserted, the *raśmís* with which the stick is rotated and a woman who rotates it.

This mortar is called somewhat conspicuously *grā́vā pṛthúbudhnaḥ* in v. 1 : "There where the stone with a broad base is raised high for pressing Soma, drink eagerly, O Indra..." However, while discussing the difference between *ádri* and *grā́van* we have seen that the main characteristic of the *grā́van* is its "talking" and "ringing." There are unmistakable evidences for the fact that the *grā́van* was not necessarily made of stone, but also of wood,[38] which of course depended upon the sacrificer's preference. First of all, we have the evidence of VS I.14 where the ulūkhala itself is called an *ádrir vānaspatyáḥ*, a *grā́vā pṛthúbudhnaḥ.*[39] Furthermore,

AV III.10.5 : *vānaspatyā́ grā́vāṇo ghóṣam akrata*
havíṣkṛṇvantaḥ parivatsarī́ṇāṃ /

"The grāvans originating from the tree resounded, preparing

the havis for the year." *Mantra Brāhmaṇa* II.2.6.10 reads the first pāda of the same verse as follows :

aulūkhalāḥ saṃpravadanti grāvāṇo.[40]

Therefore it is probable that the ulūkhala and musala were made sometimes of stone and at other times of hard wood. Under these circumstances there is nothing remarkable about the designation of the mortar as *grā́van pṛthúbudhnaḥ* in the first verse of our hymn.

Just as in the case of the Agnimanthana here also a comparison with the act of procreation is intended. This is shown by the wording of the second verse : *yátra dvā́v iva jaghánā adhiṣavaṇyā̀ kṛtā́*, "where the two Adhiṣavaṇyas are prepared like two genitals." It is in the nature of the comparison expressed through *jaghánā* that the Adhiṣavaṇya cannot denote the mortar and pestle (much less the two pressing boards of which in fact there is no mention), but only the mortar. Probably its shape was such that it could be compared to the female genitals.[41] In the very obscure hymn X.101 there are some verses[42] which also refer in all probability to the preparation of Soma in the mortar and express similar ideas as far as can be recognized.

X.101.10 : *ā́ tū́ ṣiñca hárim īṃ drór upásthe*
vā́śībhis takṣatāśmanmáyībhiḥ |
pári ṣvajadhvaṃ dáśa kakṣyā̀bhiḥ
ubhé dhúrau práti váhniṃ yunakta ||

11 : *ubhé dhúrau váhnir āpíbdamāno*
antár yóneva carati dvijā́niḥ |
vánaspátiṃ vána ā́sthāpayadhvam
ní ṣū́ dadhidhvam ákhananta útsam ||

"Pour the golden [juice] into the womb of the wood. Prepare it with knives made of stone. Encircle it with ten girdles. Attach the draught animal (pestle) to the fork.

"Pushing at the fork, the draught animal moves in the *yoni* like one who has two wives. Put the tree in the wood. Make a well without digging." However, these verses are not very clear since we do not know the instruments.

vánaspáti and *vána* are the pestle and mortar, the former corresponding to the *mántha* and the latter to the *ulū́khala* of hymn I.28. Other designations of symbolic nature are *váhni*[43] and *yóni*. The former is again the pestle and the latter the mortar as compared to the female genitals. I think *dhúrau* are a fork-like contraption attached to the mortar, into which the pestle is inserted (corresponding roughly to the *dvā́v iva jaghánā adhiṣavaṇyā̀ kṛtā́*), i.e., two side pieces or handles alongside the mortar going up like shanks.[44] The expression *dvijā́ni* probably refers to these. The *daśa kákṣyāḥ* should, as they are ten in number, be certainly the fingers of the one who crushes; or they would be like the *raśmis*.

The last three verses of I.28 still remain to be discussed. The ulūkhala, however, is not mentioned in these, but the dual *vánaspátī* shows that here also the reference is to the crushing of Soma in the same way. *vánaspátī* corresponds to the *vána* and *vánaspáti* of X.101.11 and denotes the mortar and pestle. This seems to be contradicted by v. 9 which mentions, apart from the cowhide to be discussed later, and the Pavitra, also the two *camū́-s*. A cowhide is spread under the Soma stones as well as under the mortar — under the latter so that nothing of the corn etc. that jumps out is lost. A Soma strainer is required in every form of pressing Soma.

An objection can be raised against my interpretation only on the basis of *camvòr* which have been explained as the "pressing boards." It can be shown that this is not the meaning of *camū́*.

Camū́

It is best to begin this inquiry by establishing two facts. First, it is evident from the description given in the ritual texts that the two boards do not rest upon one another but one beside the other; that is to say, Soma is not pressed between them but upon them. Even if this fact does not necessarily rule out a different custom in the Vedic period itself, yet it reduces the probability of such a custom; all the more so because except for this word *camū́* itself no further allusion to the pressing of Soma between two boards can be found in the Vedic hymns. The ritual act of placing two boards underneath has its reason because this creates a firm base for the stones which ought not to shift from their fixed positions. Furthermore, the Soma juice is always called *camū́ suta* or *camvòḥ sutá*, but never *camū́bhyāṃ sutá*. Even if we were to concede that *camū́* means "board," the locative dual refers to the fact that in the Veda as in the entire ritual Soma was not pressed between the boards. The expressions *grā́vṇā tunná* IX.67.19, *suvānó ádribhiḥ* IX.107.10, etc. show that in the ṚV also the stone, and not the board, was used for crushing the stalks.[45]

A second factor that leads us to the correct interpretation of the word *camū́* is X.91.15, the interpretation of which is indisputable.

X.91.15 : *áhāvy agne havír āsye te*
srucī́va ghṛtáṃ camvī̀va sómaḥ

"In your mouth, O Agni, the havis was offered in sacrifice, as butter in the sruc, as Soma in the camū."[46]

The sruc is a laddle for offering butter; the camū accordingly must be a vessel for offering the Soma juice in the sacrifice. In the latter period it is primarily the Grahapatras that serve this purpose. These are known to the ṚV also. It is said in

X.114.5 : *chándāṅsi ca dádhato adhvaréṣu*
gráhān sómasya mimate dvā́daśa //

"Determining the metres in the sacrifices, they measure out twelve cups of Soma."

Furthermore, in X.119.13 where *gṛhá* occurs for *grahá* the former should not be regarded as a corrupt reading but a cognate name for the same thing :

gṛhó yāmy áraṃkṛto devébhyo havyavā́hanaḥ /

"A cup, well prepared, was filled, which carries the oblations to the gods."[47]

In view of the important position occupied by the Soma cult in the Vedic hymns, it is strange that the Grahas with which Soma is offered are mentioned so rarely. This suggests the possibility that these might have been known to the ṚV under a different name. This name was, as ṚV X.91.15 demonstrates, *camū́*. Thus the following verse can be explained very easily when we assume that it refers to the filling of the Grahas and arranging them in appropriate places.

IX.99.8 : *sutá indo pavítra ā́ nṛ́bhir yató ví nīyase* /
índrāya matsaríntamaś camū́ṣv ā́ ní ṣīdasi //

"Having been pressed, O Indu, [and poured] over the Pavitra, you are drawn [in the cups] by men and are carried away. Most exhilaratingly for Indra, you sit in the Grahas."[48] *vána*, "wooden vessel," occurs in quite general sense in one of the almost parallel verses, viz.,

IX.27.3 : *eṣá nṛ́bhir ví nīyate divó mūrdhā́ vṛ́ṣā sutáḥ* /
sómo váneṣu viśvavít //

"The head of heaven, the strong, the pressed, the omniscient Soma, is conducted by men [to the Barhis] in the wooden vessels." The camū is employed only for the gods to drink and not for men. This is also an evidence for the fact that the camū is to be explained as a Graha-vessel.

The vessel that served the priests for drinking, which followed the libations to the gods, was *kalaśa* and probably also *camasá.* For *kalaśa* this is attested by

X.167.3 : *távāhám adyá maghavann úpastutau*
dhā́tur vídhātaḥ kaláśāṅ abhakṣyam |

"In your praise, O Maghavan, I enjoyed today, O creator and ruler, the kalaśas (jars)." IV.32.19 can also be cited here :

dáśa te kaláśānām híraṇyānām adhīmahi

"We received from you ten golden jars." This number "ten" corresponds to the ten *camasás*[49] used in the ritual, from which the priests enjoy Soma. This correspondence can be accidental. But one cannot argue that the use of so many types of vessels cannot be assumed for the period of the ṚV. For such an argument can be demolished by a reference to I.15 and II.36, 37 where jars like *hotra, potra* etc., belonging to individual priests are already mentioned by name.

The other designation for the drinking vessels of priests is *camasá.* This designation is in conformity with the linguistic usage of the later period, the traces of which can be seen even in the ṚV itself. However, in the ṚV it has primarily the more general meaning of "vessel" or "jar," used most frequently for that vessel which the Ṛbhus make "new" or "fourfold." We learn from X.68.8 that *camasá* is made of wood. In X.25.4 and 101.8 also the general meaning is sufficient, but not in VIII.82.7 where it clearly denotes a vessel for Soma as distinct from the *camū́* :[50]

yá indra camasésv ā́ sómaś camū́ṣu te sutáḥ |

"Which Soma, O Indra, pressed for you, stands in the camasas and camūs." Since the camū is used for the offering of Soma and thus corresponds to Graha, the necessity to understand *camasá* here in accordance with the later ritual is quite obvious. Indeed, libations are made to the gods from the camasas also before they are consumed. Therefore Sāyaṇa has explained quite correctly *cameséṣu* in this passage as *etannāmakeṣu pātreṣu* and *camū́ṣu* as *graheṣu.*[51] Hence, I propose to translate *camū́* as "cup" and *camasá* as "jar" in order to make a rough distinction.[52]

Through this meaning of *camū́* which has been firmly established in a certain number of passages the possibility of interpreting this word as the Soma boards in other passages is ruled out; for such a change in meaning would not at all be recognizable.

If we examine the individual passages with reference to the verbs accompanying the word *camū́*, then a clear distinction between the singular and the dual on the one hand and the plural on the other becomes obvious. Of the thirteen occurrences of the locative plural, in seven cases there is *sad* (said of Soma), once *sru*,[53] once *apibat*,[54] once *śrī*[55] (said of mixing Soma with milk), once *dṛś*,[56] once *asti*[56a] that is implied, and once *pū*.[57] In all these verses *camū́* means "cup."[58]

This is not so with the singular. Here *sad* does not occur at all. In five of the seven passages there is *sutá*,[59] which, however, does not occur with the plural at all.[60] The remaining two passages are X.91.15 where *camū́*, as we have shown already, definitely means Graha and IX.107.18 : *punānáś camū́ janáyan matím...sómaḥ*, where *camū́* — on the analogy of IX.97.46 (*pavate camū́ṣu*) — has probably the same meaning. It is obvious that in the above five passages *camū́* cannot mean the same as in the other two passages or in the plural, but that it should be connected with the Soma pressing itself. Here *camū́* is a locative form and not instrumental. This is attested by the locative dual which alternates with *camū́* and is likewise connected with the verb *su* in some examples :

IV.18.3 : *apibat sómam índraḥ*
śatadhanyàṃ camvòḥ sutásya /

VI.57.2 : *sómam anyá úpāsadat pā́tave camvòḥ sutám* /

IX.31.1 : *ásarji ráthyo yathā pavítre camvòḥ sutáḥ* /

In all these passages *camvòḥ* is locative, consequently *camū́* is also one. As has already been remarked, *camū́bhyām* never occurs; we should expect it on the analogy of *ádribhiḥ*, *grā́vṇā* etc., if *camū* really meant a board and if Soma was pressed with these "boards." This means the pressing is done on, or in, the *camū́* as the case may be. Therefore, *camū́* in these cases cannot be a vessel into which Soma flows, but rather one from which Soma flows out.

Now we may pose the question : what does *camū́* mean in *camū́ sutá* and *camvòḥ sutá*, because here it is definitely connected with the pressing of Soma ? We have a clue to its meaning in the fact that this word occurs precisely in that hymn which speaks of the pressing of Soma in the mortar, namely in I.28.9. In this verse *camòḥ sutá* means as much as *ulū́khalasuta* in the first verse. Probably *camvòḥ* is one of the elliptical duals and denotes the mortar as well as the pestle at the same time, just as *aulūkhalau* in MS I.4.10 (58.11) denotes both of them.[61]

The reason why *camū́* could at times be the designation of the mortar and at others the designation of the Graha lies apparently in the similarity in their external forms.[62] The authors of the Indian ritual texts explain frequently that the Grahas resemble the mortar in shape. The commentary on KŚS IX.2.14 has the following to say on the injunction of the text according to which the individual vessels for Upāṅśu, Antaryāma, Śukrāmanthinau etc. (i.e., the Grahapātras) must be narrow in the middle : *evaṃvidhāś colūkhalā eva bhavanty ata etāny ulūkhalarūpāṇi bhavantīty arthaḥ.* Later the same commentary says of these vessels that they are "nine mortars."

This meaning of mortar and pestle, which we have obtained here for the dual *camvòḥ*, does not, of course, rule out for the dual the meaning of Graha which occurs in the plural and also in the singular. On the contrary, such a meaning for the dual is absolutely necessary in several passages.

IX.72.5 : *vér ná druṣád camvòr ā́sadad dhárih ||*
103.4 : *sómaḥ punānáś camvòr viśad dhárih ||*
107.10 : *jáno ná puri camvòr viśad dhárih...||*
97.48 : *pári srava camvòr pūyámānaḥ |*
96.21 : *krīḷañ camvòr ā́ viśa pūyámānaḥ*
indraṃ te ráso madiró mamattu ||
97.2 : *ā́ vacyasva camvòḥ pūyámānāḥ...*[63] *||*
108.10 : *ā́ vacyasva sudakṣa camvòḥ sutáḥ... |*

In all these cases *camū́* is that vessel into which Soma, already pressed and purified, flows, i.e., as before, a Graha, perhaps a double Graha. Besides these, there are some other verses which give more detailed information. They state that in these Grahas milk is added to the Soma juice.

IX.86.47 : *yád góbhir indo camvòḥ samajyása ā́*
suvānáḥ soma kaláśeṣu sīdasi ||

69.5 : *divás pṛṣṭhám barhánā nirṇíje kṛta*
upastáraṇaṃ camvòr nabhasmáyam ||
71.1 : *hárir opaśáṃ kṛṇute nábhas páyaḥ*
upastíre camvòr bráhma nirṇíje ||[64]

The following two verses show us the right path,

IX.97.21 : *pári srava nábho árṇaś camū́ṣu* |
93.3 : ...*mūrdhā́naṃ gā́vaḥ páyasā camū́ṣu*
abhí śrīṇanti vásubhir na niktaíḥ ||

because in these verses *camū́ṣu* can, without any difficulty, refer to those Grahas in which milk is mixed. It is probable, therefore, that in the first three passages also *camvòr* denotes one or two Grahas in which milk is mixed to Soma.[65]

Thus the following meanings have been established for *camū́* :

1. In the plural throughout and occasionally in the singular and in the dual a vessel corresponding to the later Grahapātras which were used for drawing out and offering Soma and which had probably a mortar-like shape — in other words, a Graha.

2. Besides this, in the singular and in the dual (but never in the plural) a mortar used for crushing the plant.

camū́ denotes the Soma mortar in the following passages :

Singular *camū́* : V.51.4; VIII.4.4; 76.10; IX.46.3; X.24.1.

Dual *camvòḥ* : I.28.9; IV.18.3; VI.57.2; IX.36.1. Thus in nine passages.

On the other hand, it denotes Graha in the following :

Singular *camū́* : IX.107.18 (see p. 279); *camvì* X.91.15.[66]

Dual *camvoḥ* : IX.69.5; 71.1; 72.5; 86.47; 97.2, 48; 103.4; 107.10; 108.10; 96.20, 21; thus in thirteen passages.[67]

When we examine these numbers, it will be seen that the second meaning occurs, with the exception of X.91.15, in the ninth maṇḍala only and that too in the second half (i.e., starting from hymn 69) and that the first meaning does not occur precisely in this second half. Now we know from IX.67.32[68] that this hymn forms the end of a group; hence we may safely assume that there is a difference in the linguistic usage. The differentiation is not so clear in the case of the plural; nevertheless it can be recognized. It is never said here *camū́ṣu sutā́ḥ*. In all, there are fourteen passages with the plural form : III.48.4; VIII.2.8; 82.7, 8; IX.20.6; 62.16; 63.2; 92.2; 93.3; 97.21, 37, 46; 99.6, 8.

As can be seen, the plural is distributed throughout the ṚV somewhat more evenly than the dual which denotes Graha. All the same, seven out of the fourteen passages belong to that half of the ninth maṇḍala where the dual *camvòḥ* in the sense of Graha also occurs.

camū does not occur at all in the second and seventh book, and only once each in the fourth, fifth and sixth books. The two passages of the third book have been discussed above. In the tenth maṇḍala *camū́* denotes Graha (X.91.15) as well as mortar (24.1); but these hymns are by different composers. Similarly in the first half of the ninth maṇḍala 20.6; 62.16; 63.2 contain one meaning while 36.1; 46.3 contain the other; but all the five hymns belong to different composers. It is only in the eighth book of the Kaṇvas that the sense of Graha coexists side by side with that of mortar, the latter occuring in 4.4 ; 76.10 and the former in 2.8; 82.7, 8.[69]

camū does not denote the "boards for pressing Soma," nor does another much misinterpreted word, viz., *dhiṣáṇā*.

Dhiṣáṇā

It is difficult to find its correct meaning. The PW says that it is firstly a specific vessel used for the preparation and drinking of Soma — a jar, cup, bowl — and also a press according to isolated statements of the commentaries. Furthermore, says the PW, it is used metonymically for the Soma juice itself and its effect. But the correct meaning is the one given in the PW itself : heaven and earth (in the dual), or heaven, atmosphere and earth (in the plural). There are some verses which positively establish that *dhiṣáṇā* does not mean a bowl, e.g.,

X.17.12 : *yás te drapsáḥ skándati yás te aṅśúḥ*
bāhúcyuto dhiṣáṇāyā upásthāt /

"which drop of yours splashes out, which stalk, moved by the arms, [falls] down from the lap of the *dhiṣaṇā*." Accordingly, *dhiṣáṇā* cannot denote a cup, for no stalks are kept in a cup. It must, therefore, be some sort of a base on which the Soma stalks are placed.[70]

This is demonstrated more clearly by

I.109.3 : *mā́ chedma raśmī́nr íti nā́dhamānāḥ*
pitṝṇā́ṃ śaktī́r anuyácchamānāḥ /
indrāgníbhyāṃ káṃ vṝṣaṇo madanti
tā́ hy ádrī dhiṣáṇāyā upásthe //

4 : *yuvā́bhyāṃ devī́ dhiṣáṇā mádāya*
índrāgnī sómam uśatī́ sunoti /

According to these verses it might appear as though *dhiṣáṇā* actually denotes either the skin or the boards. Against the second possibility speaks the use of the singular (and not the dual) in the very passage where it is supposed to denote these boards. Wherever this word occurs in the dual it always means "heaven and earth." Against the meaning "skin" we may cite the linguistic usage in other texts. In VS I.19[df] and in other Yajus texts[71] the Adhvaryu says to the Upalā stone and to the Dṛṣad stone *dhiṣaṇāsi parvatī* and *dhiṣaṇāsi pārvateyī* respectively. Moreover, in VS VI.35 he says to both the boards before he begins to press *dhiṣaṇe vīḍvī.*[72] In either example the meaning of "skin" would be inappropriate.

We come closer to the true meaning of this word through another approach. It is obvious and absolutely certain that it means "heaven and earth" in the dual.[73] If the basic meaning was "cup," then it would be impossible, in my view, for the poet of VI.8.3 to say that the god Agni spreads these *dhiṣaṇé* like two skins.

The plural of this word also occurs, e.g., in

V.69.2 : *tráyas tasthur vṛṣabhā́sas tisṛṇā́m*
dhiṣáṇānāṃ retodhā́ vi dyumántaḥ

"There stand the three bulls, shining, who impregnate the three dhiṣaṇās." What is meant are the three "planes" : heaven, atmosphere and earth. Likewise IV.36.8; IX.59.2.

Heaven and earth are the symbols of stability. In hymn X.173, where the poet wishes a secure rule for the king, it is said in v. 4 : "Firm is heaven, firm is the earth, firm are these mountains here, firm is this whole world. May this king of tribes stand firm." In X.121.5 the earth is called *dṛḍhā́.* From this we can understand why it is said to the pressing boards *dhisaṇe vīḍvī* and to the pressing stones *dhiṣaṇā parvatī.*

Consequently, *dhiṣáṇā* in the singular should be able to denote heaven or atmosphere or earth in that order, but actually it denotes earth only. We should understand I.22.10 in this sense :

ā́ gnā́ agna ihā́vase hótrāṃ yaviṣṭha bhā́ratīm |
várūtrīṃ dhiṣáṇāṃ vaha |

"Lead here the protecting goddess earth." Furthermore, X.35.7 : *rāyó jánitrīṃ dhiṣáṇām úpa bruve*, "I invoke the earth, the begetter of wealth," with which we may compare VII.38.5 : *rātíṃ divó rātiṣā́cah pṛthivyā́ḥ.*

VIII.15.7 : *táva tyád indriyáṃ bṛhát*
táva śúṣmam utá krátum /
vájraṃ śiśāti dhiṣáṇā váreṇyam //[74]

"The earth sharpens your excellent thunderbolt." Therefore, I.102.7 : *amātráṃ tvā dhiṣáṇā titviṣe mahī́*, "the great *dhiṣaṇā* has inspired you who are boundless," does not refer either to "longing" or to a "Soma cup"' but to the earth. Further, we may compare I.102.1; III.31.13; 56.6; VI.19.2; VII.90.3;[75] X.96.10.

I.96.1 also can be explained in this way :
ápaś ca mitráṃ dhiṣáṇā ca sādhan
devā́ agníṃ dhārayan draviṇodā́m

"The waters and the earth led the friend to the goal. The gods kept Agni Draviṇodas." In X.30.6 also *dhiṣáṇā* and *ápaś ca devī́ḥ*, earth and the divine waters, occur together.[76]

In X.17.12; I.109.3, 4 (see p. 282 above), the passages which formed the starting point of this discussion, the meaning "earth," ascertained so far, does not fit readily. However, the meaning becomes clear if we keep in mind that these passages refer to the objects on the sacrificial place. The pressing did not take place outside the sacrificial ground but within its boundaries. In all the mythical sacrifices the earth plays the role of the vedi. It is said in

AV XIII.1.46 : *urvī́r āsan paridháyaḥ védir bhū́mir akalpata* /
and 52 : *védiṃ bhū́miṃ kalpayitvā́ díváṃ kṛtvā́ dákṣiṇām*

"having prepared the earth as the vedi and having made heaven the sacrificial fee." ŚBr I.2.5.7 states : "having enclosed [the sacrifice] with metres all around and having installed Agni in the east, they went on singing and working with it. Through it they obtained (*avindanta*)[77] this entire earth. As they obtained the entire earth through it, vedi is the name [for the sacrificial place]. Therefore it is said : as great as the vedi is so great is the earth."[78]

The vedi is well known to the ṚV. It is mentioned in eleven passages distributed over different maṇḍalas.[79] Already there it is regarded as a privileged place on earth[80] and conceived as a person. In X.114.3 the maiden with four braids from whom the gods receive their share is to be understood as the vedi. The continuation of this verse in the TBr[81] calls her *devī́*, implores her to fulfil the wishes of the sacrificer and identifies her with the earth. ṚV VII.35.7 says : *śáṃ naḥ prasvàḥ śám v astu védiḥ.*

Now in the ṚV the vedi was the place where the Soma stones are kept. This is stated in the verse cited on p. 272 : "the speaking stone should be placed on the vedi."

With this we have arrived at our starting point once again. ṚV I.109.3 : *tá hy adrī dhiṣáṇāyā upásthe* means, "for, the two stones are on the lap of the vedi," and X.17.12 "which stalk [falls] down from the lap of the vedi."[82] The wording in I.109.4 *dhiṣáṇā sómam uśatī́ sunóti* broadly states as much as *dhiṣáṇāyā upásthe sómaḥ sūyate.* With equal felicity says *Rāmāyaṇa* I.32.9 (33.8) : *prajajvāla tadā vediḥ.*

Agni is seated on the vedi and is, therefore, called *vediṣád.* Hence

III.2.1 : *vaiśvānaráya dhiṣáṇāṃ ṛtāvṛdhe*
ghṛtáṃ ná pūtám agnáye janāmasi |

is to be translated thus : "We prepare the vedi for Agni."

VI.11.3 : *dhányā cid dhí tvé dhiṣáṇā váṣṭi prá...yajadhyai* |

"The opulent vedi longs for you...in order to worship."

V.41.8 : *dhányā sajóṣā dhiṣáṇā námobhir*
vánaspátīṅr óṣadhī rāyá éṣe |

"The opulent vedi unites herself with the venerations."[83] Furthermore, IV.34.1; III.49.4.[84]

To sum up, *dhiṣáṇā* has only the following meanings throughout the ṚV :

1. earth; in the dual heaven and earth; in the plural heaven, atmosphere and earth.
2. vedi.

All other supposed meanings like "pressing boards" or even "enthusiasm" are wrong and superfluous.

Against this Johansson emphasizes the necessity of a more abstract conception of *dhiṣáṇā*, whom he regards as a vegetation goddess and identifies with the earth.[85] My own investigation is not opposed to this. The vedi itself, which represents the earth and which through the shoulders and hips (*áṅsa, śróṇi*) indicates the body of the earth, has mystic power, as is suggested by the mantras recited during the preparation of the vedi. Therefore, like *hotrā, iḍā* etc., vedi can be regarded with Johansson as a goddess.[86]

C. THE COWHIDE

As we have seen, the ritual texts state that the stones rest on a cowhide spread over the two boards which serve as the base and that the juice flows on to this cowhide. In the ṚV the cowhide is frequently mentioned under the designation *tvac*.

IX.79.4 : *ádrayas tvā bapsati gór adhi tvací*
apsú tvā hástair duduhur manīṣíṇaḥ ||

"The stones chew you on the cowhide; with their hands the wise men milked you into the water."

IX.66.29 : *eṣá sómo ádhi tvací gávāṃ krīḍaty ádribhiḥ* ||
70.9 : *gavyáyī tvág bhavati nirṇíg avyáyī* ||

"From the cow is the hide, from the sheep the ornament."

Also 65.25; 101.11, 16. Furthermore, I.79.3 deserves a few words.

I.79.3 : *aryamā́ mitró váruṇaḥ párijmā*
tvácaṃ pṛñcanty úparasya yónau ||

IX.65.25 states that Soma is sent on to the hide of the cow;[87] our verse also is to be understood in the same sense : "they fill the hide on the lap of the upara," that is to say, the juice flows over the upara on to the hide. Grassmann and Ludwig have understood this correctly long ago.[88]

Apart from *tvác góḥ* and *gavyáyī*, *go* alone occurs in one or two passages.

X.94.9 : *aṅśúṃ duhánto ádhy āsate gávi* |

"Milking the stalk, [the stones] sit on the cowhide." Perhaps also

X.116.4 :[89] *gávy ā́ sutásya prábhṛtasya mádhvaḥ*
satrā́ khédām aruśahā́ vṛṣasva |

However, the admixture of milk might have been meant by this word here.

Thus it has been established that Soma was prepared either with a mortar or with stones, under which a cowhide was spread, and that the view that Soma was crushed between two boards, or that it was pounded on the boards with stones, is without any foundation. As far as I can see, the two boards of the ritual, which were placed under the pressing apparatus so that the latter does not shift from its position are not mentioned in the ṚV at all.

B. ON SOME SOMA VESSELS IN THE ṚGVEDA

camū́ and *camasá* have already been discussed. In addition to these, the following are mentioned more frequently.

1. *Kóśa* and *Kaláśa*

There is an unmistakable difference between the two words. I cannot explain away with Foy[89] this difference as a mere accident caused by the more frequent occurrence of *kaláśa*. *kóśa* throughout denotes a big vessel. IV.17.16 speaks of the *kóśa*, "the pail at the well" (*avaté ná kóśa*). V.53.6; 59.8; 83.8 mention the *diváḥ kóśa*, or *divyá kóśa*, or *mahát kóśa* which the Maruts set in motion. IX.86.3 has *kóśaṃ divó ádrimātaram*. It is evident from other passages also that it is a big vessel. In VII.101.4 *víśvāni bhúvanāni tisró dyā́vaḥ* occur by the side with *tráyaḥ kóśāsa upasécanāso*. VIII.20.8; 22.9 speak of a *ráthe kóśe hiraṇyáye* etc. Thus the word is used in comparisons that suggest abundance.[90] But *kaláśa* is used neither in one way nor in the other. There is no lack of verses which indicate the difference between *kaláśa* and *kóśa* quite clearly. In AV XVIII.4.30 *kóśa* and *kaláśa cáturbila* occur side by side.

ṚV IX.75.3 : *áva dyutānáḥ kaláśāṅ acikradat*
nṛ́bhir yemānáḥ kóśa ā́ hiraṇyáye |

"Caught by men in the golden pail, he bellowed shining (?) in the kalaśas." Probably the singular of the one and the plural of the other should be understood thus : the *kóśa* denotes a bigger container from which Soma is distributed into the *kaláśas*.[91] III.32.15 should be understood in this sense :

ā́pūrṇo asya kaláśaḥ svā́hā sékteva kóśaṃ sisice píbadhyai |

kaláśa contains, as is evident from the use of the term *svā́hā*, a portion meant for libation and corresponds to the Grahapātra or more correctly to the *camasá*. It is filled from the *kóśa* : "The jar has been filled for him. Svāhā ! Like a cup-bearer he poured from the pail for drinking."[92] It is in conformity with the distinction noticed here between the *kóśa* and *kaláśa* that *kóśa* occurs primarily in the singular whereas *kaláśa* occurs sometimes in the singular and some other times in the plural. *kóśa* is used in the plural, as far as it has any ritual significance, in two passages only : IX.86.20 and VIII.2.8. The first, *nṛ́bhir yatáḥ pári kóśāṅ acikradat*, can probably be eliminated.

Elsewhere it is said constantly *pári kóśam arṣ*;[93] therefore, we should perhaps read *kóśam* here also instead of *kóśān*. The other verse has no significance.[94]

Furthermore, a distinction between *kóśa* and *kaláśa* can be seen in the selection of the verbs that go with them. *kóśa* is accompanied by *pári-arṣ* (four times), *abhi-arṣ*, *páry-ās*, *pári-ni-sad* (*vi-yu*), *sic* (*kośam* and *kośena*), *pári-acikradat* (*kośān*), *jinv*, *cyu*, *yam* (*kośe*), *pūrṇá*, *nyṛṣṭá* as transitive verbs, and *kṣar*, *pū* (three times of which twice with *abhi*) as intransitive verbs. The first group is more characteristic than the second. What is remarkable is the frequent occurrence of *pári* which, if I am not much mistaken, accompanies the verbs of kalaśa in IX.67.15 only.

On the other hand, *kaláśa* (singular as well as plural) is accompanied by *sad* and *āsad* nine times;[95] *kṣar* (*kalaśe*) IX.63.3; *abhikrandan arṣ* (only once) IX.86.11; *i* IX.97.22; *yā* IX.92.6; *ā-viś* IX.62.19; 96.22; 97.33; *dhāv* IX.17.4; 60.3; 67.14; *nū* IX.65.14; *vāś* (*kalaśe*) IX.96.14; *vāś* (causative) IX.86.19; *krand* (causative) IX.18.7; 75.3; *kram* IX.74.8; *syand* IX.81.2; *sṛj* (*kalaśe*) IX.67.15; 86.22; *abhi-sṛj* IX.88.6; 106.12; *dhā* (*kalaśe*) IX.63.13; 12.5 (?); *mṛj* (*kalaśe*) IX.85.7. As we can see, almost all these verbs are different from the ones used with *kóśa*. The reason for this is not clear.

Another distinguishing factor is that the mixing of Soma with milk in the *kóśa* is not mentioned clearly in any passage,[96] whereas it is twice stated that the Soma is mixed with water in the *kóśa*.

IX.76.5 : *vṛ́ṣeva yūthā́ pári kóśam arṣasi*
apā́m upásthe vṛṣabháḥ kánikradat

"As a bull rushes to the herd so do you flow to the pail, you, a roaring bull in the lap of the waters." Furthermore,

IX.107.26 : *apó vásānaḥ pári kóśam arṣati*
índur hiyānáḥ sotṛ́bhiḥ

"Urged by the pressers, clothed in the waters, Indu flows into the pail."

On the other hand, I find that only once water is mentioned in connection with the *kaláśa*.[97] More often it is the admixture of milk that Soma receives in the *kaláśa*.

IX.85.5 : *kaláśe góbhir ajyase*; 72.1 : *sáṃ dhenúbhiḥ kaláśe sómo ajyate*; IV.27.5 and IX.74.8 : *śvetáṃ kaláśaṃ góbhir aktám*; IX.8.6 : *punānáḥ kaláśeṣv ā́ vástrāṇy aruṣó háriḥ* / *pári*

gávyāny avyata; 93.2 : *sáṃ gacchate kaláśa usríyābhiḥ*; (86.16 : *márya iva yuvatíbhiḥ sám arṣati kaláśe*); 96.22 : *aktó góbhiḥ kaláśāṅ á viveśa*; also 96.14 cited in note 97. We should keep in mind that the kalaśa contains *gávas*, while explaining the following passages also — IX.86.19 : *kaláśāṅ avīvaśat*; 65.14 : *á kaḷáśā anūṣata*; IX. 18.7; 75.3: *acikradat*. Soma comes purified into the *kaláśa* : 60.3; 17.4; 88.6; 97.4 etc.

However, in the ṚV *kaláśa* also denotes a big vessel a few times. But these are isolated passages limited to one hymn of the sixth book.[98] Therefore, this does not affect the overall result. The distinction is to be established by translating *kóśa* as "pail"[99] and *kaláśa* as "jar."

The use of *kaláśa* also in the sense of pail, beginning in the sixth book, comes into its own outside the ṚV only. MS IV.5.9 (77.12, 13) says that the *droṇakalaśa* is the head and the two *kalaśas* the hips. Thus here we have the three big vessels, Droṇakalaśa, Pūtabhṛt and Ādhavanīya, used in the Soma sacrifice.[100] The pails filled with water and carried by women around the fire in the Mahāvrata are likewise called kalaśas.[101] The vessels used for drawing the ekadhanā waters are also called kalaśas occasionally,[102] and so on.

I think the reason for this change in the linguistic usage is that in the later period *camaśa* was substituted for *kaláśa* in the sense of the "drinking jar of the priests" and *kaláśa* became free for other uses.

camū́ and *kaláśa* are quite close in meaning but not identical. *camū́* is used for offerings to the gods and *kaláśa*, according to the testimony of X.167.3 (see p. 278 above), for the priests. Milk can be added to Soma in both these vessels.[103] When it is said in VI.47.6 : *dhṛṣát piba kaláśe somám indra*, this contradiction can be removed by arguing that from *camasás* also libations were offered to the gods beforehand and that this linguistic usage belongs anyway to the sixth book, which is characterized by many peculiarities.

That we are right in separating *camū́* from *kaláśa* is proved by IX.86.47 : *yád góbhir indo camvòḥ samajyása á*
suvānáḥ soma kaláśeṣu sīdasi

"While you are anointed with milk in the Graha, O Soma, you sit, having been pressed, in the kalaśas."[104]

Apart from its size, *kóśa* has two other qualities which

distinguish it from other vessels. One is the epithet *hiraṇyáya*, "golden,"[105] attributed to it in IX.75.3. Wherever there is a mention of *yóni hiraṇyáya* or *áyohata*, it should be understood that these terms refer to the *kóśa* because no other golden Soma vessel is known.[106] I do not, however, notice any golden vessel in the Agniṣṭoma, but it is used in the Vājapeya in circumstances that deserve a brief discussion later on.[107]

Another peculiarity of *kóśa* is that it is called *madhuścút*, "dripping of honey or sweetness." Thus it is called six times[108] to which we should add VII.101.4 and also I.87.2; 112.11.[109] This epithet would have been meaningless if it was used for every other Soma vessel. But it is only kośa which is called thus and not kalaśa or camasa or camū. Therefore, it would be necessary to examine *madhuścút* more closely than has been done so far. It will be seen that this word may be translated as "rich in honey" and not merely as "rich in Soma."[110]

2. *Drú*

This word occurs rarely, and that too mostly in the instrumental. Such passages can be divided into two groups. In the first group this word is used in the general sense,[111] whereas in the second it has some connection with the Soma juice since all these passages refer to the Soma juice. This second group deserves a few words,[112] for in all these passages *drú* is apparently an object through which Soma flows into other vessels. Through the use in the instrumental, *drú* is distinguished from *camū́*, *kaláśa*, *kóśa*[113] and *dróṇa*. Therefore, it must have served a different purpose. I presume that it was used to catch the juice flowing out of the strainer. More cannot be ascertained. Perhaps it is also synonymous with *srúva*.

3. *Dróṇa*

It has no specific meaning other than "wooden vessel." It occurs in the singular as well in the plural — more often in the latter. It appears that it can denote all vessels made of wood, whether small or big. That it can be a big vessel is shown by the expression *dróṇāhāva avatá* X.101.7. On the other hand from IX.33.2; 15.7 (cf. 85.7); 67.14 it appears that it means as much as kalaśa. We learn from IX.96.13 that droṇas contain butter, that they are *ghṛtávānti*.

The verbs[114] that accompany the word droṇa are not very significant. They rather agree with those used with the word kalaśa.

4. *Vána*

This, as the name itself shows, is a wooden vessel like droṇa. Several verses state that in a *vána* Soma is mixed with milk.[115] This, as well as the comparison in IX.96.23,[116] show that *vána* can be similar to kalaśa. But its meaning is wider. It follows from II.14.9 : *váne nípūtaṃ vána ún nayadhvam* that among the Gṛtsamadas this word denotes a vessel in which Soma is kept after purification as well as that with which Soma is drawn out. I think it is unnecessary to go into further details. It denotes nowhere a specific vessel.

5. *Srúva*, LADLE

In I.116.24 this is stated to be the means for ladling out Soma. One may compare it with a ladle called pariplavā in the ritual (e.g., ĀpŚS XII.20.20). Sāyaṇa on IX.65.6 states : *drumamayena pārīplavena pātreṇa gṛhyamāṇaḥ.*

The expressions *ararínda* I.139.10; *khārī* IV.32.17; *camríṣ* I.56.1 are obscure.[117]

It is not necessary to go into the common names like *āhāva, dhāman, pātra, sadana, sadhastha* (seat).

C. THE SWELLING OF SOMA

During the pressing, Āpyāyana, "causing to swell," is done repeatedly. This Āpyāyana, as we have remarked earlier, is an auxiliary means. We have seen that the Soma plant must be full of juice. Juicy plants, however, need not be soaked in water. This is required only when the plants contain too pungent a juice to be enjoyed without diluting, or when they are dried up, or when much of their juice has already been extracted. In the last event the process is required only to extract the juice still remaining in the pulp.

The authors of the ritual texts differ about the meaning of the Āpyāyana. Some think it is mere touching, other regard it as soaking in water. The first view is based on a forced explanation unknown to the older texts. The MS says at IV.5.5 (69.11) : *vasatīvarībhiḥ*[118] *somam āpyāyayanti / na hi somena soma āpyāyate* and similarly somewhat earlier.[119] The commentary on ABr I.26 also says : *jalena prokṣaṇam āpyāyanam.* As against this the commentator on KŚS VIII.2.6; IX.5.2 states that it is a mere touching, *ālambhanamātra.* The same is the view of the commentators on ŚŚS V. 8.3 and ĀpŚS XI.1.11. The last one, however, knows the other view also.[120]

The question whether the ṚV mentions the custom of Āpyāyana is to be treated with caution. Verses I.91.16-18; X.85.5, which speak of the swelling of Soma, refer not to the plant, but to the god, or to both, as has been recognized long ago. The same applies probably to another passage, IX.67.28, as we have stated on p. 204. Even if one would want to relate this passage to the plant, the wish "be full of juice" would not immediately imply the soaking of the plant. On the other hand, there is one verse which probably does not rule out the possibility of assuming that Āpyāyana was known to the ṚV. By this I have in mind IX.74.9 :

adbhíḥ soma papṛcānásya te ráso
ávyo vā́raṃ ví pavamāna dhāvati /[121]

D. EXTRACTION AND PURIFICATION

1. In the Ritual

In the method of pressing Soma usually adopted by the ritual, the Upāṅśusavana and the Mahābhiṣava, i.e. the preliminary and the main pressings, are distinguished from one another. Kātyāyana enjoins how these pressings are to be performed. I give below his rules in a slightly abridged form.

KŚS IX.4.1 : "They sit around the skin.

2-3 : "To the north of it the Adhvaryu and the sacrificer. The Adhvaryu to his left.

4 : "The three others (Pratiprasthātṛ, Neṣṭṛ and Unnetṛ), after having gone around behind [the skin, sit in the south].

5 : "The Adhvaryu takes a stone with the words, 'by the order of god Savitṛ' etc., and remains silent until the hiṃkāra.

6 : "This [stone meant for pressing the Upāṅśugraha] is called Upāṅśusavana.

7 : "Over the so-called Nigrābhyā waters[122]...he makes the sacrificer speak the words, 'You are the Nigrābhyās' etc.

8 : "[After these words the Adhvaryu places the Upāṅśusavana

stone on the skin and] on it measures out the Soma five times, each time with one of the following mantras:[123]

i. 'you (accusative) for Indra with the Vasus and the Rudras.'
ii. 'you for Indra with the Ādityas.'
iii. 'you for Indra, the subduer of the Abhimātis.'
iv. 'you for the eagle who brings Soma.'
v. 'you for Agni who bestows wealth.'

10-11 : "The Pratiprasthātṛ takes six aṅśus [from the Soma thus measured out] and puts two each between the fingers [of the left hand].

12 : "With the words, 'you are delicious...,' [the Adhvaryu] pours the Nigrābhyās [upon the Soma with the Hotṛ's jar].

15 : "He says : 'do not break, do not skid,' and strikes [the Soma] with the stone.[124]

16 : "Thus he presses three times, pouring water each time.

17 : "In the first round he strikes eight times, in the second eleven times and in the third twelve times.[125]

20 : "In each round he throws the stalks from which juice is dripping meagerly into the jar of the Hotṛ and causes the Nigrābha formula to be uttered : 'from east and west' etc.[126] [Having pressed them out he throws them back].

23 : "He draws the Upāṅśugraha, reciting each time one of the three mantras, 'for Vācaspati,' 'the god for the gods,' 'the sweet ones,' [each time one third].

24 : "[While drawing with the right hand] the Pratiprasthātṛ holds the Upāṅśu cup below [near the Adhvaryu].

25 : "Of the six aṅśus taken [from the previously measured out Soma] he puts two each in between, by holding them between the fingers over the vessel while drawing the Graha.[127]

28 : "Then he puts these six down on the Soma.

29 : "Thereupon he wipes the Upāṅśu [with the woollen strainer, and also] the Antaryāma all around without putting it down...[Having offered a libation with it].

40 : "he pours a part of the remnants contained therein into the Āgrayaṇīsthālī and throws a Soma stalk [into the Upāṅśu cup] for the third pressing..."

A special significance is attributed to this Upāṅśugraha. On this ŚBr IV.1.1.5 says : *sarvaṃ vā eṣa grahaḥ sarveṣām hi savanānāṃ rūpam.* The reason is obviously this : its three rounds with their numbers of eight, eleven and twelve strokes correspond exactly to the sequence of numbers occurring frequently in the Savanas — a sequence which influences even the selection of metres. The ŚBr explains this in further detail at IV.1.1.8, 10, 12.

This preliminary pressing is followed by the main pressing, the Mahābhiṣava.[128]

This pressing is done not by one person only as before but by four, that is, by Adhvaryu, Pratiprasthātṛ, Neṣṭṛ and Unnetṛ according to their position.[129]

KŚS IX.5.2 : "Each pressing consists of three rounds and ends with the Āpyāyana.

3 : "[The number of strokes is] according to [one's] inclination.[130]

4 : "At the beginning of each round he adds the Nigrābhyā water [in order to release the juice].[131]

5 : "Or, only in the first round because this is sufficient.

6 : "At the end of the recitation of the Nigrābha verses, he puts the juicy stalks with the help of a vessel suited for this purpose, the so-called Saṃbharaṇi,[132] into the Ādhavanīya[133] [that has been filled with water], washes them, [presses them out and] and brings them back [again with the Saṃbharaṇi] in order to throw them on the press.[134]

7 : "Thus two more times.

8 : "The Nigrābhyās as before."[135]

According to a subsequent sūtra of Kātyāyana, the Upāṅśusava and the Mahābhiṣava can also be combined, but the separation of the two seems to be more customary since this is enjoined by Āpastamba and Hiraṇyakeśin as well. A change in the sequence of the Upāṅśusava and the Mahābhiṣava is also mentioned, but it is pointless to go into such minor details.

The pressing is followed by the purification of Soma. Kātyāyana enjoins the following procedure.

KŚS IX.5.14-15 : "Having brought the Droṇakalaśa[136] forward, the Udgātṛs place it on the stones, the pounding surface of which has been previously covered with the husk of the Soma stalks, and spread the woollen strainer upon it in such a way that the fringe is upwards and the nābhī downwards.

17 : "With the Udañcana the Unnetṛ draws the Soma from the Ādhavanīya [and] pours it on the Nigrābhyās [contained in the Hotṛcamasa]. Thereupon the sacrificer pours these [Nigrābhyās with the Soma] in one stream upon the strainer [held above the

Droṇakalaśa by the Udgātṛs]. From this [continuous stream] all the [eight] Grahas up to the Dhruva [are drawn].[137]

18 : "In the midday pressing the first five (Śakra and Manthin, Āgrayaṇa, Marutvatīya, Ukthya).

19 : "In the Droṇakalaśa is placed the purified Soma (*śukra*) [in all the three Savanas].

20 : "The remaining Grahas are drawn from it [or from the Pūtabhṛt to be mentioned in 24] as long as there is no special injunction.

21 : "[In the third Savana] the Graha for Savitṛ, the Pātnīvata and the Hāriyojana, as well as those which have become dry [due to the length of time], are drawn from the Āgrāyaṇa; all the camasas from the Pūtabhṛt.

23 : "From the same a Vaiśvadevagraha [in the evening].

24 : "Similarly those for which there is no special injunction.

25 : "With the woollen strainer he wipes each Graha and puts it in its place with the words, 'this is your place.'

6.26 : "Having filled the Grahas [beginning with the Antaryāma up to the Dhruva from that continuous stream] completely, and the Droṇakalaśa up to half [with the Soma flowing out during this], the sacrificer (*sunvat*) pours all [that is in the Hotṛcamasa].

27, 28 : "Holding each other, the Adhvaryu, the Pratiprasthātṛ, the Prastotṛ, the Udgātṛ, the Pratihartṛ and the sacrificer go out — the Adhvaryu first and others according to their number.

30 : "They offer the Vipruṣ homa with the verse, 'which drop' etc. (VS VII.26).

32 : "The Adhvaryu takes two blades of grass from the vedi.

33 : "Bending down, they go north [south of the pit to the Bahiṣpavamānadeśa in the middle of the vedi].

34 : "He throws one of the blades of grass on the pit with the verse 'of the gods' etc. (VS VII.26).

35 : "The other silently in front of the Udgātṛs [seated at the Bahiṣpavamāna place].

36 : "While [the Udgātṛs] mutter [the preliminary portion, the Adhvaryu], as he gives the Prastotṛ two blades of grass, leads [the singing of the verses of purification with the following mantra : 'Soma purifies himself; Soma purifies himself for this brahmin, for this Kṣtra, for the Soma sacrificer; he purifies himself into food' etc.

7.2 : "[The Adhvaryu and the Pratiprasthātṛ] sit down [in front of the Udgātṛs who are seated] facing the west.

3 : "The sacrificer to the south.

4 : "During the singing of the Stotra, the Unnetṛ pours the Ādhavanīya into the Pūtabhṛt upon which he has placed the strainer.[138]

8 : "[Immediately after the Bahiṣpavamāna Stotra the Adhvaryu draws with the Pariplavā ladle] the Āśvinagraha from the Droṇakalaśa or from the Pūtabhṛt with the words, 'which whip' etc. (VS VII.11)."[139]

2. In the Ṛgveda[140]

It cannot be maintained that this form of extracting Soma and distributing it into the individual vessels as described in the ritual literature was already known to the same extent in the period of the ṚV. Nor can we deny it altogether. While deciding such questions, we should keep in mind that there was no motivation for describing the activities of the Adhvaryus more closely in the Vedic hymns, which were primarily devoted to the activities of the Hotṛs, and that a long period of development of the ritual must be anticipated. Even from the great number of priests in the ṚV — Hotṛs as well as Adhvaryus[141] — it is evident that the ceremonial pressing of Soma was no longer a simple affair and that, with regard to the number of rites, the ṚV probably did not lag considerably behind the later period. Concerning the details of the ceremonies, I have nothing to add to what I have stated earlier about *grávan.* It seems that the bursting stalks, or the falling drops, emitted a loud hissing sound (see pp. 141 f., 222 f. above). The process of purification deserves some words. We have seen that Soma was purified in two different ways in the preliminary and main pressings : in the former with some of the aṅśus held in the hand, in the latter with a strainer made of wool. It cannot be determined whether the ṚV knew the former. This method is suggested by some expressions like ṚV II.14.8, "Offer Soma purified in the hands to the famous one,"[142] and IX.71.3, "pressed by the stones, he purifies himself in the hands."[143] These expressions correspond with the verse used precisely in this form of purification:[144] *vācáspátaye pavasva vṛ́ṣṇo aṅśúbhyāṃ gábhastipūtaḥ*, "O Lord of Speech, purify yourself, purified with the two stalks in the hands of the strong one." Nevertheless, there is the possibility that *gábhastipūta* is not a technical term in the ṚV, but only a general expression which could be applied equally to the purification with a woollen strainer, where also the hands are active.[145] The familiarity with the second method, the requisite for which is the Soma strainer made of sheep's wool is all the more certain. The strainer is mentioned very often and under different names : *áṇva* IX.16.2; *áṇvāni meṣyàḥ* 86.47; 107.11; *ávi* (plural),[146] *tvác* (*ávya, avyáya*), *pavítra* with and without *ávya* (*avyáya*), *meṣī́* (plural),[147] *rūpá* (*avyáya*),[148] *róman* with and without *avyáya*, *vā́ra* with and without *ávya* (*avyáya*), with the genitive *ávyaḥ*, *sā́nu* with and without[149] *ávya* (*avyáya*), *ádhi ṣṇúbhir ávīnām*, *hváras* (plural). IX.66.9 : *ávye jīrā́v ádhi ṣváṇi* is not quite plain. There is no evidence to say that small sticks were used for making the strainer. The explanation of *vip* in this sense by the PW is doubtful.

Soma is poured on the strainer. In IX.63.10 and 19, it is said : *ávyo vā́reṣu siñcata*; there are other similar expressions.[150] The most frequent designation for the Soma juice that is passing through the strainer is *pávamāna* or *punāná*. The word used most frequently to denote this action is, as is well known, *pū*. Besides this there is a second verb, *mṛj*,[151] which is more general and less specific than the former. For it is used not only for the purification with the woollen strainer but also for the admixture of water and milk. Thus IX.91.2 : *marmṛjanó 'vibhir góbhir adbhíḥ* ; 68.9 : *adbhír góbhir mṛjyate* ; 86.11 : *marmṛjānó 'vibhiḥ sindhubhíḥ*. It is used even for the stones in X.76.7 : *marjayanta āsábhiḥ*.[152]

E. PURE UNMIXED SOMA JUICE

The ritual makes a distinction between *sóma śuddhá* and *sóma śukrá*. There the former denotes the Soma plants from which all extraneous matter has been sorted out[153] and the latter the Soma juice purified through the strainer. However, *śuddhá* does not yet have this meaning in the ṚV. IX.78.1 (p. 149) shows that there *śuddhá* refers to the juice purified through the strainer. Perhaps it is the same in VIII.95.7[154] also, although the play on words in this verse[155] rules out a positive interpretation. Two other adjectives are used more frequently than *śuddhá* to denote the purified — or, at least still unmixed — drink,[156] namely *śukrá* and *śúci*.

For *śukrá* this is attested by juxtapositions like *gávāśir, manthín* and *śukrá* in III.32.2[157] or *śukrá manthínā* in IX.46.4 on the one hand and by those like *śukrá gávāśirah* I.137.1; I.X64.28; Vāl 4.10 etc. on the other; also by verses like VIII.2.10 : *śukrá āśiram yācante*, "the pure [drops] long for the admixture, IX.33.2: *babhrávah śukrá...vájam gómantam akṣaran*, "the brown pure [drops] flowed...towards the food made of cow's milk."[158]

Synonymous with *śukrá* is *śúci*. He flows on to the strainer, *śúcih punānás tanvàm arepásam* (IX.70.8; 72.4). This *śúci* also is often contrasted with the Soma juice to which admixtures have been added. In I.5.5 *sómāso dádhyāśirah* are contrasted with *sutáh śúcayah*. Similarly I.30.2 :

śatám vā yah śúcīnām sahásram vā sámāśirām /
éd u nimnám ná rīyate //

"He who drinks a hundred of the pure or a thousand of the mixed Somas — it flows down in him as into a valley." Vāl. 4.10, or

VIII.2.9 : *śúcir asi puruniṣṭháh kṣīraír madhyatá áśīrtah /*
dadhná mándiṣṭhah śūrasya //

"Unmixed are you at many places, mixed with milk in the middle [of the day ?], but with curd you are most pleasing to the hero."

VIII.101.10 :... *piba śúcim sómam gávāśiram //* etc.

Of all the gods Vāyu has the foremost claim to the unmixed Soma. He alone is called *śucipá* VII.90.2; 92.1; X.100.2 and *śukrapūtapā* VIII.46.26. In the hymns unmixed Soma is mentioned often directly as his drink.[159] Besides him only Indra, who is closely connected with the former in mythology and in ritual, gets a share of this almost to the same extent. Indra receives the unmixed drink I.84.4; IX.72.4; 86.13; Vāl 4.10; AV. IV.24.4; more often together with Vāyu I.135.5,6; II.41.3; VII.90.1; 91.4. In the last passage they are called *śucipá* jointly.

Of instances where pure Soma is offered to gods other than Vāyu or Indra-Vāyu, I have noticed only I.137.1 which mentions an offering for Mitra-Varuṇa and IX.97.20 where Viśve Devāḥ are invited to come to the *śukrásah sómāh*. Thus the Ṛgvedic ritual makes a clear distinction between pure and mixed Soma.

The offering of unmixed Soma to Indra-Vāyu is in complete accord with the practice of the later ritual. For of the Dvidevatya

Grahas the first is offered to Vāyu and Indra-Vāyu without any admixture,[160] whereas the Graha for Mitra-Varuṇa contains an admixture of milk and that for the Aśvins an admixture — at least in theory, if not any more in reality — of honey.[161]

There is no lack of indications to show that many Śrotriyas of the Vedic period spurned the offering of unmixed Soma completely. These appear to have been primarily the descendants of Kaṇva because almost all the passages I could find on this belong precisely to book VIII.[162] The Kaṇvas did not enjoy the same prestige everywhere. The magic formula directed against a Kaṇva *arā́ya asṛkpā́van* in AV II.25.3 does not show much respect for this name. In ĀpŚS XIII.7.5 it is prohibited to give dakṣiṇā to a Kaṇva or to a Kaśyapa; "the reason is in dispute," says the commentary.[163]

The Kaṇvas were connected with the "five peoples."[164] This could very well have been the cause for the differences in the ritual and others. It cannot be ruled out that the strong emphasis laid by the Kaṇvas, or at least by the composers of hymn VIII.2, on the necessity of an admixture had its origin in the employment of a different kind of plant the juice of which taken alone did not have pleasing taste. VIII.2.3 states : *tám te yávaṃ yáthā góbhiḥ svādúm akarma śrīṇántaḥ*, "We have made it sweet for you like barley, mixing it with milk." However, we cannot establish anything positive on this.[165]

The colour of the Soma juice coming out of the press is often mentioned. The juice is called *babhrú*,[166] *aruṇá*,[167] most frequently *hári*;[168] it must have been reddish or light yellow exactly like the stalks themselves. Milk takes on its colour.[169]

The juice has the same scent as the plant. As we have stated earlier, the plant is called *hubaoiδiš* in the *Avesta*. *Mantra Brāhmaṇa* II.4.14 states that its main characteristic is its fragrance. The same is said about the juice in two passages of the ṚV.

IX.97.19 : *sahásradhāraḥ surabhír ádabdhaḥ pári srava*...
and 107.2 : *nūnáṃ punānó 'vibhiḥ pári srava*
ádabdhaḥ surabhíntaraḥ //

We have an evidence from the later period also about the smell emanating from Soma. However, the smell does not seem to have been always pleasant, either because different plants were used or because the drink itself had gone bad. Thus ŚBr IV.1.3.6 narrates :

"He stank putrid to them. Sour and putrid he blew towards them. He was fit neither for offering nor for consuming.

7 : "The gods said to Vāyu: 'Vāyu, blow through him. Make him palatable to us.' 'What shall I get for this ?' 'These bowls shall be called after you.'

8 : " 'So be it,' he said, 'but you blow along with me.'

9 : "All the smell the gods removed they placed in the cattle. Therefore, there is putrid smell in [dead] cattle. Hence, one should not close one's nose because of the putrid smell, since it is the smell of king Soma."[170]

F. ADMIXTURES TO THE SOMA JUICE

ṚV V.27.5 speaks of the *sómās tryàśiraḥ*[171] and thus shows that three kinds of admixtures (*āśír*) were added to Soma. These three are specified more exactly by the words *gávāśir, dádhyāśir, yávāśir* — sweet milk, curd and barley.[172] In addition to these there is also the mixing with water. Besides *āśír*, the ṚV has various general expressions for all these admixtures or for some individual ones. I have noted *vástra, vā́sas* and *átka*.

IX.8.6 : *punānáḥ kaláśeṣv ā́ vástrāṇy aruṣó háriḥ |*
pári gávyāny ávyata ||

"Purifying himself, the reddish and golden one clothed himself with the garments of milk in the jars." Also 96.1; 101.14; 107.13;[173] 104.4.[174]

69.4 : *átkaṃ ná niktáṃ pári sómo avyata ||*
5 : *ámṛktena rúśatā vā́sasā hárir*
ámartyo nirṇijānáḥ pári vyata |

Therefore, these admixtures of milk are compared to an ornament or a splendid robe which Soma puts on — IX.14.5 : *gā́ḥ kṛṇvānó ná nirṇíjaṃ*; similarly 86.25; 95.1; 107.26; 68.1; 82.2.

It follows from this that we should translate the word *śrī́* also, which is used a few times in the same context, as "beauty" or "ornament."

IV.41.8 : *śriyé ná gā́va úpa sómam asthuḥ*
índraṃ gíro váruṇaṃ me manīṣā́ḥ ||

"Just as the milk has gone to Soma to become his ornament, so have my songs to Indra, my thoughts to Varuṇa."

IX.16.6 : *punānó rūpé avyáye víśvā árṣann abhí śríyaḥ |*
śū́ro ná góṣu tiṣṭhati ||

"flowing towards all the beauties..."

VIII.72.13 : *á suté siñcata śríyam ródasyor abhiśríyam |*
rasā́ dadhīta vṛṣabhám ||

"Pour into Soma that which beautifies him..."[175]

A few times *abhiśrī́*[176] occurs. However, perhaps it should not be understood in the same sense as *śrī́* but, as derived from the root *abhi-śrī́*,[177] as an admixture. Nevertheless, this etymology can also be deceptive because *abhiśrī́* is used several times in such a way that it supports the assumption that it is only an intensification of *śrī́*.[178]

A third word is *rūpá*, employed in the same sense as *nirṇíj* and *śrī́* in so far as it does not refer to the various forms of the admixtures.

IX.25.4 : *víśvā rūpā́ṇy āviśán punānó yāti haryatáḥ |*

"Entering all the beauties, purifying himself, the desirable one moves forth." 34.4 : *sáṃ rūpaír ajyate háriḥ*;[179] 64.8; 111.1. Therefore, it is said in IX.81.1 that the richly adorned (*supéśas*) Somas enter into Indra's body.

Furthermore, there is also *sū́da*, since Pischel's discussion of this word (VSt I.73) is mainly correct.

Another general expression is *práyas*. In individual cases like II.19.1 it denotes Soma itself, in others the offerings that accompany the libation of Soma as in III.30.1 : *sunvánti sómaṃ dádhati práyāṅsi*,[180] or X.42.5 : *yó asmai tīvrā́n sómān āsunóti práyasvān*. Therefore the Veda speaks of him as *sóma práyasvat* (eg., IX.46.3; 66.23).

In the following passages probably *nábhas* also has the general meaning of admixture.

IX.83.5 : *nábho vásānaḥ pári yāsy adhvarám |*
97.21 : *pári srava nábho árṇaś camū́ṣu |*[181]
69.5 : *upastáraṇaṃ camvòr nabhasmáyam ||*
71.3 : *...pavate gábhastyor | vṛṣāyáte nábhasā...*

1. Mixing with Water

The ritual makes a distinction between the Vasatīvarī and the Ekadhanā waters. The former should be collected as far as possible from a river that breaks through a mountain. One should do this when the sun is hidden by a cloud, or at least in the shadow of one's person or of a tree or of a hill. If the sun sets before the waters are collected, one should, after making some offerings to the sun, hold a fire brand over the vessel, put a piece of gold in it and then fill it. Water from the vat of a brahmin also serves the purpose if that brahmin had already performed the Soma sacrifice.[182]

These Vasatīvarīs are meant for pouring over the Soma plant.[183] They are divided into three parts for the three Savanas.[184] Before the preliminary pressing begins, the Hotṛcamasa is filled with these Vasatīvarīs.[185] The waters in the Hotṛcamasa, employed for soaking the plants, are called Nigrābhyās.

The second variety, the Ekadhanās,[186] are collected early in the morning[187] (of course, before the pressing of Soma) from flowing water at such a distance from the sacrificial place that one can still hear the voice of the Hotṛ reciting. One fills three or more vessels and also the Maitrāvaruṇacamasa[188] with the words, "I take you, the juice, for the Soma of the Mūjavat."

These Ekadhanās serve exclusively the purpose of diluting the Soma and are added to the juice itself.[189] That is to say, these waters are needed to fill the Ādhavanīya pail. Thus it is said, for instance, in ĀpŚS XII.16.11 : "According to the need[190] he pours from the Ekadhanās — besides these, all the water in the Maitrāvaruṇacamasa — in the Ādhavanīya. Then he pours the Soma which is in the Ādhavanīya and is mixed with water partly[191] into the Pūtabhṛt, having spread the woollen strainer over it previously."

It is not possible to trace all these details of the ritual back to the ṚV. But in X.30 we have a hymn which is recited at the time of fetching the water and which, according to its content, has been composed for this very purpose. See, for instance, the wording of the third verse : "Go to the samudra for waters. Worship the son of the waters with havis. May he give you a pure way now. Press sweet Soma for him." Therefore, it is to be assumed that already in the ṚV the activity of drawing water took place in a ceremonial way. It has been mentioned earlier that the custom of Āpyāyana was probably known to the ṚV also, although it was not employed as regularly as in the later period. On the other hand, our texts leave no doubt about the dilution of the juice with water. There are quite a number of verses in which a procedure similar to that of the later period, namely rinsing and squeezing the Soma stalks in a vessel filled with water, or pouring the Soma juice in a water pail, is anticipated. As examples I quote the following.

IX.30.5 : *apsú tvā́ mádhumattamaṃ haríṃ hinvanty ádribhiḥ* /

53.4 : *táṃ hinvanti madacyutaṃ hariṃ nadī́ṣu vājínam* /

86.8 : *rā́jā samudráṃ nadyò ví gāhate*
apā́m ūrmíṃ sacate síndhuṣu śritáḥ /

86.25 : *apā́m upásthe ádhy āyávaḥ kávim*
ṛtásya yónā mahiṣā́ aheṣata /

96.19 : *apā́m ūrmíṃ sácamānaḥ samudrám* etc.[192]

The Soma drops dissolve on the surface of the water. IX.21.3 : *síndhor ūrmā́ vy àkṣaran*; 12.3; 39.4. They spread a bright glimmer in the water.[193]

In many cases mythological allusions come into play. The king who dives into the streams in IX.86.8 is the god Soma in heaven as well as the terrestrial drink, which indeed is a part of the former. The same is the case in IX.68.6.

A frequent expression that characterizes the act of rinsing and squeezing is *mṛj*. Actually this expression is ambiguous.[194] According to the context it could refer equally to the pressing[195] as well as to the purification or to the squeezing in water of the Soma stalks that have already been pounded. Examples for the latter are to be found in IX.2.5 *samudró apsú māmṛje*; 63.17 : *tám ī mṛjanty āyávo hárim nadī́ṣu vājínam* etc.[196] Here *mṛj* has roughly the same meaning as in IX.98.6 :

dvír yáṃ páñca sváyaśasaṃ svásāro ádrisaṃhatam /
priyám índrasya kā́myam prasnā́payanty ūrmíṇam//[197]

The causative of *pra-snā* denotes clearly an act which follows the pressing and which certainly corresponds to the one that takes place in the Ādhavanīya of the later ritual. The same is the case in

IX.79.4 : *ádrayas tvā bapsati gór ádhi tvací*
apsú tvā hástair duduhur manīṣíṇaḥ //

"The stones chew you on the cowhide; with their hands the wise men milked you into the water."

In the same sense we should understand

IX.97.57 : *hinvánti dhī́rā daśabhiḥ kṣípābhiḥ*
sám añjate rūpám apā́ṃ rásena //

"The wise men send him forth with ten fingers and decorate his form with the juice of the waters."

Besides *mṛj*, the verb *dhāv* also occurs in the same meaning. Thus in the oft-quoted verse,

VIII.1.17 : *sótā hí sómam ádribhiḥ ém enam apsú dhāvata |*
gavyā́ vástreva vāsáyanta ín nára ḥ
nír dhukṣan vakṣáṇābhyaḥ ||

The sequence of *su* and *ā-dhāv* here is not accidental. It occurs exactly in the same way again in VII.32.6; VIII.31.5; AV VI. 2.1[198] and makes it clear that the Ādhavana must follow the Savana, that is to say, it must correspond to the procedure of the later ritual. At the same time the first of the verses mentioned here, VIII.1.17, suggests by connecting *ā́ dhāvata* with *apsú* that here it cannot mean purifying the Soma since this takes place on the Pavitra, on the *ávyo vā́rāṇi.* The PW has explained *ā-dhāv* quite correctly.

dhūtá does not belong to the same category because in two out of the three passages it can be seen from the sequence of the words that the activity expressed by the word *dhūtá*, unlike *ā-dhāv*, must have preceded the pressing.

VIII.2.2 : *nṛ́bhir dhūtáḥ sutó áśnaiḥ |*
ávyo vā́raiḥ paripūtáḥ ||

Here we see that before Soma is pressed by the stones and purified by the wool it is *nṛ́bhir dhūtā́ḥ.* Similarly

IX.62.5 : *śubhrám ándho devávātam apsú dhūtó nṛ́bhiḥ sutáḥ |*
svádanti gā́vaḥ páyobhiḥ ||

The same sequence is maintained in X.104.2 also, though it is not very pertinent in this case.[199] It can therefore be assumed that this *dhūtá* refers to the Āpyāyana discussed earlier.[200] See verse IX.74.9 above (p. 292).

In spite of those passages cited above (pp. 300, 303), the waters do not belong to the *āśiras* proper. As we have said on p. 300, the Veda counts among them only sweet milk, curd and barley : *gávāśir, dádhyāśir, yávāśir.*[201]

Such admixtures are well known to the ritual. This is evident, for instance, from the Praiṣas, which are employed in the morning, at noon, and in the evening during the offering of the Grahas for Indra and which read, according to Āpastamba, as follows.

ĀpŚS XII.23.4 : *prātaḥ prātaḥsāvasya śukravato manthivato madhuścuta indrāya somān prasthitān preṣya;*

XIII.4.14 : *mādhyandinasya savanasya niṣkevalyasya bhāgasya śukravato manthivato madhuścuta indrāya somān...*

and XIII.12.2 : *tṛtīyasya savanasyarbhumato vibhumato*

vājavataḥ savitṛvato bṛhaspativato viśvadevyāvatas tīvrāñ āśīrvata indrāya somān...

According to these formulas, there is a clear distinction between the first two pressings and the third one in so far as in the morning and at noon the Somas are used with *śukra* and *manthin* whereas in the evening they are called only *tīvrāḥ* and *āśīrvantaḥ*. According to Āpastamba's ritual, the offerings for Indra are mixed with *āśiras* in the evening only. This is also attested by some passages of other texts. For example, ŚBr IV.3.3.19 states : "These two Savanas, the morning Savana and the noon Savana, are rich in pure Soma, rich in juice; but the third Savana is devoid of it."

2. Mixing with Milk

Different varieties of milk are used in the ritual. In the very detailed rules of the ĀpŚS the relavant injunctions read as follows.

XI.21.8 : *yā yajamānasya vratadhuk tasyā āśiraṃ kuruta ! yā patniyai tasyai dadhigrahāya ! yā gharmadhuk tasyai dadhigharmāya ! taptam anātaktaṃ maitrāvaruṇāya ! śṛtātaṅkyaṃ dadhi kurutādityagrahāya !*

"From the cow which supplies the milk for the vrata of the sacrificer make the āśir;[202] from the cow for the wife the milk for the Dadhigraha; from that which gives the milk for the Pravargya the milk for the Dadhigharma; boiled, uncurdled milk for the Maitrāvaruṇagraha; prepare curdled milk in boiled milk for the Ādityagraha."

Here we find milk being used in many different ways — sweet and sour, offered alone or mixed with Soma. As far as I can see, according to Āpastamba, sweet milk is usually added only to the Maitrāvaruṇagraha in the ritual;[203] on the other hand, if substitutes for the Soma plant are employed, sweet and raw milk is added to all the Grahas in the morning, boiled milk at noon, curd with or without the addition of butter in the evening.[204] It is not my intention to go into the minute details more closely and to discuss their differences; for us this has no value because in the ṚV differentiation in such a detailed manner does not seem to have taken place[205] and sweet milk must have been added in much greater quantities to Soma. Nowhere is it stated whether this was done to improve the taste of Soma or to lessen what was probably a strong effect of the drink. At one place the ŚBr tells us that Indra complained that Soma did not agree with him whereupon it was mixed with boiled milk.[206] Another verse ṚV (VIII.2.3, p. 299) states explicitly that like barley Soma is sweetened with milk.

Earlier (pp. 280f., 288f.) we have given a number of examples to show that Soma is mixed with milk. It is sufficient to refer to these as well as those collected by Ludwig.[207] From one passage — IX.91.3 : *pávamāno rúśad īrte páyo góḥ*, "he excites the milk of the cow" — it seems to follow that milk begins to ferment when it is mixed with Soma. Nevertheless this verse can also be explained differently.

This custom goes back to very ancient times; it is not merely a Vedic custom but Iranian as well. *Yasna* 10.13 states : *yasə tē bāδa haoma zāire gava iristahe baxšaiti*, "he who drinks of you, O golden Haoma, after you have been mixed with milk." Geldner cites a passage from the *Nīrangistān*[208] which says : *āaṭ raēθwiškarahe yaṭ haoməm ča gava raēθwayāṭ baxšayāaṭ ča*, "and the duty of Rawəθiṣkara is that he mixes Haoma with milk and gives it for drinking." Hence I think that *gaoma* in *Yasna* 10.13 should be translated not as "milky" but directly as "mixed with milk." The formula *haoma yō gava* also belongs in this context; it has been discussed by Caland and de Harlez; howsoever one might interpret it, it refers nevertheless to the mixing of Haoma with milk.[209]

Different from *go* is curd, *dadhi*. In the ritual it is used alone in the Dadhigraha offered during the morning pressing as well as in the Dadhigharma[210] offered additionally during the Soma sacrifices at noon. Thus it is connected with the Soma sacrifice in a loose form like the Pravargya ceremony.[211]

The ṚV knows the Dadhigharma as well as mixing Soma with curd. Familiarity with the former is attested by hymn X.179, which is recited in fact during the Dadhigharma ceremony according to the testimony of ĀpŚS XIII.3.4 and others. From the wording of the third verse — *mādhyandinasya savanasya dadhnaḥ pibendra*, "drink, Indra, of the curd of the noon's libation" — it follows that the Ṛgvedic ritual corresponds to the later custom even in regard to the time of offering. That the Soma juice is also mixed with curd is suggested by some verses like VIII.2.9 : *dadhnā́ mándiṣṭhaḥ śū́rasya,* "with curd [Soma is] most pleasing to the hero."

IX.11.6 : *námased úpa sī́data dadhnéd abhí śrīṇītana* | "Approach him with reverence, mix him with curd," and so on.[212]

I think it is superfluous to enquire at this stage as to which gods receive a share of this mixture.

3. Yavāśir

The ritual mentions, as far as I can see, two occasions on which flour is added to a Graha, namely to the Hāriyojanagraha and to the Manthingraha. A part of the dhānās[213] — the barley grains used in the sacrifice — is husked, mixed with butter and added after the evening pressing to the Graha that is offered to Indra and his horses.[214] One would not go wrong if one rediscovers it in the *pā́traṃ hāriyojanáṃ pūrṇám* of the ṚV.[215]

In all the three pressings the Manthingraha is drawn together with the Śukragraha for the two demons Śaṇḍa and Marka (i.e., death). The rules pertaining to this custom deserve a thorough discussion.

ĀpŚS XII.14.13 : "Reciting the verse ṚV X.123.1,[216] he draws the Śukragraha, adds a piece of gold to it and sets it down with the words : 'This is your womb; protect the manliness.'

14 : "For an enemy [he says] : 'You are drawn; [I take] you for Śaṇḍa.'

15 : "When he hears the verse ṚV V.44.1,[216a] he draws the Manthingraha, recites ṚV X.61.3 and mixes barley flour to the Graha without dropping the flour on himself or on the other Grahas.

16 : "He sets it down with the words : 'This is your womb; protect the progeny.'

15.1 : "For an enemy [he says] : "You are drawn; [I take] you for Marka.' "[216b]

Śaṇḍa and Marka, for whom the two Grahas are drawn, are considered to be the priests of the Asuras.[216c] ŚBr IV.2.1.6 narrates thus : "The gods said : 'See to it that we drive away the two.' They said : 'Let us draw two Grahas for them; they will come down to us, and we shall seize them and drive them away.' They drew the Grahas for the two...therefore, they (Grahas) are drawn nominally for Śaṇḍa and Marka, but are offered to the gods."

Actually these two Grahas are not offered to Śaṇḍa and Marka, but to Indra.[217] That is why Yājñavalkya asks if these should not be drawn rather for the gods themselves.[218]

The formulas of exorcism connected with the offering of these Grahas[219] indicate that originally the demons or gods of hostile cults or tribes must have found somehow a place in this rite. The MS says that one who wants to exorcize should let the Manthin cup precede the other.[220] ĀpŚS XII.23.12 says that the Manthin cup brings disease, and the commentary adds that it should not be brought close to a Tānūnaptrin.

marka is the same as Avestan *mahrka* and denotes "death." The employment of this word in the place of the usual *mṛtyu* also suggests that extraneous influences have not been absent in the evolution of the Vedic ritual.[221]

The offering of the Śukragraha and the Manthingraha is known to the ritual of the ṚV also. This is evident from

III.32.2 : *gávāśiraṃ manthínam indra śukráṃ pibā́ somam*

and still more clearly from

IX.46.4 : *ā́ dhāvatā suhastyaḥ śukrā́ gṛbhṇīta manthínā |*
góbhiḥ śrīṇīta matsarám...

Here the connection between the two words through the dual indicates that their intimate relation can be traced back even to the time of the ṚV. In both cases Indra is the presiding deity.[222] It is not certain if these two Grahas are drawn nominally for a demon in the ṚV also as in the later ritual. However, we find a *gṛ́dhra* mentioned in V.77.1 who, according to the content of the passage, must have had a place in the Ṛgvedic sacrifice just like Śaṇḍāmarkau.

V.77.1 : *prātaryā́vāṇā prathamā́ yajadhvam*
purā́ gṛ́dhrād áraruṣaḥ pibātaḥ ||

"First worship the two who come in the morning (the Aśvins). May they drink before the niggardly vulture."

While discussing this passage, Ludwig[223] at first thought of the two demons of the Śrauta Sūtra, but later discarded the idea. I think that these two, as a matter of fact, have the same position as the *gṛ́dhra* of the ṚV. I am supported in this view by the fact that according to the testimony of this verse the Aśvins drink before the *gṛ́dhra*. Precisely in the same way, in the ritual of some Yajus schools[224] also the Aśvins — as the last pair of gods — drink before Śaṇḍa and Marka.

The *gṛdhra* of the ṚV corresponds to Marka. The TĀr[225] contains a verse, which is to be recited at the call of an inauspicious bird :

ásṛṅmukho rudhiréṇābhyaktaḥ[226]
yamásya dūtáḥ śvápād ví dhāvasi /
gṛdhraḥ suparṇáḥ kuṇápaṃ ní ṣevase
yamásya dūtáḥ prahito bhavásya cobháyoḥ //

"[You have a] bloody face; [you are] anointed with blood. As the messenger of Yama, you run around tearing. [You are an] eagle; [yet you] enjoy carrion. [You are] sent as messenger of both Yama and Bhava." Similarly the *gṛdhra* of the ṚV is probably a bird of death, an inauspicious bird which might have been regarded as the messenger of Yama. The *gṛdhra* (as *yamásya dūtá*) corresponds almost exactly to the demon Marka of the Śrauta ritual.

Certain remarks of our sources take us still further. The two Grahas are called the two eyes.[227] The ŚBr as well as the MS state in so many words that the Śukra is the sun and the Manthin the moon. This is not a fanciful interpretation by the Brāhmaṇa texts, but in the mantras connected with the Grahas an allusion to the "radiance" of these "eyes" — based certainly on the same outlook — can be seen.[228] For the priest says to the Śukra : "Uniting himself with heaven and earth, the brilliant one (*śukra*) [shines] with brilliant (*śukra*) radiance;" and to the Manthin : "Uniting himself with heaven and earth, the Manthin [shines] with mixed (*manthin*) radiance." The mystic significance of the first Graha can be recognized further from the fact that a piece of gold is added to the cup of pure Soma as we have mentioned earlier. The meaning of the name Śaṇḍa itself is obscure.

However, from the fact that "Marka" is connected with the Manthin, we can easily guess the reason why the Manthin with its "manthin-radiance" was conceived in association with the moon; for the moon is the abode of the Manes. This is slightly reflected in the myth of Yava being created from a tear of Soma, which the ŚBr[229] invents in order to justify the mixing of Soma with Yava : "He mixes it with Saktus...Varuṇa once struck king Soma in the eye, and it swelled. Therefrom a horse arose... A tear fell down from this [eye]. Barley grew from this [tear]... Thus whatever was destroyed of the eye he made whole again."[230]

If this interpretation based on some statements of the

Brāhmaṇas is correct, then we have in the middle of the Soma sacrifice the offering of libations to the sun and the moon, which through its use of the names suggests that it is an accretion, that it originated outside the Brahmanical ritual proper, but has been given a Brahmanical colouring through the very early substitution of Indra for Śaṇḍa-Marka.

Whether flour was added to the Manthingraha at the time of the ṚV also cannot be deduced from the ṚV. But the mixing of Soma with flour is known to the ṚV. This can be seen from two passages, viz.,

VIII.92.4 : *ápād u śipry ándhasaḥ índor índro yávāśiraḥ*[231]*...*//
IX.68.4 : *aṅśúr yávena pipiśe yató nṛ̥bhiḥ*
sáṃ jāmíbhir násate rákṣate śíraḥ //[232]

Yava enjoys a high reputation. In AV VIII.7.20 it is mentioned along with Vrīhi, Aśvattha and Soma; Yava and Vrīhi together are stated to be *bheṣajaú divás putrā́v ámartyau.* In AV IX.1.22 Brāhmaṇa, Rājan, Dhenu, Anaḍvaḥ, Vrīhi, Yava and Madhu occur together. Furthermore, it should be mentioned that in AV II.8.3 Yava is said to be *babhrú árjunakāṇḍa,* that is to say, it has the same colour as the Soma plant.

In the *Avesta* also Haoma is mixed with the fruits of another plant, the so-called *haδānaēpātā.*[223] This is explained as the "pomegranate."[234]

4. Admixture of Butter[235]

As far as I know, this occurs very rarely. The vessels were smeared with butter or filled partly with it. We have *dróṇāni ghṛtávānti* IX.96.13; *yóni ghṛtávat* 82.1. Hence it is said of the Soma flowing into the vessels in IX.82.2 : *ghṛtáṃ vásānaḥ pári yāsi nirṇíjam,* that he clothes himself with butter; X.29.6 : *várāya te ghṛtavántaḥ sutāsaḥ.*[236]

5. Food Offered with the Soma Drink

Among the sacrificial foods, the Puroḍāśas or Carus, made of grains, play a greater role. These are offered along with Soma and formed already in the ṚV an integral part of the Soma sacrifice. The MS[237] offers a practical reason for such additional foods. It states that these are necessary "for holding the Soma drink." The great quantities of Soma that were consumed make the desire for a somewhat more substantial food appear quite understandable.

We learn from the Viśvāmitra hymn, III.52, what the custom of this family during the sacrifices was. This hymn is composed of different metres. Verses 1-4 are in Gāyatrī metre; vv. 5, 7, 8 in Triṣṭubh and v. 6 in Jagatī. The first group deals with the morning pressing, v. 5 with the noon pressing and v. 6 with the evening pressing. The metres are chosen exactly in conformity with the rules of the Brāhmaṇas, which prescribe the series with eight syllables for the morning sacrifice and those with eleven syllables for the noon sacrifice.

Now vv. 1, 5, 6 are the **Puronuvākyā** verses to be recited during the cake-offerings of the three Savanas. They show that in the ritual of the Viśvāmitras the three pressings are differentiated through the fact that in the morning, besides Puroḍāś and Dhānās, a Karambha and an Apūpa was offered, whereas at noon only Dhānās and Puroḍāś were offered. This is not important in itself, but it shows that already at the time of the ṚV there were detailed rules. It is twice stressed in the ṚV that the correct way of worshipping Indra is to press Soma, to bake and to fry grains; pressing and baking are often mentioned together.[238] Indra accepts the cakes of only those who press Soma.[239] In X.28.1 eating the Dhānās and drinking Soma are on the same footing. Pakti is rarer than Puroḍāś and was probably not identical with it. For both occur side by side, for instance, in VS XXI.59 etc., in the expression *pácan paktī́ḥ pácan puroḍā́śān*; similarly in

ṚV IV.24.5 : *ā́d ít paktī́ḥ puroḍā́śaṃ riricyāt /*
ā́d ít sóma ví papṛcyād ásuṣvīn...//

"Then let Pakti leave Puroḍāś behind,[240] let Soma exclude those who do not press."

How detailed the rules of the Ṛgvedic period are can be seen from the following fact. The Savanīya Puroḍāś, the cake-offerings belonging to the pressing, end always with an offering to Agni Sviṣṭakṛt.[241] These are accompanied by the first, fourth and fifth verses of hymn III.28, which correspond to the three Savanas completely with regard to their content as well as to the changing metre, and thus prove that this offering to Agni Sviṣṭakṛt at the end of the Savanīya Puroḍāś is an ancient custom.

Apart from the cakes, there are other offerings which accompany Soma. To these belong Dhānās for Indra Harivat, a Karambha for Indra Pūṣaṇvat, a Payasyā for Mitra-Varuṇa and a Parivāpa for Sarasvatī Bhāratī.[242] By and large, these are also known to the ṚV. The Dhānās for Indra Harivat, or the feeding of Indra's horses and the Karambha for Pūṣan are mentioned at various places. We may refer to

III.35.7 : *stīrṇáṃ te barhíḥ sutá indra sómaḥ*
kṛtā́ dhānā́ áttave te háribhyām /

"The barhis is strewn for you, O Indra, pressed is Soma, prepared are the Dhānās for your horses to feed on."

Indra also receives a share of the Dhānās. III.35.3: *divédive sadṛ́śīr addhi dhānā́ḥ*; III.43.4; I.16.2.

Also III.52.7 : *pūṣaṇváte te cakṛmā karambhám*
hárivate háryaśvāya dhānā́ḥ /
apūpám addhi ságaṇo marúdbhiḥ sómaṃ piba...

"We have prepared gruel[243] for you in league with Pūṣan, Dhānās for you, the lord of bay horses in league with the Haris; eat a cake with the Maruts, drink Soma" etc.

Furthermore III.52.1; VI.57.2; TS III.1.10[d]; MS III.10.6 (137.16); VS XIX.21 etc.

In the ṚV, the Karambha appears only during the morning libation and it is only in the later period that this is offered at other times of the day. The cake for Indra Marutvat has probably been replaced by the Parivāpa for Sarasvatī. I cannot establish a Payasyā for Mitra-Varuṇa. But twice they are called *ghṛtā́suti*, and also *ghṛtánna*.

That the *Avesta* knows side-dishes for the Haoma drink, which were known under the name Draona and consisted partly of pieces of meat,[244] is disputed by Bartholomae in the *Altiranisches Wörterbuch*.

6. Soma Tīvra

tīvrá is an epithet that occurs more frequently. The general meaning "sharp, stinging" does not suffice to give a clear idea of what the word means.

In the ritual there is a *tīvrasava* offered by one who wishes to become *tīvra*, "outstanding," in progeny, cattle etc. A previous section of this study (p. 153) gave us the occasion to show that *tīvrānta* meant "pointed at the ends" in contradistinction to *bahuramadhya*, "thick in the middle." Hence *tīvrasút* in ṚV VI.43.2 should probably be understood in the same way.[245] Here the contrast between this word on the one hand and the *mádhya* and *ánta* on the other is so clear that, in my opinion, the last two words should be construed as *madhyasuta* and *antasuta* respectively : the Soma juice in the stalks, i.e., at the top, in the middle and at the bottom. My interpretation would become all the more probable when we consider that the word *tīvrasút* occurs in the verse cited in the ŚŚS, to be recited during this very *tīvrasava*.[246]

But we cannot apply the meaning "pointed" everywhere. Often it has a figurative sense. We find in ṚV VI.75.7 *tīvrā́s ghóṣās* "loud noise," X.72.6 *tīvró reṇús* "thick dust," VS XXIX.39 *tīvrā́s samádas* "voilent fights." It is attributed to liquids also. *ghṛtáṃ tīvráṃ juhotana* V.5.1; the waters are called *tīvrā́ aruṇā́ lóhinīs tāmradhūmrā́ḥ* in AV X.2.11.

Just as the meaning of *tiktá*, a word from the same root, changed from "bitter" to "fragrant"[247] so also in the case of *tīvrá* we should assume a similar evolution from the original meaning of "pointed, sharp."

What then does the *tīvrá sóma* mean ? In the formulas for the Indragraha, cited on p. 304 f. only those cups that are offered in the evening carry the epithets *tīvrá* and *āśī́rvat*. The others are filled with pure Soma. Now we see that in the ṚV also *tīvrá* occurs often along with *āśír* or similar other expressions.

I.23.1 : *tīvrā́ḥ sómāsa ā́ gahi āśī́rvantaḥ sutā́ imé |*
vā́yo tā́n prásthitān piba ||

VIII.2.10 : *imé ta indra sómās tīvrā́ asme sutā́saḥ |*
śukrā́ āśíraṃ yācante ||

Instead of *āśír* there is *práyas* in

X.42.5 : *yo asmai tīvrā́n sómāñ āsunóti práyasvān*[248]

or *rása* in

VI.47.1 : *svādúṣ kílāyáṃ mádhumāñ utā́yám*
tīvráḥ kílāyáṃ rásavāñ utā́yám |

or more specifically *go* in

V.37.4 : *tīvráṃ sómaṃ píbati gósakhāyam*

or *abhívayas* in

X.160.1 : *tīvrásyābhívayasa asyá pāhi*
sarvarathā́ ví hárī ihá muñca.

As Sāyaṇa[249] has noted on this verse, *abhívayas* is probably derived from *vayas* "food," and means as much as *práyasvat*.

Just as *go* accompanies *tīvra* in one passage so does *mádhu*, "honey," in several passages — we shall discuss the use of honey in the Soma sacrifices later on.

IX.17.8 : *mádhor dhā́rām ánu kṣara tīvrā́ḥ sadhástham ā́sadaḥ* /

II.41.14 : *tīvró vo mádhumān̐ ayáṃ śunáhotreṣu matsaráḥ* /[250]

From the verse in ĀśvŚS VI.5.24 : *ime somāsas tiroahnyāsas tīvrās tiṣṭhanti* also a similar conclusion can be drawn about *tīvrá,* since this verse is recited during the Āśvinagraha which is connected with a cake-offering according to sūtra 23.

In two further passages of the ṚV[251] *tīvrá* occurs as an epithet of the Soma of the evening offering, that is to say, of that very Savana in which the Soma is *tīvrá* and *āśī́rvat* according to the formulas mentioned above. Thus we have once again a full agreement between the Vedic ritual and that of the later period.

Hence, we may conclude that *tīvrá* is a quality of the Soma juice produced by the admixture or addition of other things like milk, honey and cakes — roughly "piquant, astringent."

In order to determine the meaning more precisely we may refer to several other passages of the Vedic literature. *Tāṇḍya Mahā Brāhmaṇa* XVIII.5.12 : *śatam āśiraṃ duhanti tīvrayanty evainam.* Mahīdhara explains this word in VS XIX.1, where Soma and Surā are called *tīvra,* as *kaṭuvacana* and adds that the *surā tīvrā* is "quickly intoxicating."[252] ŚBr II.4.4.16 states as follows : *atha yad pūrvedyur agnīṣomīyeṇa yajate paurṇamāsyām abhiṣuṇoty evainam etat, tasminn abhiṣuta etaṃ rasaṃ dadhāty, etena rasena tīvrīkaroti / svadayati ha vai devebhyo havyam* etc. and XII.7.3.5 : *tīvrāṃ tīvreṇetīndriyam evāsmin dadhāti.*[253] Thus these testimonies can corroborate the outcome of our study based on the ṚV, that *tīvrá* must denote "astringent, seasoned" when it is applied to the Soma juice. This meaning is suitable for *ghṛta* and *āpas* also. Hence *tīvrá* seems to have the following meanings :

1. sharp, pointed
2. powerful (*reṇu, ghoṣa* etc.); seasoned, astringent (Soma juice with admixtures).

7. Ṛjīṣa, Ṛjīṣin

In the Brāhmaṇas and the Sūtras, *ṛjīṣá* is a very common word for the Soma stalks that have been completely pressed out, i.e., the husks or residue.[254] This sense of the word extends up to the Saṃhitās of the *Yajurveda* also since the MS says, for instance, at IV.8.5 (112.3) : *átiriktaṃ vā́ etád yajñásya yád ṛjīṣáḥ*;[255] we find it in a prose passage of AV IX.6.16, which however is a late composition.

Now the same word occurs in the ṚV also. Apparently derived from it is *ṛjīṣín*, which is used almost exclusively as an epithet of Indra and the Maruts.

From no verse could I gain the impression that the meaning "rushing forth" — which has been arrived at merely through etymology and has been attributed to the word in the ṚV (in opposition to the later linguistic usage) — is either indicated in that verse or warranted by it. The only verse which might support such a theory is VIII.79.4;[256] but there also the genitives *diváḥ* and *pṛthivyā́ḥ* need not depend on *ṛjīṣín* at all.

Under these circumstances it is hazardous to make a complete departure from the traditional meaning of this word. I think Ludwig (499.1) was more correct when he turned to the native interpretation for verse III.32.1, according to which *ṛjīṣín* means "the enjoyer of the husks." Thus, for example, the commentary on Yāska (III.68.9) says : *ṛjīṣī yadi somo 'bhipretaḥ tasya ṛjīṣitvam upapadyate / athendro 'bhipretaḥ / tasya tayor aśvayor ṛjīṣabhāgā ity anayāpekṣayā ṛjīṣatvam*; ibid. p. 69, last line : *ṛjīṣī* : *vajrī vṛṣabhaḥ* (ṚV V. 40.4)...*ṛjīṣeṇa tadvān ṛjīṣī*. Cf. among others, also TS III.2.2.1. But even this meaning is not sufficient for the ṚV.

In the ṚV, *ṛjīṣá* occurs only once and that too in a context which does not leave any doubt that here it is an adjective.[257] The view of the PW that here it has the same sense as *ṛjīṣín* seems to be justified. However, in interpreting *ṛjīṣín* itself I differ from these authorities for reasons given just now. On the other hand, the meaning "equipped with husks" is too narrow for the ṚV since Indra is called thus not only during the evening offering, but also in verses which do not refer to the time of the day.[258] Soma himself is called thus in two passages. Therefore, we should attribute to *ṛjīṣá* — which is the basis for *ṛjīṣín* — a meaning like *aṅśú*, "Soma stalk," denoting originally its outer covering as well as the juice contained therein. From this is derived *ṛjīṣín*, "one who possesses the young shoots" or "one to whom they belong." That is why Indra and the Maruts, who particularly have a share in the Soma drink apart from

Vāyu, are called precisely by this word. From this general meaning of *ṛjīṣá* there evolved the specific sense of *śárya*, "skin of the Soma plant" or "husks," that is current in the later period.

8. Soma Tiroahnya

In the ṚV, *tiróahnya* is an epithet of the Puroḍāś offered to Agni sviṣṭakṛt and of the Soma drink. The commentary on the KŚS states very precisely what should be understood by Soma *tiróahnya;* its explanation corresponds to the meaning that can be obtained from the word itself.[259] It is the Soma that has been pressed the day before and is offered during the Āśvinaśastra, according to KŚS XII.6.10; XXIV.3.42 and its commentary, to the Aśvins. This is in conformity with the testimony of the ṚV because in several passages like I.47.10; III.58.7, to which we may add the verse *imé sómāsas tiróahnyāsas* ĀśvŚS VI.5.24; ŚŚS IX.20.31 etc., it is exactly the Aśvins who are invited to the drink of *tiróahnya*; only in I.45.10 the gods in general are invited and in VIII.35.19-21 Uṣas and Sūrya are specially mentioned besides the Aśvins.[260]

G. SOMA, MADHU AND SURĀ

In Indian literature the use of honey during the festive occasions is amply recorded. Manu, for instance, enjoins at III.119 the entertainment of the king, the priest and other guests of honour with a Madhuparka, i.e., a mixed dish consisting of honey and curd. The Gṛhya Sūtras mention it often. On his arrival at the abode of the god of the mountains,[261] Śiva receives milk and honey from the former.[262] The ṚV also knows a drink consisting of milk and honey. In VIII.4.8, a verse addressed to Indra, it is said :

mádhvā sáṃpṛktāḥ sāragheṇa dhénavas
tū́yam éhi drávā píba /

"The milk is mixed with the honey of the bee; come quickly, rush and drink."

According to IX.11.2, it is the custom of the Atharvans to prepare this drink : *abhí té mádhunā páyaḥ átharvāṇo aśiśrayuḥ*, "The Atharvans mixed milk with honey for you."

According to MS IV.9.7 (128); VS XXXVIII.6 etc., a mantra recited during the Pravargya ceremony runs as follows : *indrāśvinā madhunaḥ sāraghasva gharmaṃ pāta.*[263]

In the *Avesta* madhu occurs rarely. In both passages it means merely honey, as Windischmann has noted.[264] In *Vendidād* 8.22 : *myazdəm gaoməntəm maδumantəm*, milk and honey are mentioned together as in the Indian texts.

The concept of the bees being sacred, or the important role assigned to honey in mythology, is not Indian, nor is it Indo-Iranian; it is even prehistoric according to the testimony of the Greek concepts.[265] Thus the occasional use of honey in the Veda is based on an ancient tradition, which was incorporated into the ritual but which gradually yielded its place to the Soma cult.

1. The Aśvins and Honey

There is one point that we should consider at first. It is obvious that among all the gods the Aśvins must have been the foremost to be connected with the Madhu cult. In I.117.6 it is they who pour out hundred pots of madhu.[266] The *madhukaśā*, the honey goad, belongs to them exclusively; their chariot alone is called *mádhuvarṇa* and *mádhuvāhana*; they are called *madhūyu*, *madhupā́*, *mādhvī*, but never *somapā́* although Soma is offered to them also. In a large number of passages, eg., I.180.1, 2; 182.2; 183.4cd; III.58.4; X.40.6; 41.3, the word *mádhu* is connected precisely with them. The Adhvaryu to whom they are invited to come in X.41.3 is called *mádhupāṇi* there. We may conclude from this that even though *mádhu* has already acquired in many passages of the ṚV the general sense of "sweet liquid," attributed also to Payas, Ghṛta and Soma, yet at several places, particularly where the Aśvins are referred to, it must still mean honey, or at least the drink the important constituent of which was honey. The Aśvins bestow honey on the bees.

I.112.21 : *mádhu priyáṃ bharatho yát sarádbhyaḥ*
"as you brought the sweet honey to the bees,"
or X.40.6 : *yuvór ha mákṣā páry aśvinā mádhu*
āsā́ bharata niṣkṛtáṃ ná yóṣaṇā //
"The bee[267] has carried in its mouth the honey from you [to its hive] like a woman going to her tryst [with her mouth full of honey]."[268] The Aśvins themselves are compared to the bees in
X.106.10 : *āraṅgaréva mádhv érayethe*
sāraghéva gávi nīcīnabāre /
"Like two bees you create honey in the udder of the cow."[269]

They are requested to anoint the singer with honey so that he could speak happily in front of men.[270] Therefore, even in those passages where the bee is not specially mentioned, *mádhu* in association with the Aśvins must have meant originally "honey" and only later, when the Aśvins had been included in the Soma cult, it must have been employed in a wider sense to denote the Soma drink. Several statements of the Vedic literature support the assumption that the Aśvins were admitted very late into the circle of those gods who were worshipped with the Soma drink. MS IV.6.1 (79.20) states that the Aśvins were the healers of the gods and that they did not have a share in the Soma.[271] Asked by the gods to heal the sacrifice, they did so under the condition that they should be allowed to partake in the Soma drink. This legend is certainly not without significance because the well known legend of the ŚBr about Cyavana and the Aśvins deals with the same motif, and it does so in such an individualistic way that one is struck by the underlying idea that these Aśvins were originally non-Brahmanical gods, who were taken into the cult later. As a matter of fact, on the advice of Cyavana, Sukanyā tells the Aśvins : "You are neither quite complete, nor quite perfect." It is said that the gods performed a sacrifice in Kurukṣetra and excluded the Aśvins from it. The Aśvins implored the gods, but the latter refused them admission because as healers the Aśvins moved much among men.[272]

There is another factor which points to the same direction. Apart from the bee, the donkey is the animal of the Aśvins, e.g., ṚV VIII.85.7. In the running race held in honour of Sūryā, the Aśvins become the winners in their chariot drawn by donkeys.[273] But the donkey is an inferior animal. In PGS III.15 the donkey is addressed as *śūdro 'si śūdrajanmā* — this fact also leads us to the assumption that the Aśvins were the gods of a lower stratum of people and that too of non-Brahmanical people.[274]

2. Honey in the Śrauta Ritual

The use of honey is very rare in the Śrauta ritual. Honey has a place in the Vājapeya sacrifice, where a Madhugraha is drawn in a golden bowl, after the Surāgrahas and the Somagrahas have been filled.[275] Kātyāyana gives the following rules on this Madhugraha.

KŚS XIV.4.15 : "The Adhvaryu and the sacrificer give the Madhugraha to [a Rājanya or a Vaiśya] who sits on the northern śroṇī of the vedi to receive the Surāgrahas.

16 : "The Neṣṭṛ takes the Surāgrahas through the back door of the Havirdhāna, carries them forth behind the hut and gives one [to that Rājanya or Vaiśya as the case may be] with the words : 'with this I buy [the Madhugraha] from you.' [Thereupon he gives him all the Surāgrahas and takes the Madhugraha.]

17 : "He gives the Madhugraha along with the vessel to the Brahman.

18 : "The latter does whatever he pleases with it," (i.e., according to the commentary, he either gives it away, or pours it elsewhere, or drinks it).

This mode of employment of the Madhugraha — described in the ŚBr also in a similar way — is quite peculiar; it is not offered to any deity, and even otherwise it does not serve any apparent purpose. We get the impression as if the Śrotriyas did not know any more what to do with it, but retained it all the same at this place because it was an old custom.

The fact that the vessel used for this had to be of gold leads us to an assumption with regard to its original significance.

We have seen on p. 290 that the ṚV also knows a golden vessel used at the Soma sacrifice — the *kóśa hiraṇyáya* which is also called *yóni hiraṇyáya* or *áyohata*. At the same place it has been established that *madhuścút* is an epithet frequently attributed to *kóśa*. In the light of the present discussion we can translate *madhuścút* as "dripping of honey." It is likely that there is an innate connection between this *kóśa madhuścút, hiraṇyáya* and the Madhugraha of the Vājapeya drawn in a golden vessel and that the filling of the Madhugraha during the Vājapeya is based on an old custom which is not understood correctly any more. The purpose of *kóśa madhuścút* becomes clear when we consider that it is the Soma juice which flows into it.

E.g. IX.103.3 : *pári kóśaṃ madhuścútam avyáye vā́re arṣati* / In other words, this *kóśa* was used in the ritual of the ṚV for mixing Soma with honey.

Having established this, we can interpret easily some other verses as referring to the mixing of Soma and Madhu, e.g.,

IX.17.8 : *mádhor dhā́rām ánu kṣara tīvráḥ sadhástham ā́sadaḥ* /

86.48 : *ávyo vấre pári dhāva mádhu priyám* /[276]
97.11 : *ádha dhấrayā mádhvā pṛcānás*
tiró róma pavate ádridugdhaḥ /
109.20 : *añjánty enaṃ mádhvo rásena*
índrāya vṝṣṇa índum mádāya //

Therefore, *madhumat soma* did not mean originally "sweet" Soma, but "sweetened" Soma, i.e., Soma mixed with honey. This is what is meant, for example, in II.41.14 where the addition of the epithet *tīvrá* especially points to this.

tīvró vo mádhumāñ ayáṃ śunáhotreṣu matsaráḥ /

"Well seasoned is the [draught] mixed with honey, exhilarating among the Śunahotras."[277]

Thus the word *madhuścut*, used next to *śukravat* and *manthimat* in the above-mentioned Indrapraiṣa formulas, acquires its meaning, although in the actual performance of the sacrifice this meaning does not have a significance any more. Often such formulas are products of a much earlier age, and hence this designation in these formulas has probably its origin in a very ancient custom.

I cannot find any evidence in the later literature for the mixing of Soma with honey; its place is taken by Soma and Surā.

3. Surā[278]

The views of the Vedic texts differ on the merits of Surā. In ṚV VIII.21.14 the poet laments thus :

nákī revantáṃ sakhyấya vindase pī́yante te surāśvàḥ /

"You do not find a rich man for friendship; they talk arrogantly, drunk with Surā." VII.86.6 and VIII.2.12 also speak of the intoxication caused by Surā.

VII.86.6 : *ná sá svó dákṣo varuṇa dhrútiḥ sấ*
surấ manyúr vibhī́dako ácittiḥ /

"[Our sin is] not of our doing, O Varuṇa; it is seduction, Surā, passion, game of dice and infatuation."-

VIII.2.12 : *hṛtsú pītā́so yudhyante durmádāso ná súrāyām* /

"[The draughts of Soma] which have been drunk are fighting within the stomach like those intoxicated with Surā."

In these two verses Surā is regarded as an intoxicating drink, though not yet objectionable. But a disapproval is expressed in VIII.21.14 because the drinkers of Surā are no friends of Indra. On the other hand, there is no dearth of passages which suggest that this drink is held in high esteem — particularly I.116.7 where it is said that the Aśvins caused hundred pots of Surā to stream out of the hoof of a horse. This verse is completely identical with I.117.6 cited earlier, except that *súrāyāḥ* takes the place of *mádhūnām*. From this we may conclude that both the words denote the same thing or similar things. There are two other verses which mention Surā quite favourably.

X.131.4 : *yuvám surā́mam aśvinā námucāv āsuré sácā*
vipipānā́ śubhaspatī́ índram kármasv āvatam //
5 : *putrám iva pitárāv aśvínobhā́*
índrāvathuḥ kā́vyair daṅsánābhiḥ /
yát surā́mam vy ápibaḥ śácībhiḥ
sárasvatī tvā maghavann abhiṣṇak //

surā́ma is — as Garbe,[279] following the example of Roth, has shown, — certainly related to Surā. This is attested also by the fact that these two verses are recited during the Sautrāmaṇī, to be discussed below, on which occasion Surā and Soma are mixed together. The commentary on TBr I.4.2.1 explains *surā́ma* as "prepared with Surā."[280] I think this explanation points in the right direction because this is corroborated by the expressions *surāmṇām somānām pibatu* MS IV.12.5 (191.2) or *somāḥ surāmāṇaḥ* VS XXI.42. *somāḥ surāmāṇaḥ* means as much as *surāsomāḥ*, Somas prepared with Surās, in VS XXI.60.[281] Since our two verses are recited precisely in the Sautrāmaṇī and since they also contain the same gods (i.e., Indra, Sarasvatī, Aśvins) who are worshipped in the Sautrāmaṇī, there is no other way to interpret *surā́ma* but as a derivative of Surā. Therefore I translate these verses as follows :

"When you, O lords of light, had drunk [the draught] prepared with Surā at Asura Namuci, you helped Indra with your deeds.

"As parents help the son, so did you, O Aśvins, both help Indra with your wisdom and marvellous powers. When you drank skilfully [the draught] prepared with Surā, O bountiful one, Sarasvatī healed[282] you."[283]

This vacillation of the ṚV between praise and censure of Surā is continued in the other Vedic texts also. Surā is mentioned repeatedly together with Soma; it is also held in slightly less esteem than Soma; but by no means is it considered despicable all the time. In TBr I.3.3.2 ff. these two are called "husband and wife — Soma is the best food of the gods, Surā the best food of men." In ŚBr XII.7.3.8 it is said : *payaś ca surā ca bhavataḥ / somo vai payo 'nnaṃ surā payasaiva somapītham avarunddhe surayānnādyam.* ŚBr XII.7.3.12 states that both are meant for intoxication : *madāya somaḥ, madāya surā.* AV IV.34.6 mentions *ghṛtahradā madhukūlāḥ surodakāḥ kṣīreṇa pūrṇā udakena* etc. In ṚV X.6.5 *surā, ghṛta* and *madhu* are mentioned together.

Also in the oft narrated legend of Viśvarūpa, the son of Tvaṣṭṛ, who had three mouths — one for drinking Soma, one for drinking Surā and the third for the enjoyment of other foods — Surā is, of course, treated as an inferior drink, but certainly not a despicable one.[284] On the other hand, MS I.11.6 (167.14) states : *śrīr vai somaḥ. pāpmā suropayāmāḥ*; II.4.2 (39.4) : *anṛtaṃ surā* etc. Surā appertains to the Asuras, say MS IV.2.1 (21.16) etc. The rivalry between the two drinks has obviously been judged variously and has never been settled. Where does the rivalry arise from ? We find an offering of Surā and Soma in a great sacrifice, the Vājapeya. *vājapeya* (i.e. *somaḥ*), "the drink of victory," is a festival which, like the Aśvamedha and the Mahāvrata, shows us what a wealth of folkloric customs has been preserved in Indian ritual that embraces all facets of life. The chariot races[285] held on the same occasion with a great pomp make this festival a sort of Olympic games of the ancient Indians. The rules for the Vājapeya sacrifice are found in the ŚBr[286] and in the KŚS.[287] I give below what is relevant here.

KŚS XIV.1.16 enjoins that "one should buy for a piece of lead the Parisrut,[288] or the ingredients required for it[289] from a long-haired man to the south of Soma. While Soma is being conveyed on a cart, he carries the Parisrut, or the ingredients, behind it.

17 : "The Neṣṭṛ enters through the southern door, cooks on the southern fire and brings the Surā to the back part of the hut.

26 : "At the time when the Ekadhanā waters are brought, the Neṣṭṛ fetches the Surā in from behind and puts it on the earth-mound.

27 : "Through a small opening [made to the south of the Havirdhāna] he fetches the Surāgraha vessels and cleans the Surā with a horse's hair in a [big] vessel.

2.3 : "The Adhvaryu draws seventeen Somagrahas.

4 : "and the Neṣṭṛ the same number of Surāgrahas.

5 : "The Grahas are drawn alternately.

6 : "The Grahas should not be carried above the axle of the cart.

7 : "The Adhvaryu holds his Graha high over the axle, the Neṣṭṛ holds his deep below it with the words : 'you are united.'

8 : "They withdraw them again with the words : 'you are separated.' " Thereupon follows the drawing of the honey-graha, which we have discussed earlier.

The injunctions of the ŚBr are somewhat more detailed. I give them below as far as it is necessary to complete the picture.

ŚBr V.1.2.10 : "He draws seventeen Somagrahas and seventeen Surāgrahas. Soma and Surā are the two drinks of Prajāpati. Therefore Soma is truth, excellence, light; Surā is untruth, baseness, darkness.[290] These two drinks (*andhasī*) he wins there.

14 : "To the south of the place where he buys king Soma, he buys for a piece of lead the Parisrut[291] from a long-haired man.[292] A long-haired man is neither man nor woman...Lead is neither iron nor gold. Parisrut is a neither Soma nor Surā. Therefore he buys for a piece of lead the Parisrut from a long-haired man.

15 : "On the preceding day they prepare two earth-mounds, one in front of the axle and other behind it, with the thought : 'we must not deposit the Somagrahas and the Surāgrahas together.'

16 : "When they bring the Vasatīvarī waters inside through the eastern door, the Neṣṭṛ brings the Parisrut in through the opposite door. From the south they bring the vessels in. The Adhvaryu, seated in front of the axle and facing the west, draws the Somagrahas; the Neṣṭṛ, seated behind the axle and facing the east, draws the Surāgrahas. The Adhvaryu draws a Somagraha, the Neṣṭṛ a Surāgraha, the Adhvaryu again a Somagraha and the Neṣṭṛ again a Surāgraha — in this way they draw them alternately.

17 : "The Adhvaryu does not bring the Somagraha westwards beyond the axle, the Neṣṭṛ does not bring the Surāgraha eastwards, thinking : 'lest we should mix light and darkness.'

18 : "The Adhvaryu holds the Somagraha over the axle and the Neṣṭṛ below it with the mantra : 'you are united; unite me

with my happiness' etc. Thinking 'lest we should speak evil' they withdraw the Grahas again and recite the mantra : 'you are separated; separate me from the evil...' " Thereupon follows the Madhugraha.

Thus there exists an unmistakable rivalry between Soma and the Surā. Yet the fact that both of these were admitted into the sacrifice shows that a reconciliation of the differences took place. The injunction that the ingredients for Surā should be bought from a "long-haired" man indicates the direction where we should look for an explanation for these differences. The words "light and darkness" mean as much as Brahmanical and non-Brahmanical. Surā was the drink of the Aryans who did not follow the Brahmanical customs. The strange figure of Neṣṭṛ suggests similarly an accretion from the cult of Barbarian or non-Brahmanical tribes.[293]

The high repute which Surā enjoys, contrary to the normal Brahmanical attitude, is evident most clearly in the Sautrāmaṇī, a festive sacrifice in honour of Indra, through which the Aśvins, who were called by the gods, and Sarasvatī cure Indra who had become ill from the consumption of Soma.[294] It is quite clear that Soma does not have the same significance in this ceremony as elsewhere[295] because this ceremony is not flattering to the worshippers of Soma; on the contrary, it amounts to the triumph of the Surā-worshippers, whose drink cured Indra when he was in distress. That there are many elements in the Sautrāmaṇī which differ from the usual ritual is suggested by Śāṅkhāyana when he says that some authorities are in the habit of changing all the Praiṣas during the Sautrāmaṇī;[296] he adds that it is the practice of the Asuras.

We have seen that the Aśvins caused a hundred pots of Surā or Madhu to flow out of the hoof of a horse. We have also seen that the two verses, X.131.4, 5, containing the word *surā́ma* and recited in the Sautrāmaṇī, are closely connected with Surā. There is further evidence in several Atharva verses which, though not important in themselves, contribute in making the picture complete.

AV IX.1.18-19 : *yád giríṣu párvateṣu góṣv áśveṣu yán mádhu /*
súrāyāṃ sicyámānāyām yát tátra mádhu tán máyi //[297]

"Whatever sweetness is in hills and mountains, in cows and

horses, whatever sweetness is in the Surā that is poured out, may that be in me."

XIV.1.35 : *yác ca várco akṣéṣu súrāyāṃ ca yád áhitam /*
yád gōṣv aśvinā várcas ténemáṃ várcasāvatam //

"Whatever splendour is in the dice, whatever is placed in Surā, whatever splendour, O Aśvins, is in cows, with that help this woman." This almost indiscriminate association of the Aśvins at times with Surā and at others with Madhu makes it likely that both the drinks were of similar nature and that probably Surā also consisted partly of honey.[298]

In order to have a clear idea of the position of the Sautrāmaṇí and Surā in the Indian sacrifice, we should recollect what has been said earlier about the exclusion of the Aśvins from the Soma sacrifice : they are not entitled because they move too much among the human beings; the donkey is their sacred animal and the donkey is "Śūdra by birth." Thus we are led to a stratum of people who were not Brahmanical and to localities where one did not drink Soma but Surā. Surā and Sabhā, Surā and the dice are mentioned more often together.[299] Like the Aśvins, their sacred drink also — be it Surā or Madhu — was probably not recognized by the wise men of Kurukṣetra as fully entitled to respect.

It is worth noting that in the group of sagas connected with Surā and the Aśvins it is not Vṛtra who is regarded as the evil force, but it is primarily Namuci Āsura;[300] of course, there are other demons also like Viśvarūpa, the son of Tvaṣṭṛ, but, if I understand correctly, they are not mentioned so frequently.[301]

We can trace the gradual decline in the reputation of Surā when we study the periods preceding and following the Brāhmaṇas.

At the end of *Vendidād* 14, *hurā* and *maδu* are mentioned as the alms for a pious man. Bartholomae[302] cites from the *Nīrangistān* the words : *dahmō hurąm xvaraiti; maδō aspya-payaŋho*, "the faithful enjoys the hurā; a Madha out of horse's milk."[303] We need only to compare this estimation of Surā with the statement of ṚV I.116.7 that the Aśvins created Surā to see that the latter concept is the older one. In the Brāhmaṇas opinions vary. However, when Brahmanism became supreme the Surā drink was denounced in the strongest possible terms. GDS 23.1 as well as ĀpDS 1.9.25.1 enjoin that hot

Surā should be poured into the mouth of the brahmin who has drunk Surā. If this happened unintentionally, they say, the sinner should drink for three days hot milk, clarified butter and water, and inhale hot air. According to Manu IX.235, the killer of a brahmin, the drinker of Surā, the thief and the one who defiles the marital bed of his teacher are *mahāpātakins*, i.e., people who have committed mortal sins. Yājñavalkya III.207 (and likewise Manu XII.56) makes the prophecy that the Surāpa will be reborn in the womb of a donkey, or as a Caṇḍāla or a Veṇa.[304] We may suppose that the contempt for, and the gradual suppression of, Surā totally coincide with the spread of Brahmanism; Soma-drinker was opposed to Surā-drinker. With the political superiority of the former, the prestige of his national drink also increased.

Therefore, the ceremonies of the Sautrāmaṇī appear all the more strange. The Brahmanical scholiasts attempted to explain it as a Soma sacrifice; but without any success. For the dialogue between two theologians, Suplan Sārñjaya and Pratīdarśa Aibhāvata, only goes to show how difficult it was for them to come to terms with this Sautrāmaṇī which requires Surā. Suplan asks : "How can then the Sautrāmaṇī be a Soma sacrifice when one neither consecrates himself with dīkṣā, nor throws down the Soma shoots ?"[305] The one thus addressed replies : "The Soma shoots at this sacrifice are the young blades of grass, fresh sprouts of corn and parched grain. The form of the morning pressing are the young blades of grass"[306] etc.

How is the acceptance of this Sautrāmaṇī to be explained ? We know that, apart from Indra, the Aśvins and Sarasvatī are associated with the Sautrāmaṇī.[307] These Aśvins, who are regarded as non-Brahmanical because they are the lords of Surā and Madhu, point to a non-Brahmanical land; where we should look for it is indicated by the name of the river : Sarasvatī. In the ŚBr[308] Soma and Surā are repeatedly called the two *andhas*. As we have stated earlier these *andhasī* occur in ṚV VII.96.2, and that too in association with Sarasvatī. No matter whether this was the eastern or western Sarasvatī, contacts must have taken place on its banks between the Indians who followed Brahmanical customs and those who did not. The Sautrāmaṇī is the ritual expression of these contacts.

The rivalry between the Somapa and the Surāpa, which we have established here, is in accordance with a later point of my discussion. I mean, there is a faint, yet perceptible, difference between the seventh maṇḍala and the rest concerning the Soma cult in so far as the Vasiṣṭhas do not seem to have practised it to the same extent as the other clans. These Vasiṣṭhas were settled on the Sarasvatī in Madhyadeśa. Now it is pertinent to ask whether the Soma drink has been brought to the Vasiṣṭhas for the first time by those tribes who reached there later.[309]

It is interesting that the views of the Brahmanical Indians about the ignominy of Surā did not spread everywhere. That must be because old customs die hard. After all, the Brahmanical Indians were not all-powerful. Lāṭyāyana V.4.20 states that there are two kinds of Sautrāmaṇī, the Kaukilī[310] and the Caraka-Sautrāmaṇī. This ceremony must therefore go back to specific schools or systems which might have been originally of local nature. Of these two names, the latter deserves our special attention because it recalls that school of medicine which brought out the *Carakasaṃhitā*. As a matter of fact, Surā enjoys a high esteem in this Āyurvedic text, which is traced to the Aśvins. The *Carakasaṃhitā* describes the preparation of Surā and recommends its drinking :

yā surā suragandharvayakṣarākṣasamānuṣaiḥ
ratiḥ surety abhihitā tāṃ surāṃ vidhinā pibet /[311]

Thus we see a clear difference between this attitude and the statements of the law books, the prohibition by which could not have been observed in reality.

In the ṚV, Surā does not occur as often as Madhu. We have stated already that the close association of the Aśvins with these two drinks leads us to the assumption that these two should not have been very different from each other and that one of them might have been substituted for the other. In any case, it is worth noting that honey also was not regarded throughout as fit for the ritual. This is evident from the curious discussion in the ŚBr on the question whether a Brahmacārin may eat honey or not.[312]

Nowhere in the ṚV have I encountered a statement to the effect that Soma is cooked. All that I could cite is only one passage from the ŚBr (XII.7.3.6) where it is said : *somo 'sy aśvibhyāṃ pacasva.*

H. THE THREE SAVANAS

The Soma pressing takes place three times a day — in the morning, at noon and in the evening. The statements of the ṚV are in full agreement with this practice of the ritual. Among the Iranians the number of the Savanas was only two according to the testimony of *Yasna* 10.2[313] ; the Vedic Aryans have increased the number by one.

We are in a position to enumerate not only the number of the Savanas but also the names of the gods invoked on these occasions in the Ṛgvedic period; in this respect also we see that posterity merely continues and elaborates what has already existed in earlier times.

Already in the ṚV all the gods get a share in the Soma drink. Most frequently invoked are Indra and Vāyu who have a foremost claim on Soma by their very nature. Others like Pūṣan are invoked only occasionally.[314] Again there are others like the Aśvins who, of course, have a place in the Soma cult, but whose original drink must have been Madhu and Surā.

The information we possess about the evening pressing is quite positive. With greater uniformity the Vedic hymns state that the Ṛbhus are invited to it.[315] From this it may be concluded that ṚV III.60.1 also, which in fact speaks only of a Savana in general, must refer to the evening pressing. Similarly in the ritual also the Ṛbhus drink in the evening. According to ABr III.30.1 ff., they were assigned a place there after a long dispute with the gods.[316] Accordingly, in the invocation formula addressed to Indra, the Savana is referred to as *savana ṛbhumat, vibhumat, vājavat* (see p. 304 f.). Almost similarly ṚV III.52.6 speaks of *indra ṛbhumat, vājavat*. In ṚV IV.34.7, 8 besides the Ṛbhus, Indra, Varuṇa, Gnāspatnīs, Ādityas, Savitṛ etc.[317] are mentioned. As against this, Vālakhilya 9.1 ff. drops the Ṛbhus completely and mentions only the Aśvins as the gods of the evening offering. VS XIX.26 has Vāc and Sarasvatī.

The midday pressing is done in honour of Indra. Four Grahas are drawn; three for "the one who is accompanied by the Maruts" and one for Mahendra. The same position is reflected in the ṚV; for it is said in III.32.1-2 : "Indra, drink this Soma...the midday pressing which you love. Drink the milk-mixed, the flour-mixed and the pure. We offered it to you for your exhilaration; in concert with the host of Maruts, who created the Brahman,...drink."[318]

However, IV.34.4; VIII.37.1; also X.96.13 and VS XIX.26 make a departure in so far as they assign the midday pressing to Indra alone : *mádhyandinaṃ sávanaṃ kévalaṃ té*. This difference is understandable in view of the original, or at least occasional, rivalry between Indra and the Maruts, which I have attempted elsewhere[319] to explain on the basis of cult differences or clan differences. It is through the fusion of these different attitudes that Indra became Indra Marutvat.

AV VI.47 adds Viśve Devāḥ to these gods; AV IX.1.11 differs from this completely by substituting the above-mentioned gods by Indra and Agni; perhaps this refers to a different sacrifice.

In the later ritual, the Grahas are most numerous in the Prātaḥsavana of the Agniṣṭoma. Apart from the Upāṅśu and the Antaryāma, the following are drawn there : Aindravāyava, Maitrāvaruṇa, Āśvina, Vaiśvadeva, Māhendra, Vaiśvānara, Ṛtugrahas etc. This great number makes it abundantly clear that in the formation of these Grahas different cults, sacrifices and seasons have had their contribution. It seems that the Grahas were not so numerous in the older period. ṚV IV.35.7 says :

prātáḥ sutám apibo haryaśva
mádhyandinaṃ sávanaṃ kévalaṃ té /[320]

X.112.1 : *prātaḥsāvás táva hí pūrvápītiḥ* / (Indra)

AV VI.47 mentions Agni Vaiśvānara as the recipient of the morning libation; but according to AV IX.1.11 ff. and VS XIX.26, it is only the Aśvins. A Brāhmaṇa[321] states that the pressing appertains to Agni in the morning, to Indra at noon, and to All Gods in the evening.[322]

I have not investigated further the reason for these differences which might be traced back to the diversities in the sacrifices and in the family customs. That would lead us more deeply into the details of the ritual than is necessary here. The endeavour not to ignore any of the gods who were gradually becoming important might have been one of the causes that brought about a superficial compromise in the sacrificial repertory.

I shall limit myself here to show, on the basis of two examples, what sort of perfection the grouping of gods in sacrifices had attained already at the time of the ṚV. Our hymn-collection contains a series of hymns which are scattered over various maṇḍalas and are addressed to dual gods. These hymns vary in minor details but agree in the main as is evident from the following table.

	I.2, 3		II.41
I.2. 1-3	Vāyu	1-2	Vāyu
4-6	Indra-Vāyu	3	Indra-Vāyu
7-9	Mitra-Varuṇa	4-6	Mitra-Varuṇa
I.3. 1-3	Aśvins	7-9	Aśvins
4-6	Indra	10-12	Indra
7-9	Viśve Devāḥ	13-15	Viśve Devāḥ
12-10	Sarasvatī	16-18	Sarasvatī
		19-21	Dyāvāpṛthvī, Agni
	I.23		I.135, 136
1	Vāyu	I.135.1-3	Vāyu
2-3	Indra-Vāyu	4-8	Indra-Vāyu; 9 Vāyu
4-6	Mitra-Varuṇa	136.1-5	Mitra-Varuṇa, also Aryaman
7-9	Indra, Maruts		
10-12	Viśve Devāḥ	6-7	Mitra-Varuṇa, Indra, Agni etc. (also Viśve Devāḥ)
13-15	Pūṣan; 16 ff. Āpas[323]		

We see a very detailed arrangement in the sequence of gods here. Vāyu is always in the forefront. He is the *agrepá*, who as a rule, has precedence even over Indra.[324] The variation in the number of verses addressed to Indra-Vāyu betrays a difference in outlook as to the relative importance of the Aindravāyavagraha at this place. The question whether Indra or Vāyu should have a share in this Graha is in dispute from time immemorial. ŚBr IV.1.3.11 ff. narrates that an altercation took place between these two gods because Indra wanted to have a share in this Graha. It ended with a compromise between the two, and the Brāhmaṇa remarks thus 12 : "henceforth the Graha belonged to Indra-Vāyu; previously it belonged to Vāyu alone."

The sequence of the names of the gods in the hymns mentioned above corresponds partially to that of ABr II.25 which enumerates Vāyu, Indra-Vāyu, Mitra-Varuṇa, and Aśvins in this order;

or more exactly to that of ŚŚS VII.10.9 ff. where verses are prescribed for Vāyu, Indra-Vāyu, Mitra-Varuṇa, Aśvins, Indra, Viśve Devāḥ and Sarasvatī, i.e., just the same sequence as in ṚV II.41.

The second example is offered — if we overlook the Āprī hymns — by the Ṛtupraiṣas which are recited during the selection of the priests as well as during the offering of the Ṛtugrahas.[325]

In the ritual, gods and priests are grouped in the following way : 1. Indra and Hotṛ, 2. Maruts and Potṛ, 3. Tvaṣṭṛ with the wives of the gods and Neṣṭṛ, 4. Agni and Āgnīdhra, 5. Indra-Brahman and Brāhmaṇācchaṅsin, 6. Mitra-Varuṇa and Maitrāvaruṇa (Praśāstṛ), 7-10. Deva Draviṇodas and Hotṛ, Potṛ, Neṣṭṛ and Acchāvāka respectively, 11. Aśvins and Adhvaryu, 12. Agni Gṛhapati and Gṛhapati.

Here it is immaterial for us whether the Ṛtugrahas were the original constituent parts of the Agniṣṭoma or not (probably they were not); nevertheless, ṚV I.15; II.36, 37[326] show that they were known already to the oldest of our sources, and that they anticipate the same connection between the individual gods and priests in the ṚV as in the Śrauta ritual; thus Maruts and Potṛ (I.15.2; II.36.2), wives and Neṣṭṛ[327] (I.15.3)[328], Indra and Brahman (I.15.5; II.36.5), Mitra-Varuṇa and Praśāstṛ (i.e., Maitrāvaruṇa) etc.[329]

The connection noticed here between the individual gods and specific priests is a remarkable phenomenon which needs an explanation. For instance, when ṚV II.36.6 states that Mitra-Varuṇa drink from the cup of the Praśāstṛ, we should treat this as an allusion to the fact that at the time of the ṚV, or in an earlier period, the cult of individual gods was connected with specific priests. The Praśāstṛ is called Maitrāvaruṇa after his deities;[330] Acchāvāka's case is also somewhat similar. Originally he was excluded from Soma, but he received admission through Indrāgnī, and is therefore called Aindrāgna.[331]

The connection between the Neṣṭṛ and Tvaṣṭṛ was touched upon above. Tvaṣṭṛ drinks from the cup of this priest, and in I.15.3 Neṣṭṛ himself is substituted for Tvaṣṭṛ.

If specific priests belonged to the cults of specific gods, then such a grouping might have been a relic from a period when tribal or Gotra-peculiarities were much more sharply in focus than in the period of the colourless Veda and its ritual. The most natural explanation for the rich variety of the Vedic period is that there took place a gradual acceptance and fusion of gods and priests of different systems, of different times and clans. When ŚBr XII.6.1.41 states that only the Vaśiṣṭhas, i.e., the priests of the Tṛtsu-Bharatas, had the right to assume the duties of the Brahman because they alone knew certain formulas, this implies that a particular priestly activity was associated authentically with a certain Brahmanical family — a clear pointer to the possibility assumed by me.

Sequences of gods other than the examples given here can be adduced from other passages like V.43. Thus even for the period of the ṚV a number of clearly defined sacrifices can be established, which were developed, increased and dogmatized in the later Śrauta literature. Indeed, the ṚV contains very clearly specific names like Trikadruka, Kuṇḍapāyya,[332] Atirātra; also a sacrifice of fifteen days duration is probably mentioned.[333] It is beyond the scope of this work to follow the traces of this development of the ritual.

With this I conclude the study of the procedures of the Soma cult. I am afraid I have been too detailed for many a reader who would have liked, not without justification, a shorter account; even then there remains much that has not found mention here. This refers particularly to the many individual customs — partly very old — which the Indians incorporated into the Agniṣṭoma. The Indian sacrifice contains — as my *Rituallitteratur* as well as *Sonnenwendfeste*, and especially Oldenberg's *Religion des Veda* have shown — such a rich treasure of old and oldest traditions that one person cannot master it alone. To dwell further upon this would have led me away from my goal.

APPENDIX II

THE PAṆIS IN THE ṚGVEDA[1]

About the Paṇis the *Petersburger Wörterbuch* has the following to say : "Paṇi (properly trader, barterer, who will give nothing without return) the niggard, miser, skinflint; thus are called especially those sparing in sacrifice, or unbelievers who want to retain their own faith completely...Thus are called also the grudging demons who guard the treasures and who are overpowered by the gods and the Aṅgiras'." According to Ludwig (III.34 and especially 51) the Paṇi was "a trader and belonged to the aboriginal population, with which he is occasionally identified. He was a travelling trader, who was of course quite useful, yet must have caused, above all, aversion and mistrust...He certainly never travelled alone but in caravans with armed servants; if he were in majority, his commercial expeditions must have occasionally turned into raids; we may compare the description of the activities of the bigger caravans of the Arabian merchants from Tunis, Tripoli and Murzuk on their incursions into the interior of Africa."

Bergaigne, II, p. 329 thinks that "the word Paṇi signifies literally 'a greedy, miserly person' and designates the man who does not make any gifts to the priests...the demons who withhold the celestial treasures are also regarded as greedy and miserly. We shall not therefore be surprised if the word *paṇi* denotes also the mythical enemy. The Paṇis are the miserly guardians of the celestial cows, or, which comes to the same thing, of butter, which they conceal, but which is discovered by the gods" etc.[2]

The Ṛgvedic passages which mention the Paṇis are distributed all over the entire collection — but unevenly; for in maṇḍalas II and III they are mentioned only once each; in V and IX twice each, in IV and VII three times each and in VIII six times. In maṇḍala X there are four more occurrences apart from those in hymn 108; in maṇḍala I there are nine passages, whereas they occur twelve times in maṇḍala VI, or if we count hymn-wise, nine times. From these statistics — given in detail in ZDMG, LXX, p. 512 ff. — it is evident that the number in the book of the Bharadvājas surpasses those in the other books considerably — absolutely if we do not count the voluminous first maṇḍala, or relatively if we include it also. This has its natural reason[3] in the fact that the statements about the Paṇis in the sixth maṇḍala are based on a more real foundation than elsewhere.

Before we examine the individual passages it would be good to eliminate the entirely mythical hymn X.108 for the time being because the Paṇis appear to its composer as a defiant tribe of demons living at a hazy distance, "on the other side of the Rasā." This is rarely the case in other passages where they are mostly persons with flesh and blood, their most peculiar trait of character being that they do not press Soma for Indra in spite of their wealth.

IV.25.7 : *ná revátā paṇínā sakhyám índro*
ásunvatā sutapā́ḥ saṃ gṛṇīte /

"Indra, the Soma-drinker, does not make friends with the rich Paṇi who does not press."

VIII.64.2 : *padā́ paṇī́ṅr arādháso ní bādhasva mahā́ṅ asi* /

"With your foot strike down the miserly[4] Paṇi : you are mighty."

VIII. 97.2 : *yám indra dadhiṣé tvám áśvaṃ gā́ṃ bhāgám ávyayam* /
yájamāne sunvatí dákṣiṇāvati tásmin táṃ dhehi mā́ paṇaú //

"Whatever, O Indra, you have of horses, cows and sheep, grant that to the sacrificer who presses and gives dakṣiṇā; but not to the Paṇi."

X.60.6 : *agástyasya nádbhyaḥ sáptī yunakṣi róhitā* /
paṇī́n ny àkramīr abhí víśvān rājann arādhásaḥ //

"For the sons of Agastya you harness the two red steeds; you trampled down all the miserly Paṇis, O King."

I.83.3cd : *ásaṃyatto vraté te kṣeti púṣyati*
bhadrā́ śaktír yájamānāya sunvaté //
4a : *ā́d áṅgirāḥ prathamáṃ dadhire vā́yaḥ*.../
c : *sárvaṃ paṇéḥ sám avindanta bhójanam*
áśvāvantaṃ gómantam ā́ paśúṃ náraḥ //

"Unchecked, he lives and flourishes in your realm; auspicious is your might to the sacrificer. There the Aṅgiras' attained the energy for the first time. The men together found all the food of the Paṇi, and they [drove] hither his horses and cattle."

V.34.5b : *nā́sunvatā sacate púṣyatā caná* /...
6 : ...*ásunvato viṣuṇaḥ sunvató vṛdháḥ* /
índro víśvasya damitā́ vibhī́ṣaṇo
yathāvaśáṃ nayati dā́sam ā́ryaḥ //
7 : *sám īṃ paṇér ajati bhójanaṃ muṣé*
ví dāśúṣe bhajati sūnáraṃ vásu /

"[Indra] is not with him who, though prosperous, does not press. Averse to the non-presser and promoting the presser, Indra the terrible, tamer of every man, the Ārya, leads away the Dāsa at his will. As booty he gathers all the food of the Paṇi and distributes the excellent possession to his worshippers."

VS XXXV.1 : *ápetó yantu paṇáyo ásumnā devapīyávaḥ* /
asyá lokáḥ sutā́vataḥ //

"Let the adverse Paṇis clear off, who scorn the gods. The world belongs to the Soma-presser."

AV XX.128.4 : *yáś ca paṇír ábhujiṣṭho yáś ca revā́ṇ ádāśuriḥ* /

As in this passage, their wealth is emphasized repeatedly elsewhere also : "We pride ourselves in being the true singers of your praise, unlike the rich Paṇi" ṚV I.180.7.[5] It is said in ṚV I.151.9 that even the Paṇis do not attain the wealth of Mitrāvaruṇa.[6]

From the preceding it is evident that there is a clear distinction between the *paṇí ásunvat*, "who does not press Soma," and the worshipper of Indra. Whosoever invokes Indra gets himself rid of the Paṇi.[7] What we see here is not the portrait of a travelling trader who sells his wares with persuasion or at a great profit to himself, or even lives among the Indians, but a cult-difference between the followers and opponents of that god, between believers and such unbelievers who certainly do not lack the means to press Soma and to give sacrificial honorarium to the brahmins.

For the worshippers of Indra the act denoted by the word *su*, "to press," is more than an ordinary action; it is the watch-word of an Aryan true-believer. Therefore, Indra, the god of national wars, is also the one who wields his weapon against the Asunvat.[8] In one of the passages cited above, i.e., V.34.5 ff., the Dāsa is on the same level with the Paṇi, and the Dāsa is an enemy of the Aryan; the Paṇis, similarly, must have been the enemies.

In ṚV VII.6.3 we have a verse which should be interpreted in this sense :

ny àkratū́n grathíno mṛdhrávācaḥ
paṇī́ṅr aśraddhā́ṅ avṛdhā́ṅ ayajñā́n |
prápra tā́n dásyūṅr agnír vivāya
pū́rvaś cakārā́parāṅ áyajyūn ||

In this verse the Paṇis are called not only unbelievers and without sacrifice but also *mṛdhrávāc* and *grathín*. Zimmer has attempted to show that the former denotes "one who uses offensive speech, slanderer"; I do not think that he succeeded in this. In ṚV IV.25.6 the *ásuṣvi* is called, besides *duṣprāvī́*, also *ávāc*, "dumb"[9]: "He is no kinsman of the one who does not press, nor friend, nor brother. He destroys the unfriendly and dumb one."

Dumb is one who does not understand my language. Thus the Slav calls the German "stumm" (dumb). Indeed, the fifth verse of hymn VII.6 speaks also of the tributes paid by the other tribes. One who does not press Soma and does not speak the language of the Indra-worshipper is his natural enemy. Yet it does not follow from this that such tribes have always been non-Aryan as we understand the word today. Not everybody whom the Indians counted among their enemies belonged to a Barbarian tribe. Even under the name Asura people were included who, in my view, were quite Indian. According to ŚBr III.2.1.23 ff., the Asuras cry out during their flight *he 'lavo, he 'lavo*; this means that they speak an Indian dialect.[10] Thus it is likely that those Indians who did not press Soma and spoke a strange dialect were called *ávāc*, "dumb." I regard *mṛdhrávāc* as a synonym for *ávāc* in this sense. *mṛdhrá* means "despiser" as well as "enemy"; both meanings are close to each other, and *mṛdhrávāc* could in itself mean "language of the enemy" as well as "one who uses despicable language." The latter meaning is not required in any passage, not even in X.23.5;[11] the former recommends itself through the comparison with *ásuṣvi ávāc* and through the consideration that wherever *mṛdhrávāc* occurs in the ṚV it is not merely the scoffers but it is the real enemies of Indra and his worshippers who are described by this word. If it meant only "slanderer" in the general sense, then we should expect to find it being used in other contexts also.

Besides *mṛdhrávāc*, "speaking the language of the enemy," or in other words, "barbarian," the Paṇis are styled *grathín*; there is no positive explanation for this word. I think it is derived from *grath*, "to string together" or "to fasten." One cannot easily differentiate the separate words in a foreign language : it appears to be a continuous flow of speech, and *grathín* could easily refer to this. Sāyaṇa renders it not incorrectly with *jalpaka.* Therefore, the Paṇis could have been Aryans all the same, and not aborigines.

One who does not press Soma does not offer any dakṣiṇās either; in VIII.97.2 *sunvát dákṣiṇāvat* stands in contradistinction to the Paṇi. The Paṇis are therefore branded as misers, and the gods are requested to be generous and not be equal to, or surpass, the Paṇis in miserliness. Thus

ṚV I.33.3 : *coṣkūyámāṇa indra bhū́ri vāmám*
mā́ paṇír bhūr asmád ádhi pravṛddha //

"Gathering great wealth, O Indra, do not become a Paṇi towards us, you mighty one."

In AV V.11.7 Varuṇa is addressed in the following words :

mó ṣu paṇī́ṁr abhy etā́vato bhūt
mā́ tvā vocann arā́dhasaṃ jánāsaḥ //

"May he not surpass these Paṇis; may not men call you stingy." In VIII.45.14 the poet is quite dissatisfied with Indra and calls him a Paṇi. In I.124.10; IV.51.3 the word is used in the general sense of miser, but that is not its original meaning.

There is one more reason why the Paṇis could not have been miserly traders or merchants. The ṚV speaks repeatedly of their wealth in cattle and horses; Indra and also Agni-Soma rob them of their wealth in order to distribute it among the pious Soma-pressers. Therefore, it seems that looting expeditions, *gáviṣṭis*, which play quite an important role in the thinking of the Vedic Indians, have been organized against the Paṇis, and the pious friends of Indra seem to have given the Paṇis no less reason for complaint than the Paṇis themselves have given the former. Of the typical passages, several like I.83.4; V.34.7 have been cited above; either the Aṅgiras' themselves find the food of the Paṇis, or Indra drives the food towards his kin. To such passages I shall add the following.

VI.13.3 : *sá sátpatiḥ śávasā hanti vṛtrám*
ágne vípro ví paṇér bharti vā́jam /
yáṃ tváṃ praceta ṛtajā́ta rāyā́
sajóṣā náptrāpā́ṃ hinóṣi //

"The hero kills the enemy with all his might; O Agni, the singer carries away the possessions of the Paṇi — [the singer] whom you in league with Apāṃ napāt, O wise son of truth, incite with wealth."

VI.33.2 : *tvā́ṃ hīndrā́vase vívāco*
hávante carṣaṇáyaḥ śū́rasātau |
tvā́ṃ víprebhir ví paṇī́ṅr aśāyas
tvóta ít sánitā vā́jam árvā ||

"With different utterances men implore you, O Indra, to help them in the battle of heroes. Along with the singers you pierced through the Paṇis. Favoured by you, the charger carries away the booty."

VIII.75.7 : *paṇíṃ góṣu starāmahe*

"We will knock down the Paṇi amidst his cattle."

The eleventh verse of this hymn speaks of a Gaviṣṭi, v. 15 of the *párā saṃvát*, the hostile side (tract of land).

It appears that the battles had been very severe. According to VI.20.4, the Paṇis fell in hundreds :

śataír apadran paṇáya indrā́tra
dáśoṇaye kaváye arkásātau |
vadhaíḥ śúṣṇasyāśúṣasya māyā́ḥ
pitvó nā́rirecīt kíṃ caná prá ||

"There, O Indra, the Paṇis fell in hundreds[12] for the singer Daśoṇi in the battle; through the blows of the club the magic devices of the voracious (?) Śuṣṇa. He did not leave any of the food remaining."[13]

The Paṇis apparently did not fail to retaliate these raids. In V.61.8 they are remembered with contempt :

utá ghā némo ástutaḥ púmāñ íti bruve paṇíḥ |
sá vaíradeya ít samáḥ ||

"Thus quite a few have become unpopular. The Paṇi calls himself a 'man.' He is equal to a man merely in so far as he has to pay blood money."[14]

The Paṇis must have certainly killed quite a few people. In III.58.2 the singer implores the Aśvins to ward off the assault of the Paṇis.[15] In VI.51.14 the Paṇi is even styled a wolf : *jahī́ ny àtríṇaṃ paṇíṃ vṛ́ko hí sáḥ*, "destroy the voracious Paṇi because he is a wolf." The word is well-chosen for a tribe which was feared for its predatory invasions.

It is characteristic that in the same sixth maṇḍala where the Paṇis are remembered most often, it is precisely Pūṣan who plays an important role.[16] Pūṣan is the lord of paths (53.1); he brings the lost cattle back (54.10) and shows the houses where it is hidden (54.1, 2). Throughout an entire hymn (53.3, 5, 6, 7) Pūṣan is invoked as the protector against the Paṇis, whom he is asked to defeat and hand over to the tribe of the singer.[17] In the same book we encounter proper names which remove all the doubts about the historicity of these events. In the Dānastuti VI.45.31ff. it is said of Bṛbu, who is praised for his magnificent generosity, that "he stepped on the thickest skull of the Paṇis," with which title of honour the leader of the enemies must have been characterized. In hymn 61, again of the sixth maṇḍala, the historical basis is even more firm.

After the above discussion it seems indubitable that the Paṇis must be regarded not as a tribe of traders but a tribe that was hostile towards the Indians. Nowhere do we find a mention of their trade, but only of their predatory expeditions, of their wealth, of the booty that was taken away from them with the help of Indra. It is clear that it is merely etymology — the purely superficial connection with the verb *paṇ*, "to buy" — which gave rise to the theory that they were traders.

WHO WERE THOSE PAṆIS AND WHERE WERE THEY SETTLED ?[18]

No other tribe seems to be more suitable for identification with the Paṇis than those who were known to the antiquity as the Parnians. This identification has already been stressed by Brunnhofer in his book, *Iran und Turan*. It will be seen that this is correct and that there were really contacts between the Indians and that tribe of nomads from whose midst, much later, one of its sons has ascended to one of the proudest thrones of the old world. The mention in the ṚV of tribes from such far off western lands is no more extraordinary in itself than the mention of the Gandharas situated on the western bank of the Indus, or of the Derbikes, or of the Alinas who were probably settled on both the banks of the Oxus.[19] We do not often find the Paṇis mentioned together with other tribes; however, some of these occurrences are of importance.

In the Ṛgvedic passage V.34.6d,7a, cited on p. 335, they are mentioned together with the Dāsas :

yathāvaśáṃ nayati dā́sam ā́ryaḥ ||
sáṃ īṃ paṇér ajati bhójanaṃ muṣé...

and once again in AV V.11.6 :

tát te vidvấn varuṇa prá bravīmi |
adhóvarcasaḥ paṇáyo bhavantu
nīcaír dāsấ úpa sarpantu bhū́mim ||

"This I proclaim to you, O Varuṇa, as one who knows. Let the Paṇis be humiliated and let the Dāsas creep deep down on the earth."

Furthermore, a third passage, VII.6.3 (p. 336), may be considered, where the Paṇis are mentioned together with the Dasyus or called directly the Dasyus.

I do not think that the association of the Paṇis with the Dāsas, which we have ascertained from two passages, is purely accidental; for this recalls the close connection that existed between the tribes of the Dahae (Gr. *Daoi*, also *Dasai*) and the Parnians who were a sub-tribe of the former. Referring to Arsakes, Strabo (XI.315) states : "Later on, Arsakes, a Skythian, commanding a group of the Dahae, viz. the nomads called Parnoi who dwelled along the river Ochos, attacked Parthia and conquered it."[19a]

That the Dāsas or Dahae were inhabitants of the steppes supports the assumption that the Parnians dwelt in historical times on the Ochus, i.e., the modern Tejene.[20]

If the identification of the Paṇis with the Parnians and of the Dāsas with the Dahae is to be valid, it will be necessary to show that either these tribes advanced so far away from their homelands to harass the Indians in their settlements on the Indus, or that some of the Indian tribes lived farther west of the Indus than has been assumed so far or, at least, preserved the reminiscences of this period in their hymns.

It can be shown that the second possibility is almost certain.

I cannot share the oft-repeated theory that the name Dāha has the general sense of "enemy" and that it is found among the Indians as Dāsa with the same meaning. I believe that, on the contrary, Dāsa was at first a proper name and later came to acquire the general sense of "enemy."[21] In the ṚV there is a king called Divodāsa, that is "Heavenly Dāsa." If Dāsa was anything but a proper name, if it really meant "enemy," then it is unbelievable that this prince should be designated as an "enemy of heaven" in those very hymns which glorify his fame. But Dāsa does not yet mean "slave" in the entire sixth book; it does so only in three passages in the whole of the ṚV. Therefore, it is wrong to render the word as "slave of heaven." Certainly we have to regard Dāsa here as a proper name which received an honorific prefix in the genetive *divás* — "Heavenly Dāsa."

We encounter this Divodāsa[22] in a hymn of the same sixth maṇḍala, where the information about the Paṇis comes closest to concrete realities. The first three verses of this 61st hymn are of such great importance that I shall quote them in full.

VI.61.1 : *iyám adadāt rabhasám ṛṇacyútam*
dívodāsaṃ vadhryaśvā́ya dāśúṣe /
yā́ śáśvantam ācakhā́dāvasáṃ paṇím
tā́ te dātrā́ṇi taviṣā́ sarasvati //
2 : *iyáṃ śúṣmebhir bisakhā́ ivārujat*
sā́nu girīṇā́ṃ taviṣébhir ūrmíbhiḥ /
pārāvataghnī́m ávase suvṛktíbhiḥ
sárasvatīm ā́ vivāsema dhītíbhiḥ //
3 : *sárasvati devanído ní barhaya*
prajā́ṃ víśvasya bṛ́sayasya māyínaḥ /
utá kṣitíbhyo 'vánīr avindo
viṣám ebhyo asravo vājinīvati //

"To the pious Vadhryaśva she gave the impetuous Divodāsa, who redeems all debts. These mighty gifts come from you, O Sarasvatī, who consumed the obstinate, intractable[23] Paṇi.

"Like one digging for roots, she violently broke through the ridge of the mountains with her mighty waves. With hymns and thoughts, let us invite the help of Sarasvatī, who slew the Pārāvatas.

"Sarasvatī, cast you down the enemies of the gods, the progeny of every sly Bṛsaya. O you rich in horses, you gave the streams back to our abodes and made poison flow towards them."

We see that Divodāsa is the son of Vadhryaśva and lives on the banks of the Sarasvatī, the sacred stream of the land, and that his enemies are called Paṇi, Pārāvata and Bṛsaya.

Ptolemy VI.20.3 mentions a people called *Paroyētai*, whom Lassen[24] attempts to locate in the southern part of the Paropamisadian country on the northern border of Gedrosia. It is quite likely that this name denotes "mountaineers" as Lassen believes and that it is related to the above-mentioned Pārāvata. I think, therefore, that Ludwig (ṚV III.162, 197) and Brunnhofer[25] are justified in considering with Lassen the two words as synonymous and in explaining the Pārāvatas as an "alien" Iranian tribe.[26]

If this assumption is valid, then we would find Divodāsa as the enemy of a tribe settled in the northern part of Arachosia. After establishing this, it should not be difficult to look for the Parnians mentioned in the first verse in the same direction, that is to say, roughly in the same region which they occupied in historical times, namely on the Oxus. When we hear that Antiochus I built a 1500 stadia long rampart around the region of Margiana on the Murgāb as a protection against the nomads of the northern desert, viz., the Dahae, the Parnians and the Massagetae,[27] then we can also assume that in still earlier times these tribes had penetrated during their predatory expeditions a bit further southwards into the territory of that king who calls the Paṇis and Parnians his enemies. We do not know how far north they had reached in their migrations. Their earlier settlements are quite in accordance with the view of the poet of X.108, who looks for them on the other side of the Rasā, which is mythical for him, but is probably identical with the Oxus.[28] Their territories can very easily have extended up to that river.[29]

One factor seems to speak against this theory, namely the statement of our hymn that Divodāsa lives on the banks of the Sarasvatī. For, since the remarks of Roth in the PW and the detailed reasoning by Zimmer[30] in support of the former's view, it looks as if Sarasvatī is undoubtedly another name for the Indus. But this is not true; this theory is incompatible with the fact that the Western writers never call the Indus, which was well known to them, by that name. Furthermore, the passage cited by Zimmer as significant (VII.95.2) does certainly not prove what it is supposed to prove; we have to explain it differently. ṚV VII.95.1 reads as follows :

prá kṣódasā dhā́yasā sasra eṣā́
sárasvatī dharúṇam ā́yasī pū́ḥ |
prabā́badhānā rathyèva yāti
víśvā apó mahinā́ síndhur anyā́ḥ ||

If we adopt the very common and simple meaning "stream" for *síndhu*, then all the significance of this passage disappears.[31]

Therefore, I think that we must depart from the identification of the Sarasvatī with the Indus which has been arrived at merely through conjecture, and restrict the name to those two rivers only which have a historical claim upon this name : the insignificant little stream in the interior of India which loses itself in the desert, and secondly the stream in Arachosia, known to the Greeks as Arachotos and to the Iranians as Haraxvaitī. Wherever we encounter the name Sarasvatī it would primarily mean these two streams; very rarely or as an exception could such a transfer of name to the Indus have taken place. But I consider even that improbable.[32]

Because of the mention of the Pārāvatas and the Paṇis, there can be no doubt as to which of the two streams is meant in our hymn. Divodāsa must have dwelt on the Haraxvaitī in Arachosia, i.e., in a territory which could have easily been exposed to the raids of the Parnians who were living as nomads in the north or north-west. The content of our hymn might have had its origin there.[33]

Besides the Paṇis and the Pārāvatas, a third name is also mentioned : Bṛsaya. If my reasoning is correct, then this name also can be located in the vicinity of Divodāsa. That this name is not Indian is evident from the fact that the *s* is not cerebralized.

The expression *prajā́ viśvasya bṛ́sayasya* requires that we interpret the word as the name of a tribe. The offspring of Bṛsaya and the Paṇis seem to belong together, since they are mentioned together — besides in VI.61 — once more in

I.93.4 : *agnīṣomā céti tád vīryàṃ vām*
yád ámuṣṇītam avasáṃ [°*śaṃ*] *paníṃ gā́ḥ*/
ávātiratam bṛ́sayasya śéṣo...

"O Agni-Soma, your prowess manifested itself as you robbed the intractable Paṇi of his cattle; you overpowered the progeny of Bṛsaya."

Therefore, we may assume that these Bṛsayas lived, like the Pārāvatas, to the west of the Sarasvatī in Arachosia, or in Drangiana, or in a neighbouring region. It seems to me that there is an indication for this in the name Barsaentēs of the Satrap of Arachosia and Drangiana, who marched in support of Darius and later was excuted by Alexander because of his disloyalty towards Darius. About him Arrian reports thus in his *Anabasis*, III.8.4 : "Barsaetes [Barzaentes] governor of Arachoti brought thither his Arachoti, and Indian mountaineers.

21.1 : Brazas [Barzaentes] prefect of Arachoti and Drangae...

25.8 : Alexander...marching against the Zarangaei, came

to the imperial city; but Barsaentes, one of those who murdered Darius in his flight, and was then prince of that country, hearing of his approach, fled to the Indians, on the other side of the river Indus; but they having seized him, sent him to Alexander, who, for his treachery to Darius, commanded him to be put to death."[33a]

In its first part this personal name corresponds so completely to that of the Bṛsayas that it is not too far-fetched to suppose that here we have an indigenous proper name adapted from the name of the tribe. Perhaps Barsaentēs belonged to a dethroned noble clan of his country. Then the territory of the Bṛsayas would lie close to the territories of the Pārāvatas, Paṇis and Divodāsa.

The outcome of this discussion is of great significance for determining the geography and date of the ṚV. We see that a part of the events described in the ṚV took place to the west of the Indus in Iranian territories in Arachosia and its neighbourhood and that one of the enemies was the nomadic tribe of the Parnians, mentioned very often in the later periods. A wide gulf that cannot be bridged by mere decades separates the singer of our hymn, for whom as well as for the majority of the hymns of the Bharadvājas the Paṇis were still a historical reality, and the poet of the Saramā-hymn X.108,[34] who sees the Paṇis in the twilight of saga and who looks for them in the remotest distance beyond the mythical Rasā.

If we are right in concluding from Divodāsa's name that he was himself a Dāsa, then it will be obvious that he was in feud with the members of his own tribe. This recalls to mind the distinction made by Darius in his inscriptions between the *Sakā Humavarkā* (the *Amyrgioi Sakai* of Herodotus) and the *Sakā tigrakhauda*. Rawlinson[35] says that the first name obviously refers to the eastern Skythians on the borders of India, "the latter those scattered through the empire, who are known simply as 'bowmen.' According to Hellanicus, the word 'Amyrgian' was strictly a geographical title, Amyrgium being the name of the plain in which these Scythians dwelt." Accordingly Divodāsa should be counted among the Sakā Humavarkā.[36] We do not know what divided these tribes. When we recall that the Paṇis were accused of not being Soma pressers, then the idea of religious difference, in addition to other differences, is not to be dismissed easily.

The above-mentioned tribes, i.e., the Paṇis, Pārāvatas and Bṛsayas, were not the only enemies of the "Heavenly Dāsa." In the hymns of the sixth book, where quite a number of names occur which do not sound like Sanskrit, there are three passages (22.10; 33.3; 60.6) in which a distinction is made between the Dāsa enemies and the Aryan enemies. Such a statement about a Dāsa is as little surprising as about the Aryans who had certainly their Aryan enemies and Dāsa enemies. One of the greatest enemies of Divodāsa must have been Śambara, a mountain chief, who is also styled a Dāsa in VI.26.5, and who is referred to six times in five hymns of the sixth book.[37] Several times Varcin, who was likewise a Dāsa, is associated with Śambara.[38]

The singers who lived at the court of Divodāsa must have belonged to the family of the Bharadvājas. This can be inferred not only from the fact that the most important of our evidences come from the sixth book, which is called after this family, but also from some statements in the same book which are more precise. In the Dānastuti VI.47.22 ff., which praises several benefactors of the Bharadvājas, the bountiful gifts received from Divodāsa are enumerated in great detail. In VI.16.5; 31.4 Bharadvāja and Divodāsa occur together,[39] and also in I.116.18 (and perhaps in I.112.13, 14 if we may combine the two verses). Thus Vedic tradition has preserved the two names in a close association.

Divodāsa was not the only ruler whom they served. In the sixth book several other names occur which are of interest. On p. 339 we have referred to a prince called Bṛbu, of whom it was said that he had stepped on "the thickest skull of the Paṇis." VI.45.33 states that he was also a generous prince. However, according to the *Anukramaṇikā*, the poet of this hymn was a Śamyu Bārhaspatya, but he must have been close to the family of the Bharadvājas since his hymns are included in their collection. ŚŚS XVI.11.11 names a Bharadvāja directly as the recipient of dakṣiṇā from Bṛbu.[40] Śāṅkhāyana mentions a third name, that of Prastoka Sārñjaya, who was also a patron of the Bharadvājas. He is also alluded to in the ṚV in the same Dānastuti which praises Divodāsa. Besides him, the Dānastuti includes an Aśvattha also whom I cannot identify at all. Prastoka from the clan or tribe of Sṛñjaya was a prince like the other patrons of our family of singers. This is attested by several statements of Vedic texts in which Sṛñjaya occurs frequently. Vītahavya in VI.15.2,3; VII.19.3 is probably a Sṛñjaya. In VI.27.7 — it is not an insignificant fact that this occurs in the sixth book — a Sṛñjaya Daivavāta is stated to be the conqueror of Turvaśa and of the Vṛcīvats.[41] According to the next verse, his real name is Abhyāvartin Cāyamāna and he is himself a lord of the Parthians. Indian priests must have been associated with the king of the Parthians.[42]

Furthermore, in IV.15.4 a Sṛñjaya Daivavāta is remembered as a follower of the fire cult.[43] Since v. 6 ff. of this hymn refers to a Kumāra Somaka Sāhadevya, this hymn seems to have been written for a Sṛñjaya prince. ABr VII.34 speaks of Somaka Sāhadevya and Sahadeva Sārñjaya. Sahadeva Sārñjaya is said to have been called earlier Suplan Sārñjaya, which sounds foreign.[44] A Sahadeva who won victory over Dasyus and Śimyus is mentioned in ṚV I.100.17 — a clumsily composed hymn — in the midst of names like Vārṣagirāḥ and Ambarīṣa; I am not certain that these are of Indian origin. Finally, in ŚBr II.4.4.5 a Ṛṣi Devabhāga Śrautarṣa is mentioned, who was the Purohita of two kingdoms, namely, of the Kurus and of the Sṛñjayas. From all this it is evident, I believe, that Sṛñjaya was the name of a prince or — what is perhaps the same — of a tribe and that there is nothing in principle which speaks against the assumption that they could have lived, like Divodāsa, to the west of the Indus in the neighbourhood of the Dāsa tribes.

From this discussion we may conclude that the family of the Bharadvājas held the priestly office at the court of Divodāsa as well as at that of Sṛñjaya, and most likely also at the court of Bṛbu. In principle, such a double office would not have been impossible; for from the passage of the ŚBr cited above we know of Devabhāga Śrautarṣa that he was the Purohita of two tribes.[45]

Thus the kingdom of Divodāsa was situated on the Sarasvatī in Arachosia. I cannot say precisely where the homes of the other princes were. Since the Bharadvājas acted as the priests at all the three courts, we can assume that they were in the vicinity of one another. Brunnhofer was the first to state the view that Sṛñjaya was the same as that country on the river Helmend bordering on Arachosia, viz., Drangiana, Old Persian Zaraṅka, whose inhabitants were known to the Greeks as *Zaraggai*, to Herodotus as *Saraggai* and *Saraggees* and to Strabo and Arrian as *Daraggai*.[46] This theory has the advantage of doing complete justice to the geographical position which we may assume for the Sṛñjayas.[47] However, this is contradicted by the fact — which is important enough to make this identification appear dubious — that the Sanskrit name has an initial *s*. It could, of course, be a loan word in Sanskrit; but we know still too little about the corruption which the old loan words must have undergone in Sanskrit to make such a claim.

Notwithstanding the last consideration, there remains still, I believe, as an ascertained core of information the fact that the Dāsa prince Divodāsa fought against the tribe of the Parnians on the banks of the Arachotos and that the Bharadvājas were in his entourage.

This is the state of affairs in maṇḍala VI. Since I wrote this our knowledge of the Vedic period has altered considerably and that too in favour of my views. The discovery of Vedic names for gods in the records of the Mitanni, Indian numerals and allusions to equestrian sport prove the existence of Indian (not proto-Indian) influences in the western kingdoms. To these we may add the occurrence of the name *In-tar-u-da* or *En-dar-ú-ta* in the el-Amarna letters; Jirku (*Zeitschrift für Assyriologie*, NF, II, p. 74 ff.) explains this word as *Indar-uta* and Sieg (ibid, p. 164) as *Indra-uta* (*Indrota*), "beloved of Indra." Hence, Indian tribes were settled on this side of the Hindukush and Suleman.[48]

That is why I cannot see how my attempt to transfer a group of Indians into the west has been a "failure" (Keith, p. 91). At the most, I am prepared to concede that book VI was not composed in the west but, all the same, its reminiscences are derived from there.[49]

Book VII takes us into quite different circumstances. Its centre of focus is Sudās, a descendant of Divodāsa — perhaps his son or, because of the epithet Paijavana, more likely his grandson or some other descendant. The ancient clan of singers, the Bharadvājas, have completely receded into the background; now the star of the Vasiṣṭhas who support the descendant of Divodāsa shines brightly. The scene of the deeds of Sudās and the Bharatas whom he leads is laid in another country. On the Irāvatī they win a victory over their enemies, on the *Yphasis* and *Zadadrēs* they encounter the Ten Kings, and on the Yamunā they defeat Bheda. But the most powerful enemies of Divodāsa have almost been forgotten. Śambara is remembered in two passages only (18.20; 99.5), whereas the sixth maṇḍala mentioned him six times in five hymns.

When we examine the first of the two passages, we find the name of Śambara in a context which is nothing but a dry enumeration of all the achievements of Indra and of the Vasiṣṭhas, a kind of family chronicle of Sudās which the Vasiṣṭhas made use of. Many of the enemies mentioned there — like Pakthas, Bhalānas, Alinas and others — were situated so far away from the Irāvatī that we are justified in doubting whether Sudās himself has ever come into contact with them. Not does the verse say that Sudās himself won victory over Śambara; it only praises Indra as the destroyer of Śambara who considered himself a god. Therefore, I think that this is only a reminiscence of the dynastic history of our prince. The case is no better with the other hymn, VII.99. Of course it contains no dynastic history, but there is much else that is remarkable.

VII.99.5 : *índrāviṣṇū dṛṅhitā́ḥ śámbarasya*
náva púro navatíṃ ca śnathiṣṭam /
śatáṃ varcínaḥ sahásraṃ ca sākáṃ
hathó apraty àsurasya vīrā́n //

"You have, O Indra-Viṣṇu, destroyed the ninety-nine fortified castles of Śambara; at the same time you have routed, without any resistance, hundred and thousand heroes of Varcin, the Asura." Elsewhere the victory over Śambara is attributed solely to Indra; here we have Indra-Viṣṇu who are, mostly or always, engaged in cosmogonic activity. In the eyes of the poet of our hymn Varcin, the ally of Śambara, was a mere Asura. Similarly, for the poet Śambara also must have been no longer a real person. This assumption is supported by the content of the preceding verses in our hymn, which praise Viṣṇu, stating that he supported the world-halves, that together with Indra he created Sūrya, Uṣas and Agni and that in his battles he conquered the wiles of the "bull-jawed" Dāsa; all this is a late addition. In this context the mention of Dāsa also sounds mythical. Our poet has the same relation to those of the sixth book as the author of the Saramā hymn to the author of the Divodāsa hymn VI.61. These composers of the seventh book had no longer a knowledge of the actual events, and they saw only through the haze of saga what was very real generations ago.[50]

It is the same case with the Paṇis. While this name occurs twelve times in nine of the seventy-five Bharadvāja hymns, it is referred to only three times in the compilation of the Vasiṣṭhas : 6.3; 9.2; 19.9. And only in one passage (6.3) it must denote the people of the Paṇis, whereas in the other two passages it does not have this concrete meaning any longer.[51]

Therefore, we can assume that the Vasiṣṭhas had no longer any precise knowledge of the wars which the ancestors of Sudās had waged against the mountain chief.

Their statements are based on what they had heard from others; yet they preserved an old memory in as much as they mentioned Śambara and Varcin together at least once. Without doubt this accords with the fact that the Viśvāmitras of book III do not mention Śambara at all, the Paṇi only once — that too in a context which does not exclude the very general meaning of the word "enemy" or "unbeliever." According to Roth,[52] these singers were the followers of Sudās until they were driven out by the more adept Vasiṣṭhas. This explains why there is no allusion at all to Śambara who belonged to the past and who was perhaps completely unknown in their homeland.

The fact that Śambara is not mentioned at all in book III and only casually in book VII is consistent with the further fact that Divodāsa's name also does not occur at all in book III[53] and only once in book VII as the "father" of Sudās. The dynastic history of Sudās was quite certainly very remote from the thoughts of these singer-families.

How was it possible that at the court of Sudās quite different priests were officiating from those at the court of his ancestors ? I see only one answer to this : Sudās, advancing farther into the east as a conqueror, reached those regions where the families of the Viśvāmitras and Vasiṣṭhas dwelt,[54] of whom especially the latter knew how to find the favour of the powerful foreigner.

This conjecture explains why these singers so seldom refer to the most important enemies of the homeland of his ancestors such as the Paṇis and Śambara, and why they have little or nothing to say about them. Furthermore, it would follow from my assumption that a new wave of immigration led by a Dāsa followed the earlier one of the Aryan tribes. We can probably regard the Tṛtsus as the representatives of these earlier settlers. The name Tṛtsu would be dropped, but my hypothesis as such would remain valid, if Ludwig and Oldenberg[55] were right in considering the Bharatas and the Tṛtsus as one and the same tribe. Later on Oldenberg[56] changed his view to say that the Tṛtsus were identical with the Vasiṣṭhas who were the priests of the Bharatas. I consider both the equations improbable because I cannot set aside the doubts caused by the following verse.

VII.33.6 : *daṇḍā́ ivéd goájanāsa āsan*
páricchinnā bharatā́ arbhakā́saḥ /
ábhavac ca puraetā́ vásiṣṭhaḥ
ā́d ít tṛ́tsūnāṃ víśo aprathanta //

In this verse *tṛ́tsūnāṃ* and *bharatāḥ* can hardly be identical; one would not understand the transference of the names, much less can one call priests the "regions of the Tṛtsus." The difficulties seem to disappear when we regard Sudās as an invader marching in the vanguard of the Bharatas, whom for some reason or other the Tṛtsus headed by the Vasiṣṭhas supported in his troubles and helped in his conquests. In the kingdom of Sudās the two tribes merged together, and the Vasiṣṭhas became his singers.[57]

We have yet to add a few remarks about the Pūrus. According to IV.38.1, they were ruled by a king called Trasadasyu.[58] IV.42.8ff. states that he was a descendant of Durgaha and son of Purukutsa, to whom he was granted by Indra-Varuṇa at the request of the pious Purukutsānī at a time of great distress due to enemies from without. Trasadasyu was a mighty warrior. He is styled as *ardhadevá* and *vṛtrahán*. He conquered new territories for the Pūrus. If we are to trust the statement of I.62.7, his father Purukutsa was an ally of Sudās, or if we accept Ludwig's conjecture, for which I do not see any convincing reason, his enemy; in either case Purukutsa was a contemporary of Sudās.[59]

It is significant that Trasadasyu is not mentioned in maṇḍala VI. After what has been stated so far, such a mention is unlikely, or had he been mentioned, the passage would be a late one because

Trasadasyu was a son of a contemporary of Sudās, and Sudās himself was a descendant of Divodāsa who plays a prominent role in book VI. Therefore Trasadasyu lived two or three generations later than Divodāsa. On the other hand, Purukutsa is remembered once in VI.20.10, but it is never said that he came into contact, either as a friend or as an enemy, with Divodāsa. It is said of Purukutsa that he destroyed the autumnal forts of the Dāsa.[60] But this Dāsa need not necessarily be the son of Vadhryaśva, who himself fought against the Dāsas. On the contrary, VI.20.6 states that a Dāsa Namuci was his enemy; from a reference to a victory over the Paṇis (VI.20.4) it follows clearly that he had partly the same enemies as Divodāsa, either during Divodāsa's time or afterwards.

That this hymn, which seems to have been composed after the time of Divodāsa,[61] is an interpolation into the book of the Bharadvājas can be explained by the fact that its composer is a Bharadvāja and that the Bharadvājas must have served the Pūrus as well. I.59.6,7 states that the Pūrus defeated the Dasyu Śambara with the help of Agni Vaiśvānara and that this god was held in high regard among the Bharadvājas.[62]

The association of the Bharadvājas with the Pūrus, with Divodāsa, Sṛñjaya and Bṛbu leads to the assumption that the Pūrus or a part of them were settled not far away from the kingdom of Divodāsa. From maṇḍala VI it is not clear whether Divodāsa knew the Pūrus or not. As we have seen, VI.20.10 need not necessarily have anything to do with Divodāsa. VI. 46.8, the only other passage where the name of the Pūrus appears again in this book, is probably still younger because it mentions, apart from the Pūrus, a man named Tṛkṣi who, according to the testimony of VII.22.7, is a descendant of Trasadasyu, provided these two persons are not identical.[63]

However, there is one verse which mentions Divodāsa and Pūru together, I.130.7 :

bhinát púro navatím indra pūráve
dívodāsāya máhi daśúṣe nṛto...atithigvāya...

But this is such a chronicle-like enumeration that much significance should not be attached to the fact that Divodāsa and Pūru occur together. The value of such enumerations can be judged from I.112.14 where Divodāsa is immediately followed by the much later Trasadasyu.[64]

If in Divodāsa's time the Pūrus inhabited a region which was, as I suppose, close to the kigdom of this prince, book VII places them again in quite different surroundings. VII.5.3 ff. describes their wars against the "black tribes"; Agni Vaiśvānara still helps them as before, but clearly it is no more a Bharadvāja who sings for them. We do not know who composed hymn VII.5. It is included among the Vasiṣṭha-hymns; but, as Ludwig (III.131, 175) has noticed, precisely because of its partiality towards the Pūrus it cannot have belonged originally to the Vasiṣṭhas. The same is true of VII.6, also noticed by Ludwig. The clear reference to the Paṇis in v.5, which shows that the poet meant the tribe of the Paṇis, is one more reason to doubt that this hymn belonged to the Vasiṣṭhas, and to seek its origin or its content still farther westwards. It is significant that the word *dásyu*, which occurs eight times in book VI, appears in book VII in hymns 5, 6, 19 only, which should be judged similarly. A different homeland is clearly indicated in VII.8.4, where a Vasiṣṭha proclaims the victory of the Bharatas over a Pūru. Hence, the Pūrus must have extended their territories up to the Yamunā and Paruṣṇī, and seem to have spoken a different dialect than that of the Bharatas. In VII.18.13 they are called *mṛdhrávāc*, which means "speaking a Barbarian tongue" rather than "talking disdainfully."

Such a difference in language would not be surprising, the less so if they, like Sudās, migrated to those lands later than the Tṛtsus did.[65]

The events described in books III and VII which take place mostly farther in the east on the Paruṣṇī, Yamunā, Vipās and Śutudrī make it improbable that the Sarasvatī mentioned in VII.95, 96, on the banks of which the Pūrus dwelt, can still be identical with the Arachotos. Howsoever exuberant the description might appear, there is no other possibility but to locate them on the small river in the Madhyadeśa, which was considered sacred in later periods.[66] Precisely the emphasis on its sacredness as early as in the Brāhmaṇa period, and the sacrificial sessions held on its banks by wise Ṛṣis suggest that Indians thought differently about the Sarasvatī than might appear natural to us. I do not see why we should not read a tradition which reaches upto the ṚV into the ṚV itself or why we should not be permitted to consider a river which is called sacred in the ṚV and which, according to other indications, conforms to the later Sarasvatī in its geographical position as really identical with the later Sarasvatī.[67]

Our hymns are addressed as much to the celestial Sarasvatī as to her terrestrial counterpart. The poet turns his attention from the one to the other so frequently that it is difficult to determine in each case which of the two he is speaking about.[68]

NOTES

INTRODUCTION

1. ARW, I, p. 89.

2. *Die Religionen*, I, 1923, p. 425.

3. E. B. Tylor, *Anfänge der Kultur*, I, pp. 347, 350; II, p. 323; A. Lang, *Myth, Ritual and Religion*, I, p. 122 ff.; Franz Cumont, *La Théologie Solaire*, 1909, p. 3; K. Th. Preuss, "Das Problem der Mondmythologie" in ARW, XXIII, p. 1 ff.

4. On the Sauras see R. G. Bhandarkar, *Vaiṣṇavism, Saivism and Minor Religious Systems* (Grundriss III, 6), p. 152 ff.

5. Böhtlingk, *Chrestomathie*, 2nd ed., p. 101.

6. R. E. Enthoven, *Folklore of Bombay*, Oxford, pp. 29-62; William Crooke, *Religion and Folklore of Northern India*, (prepared for the press by R. E. Enthoven), pp. 29-42.

7. *Hindu Gods and Heroes*, London, 1922, Preface.

8. *Revue Critique*, 1902, p. 3.

9. A. Lang, *Modern Mythology*, pp. 133, 135. See also Brinton, *Religions of Primitive Peoples*, p. 138 ff.

10. Hillebrandt, ZII, IV, p. 219.

11. *Der arische Weltkönig und Heiland*, pp. 51, 120, 123.

12. Neisser translates differently: "benevolent, benefactor." But the word can hardly be separated from *ghṛṇá* and *ghṛ́ṇi*. Geldner (Glossar) also translates *ghṛ́ṇi* as "sunshine, blaze of the sun, the sun."

13. Cf. also von Bradke, *Dyaus Asura, Ahura Mazda und die Asuras*, p. 16.

14. Cf. Arbman, *Rudra*, p. 127.

15. In his foreword to W. Crooke's *Religion and Folklore of Northern India*, p. 2, Enthoven says quite rightly that "the student should be prepared to accept with caution the picture of the common beliefs of Hindus drawn by scholars from a study of Sanskrit literature. Spirit-scaring rites are to be traced in the Vedas; but primitive thought and practice in India rest largely on a system of godling worship and spirit scaring that is older than the Vedas."

16. A. Lang, *The Making of Religion*, 2nd ed., p. 173 ff. (p. 185: "We must try to get rid of our theory that a powerful, moral, eternal Being was, from the first, *ex officio*, conceived as 'spirit': and so was necessarily derived from a ghost;" p. 189 : "The ghost-theory, therefore by the evidence of anthropology itself, is not needed for the evolution of the high gods of savages.")

17. Keith raises two "fatal objections" against my use of the words, Devayāna and Pitṛyāṇa. He thinks that "it is not in accord with tradition which does not thus connect the Ṛigveda with the ceremonies of the Devayāna or the Uttarāyaṇa, with which Hillebrandt, without warrant, identifies that term, and, as a matter of fact, the Rigveda does contain, along with other

matter not appropriate to its supposed purpose, a most important section of hymns dealing with the worship of the Fathers" (*Religion and Philosophy of the Veda*, I, p. 15). I have always said that the ṚV serves "primarily" the Devayāna. Of course, I have not overlooked the Pitṛsaṃhitā in book X, the number of hymns of which is insignificant and which is not included in any of the family-books, but precisely in the book of additions which contains much other material also. At various places in the first edition of this work (II.29n, 30, 82, 138, 141; III.297, 299, 420) I have emphasized the reasons for choosing the very appropriate expression, and I do not see any reason to change it now.

18. *Die Religion des Veda*, 1st ed., p. 605.

19. *Anfänge der Kultur*, II, p. 299.

20. K. Th. Preuss, *Zeitschrift für Ethnologie*, 1910, p. 800.

21. Reproduced in my *Vedische Mythologie* (smaller ed.), p. 17.

22. (Contrary to what has been stated in VSt, II, 288) nothing is proved by the verse ṚV X.14.2 :

yátrā naḥ pū́rve pitáraḥ pareyúḥ
enā́ jajñānā́ḥ pathyā ánu svā́ḥ ||

"Whither, along their own path, our Fathers, who were born here, went once." "Their own path" is the path of death, or the *pitṛyā́ṇo "itaro devayā́nāt"* (Cf. X.18.1). Nor can I agree with the interpretation which Böhtlingk, following Roth (ZDMG, XLVI, 759), gives for the verses ṚV I.164.30, 38 (SBKSGW, 1893, 92).

23. SBE, XI, pp. 162-3.

24. *Divyāvadāna*, p. 83 ff. *Śakro devānām indro* or *devendro*.

25. *Saṃyuttanikāya*, 4, 201.

26. Oldenberg, *Buddha*, 5th ed., p. 65.

27. Cf. ZDMG, XLIX, p. 287 ff.; Hillebrandt, *Zur Bedeutung von Gandharva*, Breslau, 1906.

28. When they are mentioning Brahmanical gods, Buddhist texts, as a matter of fact, enumerate very few names only. The *Tevijjasutta* (I, p. 244) mentions Indra, Soma, Varuṇa, Īśāna, Prajāpati, Brahman, Mahiddhi and Yama; *Saṃyuttanikāya*, I, p. 219, has Prajāpati, Varuṇa and Īśāna besides Sakka and the *devā tāvatiṃsā*; *Therīgathā* 87: *aggiṃ candañ ca sūriyañ ca devatā ca namassi 'ham*; also *Dīghanikāya* XIII, 17; *Jātaka* 543 : Kuvera, Soma, Varuṇa, Dhātā and Vidhātā as sacrificers. A Mahārāṣṭrī legend (Jacobi, *Ausgewählte Erzählungen in Mahārāṣṭrī*, p. 30, 207) narrates that many people gathered at one place; some said that Brahman is the highest god because he with his four faces brings perfection to all the world and is the teacher of the Vedas; others said that Viṣṇu is the important one because he goes everywhere, destroys the Dānavas who bring ruin to the world and at the time of universal destruction he preserves the world within himself; still others say that Maheśvara is the highest deity because he creates and destroys and has no origin.

29. ZDMG, XLIX, p. 173.

30. H. D. Griswold, *The Religion of the Ṛgveda*, p. 82, agrees with my view.

31. The same is the case among the Mexicans: K. Th. Preuss, "Phallische

Fruchtbarkeitsdämonen" in *Archiv für Anthropologie*, NF, I, 1903, p. 144.

32. von Bradke, ZDMG, XL, p. 677 ff.; Wackernagel, *Altindische Grammatik*, I, p. XX ff.

33. Oldenberg, *Buddha*, 1st ed., Excurs.

34. Fick, *Die soziale Gliederung im nordöstlichen Indien zu Buddhas Zeit*, p. 138 ff., 157 ff.

35. OST, IV, 1st ed., pp. 317[281], 320, 321.

36. *The Religion of the Ṛgveda*, p. 30 ff.

37. Not to be ignored is the absence of the actual Indian landscape — its fauna as well as flora — as pointed out by C. Formici, *Pensiero religioso nell 'India*, Bologna 1926, p. 21 ff.

38. *Indian Thought*, I, p. 112.

39. Griswold agrees with me. Cf. *The God Varuṇa in the Ṛgveda*. Ithaka 1910, p. 31 and *The Religion of the Ṛgveda*, p. 86. Cf. also the statement of Boas (*Zeitschrift für Ethnologie*, XXVII, p. 512) that we must regard the mythology of each tribe as the product of a fusion of material from the most varied sources. This material, he adds, is developed by each tribe according to its genius, its social institutions and the older concepts which govern its thought-process. Nietzsche (X, Leipzig 1896, pp. 350, 356) says of the Greek gods that almost all of them are "assembled one layer upon the other, sometimes fused together, sometimes joined in a make-shift way."

40. *Vedische Mythologie* (smaller ed.), p. 39.

41. See also M. Bloomfield, *Contributions*, III, p. 185; Oldenberg, *Die Religion des Veda*, 2nd ed., p. 52: "If such myths, which one would like to call myth-molecules or monads in contrast to the more complex new formations, undergo a fusion, one should not expect to find in the resulting product the mythical image of a long involved natural event...fantasy utilises the old motifs for its independent creation."

42. Oldenberg is right when he says in *Die Religion des Veda*, 2nd ed., p. 100: "While glorifying Indra and Agni together, people extended what was due to one god to the other also. ...Thus the myth wanders from one god to the other; scholars must be cautious enough not to ascribe to the myth the same importance at both the places; on the contrary they must distinguish between what was original and what was transferred, Cf. Vodskov, *Syaeledyrkelse og Naturdyrkelse*, p. 497.

43. At first the agent and the object are identical; then the former is separated from the object, becomes its beast of burden, leader, bearer and creator; thirdly the agent and the object become completely separate; the agent becomes a free deity whose exit is forgotten and is connected with other gods. Thus Pūṣan, without any objective motivation, comes into the marriage celebrations of Sūryā, the Aśvins drive around the sun and Mitra is separated from the sun.

44. KŚS V.13.1 : *agni annapati, soma rājapati, varuṇa samrāṭpati, mitra kṣatrapati, indra balapati, bṛhaspati brahmapati, savitṛ rāṣṭrapati, pūṣan bhagapati, sarasvatī puṣṭipati.* Or, the gods are assigned to separate classes of men; the animal for a friend, for instance, belongs to Mitra, that for the king belongs to Indra, that for the teacher to Agni, that for the priest to Bṛhaspati, that for the Snātaka to Indrāgnī (ŚGS II.15). Just as certain qualities

are assigned to them so also specific cardinal points are assigned to them to some extent in accordance with their historical evolution. *Gobhila Gṛhya Sūtra* IV.7.41 etc. A remarkable phenomenon is the late formation of a special class of *viśve devāḥ*, who appear along with the *sarve devāḥ*.

We find also isolated instances of attempts to divide the gods according to caste; in this form it is a theological product.

1. Kṣatra : Indra, Varuṇa, Soma, Rudra, Parjanya, Yama, Mṛtyu, Īśāna.
2. Vaiśya : Vasus, Rudras, Ādityas, Viśvedevāḥ, Maruts.
3. Śūdra : Pūṣan.

Cf. ŚBr XIV.4.2.23 ff.; Weber, Ist, X, 10.

45. Already in the ṚV the gods have been divided according to the three realms. Deviating from the later arrangement, I.139.11 distinguishes between eleven *diví*, eleven *pṛthivyā́m ádhi* and eleven *apsukṣít*. About the later period, cf. Oertel, JAOS, XV, p. 239: 33 gods, namely a) 8 Vasus : Fire, Earth, Wind, Atmosphere, Sun, Sky, Moon, Nakṣatras; b) 11 Rudras : ten breaths and the self is the eleventh; c) 12 Ādityas = 12 months.

46. *Arische Urzeit*, p. 147 ff.

CHAPTER 1

UṢAS

1. *Der Rigveda*, IV. p. xi; VI, p. 173 a, s.v. Uṣas.

2. Krichenbauer, *Theogonie und Astronomie*, Vienna 1881, p. 348. Krichenbauer's work contains nothing that is useful for Indian mythology — it is not my task to judge it on other aspects. There he says: "The goddess Uṣas, Gr. *ēōs*, became the bringer of dawn, of the light; in the hymns of the Veda she is compared to a reddish cow and stands by the side of Agni, the ram, as Thetis stands by the side of Hermes. Thetis was also a bringer of spring, of light, and the cow was consecrated to her just as to Uṣas."

3. *Rituallitteratur*, p. 125.

4. ŚŚS VI.5.2 ff. : I.30.20-22 (Gāyatrī); I.48 (Bṛhatī); I.49 (Anuṣṭubh); I.92.1-4; (Jagatī); 13-15 (Uṣṇiḥ); IV.52 (Gāyatrī); V.79 (Paṅkti); VII.77-80 (Triṣṭubh); 81 (Bṛhatī). ĀśvŚS IV.14 : I.30.20-22; I.48, 49; 92.1-4, 5-12, 13-15; 113, 123; III.61; IV.51, 52; V.79, 80; VI.64; VII.75.1-6; 81. I have arranged these passages according to their position in the Saṃhitā. Remarkably enough our Sūtras vary in their selection of the Triṣṭubh verses. Śāṅkhāyana chooses them exclusively from the book of the Vasiṣṭhas (VII. 77-80), whereas Āśvalāyana takes from there only verses VII.75.1-6 and the rest from the other books : I.92.5-12; 113, 123; III.61; IV.51; V.80; VI.64. Here it is worth noting that Śāṅkhāyana does not choose the Triṣṭubh verses 5-12 from hymn I.92, whereas both Śāṅkhāyana and Āśvalāyana enjoin the recitation of the Uṣṇiḥ and Jagatī verses of the same hymn.

5. I.44.1, 2 : Agni, Aśvins, Uṣas; 3-14: Agni.

I.45.1-10a : Agni; 10b : Devāḥ; 46, 47 : Aśvins; 48, 49 : Uṣas; 50 : Sūrya.

I.92.1-15 : Uṣas; 16-18 : Aśvins.

V.73-78 : Aśvins; 79-80 : Uṣas.

VI.62-63 : Aśvins; 64 : Uṣas.

VII.67-74 : Aśvins; 75-81 : Uṣas, both here with changing metres. Thus we find here litanies corresponding to the Agniṣṭoma almost with the same sequence.

6. AV III.10; VIII.9; TS IV.3.11; MS II.13.10.

7. Weber, *Naxatra*, II, pp. 337, 341 ff. For further quotations see *Ritualliteratur*, p. 94.

8. *Ritualliteratur*, p. 6.

9. *vānaspatyā grāvāṇo ghoṣam akrata haviṣ kṛṇvataḥ parivatsarīṇām.* I translate *parivatsarā* here as the New Year. Sāyaṇa on ṚV X.62.2 makes the equation *parivatsaré* = *paryāgate vatsare sampūrṇe* (*sattrānte*); from this the meaning of a full year can easily develop, and perhaps this meaning suited here also.

10. AV III.10.8 : *āyam agant saṃvatsaraḥ patir ekāṣṭake tava* /

11. MS II.13.10 : *ṛtūnāṃ patnī prathameyam āgāt*
ahnāṃ netrī janitry uta prajānām /
ekā satī bahudhoṣā vyuccha
ajīrṇā tvaṃ jaraya sarvam anyat // = TS IV.3.11.

12. ṚV I.49.3 : *úṣaḥ prấrann ṛtū́ṅr ánu divó ántebhyas pári* /
IV.51.6 : *kvà svid āsāṃ katamā́ purāṇī́ yáyā vidhā́nā vidadhúr ṛbhūṇā́m.* Cf. *Kauśika Sūtra* 101 : *ṛtūn bibharti bahudhā virūpān.*

13. Cf. ŚBr VI.1.3.8 : *bhūtānāṃ patir gṛhapatir āsīd uṣāḥ patnī* / *tad yāni tāni bhūtāni ṛtavas te 'tha yaḥ sa bhūtānāṃ patiḥ saṃvatsaraḥ so 'tha yā soṣāḥ patny auṣasī sā* / *tānimāni bhūtāni ca bhūtānāṃ ca patiḥ saṃvatsara uṣasi reto 'siñcan...*

14. The return of Sūrya, the sacrifice and Agni can, of course, refer to the individual day; the renewal of the Uttarāyaṇa appears to be the more appropriate prerequisite.

15. Wilson, *Religious Festivals of the Hindus, Essays*, vol. II, 1862, p. 158 ff.; Nateśa Sāstrī, *Hindu Feasts, Fasts and Ceremonies*, Madras, p. 115; Dubois and Beauchamp, *Hindu Manners*, 2nd ed., p. 575; Charles E. Gover, JRAS, 1871, NS, vol. V, p. 91 ff.; L. Scherman, "Zum indischen Neujahrsfest" in *Einkehr* (1920 No. 51; 1921 No. 1); Nariman-Jackson, *Priyadarśikā*, p. 98, n. 13; Hillebrandt, *Vedische Mythologie* (smaller ed.), p. 27 (description of the New Year festival in Banaras); W. Crooke, "The Holi," *Folklore*, 25, p. 55 ff.

16. *Zeitschrift für deutsche Wortforschung*, II, p. 42.

17. "Lihgo — Refrain der lettischen Sonnenwendlieder" (in *Mitteilungen der Anthropologischen Gesellschaft in Wien*, 32), p. 1 ff.; *Mysterium und Mimus*, p. 45 ff.

18. VII.76.4 : *tá íd devā́nāṃ sadhamā́da āsan*
ṛtā́vānaḥ kaváyaḥ pūrvyā́saḥ /
gūḷhā́ṃ jyótiḥ pitáro ánv avindan
satyámantrā ajanayann uṣā́sam //

X.62.2 : *yá udā́jan pitáro gomáyaṃ vásu*
ṛténā́bhindan parivatsaré valám //

3 : *yá ṛténa sū́ryam ā́rohayan diví*
áprathayan pṛthivī́ṃ mātáraṃ ví /
7 : *índreṇa yujā́ níḥ sṛjanta vāgháto*
vrajáṃ gómantam aśvínam /
107.1 : *āvír abhūn máhi mā́ghonam eṣām*
víśvaṃ jīváṃ támaso nír amoci /
máhi jyótiḥ pitṛ́bhir dattám ā́gāt
urúḥ pánthā dákṣiṇāyā adarśi //

Cf. also VII.79.4 and perhaps X.15.7 : *ā́sīnāso aruṇī́nāṃ upásthe rayíṃ datta...*

19. Cf. ŚBr I.9.3.2 and Eggeling's note on this (SBE, XII, p. 267).

20. X.2.1-6 speaks of the gods (v. 3 : *ā́ devā́nām ápi pánthām aganma*, v. 6 : *víśveṣāṃ hy àdhvarā́ṇām ánīkam...*), v. 7 of the *pitṛyā́ṇa* (*pánthām ánu pravidvā́n pitṛyā́ṇam*). As *pravidvā́n* occurs only in this verse, but in vv. 1, 3, 4 *vidvā́n* occurs as referring to Agni, a contrast must have been intended, and *pravidvā́n* should perhaps be understood as a perfective. Cf. ŚBr II. 1.3.1 : *vasanto grīṣmo varṣāḥ te devā ṛtavaḥ / śarad dhemantaḥ śiśiraḥ te pitaraḥ* [*ṛtavaḥ*].

21. *Ritualliteratur*, p. 95. It should be noted that accordingly during the Agniṣṭoma, which follows the movement of the sun, an Ārbhava Pavamāna-stotra and a sacrifice to the Manes is included in the evening Savana.

22. *Hiraṇyakeśi Gṛhyasūtra*, II.15.9 : *ekāṣṭakā tapasā tapyamānā saṃvatsarasya patnī duduhe prapīnā / taṃ doham upajīvātha pitaraḥ saṃvidānāḥ...*

23. Besides VII.80.2, quoted on p. 23f., cf. VII.78.3 : *ájījanan* [*uṣáso*] *sū́ryaṃ yajñám agním...*, perhaps also I.113.12 : *sumaṅgalī́r bíbhratī devávītim...*VII.75.3 : *janáyanto* [*bhānávo*] *daívyāni vratā́ni...*VI.65.2 : *ágraṃ yajñásya bṛható náyantīr. ...*Perhaps because of this reason she is called dakṣiṇā (Cf. Bergaigne I, p. 128 ff., 243) as a symbol of the cows that are given as gifts during the sacrifice. In view of the parallelism between the day and the year, it is impossible to say positively whether certain verses refer to the individual day or to the New Year. But the latter is more frequent if we look from the ritual point of view, because the ṚV serves only the major sacrifices and hardly takes into account the individual days as long as they do not represent any significant periods of time.

The individual verses of IV.1, particularly 13-17, read like a hymn to the spring or to the beginning of the year — even this is difficult to determine. 13 : "Here did our Fathers, the men, sit (sattra) eagerly [for the sacrifice]. ... With a loud call, they drove out the reddish Dawns, whose shed was a rock, who were rich in milk and were in the cavern." 17 : "The darkness disappeared, the sky lit up and up rose the ray of the divine Dawn. Sūrya entered the high domains, beholding the good and evil in men."

24. Bergaigne I, p. 297. — Cf. I.71.2; II.34.12 : *té dáśagvāḥ prathamā́ yajñám ūhire té no hinvantūṣáso vyùṣṭiṣu* / IV.3.11 : *ṛtenā́driṃ vy àsan bhidántaḥ sám áṅgiraso navanta góbhiḥ / śunáṃ náraḥ pári ṣadann uṣā́sam āvíḥ svàr abhavaj jāté agnaú* // 51.4; V.45.7 : *ánūnod átra hástayato ádrir ā́rcan yéna dáśa māsó návagvāḥ / ṛtáṃ yatī́ sarámā gā́ avindad víśvāni satyā́ṅgirāś cakāra* // v. 8; VI.65.5 : *idā́ hí ta uṣo adrisāno gotrā́ gávām áṅgiraso gṛṇánti / vy àrkéṇa bibhidur bráhmaṇā ca...*VII.79.4 : *tā́vad uṣo rā́dho asmábhyaṃ*

rāsva yā́vat stotṛ́bhyo árado gṛṇānā́ / yā́ṃ tvā jajñúr vṛṣabhásyā rávena vi dṛḷhásya dúro ádrer aurṇoḥ // X.62.2, 3 and particularly the Bṛhaspati hymns like X.67,68. In view of the close association between Ekāṣṭakā — or Uṣas as the case may be — and the Manes, *svadhā́* in I.113.13 : *ajárāmṛ́tā carati svadhā́bhiḥ*; VII.78.4 : *ásthād rátham svadháyā yujyámānām* (cf. also IV.52.6) has the meaning of "offering to the Manes" and not of "by itself." The ritual distinction between the offerings to the gods and those to the Manes is known to the ṚV (cf. X.14.3).

25. Cf. e.g., TS VII.3.10.1 or TMBr VII.10.6 : *chandobhir vai devā ādityaṃ lokam aharan.*

26. *Ritualliteratur*, p. 106.

27. III.19.3 : *atha yad tad ajāyata so 'sāv ādityaḥ taṃ jāyamānaṃ ghoṣā ulūlavo 'nūdatiṣṭhan sarvāṇi ca bhūtāni sarve ca kāmāḥ / tasmāt tasyodayaṃ prati pratyāyanaṃ prati ghoṣā ulūlavo 'nūttiṣṭhanti* etc.

28. V.45.8 : *víśve asyā́ vyúṣi máhināyāḥ*
sáṃ yád góbhir áṅgiraso návantaḥ /
10 : *ā́ sū́ryo aruhac chukrám árṇo.../*
udnā́ ná nā́vam anayanta dhī́rāḥ
āśṛṇvatī́r ā́po arvā́g atiṣṭhan //
VI.7.4 : *tvā́ṃ víśve amṛta jā́yamānam*
śíśuṃ ná devā́ abhí sáṃ navante /
X.88.10 : *stómena hí diví devā́so agním*
ájījanañ cháktibhī rodasiprā́m /

Cf. Scherman, *Philosophische Hymnen aus der Ṛg- und Atharva-Veda-Saṃhitā*, p. 82; Brunnhofer, ZDA, 53 (1911), p. 298.

29. E. H. Meyer, *Deutsche Volkskunde*, p. 254.

30. Hanusch, *Die Wissenschaft des slavischen Mythus*, pp. 193-94 : "As singing was an important aspect of this festival [of winter solstice], the Koleda festival also became a festival of song among the Slavonic peoples... Valvasor also...says : 'It is also the custom [in Carniola] that certain people go around and sing from St. Nicholas' day till Candlemass...They go around in the whole country as they please like the Sternsinger in Germany, to whom they can rightly be compared' "; L. von Schroeder, *Arische Religion*, II, p. 97 ff.

31. VIII.41.3 : *sá kṣápaḥ pári ṣasvaje ny ùsró māyáyā dadhe sá víśvaṃ pári darśataḥ / tásya vénīr ánu vratám uṣás tisró avardhayan*...III.17.3: *trī́ṇy ā́yūṃṣi táva jātavedas tisrá ājā́nīr uṣásas te agne* : "You have three ages, O Jātavedas, the three Uṣas are your mothers" (*mātaraḥ* i.a. Sāyaṇa). VIII.101.6 : *té hinvire aruṇáṃ jényaṃ vásv ékaṃ putráṃ tisṝṇā́m /*. With Ludwig, I count the following also among these passages. I.174.7 : *kárat tisró maghávā dā́nucitrā ní duryoṇé kúyavācaṃ mṛdhí śret /*, said of Indra, and X.67.4 : *avó dvā́bhyāṃ pará ékayā gā́ gúhā tíṣṭhantīr ánṛtasya sétau / bṛ́haspátis támasi jyótir icchán úd usrā́ ā́kar ví hí tisrá ā́vaḥ. vi-āvar* is to be explained as in I.68.1 : *aktū́n vy ū̀rṇot*, I.105.15 *vy ū̀rṇoti matím*, VI.44.8 : *vápūr dṛśáye venyó vy ā̀vaḥ*, that is to say, "he made the three manifest." Geldner, VSt, 2, p. 286 adds, with Sāyaṇa, "*dvārāḥ*."

32. Bergaigne, *Vedic Religion according to the Hymns of the Ṛgveda* (translated by V. G. Paranjpe), I, p. 314. (This and the subsequent quotations

from this work with the kind permission of Professor V. G. Paranjpe — Tr.)

33. JAOS, XV, p. 270; *The Religions of India*, p. 77.

34. Böhtlingk, SBKSGW, 23, 4 (1902), p. 17.

35. Other passages that can be cited are uncertain. The *tisráḥ prajā́ ā́ryāḥ* in VII.33.7 deserve our attention : *trayás kṛṇvanti bhúvaneṣu rétas tisráḥ prajā́ ā́ryā jyótiragrāḥ / tráyo gharmā́sa uṣásaṃ sacante sárvāṅ ít tā́ṅ ánu vidur vásiṣṭhāḥ //* "Three place the semen in the worlds; the Aryan progeny, which is preceded by the light, consists of three; three hot vessels follow Uṣas" — (cf. Oertel, *Contributions*, I.33). The verse makes great difficulties. For the "three who place the semen in the worlds," one may refer to V.69.2 : *tráyas tasthur vṛṣabhā́sas tisṛṇā́ṃ dhiṣáṇānāṃ retodhā́ḥ...* VII.101.4 : *tráyaḥ kóśāsa upasécanāsaḥ*; VIII.2.8 (?); I.164.10 : *tisró mātṝ́s trī́n pitṝ́n bíbhrad éka ūrdhvás tasthau*; II.27.8 : *tisró bhū́mīr dhārayan tṝ́ṇr utá dyū́n...*

It is different with the three *gharmas*. In TS IV.3.11a three *mahimans* replace them (*vadhūr jajāna navagaj janitrī, traya enām* [*uṣāsam*] *mahimānaḥ sacante*). AV VIII.9.11 : *mahānto asyāṃ mahimāno antar vadhūr jigāya navagaj janitrī*. These three Mahimans are explained in TS IV, comm., p. 379 as Agni, Sūrya and Candra; this is quite correct and applies to the three Gharmas also; see comm. on TS IV.3.11c, p. 380 (*ṛtasya panthām anu tisra āgus trayo gharmāso anu jyotiṣāguḥ / prajām ekā rakṣaty ūrjam ekā vratam ekā rakṣati devayūnām*; AV VIII.9.13; MS II, p. 160, 5). But quite differently MS IV.2.12 (35.8); TMBr XX.15.3 (*agnir uṣasaṃ sacate vāyur uṣasaṃ sacate 'sāv āditya uṣasaṃ sacate*). This is also correct as will be shown below s.v. Agni.

36. *agnis tigmena śociṣā...*

37. v. 6 : *yát púruṣeṇa haviṣā devā́ yajñám átanvata vasantó asyāsīd ā́jyaṃ grīṣmá idhmáḥ śarád dhavíḥ /*. For *varṣāḥ* VII.103 has *prā́vṛṣ*. According to ŚBr I.5.4.1 ff.; II.1.3.1; TS II.6.1.1 ff. the five seasons are to be understood by *samidh, tanūnapād, iḍ, barhiḥ* and *svāhā*. According to KBr III.4 *samidh* (that is, the kindling) = *vasanta, tanūnapād* = *grīṣma, iḍ* = *varṣāḥ barhiḥ* = *oṣadhi, svāhā* = *hemanta*.

38. V.14.4 : *agnír jātó arocata ghnán dásyūñ jyótiṣā támaḥ / ávindad gā́ apáḥ svàḥ*; X.91.6 : *evā́ punānó apáḥ svàr gā́ḥ.../*

39. VI.60.2: *tā́ yodhiṣṭaṃ abhí gā́ indra nūnám apáḥ svàr uṣáso agna ūḷhā́ḥ...;* IX.90.4: *apáḥ siṣāsann uṣásaḥ svàr gā́ḥ sáṃ cikrado...*

40. Her chariot (Sing. or Plur.) I.48.7; 113.14; 123.1, 7; IV.14.3; VI.65.2; VII.75.6; 78.1, 4.

41. Cf. VII.77.2 : *gávāṃ mātā́ netry áhnām aroci* and 76.6.

42. V.80.1; VIII.5.1; 73.16 attribute the epithet *aruṇápsu* to Uṣas. As the meaning of *psu* as "food" is not quite clear, in spite of the statement of Hopkins (JAOS, XV, p. 267 : "the word *aruṇápsu* gives a combination of 'bearing food' and 'the food is red' "), it is but logical to assume — taking into account *ruśadgo* and *ruśatpaśu* — that here it is synonymous with *aruṇápasu* = *aruṇápaśu* (cf. Avestan °*fšu* and the short forms *frafšu* and *drvafšu* mentioned by Joh. Schmidt, KZ, 25, 57) and that the earliest evidence for the pronunciation of *ś* as *s* occurs here (Wackernagel, §197, 198). Uṣas neither brings nor receives any reddish food; reddish are only the horses of her chariot.

The same meaning applies to other compounds, e.g., VIII.20.10 : *vṛṣaṇaśvéna maruto vṛ̥ṣapsunā ráthena*; or VII.4.6 : *mā́ tvā vayám...avīrā́ mā́psavaḥ pári ṣadáma.* (To I.49.1 : *vahantv aruṇápsava úpa tvā somíno gṛhám* we may add *rathā́saḥ*, cf. I.48.7). Perhaps this meaning is not suitable to *viśvápsu, pruṣitápsu,* epithets of the eagle, of the birds etc. But it is not necessary to explain the second part of all these compounds in the same way; here we can think of *psu* (food) derived from *bhas* "to eat," or of *bhās* "to shine," from which Kretschmer, KZ, 31, p. 413, wishes to derive *aruṇápsu* also. Bloomfield, AJPh, 29, p. 81; IF, 25, p. 185 ff. sees in *γu* and *βu* a representative of Indo-European *gᵘu* and thinks that "the weak stemforms of Sanskrit *paśu* are present in Vedic *kṣu, kṣumát*" etc. — I think that *aruṇápsu* is a nearer example. *ṛtapsu* might also belong to the same category. Cf. Neisser, WB.

43. On *étagva* "having bright rays," "shining brightly" see Bloomfield, *Contributions to the Interpretation of the Veda*, 7, p. 427.

44. *Nighaṇṭu*, 1.15 : *aruṇyo gāva uṣasām.* Cf. also ABr IV.9.2.

45. Cf. Bergaigne, I, p. 242 ff. — I.92.5 : *ví tiṣṭhate bā́dhate kṛṣṇám ábhvam*; 113.16b : *ápa prā́gāt táma ā́ jyótir eti*; IV.51.9 : *gū́hantīr ábhvaṃ ásitaṃ rúśadbhiḥ*; 52.6 : *vy ā̀var jyótiṣā támaḥ*; VI.64.3; 65.1 : *yā́ bhānúnā rúśatā rāmyā́sv ájñāyi tirás támsaś cid aktū́n*; 65.2; VII.71.1; VII.75.1 : *ápa drúhas táma āvor ájuṣṭam*; 77.1 : *ákar jyótir bā́dhamānā támāṅsi*; 78.2 : *uṣā́ yati jyótiṣā bā́dhamānā víśvā támāṅsi duritā́pa devī́*; 3 : *apācī́naṃ támo agād ájuṣṭam*; 80.2 : *eṣā́ syā́ návyam ā́yur dádhānā gūḍhvī́ támo jyótiṣoṣā́ abodhi*; 81.1 :... *jyótiṣ kṛṇoti sūnárī.*

46. The verse gives no occasion for assuming it to be a much shortened comparison (Geldner, VSt, 2, p. 286, n. 5). Cows as well as horses break through their fences often enough in reality. Cf. also VII.79.4.

47. III.5.1 : *práty agnír uṣásaś cékitānó 'bodhi...* /
...sámiddhó 'pa dvā́rā támaso váhnir āvaḥ //
V.45.1 : *vidā́ divó viṣyann ádrim ukthair*
āyatyā́ uṣáso arcíno guḥ /
ápāvṛta vrajínīr út svàr gāt
ví dúro mā́nuṣīr devá āvaḥ //

Spring opens the doors of the houses.

VI.17.6 : *aúrṇor dúra usríyābhyo vi dṛlhā́*
úd ūrvā́d gā́ asṛjo áṅgirasvān // (Indra)
VII.75.7 : *rujád* [*uṣā́*] *dṛḷhā́ni dádad usríyāṇām*
práti gā́va uṣásaṃ vāvaśanta /

IV.1.13; VII.79.4 etc. It is unnecessary to cite additional passages here. They will be discussed in connection with Indra, who breaks open the caves of Vala and frees the enclosed cattle which are distinguished from the enclosed waters. About the Manes cf. p. 24 ff. above.

48. Weber, *Zwei Vedische Texte über Omina und Portenta*, p. 351; Schlagintweit, *Reisen in Indien und Hochasien*, I, p. 113 (cited by Brandes, p. 78, n. 1). Hopkins, "The Punjab and the ṚV" in JAOS, 19, p. 28.

49. According to a calculation which Prof. Neugebauer was good enough to make, the ratio for Punjab is as follows :

	Geographical Latitude	Longest Day	Shortest Day
Multan	30°	13 h 56 m	10 h 4 m
Lahore	32°	14 h 6 m	9 h 54 m
Peshawar	34°	14 h 22 m	9 h 38 m

50. Additional passages see section h. Uṣas and the Night.

51. AV XIII.3.26 : *kṛṣṇā́yāḥ putró árjuno rā́tryā vatsó 'jāyata.* Cf. TS V.4.9.3 : *naktoṣāseti kṛṣṇāyai śvetavatsāyai payasā juhoti.*

52. For the convenience of the reader, I cite the passages verbatim. I.56.4 : *yadi távisī...índraṃ síṣakty uṣásaṃ ná sū́ryaḥ*; IX.84.2; I.66.8 : *jāráḥ kanī́nām pátir jánīnām* (Agni); 69.1 : *śukráḥ śuśukvā́ṅ uṣó ná jāráḥ*; 9 : *uṣó ná jāró vibhā́vā*; 92.11 : *yóṣā jārásya cákṣasā ví bhāti*; 123.10: *kanyèva tanvā̀ śā́śadānāṅ éṣi devi devám íyakṣamāṇam*; 152.4 : *prayántam ít pári jāráṃ kanī́nāṃ páśyāmasi nópanipádyamānam*; VII.9.1 : *ábodhi jārá uṣásām upásthāt*; 10.1 : *uṣó ná jāráḥ pṛthú pā́jo aśret;* VII. 63.3 : *vibhrā́jamāna uṣásām upásthād rebhair úd ety anumadyámānaḥ*; VII.76.3 : *yátaḥ pári jārá ivācáranty úṣo dadṛkṣé ná púnar yatī́va*; X.3.3 : *bhadró bhadráyā sácamāna ā́gāt svásāraṃ jāró abhy èti paścā́t*; cf. also TBr III.1.6.3 : Uṣas wished "*priyādityasya subhagā syām.*"

53. I.113.9 : *úṣo...ví yád ā́vaś cákṣasā sū́ryasya |*
122.2 : *sū́ryasya śriyā́ sudṛ́śī híraṇyaiḥ ||*
123.12 : *yátamānā raśmíbhiḥ sū́ryasya |*
124.8 : *vyucchántī raśmíbhiḥ sū́ryasya...*
II.23.2 : *usrā́ iva sū́ryo jyótiṣā mahó*
víśveṣām ij janitā́ bráhmaṇām asi |
V.79.8 : *...íṣa ā́ vahā duhitar divaḥ |*
sākáṃ sū́ryasya raśmíbhiḥ śukraíḥ śócadbhiḥ...
VI.49.3 : *aruṣásya duhitárā vírūpe*
stṛ́bhir anyā́ pipiśé sū́ro anyā́ |
VII.36.1 : *ví raśmíbhiḥ sasṛje sū́ryo gā́ḥ |*
VIII.9.18 : *yád uṣo yā́si bhānúnā sáṃ sū́ryeṇa rocase |*
X.3.2 : (Agni separated from Sūrya) *kṛṣṇā́ṃ yád énīm abhí várpasā bhū́j janáyan yóṣāṃ bṛhatáḥ pitúr jā́m* (cf. Bloomfield, *Contributions*, 7, p. 408)
35.5 : *prá yā́ḥ sísrate sū́ryasya raśmíbhir*
jyótir bhárantīr uṣáso vyùṣṭiṣu |

54. i.e., the sun conceived as a woman. But according to Patañjali, II.220, it means as much as *sūryasya strī*, i.e., wife of the sun, thus confirming what was said above.

55. Oldenberg, *Die Religion des Veda*, 1st ed., p. 213 ff.; 2nd ed., p. 245 ff. etc. L. v. Schroeder, *Arische Religion*, II, pp. 14, 392 ff.

56. I have come across only one instance where the moon is feminine (*candrā*), IA, 22, p. 315 ff.

57. IX.71.7 : *rebhó ná pūrvī́r uṣáso ví rājati*; 75.3 : *uṣáso ví rājati*; 86.19, 21 : *uṣáso ví rocayat*, and (of Bṛhaspati) 83.3.

58. Andrew Lang, *Custom and Myth*, p. 210. Contra Hopkins, *The Religions of India*, p. 77.

59. Does VI.59.6 also belong here : *índrāgnī apā́d iyám pū́rvā́gāt padvátībhyaḥ | hitvī́ śíro jihváyā vā́vadat* etc. ?

60. I think that it will not be superfluous to collate all the verses here for the sake of clarity. I.92.11 : *vyūrṇvatī divó antāň abodhy ápa svásāraṃ sanutár yuyoti;* 113.1d : *evā́ rā́try uṣáse yonim āraik*; 2: *rúśadvatsā rúśatī śvety ā́gād ā́raig u kṛṣṇā́ sádanāny asyāḥ / samānábandhū amṝte anūcī dyā́vā várṇaṃ carata āminānė́*; 3 : *samānó ádhvā svásror anantás tám anyā́nyā carato deváśiṣṭe / ná methete ná tasthatuḥ suméke nā́ktoṣā́sā sámanasā vírūpe //*; 14b : *ápa kṛṣṇā́ṃ nirṇíjaṃ devy ā̀vaḥ*; 123.1cd : *kṛṣṇā́d úd asthād aryā̀ vihāyās...;* 6cd : *spārhā́ vásūni támasā́pagūlhāvíṣ kṛṇvanty uṣáso vibhātī́ḥ //*; 7 : *ápānyád ety abhy ànyád eti víṣurūpe áhanī sáṃ carete / parikṣítos támo anyā́ gúhākar ádyaud uṣā́ḥ śóśucatā ráthena //*; 9b : *śukrā́ kṛṣṇā́d ajaniṣṭa śvitīcī́ /*; 124.8 : *svásā svásre jyā́yasyai yónim āraig ápaity asyāḥ praticákṣyeva /*; 142.7; 185.1 : *katarā́ pū́rvā katarā́parāyóḥ kathā́ jāté kavayo kó ví veda / víśvaṃ tmánā bibhṛto yád dha nā́ma ví vartete áhanī cakríyeva* (cf. VI.9.1 : *áhaś ca kṛṣṇám áhar árjunaṃ ca ví vartete*); 186.4 : *úpa va éṣe námasā jigīṣóṣā́sānáktā sudúgheva dhenúḥ / samāné áhan vimímāno arkáṃ víṣurūpe páyasi sásminn ū́dham //*; 188.6 : *surukmé hí supéśasā́dhi śriyā́ virā́jataḥ / uṣā́sāv éhá sīdatām//*; II.3.6 : *tántuṃ tatáṃ saṃváyantī samīcī́ yajñásya péśaḥ sudúghe payasvatī //*; 31.5 : *utá tyé devī́ subhága mithūdṝśoṣā́sānáktā jágatām apījúva /*; III.4.6 : *ā́ bhándamāne uṣásā úpāke utá smayete tanvā̀ vírūpe /* 54.6, 7; 55.11 : *nā́nā cakrāte yamyā̀ vápūṃṣi táyor anyád rócate kṛṣṇám anyát / śyā́vī ca yád áruṣī ca svásārau...;* 12 : *mātā́ ca yátra duhitā́ ca dhenū́ sabardúghe dhāpáyete samīcī́...*; IV.52.1 : *práti ṣyā́ sūnárī jánī vyucchántī pári svásuḥ*; V.5.6 : *suprátīke vayovṛdhā yahvī́ ṛtásya mātárā / doṣā́m uṣā́sam īmahe //*; 41.7; VI.49.3 (see n. 53 above); VII.2.6 : *utá yóṣaṇe divyé mahī́ na uṣā́sānáktā sudúgheva dhenúḥ*; 71.1 : *ápa svásur uṣáso nág jihīte;* X.36.1 : *uṣā́sānáktā bṛhatī́ supéśasā:* 70.6 : *devī́ divó duhitárā suśilpé uṣā́sānáktā...*; 110.6 : *...divyé yóṣaṇe bṛhatī́ surukmé ádhi śríyaṃ śukrapíśaṃ dadhāne //*; 172.4 : *uṣā́ ápa svásus támaḥ sáṃ vartayati vartaníṃ sujātátā //.* To these passages we may perhaps add X.61.4 also : *kṛṣṇā́ yád góṣv aruṇī́ṣu sī́dad divó nápātāśvinā huve vām.* The Aśvins are invoked, among other occasions, during the Prātaranuvāka, i.e., in the earliest hour of the morning. Ludwig and Geldner have interpreted the verse as referring to the day time. That some one should wish for "a black cow among the red ones" as Dakṣiṇā (Pischel, VSt, I, p. 75) is not probable if we take the significance of the black colour into account. On *yad* "if, when" see Delbrück, *Altindische Syntax*, p. 322. Bergaigne, I. p. 250 refers the *kṛṣṇé vásudhitī* in III.31.17; IV.48.3 to the day and the night. Cf. further TS III.2.1 : *dvau samudrau vitatāv ajūryau* etc.; TBr II.5. 5.3 : *ávānyā́ṅs tantū́n kiráto dhattó anyā́n / nā́papṛjyáte ná gamāte ántam*; 7.12.6; AV X.7.42; MBh I.3.146 ff. — Cf. Ludwig, VI, 173a s.v. Uṣas.

61. *vi dyā́m eṣi rájas pṛthv áhā mímāno aktúbhiḥ / páśyañ jánmāni sūrya //.* Cf. AV XIII.2.5 : *ahorātre vimimāno yad eṣi* or about Savitṛ in ṚV IV.53.7 : *sá naḥ kṣapā́bhir áhabhiś ca jinvatu.*

62. I.115.4 : *yadéd áyukta haritaḥ sadhásthāt*
ā́d rā́trī vā́sas tanute simásmai /
(differently VSt, II, p.189).

63. I.115.5cd : *anantám anyád rúśad asya pā́jaḥ*

kṛṣṇám anyád dharítaḥ sáṃ bharanti ||

Cf. also X.3.2 (n. 53 above).

64. IV.13.4 : *vahiṣṭhebhir viháran yāsi tántum*
avavyáyann ásitaṃ deva vásma |
dávidhvato raśmáyaḥ sū́ryasya
cármevā́vādhus támo apsv àntáḥ ||

65. X.37.3 : *prācī́nam anyád ánu vartate rájaḥ*
úd anyéna jyótiṣā yāsi sūrya ||

It is the two *rūpé* about which AV XIII.2.28, 42 says : " 'Day and night,' the two *jyótiṣī*" (*Zeitschrift für Buddhismus*, VI, p. 114, n. 2). Cf. the Savitṛ verses I.35.4,9; further I.164.14 and III.55.11 (n. 60 above). (Cf. Bergaigne, *Quarante Hymnes*, p. 63).

66. Cf. III.55.12 (see n. 60 above); V.1.4 : *yád īṃ súvāte uṣásā virūpe* (I.113.3) *śvetó vājī́ jāyate ágre áhnām*. Similarly the two *mātúr anyé yamyā̀ sábandhū* in V.47.5 appear to be Uṣāsānaktā :
dvé yád īṃ bibhṛtó mātúr anyé
ihéha jāté yamyā̀ sábandhū ||

67. Perhaps the two persons "of the same age" in I.114.4 also denote the day and the night.

68. *pátnīva pūrváhūtiṃ vāvṛdhádhyā uṣā́sānáktā purudhā́ vidāne starī́r nā́tkaṃ vyùtaṃ vásānā sū́ryasya śriyā́ sudṛ́śī híraṇyaiḥ*. Not all the difficulties of this are removed in VSt, II, p. 197 ff. The *parivṛktā* appears during the twelve *ratnāhavis* of the Rājasūya, one of which is offered in her house; furthermore, she appears with a great entourage, decorated and with other women during the Aśvamedha; *àtka vyùta* must somehow or other refer to her clothing.

69. AV VIII.9.12 : *chándaḥpakṣe uṣásā pépiśāne*
samānáṃ yóniṃ ánu sáṃ carete |
sū́ryapatnī sáṃ carataḥ prajánatí
ketumátī ajáre bhū́riretasā ||

70. AV XIII.2.32 : *ahorātré pári sū́ryaṃ vásāne*. Cf. ŚBr X.5.2.4 : *asau vā āditya vivasvān eṣā hy ahoratre vivaste*...

TS III.2.2 : *dvé drádhasī satátī vasta ékaḥ*
keśī́ víśvā bhúvanāni vidvā́n |
tirodhā́yaity ásitaṃ vásānaḥ
śukrám ā́ datte anuhā́ya jā́ryai ||

In a quite different metaphor, it is said in TS VII.5.25.2 : *ahar vā aśvasya jāyamānasya mahimā purastāj jāyate rātrir enam mahimā paścad anu jāyate*| *etau vai mahimānāv aśvam abhitaḥ sambabhūvatuḥ* |. Again we find another metaphor in TBr 1.5.10.7 : *te kuśyau vyaghnan te ahorātre abhavatām* | *ahar eva suvarṇābhavat* | *rajatā rātriḥ* | *sa yad āditya udeti etām eva tat suvarṇāṃ kuśīm ānusameti* | *atha yad astam eti etām eva tad rajatāṃ kuśīm anusaṃviśati* | . Further material under Vivasvat.

71. I.62.3 : *indrasyā́ṅgirasāṃ ceṣṭaú*
vidát sarámā tánayāna dhāsím |
bṛ́haspátir bhinád ádriṃ vidád gāḥ
sám usríyābhir vāvaśanta náraḥ ||

III.31.6 : *vidád yádī sarámā rugṇám ádrer*

máhi pā́thaḥ pūrvyáṃ sadhryàk kaḥ |
ágraṃ nayat supády ákṣarāṇām
ácchā rávaṃ prathamā́ jānatī́ gāt ||
V.45.7 : *ánūnod átra hástayato ádriḥ*
árcan yéna dáśa māsó návagvāḥ |
ṛtáṃ yatī́ sarámā gā́ avindat
víśvāni satyā́ṅgirāś cakāra ||
8 : *víśve asyā́ vyúṣi máhināyāḥ*
sáṃ yád góbhir áṅgiraso návanta |
útsa āsāṃ paramé sadhásthe
ṛtásya pathā́ sarámā vidad gā́ḥ ||

To these belong the legends of the Brāhmaṇa literature also (cf. Oertel, "*Contributions* II" in JAOS, XIX, p. 97 ff.), in which myth, ritual and new elements are fused together into a mythologically inextricable mixture. The waters, Indra, Saramā and Gotra are mentioned together in ṚV IV.16.8.

72. Geldner, *Auswahl,* II, p. 199 : "perhaps originally the voice of the gods"; Charpentier, *Suparṇa Sage,* p. 92 : "voice (*vāk*) of the middle region," following Yāska. Charpentier refers to *ágraṃ nayat supády ákṣarāṇām* III.31.6, but is that not also Uṣas in I.92.9 : *víśvasya vā́cam avidan manāyóḥ* (Bergaigne, I, p. 286) ? And above all there must be an inner connection between Saramā and Sārameyau, the "two dogs," which I fail to see in the case of Vāc. But this inner connection becomes evident when we think of Uṣas, no matter whether we follow Bloomfield (Cerberus) in explaining Sārameyau as the sun and the moon or not.

73. "Go away from here, O Paṇis; the cattle vanishing away [among you] should come out according to the Law — the cattle which Bṛhaspati, Soma, the Soma stones and the wise Ṛṣis found in the hide-out."

74. Cf. further the second verse of this hymn : *órvā́d gávāṃ mātā́ jānatī́ gāt* and III.31.6 : *ágraṃ nayat supády ákṣarāṇām ácchā rávaṃ prathamā́ jānatī́ gāt* (Saramā). The ṚV explains sufficiently who this *gávāṃ mātā́* is.

75. JAOS, XV, p. 163; contra Tilak, *Orion*, p. 109; Ehni, *Der vedische Mythus des Yama*, 2nd ed., p. 83 ff.

76. Cf. Bloomfield, JAOS, XV, p. 172 ff., who came to the same conclusion about Saraṇyū (p. 186) at the same time as I did; Macdonell, p. 125. —Sāyaṇa on III.39.3 : *yamā́ cid átra yamasū́r asūta* explains the mother as Uṣas and the twins as the Aśvins.

77. AV XIII.1.33 : *vatsó virā́jo vṛṣabhó matīnā́m*
ā́ ruroha śukrápṛṣṭho 'ntárikṣam |
ghṛténārkám abhy àrcanti vatsám
bráhma sántaṃ bráhmaṇā vardhayanti ||

"The calf of Virāj, the bull of hymns, climbed the atmosphere; its back is white. With libations of butter they sing a hymn to the calf; it is Bráhman, and they strengthen it with Bráhman."

78. SBE, XLII, p. 667 : "another personification of the shining female heaven (dawn)." Cf. Henry, *Les Hymnes Rohitas*, p. 31.

79. AV VIII.9.1 : *kútas taú jātaú katamáḥ só árdhaḥ*
kásmāl lokā́t katamásyā pṛthivyā́ḥ |

vatsaú virā́jaḥ salilā́d úd aitām
taú tvá pṛcchāmi kataréṇa dugdhā́ ||

"From where were the two born ? Which is the half [of the world] ? From which place, from which land ? The two calves of Virāj climbed out of the ocean. I ask you about the two. Which of them has milked her (Virāj) ?"

80. *Les Livres VII et IX* (Paris 1894), p. 65. Henry refers to AV XIII.1.41 : "...bearing the calf with her foot, the cow rose up. Where has she turned to ? To which half [of the world] has she gone away ? Where does she give birth ? Certainly not in our herd." Bloomfield also sees here "sun" and "dawn" in the calf and cow (SBE, XLII, p. 667).

81. AV VIII.9.8 : *yā́ṃ prácyutām ánu yajñā́ḥ pracyávante*
upatíṣṭhanta upatíṣṭhamānām |
yásyā vraté prasavé yakṣám éjati
sā virā́ḍ ṛṣayaḥ paramé vyòman ||
9 : *aprāṇaíti prāṇéna prāṇatī́nām*
virā́t svarā́jam abhyèti paścā́t |...

82. The beginning and the end of the ritual year. Cf. TS III.4.10.2 : *virājy eva yajñam āpnoti* and the commentary on it (p. 289) : *agnihotrī virājam eva prāpya tāṃ virājam ekāṣṭakāṃ kṛtvā upadhānaṃ kṛtavān bhavati.* Uṣas restores Sūrya, Agni and Yajña; see p. 23 f. above.

83. Virāj, Svarāj and Samrāj occur together in AV XVII.1.22, 23.

84. From the semen arose Rudra (for the continuation of this legend see s.v. Rudra in vol. II).

85. Muir, OST, 1st ed., IV, p. 39.

86. Cf. TMBr VIII.2.10; MS IV.2.12 (35.11 ff.).

87. ṚV I.71.5 : *mahé yát pitrá īṃ rásaṃ divé kár*
áva tsarat pṛṣaṇyàś (gen.) *cikitvā́n |*
sṛjád ástā dhṛṣatā́ didyúm asmai
svā́yāṃ devó duhitári tvíṣiṃ dhāt ||

The archer is Rudra. Other passages where the incest is mentioned are
I.71.8ab : *ā́ yád iṣé nṛpátiṃ téja ā́naṭ*
śúci réto níṣiktaṃ dyaúr abhī́ke |

III.31.1; V.42.13; X.10.1 (cf. Geldner, VSt, II, p. 34; *Festgruss für Weber*, p. 19 ff.); X.61.5 ff. The punishment for the violation by Rudra must have been known also to the author of this hymn, the seventh verse of which is quoted in ŚBr I.7.4. Cf. v. 1 : *raúdraṃ bráhma.* — Andrew Lang, *Custom and Myth*, p. 134.

CHAPTER II

THE AŚVINS

1. Special mention must be made of the studies by Baunack, KZ, XXXV, p. 485 ff.; ZDMG, L, p. 263 ff. Cf. also Scheftelowitz, ZDMG, LXXIV, p. 200 ff. E. W. Hopkins shows, on the example of Cyavana and the Aśvins, the wide popularity of some of these sagas, "The Fountain of Youth" in JAOS, 26 (1905), p. 1 ff.

2. Müllenhof, ZDA, 30, p. 217 ff.; Nieder, ZDA, 42, p. 229 ff.; Mogk, *Deutsche Mythologie,* 2nd ed., pp. 678-79; Bethe in Pauli, V, p. 1087; bibliographical references ibid, p. 1111 § 15.

3. The name *nāsatyau,* which is often attributed to them in the Veda and which remains unexplained (Güntert, *Der arische Weltkönig und Heiland* p. 259, derives it from *nasati* — from *násate* — "rescue by hurrying to the place," therefore, "the two helpers in distress, rescuers, saviours"), is preserved in Iran in the designation of a demon *nā̊ṅhaiθya,* about whose origin and significance we know nothing. It is still more uncertain when Nieder wants to recognize the Dioscuri in the Beowulf. ZDA, 42, p. 229 ff. — That the individual names were *dasra* and *nāsatya* in antiquity (Geldner, VSt, III, p. 72; Henry, MSL, IX, p. 105 ff.) cannot be proved either.

4. Cf. the compilation in Miller, *Aśviny-Dioskury,* p. 325 ff.; Myriantheus, *Die Aśvins oder die Arischen Dioskuren,* Munich 1876, p. 23 ff.; Vodskov, *Syaeledyrkelse og Naturdyrkelse,* p. 485 ff.

5. Renel, *L'évolution d'un mythe,* p. 67.

6. O. Gruppe, *Bursians Jahresberichte,* Supplementsband 137, Leipzig 1908, p. 16.

7. I.34.5; 44.14; 116.17; 117.13; 118.5; 180.2 (and Pūṣan I.184.3); IV.14.4; 52.2; V.51.8; 73.5; VII.69.4; VIII.5.1, 2; 9.17, 18 etc. (Uṣas is substituted by *sūryasya duhitā́* etc., see p. 29 above) Like Aryaman, they are divine suitors and, therefore, in the Indian marriage ritual they solicit the bride X.40.11ff. Cf. Myriantheus, *Die Aśvins oder die Arischen Dioskuren,* p. 114 ff.

8. ŚŚS VI.6.1 ff. This arrangement occurs in some hymns of the ṚV also. These hymns can thus be regarded as the old constituents of the morning litany. See p. 22 above.

9. The Śastra to be recited as the Prātaranuvāka during the Atirātra consists of more than 1000 Aśvin verses and is recited, according to ĀśvŚS VI.5.4, by the Hotṛ "in the position of a soaring bird." ŚŚS IX.20.29 speaks of a Bṛhatīsahasra artificially constructed with different metres. (*Rituallitteratur,* p. 138).

10. I.730 ff. (I.3.57 ff.; Bombay ed., p. 29 ff.) :

> *ṣaṣṭiś ca gāvaḥ triśatāś ca dhenava ekaṃ vatsaṃ suvate taṃ duhanti |*
> *nānāgoṣṭhā vihitā ekadohanās tāv aśvinau duhato gharmam ukthyam ||*
> *ekāṃ nābhīṃ saptaśatā arāḥ śritāḥ pradhiṣv anyā viṅśatir arpitā arāḥ |*
> *anemi cakraṃ parivartate 'jaraṃ māyāśvinau samanakti carṣaṇī ||*

11. Their chariot also has "three seats" (*vandhúr* I.34.9), or they drive in three chariots, which have six horses and "hundred feet." Cf. Baunack, KZ, XXXV, p. 544. The three day watches and the three night watches are also connected with them. I.34.2 : *trír náktaṃ yāthás trír v aśvinā dívā ||*; "the three night watches" VIII.5.8 (Ludwig, *Der Rigveda,* and Geldner, VSt, II, p. 31). The number "three" has become so typical for them that the entire hymn I.34 is a play upon the number three. Keith's view (p. 114) "that the three wheels are connected with the fact that, unlike other gods. the Aśvins in their chariot bear with them Sūryā, for whom, therefore, there must be provided a third seat" is very improbable; after all they did not sit on the wheels ! Besides the number three, the numbers nine or ten, as the

case may be, are characteristic for them. The ṚV speaks of nine days and nights (I.116.24; 117.2; cf. Baunack, loc. cit). Besides the chariot, they possess a ship with hundred oars.

12. I.180.1 : *...rátho yád vāṃ páry árṇāṅsi dī́yat* |
10 : *áriṣṭanemiṃ pári dyā́m iyānám...*
IV.45.7 : *ráthaḥ sváśvo ajáro yó ásti* |
yéna sadyáḥ pári rájāṅsi yātháḥ...
VI.62.1 : *yā́ sadyá usrā́ vyúṣi jmó ántān*
yúyūṣataḥ páry urū́ várāṅsi ||
VII.69.1 : *ā́ vāṃ rátho ródasī badbathānó*
hiraṇyáyo vṛ́ṣabhir yātv áśvaiḥ |
2 : *sá paprathānó abhí páñca bhū́mā*
trivandhuró mánasā́ yātu yuktáḥ |
3 : *ví vāṃ rátho vadhvā́ yā́damāno*
ántān divó bādhate vartaníbhyām |
III.58.8; IV.43.5; VIII.22.4, 5.

We may compare these with the following with reference to the chariot, horses or cattle of the sun.

I.115.3 : *pári dyā́vāpṛthiví yanti sadyáḥ* [*áśvāḥ*] ||
III.43.6 : *prá yé dvitā́ divá ṛñjánty ā́tāḥ ... vṛṣbhasya mūrā́ḥ* ||
IV.36.1 : *ráthas tricakráḥ* [*ṛbhūṇām*] *pári vartate rájaḥ* |
45.1 : *eṣá syá bhānúr úd iyarti yujyáte*
ráthaḥ párijma divó asyá sā́navi |
51.5 : *pariprayāthá bhúvanāni sadyáḥ* [*uṣasaḥ*] |
V.47.4 : *...gā́vo diváś caranti pári sadyó ántān* ||
VI.48.21 : *sadyáś cid yásya cakṛtíḥ pári dyā́ṃ devó naiti sū́ryaḥ* |
13. I.30.19 : *ny àghnyásya mūrdháni cakrám ratbásya yemathuḥ* |
pári dyā́m anyád īyate ||

This recalls the concept according to which the sun, moon and stars are fixed to the Pole Star : *dhruve baddhāni, Viṣṇu Purāṇa* II.9.3. Since the stars are often styled cattle, I think that it is not impossible that *aghnyá* means the Pole Star. In this connection we may perhaps cite the following also.

V.73.3 : *īrmā́nyád vápuṣe vápuś cakráṃ ráthasya yemathuḥ* |
páry anyā́ nā́huṣā yugā́ mahnā́ rájāṅsi dīyathaḥ ||
and VIII.22.4 : *yuvó ráthasya pári cakrám īyata īrmā́nyád vām iṣaṇyati* |.

14. Mannhardt, *Zeitschrift für Ethnologie*, VII, p. 312 ff.; Bollensen, ZDMG, XLI, p. 497; Oldenberg, *Die Religion des Veda*, 2nd ed., p. 207 ff.; L. v. Schroeder, WZKM, IX, p. 129 ff; lastly H. Güntert, *Der arische Weltkönig und Heiland*, p. 266 ff. Contra Hopkins, PJAOS, XVI, p. cxlix.

15. *Die Religion des Veda*, 2nd ed., p. 210.

16. This is only the view of an Atri. Other passages show that the Aśvins were worshipped in the evening also. V.76.3; VIII.22.14; 57.1; X.39.1; 40.4. Bergaigne, II, p. 512.

17. Littrow, *Wunder des Himmels*, 5th ed., pp. 129, 320. Even if one sees in Mars a second morning star or evening star, the situation is not much different. See my comments in ZII, IV, p. 213 ff.

18. In Saules meita Mannhardt sees the twilight, E. H. Meyer the cloud-woman, Oldenberg a feminine designation for the sun. Here Oldenberg

gets completely lost in academic constructions : "The Lettic sun-daughter marries the moon besides the morning star; the Vedic Sūryā is not only the wife of the Aśvins, but also of Soma, the moon. Whom else should the moon have married if not the sun ? The sun comes closest to the one who could be understood under the name of Sūryā [?]; but when in India the daughter of the sun is mentioned besides Sūryā and when similarly the daughter of the sun is mentioned among the Letts, can this not be explained as an expedient of an age which is accustomed to conceive the sun as masculine?" (*Die Religion des Veda*, p. 213). I do not think so. It should be mentioned that the view of Mannhardt is contested by H. Bielenstein, "Die deeva dēli (Gottessöhne) des lettischen Volksliedes" (*Magazin*, herausgegeben von der Lettisch-Literarischen Gesellschaft, XIX, 4, p. 240 ff. 1896).

19. Weber, ISt, V, pp. 234, 266; IStr, III, pp. 39, 468; *Rājasūya*, p. 100.
20. SBKPAW (1898), p. 566; see O. Gruppe, op. cit., p. 56 ff.
21. *Verhandlungen der Berliner Anthropologischen Gesellschaft* 1899, p. 478 ff.; 1900, p. 80ff; cf. ZDMG, LXXXI, p. 53.
22. *Aśviny-Dioskury*, p. 341.
23. Vodskov, op. cit., p. 485 ff.
24. Macdonell, *Vedic Mythology*, p. 25.
25. *Syaeledyrkelse og Naturdyrkelse*, p. 498 : "Now the Vedic rain gods are, all in all, bringers of light, so that the morning ride of the Aśvins can very well be explained as a transformed memory of their old full function as rain gods. However, one should rather like to have a more specific foundation for their so characteristical and recurring nature as morning gods, and it is possible that they have had their own relation to the sun, and that we are indirectly informed about this in the old sources of miracles." (The Translator is grateful to Dr Asko Parpola of the Scandinavian Institute of Asian Studies, Copenhagen, for translating this and the next passage from the Danish).
26. Ibid., p. 522 (translated by Dr Asko Parpola).
27. *Der Rigveda*, III, p. 224; V, p. 195 on X.24. Cf. Hardy, *Die Vedisch-brahmanische Periode der Religion des alten Indiens*, Münster 1893, p. 47 ff., and Sāyaṇa on I.181.4.
28. *Aśviny-Dioskury*, p. 335.
29. Ibid., p. 338.
30. Further Yāska XII.2. See Oldenberg, *Religion des Veda*, p. 211. The reading *rajatam* (cf. TĀr I.10.1) is not at all objectionable and should not be replaced by *yajatam* : *śukraṃ vām anyad rajataṃ vām anyad viṣurūpe ahanī dyaur iva sthaḥ* ||
31. See my comments against Güntert, (*Der arische Weltkönig und Heiland* p. 268), in ZII, IV, p. 213 ff.
32. I.22.1-4 Aśvins, 5-8 Savitṛ, 9-12 wives of the gods, 13-15 Dyāvāpṛthivī, 16-21 Viṣṇu; see p. 22 above.
33. III.58.7, 9; IX. 7.7; 8.2; cf. Renel, *L'évolution d'un mythe*, p. 127, n. 1.
34. In the ritual, the Aśvins receive a graha of *tiróahnya sóma* during the Atirātra (*Rituallitcratur*, p. 138).
35. I.119.2; V.73.6; 76.1; VII.70.2; VIII.9.7; 87.2. The gharma-offering

for the Aśvins during the Pravargya corresponds to this (*Ritualliteratur*, p. 135).

36. Renel, op. cit., pp. 125-6 has raised an objection against this. But his statistics are inadequate and some of my arguments are not sufficiently appreciated. About my statement that the Aśvins are never called *somapā* he says : "We answer that this epithet, like the epithet *sómapati*...could be peculiar to certain gods in the same manner as the epithet *śubháspátī* (lords of splendour) was peculiar to the Aśvins." After all, since this has to do with an activity, this epithet should definitely be attributed especially to those only who were special drinkers of Soma and be absent from those who were not Soma drinkers. Renel says further : "As against this, Hillebrandt cites words which are derived from *madhu* and are applied to the Aśvins; for example, *madhupā, madhūyu* and *mādhvī*. In reality, only *mādhvī* is peculiar to them just as *sómapati* is peculiar only to Indra. But *madhupā* does not particularly belong to them, and *madhūyu* occurs only twice in the ṚV..." Indra is called Sómapati precisely because he is the most important recipient of Soma, and thus a god who is pre-eminently a recipient of honey should be called *mādhvī*; this word occurs seven times and refers always to the Aśvins. *madhupā* refers to the Aśvins in four passages, and only in one of the five passages of the ṚV it refers to Śuṣṇa in an easily intelligible way. Although *madhūyu* occurs only twice, yet these two passages are to be counted along with the seven containing *mādhvī* and the four containing *madhupā*. Moreover, the Aśvins and their chariot are called five times *mádhuvarṇa* and *madhuvā́hana* respectively.

37. MS IV.6.1 (79.20). Also ŚBr XIV.1.1.1. They turn to Dadhyañc so that he may tell them how "the head of the sacrifice can be replaced again, and how the sacrifice will become complete." Occasionally they are also called *devānām ānujāvarau* TS VII.2.7.2.

38. The plural *aśvibhiḥ*, without referring to the Aśvins, occurs in VI. 45.21. Maṇḍala II also contains a hymn to them (39); otherwise the dual form occurs there in insignificant passages like 31.4; 41.7, 9. *nāsatyā* occurs, almost without any significance, in VI.11.1; 50.10.

39. TS II.6.3.3 mentions a *dvikapāla puroḍāśa* as Prāyaścitta (ABr VII. 9.2) in order to "cure" the broken kapālas.

40. See below the section on "The Aśvins and Honey" in the chapter on Soma, p. 317 f.

41. The animals assigned to them in the Aśvamedha are *śuddhavāla*, *sarvaśuddhavāla* and *maṇivāla* TS V.6.13.

42. TS, vol. II, p. 320 *dhūmralalāma*. Comm.: *malinaśvaityaṃ dhūmratvaṃ lalāṭe śauklyena lāñchito 'vaśiṣṭe śarīre dhūmravarṇaḥ paśur aśvinoḥ priyaḥ*.

43. *durbrāhmaṇa*; the commentary on this cites from Baudhāyana : *yasya vedaś ca vedī ca vicchidyete tripūruṣam / sa vai durbrāhmaṇo nāma yaś caiva vṛṣalīpatiḥ*.

CHAPTER III

AGNI

1. NVO, pp. 81, 89, n. 1.

2. *The Tribes and Castes of the North-Western Provinces and Oudh,* Calcutta 1896, vol. I, p. 30 (cf. also Bhandarkar, IA, III, 135); for further details see my *Vedische Mythologie* (smaller ed.), p. 54, n. 1. On ancient clans in Tamil country, whose heads claimed to have originated from the sacrificial fire, see S. Kṛshṇasvāmi Aiyangar, IA, 34, 261 ff. (in continuation of Hoernle, JRAS, 1905, p. 1 ff.).

3. RdV, 2nd ed., p. 110; Bergaigne, I. 141 ff. See ŚBr II.3.1.5.

4. RdV, 2nd ed., p. 105; further L.v. Schroeder, *Arische Religion,* II, pp. 82, 84.

5. WZKM, IX, p. 229; XIII, p. 288 ff.; *Arische Religion,* II, p. 482.

6. See below under section G.

7. JRAS, 1900, p. 382.

8. I do not know if the atmosphere was ever conceived or drawn as a bow. Kirfel has nothing on this. Since it was difficult to represent the atmosphere, it seems that it became necessary to suggest it through the overlord of the atmosphere, i.e., Vāyu (winnowing basket) or the moon (half moon).

9. Geldner, VSt, II, p. 250, n. 2.

10. I.58.4 : *kṛṣṇáṃ ta éma ruśadūrme ajara*; IV.7.9 : *kṛṣṇáṃ ta éma rúśataḥ puró bhā́ḥ*; VI.6.1 : *kṛṣṇáyāma*; 10.4 : *kṛṣṇā́dhvan*; I. 141.7: *kṛṣṇájaṅhas*; II. 4.7 : *kṛṣṇávyathiḥ*; VII.3.2; 8.2 : *kṛṣṇápavi*; 23.19 : *kṛṣṇávartani*; VI.60.10 : *kṛṣṇā́ kṛṇóti jihváyā*; VIII.43.6 : *kṛṣṇā́ rájāṅsi patsutáḥ prayā́ṇe jātávedasaḥ.*

11. *go*=song, voice. Cf. also III.57.1; (IV.41.5; VIII.27.11).

12. Tylor, *Anfänge der Kultur*, II, 278; *Researches into the Early History of Mankind*, 233; Max Müller, *Physische Religion*, p. 296.

13. Bastian, *Zeitschrift für Ethnologie*, I, 383; Tylor, *Anfänge der Kultur*, II, pp. 280-81 : "Mother Ut, Queen of the Fire, you who were created from the elm tree growing yonder on the peaks of the mountains Changgi-Chan and Burchatu-Chan, you who arose as heaven and earth separated from each other, you came out of the footprints of the mother earth and were formed by the king of gods. Mother Ut, you whose father is the hard steel and whose mother the flint stone, whose ancestors the elm trees and whose lustre reaches up to heaven and pervades the whole earth..."

14. AV. III.21.1. See Oldenberg, RdV, p. 121.

15. VI.16.39 : *yá ugrá iva śaryahā́ tigmáśṛṅgo ná vánsagaḥ / agné púro rurójitha;* VII.5.3 : *tvád bhiyā́ víśa āyann ásiknīr asamanā́ jáhatīr bhójanāni / vaiśvānara pūráve śóśucānaḥ púro yád agne daráyann ádīdeḥ //*

16. X.156.2 : *yáyā gā́ ākárāmahe sénayāgne távotyā́ / tā́ṃ no hinva.* Cf. also *Ritualliteratur*, p. 176; TĀr. I.28.1 etc.

17. I.65.8: *...íbhyān ná rā́jā vánāny atti / yád vā́tajūto vánā vy ásthād agnír ha dāti róma pṛthivyā́ḥ;* I.94.10,11 :*...ádha svanā́d utá bibhyuḥ patatríṇo drapsā́* (spark) *yát te yavasā́do vy ásthiran /*; I.95.10; II.4.6,7 :*...sá yó vy ásthād abhí dákṣad urvī́ṃ paśúr naíti svayúr ágopāḥ...atasā́ny uṣṇán kṛṣṇávya-*

thir asvadayan ná bhū́ma / (On this cf. ŚBr I.4.1.10ff.); VI.6.4; 12.5; VII.8.2; X.142.3, 4 : *utá vā́ u pári vṛṇakṣi bápsad bahór agna úlapasya svadhāvaḥ utá khilyā́ urvárāṇām bhavanti*..."consuming the abundant grass, sometimes you leave out [spaces], sometimes gaps (isolated places) appear in the fields of corn." In spite of what VSt, II.180; II.207 states, I do not think that *pari vṛṇakṣi* here should be extended by *aśmanaḥ*. I believe that the verse refers to the irregular burning by the fire, which at times leaves out individual places and at other times burns only individual places as one could see in the case of the bushfire. See also the comparison in v. 4 : *pragardhínīva sénā* "like a marauding army" (Sāyaṇa : *pararāṣṭraṃ gacchato rājñaḥ senā tatratyaṃ dhanajātam abhikāṅkṣamāṇetas tataḥ saṃghaśo gacchati tadvat*). (Incidentally, the forest fire is not always a source of fear. Cf. K. von den Steinen, *Unter den Naturvölkern Zentral-Brasiliens*, p. 222).

18. Cf. E. W. Hopkins, JAOS, XX, p. 218. Crooke, *The Tribes and Castes of the North-Western Provinces and Oudh*, I, p. 35 : "The chief danger to the timber is from forest fires. When all the undergrowth is parched in the fierce heat of an Indian summer, a spark from a herdsman's pipe, or even the very friction of the branches against each other by the wind, is sufficient, on the authority of Thucydides, if it were not corroborated by Indian evidence, to start a destructive conflagration. No more awful sight than a mountain side, on the Vindhyan or Siwālik range, in the grasp of the fire demon can well be imagined. In 1893-94 attempts were made to protect 2807 square miles, of which 186 were burned."

19. There is evidence that fire brands were also thrown. I.66.8 : *ástur ná didyút tveṣápratīkā*; IV.4.1, 2; VII. 5.3.

20. *Ritualliteratur*, p. 87.

21. TS III.3.8.3 and the commentary on p. 208; ĀPŚS XIII.24.16, commentary.

22. ĀpŚS XIII.24.15,16.

23. ŚŚS III.4.3 ff.; ĀpŚS IX.3.22; KŚS XXV.4.29 ff.; ABr VII.7.1 ff. *vīti=vi+iti*.

24. ĀśvŚS III.13 prescribes these verses for Agni *saṃvarga* during the mixing of the fires *grāmāgninā*.

25. E. B. Tylor, *Researches into the Early History of Mankind*, 3rd ed., p. 229 ff.; Alsberg, *Anthropologie*, 2nd ed., pp. 155, 345; L. v. Schroeder, *Arische Religion*, II, p. 589 ff. See also the bibliography given by Roth, ZDMG, XLIII, p. 590 ff.

26. Terrien de Lacouperie, *The Babylonian and Oriental Record*, VI, 42.

27. ĀpŚS V.1.2. TBr I.1.9.1; 2.1.8. ĀśvŚS II.1.16, 17 : "He should fetch the Araṇis from an Aśvattha that has grown upon a Śamī, *without looking around.*" The Vājasaneyins permit also another variety of Aśvattha in an emergency — KŚS IV.7.22, 23. Probably the circumstance that the Aśvattha grows neither on the earth nor in the sky makes it holy. Frazer, II, p. 361 cites the instance of the holiness of such plants like the mistletoe or the mountain-ash in Jutland, which grows on the top of another tree.

28. See Kātyāyana, pp. 355, 356 and TS I, p. 503 ff.

29. Described in my *Ritualliteratur*, p. 106. For a more exact description see Roth, ZDMG, XLIII, p. 590 ff. On the implements used today see W.

Crooke, *The Tribes and Castes of* the *North-Western Provinces and Oudh*, I, p. 33; *The Popular Religion and Folklore of Northern India*, 2nd ed., II, pp. 194, 5.

30. ĀpŚS V.7.4 ff. See *Rituallitteratur*, p. 105 ff.
31. TBr I.2.1.15.
32. ṚV III.29.10.
33. TBr I.1.2.13.
34. *śakvarīḥ*; commentary on TBr : *śaktiyuktā aṅgulayo ye santi teṣāṃ daśatam.*
35. Cf. ŚŚS, Index, s. v. *ruh*; ĀśvŚS III.10.4 ff., etc.
36. Thus I conclude from the context of the passages. Wenle, *Die Kultur der Kulturlosen*, p. 73 : "When the dockyard is moved away or shifted to some other place, the burning sacred fire is taken along, as the Missionary Irle reports in his excellent book, *Die Herero*."
37. *araṇibhāṇḍe*, commentary.
38. Cf. also the description in ĀpŚS VI.28.8 ff., which is slightly different, and TS III, p. 292. When the Agnihotrin goes on a journey he bids farewell to his fires thus : "May you carry my first name, which my father and mother gave me at the beginning, until I return. I wish to carry your name, O Agni" (TS I.5.10a). It is explained that the worship of the fire at the time of farewell is "like appointing a brahmin for the protection of the house and handing the house over to him" (TBr I.1.10.6, commentary, p. 67). He hands his cattle over to the Āhavanīya for protection, his kin to the Gārhapatya and his food to the Anvāhāryapacana (ĀpŚS VI.24.3). During the journey, at the time of the Agnihotra, he turns his face towards the direction of his household fires and whispers the verses meant for the worship of Agni (ibid., 25.1). And when he returns, he brings firewood for them as a present (just as one brings fruits for children). "Just as children run towards the father returning from his journey, so do the fires run towards him" (ibid,25.4).
39. At the end of the ceremony. The intermediate verses also describe the individual stages; v. 9 : *kṛṇóta dhūmam* (the feeding of the flame). Cf. also the Sāmidhenī hymns, *Rituallitteratur*, p. 16, and other verses like VI. 15.6 : *agníṃ...samidha duvasyata*; 10 : *sapema*; 19 : *ákarma*.
40. IV.7.2 : *ádhā hí tvā jagṛbhriré mártāso*; VII.4.3 : *yáṃ mártāsaḥ śyetáṃ jagṛbhré.*
41. X.4.6 : *tanūtyájeva táskarā vanargū́ raśanā́bhir daśā́bhir abhy àdhītām.*
42. I.95.2 : *dáśemáṃ tvā́ṣṭur janayanta gárbham átandrāso yuvátayo víbhṛtam*; I.141.2; III.26.3 : *jánibhiḥ sám idhyate*; 29.13; IV.6.8.
43. IV.7.9. Sāyaṇa on III.29.3 : *pravītā niṣiktaretaskā.*
44. X.31.10; according to Sāyaṇa *ajyamānā* is the same as *niṣicyamāna-retaskā.*
45. V.7.9. But V.19.1 is obscure.
46. II.10.3; III.29.1, 3. See Kuhn, *Herabkunft des Feuers*, 2nd ed., p. 64.
47. X.32.3. Baunack, KZ, XXXIV, 562.
48. X.31.10 and 32.3. Baunack, loc. cit.
49. E.g., III.3.11. Cf. Macdonell, *Vedic Mythology*, p. 90.
50. TS I.3.7k; ŚBr III.4.1.22; *Kauśika Sūtra* 69.20 etc.
51. Thus also Geldner : Leitseil (Guide-rope). Does *śvātra* in I.31.4 : *śvātréṇa yát pitrór múcyase pári* also belong here ? Sāyaṇa explains it as *kṣipramanthanena.* X.46.6 is also obscure : *ayantraír īyate nṝn.*

52. Like elsewhere, here also we should distinguish *pra-nī* from *pari-nī* (carrying the fire brand around the Havis, *Rituallitteratur*, p. 14, n. 19. See also ṚV I.95.2d; III.2.7). However, in our ritual *pra-nī* has a different connotation from the escorting of the fire as, e.g., in Agnīṣomapraṇayana (*Rituallitteratur*, p. 128). But since there is no question of a rope in the above rite and since our passage has *rasanáyā*, it looks as though our passage is using *pra-nī* in another sense, namely, to "extract" from the Araṇis, Latin, *educitur*. See also I.141.4 : *prá yát pitúḥ paramā́n nīyáte pari*; 148.3; III.27.8; X.4.5; X.176.3.

53. I.31.2; III.55.6,7.

54. Bergaigne, I, p. 27; II, 52; Oldenberg, RdV, p. 105; Macdonell, *Vedic Mythology*, p. 90. E.g., in III.6.4 heaven and earth are called *urugāyásya dhenū́*.

55. I.60.1; 140.2; 149.4.

56. I.95.1.

57. V.11.3 : *ásammṛṣṭo jāyase mātróḥ śúcir mandráḥ kavíḥ*; VII.3.9; VIII.60.15.

58. Cf. Roth, ZDMG, XLIII, p. 595. Further compare also I.70.2 : *gárbho yó apā́ṃ gárbho vánānāṃ...| ádrau cid asmā antár duroṇé*; II.12.3 : *yó áśmanor antár agníṃ jajā́na*; VI.48.5 : *yám ā́po ádrayo vánā gárbham ṛtásya píprati | sáhasā yó mathitó jā́yate*; VII.6.2.: *kavíṃ ketúṃ dhāsíṃ bhānúm ádrer hinvánti*; X.20.7 : *ádreḥ sūnúm āyúm āhuḥ*. II.24.7 is mystical. I do not think that *aśman* and *adri* here can be understood in the sense of cloud. In some cases the stones of the hearth could have been meant; thus III.29.6 : *pári vṛṇakty áśmanas tṝṇā dahan*; VIII.60.16 : *bhinátsy ádriṃ tápasā ví śocíṣā*; 72.4 :...*aruhad vánam | dṛṣádaṃ jihváyā́vadhīt ||*

59. VI.16.13 : *tvā́m agne púṣkarād ádhi átharvā nír amanthata |*
mūrdhnó víśvasya vāghátaḥ ||

60. TS IV.1.3.2c, comm. p. 41.

61. TS, loc. cit. The comm. explains *viveṣṭya* (Text *viceṣṭya*) as *mṛdaṃ prakṣeptuṃ puṭikāṃ kṛtvā*.

62. *apāṃ pṛṣṭham asiti puṣkaraparṇam āharati, apāṃ vā etat pṛṣṭhaṃ yat puṣkaraparṇam | ...yonir vā agneḥ puṣkaraparṇaṃ sayonim evāgniṃ saṃbharati |*

63. *agnir devebhyo nilāyata | tam atharvānvapaśyat...puṣkaraparṇe hy enam upaśritam avindat.* ŚBr VII.3.2.14 : *tam abhya upodāsṛptam puṣkaraparṇe viveda.*

64. ĀpŚS XVI.13.10; 22.2 ff.; TS V.2.6.5.

65. Cf. also TS IV, comm., p. 255.

66. Incidentally, it may be mentioned here that the lotus leaf plays a role in cosmogony. According to TS V.6.4.2, Prajāpati in the form of wind swings on a lotus leaf on the waters, before he finds a firm support and creates the earth. According to TBr I.1.3.6, Prajāpati spreads out the earth on a lotus leaf : "He saw a lotus leaf standing and thought, 'this is it upon which it stands.' He became a boar and dived. He reached the earth below. He knocked off [a piece] from it and came up. This he spread out on the lotus leaf. Since he spread it out (*aprathayat*) the earth (*pṛthivī*) is called

accordingly. (Böhtlingk, SBKSGW, 1892, p. 211, translates thus : "He spread out this piece next to the lotus leaf"). Cf. TBr I.2.1.4 : *parṇaṃ pṛthivyāḥ prathanaṃ harāmi*, and the comm., p. 73 : *tat puṣkare prathayati*. A lotus garland symbolizes the dominion of Vṛtra : TMBr XVIII. 9.6 : *avakāśena puṇḍarīkaṃ jāyate / yat puṣkarasrajaṃ pratimuñcate vṛtrasyaiva tadrūpaṃ kṣatraṃ pratimuñcate*. Comm. : *antarikṣeṇa vṛtrarūpātmakam eva puṇḍarīkaṃ jāyate*.

67. Did the lower part of the fire drill have the shape of a lotus bud in this case ?

68. On "the fetching of the fire" from the neighbour, see W. Schulze, *Beiträge zur Wort- und Sittengeschichte* III, SBKPAW, 1918, pp. 769, 772 (Gr. *pyr ayein*, Lat. *lumen acendere*), 777 (*agnida*, Manu IX.278).

69. Oldenberg, RdV, p. 352; *Ritualliteratur*, p. 69.

70. Others exclude the Śūdra.

71. Cf. also Eggeling, SBE, XLIII. Introduction.

72. Cf. KŚS XVI.5.3,4 and the verses recited there, viz. VS XII.2, 3, although not all the verses used in the ceremony are appropriate.

73. TS IV, p. 120; V.1.9.4; ĀpŚS XVI.9.7 ff.; KŚS XVI.4.33.

74. ĀpŚS XVI.9.1.

75. ĀpŚS V.7.7; TBr I.1.9.7.

76. Among others, B. W. Leist, *Altarisches jus gentium*, p. 59 ff.

77. TBr I.1.2 ff. (cf. Böhtlingk, SBKSGW, 1892, p. 199 ff.; Lang, *Mythes, Cultes et Religion*, p. 127); 5.1; III.1.4; ŚBr II.1.2.

78. According to the comm. on ĀpŚS V.3.18, 19, ostensibly a particular caste of lower origin is not meant here, but those among the three castes who, being in reduced circumstances, follow this occupation.

79. *yathā vai puruṣo 'śvo gaur jīryaty evam agnir āhito jīryati, saṃvatsarasya parastād āgnipāvamānībhir upa tiṣṭhate, punarnavam evainam ajaram karoti* — MS I.5.6 (74.12). Keith, *Religion and Philosophy of the Veda*, pp. 289, 318, underestimates the significance of this passage. MBh XII.165.15 : *iṣṭiṃ vaiśvānarīṃ nityaṃ nirvaped abdaparyaye*. The custom of kindling a new fire at the beginning of the year can be noticed even today in India. William Crooke, *Religion and Folklore of Northern India*, 1926, pp. 337, 342 ("the burning of the old year"), 345; "The Holi" in *Folklore*, XXV, p. 55 ff. I think that the possibility is not ruled out of seeing a historical connection between the customs of today and the Vedic ritual, which is, after all, based partly on folk customs. Then the Agnyādheya would be related to the modern "lighting of the fire on the full moon of Phālguṇa" precisely in the same way as the celebration of Uṣas is connected to the Vasantotsava.

80. Grimm, *Deutsche Mythologie*, 4th ed., p. 501.

81. I.5.7.2 : *ṣaḍbhir upa tiṣṭhate ṣaḍ vai ṛtava ṛtuṣv eva prati tiṣṭhati ṣaḍbhir uttarābhir upa tiṣṭhate dvādaśa sam padyante dvādaśa māsāḥ saṃvatsaraḥ saṃvatsara eva prati tiṣṭhati*. Cf. ĀśvŚS II.4.1.

82. TS I, comm. p. 507 : *kalpaḥ bhavataṃ naḥ samanasāv ity agreṇottaraparidhim āhavanīye praharati sandhinā vā, agnāv agniś carati 'praviṣṭa iti prahṛtya.../ yo 'gniḥ purāhavanīye vartate yaś cedānīṃ mathitas tasmin prahriyate*...Quotations in Oldenberg, RdV, p. 353.

83. Oldenberg, op. cit., p. 77; *Ritualliteratur*, pp. 106, 7.

84. And of fertility.

85. TBr III.7.3.1,2. However, he should not consume anything of the goat. (If he does not find a goat, then he should make the offerings in the hand of a brahmin). It may be pointed that the animal of Pūṣan is a ram or a goat and that it is Pūṣan who is called *ắghṛṇi*.

86. TMBr XII.10.12 : *dakṣiṇa ūrāv udgātur agniṃ manthanti dakṣiṇato hi retaḥ sicyate.* Cf. comm. — However, I do not know exactly whether this happens in the Agnyādheya itself or in a connected ceremony; but this seems to follow from the context in the TMBr where this injunction is given along with the Vairāja Sāman; for, according to Lāṭyāyana IV.10.9, this is used in the Agnyādheya among others.

87. Cf. also the series, *āhavanīya, udgātṛ,...svar* (*sūrya*) in KŚS XXV.1.8, comm.; MS IV.4.8 (59.1 ff.).

88. *Rituallitteratur*, p. 107. Cf. ĀpŚS V.14.6,7. TBr I.1.6.8 : *rathacakraṃ pravartayati / manuṣyarathenaiva devarathaṃ pratyavarohati.*

89. ĀpŚS V.22.13. Cf. 23.3; ĀśvŚS II.1.35.

90. ĀpŚS V.20.12 ff. Or one can offer a smaller number.

91. ĀpŚS V.21.1 among others. *Rituallitteratur*, p. 108.

92. I.1.6.10 : *agnimukhān evartūn prīṇāti.*

93. In this context we may also mention the frequently occurring connection between Agni, Gāyatri, Rathaṃtara, Vasanta (as against Indra, Triṣṭubh, Bṛhat, Grīṣma etc.). TS VII.5.14; MS II.5.2 (49.6); 7.20 (104.16); III.15.10 (180.7); TMBr VI.1.6 etc. In other passages *samidh* occurs in the Agni series for obvious reasons. Cf. TS I.8.13; II.6.1.1 : *samidho yajati, vasantam evartūnām ava runddhe.../ samidho yajati uṣasa eva devatānām ava runddhe.../*

94. X.88.2 reads thus :

gīrṇáṃ bhúvanaṃ támasắpagūḷham
āvíḥ svàr abhavaj jāté agnaú /

Pāda *b* occurs again in IV.3.11, in a verse which, like the greater part of this hymn, refers to the recovery of light. vv. 9-12 praise the Ṛta and v. 11 the opening up of the rock : *śunáṃ náraḥ pári ṣadann uṣắsam āvíḥ svàr abhavaj jāté agnaú* (cf. I.71.2). Probably II.18.1 : *prātắ rátho návo yoji sásniś cáturyugas trikaśáḥ saptáraśmiḥ* also belongs here, and also several verses used in connection with the Ukhya-Agni, like TS IV.2.1[1k].

ṚV III.10.9 : *jāgṛvấṅsaḥ sám indhate* suggests a greater celebration which begins with a vigil at night. I do not agree with Bloomfield, who says (in *Contributions* V, JAOS, XVI, p. 36, note) that *jāgṛvấṃsaḥ* "means simply 'having awakened (in the morning).'" We know that it was enjoined that the participants should keep a vigil during the Agnyādheya, playing flutes and lutes (see p. 56 above; *Rituallitteratur*, p. 106).

95. ŚBr II.3.1.5 : *atha yat prātar anudite juhoti prajanayaty evainam etat so 'yaṃ tejo bhūtvā vibhrājamāna udeti śaśvad dha vai nodiyāḥ yad asminn etām āhutiṃ na juhuyāt tasmād vā etām āhutiṃ juhoti.* See p. 49 above.

96. ŚBr III.4.1.19 ff. Cf. ĀpŚS VII.3.3.

97. Cf. von den Steinen, *Unter den Naturvölkern Zentral-Brasiliens*, p. 228.

98. P. 366, 20.

99. KŚS IV.8.29; ĀpŚS V.11.5.

100. ĀpŚS V.1.4, 5; KŚS IV.8.16; TBr I.1.3.

101. *sūda.* ĀpŚS V.2.1 comm. : *jalāśayasya mṛd aśoṣyasya.* The Sūtra of Baudhāyana (II.12) cited there gives other rules.

102. Thus ĀpŚS V.9.4 ff.

103. KŚS IV.8.16, 17; ĀpŚS V.10.3.

104. Cf. also TBr I.1.3.9 ff.

105. Comm. on ĀpŚS : *aśanihatābhāve śītahataṃ vātahataṃ vā.*

106. ĀpŚS V.17.2 ff.

107. According to Ludwig (VI, p. 168, s.v. anblasen "blowing the fire") also in VIII.102.13 and V.73.6 (V, p. 584 on 44.6).

108. VI.16.40 : *ā́ yáṃ háste ná khādínaṃ śíśuṃ jātáṃ ná bíbhrati |*

109. VI.16.41 : *prá deváṃ devávītaye bháratā vasuvíttamam |*
ā́ své yónau ní ṣīdatu ||

pra-nī should be distinguished from *pra-bhṛ*; the former denotes the extraction of the fire from the Araṇis (see n. 52 above); on *pari-nī* ibid.

110. Because Agni is called *vediṣád* in I.140.1, thus corresponding to the Uttaravedi of the ritual.

111. *dáma* etc.; once *agnidhāna* X.165.3; *nābhi* X.62.4 etc.

112. Agni's epithet *párivīta* is obscure : I.128.1; IV.1.7; 3.2; X.6.1; 46.6. Sāyaṇa explains it as *tejobhiḥ parivītaḥ jvālābhiḥ vyāptaḥ* and so on. Only while commenting on I.128.1 he explains the epithet as *ṛtvigbhiḥ paridhibhir vā parito veṣṭitaḥ.* However, it is said in VI.4.3 : *bhā́sāṅsi vaste sū́ryo ná śukráḥ* and in I.26.1 : *vásiṣvā vástrāṇi* (Sāyaṇa : *tejāṅsi*); but *pari-vyā* and *vas* are not synonyms. Cf. also X.4.4 *vavrí.* Geldner translates *párivīta* in I.128.1 as "umhegt" (enclosed, fenced in). Oldenberg (SBE, XLVI, p. 254) sees in *párivīta* III.8.4 an allusion to the Upanayana. Geldner agrees with this view (ZDMG, LII, p. 759), though I find it unconvincing.

113. Cf. VII.16.3 : *úd asya śocír asthād...úd dhūmā́so* etc. On the other hand, V.77.4 : *ánūrdhvabhāsaḥ śadam ít tuturyāt.* Therefore, not burning brightly is a bad omen. (Cf. MBh III.46.25 in Ludwig, IV, p. 137).

114. IV.2.6 : *yás ta idhmáṃ jabhárat siṣvidānó mūrdhā́naṃ vā tatápate tvāyā́*; IV.12.2 : *idhmáṃ yás te jabhárac chaśramāṇó*; V.7.5 : *áva sma yásya véṣaṇe svédaṃ pathíṣu júhvati*; VI.1.9 : *só agna īje śaśamé ca márto yás ta ā́naṭ samídhā havyádātim*; VI.2.4 : *yás...dhiyā́ śaśámate.*

115. V.8.7 : *ā́hutaṃ ghṛtaíḥ...suṣamídhā sám īdhire sá vāvṛdhānó óṣadhībhiḥ.* Cf. VI.1.10 : *námobhiḥ, samídhā, havyaíḥ, védī, gīrbhíḥ, ukthaíḥ*; VII.14.1 : *samídhā, deváhūtibhiḥ, havírbhiḥ*; 2 : *samídhā, suṣṭutí, ghṛténa, havíṣā* etc.

116. III.5.8 : *jātá...óṣadhībhir vavakṣe*; V.8.7; VII.8.2. Of course, the wood and the twigs must be dry. III.23.1 : *jū́ryatsu...vánesu*; X.92.1 : *śócañ chúṣkāsu hárīṇṣu.* In several passages this meaning accrues also to the epithet of Agni's food, *tṛṣú* (for examples, see Oldenberg, SBE, XLVI, p. 345).

117. In II.35.12 they are called *bílma* (chips).

118. Other foods are mentioned only occasionally (Macdonell, *Vedic Mythology*, p. 89); often in connection with other gods. The *ṛtvij* are called *práyasvat* I.60.3, and the *viś* are called *pitubhṛ́t* X.1.4; I.36.7 states in general terms : *hótrābhir agníṃ mánuṣaḥ sám indhate.*

119. V.14.3 : *srúc ghṛtaścút*; 28.1 : *éti prắcī viśvávārā námobhir devắn īḷānā haviṣā ghṛtắcī*; VI.11.5 : *áyāmi srúg ghṛtávatī*; VIII.23.22 : *práti srúg eti námasā havíṣmatī*; in I.84.18 *havíṣā, ghṛténa, srucắ* are mentioned together. The *dárvī* occurs in two passages; in V.6.9 in association with *sarpis* and that too in the dual (*ubhé...sarpíṣo dárvī*).

120. i. With *ghṛtá* — V.1.7 : *nítyaṃ mṛjanti vājínaṃ ghṛténa*; 8 : *mārjālyò mṛjyate své dámūnāḥ*; VII.3.5 : *tám íd doṣắ tám uṣási...agním átyaṃ ná marjayanta náraḥ*; as in this passage, he is compared in other passages also frequently with a steed or with a youth. ii. With *gīrbhiḥ* — VIII.103.7 : *áśvaṃ ná gīrbhí rathyàṃ...marmṛjyánte*. (Cf. Oldenberg, SBE, XLVI, pp. 462-3; Index s.v.) In I.61.2 *dhíyaḥ* refers to Indra.

121. ŚŚS II.6.5; ĀpŚS VI.2.12; ĀśvŚS II.1.36.

122. Oldenberg, RdV, p. 348.

123. Crooke, *The Tribes and Castes of the North-Western Provinces and Oudh*, I, p. 30 ff., s.v. Agnihotrin; *Vedische Mythologie* (smaller ed.), p. 54.

124. *Ritualliteratur*, p. 108.

125. ŚŚS, vol. II, comm. p. 86.

126. "Mythological Studies," JRAS, 1893, p. 468, n. 2.

127. NVO, pp. 41, 65, n. 4.

128. ĀpŚS IV.1.10.

129. *Ritualliteratur*, pp. 114, 118, 160. Cf. also Oldenberg, RdV, p. 350 ff.; TBr III.7.4.5; ĀpŚS I.8.3; VIII.13.8, 9, 18; XIX.3.11; KŚS IV. 1.2, 3, 8; V.8.6, 16, 21, 22; XV.10.17; XIX.3.20, 23 etc.

130. ĀpŚS I.8.7. Almost all the texts associate the Dakṣiṇa fire with the Manes during the cremation (Caland, *Die altindischen Todten- und Bestattungsgebräuche*, p. 59, n. 230) whereas these texts differ considerably with reference to the worlds to which the other two fires belong.

131. During the installation of the Dakṣiṇa the Yajñāyajñīya Sāman is sung, which belongs to the evening Savana and calls for quite special rites there. It is remarkable that the Anvāhārya is cooked on the southern fire. One would think that the brahmins who receive the gruel are thought of as the representatives of the Manes. *Ritualliteratur*, p. 93.

132. ABr II.34.1 : *agnir deveddha iti śaṅsaty, asau vā agnir deveddha, etaṃ hi devā indhate, etam eva tad etasmiṅl loka āyātayati*; 2 : *agnir manviddha iti śaṅsaty, ayaṃ vā agnir manviddha, imaṃ hi manuṣyā indhate 'gnim eva tad asmiṅl loka āyātayati*; 4 :...*asau vai hotā devavṛtaḥ*...; 5 :...*ayaṃ vā agnir hotā manuvṛtaḥ*. — TS VI.1.8.5; 4.2.5 : *asmai vai lokāya gārhapatya ā dhīyate 'muṣmā āhavanīyaḥ* (V.7.4d : *brahmavādino vadanti yad eṣa gārhapatyaś cīyate 'tha kvāsyāhavanīya ity asāv āditya iti brūyāt / etasmin hi sarvābhyo devatābhyo juhvati*); IV.6.5h : *pṛthivyāṃ sīda, pṛṣṭhe pṛthivyāḥ sīda, bhāsāntarikṣam ā pṛṇa jyotiṣā divam ut tabhāna* (at the Citi). — TS II.6.5.5 : *tasya kva suvargo loka ity āhavanīya iti brūyāt*; TBr I.1.4.6; 5.2; 6.3.6 : *suvargo loka āhavanīyaḥ*; III.9.23.2 : *asau vā ādityo 'śvaḥ, sa āhavanīyam āgacchati*.

133. Occasionally the Āgnīdhrīya takes its place, TS V.4.6.4.

134. TBr I.1.8.1 : *ime vā ete lokā agnayaḥ / te yad avyāvṛttā ādhīyeran śocayeyur yajamānam / gharmaḥ śira iti gārhapatyam ādadhāti / vātaḥ prāṇa ity anvāhāryapacanam / arkaś cakṣur ity āhavanīyam ... rathaṃtaram*

abhigāyati gārhapatya ādhīyamāne | rāthaṃtaro vā ayaṃ lokaḥ; 2 :...*vāmadevyam abhigāyata* (*anvāhāryapacane*) *uddhriyamāṇe | antarikṣaṃ vai vāmadevyam...| bṛhad abhigāyata āhavanīya ādheyamāne | bārhato vā asau lokaḥ*. In the preceding Anuvāka, the same Brāhmaṇa says (7.1, 2) : *gharmaḥ śiras tad ayam agniḥ...vātaḥ prāṇas tad ayam agniḥ...arkaś cakṣus tad asau sūryas tad ayam agniḥ*; on this the comm. remarks on p. 48 : *ayaṃ purovartī gārhapatyo 'gniḥ* (1) and *yo 'yam agnisakho vāyuḥ so 'gneḥ prāṇaḥ, tat prāṇarūpam ayam ādhīyamāno 'nvāhāryapacano 'gniḥ* (2), and *asau divi dṛśyamānaḥ sūryarūpaḥ sa sūrya ayam ādhīyamāna āhavanīya 'gniḥ* (3) respectively. Cf. also ABr V.32.1; 34.4.

135. Cf. e.g., TS III.1.6b; 2.4h; IV.4.5c-e, TBr I.3.6.4; II.1.6.1; 3.3.2; 3.6.1; III.7.7.5; 8.18.1 : *ambhāṅsi...ayam loko...agni | nabhāṅsi* etc. | *mahāṅsi* etc.; TĀr I.1.2; TMBr I.2.1; 3.2; XX.15.2, 3; ABr IV.25.10; V.25.22.

136. ŚBr II.4.2.2.

137. Some other examples in Ehni, *Der vedische Mythus des Yama*, 2nd ed., p. 84.

138. ŚBr XIV.8.12.1 : *yadā vai puruṣo 'smāl lokāt praiti sa vāyuṃ āgacchati* etc.

139. The square represents, as one comm. (*Pandit*, X, p. 22) explicitly states, heaven, and the circle the earth. Although the sun also is regarded as *catuḥsrakti* (Weber, ISt, IX. p. 359), the Āhavanīya hearth should not be regarded as identical with the sun himself on the basis of this view which occurs but rarely. Here also we cannot expect a complete unanimity of views. For instance, occasionally the earth also is regarded as a square. Weber, loc. cit.; Wallice, *The Cosmology of the Ṛgveda*, p. 112.

140. Preface, p. 1 (Benares Saṃvat 1944, reprint from the *Pandit*).

141. Circles are drawn in a specific way. It is said on p. 5 : *maṇḍalasya dakṣiṇato vidyamāno bhāgaḥ pūrvakṛtamaṇḍalasya ca dakṣiṇo bhāgaḥ śūrpākāraḥ saṃpadyate sa dakṣiṇāgner āyatanaṃ bhavati* etc. I do not find this statement in the *Baudhāyana Śulva Sūtra*, edited by Thibaut, *Pandit*, X.

142. NVO, p. 30.

143. X.4.5.1 : *athādeśa upaniṣadām | vāyur agnir iti ha śākāyanina upāsata, ādityo 'gnir ity u haika āhuḥ | atha ha smāha śraumatyo vā hāliṅgavo vā vāyur evāgniḥ*.

144. KŚS, p. 356; NVO, p. 188; *Pandit*, New Series, IV, p. 338 : *rathacakrākṛtiḥ paścāt, candrārdha iva dakṣiṇaḥ* (*Yajñapārśvapariśiṣṭa*).

145. *ayaṃ sa devayānānām āditryo dvāram ucyate, ayaṃ sa pitṛyāṇānāṃ candramā dvāram ucyate*. Cf. inter alia, Monier-Williams, *Brāhmanism and Hinduism*, p. 343; *Folklore Journal*, II, p. 221; Crooke, *Popular Religion* etc., 2nd ed., I, p. 18. I notice that Crooke, from his material, has come to the same interpretation of Yama as I did ("hence the realm of Yama would naturally be fixed in the moon"); PW, s.v. pitṛyāṇa.

146. According to the comm. on the *Baudhāyana Śulva Sūtra*, *Pandit*, X, p. 22, the reason is different : *antarikṣasaṃstavād dhanurākṛtiḥ*. Is this concept that the Antarikṣa has the shape of a Dhanuḥ known elsewhere also ?

147. Thus ABr VIII.24.4 : *purohita evāhavanīyo bhavati, jāyā gārhapatyaḥ, putro 'nvāhāryapacanaḥ*.

148. Cf. eg., also ĀśvŚS II.2.13 : *pitā vā eṣo 'gnīnāṃ yad dakṣiṇaḥ putro gārhapatyaḥ pautra āhavanīyaḥ.* In the sources cited by Caland, *Die altindischen Todten- und Bestattungsgebräuche*, p. 58, n. 250, the *gārhapatya* is assigned to the *brahmaloka* (*Mānava Śulva Sūtra*), or the *āhavanīya* to the *devaloka* and *gārhapatya* to the *gandharvaloka* (*Baudhāyana Śulva Sūtra*), and so on.

149. Except in one passage : *Chāndogya Up.* IV.12, 13 where *āpaḥ, diśaḥ, nakṣatrāṇi* and *candramas* are mentioned together with the *anvāhārya-pacana*; and *prāṇa, ākāśa, dyaur* and *vidyut* with the *āhavanīya.* Nobody would attribute any importance to this. It will be shown later that the sun and lightning are thought of as closely connected.

150. VII.1.9 : *ví yé te agne bhejiré ánīkam*
mártā nárah pítryāsaḥ purutrā́ |

This passage can be interpreted in a different way also. It seems that in the Ṛgvedic period — contrary to the ritual custom of the Sūtras — there was, besides the usual method, also the custom of distributing the fire, once kindled in a common hearth, to all the others. This is suggested primarily by V.11.4 : *agníṃ náro vi bharante gṛhégṛhe.* Just as in the later period so also in earlier times the maintenance of the three fires could not have been a simple and inexpensive affair. Hence, I think that in the Vedic period also it might not have taken place *gṛhégṛhe*. Perhaps we should assume that the ceremonial transfer of the fire into the houses was done from a Gr. *koinē estia.* That such a *koinē estia* existed in the Vedic period is attested by other factors which we shall discuss later on. From the term *vi-bhar* is derived Agni's epithet *víbhṛtra* I.95.2; II.10.2 (Cf. on this *víbhṛtaḥ purutrā́* III.55.4 — not identical with the designation *purudhá prásūtaḥ* III.54.19 — and also *víbhṛta oṣadhīṣu* TS IV.1.4e).

151. I.31.4 : *śvātréṇa yát pitrór múcyase pári*
ā́ tvā pū́rvam anayann ā́paraṃ púnaḥ |

152. *uśán hotar ní ṣadā yóniṣu triṣú.* Cf. I.15.4 : *ágne deuā́ṅ ihā́ vaha sādáyā yóniṣu triṣú.*

153. V.11.2 : *agníṃ náras triṣadhasthé sám īdhire.* Cf. III.20.2 : "... three are your seats (*sadhástha*), three your tongues... three your bodies..." Incidentally, it is well known that Agni, the god, is distinguished from the fire, the element (singular as well as plural). Cf. I.26.10; III.24.4; V.6.6; VI.10.2; 11.6; VII.1.4; VIII.18.9; 19.33. Another word for *sadhástha* is *dhā́man* (Hillebrandt, IF, XLIV, p. 141). On

X.70.7 : *ūrdhvó grā́vā bṛhád agníḥ sámiddhaḥ*
priyā́ dhā́māny áditer upásthe |

it should be noted that the hearths of Agni, who is seated on the vedi (*vediṣád* I.140.1) are meant here, and that Pischel might be right when he supposes that *dhiṣáṇā* and *áditi* are identical in some passages.

154. X.88.10 : *stómena hí diví devā́so agním ájījanan...| tám ū akṛṇvan tredhā́ bhuvé....* In X.105.9 the threefold distribution is called *tretínī* (Ludwig. Cf. Sāyaṇa).

155. Cf. also III.2.9 : *tisró yahvásya samídhaḥ...| tā́sām ékām ádadhur mártye bhújam u lokám u dvé úpa jāmím īyatuḥ ||* = Agni of the earth, of the atmosphere and of the sky ?

156. Ludwig, III, p. 355. Oldenberg, SBE, XXX, p. x, n. 1.

157. *Ritualiteratur*, p. 11, § 3.

158. The idea that Narāśaṅsa is one of the sacrificial fires was stated by Ludwig, loc. cit., who supposed that Narāśaṅsa is a name of the Āhavanīya.

159. Nersch, Gr. *Narsēs.* Lagarde, "Zur Urgeschichte der Armenier," *Symmicta* (private ed.), pp. 461, 2245. F. Justi, *Iranisches Namensbuch*, s.v.

160. Oldenberg (NGGW, 1915, p. 217, n. 3) objects to this statement thus : "Hillebrandt speaks repeatedly of Nairyōsaŋha's 'position in the midst of the other names of the fire in *Yasna* 17.11' (*Vedische Mythologie*, 1st ed., II, p. 106 ff.; III, p. 445). Not in the midst, but after those names. And the way he describes the passage by passing over the absence of the epithet 'fire' for Nairyōsaŋha only, which is used otherwise, gives a wrong impression that Nairyōsaŋha is akin to the fire." Here Oldenberg is quite wrong. *Yasna* 17.11 reads thus : *ātrəm spə̄ništəm yazamaide / xšaθrəm nafəδrəm nairyōsaŋhəm yazatəm yazamaide / ātrəm vīspanąm nmānanąm mazdaθātəm ahurahe mazdå puθrəm ašavanəm ašahe rātum yazamaide· maṭ vīspaēibyō ātərəbyō.* Here Nairyōsaŋha is followed by the "fire which rules over all the dwellings along with all the fires." Certainly, one could say in ordinary parlance — though not, of course, in mathematical language —that Nairyōsaŋha stands in the midst of the other names of the fire (Bartholomae also, *Altiranisehes Wörterbuch*, assumes that "in fact, in *Yasna* 17, Naryōsaŋha stands among the names for fire") and add that Nairyōsaŋha receives a special position through the fire which follows him. The epithet *xšaθrəm nafəδrəm* is obscure, but it somehow connects him with overlordship and appears to make him thus a fire in a general sense. (Only in *Siroza* 2.9 he is mentioned after the other fires and spirits; 2.10 mentions the waters after him. Besides this, *Nyāyis* 5 and *Siroza* 1.9 read : *xšaθrōnaəfδrō nairyōsaŋhahe yajatahe xšnaoθra*.... Darmesteter (*Le Zend Avesta*, I, p. 152, and n. 2) translates after Neriosengh : "one who dwells in the navel of kings, that is to say, one who is transmitted hereditarily from king to king," and regards *xšaθrəm nafəδrem* as an adjective in the sense of "royal, who is in the navel"; Bartholomae : "grandson of the overlordship of the kingdom."

161. I give below all the passages in order to make this comprehensive.

II.3.1 : *sámiddho agnír níhitaḥ pṛthivyā́m*
pratyáṅ víśvāni bhúvanāny asthāt /
hótā pāvakáḥ pradívaḥ sumedhā́
devó devā́n yajatu agnir árhan //

2 : *nárāśáṅsaḥ práti dhā́māny añján*
tisró diváḥ práti mahnā́ svarcíḥ /
ghṛtaprúṣā mánasā havyám undán
mūrdhán yajñásya sámanaktu devān //

3 : *īḷitó agne mánasā no árhan devā́n yakṣi*...

V.5.1 : *súsamiddhāya śocíṣe ghṛtáṃ tīvráṃ juhotana /*
agnáye jātávedase /

2 : *nárāśáṅsaḥ suṣūdati imáṃ yajñám ádābhyaḥ /*
kavír hi mádhuhastyaḥ //

3 : *īḷitó agna ā́ vaha índraṃ citrám ihá priyám /*
sukhaí ráthebhir ūtáye //

VII.2.1 : *juṣásva naḥ samídham agne adyá*
śócā bṛhád yajatáṃ dhūmám ṛṇván |
úpa spṛśa divyáṃ sā́nu stū́paiḥ
sáṃ raśmibhis tatanaḥ sūryasya ||
2 : *nárāśáṅsasya mahimā́nam eṣām*
úpa stoṣāma yajatásya yajñaíḥ |
yé sukrátavaḥ śúcayo dhiyaṃdhā́ḥ
svádanti devā́ ubháyāni havyā́ ||
3 : *īlényam vo ásuraṃ sudákṣam*
antár dūtáṃ ródasī satyavā́cam ||
manuṣvád agníṃ mánunā sámiddham
sám adhvarā́ya sádam ín mahema ||
X.70.1 : *imā́ṃ me agne samídhaṃ juṣasva... |*
2 : *ā́ devā́nām agrayā́vehá yātu*
nárāśáṅso viśvárūpebhir áśvaiḥ |
ṛtásya pathā́ námasā miyédho
devébhyo devátamaḥ su ṣūdat ||
3 : *śaśvattamám īlate dūtyā́ya*
havíṣmanto manuṣyā́so agním |
váhiṣṭhair áśvaiḥ suvítā ráthena
ā́ devā́n vakṣi ní ṣadehá hótā ||

162. =VS XXVII.13 which, however, reads *prīṇāno* and *agne.*

163. *Nirukta* VIII.6; also *Bṛhaddevatā* III.2 ff., where different opinions are cited.

164. III.29.11 : *tánūnápāt ucyate gárbha āsuró*
nárāśáṅso bhavati yád vijāyate |
mātaríśvā yád ámimīta mātári
vā́tasya sárgo ábhavat sárīmaṇi ||

Oldenberg (RdV, p. 218, n. 5) believes to have found a contradiction between my statement in *Vedische Mythologie*, 1st ed., III, p. 446 and that in ibid., II, p. 101 f., since I have said at the former place that the Ṛgvedic hymn III.29 is by no means a mystic hymn, nor one full of fanciful identifications to the statements of which we should not give any importance, and at the latter place that this verse (III.29.11) is less useful in helping us to gain an insight (about Narāśaṅsa). Both my statements are correct : in the first place I spoke about the hymn and in the second about the verse. The verse is not clear in some points, but it is important because it sees in Narāśaṅsa a form of Agni and because it occurs in a hymn which is free of fanciful identifications. Only it does not help us in understanding the special significance of the three forms of Agni mentioned therein.

165. Caland-Henry, *L'Agniṣṭoma*, p. xxxiv : Narāśaṅsa "one of the hypostases of Agni."

166. NVO, p. 97; Schwab, *Tieropfer*, p. 90, n. 1, where additional literature is given; Bergaigne, JA, 1888, p. 18; Weber, ISt, X, p. 89 etc. — Of these hymns which serve as Prayājas in the animal sacrifice, II.3; V.5; VII.2; X.70 contain invocations to Narāśaṅsa and I.188; III.4; IX.5; X.110, on the other hand, invocations to Tanūnapāt. Only few families — Medhātithi Kaṇva (Aṅgiras) and Dīrghatamas Aucathya — invoked both the gods

in I.13 and I.142 respectively (cf. Bergaigne). The Tanūnapāt hymn of Jamadagni (X.110) seems to have finally pushed aside all others, and only the Vasiṣṭhas remained for long loyal to their Narāśaṅsa verse (Schwab, p. 91). It must, however, be stated that a connection between Narāśaṅsa and the Manes cannot be noticed any more in the Prayājas, unlike in the Soma sacrifice.

167. Verses I.106.4 and X.64.3 also are unimportant. In both cases Narāśaṅsa is not, as it was thought, an epithet of Pūṣan, but throughout an independent proper name occurring in the midst of a list of the names of gods. It is not clear whether *cáturaṅga* in X.92.11 (*nárāśáṅsaś cáturaṅgo yamó 'ditiḥ*) is an epithet of him or of Yama.

168. ABr II.24.3; KŚS IX.12.7, 8; ĀpŚS XII.25.25-27. The Āpyāyana of Soma by the Camasins is done, according to Baudhāyana, with the Vasatīvarī waters and, according to others, by the mere touch. Comm. on ĀpŚS XII. 25.25.

169. ABr VII.34 : *narāśaṅsapītasya deva soma te matividaḥ...bhakṣayāmi.* Comm. on TS III, p. 110, states : *narāśaṅsapītasya pitṛpītasyeti padadvayaṃ narāśaṅsacamasabhakṣana eva prayoktavyam / nānyatrety ekaḥ pakṣaḥ / sarvatra paṭhitavyam ity aparaḥ pakṣaḥ / naraiḥ śasyanta iti narāśaṅsāḥ pitṛviśeṣāḥ.* Cf. ĀpŚS XII.24.7 ff.; VS VIII.58; XIX.61; ŚBr XII.6.1.33; Lāṭyāyana II.5.13 ff.; Weber, ISt, IX, p. 225.

170. VII.5.22.

171. *Ritualliteratur*, p. 130.

172. I have pointed out earlier (n. 131) that the use of the southern fire for cooking the Anvāhārya seems to connect this offering with the Manes, and that it makes the priests appear as the representatives of the Manes. Moreover, the injunction of Āpastamba (XIII.5.2) and others, given in connection with the Soma sacrifice, to the effect that "the sacrificer can give all his possessions as dakṣiṇā after having made a settlement for his eldest son" is very interesting. Thus the Soma sacrifice can be associated with the passage into the next Āśrama. (Cf. also ṚV I.70.10 : *pitúr na jívrer ví védo bharanta*). Worthy of our notice is also the use of a black skin (enjoined by Āpastamba, see *Ritualliteratur*, pp. 132, 155) with which the cattle meant for the dakṣiṇā are driven into four groups; in fact, black is always the colour of the Manes.

173. *Ritualliteratur*, pp. 133, 115; ĀpŚS XIII.12.9 ff.; ŚŚS VIII.2.14 and the comm. II, p. 355; Hiraṇyakeśin IX.3.8. Cf. also verse VS XIX.61, used in the sacrifice for the Manes in the Sautrāmaṇī : *agniṣvāttān ṛtumato havāmahe nārāśaṅse somapīthāṃ ya āśuḥ.* MS IV.10.6 (157.8).

174. ŚŚS III.17.3; ĀśvŚS II.7.8. If, as Oldenberg says (NGGW, 1915, p. 220, n. 3), the context of the verse shows that it was composed for calling back the soul of a person who is seriously ill, then it is precisely the calling back from the realm of the dead, and agrees with my interpretation (cf. Nāciketas). Further, one should note that the verse speaks first of the Soma of the Narāśaṅsa and then of the hymns of the Manes.

175. Cf. the analogy of the Wajdelotes, Sigonotes and Ligustones. Thus "were called the chaplains in Poland whose duty it was to narrate to the people, or much rather sing in front of them, the history of ancestors in all

festivals, particularly at the time of the autumn festival of the ram" — Dr Weiss, *Konrad Wallenrod*, Norden 1888, 2nd ed., p. 96.

176. ŚŚS XVI.11.32; 14.11 : *puruṣo vai nārāśaṅsaḥ*. Comm. *puruṣarūpaḥ pumān nararūpeṇa praśasyata iti nārāśaṅsaḥ / narair vā paramātmadarśibhiḥ śraddhadhānair darśanasaṃpannaiḥ praśasyate*. ABr, vol. I, p. 7 : *manuṣya-vṛttāntapratipādikā ṛco nārāśaṅsyaḥ;* TBr II.7.5.2 : *manuṣyā vai narāśaṅsaḥ*; on VS VIII.58 : *pitaro nārāśaṅsāḥ sannaḥ* (*somaḥ*) the comm. remarks thus : *narā asminn āsīnāḥ śaṅsantīti* (Yāska VIII.6) *narāśaṅso yajñas tatra hitā yogyā vā nārāśaṅsā nārāśaṅsaguṇaviśiṣṭāḥ pitaraḥ*. ŚBr XII.6.1.33 : *pitṛbhyo nārāśaṅsebhyaḥ svāheti juhuyāt / pitaro hi sa tarhi nārāśaṅsā bhavanti*. TMBr XIII.7.14. See also the next note. Cf. Wundt, *Völkerpsychologie*, 2nd ed., III, p. 407 ff.. on the close connection between the glorification of heroes and the cult of ancestors.

177. AV XV.6.4; ŚBr XI.5.6.8; TBr II, p. 762 : *svayam api manuṣyarūpo devaviśeṣo narāśaṇsaḥ / tatsambandhinī yeme pañcaśatam ity ādikī nārāśaṅsī*. Weber, ISt, X, p. 53; Haug, *Aitareya Brāhmaṇa*, II, p. 430; Caland-Henry, *L'Agniṣṭoma*, Nos. 147, 153.

178. Cf. also TBr I.3.2.6 : *devā vai brahmaṇaś cānnasya ca śamalann apāghnan / yad brahmaṇaḥ śamalam āsīt sā gāthā nārāśaṅsy abhavat, yad annasya sā surā*; ZDMG, XV, pp. 136, 137; IST, loc. cit.

179. Pischel. *Die Hofdichter des Lakṣmaṇasena*, p. 4.

180. *narā aṣ̌avāno hąmbavainti nairyōsaŋho hąmbavaiti.*

181. Darmesteter, *L'Avesta*, II, p. 319.

182. Oldenberg, GGA, 1915, p. 220.

183. ĀpŚS XIV.21.11 : *ahargaṇesv āhara dahety uktvā dakṣṇāgner agnim āhṛtya nirmanthyena vā dagdhvā dakṣiṇena mārjālīye mṛtasya dahanam;* 12 : ... *kumbhe 'sthīni saṃbhṛtya mārjālīye nidadhāti;* XVII.21.8; XXII.8.19 : *sanneṣu nārāśaṅseṣu pariśrite mārjālīye pitṛyajñena caranti*; ŚŚS XIII.11.3, 4; KŚS XXV.13.33, 34 (Lāṭyāyana X.11.10).

184. *Vedic Mythology*, p. 100. Thus also Oldenberg, NGGW, 1915, p. 213. *nṛśasta*, the epithet of Narāśaṅsa would also speak in favour of this view (see p. 75). Somewhat differently, Bergaigne, I, p. 308 f. : "...the word *narāśaṅsa*, in so far as it is the name of a divine being, appears to have, as a possessive compound, the same sense as the derivative *nārāśaṅsa* ...and appears to designate Agni, not simply as the god praised by men, but as the god of human prayer, that is to say, as another Brahmaṇaspati." Fay, AJPh, XVIII, p. 11 explains *nárāśáṅsa* as "lightning and thunder or, more simply, leaping and roaring."

185. Lindner, *Altindische Nominalbildung* pp. 18, 34. Whitney, Sanskrit Grammar, 2nd ed., § 1148. 1d.

186. Bergaigne, I, p. 305 f. : "The word *śaṅsa*...denotes especially those verses to which some sort of magical efficacity is attributed, as also those formulae which are 'straight'..., that is to say, more in conformity with the religion of the ṛṣis than that of demons and sorcerers or, more generally speaking, of the enemy."

187. ṚV IX.86.42 : *dvā́ janā́ yātáyann antár īyate nárā ca śáṅsaṃ daívyaṃ ca dhartari* (Sāyaṇa : *naraiḥ śaṅsanīyaṃ mānuṣam ity arthaḥ / daivyaṃ ca divi bhavam ubhayavidhaṃ dhanaṃ dhartari dhārake yajamāne prerayan*). Here *narā*

śaṅsaṃ is opposed to *daivyaṃ* (*śaṅsam*, cf. X.31.1); *narāḥ* and *devāḥ* form the *dvā janā* (X.57.5: *púnar naḥ pitaro máno dádātu daivyo jánaḥ*). It appears to me that in our verse Narāśaṅsa denotes the lord of the dead (and thus the realm of the dead). *śáṅsa* could mean "lord" or something similar in X.31.1 also : *á no devánāṃ úpa vetu śáṅso víśvebhis turaír ávase yájatraḥ*, (cf. X.32.6 : *devānāṃ vratapáḥ*); I.185.9 : *ubhá śáṅsā náryā mám aviṣṭāṃ* (heaven and earth as rulers of men) (also IV.4.14 ?). In *uruśáṅsa* and *gambhīraśáṅsa*, the PW, its smaller edition and Grassmann understand *śáṅsa* in the sense of "ruling, governing."

188. In ṚV X.78.3, *pitṝṇáṃ śáṅsāḥ* is gen. subj.

189. Even if Yama was also a name of Agni (Ehni, *Der Vedische Mythus des Yama*, 2nd ed., p. 122 ff.), it would have to do with his identification with the fire of the Manes, in spite of ŚBr II.3.2.2.

190. MS IV.13.8 (210.13); TBr III.6.13.

191. See n. 161 above.

192. It will be evident from this explanation that in our passage, as also in II.3.2, Narāśaṅsa is connected with the gods. But Soma is the Brahman of the gods and, on the other hand, he is also *pitṛmát*. Thus Agni Vaiśvānara also, whom I identify with the Āhavanīya, receives the epithet *triṣadhasthá* from the threefold distribution that would take place later VI.8.7; so also Bṛhaspati IV.50.1. It is an open question whether at an earlier period the threefold distribution of the fire was done from the Āhavanīya in some families and from the Dakṣiṇa in others.

193. ŚBr II.6.1.30 : *havyavāhano vai devānāṃ kavyavāhanaḥ pitṝṇām*; ṚV X.16.11; TS II.6.12m : *yad agne kavyavāhana pitṝn yakṣy ṛtāvṛdhaḥ | pra ca havyāni vakṣyasi devebhyaś ca pitṛbhya ā ||* See the next note. On the *devāḥ pitaraḥ* see Caland, *Altindischer Ahnenkult*, pp. 183, 264.

194. ŚŚS III.16.3,10. There the fire is addressed as *kavyavāhana*. TBr I.6.9.6 : *agniṃ kavyavāhanaṃ yajati ya eva pitṝṇām agniḥ tam eva yad yajati*. In one passage the TS distinguishes it from the fire of the demons. TS II.5.8.6 : *trayo vā agnayo havyavāhano devānāṃ, kavyavāhanaḥ pitṛṇāṃ saharakṣā asurāṇām*.

195. ŚŚS IV.4.1 etc.

196. Baunack, KZ, XXXV, p. 512 thinks differently. Bloomfield, *Festgabe für Streitberg*, p. 13, explains the word as "the product of contamination of *kravyavāhana* and the much more common *havyavāhana*."

197. Cf. also TS I.1.7b : *apāgne 'gnim āmādaṃ jahi, niṣ kravyādaṃ sedha, ā devayajaṃ vaha |*

198. Caland, *Die altindischen Todten- und Bestattungsgebräuche*, pp. 19, 58. VS I.17 comm. *kravyāt śavadāhe kravyaṃ māṅsam attīti kravyāt citāgniḥ*.

199. The texts disagree on this point. They differ also on the question whether this is the fire of the dead. Cf. KŚS, p. 991 and *Rituallitcratur*, p. 92 where my exposition follows Kātyāyana and the comm. Caland's statement opposing me (GGA, 1897, p. 288) is wrong.

200. "I take this god for the fire of the Manes." I do not think that the translation of Bloomfield (loc. cit.) is correct : "Regarding Agni Kravyād who entered your house as another Jātavedas (holy or suspicious fire), I take

this god for sacrifice" etc. In my view, they are two different fires; cf. vv. 9, 10. Keith , *Religion and Philosophy of the Veda*, p. 160, opposes my view with the statement that it is "clearly wholly contrary to the spirit of the ritual, which regards death as requiring the extinction of all fires which are made thereby impure..." Unfortunately, he does not say how else this verse would make some sense, and he overlooks the possibility of a change in the ritual of which he himself speaks on p. 256. Cf. also Bergaigne, I, p. 79.

201. Here we find a deviation from the usual ritual as in ṚV X.18.8; 85.21. Caland (GGA, 1897, p. 290) has not shaken my view on these verses. He asks, for example, "how is it possible that a dead person is addressed with *ud īrṣvātaḥ*, 'lift up yourself away from here'? " To whom, then, are the following addressed ? X.14.7 : *prehi, prehi...*; 8 : *saṃ gacchasva...*; 10 : *ati drava*. Not to a dead person ? (Incidentally, on the antiquity of concepts contained in the Puruṣasūkta, see Lang, *Mythes, Cultes et Religion*, p. 225 ff., who defends the view of Haug that they have a primitive character).

202. *Ritualliteratur*, p. 69; Caland, *Die Altindischen Todten- und Bestattungsgebräuche*, pp. 115, 116. I take the opportunity to refer once again to ṚV X.18.8. Keith (op. cit., pp. 419, 423) repeats the wrong interpretation that the widow sits beside the dead person; there is no mention of this. How could one think of a remarriage in India right in the middle of the ceremony for the dead ? Cf. Hillebrandt, "Der freiwillige Feuertod in Indien und die Somawache," SBKBAW, 1917, p. 17 ff.

203. III.4.2 : *yáṃ devā́sas trír áhann āyájante*
divédive váruṇo mitró agníḥ |

TS IV.1.8b.; VS XXVII.12 : *tanūnapād asuro viśvavedā devo deveṣu devaḥ*. ...

204. Also ṚV III.29.11; howsoever one might explain this verse, Tanūnapāt appears to be different in nature from Narāśaṅsa and Mātariśvan.

205. TS I.2.10; MS I.2.7 : *āpataye tvā gṛhṇāmi paripataye tvā gṛhṇāmi tanūnaptre tvā gṛhṇāmi, śākvarāya tvā gṛhṇāmi śakmann ojiṣṭhāya tvā gṛhṇāmi, anādhṛṣṭam asy anādhṛṣyaṃ devānām ojo* etc. The comm. explains (TS I, p. 379) *āpati* as *prāṇa*, *paripati* as *manaḥ*, *tanūnaptṛ* as *jāṭharāgni*.

206. Cf. also TS VI.2.2.1 : *tābhyaḥ* (*tanūbhyaḥ*) *sa nir ṛchād yaḥ || naḥ prathamo 'nyo 'nyasmai druhyād iti* |

207. I.5.3.10. Likewise TS II.6.1.1 (in another context his place is taken by Viśvakarman or Indra TS IV.3.2.1; 3.1b; or by the Rudras TBr II.6.19); KBr III.4 (*samidh= vasanta, tanūnapāt=grīṣma, iḍaḥ= varṣāḥ* etc.); see p. 26 above.

208. *hotā yakṣat tanūnapātam ūtibhir jetāram aparājitam, indraṃ devaṃ suvarvidaṃ pathibhir madhumattamair narāśaṅsena tejasā* (comm. : *manuṣyaiḥ śaṅsanīyena*) *vetv ājyasya hotar yaja* |.

209. IV.13.2 (200.2) : *hotā yakṣat tanūnapātam aditer garbhaṃ bhuvanasya gopāṃ madhvādya devo devebhyo devayānān patho anaktu*. TBr III.6.2.

210. Etymology does not help us here either. I would think that *tanūnapāt* is the same as *svayaṃnapāt* (cf. *svayaṃbhū, svabhūti*). Jarl Charpentier, *Kleine Beiträge*, p. 80, explains it as *jāṭharāgni*, following the comm. on TS I.2.10, but, so far as I know, this interpretation finds no support elsewhere,

nor does it explain clearly the cult difference between Narāśaṅsa and Tanūnapāt, which appears to be rather a difference between the sun and the moon.

211. Among others, Bergaigne, II, p. 159 ff., 348; Max Müller, *Physische Religion*, p. 143; Hardy, *Die vedisch-brahmanische Periode der Religion des alten Indiens*, p. 64; Oldenberg, RdV, p. 108; Macdonell, *Vedic Mythology*, p. 93.

212. VI.7.2 : *...vaiśvānarám rathyàm adhvarā́ṇām*
yajñásya ketúṃ janayanta devā́ḥ ||
4 : *tvā́ṃ víśve amṛta jā́yamānam*
śíśuṃ ná devā́ abhí sáṃ navante |
táva krátubhir amṛtatvám āyan
Vaiśvānara yát pitrór ádīdeḥ ||
8.2 : *sá jā́yamānaḥ paramé vyòmani*
vratā́ny agnír vratapā́ arakṣata |
vy àntárikṣam amimīta sukrátur
Vaiśvānaró mahinā́ nā́kam aspṛśat ||
9.1 : *áhaś ca kṛṣṇám áhar árjunaṃ ca*
ví vartete rájasī vedyā́bhiḥ |
Vaiśvānaró jā́yamāno ná rā́jā
ávātiraj jyótiṣāgnís támāṅsi ||

Cf. also TBr III.7.8.1.

213. There the sun is represented also by Agni alone; thus in a variant of the Subrahmaṇya formula in Lāṭyāyana I.4.1 ff., which is interesting from the point of view of the history of the cult.

214. TS I.5.11.1 and II.2.5.1 respectively. Cf. also TS II.2.5.4; 5.6; 6.1; V.2.6.1; 5.1.6; 6.4.1 (V.7.6g); ABr III.41.2; MS II.1.3 (4.1, 14) etc.

215. See also TS V.4.7.7 and the comm. on TS IV.6.5 on p. 630; ŚBr IX.3.1.13. In TS II.2.11.1, in the same context Indra takes the place of Vaiśvānara.

216. *Mālavikāgnimitra*, I, v .12 (Bombay Sanskrit Series, 2nd ed., p. 21).

217. It is drawn during the Prātaḥsavana. "Originally these two grahas, the Dhruva and the Vaiśvānara, were drawn" (ISt, X, p. 157; *Ritualliteratur*, p. 129 and n. 32). It seems that in the later period these two were combined in such a way that the name was borrowed from one and the ceremonies and mantras from the other. ĀpŚS XII.16.1 : "He draws the Dhruva from the Sthālī with the verse, 'the head of the heaven...' (ṚV VI.7.1). 2 : He should draw less [than half] if he wishes for some one a shorter life [than fifty years]; more than half if he wishes for some one more [than fifty years]. 3 : For one who wishes life for oneself he should place the Dhruva on a sheet of gold with the words, 'this is your womb, you (accusative) for Vaiśvanara.' 4 : A prince protects it until it is poured out" etc. The comm. on TS, I, p. 649 says : *yathā divi nāko nāmāgnir ity āmnātaṃ tathā pṛthivyāṃ vaiśvānaraḥ*. Agni's connection with the sun becomes evident in the Pravargya also, which I explain with Oldenberg as solar magic. TĀr V.10.5 : *eṣa vā agnir vaiśvānaraḥ yat pravargyaḥ*; still more clearly in the Agnicayana. The ukhā made there serves the purpose of taking the fire that symbolizes the sun. (Comm. on TS, IV, p. 630 : *ukhyāgneḥ saṃvatsaradhāraṇena agneḥ*

saṃvatsararūpatvam). TS IV.1.5e; V.6.6d. Vaiśvānara is designated as a "chariot" also TBr II.2.5.4.

218. Cf. further I.128.3 : *sádo dádhāna úpareṣu sā́nuṣv agníḥ páreṣu sā́nuṣu*; III.5.9 : *adyaud várṣman divó ádhi nā́bhā pṛthivyā́ḥ*; III.54.1; X.88.14 : *vaiśvānarám...| yó mahimnā́ paribabhū́vorvī́ utā́vástād utá deváḥ parástāt*; 17 : *yátrā vádete ávaraḥ páraś ca yajñanyòḥ kataró nau vi véda*; AV XII.1.20 and the expression *dvijanman*, discussed on p. 58 above.

219. Bergaigne, II, p. 155. TS II.3.8.2 : *agner vai cakṣuṣā manuṣyā vi paśyanti, sūryasya devāḥ*; 6.8.5 : *na hi sūryasya cakṣuḥ kiṃ cana hinasti,... na hy agner āsyaṃ kiṃ cana hinasti*. We may recall the well known contrast in a Nigada between "*deveddha*" and "*manviddha*" (TS I.6.2h; ABr II.34; TBr III.5.3.1 etc.).

220. III.2.1 : *vaiśvānarā́ya dhiṣáṇām ṛtāvṛ́dhe*
ghṛtáṃ na pūtám agnáye janāmasi |

Cf. also the other verses of this hymn.

221. I.98.1 : *itó jātó víśvam idáṃ ví caṣṭe vaiśvānaró yatate sū́ryeṇa*; (V.4.4. : *juṣásvāgne...yátamāno raśmíbhiḥ sū́ryasya*, about Agni in general); I.59.3 : *ā́ sū́rye ná raśmáyo dhruvā́so vaiśvānaré dadhire 'gnā́ vásūni*. In any case, perhaps for this reason and because he is also a terrestrial sacrificial fire, MS IV.14.11 (234.2) says : *vaiśvānaraṃ bibhratī bhūmiḥ*, or ŚBr III. 8.5.4; TBr III.8.6.2; 9.17.3 : *iyaṃ vā agnir vaiśvānaraḥ*. Naturally, here also it would be impossible to explain all the details; for instance, in the case of Pitṛmedha the comm. explains the words *vaiśvānare havir idaṃ juhomi* (TĀr VI.6.1) as *agnisadṛśe kumbhe*. The verse occurs in the AV also (XVIII. 4.35). According to the *Kauśika Sūtra* it is recited with the offering made on the back of a cow. Bloomfield, SBE, XLII, p. 580, considers this fire in AV VIII.7.16 to be the "funeral fire"; but it is doubtful. All the three fires are used for kindling the funeral fire. In TBr II.1.4.5; III.7.3.2 Agni Vaiśvānara is like a brahmin : *eṣa vā agnir vaiśvānaro yad brāhmaṇaḥ*.

222. Bergaigne, II, p. 160 : "...in his form as the altar-fire, Agni Vaiśvānara has a celestial origin." Just as the gods kindle Agni in heaven so do men kindle him on the earth.

223. TS I.1.4p : *suvar abhi vi khyeṣaṃ vaiśvānaraṃ jyotiḥ*. Cf. the comm. on it, p. 91 : *bodhāyanaḥ "atharvaṇīyam īkṣate suvar...jyotir iti"| āpastambas tu mantrabhedam abhipretyāha "suvar abhi vi khyeṣam iti sarvaṃ vihāram anuvikṣate vaiśvānaraṃ jyotir ity āhavanīyam iti."* Likewise in the case of the Soma sacrifice, see TS I.3.41 and the comm. on p. 480. Cf. also TBr II.5.8.8 (comm. p. 644); MS IV.1.5 (7.10). — In TBr I.2.1.27 all the fires are worshipped with the mantra : *jyotiṣā vo vaiśvānareṇopa tiṣṭhe*. Cf. the following note.

224. Of Vaiśvānara, it is said in I.59.1 : *vayā́ id agne agnáyas te anye tvé víśve amṛ́tā mādayante* (ŚBr VI.1.2.35 : *vaiśvānaro vai sarve 'gnayaḥ...*); hence, he is the trunk, and the others the branches spreading out from him.

225. V.45.9.

226. GDS XV.28; Baudhāyana II.14.2; ĀpDS II.7.17.22; Manu III.185.

227. *Rituallliteratur*, p. 108. The Āvasathya fire is that of the rest house.

228. XIX.55.6.

229. Ananta (on Kātyāyana) remarks on p. 370 : The installation of the

Sabhya is the duty of a Kṣatriya because the convoking of a Sabhā is his privilege.

230. ĀpŚS V.17.1 and the comm.

231. *Rituallliteratur*, p. 108. The question whether it was the Kṣatriyas or the priests who played the game of dice is controversial. Lüders, *Daş Würfelspiel im alten Indien*, p. 51 ff.; Caland, ZDMG, LXII, p. 123 ff.

232. On this point the *Dharma Sūtra* agrees with the *Śrauta Sūtra* almost with the same wording. ĀpDS II.9.25.12 : *sabhāyā madhye 'dhidevanam uddhatyāvokṣyākṣān nivaped yugmān vaibhītakān yathārthān...*

233. In my view, this has to do with the ceremonial installation of the fire of a prince, which the subjects attend, perhaps during the Rājasūya which contains many popular elements (Weber, *Rājasūya*, pp. 66, 67; *Rituallliteratur*, p. 146). Or, at least, this has to do with the consecration of the Sabhā, which, however, might have been connected with the enthronement. Along with the Sabhā, i.e., the house of assembly and of play, an Āvasatha — I translate it as "rest house" — is constructed, in which the guests from outside are accommodated and fed. Sabhā and the game of dice, and Āvasatha and food belong together. Cf. TBr I.1.10.6; III.7.4.6 (Comm., p. 456 : *ahni dyūte vijayaṃ prāptāḥ puruṣā āgatya yatra bhojanārthaṃ nivasanti sa pradeśaḥ āvasathaḥ*). The construction of the two belongs to the duties of the prince, according to the ĀpDS. II.9.25.2 : "He shall erect a palace and a town with the gates towards the south. 3 : In the middle of the town the palace. 4 : To the east of it the rest house (*āvasatha*). It is called guest house (*āmantraṇa*, Bühler : hall of invitation). 5 : To the south of the town a Sabhā shall be erected with the gates towards the north and the south, so that one can see what passes inside and outside. 6 : In all [the three places] fires shall burn constantly. 7 : And there the fire must be worshipped day after day as in the Gṛhamedha. 8 : He shall accommodate his guests, from the Śrotriyas upwards, in the rest house. 9 : They shall be given shelter, bed, food and drink according to their merit." — Cf. Leist, *Altarisches jus gentium*, p. 82. *Agnipurāṇa*, adhyāya 65 deals with the construction of the Sabhā.

234. According to TBr III.7.4.6, the following mantra is uttered in the case of the Sabhya : *ajasraṃ tvāṃ sabhāpālāḥ vijayabhāgaṃ samindhatām* etc., and in the case of the Āvasathya : *annam āvasathīyam abhi harāṇī śaradaḥ śatam / āvasathe śriyaṃ mantram ahir budhniyo ni yacchatu etc.*

235. The cow serves as the stake; it is the price for the rice to be bought. According to ĀpDS II.9.25.13, members of the three castes, "who are pure and truthful," are allowed to play in the Sabhā.

236. Hence, this has to do with the feeding of the guests at the installation of the fire. — Wagering and roasting the cow must have been probably the original practice, and the substitution with rice must have been introduced later. Here also we notice a change in the circumstances. Wagering an animal is suggested as early as in the ṚV by an allegorical verse, which anticipates a similar situation and which receives a new light here—X.27.17ab : *pī́vānaṃ meṣám apacanta vīrā́ nyùptā akṣā́ ánu dīvá āsan* / "men roasted the fat ram; the dice were thrown upon the dice board." Although the event took place in heaven, it still reflects the earthly events.

237. The idea that here it is a fusion of the three fires occurred already to Ludwig, III, p. 357, although for different reasons. Credit goes to Koulikovski, "Les Trois Feux Sacrés du ṚV," *Revue de l'Histoire des Religions*, XX. p. 151 ff., for being the first to recognize in Agni Vaiśvānara a fire in the general sense; otherwise I cannot share his views throughout.

238. VIII.30.4 : *yé devāsa ihá sthána víśve vaiśvānarā́ utá / asmábhyaṃ śárma saprátho gávé 'śvāya yacchata //* Cf. Hopkins, "Prāgāthikāṇi," JAOS, XVII, p. 46, s.v. The word occurs as an adjective also in TS III.2.8p; IV.1.5f; 6a (plural).

239. TS IV.2.3e : *prapräyam agnir bharatasya śṛṇve... / abhi yaḥ pūrum pṛtanāsu tasthau... //*

240. Cf. also VI.8.6 : *asmā́kam agne maghávatsu dhārayā́nāmi kṣatrám ajáraṃ suvī́ryam /*

241. Also in the saga of the migrations in ŚBr I.4.1.10-18, it is Agni Vaiśvānara whom Gotama Rāhūgaṇa and Videgha Māthava follow when he goes towards the east across the rivers, burning the earth, and makes the land arable. On this see TBr II.4.6.8 :*...vaiśvānara tvayā te nuttāḥ pṛthivīm anyām abhi tasthur janāsaḥ*; and also TBr I.8.4.1 : *āgneyam aṣṭākapālaṃ nirvapati / tasmāc chiśire kurupañcālāḥ prāñco yānti...vaiśvānaraṃ dvādaśakapālam / tasmāj jaghanye naidāghe pratyañcaḥ kurupañcālā yānti /* It is not clear for what reasons TS III.3.8.4 equates Agni Vaiśvānara with the forest fire (represented by the burning of the sacrificial straw) : *eṣa vā vaiśvānaro yat pradāvyaḥ.*

242. I.59.6 : *...yám pūrávo vṛtrahánaṃ sácante /*
vaiśvānaró dásyum agnir jaghanvān
ádhūnot kā́ṣṭhā áva śambaraṃ bhet //

"Vaiśvānara Agni, whom the Pūrus follow as the destroyer of their enemies, struck down the Dasyu, shattered the fences (? Ludwig), and pierced Śambara."

243. X.91.2 distinguishes between *gṛhegṛhe, janaṃjanam, viśaṃviśam.*

244. Cf. e.g., TS VII.5.23.2.

245. Cf. VI.1.5 : *tvā́ṃ vardhanti kṣitáyaḥ pṛthivyā́m...*; 6 : *saparyéṇyaḥ sá priyó vikṣv ágniḥ...*; 7 : *tváṃ víśo anayo dī́dyāno...*; 8 : *viśā́ṃ kavíṃ viśpátiṃ śáśvatīnām.* IV.49.2; V.3.5; VII.7.4.6; VIII.23.20; MS IV.12.5 (192.13) : *varṣman pṛthivyāḥ=nābhau.*

246. Foy, *Die Königliche Gewalt*, p. 10; Hillebrandt, *Altindische Politik*, p. 60.

247. Bühler, ZDMG, XXXVII, p. 278; XLVIII, pp. 55, 56.

248. Zimmer, *Altindisches Leben*, p. 158 ff.; Foy, op. cit., pp. 6, 7. I cannot distinguish clearly the Sabhā from the Samiti, since, after all, the king builds the Sabhā, and from this we may conclude that a legal relationship existed between the king and the assembly that met there. Perhaps the Samitis also met in such a Sabhā house.

249. Probably the chieftains or Aryans as opposed to the lower strata. Cf. also VII.97.1 : *yajñé divó nṛṣádane pṛthivyā́ náro yátra devayávo mádanti.*

250. MS IV.7.4 (97.17) : *pumāṅsaḥ sabhāṃ yanti na striyaḥ.*

251. I come back once more to *nṝ́n* here. In ṚV I.181.8 : *utá syā́ vām...*

gīs tribarhíṣi sádasi pinvate nṝn (cf. ZDMG, XLVIII, p. 421), *nṝn* is to be connected as genitive with *sádasi* and not with *vām*. About my translation of VI.39.5 where *nṝn* as accusative occurs with *gā́ḥ* and *árvato*, cf. VI.22.3 : *rāyā́ḥ puruvīrasya nṛvátaḥ purukṣóḥ*; in the Vedic view, wealth consists of "men" also.

252. III.23.4 : *ní tvā dadhe vára ā pṛthivyā́ḥ*
ílāyās padé sudinatvé áhnām /

253. Cf. *Festgruss für Böhtlingk*, p. 43.

254. Spiegel, *Eranische Altertumskunde*, 3, p. 575; Geiger, *Ostiranische Kultur im Altertum*, p. 472.

255. X.45.1 : *divás pári prathamáṃ jajñe agníḥ*
asmád dvitī́yaṃ pári jātávedāḥ /
tṛtī́yam apsú nṛmáṇā ájasram...

VIII.43.28 runs quite parallel to this : *yád agne divijā́* (1) *ásy apsujā́* (2) *vā sahaskṛtā* (3); *sahaskṛtā* here corresponds to the *asmád jātá* in the former. Cf. further VI.49.2 : *diváḥ śíśum* (1); *sáhasaḥ sūnúm* (3). Also VIII.44.16; X.2.7; (46.9). Cf. Macdonell, *Vedic Mythology*, p. 93; ĀpŚS V.16.4. Sāyaṇa on X.45.1 explains *apsu* as *antarikṣe vaidyutātmanā*.

256. *trī́ṇi jā́nā pári bhūṣanty asya samudrá ékaṃ divy ékam apsú.*

257. I.95.2 : *tigmā́nīkaṃ sváyaśasaṃ jáneṣu*
virócamānaṃ pári ṣīṃ nayanti //

Oldenberg, RdV, p. 107, n. 1, has recognized this correctly.

258. TS IV.7.13c : *cíd asi samudráyonir índur*
dákṣaḥ śyená ṛtā́vā /

259. I.164.1 : *asyá vāmásya palitásya hótuḥ*
tásya bhrā́tā madhyamó asty áśnaḥ /
tṛtī́yo bhrā́tā ghṛtápṛṣṭho asya
átrāpaśyaṃ viśpátiṃ saptáputram //

260. ŚBr I.6.4.19; IV.6.7.12 : *candramā hy etasyānnaṃ ya eṣa tapati.*

261. *agnir vai devānām annadaḥ.*

262. *Vedisch-brahmanische Periode der Religion des Alten Indiens*, p. 64.

263. RdV, pp. 111, 116; 2nd ed., pp. 108, 111.

264. *Religions of Primitive Peoples*. Cf. there on p. 138, the categories of gods actually worshipped. *Myths of the New World*, 3rd ed., pp. 126, 181 ff; also his article on the Thunderbird, ERE, I, p. 529. The aborigines of the North-West coast see the thunder as the flapping of wings of a huge bird and the lightning as the flash of its eyes; the Caribbeans conceived the thundercloud as a bird which produces the lightning by blowing through a hollow tube. One can directly regard it as a bird, or describe it in some other way. On the mythical relationship between *ākhu* (mole, rat, mouse) and the lightning (doubtful on my view), see Eggeling, SBE, XII, p. 278, n. 3.

265. *Die allgemeine Mythologie und ihre ethnologischen Grundlagen*, p. 136.

266. *Mythes, Cultes et Religion*, p. 103 ff; Cf. K. von den Steinen, *Unter den Naturvölkern Zentral-Brasiliens*, p. 222. Obviously, there is a great difference whether one conceives the lightning as a living being or as a deity. One can regard the clouds as "cows," yet one may be far from deifying them.

267. Thus also W. Crooke, *Religion and Folklore of Northern India*, ed.

Enthoven, 1926, p. 53 ff.; Enthoven, *Folklore of Bombay*, 1924, p. 76 ff. All this should prevent us from looking for the personifications of the lightning in the Vedic gods — a mistake which Keith has committed again recently (*Religion and Philosophy of the Veda*, pp. 147, 156 ff.).

268. In his review of E. H. Meyer, *Indogemanische Mythen*, Mogk, AISAK, III, p. 25, n. 1 : "in the entire saga literature, I know only two examples where lightning was mentioned at all..." Greek Mythology offers a bigger booty, see Usener, *Götternamen. Versuch einer Lehre von der religiösen Begriffsbildung*, p. 286 ff.

269. We find *vanadevatās*, *rukkhadevatās*, worship of rivers etc., see Oldenberg's Index to the *Vinaya Piṭaka*, II, 336; V, 237; *Dígha Nikāya* (*Tevijja*) XIII.17.25; *Divyāvadāna* I.1; *Ritualliteratur*, p. 18 etc. In Jacobi, *Ausgewählte Erzählungen in Mahārāṣṭrī*, p. 30, also where different gods are enumerated, a god of lightning is not mentioned. Similarly, a survey of all the Ṛgvedic passages where *vidyut* is mentioned would not support the lightning theory.

270. E.g., TS IV.1.4k : *apāṃ garbham*; comm. on p. 61 : *meghasthānāṃ jalānāṃ madhye vidyudrūpam "samudriyaṃ" samudre vaḍavāgnirūpeṇotpannam...*

271. *India*, tr. Sachau, I, p. 42 : "Brahman, on seeing sparks under the earth, brought them forward and divided them into three parts : the first *pārthiva*, is the common fire...; the second is *divya*, *i.e.* the sun; the third, *vidyut*, *i.e.* the lightning. The sun attracts the water; the lightning shines through the water" etc. Holtzmann, *Agni nach den Vorstellungen des Mahābhārata*, p. 3. Hemādri, in his comm. on *Raghuvaṃśa* VI.5 associates the colours of lightning with certain natural events : yellow augurs good crop, white famine etc.

272. Quotations in Oldenberg, RdV, p. 112, n. 1.

273. Bloomfield, *Seven Hymns*, p. 4 (on AV I.12); SBE, XLII, pp. 7, 246 ff. AV VII.11 contains a spell against the lightning which is dangerous to the crop. There the lightning is only a weapon in the hand of the god.

274. In ṚV VI.21.7 as "his old comrade in arms"; 47.28 as chariot. Cf. also X.92.7. Above all, one should remember the *vazra* in the hand of *Miθra*.

275. IX.67.30 : *alā́yyasya paraśúr nanāśa.* See ZDMG, XLVIII, p. 418 : "his axe was hidden; it was lost," if we decide upon changing the accent signs. Thōr's hammer was also lost. On this one can cite TBr I.1.3 — as far as I know, these are the only passages where Agni who was running away from the gods can be interpreted as the lightning — : *agnir devebhyo 'nilāyata / ākhurūpaṃ kṛtvā sa pṛthivīṃ prāviśat / sa ūtīḥ* (*bilāni*) *kurvāṇaḥ pṛthivīm anusamacarat / tad ākhupurīṣam abhavat* and TBr I.2.1.2 :

ūtīḥ kurvāṇo yat pṛthivīṃ acaraḥ
guhākāram ākhūrūpaṃ pratītya...

However, I admit that my interpretation is uncertain (see Oldenberg, *Die Hymnen des Ṛgveda*, II, p. 167).

276. Not *apsú* !

277. During the Ādityopasthāna. Cf. also ṚV VIII.67.20 :

mā́ no hetír vivásvataḥ ā́dityāḥ kṛtrímā śáruḥ /
purā́ nú jaráso vadhīt // (Vivasvat=sun).

278. Cf. also TBr III.8.4.2 : *vajrī vā aśvaḥ prājāpatyaḥ*; ŚBr XIII.1.2.9 : *vajro 'śvaḥ*.

279. ṚV I.39.9; V.84.3; VII.56.13; X.91.5 in Bloomfield, *Contributions* V, p. 11, n. 2. On lightning and cloud see Bloomfield, *Contributions*, I, p. 5; V, p. 15; VI (in ZDMG, XLVII), p. 565 : on the meaning of the word *śuṣma*.

280. E.g., TS II.2.8.5 : *vajro vai śakvarī* (cf. Gobhila III.2.22); V.2.7.4 : *vajro vā ājyaṃ vajraḥ kārṣmaryaḥ*; VI.3.3.2 : *vajro vai svadhitiḥ*; 6.11.3 : *vajro vai ṣoḍaśī*; 11.6 : *aruṇapiśaṅgo 'śvo dakṣiṇaitad vai vajrasya rūpam*; VII.4.7 and elsewhere : *pañcadaśo vajraḥ*; ABr II.35.5 : *ārambhaṇato vai vajrasyāṇimātho daṇḍasyātho paraśoḥ*; 41.10 : *vṛṣṭir vai yājyā vidyut*; TBr I.1.3.12 : *maruto 'dbhiḥ agnim atamayan | tasya tāntasya hṛdayam ācchindan | sāśanir abhavat*; III.2.4.2 : *vajraḥ vai āpaḥ*; 10.1 : *vajro vai sphyaḥ*; 12.5.6 : *vajro vai rathaḥ* (=TS V.4.9.3 etc.); MS IV.4.1 (51.2) : *vajro vai paśavaḥ* etc. ABr III.6.1 : *vajro vā eṣa yad vaṣaṭkāraḥ*. Cf. inter alia, the interpretation of the sacrificial invocations in TS I.6.11.3, 4 (*astu śrauṣad ity abhraṃ sam aplāvayan, yajeti vidyutam ajanayan* etc.). Or, the Anumantraṇas connected with the three Anuyājas in the case of an exorcism : "*aśanī*, strike NN !" "*hrādunī*, strike NN !" "*ulkuṣī*, strike NN !" (NVO, pp. 138, 9). Of course, I concede that the arguments adduced by Bloomfield (JAOS, XVI, p. 11 ff.) while interpreting the eagle that brings Soma as the lightning are correct; but the lightning is not a god and should be clearly distinguished from Agni who is otherwise described as a bird (*divya suparṇa* etc.). Probably the lightning was also occasionally thought of as the bringer of fire from heaven.

281. Perhaps TBr III.10.5 : *jātavedā yadi vā pāvako 'si vaiśvānaro yadi vā vaidyuto 'si*.

282. Perhaps AV VII.41. Bloomfield, *Contributions*, V, in JAOS, XVI, p. 13.

283. Quite colourless are AV III.21.7; VS XXV.1.

284. X.30.4 : *yáṃ víprāsa ílate adhvaréṣu*; 8 : *íḍyaṃ adhvaréṣu* show merely that *apāṃ napāt* is not the lightning.

285. ABr I.15.6. According to ŚBr XIII.2.7.13 ff., Agni, Vāyu and Sūrya are "*paśu-s*."

286. Cf. also I.26.8; 31.11; 36.4, 5, 10; 59.2, 5; II.1.13 : *tvám agna ādityā́sa āsyàm tvā́ṃ jihvā́ṃ śúcayaś cakrire kave | ...tvé devā́ havír adanty ā́hutam ||*; 14; II.4.3; III.1.4, 13; 3.5; 11.4; 17.4; 29.7; IV.1.1; V.3.4; 8.6 : *urujráyasaṃ ghṛtayonim...cákṣur dadhire*; 21.3; 25.2; VI.15.8; 16.1; VII.11.1, 4; VIII. 84.2; X.12.2 : *devó devā́n paribhū́r*; 3; 46.9, 10 etc. —TBr II.4.6.7 : *nahi spaśam avidann anyam asmāt | vaiśvānarāt puraetāram agneḥ | atheme 'manthann amṛtam asurāḥ vaiśvānaraṃ kṣetrajityāya devā́ḥ...*

287. ṚV VI.7.1 : *mūrdhā́naṃ divó aratíṃ pṛthivyā́ḥ*
vaiśvānarám ṛtá ā́ jātám agním |
kavíṃ samrā́jam átithiṃ jánānām
āsánn ā́ pā́traṃ janayanta devā́ḥ ||

2 : *nā́bhiṃ yajñā́nām...abhí sáṃ navanta |*
vaiśvānaráṃ rathyàm adhvarā́ṇām
yajñásya ketúṃ janayanta devā́ḥ ||

288. *yadéd enam ádadhur yajñíyāso diví devā́ḥ sū́ryam ādityám |* The realistic conception of the sun occurs outside India also. Lang, *Mythes, Cultes et Religion*, p. 117, cites the following from Brough Smyth, *Aborigines of Victoria*, I, p. 430 : "Sun, Sun, burn your wood, burn your internal substance and go down." In X.28.8 gods carry axes with which they split wood.

289. X.88.10 : *stómena hi diví devā́so agním ájījanan...|*
tám ū́ akṛṇvan tredhā́ bhuvé kám...

290. VIII.101.12 : *baṭ sūrya...| mahnā́ devā́nām asuryàḥ puróhito vibhú jyótir ádābhyam ||*

291. TMBr V.3.9 : *agnir vā idaṃ vaiśvānaro dahann ait tasmād devā abibhayuḥ.*

292. Cf. also TBr II.4.6.7 cited in n. 286 above; ṚV I.59.5 etc.

293. Hillebrandt, "Die Sonnenwendfeste in Altindien," *Romanische Forschungen*, V, 1889, pp. 299-340. TMBr IV.5.9; VI.7.24; VII.4.7; XII. 10.6; XXV.10.11.

294. TS VI.2.8.4: *sa yāṃ vanaspatiṣv avasat tāṃ pūtudrau, yāṃ oṣadhīṣu tāṃ sugandhitejane yāṃ paśuṣu tāṃ petvasyāntarā śṛṅge.* (In TBr III.8.12.2, this legend is transferred to Prajāpati who takes the place of Agni there : *āśvattho vrajo bhavati | prajāpatir devebhyo 'nilāyata | aśvo rūpaṃ kṛtvā so 'śvatthe saṃvatsaram atiṣṭhat, tad aśvatthasyāśvatthatvam...*) ŚBr I.2.3.1; 3.3.13 ff. also narrates this legend without any substantial variations. MS III.8.5 (101.3 ff.). On the form of this legend in the later period, see A. Holtzmann, *Agni nach den Vorstellungen des Mahābhārata*, p. 11. Cf. inter alia, *Anuśāsanaparva* 85.20 ff.

295. In the *Kāṭhaka*, he is the fourth Hotṛ himself; Macdonell, *Vedic Mythology*, p. 95.

296. Cf. I.65.1 : *paśvā́ ná tāyúṃ gúhā cátantam...|*
sajóṣā dhī́rāḥ padaír ánu gman úpa
tvā sīdan víśve yájatrāḥ ||
65.4; 67.6, 7; 72.2 :
asmé vatsáṃ pári sántam ná vindan
icchánto víśve amṛ́tā ámūrāḥ |
III.1.9, 14 (*gúheva vṛddhám*); IV.5.9; 7.6; V.8.3; 11.6; 15.5; VI.1.2, X.46.2.

297. Jarl Charpentier, *Suparṇasage*, p. 115.

298. V.2.8 : *hṛṇīyámāno ápa hí mád aíyeḥ*
prá me devā́nāṃ vratapā́ uvāca |
índro vidvā́ṅ ánu hí tvā cacákṣa
ténāhám agne ánuśiṣṭa ā́gām ||

Cf. v. 12 of this hymn, and more particularly, X.32.6 ff. where the same verse occurs with a variant; there pāda *a* is replaced by *nidhīyámānam ápagūḷham apsú.*

299. Cf. Oldenberg, ZDMG, XXXIX, p. 71 ff.; RdV, p. 124.

300. Agni wants a long life for himself; cf. X.51.7 : *kurmás ta ā́yur ajáram yád agne...*; 8 : *agnéś ca dīrghám ā́yur astu devā́ḥ.*

301. X.124.1 : *imáṃ no agna úpa yajñám éhi*
páñcayāmaṃ trivṛ́taṃ saptátantum |
áso havyavā́ḍ utá naḥ purogā́
jyóg evá dīrghám táma ā́śayiṣṭhāḥ ||

302. X.181.3 : *té 'vindan mánasā dī́dhyānā yájuḥ*
ṣkannáṃ prathamáṃ devayā́nam |

303. See pp. 24, 63 above.

304. KBr V.7.

305. Caland, *Altindischer Ahnenkult*, p. 179. (This speaks against interpreting Yama as the sun who went down, i.e., the "night sun").

306. Caland, op. cit.

307. X.88.15 : *dvé srutī́ aśṛṇavaṃ pitṝṇā́m*
aháṃ devā́nām utá mártyānām |
tā́bhyām idáṃ víśvam éjat śam eti
yád antarā́ pitáraṃ mātáraṃ ca ||

Cf. TBr I.3.10.1 : *pitṝn yajño 'gacchat | taṃ devāḥ punar ayācanta* etc.

308. VI.48.5 : *yám ā́po ádrayo vánā gárbham ṛtásya píprati |*
sáhasā yó mathitó jā́yate nṛ́bhiḥ pṛthivyā́ adhi sā́navi ||

309. Cf. AV XIII.1.50 : *satye anyaḥ samāhito 'psv anyaḥ samidhyate brahmeddhāv agnī ījate rohitasya...*; TS I.4.45d : *agner anīkam apa ā viveśa.*

310. Cf. I.70.2; 141.5; 144.2; 145.5; II.4.2; III.5.3; 25.5; IV.7.6; V.34.9; 85.2; VII.9.3; VIII.39.8; X.8.1; 32.6; 46.2; 51.1; 121.7; 177.1. X.91.6 has a graphic description : *tám óṣadhīr dadhire gárbham ṛtvíyaṃ tám ā́po agníṃ janayanta mātáraḥ | tám ít samānáṃ vanínaś ca vīrúdho 'ntárvatīś ca súvate ca viśváhā ||*

311. I have no objection against assuming with other scholars that the Vedic concepts include an Agni in the waters of the earth also (AV XII.1.37; cf. Oldenberg, RdV, p. 115, who collected the passages, which are, however, of late origin; with regard to "Agni in the waters" he thinks of the ordinary water and the fire latent in it). But here I cannot count among the evidence the usages of the later literature, since they have only a symbolical meaning. In spite of Geldner, VSt, II, p. 271, I doubt that the Ṛgvedic period was acquainted with the later concept of the "ocean fire."

312. X.72.7 : *yád devā yátayo yáthā bhúvanāny ápinvata |*
átrā samudrá ā́ gūlhám ā́ sū́ryam ajabhartana ||

313. MS IV.12.4 (194.3) : *sūryo apo vigāhate.* For our present purpose the following are not significant — ṚV IV.38.10 : *ā́ dadhikrā́ḥ...sū́rya iva jyótiṣāpás tatāna* (VII.47.4; X.178.3); V.45.10.

314. Ludwig thinks differently, No. 240 (vol. IV, p. 238).

315. X.27.17 : *dvā́ dhánuṃ bṛhatī́m apsv àntaḥ*
pavítravantā carataḥ punántā ||

The two "calves of the Virāj, which emerge out of the ocean," AV VIII. 9.1 (see p. 34 above) can only be the sun and the moon in their diurnal risings. The wind is also closely connected with the waters :

ṚV I.122.3 : *mamáttu vā́to apā́ṃ vṛ́ṣaṇvān;* VII.40.6 : *vṛṣṭíṃ párijmā vā́to dadātu*; X.168.3 : *apā́ṃ sákhā*; TS VII.4.20c; TMBr VII.8.1 and AV X.8.40 : *apsv ā̀sīn mātaríśvā právíṣṭaḥ právíṣṭā devā́ḥ...*

316. VII.49.4 : *yā́su rā́ja váruṇo yā́su sómo*
víśve devā́ yā́sūrjaṃ mádanti |
vaiśvānaró yā́sv agníḥ právíṣṭas...

317. Cf. verse X.72.7 cited earlier in n. 312 above, which states that

the gods brought forth the Sūrya who was hidden in the ocean. The verse can be regarded as a twin of the present one.

318. Cf. also I.146.4 : *dhírāsaḥ padáṃ kaváyo nayanti...| siṣāsantaḥ páry apaśyanta síndhum āvír ebhyo abhavat sū́ryo nṝn ||*. *Hiraṇyakesi Gṛhya Sūtra* II.3.10 : *sūryam ṛtaṃ tamaso grāhyā yad devā amuñcann asṛjan vy enasaḥ*. ṚV I.117.5 : *sū́ryaṃ ná támasi kṣiyántam*. L. v. Schroeder, *Arische Religion*, II, pp. 557, 585 suspects, as mentioned above, an old Aryan myth in the strange flight of Agni or his hiding in the waters. Like him, Foy (AISAK, 12, p. 41) also thinks that this legend developed from the phenomenon that a fire-brand when put into water is extinguished with a hissing sound. I do not understand how one could deduce Agni's stay in the waters from the extinction of the fire.

319. Cf. ṚV V.59.5 : *sū́ryasya cákṣuḥ prá minanti vṛṣṭibhiḥ* (*marútaḥ*); 63.4 : *tám* (*sū́ryam*) *abhréṇa vṛṣṭyā́ gūhathaḥ*; X.72.7 : *samudrá ā́ gūḷhám sū́ryam*, see n. 312 above; MS IV.12.5 (194.3) : *sūryo apo vigāhate raśmibhir vājasātamaḥ*, *Rāmāyaṇa* (NSP ed.,) II.119.22 : *vanaṃ praviveśa... sūrya ivābhramaṇḍalam*.

320. Cf. further I.67.9; 141.4; II.1.14; III.55.4, 5; VII.4.5; X.1.2 etc. (Cf. p. 94 above; Oldenberg, RdV, p. 115; Macdonell, *Vedic Mythology*, p. 91). Thus we have a twofold division and, if we take the flint stones into account, a threefold division. ṚV II.1.1 mentions (1) *adbhyaḥ*, (2) *aśmanaḥ*, (3) *vanebhyaḥ*, *oṣadhībhyaḥ*. In a few cases *jāṭharāgni* could be added to these three. But this and the flint stone play no role in the ṚV; hence, we can remain with the twofold division of "waters" and "vegetation" for our purposes.

321. VIII.43.9 : *apsv àgne sádhiṣ ṭáva saúṣadhīr ánu rudhyase garbhe nu*; III.2.11. *jinvate jaṭháreṣu prajajñivān. citréṣu* does not refer to different men, but to the plants ("core of the plants"). Agni is *víbhṛta óṣadhīṣu* ṚV X.1.2. But these are different from the plants in the later literature, which glow at night. Cf. *Kumārasaṃbhava* I.10 and Stenzler's remarks on it.

322. As an explanation, TBr I.1.3.9 narrates thus : *aśvo rūpaṃ kṛtvā so 'śvatthe saṃvatsaram atiṣṭhat*; likewise I.2.1.5.

323. The following popular rhyme of ours is corroborated by research :

Vor den Eichen musst du weichen,
Vor den Fichten musst du flüchten,
Doch die Buchen musst du suchen.
(Avoid the oaks,
Flee from the spruce-firs,
But seek out the beeches.)

See C. Müller, *Himmel und Erde*, VIII, p. 172 : "all the recent observations agree...in the fact that, given the same circumstances, e.g., in a mixed stock, beeches are struck by lightning very rarely, but oaks disproportionately very frequently." According to the statistics collected by the Fürstlich Lippe-Detmold'sche Forstverwaltung (Ducal Forest Administration of Lippe-Detmold), "of the trees struck by lightning brought to notice between the years 1879 to 1890, the average comes to about fiftysix oaks, three to four spruce-firs, and twenty to twentyone pines that were struck before a beech tree was ever touched by lightning," while the actual proportion of beeches in the forest was "that out of every hundred trees about seventy were beeches, eleven oaks, thirteen spruce-firs, and six pines." On the physical reasons for this, see Müller, *loc. cit*, p. 178.

324. See Bergaigne, I, p. 16 ff. ; Oldenberg, RdV, p. 113. I agree with both of them in the main points.

325. Cf. (only as an analogy) *Chāndogya Up.* V.10.6 where those who attain rebirth fall down as "rain," or are born as rice, barley etc.

326. On the etymology, see the authorities cited by Richter, IF, IX, p. 247, n. 4.

327. Sāyaṇa inter alia : *vāyusaṃyogāt prajvalita ity arthaḥ.*

328. I.93.6 : *ányáṃ divó mātaríśvā jabhāra*
ámathnād anyáṃ pári śyenó ádreḥ /
I.128.2 : *yáṃ mātaríśvā mánave parāváto deváṃ bhā́ḥ parāvátaḥ* //
I.60.1; III.9.5 :...*tiróhitam* / *aínaṃ nayan mātaríśvā parāváto devébhyo mathitáṃ pári*; VI.8.4. III.2.13 also belongs here : *á yáṃ dadhé mātaríśvā diví kṣáyam* (whom Mātariśvan "took"). Charpentier, *Kleine Beiträge*, p. 75, is right when he sees these verses with their multiple points of congruence as the fragments of one or several hymns directly addressed to Mātariśvan out of which the hymnologists have filled their cups.

329. I.71.4; 141.3 :...*gúhā sántaṃ mātaríśvā mathāyáti*; 148.1.

330. The epithets of Mātariśvan in the ṚV throw no light on his nature — I.96.4 : *puruvárapuṣṭi, svarvíd, viśváṃ gopá*; I.148.1 : *viṣṭá*; 71.4 : *vibhṛta.*

331. VS XI.39 : *vāyu mātariśvan*; TS IV.1.4a : *saṃ te vāyur mātariśvā dadhātūttanāyai hṛdayaṃ yad viliṣṭam* / *devānāṃ yaś carati prāṇathena tasmai ca devi vaṣaḍ astu tubhyam*; MS II.7.4 (78.7); III.1.5 (6.22); ABr II.38.6 : *pitā mātariśvety āha prāṇo vai pitā prāṇo mātariśvā*; TĀr III.14.2; IV.42.1.

332. As the parallel cited on in n. 316 shows, the Mātariśvan "who entered the waters" can very well have been thought of as the wind.

333. Cf. Blanford, *Climates*, p. 82 : "...for an hour or more the air is calm, until violent gusts of cool air blow out in advance of the storm, raising clouds of dust. Sometimes these gusts blow with great force, blowing down trees or breaking their branches." Crooke, *The Tribes and Castes of the North-Western Provinces*, p. 52. Kipling, *Plain Tales*, Tauchnitz ed., p. 54, 57 can serve as an illustration : "the duststorm was on us and everything was roaring, whirling darkness"..."now and again we rushed through the whirling, choking 'dust devils' in the skirts of the flying storm."

334. We can safely ignore TBr II.3.9 5 where the east wind was explained as Prāṇa, the west wind as Pavamāna and the north wind as Savitṛ, and the south wind is assigned to Mātariśvan (*atha yad dakṣiṇato vāti mātariś-vaiva bhūtvā dakṣiṇato vāti* / *tasmād dakṣiṇato vāntaṃ vidyāt* etc.). All these are certainly artificial identifications. (In classical Sanskrit, the south wind is the messenger of spring; cf. *Mālavikāgnimitra*, BSS ed., III, p. 63. Raghu wins the hearts of the people like the mild southern breeze — *Raghuvaṃśa* IV.8. Cf. also *Kumārasaṃbhava* III.25 and the comm. But we are not concerned with this here).

335. RdV, p. 122, n. 1.

336. Sāyaṇa on ṚV I.95.2 from the Śruti.

337. *śvetaṃ vāyave niyutvate ālabheta tejaskāmo, vāyur vā agnes tejaḥ / tasmād vāyum agnir anveti...*

338. Cf. further IV.7.11 : *sadyó jātásya dádṛśānam ójo yád asya vāto sanuvā́ti śociḥ* (VII.3.2); from the later literature, *Raghuvaṃśa* III.37 : *vibhāvasuḥ ārathineva vāyunā*; X.40 : *svayam eva hi vāto 'gneḥ sārathyaṃ pratipadyate;* 82 : *[aikyam] yathā vāyuvibhāvasvor yathā candrasamudrayoḥ*. Manu I.77 : *vāyor api vikurvāṇād virociṣṇu tamonudaṃ jyotir utpadyate bhāsvat tad rūpaguṇam ucyate* etc. (Occasionally Anila, the wind, is called his father — Max Müller, *Physische Religion*, p. 192; cf. Holtzmann, *Agni nach den Vorstellungen des Mahābhārata*, pp. 15, 18). Cf. the trope in *Śiśupālavadha* XI.7 as an example of popularity of the concept that the fire is created by the wind :...*viviktair mātariśvāvacūrṇya jvalayati madanāgniṃ mālatīnāṃ rajobhiḥ*.

339. Crooke, *The Popular Religion and Folklore of Northern India*, 2nd ed., II, p. 194; Hopkins, "Addenda et Corrigenda I" (JAOS, XX, p. 217).

340. In ṚV X.114.1 Mātariśvan is associated with the two Gharmas : *táyor júṣṭiṃ mātaríśvā jagāma*. Sāyaṇa explains the two Gharmas as Agni and Āditya. I shall not attempt an interpretation of this verse, but would like to refer to TS I.1.3b : *mātariśvano gharmo 'sīti;* and TBr III.2.3 : *mātariśvano gharmo 'sīty āha / antarikṣaṃ vai mātariśvano gharmaḥ* (comm. on TS : *he kumbha, vāyoḥ saṃcārasthānapradānena dīpako 'yam antarikṣalokas tadrūpas tvam asi*); hence, Mātariśvan might be the wind here also.

341. See Oldenberg, RdV, p. 122, n. 1; Macdonell, s.v.

342. Sāyaṇa (who gives a different emphasis) : *vāyau kṣipraṃ vāti sati jājvalyamāno 'gnir gṛhān dahan loke dṛśyate / ato 'gnidvārā vāyor dāhakatvam*. Cf. also the remark of Merk, *Acht Vorträge*, p. 73 : "the word *loḥ*, [used to denote hot wind], means flame also."

343. Charpentier, *Kleine Beiträge*, p. 76 concludes from verses like ṚV X.48.2 etc. that in the older portions of the ṚV, Mātariśvan was actually a kind of Prometheus, a semi-divine being,...who belonged to the "fathers," who had earned such a great merit that they enjoyed almost divine pleasures, and that he was probably connected particularly with the ancient fire priests, the Atharvans and the ancient clans of the Bhṛgus. He was the first to kindle the hidden sacrificial fire for them. But I cannot see from this stage how he evolved into the wind god Mātariśvan.

344. Macdonell, *Vedic Mythology*, p. 78. If one were to explain Mātariśvan directly as a fire god, then the expressions like *āvir bhū, bhar, ānī* would contradict this (see p. 97 above).

345. ZDMG, I, p. 66 ff.

346. Bergaigne, I, p. 299.

347. Ibid., I, p. 300.

348. *Rig-Veda, ou Livre des Hymnes, traduit du Sanscrit*, I, p. 249, n. 36; p. 254, n. 83; p. 578 and Index in vol. IV.

349. *Rig-Veda-Samhita*, translated, I, XXXVIII and II, p. ix.

350. *Rigveda-Samhita*, translated, I, p. 77.

351. See Muir, OST, V, p. 282 ff.

352. Strauss, *Bṛhaspati im Veda* (Dissertation submitted to Kiel University), Leipzig 1905; Oldenberg, NGGW, 1915, p. 196 ff.; Hertel, IF, XLI, p. 185 ff.

353. *śúcikranda, mandrájihva,* particularly of Agni and Bṛhaspati, though not exclusively.

354. *svāveśá,* "with auspicious arrival," "excellent entrance." When referring to the moon, it denotes his "rise" : the appearance of the moon is *āsutíṃ káriṣṭhaḥ.*

355. It is true "that other gods also fly on their chariots," the Aśvins, Parjanya, the Maruts, the Abhva, the rivers (in whose case the speed is supposed to be described thus); but this does not speak against our argument because these are also mostly naturalistic gods, though of a different kind.

356. Similarly in other passages it is clearly the fire god or a form of fire that is meant.

I.38.13 : *ácchā vadā tánā girā́ jarā́yai bráhmaṇas pátim |*
agníṃ mitráṃ ná darśatám ||

and VII.7.5.

357. X.47.6 : *saptágu*

358. ABr III.34.1 : *yad aṅgārāḥ punar avaśāntā udadīpyanta tad bṛhaspatir abhavat.* The assumption that he was conceived as a god of light follows also from the fact that in the ritual, animals are offered to him which are to some extent bright in colour. VS XXIV.2 : *śitibāhur anyataḥśitibāhuḥ samantaśitibāhus te bārhaspatyāḥ*; AV IX.4.1 : *sāhasras tveṣa vṛṣabhaḥ bārhaspatya usriyaḥ*; ŚBr V.3.1.2 : *śitipṛṣṭho bārhaspatyasya dakṣiṇā*; MS II.6.5 (66.3); 6.6 (67.5) etc.

359. Cf. IX.86.21 : *ayáṃ punāná uṣáso ví rocayat*

360. Cf. V.47.3 : *mádhye divó nihitaḥ pṛ́śnir áśmā ví cakrame |*

361. Cf. IX.62.26; 71.4 : *agriyáḥ*; 86.12: *ágre síndhūnām, ágre vācó agriyó góṣu, ágre vā́jasya;* 86.45 : *agregáḥ.*

362. *ukṣán, vṛṣabhá* : IX.69.4; 70.7; 76.5; 85.9; 86.38 etc.

363. Cf. IX.74.2 : *divó yáḥ skambháḥ... | ...ródasī...samīcīné dadhāra;* 101.15 : *ví yás tastámbha ródasī* (about Bṛhaspati, IV.50.1 : *tastámbha ví jmó ántān*); 54.3; 62.27; 84.2; 94.3; 110.9.

364. IX.74.5 : *dádhāti gárbham áditer upástha ā́ yéna tokáṃ ca tánayaṃ ca dhā́mahe.*

Cf. the section on "Soma and the Manes."

365. In his work, *Die Anfänge der Yogapraxis,* J. W. Hauer has unravelled new insights into the spiritual conditions in ancient India, but his enthusiasm has led him too far in his investigation, which is otherwise full of interesting conclusions. He has not recognized the significance of hymn IX.83. He thinks that this hymn contains only a parallel to Soma worship and that, in reality, it describes only a ceremony of heating through the sun (p. 109). But the parallels given above show a relationship with the Soma hymns, which follows from the underlying concept of the moon in both cases. Soma (=Indu) also throws his burning shaft (VI.52.3), or hurls his weapon from the sky with Indra (VI.44.22). But such passages are less numerous in connection with the ambrosia-nature of the moon than in connection with his Agni-aspect, viz., Bṛhaspati. I do not know what to do

with the belaboured interpretation of v.1 : *pavitrasya gā́trāṇi páru eṣī viśvátaḥ*, "he himself, Brahmaṇaspati, enters his limbs from all sides, i.e., probably the limbs of the singer," or how X.98.3d : *divo drapso mádhumān á́ viveśa* could mean "that inspiration came to the poets."

366. VS XVIII.76; ŚBr 1.7.4.21; IV.6.6.7. He is the Brahman (neuter) himself : *brahma vai bṛhaspatiḥ*; TS II.2.9.1; ŚBr V.1.1.11; 4.5.11; IX.2.3.3; XI.3.1.13.

367. VS XX.11 : *devā bṛhaspatipurohitāḥ*. TS VI.4.10; ABr VIII.26.4; ŚBr V.3.1.2. One wishes to become a Purohita and, therefore, performs the Bṛhaspatisava — TS VII.4.1; TMBr XVII.11.4 ff. etc. The high position of the brahmin in the royal household is derived from Bṛhaspati since, as the celestial Purohita, he is the model for the terrestrial one. IV.50.7.9.

368. ŚBr 1.2.5.25 : *te ha devā ūcur bṛhaspatim āṅgirasam / aśraddhā vai manuṣyān avidat / tebhyo vidhehi yajñam* etc.

369. AĀr II.4.1; *Bṛhad Āraṇyaka Up.* 1.3.17; III.2.13. This is not an isolated idea based on Indian speculations only. Among the Egyptians, the moon god Thoth is regarded as the seat of intelligence.

370. I, p. 187

371. I.40.5. See also v.3; (Soma : *gṛṇīhi daívyaṃ jánam* IX.84.1).

372. In MS II.6.6 (67.10); ŚBr V.3.3.5 a Caru is prescribed for Bṛhaspati and Vāc.

373. ṚV X.130.4.

374. IV.50.1 : *yás tastámbha sáhasā vi jmó ántān*
bṛ́haspátis triṣadhasthó ravéṇa /
4 : *saptā́syas...rávẹṇa ví saptáraśmir adhamat támāṅsi /*
5 : *valáṃ ruroja phaligáṃ rávẹṇa /*
VI.73.1 : *...a ródasī vṛṣabhó róravīti /*

375. I.190.4; II.23.14; 30.4; VI.73.3; X.68.4. 6, 9. That in VI.73.3; X.68.9 *arkéṇa* or *arkaíḥ* is to be translated not as song but as ray or some similar word becomes evident from *téjiṣṭhā tapanī́* II.23.14; *agnitápobhir arkaíḥ* X.68.6. X.53.9 speaks of the axe (*paraśú svāyasá*) which Tvaṣṭṛ sharpens for him and which he takes to carve the bowl and not to fabricate hymns.

376. NGGW, 1915, p. 199.

377. I.190; II.23-26; IV.49, 50; VI.73; VII.97; X.67, 68.

378. I.190.4,5; II.23-26; IV.50.5; V.42.9; VI.73; VIII.96.15 (Indu VI.44.22); X.67.5; 68.5, 6, 9; 103.4. The conquering of Vala has become proverbial in AV IX.3.2.

379. II.23.3; 18; 24.3; IV.50.5; VI.73.3; X.67.6,8; 68-3-5; — Soma IX.87.8; 102.2.

380. VS IX.11, 12.

381. II.24.4; X.68.4, 7, 8. Soma in IX.110.5.

382. Bṛhaspati II.23.18 : *índreṇa yujā́...nír apā́m aubjo arṇavám /*
Soma IV.28.1 : *tvā́* [*sómena*] *yujā́...soma...índra apó...sasrútas kaḥ*; IX.61.22. Cf. also VIII.96.15 with VI.44.22.

383. ṚV II.24.12; IV.49: 50.10 ff.; VI.47.20. VII.97.9. 10; 98.7; X.36.5; 42.11; 100.5; 103.8; AV XI.10.9; XIV.2.42; XIX.8.6; TS III.3.11.1; TBr

II.5.6.3; ŚBr IX.2.3.3; ABr VI.36.14. In AV XV.10.4 ff.; ŚBr IX.3.4.18 the Kṣatra is assigned to Indra and the Brahman to Bṛhaspati. Strangely enough, AV XV.10.6 identifies Indra with the sky and Bṛhaspati with the earth. (Likewise TS IV.4.6). But, according to VS IX.30, Bṛhaspati is a king also. MS III.4.2 (47.10) states that he possesses a Sāmrājya. The earth was afraid when he had been consecrated the lord of all; thus ŚBr V.2.1.18. AV VII.110.3 : *úpa tvā devó agrabhīc camaséna bṛ́haspátiḥ | índra gīrbhírna ā́viśa...||* is rather obscure. Both of them receive the Soma sacrifice and certain animals. VS XXIV.7; MS III.13.8 (170.3).

384. Cf. also the *ṛ́kvan-s* VII.10.4; X.14.3.

385. In X.98.1 Bṛhaspati is called *marútvat*; in I.40.1 he is mentioned along with them.

386. I.62.3 : *índrasyā́ṅgirasāṃ ceṣṭaú*
vidát sarámā tánayāya dhāsím |
bṛ́haspátir bhinád ádriṃ vidád gā́ḥ
sám usríyābhir vāvaśanta nárah ||
v. 5; VI.18.5 etc. state that the Aṅgiras' help Indra.

387. IX.86.23 : *...índav índrasya jaṭháreṣv āviśán |*
...sóma gotrám áṅgirobhyo 'vṛṇor ápa ||

388. Oldenberg, ZDMG, IL, p. 174; NGGW, 1915, p. 205, n. 3; Strauss, *Bṛhaspati im Veda.*

389. *devā vā oṣadhīṣv ājim ayuḥ | tā bṛhaspatir udajayat |*

390. Oldenberg, NGGW, 1915, p. 208.

391. On the meaning of *bráhman* as "magic of growth" etc., see my article, "*bráhman*" in the *Festschrift für Jacobi*, Bonn 1926.

392. Bloomfield, JAOS, XVII, pp. 180-182; *Contributions* VII, p. 426. Although, like other gods, Soma is called *aṅgirastamá* and opens the cowshed for the Aṅgiras', it is to be stated that of the seven passages where *āṅgirasa* occurs, five refer to Bṛhaspati (IV.40.1; VI.73.1; X.47.6; 68.2; 164.4), whereas *aṅgiras* is distributed equally. To these should be added AV VI.45.3; VIII.10.25; XI.10.10; XIX.4.4; *Kauśika Sūtra* 135; and passages from the Brāhmaṇas, eg., ŚBr I.2.5.25.

393. On him and his relation to magic, see W. H. Roscher, *Selene und Verwandtes* p. 84 ff.; Oldenberg, RdV, 2nd ed., p. 194; Brinton, *Religions of the Primitive Peoples*, 1897, p. 139 : "it is at first sight strange that in many mythologies the moon plays a more important role than the sun. But if we reflect that the night is the time when spirits walk abroad; when sounds strike the ear with mysterious notes; when nocturnal birds and beasts stir the senses with strange cries; when, on the other hand, the cooling zephyrs and soft moonlight bring sweet ease, and the gentle dews refresh the parched leaves; then we can understand why, both in modern folklore...and in primitive myths the moon and the stars are often fare more conspicuous than the flaming sun."

394. He is also regarded as the Devatā of the Nakṣatra called Tiṣya — Weber, *Naxatra*, II, p. 371. As early as in TS IV.4.10.1 it is said : *tiṣyo nakṣatraṃ bṛhaspatir devatā.* In the Nakṣatrahoma (*Baudhāyanaprayogamālā*, Vol. II, p. 7a, lithographic ed., Bombay Śāka 1808) also they are mentioned together. TBr III.1.1.5 contains two patchwork verses that are

used as Yājyā and Puronuvākyā for them (Pāda *a* : *bṛhaspatiḥ prathamaṃ jāyamānas* = ṚV IV.50.4).

395. Manu kindles the fire at first, ŚBr I.4.2.5. He piles up Agni, TS V.4.10.5.

396. VS I.18; TS I.1.7i; TBr III.2.7.6; MS IV.1.8 (10.10).

397. Mahādeva on KŚS IV.9.1 condemns the use of *devānām* among the Bhṛgus. Other texts (TBr I.1.4.8) do not know this in the same wording; they attribute divinity only to the Ādityas.

398. *Ritualliteratur*, p. 107; MS I.6.1; TBr I.1.4.

399. K. F. Johansson, *Dhiṣaṇā*, p. 14, n. 2 : "Originally fire priests from **engḷ-los*, cognate with agni"; Brunnhofer, *Arische Urzeit*, p. 403 makes the equation *Aṅgramainyu* = *Aṅgira-manyu* or *Aṅgirō-manyu*. H. Güntert, *Der Arische Weltkönig und Heiland*, p. 283, connects it (like others) with Perso-Greek *aggalos*, Gr. *aggelos* (yet the Aṅgiras' are neither middlemen nor messengers). Gray, JAOS, XLII, p. 323 ff. also thinks of "messengers (originally) between gods and men, very probably shamanists."

400. Weber, "Episches im Vedaritual," SBKPAW, 1891, p. 812 (46). Cf. Bloomfield, SBE, XLII, p. xxv.

401. Wilson, *Selected Works*, IX, p. 145, n. 3; Simon, *Beiträge zur Kenntnis der vedischen Schulen*, Kiel 1889, p. 11, n. 3; Weber, *Die Handschriftenverzeichnisse der königlichen Bibliothek zu Berlin. Verzeichnisse der Sanskrit Handschriften*, I, p. 55.

402. *Recherches sur l'Histoire de la Literatur Vedique*, p. 192, n. 1.

403. Cf. the enumeration of the progenitors in AV IV.29.

404. Cf. JPTS, 1888, pp. 1-2. In ṚV I.78.3 a Gotama invokes *aṅgirasvat*.

405. Cf. Macdonell, in *Festgruss für Roth*, p. 108.

406. TMBr XX.11.1; TS VII.1.4.1. "Haviṣkṛt" and "Haviṣmat" invented it.

407. And other objects; see TS V.4.2.3; TBr III.10.1.2; 11.6.2.

408. TBr III.11.1.1 ff.; MS II.13.20 (166.10). Once Prajāpati also addressed the earth in the same way as he made her into an Iṣṭakā and placed her in position TS V.5.2.4. It seems that there is an allusion to a cosmogonic myth.

409. Similarly, the Aṅgiras' are cited as authority for other individual customs, e.g., TS V.4.2.3; 3.2; VI.2.6.2; MS III.8.4 (98.20). TĀr III.8 states that "Yajus" is the characteristic of Agni, "Ukthāmada" of Indra, "Stomas" of Savitṛ, the "Āśis" of Mitrāvaruṇa, and the *dhiṣṇyā* "*agnayaḥ*" of the Aṅgiras'. Cf. their designation as *iddhágnayaḥ* in ṚV I.83.4.

410. See p. 25 above. A Sāman called *aṅgirasāṃ goṣṭha* is known to TMBr XIII.9.24.

411. Brahman once again in the same Maṇḍala, VI.35.5 : *āṅgirasā́n bráhmaṇā vipra jinva*. Cf. AV VIII.10.25 : *tāṃ* [*dhenuṃ*] *bṛhaspatir āṅgiraso 'dhok tāṃ brahma ca tapas cādhok tad brahma ca tapaś ca saptaṛṣaya up jīvanti*. They are the eyes of the Bṛahman AV X.7.18, 34. In the ṚV, Brahmaṇaspati is styled as an Aṅgiras with rēmarkable frequency. According to the Pallava inscription of Kāñcīpura, the wise Aṅgiras is born from the mind of Brahman, and from him Bṛhaspati (Hultzsch, SII, I.13; II.3, p. 354).

412. Cf. also ISt, I, *passim*; III, p. 459.

413. Cf. also XI.8.10; ŚBr XIV.4.1.21; JBr II.7.10. In the Sunaḥśepa legend he is the Udgātṛ in the mythical Rājasūya. ABr VII.16.

414. *imā́ṃ dhíyaṃ saptáśīrṣṇīṃ pitā́ na ṛtáprajātāṃ bṛhatī́m avindat |*
turī́yaṃ svij janayad viśvájanyo 'yā́sya ukthám índrāya śáṅsan ||

415. Oertel, *Contributions* I, p. 26 ff.

416. In TBr II.2.5.3 he receives a cart for carrying goods, Manu a *talpa*; II.3.2.5 he receives everything; TĀr III.10. 2, 3.

417. Clearly mythical. He drinks milk from the water, Cf. Oertel, *Contributions* II, p. 103. Lanman, JAOS, XIX, 2, p. 157.

418. According to *Chāndogya Up.* III.17.6, Kṛṣṇa Devakīputra is a pupil of Ghora Āṅgirasa. A Kṛṣṇa Āṅgirasa is regarded as the author of ṚV VIII. 85. Ghora — an epithet of the Aṅgiras' — as a proper noun seems to be an abstraction (*ghora āṅgirasa* occurs as a contrast to *bhiṣaj ātharvaṇa*; Bloomfield, SBE, XLII, p. xxi); but it is not certain. — Weber, ISt, I, p. 290.

419. In Manu III.198 the *haviṣmantaḥ* are called "*aṅgirasutāḥ*"; the *havirbhuj* are regarded as the forefathers of Kṣatriyas, ibid., III.197.

420. ṚV X.14.3 : *mā́talī kavyaír yamó áṅgirobhir bṛ́haspatir ṛ́kvabhir vāvṛdhānā́ḥ*; 5 : *áṅgirobhir ā́ gahi yajñíyebhir yáma vairūpaír ihá mādayasva.* Cf. also ĀpŚS I.8.4 : *yamāya aṅgirasvate pitṛmate*; HGS II.10.7 etc.

421. *áṅgiraso naḥ pitáro návagvā átharvāṇo* etc. Cf. ṚV I.62.2 : *yénā naḥ pū́rve pitáraḥ padajñā́ árcanto áṅgiraso gā́ ávindam*, and also I.71.2.

422. *prá bhūrjayo yáthā pathā́ dyā́m áṅgiraso yayúḥ.*

423. ṚV VIII.40.12 : *pitṛvát, māndhātṛvát, aṅgirasvát.*

424. *nákṣad dhávam aruṇī́ḥ pūrvyáṃ rā́ṭ turó viśā́m áṅgirasām ánu dyū́n.*

425. In AV XIX.54.5 : *kālé 'yam áṅgirā divó 'tharvā cā́dhi tiṣṭhataḥ* probably it is this Veda which is meant (cf. v.3).

426. *Rituallitergtur*, p. 169; Bloomfield, PAOS, XVII, p. 180; SBE, XLII, p. xviii.

427. Cf. *Kauśika Sūtra* XLVII.2.2 ff. and particularly Bloomfield, SBE, XLII, p. xxiii. — It is not clear why in AV XVIII.4.8 the *aṅgirasām ayanam* is equated with *pūrvyo agni* and the *ādityānām ayanam* with *gārhapatyaḥ*.

428. X.169.2; TS VII.4.17b.

429. In this passage they are antagonistic to the Pitaraḥ, who poison the herbs and wish for a share in the sacrifice. The plants are called *āṅgirasīḥ* in AV VIII.7.17; XI.4.16 : *ātharvaṇīr āṅgirasīr daivīr manuṣyajā uta.* In XIX.34.1 the Jaṅgida is an Aṅgiras.

430. Cf. TBr I.8.2.1.

431. *yád dha tyā́m áṅgirobhyo dhenúm devā ádattana ví tā́ṃ duhre aryamā́...* See n. 428 above.

432. *ūrg asy āṅgirasy ūrṇamradā ūrjaṃ mayi dhehi*, VS IV.10; ŚBr III.2. 1.10; TS I.2.2 f; VI.1.3.3; ĀpŚS X.9.14. The girdle in the Upanayana does not bear this name. It has one or three or five knots according to the number of the Ṛṣis among the ancestors (ŚGS II.2.2). Thus, it seems that he is thought of as related to the Manes also. In one passage the Sabhā is also addressed as *āṅgirasī* (PGS III.13.2). Cf. AV VII.12.1.

433. ŚBr VII.5.1.5 has a different explanation.

434. ṚV VII.52.1, 3; AV XII.3.43, 44; XIX.39.5.

435. Cf. also the *āditya aṅgirasyaḥ* (verse) ŚŚS XII.19.

436. Weber, *Episches im Vedaritual*, p. 46.

437. TMBr XII.11.10. Kalyāṇa turns to Urṇāyu for advice while the

latter was seated on a swing in the midst of Apsarases. He learns from Urṇāyu the *svargya sāman* under the condition that Kalyāṇa shall not mention Urṇāyu. Kalyāṇa, however, passes himself as the author and becomes a leper as punishment.

438. *ajo 'si, aja, svargo 'si tvayā lokam aṅgirasaḥ prājānan.* Incidentally, it is also occasionally said that the gods did not find the way, TBr III.8.22.1 : *aśvamedhe pavamāne suvargaṃ lokaṃ na prājānan / tam aśvaḥ prājānāt* (i.e., the sun at the end of the Pitṛyāṇa).

439. TMBr XX.11.3; TS VII.1.4.1.

440. ABr III.34; BI ed., II, p. 156.

441. ABr IV.17.6, 7, Aufrecht's ed., p. 315. The contrast is expressed differently elsewhere. Cf. ŚŚS XIII.21, 22; TMBr XXV.1.2; GBr I.4.23. It is known from TMBr XXV.16.3 that the Gavām Ayana, the Adityānām Ayana and the Aṅgirasām Ayana were performed by Para Āṭnāra, Trasadasyu Paurukutsa, Vītahavya Śrāyasa, Kakṣīvat Auśija. We encounter the same names in connection with the piling up of Agni in TS V.6.5.3 where Para Āṭnāra etc. are mentioned together. In the JUBr (ed. Orterl, II.6.11) Para Aṭnāra, Kakṣīvat, Trasadasyu are stated to have been *pūrve mahārājāḥ śrotriyāḥ*. Cf. also ŚBr XIII.5.4.4: *Para Āṭnāra Hairaṇyanābhaḥ Kauśalyo rāja.*

442. ABr VI.34, 2; KBr XXX.6; TMBr XVI.12.1; GBr II.6.14. Another legend in TBr II.2.3.5; ŚBr XII.2.2.11.

443. In ṚV X.62.5 they are called the sons of Agni.

444. KBr XXX.6 mentions Bṛhaspati as the Brahman of this sacrifice, Ayāsya as the Udgātṛ, and Ghora as the Adhvaryu — all are Āṅgirasas.

445. Cf. AV XX.135.6; TBr III.9.21.1; JBr (ed. Caland), § 136; ŚŚS XII.19.1.

446. Cf. the cow given to them by the gods (see p. 112 above).

447. This view about the Devas occurs, e.g., in TS V.3.7.1; VI.5.3.1; VII; 2.1.1; VII.4.2 (*daivīṃ saṃsadaṃ gacchema*); TBr II.2.7.3; 8.1; ABr II.1.1; TMBr II.12.2; 15.2; XVII.1.1 etc.

448. TS VII.4.6; TBr I.1.9.8; Āditya himself III.11.9.7.

449. ABr I.16.39; TBr I.3.6.1; TS V.4.2.8 etc. As Devas they reach heaven through Indra, ĀśvŚS I.3.27; ŚŚS I.6.3. We should not overlook the fact that as early as in ṚV VII.52.1, 3 the Ādityas (v. 1) and the Aṅgiras' (v. 3) are associated together. In the family books the Aṅgiras' are encountered relatively rarely. The voluminous maṇḍala VII mentions them only five times (in two cases, the word is used in superlative as referring to Uṣas, who does not carry this name otherwise); most of these passages in all these maṇḍalas contain stereotype expressions only. At times *āṅgiras* is an epithet of certain gods or refers to their customs (*aṅgirasvat*), at others the Aṅgiras' are the friends and assistants of Indra in the recovery of the cows. All the fourteen passages in book VIII are colourless. As against this, the name occurs in books I (about twentyseven times) and X (nineteen times) rather more impressively. It looks as if the literature of the Aṅgiras' lies mainly outside books II-IX and we encounter here one of the Vedic clans whose cult and tradition followed other paths.

450. Here *hemantaśiśirau* are assigned to them, *śarad* to the Viśve Devāḥ, and the rainy season to the Ādityas.

451. Cf. also TS V.6.16; TBr II.2.10.5; TĀr III.8.1.

452. AV XI.6.13 : *ādityā́ rudrā́ vásavo diví devā́ átharvāṇo áṅgiraso manīṣíṇaḥ...*; VIII.8.12.13.

453. This is seen very clearly in VII.44.4 : *saṃvidānā́ [dadhikrā́vā] uṣásā sū́ryéṇādityébhir vásubhir áṅgirobhiḥ*; VIII.35.14 : *áṅgirasvantā utá víṣṇuvantā marútvantā jaritúr gacchatho hávam* (addressed to the Aśvins), while *aṅgiras* seems to denote a gotra in I.121.3 (see p. 111 above) and VII.42.1.

454. Weber, ISt, II, p. 46; *Episches im Vedaritual*, p. 46. Probably with the exception of the "girdle"; but in India the girdle is called *āṅgirasī* only in sacrifices but not in the Upanayana. See n. 432 above.

455. Cf. Kuhn, *Herabkunft des Feuers, Mythologische Studien* I, p. 9 ff.; L. v. Schroeder, KZ, XXIX, p. 218 ff.

456. Cf. ṚV X.14.6 : *áṅgiraso naḥ pitáro návagvā átharvāṇo bhṛ́gavaḥ*; VIII.43.13 : *bhṛguvát, manuṣvát, aṅgirasvád dhavāmahe*; *Kauśika Sūtra* CXXXVII.25 (AV XIX.39.5).

457. Bloomfield, SBE, XLII, p. xxvi.

458. ŚBr XI.6.1.1; TĀr IX.1.1.6; ABr III.34.1 : *yad dvitīyaṃ [prajāpate retasā] āsīt tad bhṛgur abhavat, taṃ varuṇo nyagṛhṇīta, tasmāt sa bhṛgur vāruṇiḥ*. Cf. also the legend in TMBr XVIII.9.12; MBh VIII (*Anuśāsana*), 85.125.

459. *virurucúr váneṣu* (IV.7.1); *dadhúr vanaspátau* (VI.15.2); *upavócanta mathnántaḥ* (I.127.7); *dyā́vā yám agníṃ pṛthiví janiṣṭām...bhṛ́gavo yáṃ sáhobhiḥ* (X.46.9 and also v. 2); *yám eriré nā́bhā pṛthivyā́ḥ* (I.143.4); *adadhur* (I.58.6; II.4.2).

460. Apart from VIII.43.13 (see n. 456 above), also I.45.3; 78.3.

461. I have noticed the following only in TĀr IV. p. 557 : *ghoreṇa tvā bhṛgūṇāṃ cakṣuṣā prekṣe, raudreṇa tvāṅgirasāṃ manasā dhyāyāmi*.

462. VII.18.6 : *puroḷā́ ít turváśo yákṣur ā́sīt*
rāyé mátsyāso níśitā ápīva |
śruṣṭíṃ cakrur bhṛ́gavo druhyávaś ca
sákhā sákhāyam atarad víṣūcoḥ ||

463. VIII.3.9 : *yénā yátibhyo bhṛ́gave dháne hité yéna práskaṇvam ā́vitha* (Indra); 6.18 : *yá indra yátayas tvā bhṛ́gavo yé ca tuṣṭuvúḥ*.

464. In IV.16.20 (also X.39.14) they are praised as master chariot-makers. This seems to be an instance of confusion between the Bhṛgus and the Ṛbhus, as the PW remarks.

465. Perhaps X.122.5 also.

466. Cf. ṚV VIII.3.16 *stómebhiḥ*; 6.18 : *tuṣṭuvúḥ*.

467. Cf. also MBh III.122 ff.

468. Cf. MBh I.178 ff. Cf. Weber, *Zwei vedische Texte über Omina und Portenta*, p. 347. Moreover, Uśanas (comm. on ṚV V.31.8). Weber, loc. cit.

469. ĀpŚS IV.12.10.

470. TS I.8.18; TBr I.8.2.5; TMBr XVIII.9.2; ŚŚS XV.12.2 etc., just as the Vasiṣṭhas have the role of the Brahman in the Jyotiṣṭoma ĀpŚS XIV.8.1.

471. *Rituallliteratur*, pp. 98, 99, n. 15; GGS I.8.4; III.8.14.

472. KBr XXX.5. In the same legend, ABr VI.33 replaces the Bhṛgus with the Aurvas : *aitaśāyanā aurvāṇāṃ papiṣṭhāḥ*. The reason is not clear,

since Aurva himself is regarded as a Bhārgava. He is protected miraculously during the persecution of his clan. Cf. MBh I.178 ff.; Wilson, *Vṣṣṇupurāṇa*, pp. 290, 291. — *aurvabhṛguvát* ṚV VIII.102.4.

473. GBr I.2.8 is rather obscure because of the corrupt text.

474. Bhṛgus and Atharvan together in ṚV X.92.10; Weber, *Die Handschriftenverzeichnisse der königlichen Bibliothek zu Berlin. Verzeichnisse der Sanskrit Handschriften*, II, p. 46, cites *bhṛgubhir atharvabhir aṅgirasaḥ*; I have not seen this juxtaposition elsewhere.

475. Cf. AV X.6.20; XI.6.16; 6.13; XVI.8.12, 13.

476. Weber, *Zwei vedische Texte über Omina und Portenta*, p. 347.

477. Bartholomae, Grundriss I, § 188 (p. 101). On the necessity of distinguishing between *ātar* and *atharvan*, see Bartholomae, IF, V, p. 221; Zúbaty, KZ, XXXI, p. 2; Justi, *Preussische Jahrbücher*, LXXXVIII, p. 85.

478. Fourteen times if we do not count *atharvī*.

479. Cf. also Weber, op. cit., p. 337.

480. Cf. ŚBr VI.4.2.3.

481. Cf. also ṚV X.87.12 (=AV VIII.3.21) : *atharvaváj jyótiṣā daívyena ny òṣa*. According to *Vaitāna Sūtra*, VI.1, Prajāpati brings the horse at first to Atharvan, who receives light at first from its hoof. The verse is illustrated by the legend in GBr I.2.18, according to which the son of Kabandha Ātharvaṇa succeeds in pacifying the shy horse with Atharvan verses and Aṅgiras verses etc., after the Ṛk, Yajus and Sāman had failed.

482. Cf. ŚBr XIII.4.3.7; ŚŚS XVI.2.7 ff : *varuṇa āditya iti tṛtīye tasya gandharvā viśas ta ima āsata iti yūnaḥ śobhanān upadiśati*; 9 : *atharvavedo vedaḥ so 'yam iti bheṣajaṃ nigadet*; thus Varuṇa and the *Atharva Veda* are brought into a certain association, though this is not very significant for us here.

483. AV IV.1.7 : *yó 'tharvāṇaṃ pitáraṃ devábandhum*
bṛ́haspátiṃ námasā́va ca gacchāt/

484. AV VII.104 mentions Varuṇa and Bṛhaspati.

485. TS V.6.6c; ŚBr IV.1.5.15 ff. Cf. further Kabandha Ātharvaṇa besides Sudhanvan Āṅgirasa in *Bṛhad Āraṇyaka Up.* VI.7.1 ff. Vicārin "*kabandhasyātharvaṇasya putraḥ*" GBr I.2.9, 18. In one passage (TMBr XII.8.6) Dadhyañc is stated to be an Āṅgirasa; this could be a mistake in tradition which otherwise relates him to Atharvan. Śaṃyu, who is usually styled as a son of Bṛhaspati, is made an Ātharvaṇa in GBr I.2.18.

486. ṚV VIII.9.7 also should be taken into consideration here : *ā́ sómaṃ mádhumattamaṃ gharmáṃ siñcād átharvaṇi.* AV X.10.12 : *triṣú pā́treṣu táṃ sómam ā́ devy àharad vaśā́ / átharvā yátra dīkṣitó barhíṣy ā́sta hiraṇyáye*; this very obscure verse connects the mythical "Atharvan seated on the golden sacrificial straw" with Soma. Cf. AV XVIII.3.54 : *átharvā pūrṇám camasáṃ yám indrāyā́bibhar*; In TĀr II.10 *ṛcaḥ...payasaḥ kūlyāḥ / yajūṅṣi... ghṛtasya kūlyāḥ / sāmāni...soma / atharvāṅgirasaḥ...madhoḥ kūlyāḥ* occur together.

487. As singers of the Sāmans TMBr VIII.2.5, 6.

488. SBE, XLII, p. xxvii, n. 4.

489. *atharvāṇaś ca ha vā ā(a)ṅgirasaś ca bhṛgucakṣuṣī.*

CHAPTER IV

SOMA

Part I : The Soma Plant

1. *Zend-Avesta, Ouvrage de Zoroastre*, Paris 1771, II, p. 535.
2. *Translation of the Sanhitā of the Sāma-Veda*, London 1842, p. iv.
3. *Abhandlungen der Königlichen Bayerischen Akademie der Wissenschaften*, 1847, IV.2, p. 129.
4. MSt, I, pp. 8, 106, 171. Cf. also Muir, OST, V, p. 261; Darmesteter, *Ormazd et Ahriman*, p. 99, n. 3.
5. But the two are not the same. See the second note of Watt, to be cited later, according to which *Asclepias acida* is *Sarcostemma brevistigma*.
6. See also *Aitareya Brāhmaṇa*, II, p. 489.
7. "Über die Totenbestattung bei den Brahmanen," ZDMG, IX, p. liv.
8. See de Gubernatis, *La Mythologie des Plantes*, II, p. 351.
9. "Über den Soma," ZDMG, XXXV, p. 680 ff.; "Wo wächst der Soma ?" ibid., XXXVIII, p. 134 ff.
10. "The *Sarcostemma acidum Voigt* is a bush that grows several feet high, its peculiarity being that it has no leaves. The stalks and the numerous side branches are cylindrical in shape with joints. They are smooth and particularly the young ones are full of juice. They hang down if there is no support. They are said to be as thick as a quill or even thicker. The small white flowers growing in umbels at the end of the branches are fragrant. The quality which, above all, supports the claim of this bush to be the Soma plant is its juice. Roxburgh says that this plant contains more abundant quantity of pure milky juice than any other known to him." See also Roth's remarks in de Gubarnatis, loc. cit.
11. Eggeling, SBE, XXVI, p. xxiv ff.
12. *Arische Urzeit*, Bern 1910, p. 297 ff.
13. "What is Soma," JRAS, 1920, p. 349 ff. N. Bh. Pavgee, *The indigenous far-famed Soma and the Aryan Autochthones in India*, Poona 1921, was not available to me.
14. JRAS, 1921, p. 241 ff. I could not procure his article on the plant in the *Bulletin of the Rationalistic Society of Calcutta*.
15. Cf. also Bornmüller, "Reisebriefe aus Persien," *Mitteilungen des Thüringer Botanischen Vereins*, 1893, NF, Heft 3-4, pp. 42-43 (to which Schermann drew my attention) : "At the first glance at a Soma branch (called also Homa or Huma) in the hand of a [Parsi] priest [in Yezd] the question was solved : the sacred plant is, in all certainty, nothing but *Ephedra* (or more precisely *Ephedra distachya*). Simultaneously the importance of the question itself disappears, since the varieties of *Ephedra* occur in the entire Central Asia as well as in the coastal regions of the Mediterranean. Therefore, the knowledge of the home of this plant, spread far and wide, can contribute nothing to...the identification of the original home of the Aryans." Of course, this applies only to the plant used today.
16. These technical details are described now in Appendix I.

17. At the most, in isolated passages the Afghan grape, as Watt describes it, might have been meant.

18. *Translation of the Sanhitā of the Sāma-Veda*, p. iii.

19. See my review of Geldner's *Ṛgveda* in IF, XLII; AISAK, p. 25.

20. *Buddha*, 1st ed., p. 410.

21. Geiger, *Handbuch*, s.v. : "with soft sprouts or fresh branches"; *Ostiranische Kultur im Altertum*, p. 153, n. 6 : "with moist juicy shoots"; Bartholomae, *Altiranisches Wörterbuch* : "with supple soft young shoots"; Geldner, *Metrik*, p. 129 : "juicy shoots." Harlez, *Avesta traduit*, Liége 1875, II, 1st ed., 1875 : "its branches are soft and supple."

22. Wilhelm, BKIS, XII, p. 105.

23. SBE, XXXI, p. 235; Weber, SBKPAW, 1894, p. 787.

24. According to Caland, GGA, 1893, p. 398 with *namra*.

25. In I.8.8 "a ripe branch," *pakvā́ śākhā*, is mentioned as a comparison.

26. I did not translate *sū́bharvāḥ*, the doubtful epithet of the bulls. Grassmann renders it as "chewing well, consuming much". The smaller edition of the PW : "well-fed." I would rather think that *sū* in this passage, like *prasū* elsewhere, means "young stalk," and thus *sūbharva* "consuming the young stalks." Oldenberg, *Die Hymnen des Ṛgveda*, II, p. 301 wishes to treat *su* as a prefix .

27. *maná* (for *mā́na*)=house ?

28. MSt, I, p. 171 ff.

29. *yadi somam apahareyur vidhāvatecchateti brūyāt / sa yadi vindanti kim ādriyeran / yady u na vindanti tatra prāyaścittiḥ kriyate.* 2 : *dvayāni vai phālgunāni lohitapuṣpāṇi cāruṇapuṣpāṇi ca sa yāny aruṇapuṣpāṇi phālgunāni tāny abhiṣuṇuyāt / eṣa vai somasya nyaṅgo yad aruṇapuṣpāṇi phālgunāni tasmād aruṇapuṣpāṇy abhiṣuṇuyāt.* 3 : *yady aruṇapuṣpāṇi na vindeyuḥ śyenahṛtam abhiṣuṇuyāt / yatra vai gāyatrī somam achāpatat tasyā āharantyai somasyāṅśur apatat tac chyenahṛtam abhavat tasmāc chyenahṛtam abhiṣuṇuyāt.* 4 : *yadi śyenahṛtaṃ na vindeyur ādārān abhiṣuṇuyāt / yatra vai yajñasya śiro 'cchidyata tasya yo raso vyapruṣyat tata ādārāḥ samabhavaṅs tasmād ādārān abhiṣuṇuyāt.* 5 : *yadi ādārān na vindeyur aruṇadūrvā abhiṣuṇuyāt / eṣa vai somasya nyaṅgo yad aruṇadūrvās tasmād aruṇadūrvā abhiṣuṇuyāt.* 6 : *yady aruṇadūrvā na vindeyur api yān eva kāṅś ca haritān kuśān abhiṣuṇuyāt.* TBr I.4.7.5 does not seem to attach any importance to the colour. On the other hand, ĀpŚS XIV.24.12 agrees with what the Vājasaneyins state with minor differences : *somābhāve pūtīkān abhiṣuṇuyát / pūtīkābhāva ādārān phālgunāni ca yāni śvetatūlāni syuḥ / tadabhāve yāḥ kāś cauṣadhīḥ kṣīriṇīr aruṇadūrvāḥ kuśān vā haritān iti vājasaneyakam.* 13 : *apy antato vrīhiyāvān.* We should probably assume that the *śvetatūla* of the ĀpŚS is the same as the *aruṇapuṣpa* of the ŚBr (as opposed to *lohitapuṣpa*). Cf. also TMBr IX.5.3. (The later commentaries usually state that Soma is a creeper; thus, for example, according to Sāyaṇa on TS I.8.3, it is the young stalks of the Karīra plant (*Capparis Aphylla*) that resemble the Soma creeper. See Eggeling, SBE, XII, p. 394, n. 2. The comm. on KŚS IX.4.10 : *somalatākhaṇḍāni*; *soma iti latāsoma iti karkaḥ*; TBr I.23 etc.)

30. Roth opines that this denotes only the green, i.e., not dried, kuśa grass, the well known *Poa cynosuroides*. Eggeling translates it as "yellow."

31. On this, cf. the comm. on TBr, I, pp. 181, 182. Also KŚS I.4.10.

32. Both the colours are mentioned side by side, thus ruling out a complete identity between the two : ṚV IX.11.4; AV VI.20.3.

33. See Pischel, ZDMG, XL, p. 120.

34. In the classical period this word is used solely in the sense of "yellow"; e.g., *Kumārasaṃbhava* V.8 : *babandha bālāruṇababhru valkalam*, "a garment of bark, yellow like the young sun." The commentary equates it with *piṅgala*. Often this word is used for hair, also for the hair of the beard, eg., *Raghuvaṃśa* XV.16. Cf. also *Amarakośa* III.170 etc.

35. *yadi somaṃ na vindeyuḥ pūtīkān abhiṣuṇuyur yadi na pūtīkān arjuṇāni.* "If they do not find Soma, then they shall press Pūtīkās; if no Pūtīkas, then Arjuṇas." Pūtīkas are creepers which Roth, loc. cit., defines as *Basella cordifolia Lam.* See also Roxburgh, *Flora Indica*, II, p, 104; Drury, *Useful Plants of India*, p. 68. On the Arjuṇas our text has this to say (*Tāṇḍya Brāhmaṇa* IX.5.7) : *indro vṛtram ahan / tasya yo nastaḥ somaḥ samadhāvat tāni babhrutūlāny arjunāni / yo vapāyā utkhinnāyās tāni lohitatūlāni / yāni babhrutūlāny arjunāni tāny abhiṣuṇuyāt / etad vai brahmaṇo rūpam / sākṣād eva somam abhiṣuṇoti.* Here also of the two varieties of the Arjuna, one should choose the one with the reddish brown panicles of flowers (the commentary explains *babhrutūla* as *tūlasamababhruvarṇa mañjarīyuktāny arjunāni śyāmalāni tṛṇāni*), but not the lohitatūlas, i.e., those with red panicles. Compare this with the following statement of ŚBr VII.2.4.26 : *yā oṣadhīḥ pūrvā jātā devebhyas triyugaṃ purā* [*ṚV X*.97.1] *ity ṛtavo vai devās tebhya etās triḥ purā jāyante vasantā prāvṛṣi śaradi manai nu babhrūṇām aham iti somo vai babhruḥ saumyā oṣadhayaḥ.*

36. TS II, p. 279, line 8 from below.

37. *Yasna* IX.16, 30; X.12 etc.

38. In *Yasna* X.13 it can denote the drink.

39. The bright colour of the Soma stalk can be inferred also from ŚBr III.3.2.3 : *sa yad eva śobhanaṃ tat somopanahanaṃ syāt / vāso hy asyaitad bhavati / śobhanaṃ hy etasya vāsaḥ / sa yo hainaṃ śobhanenopacarati śobhate ha.* Cf. also ŚBr III.3.3.18 : *saśukram evaitat krīṇāti.* However, I do not attach any importance to this since particularly in the first case it is quite doubtful whether it could be interpreted in this sense : "Let the Soma wrapper (the cloth in which Soma is tied) be splendid; for it is his garment. Splendid indeed is his garment (the Stalk ?). Whosoever approaches him with a splendid [garment] will become splendid." The *ándhas* is styled *śukra* in ṚV IV.27.5 and *śubhrá* in IX.62.5; however, this can denote the drink here.

40. *Der Ṛgveda*, IV, p. 3 (on I.49.1).

41. Hillebrandt, *Tiere und Götter im vedischen Ritual*, Breslau 1905 (reprinted from the *83. Jahresbericht der Schlesischen Gesellschaft für vaterländische Kultur*).

42. 14 : *sā yā babhruḥ piṅgākṣī sā somakrayaṇy atha yā rohiṇī sā vārtraghnī yāṃ idaṃ rājā saṃgrāmaṃ jitvodākurute / atha yā rohiṇī śyetākṣī sā pitṛdevatyā yāṃ idaṃ pitṛbhyo ghnanti.* 15 : *sā yā babhruḥ piṅgākṣī sā somakrayaṇī syāt / yadi babhruṃ piṅgākṣīṃ na vinded aruṇā syāt / yady aruṇāṃ na vinded rohiṇī vārtraghnī syāt / rohiṇyai ha tv eva śyetākṣyā āśāṃ neyāt.*

16 : ***sā syād apravītā / vāg vā eṣā nidānena yat somakrayaṇī / ayātayāmnī vā iyaṃ vāg / ayātayāmny apravītā tasmād apravītā syāt / sā syād avaṇḍākūṭākāṇākarṇālakṣitāsaptaśaphā / sā hy ekarūpaikarūpā hīyaṃ vāk.*** The Kāṇva text has ***anupārṣṭakarṇā*** for ***akarṇā*** and ***aśroṇā*** for ***alakṣitā*** (See Eggeling, SBE, XXVI, p. 63, n. 1). **KŚS VII.6.14** states : ***alakṣitā*** (comm. *akṛtacihnā*), *avyaṅgā* (*anaṅgahīnā*), ***apravītā*** (*aprajātā* or ***akāmitā***), ***arajjubaddhā*** (*abaddhā*), *babhruḥ* (*kapilā*), *piṅgalā* (*piṅgākṣī, piṅgale madhuvarṇe akṣiṇī yasyāḥ*), *piṅgalābhāve 'ruṇā* (*raktabhāsurā, avyaktarāgā*), *aruṇābhāve rohiṇī* (*raktavarṇā*), *aśyetākṣī* (*araktākṣī*). The commentary quotes some more related characteristics from the *Kāṭhaka*.

43. The comm. understands *śyetākṣī* as *kṛṣṇalocanā*.

44. On this the Kāṇva text remarks thus : "For it is this [bright-coloured cow] which comes closest [to the actual Soma cow] in appearance." See Eggeling, loc. cit. Eggeling translates *aruṇa* wrongly as "a dark-red one."

45. I pass over the other statements of these texts, e.g., that it should be *akūṭa*, *akāṇā* etc., since they are not relevant here.

46. The MS, which has *svetopakāśā śucyadakṣī*, differs somewhat from the above description. The smaller edition of the PW assumes that the second word is a synonym of *śucyakṣī*. I think that it means as much as *piṅgākṣī* of other texts. On the other hand, the translation of *śvetopakāśā* there as "appearing whitelike" seems doubtful to me. The word is not quite clear. The comm. on ĀpŚS X.22.4 explains *śvitropakāśā* as *śvitrasamānavarṇā āpāṅgāpradeśe*. It is likely that of the two words, *śucydakṣī* and *śvetopakāśā*, one was an old gloss of the other and that both mean the same.

47. KŚS VII.6.14 is cited above in n. 42. BŚS VI.10 has this to say about the Soma cow : *saiṣāruṇā piṅgalyaikahāyanī bhavati*. Hiraṇyakeśin VII.2 : *upakḷptā somakrayaṇī samāṅgā bandhumatī yathāgnīṣomīyo babhrur aruṇā rohiṇī vā / upadhvastāpravītāthavā rohiṇī piṅgākṣī babhrulomnī śvitropakāśā pṛśnivālā* etc. ĀPŚS X.22.3-5. The stipulation in rule 5 about the animal to be taken by a Rājanya is certainly a later addition.

48. MS II.5.1 (46.8) : *saumyaṃ babhruṃ lomaśaṃ piṅgalam ālabheta paśukāmaḥ / saumīr vā oṣadhayaḥ...babhruḥ piṅgalo bhavati somasya rūpaṃ samṛddhyai*. 5 (53.3) : *āgneyam ajam ālabheta saumyaṃ babhrum ṛṣabhaṃ piṅgalaṃ bhūtikāmaṃ yājayed / babhruḥ piṅgalo bhavati somasya rūpaṃ samṛddhyai*; 58.18; 72.14; III.78.12; 170.8; 171.9, 12; IV.103.7; III.169.1 : *rohito dhūmrarohitaḥ karkandhurohitas te saumyās* (=VS XXIV.2); ŚBr V.5.1.9 etc. Animals are prescribed without any mention of the colour in MS III.173.3, 5 (*haṅsa, laba*), 175.3 (*kulaṅga*).

49. Cf. *vajra śataparvan* in ṚV I.80.6.

50. Comm. *avayavāḥ*.

51. Comm. *parvāṇi*. The scholiast explains *svadhitā* as *svāsthyenāvasthitāni*. I think that this is as incorrect as the translation in the smaller edition of the PW as "healthy" (*sudhita*). Provided the variant reading of *Vaitāna Sūtra* 24b, *sukṛtā* is not preferable, I take this to be a denominative of *svadhā* "sweet drink or food" so that *svadhita* would mean roughly "sweetened or sweet." For *parūṅṣi* the *Vaitāna Sūtra* reads *purūṇi* — wrongly as it is evident from the other verse of the same Sūtra cited above. Caland, VS : "well formed."

52. Geldner, *Der Ṛgveda, übersetzt und erläutert*, Göttingen 1923, I, p. 8 : "on all the Soma festival days"; according to Uvaṭācārya on VS XXX.25 : "on the occasion of the Soma sacrifices"; and according to Mahīdhara, "and on the Soma tendrils."

53. *ándhaso* and *somapárvabhiḥ* are parallel units. One would perhaps expect *ándhasā* here. But the verbs denoting drinking like *mad, pā, mand* etc. are primarily connected with the genitive of *ándhas*. I notice that *mad* governs the genitive of *ándhas* in I.85.6; IV.32.14; VIII.54.2, whereas the instrumental occurs with *saṃ-mad* in IV.20.4 and once with just *mad* (without any prefix) in IX.107.2. Likewise *pā* is connected with the genitive in I.135.4; III.40.1; VIII.17.4; 84.2 etc.; *mand* I.80.6 etc. This linguistic usage which has become almost stereotyped in the case of *ándhas* may explain the change in the construction. Otherwise, the connection with the instrumental is not so rare, e.g., I.154.4; III.4.7 *svadhayā* etc. Hence, Mahīdhara on VS XXXIII.25 equates *somaparvabhiḥ* also with *somāṅśubhiḥ*. The comm. on ŚŚS V.8.3 (my edition, II, p. 232) speaks of *triparvāṇaḥ somāṅśavaḥ*.

54. BKIS, V, p. 351 : *čyāvantō aēte asavō aŋhen* "how big should these stalks be."

55. TS I.2.6a, which cites this verse in a different context, reads *kāmam* for *somam*.

56. Besides the verses TBr III.7.13; *Vaitāna Sūtra* XXIV f., see also AV XII.5.71.: *áṅgā párvāṇi vi śrathaya*; ṚV X.97.12 : *áṅgamaṅgaṃ páruṣparuḥ*; TS II.5.6.1; ABr III.31; VS XIII.20 : *kāṇḍātkāṇḍāt páruṣaḥ-paruṣaḥ* (the comm. gives an artificial interpretation) etc.

57. In AV VIII.7.4 the poet invokes *aṅśumátīḥ kāṇḍínīr víśākhā óṣadhīr* one after the other, i.e., plants "endowed with aṅśus" along with reeds and branchless plants. However, there is not much that we can learn from this verse, since some of the other designations occurring in this verse are obscure.

58. *aṅśúr iva pyāyatām ayám*.

59. In Max Müller, *Biographies of Words*, p. 231. See above pp. 124 f., 128.

60. I am ignoring IX.74.2 because of its mystic content which will be intelligible only after the discussions that follow later. In GGA, 1875, XIX, p. 586, Haug argues against the view that *pīta āpīta* refers to the abundance of the juice in Soma. "That is to say, before the juice is pressed out, the Soma stalks are placed on the so-called Vedi and are steeped in water in order to prevent them from drying up and to keep the juice fresh. This ceremony, which must be as old as the Soma worship, is called Āpyāyana, 'the swelling of the Soma.'" I think this is not quite correct. Further below we shall discuss the Āpyāyana, which is merely an ancillary operation and which is understood variously even by those who knew the Sūtras. It is obvious, I think, that from the beginning only juicy plants were chosen. This requirement is expressly stressed during the buying of Soma.

The Āpyāyana must have become necessary when one did not have the fresh plant, or when one wished to extract the remaining juice that was still in the plant, e.g., at the offering of the husks. But I see no reason to suppose that *this* is referred to as *āpyā* in the ṚV. Through the constant comparison between the god and the plant, the word *āpyā* derives at the same time its mystic significance.

61. On this cf. the expressions *śukrám páyas* IX.19.5; 54.1; *dyumnávat páyas* IX.66.30; *pratnám páyas* IX.42.4 etc.

62. It is also said clearly that the juicy stalks give milk like the cows with udders. See VIII.9.19 cited on p. 139 above.

63. ṚV IX.72.2 and VI.49.9 respectively.

64. Oldenberg, *Die Hymen des Ṛgveda* I, p. 339, would rather see *gábhasti* as the *gábhasti* of the Soma presser; but that is not necessary. See below under *kṣip*.

65. Also "seasoned with spice" in other passages as we shall see later. In his interpretation of X.42.8 Oldenberg takes the corresponding Praiṣas into account and does not wish to separate *bahulānta* from the *bahura* in *bahuramadhya*. He refers *bahuramadhya* to the Soma drink in the sense that the "middle" offerings are compact, thick or abundant. In that case, I think, this could only denote the Soma stalks that are "thick below." Scheftelowitz, ZDMG, LXXIII, p. 42 : "pointed at the ends and thick in the middle."

66. I ignore the words *suhástya* IX.107.21 and *hástya* II.14.9 (both referring to Soma); they are not sufficiently clear. There is, however, a slight possibility that they belong here.

67. *arāvīt* IX.74.5; *róruvat* IX.91.3; *dhámat* VIII.96.13; *stanáyat* IX.72.6; *vāvaśāná* IX.95.4.

68. E.g., IX.50.1 : *út te śúṣmāsa īrate síndhor ūrmér iva svanáḥ* "like the roaring of the wave of a stream, your spray rises up." 67.18 : *té sutáso madíntamāḥ śukrá vāyúm asṛkṣata*, "the sweetest drops, the bright ones, sent forth the wind." 69.2 : *pávamānaḥ saṃtaníḥ praghnatám iva mádhumān drapsáḥ pari váram arṣati* "purifying itself, the sweet drop, like the shouts of combatants, flows over the strainer." 91.3 : *írte páyo góḥ*, "he stimulates the milk of the cow." However, even in the case of one or the other of the passages cited here it is doubtful whether they belong here.

69. *aṅśúṃ pariyántam ṛgmíyam*.

70. *divó yáḥ skambhó dhárunaḥ svàtataḥ / ápūrṇo aṅśúḥ paryéti viśvátaḥ*, unless we had a reference to a ceremony in which the stalk is transferred from hand to hand.

71. *ukṣéva yūthá pariyánn arāvīt ádhi tvíṣīr adhita sū́ryasya*.

72. *índuḥ samudram úd iyarti vāyúbhiḥ*.

73. Cf. *sugábhasti*. Bergaigne I, p. 204, explains *kṣip* differently — as an arrow.

74. I do not see any possibility of translating these words satisfactorily, nor do I find any useful suggestions from others in the summary given by Oldenberg. Ludwig (*Über die neuesten Arbeiten...*, p. 64) considers, with others, *bhūmī* in IX.61.10 as locative.

75. See p. 140 and VIII.9.19 on p. 139 above.

76. "He wanted a low price for very much; I turned back content that I had not sold; but he did not give the little for much; fools and clever ones find fault with the price".

77. However, the simple *hu* is connected several times with the accusative. Accordingly, *ahutá* should be "the one to whom no offerings were made." But this use of the accusative is hardly Vedic. The PW mentions only *tvá juhomi* AV I.31.3; *tvá hoṣyāmi* TS VI.4.5.6; probably ṚV VI.50.15. All this

notwithstanding, we can split up *ahutá* in *yasmai hutaṃ nāsti* and likewise *ávikrīta* in *yasya* (*yasmai*) *vikrītaṃ nāsti*, "one to whom no sacrifice is offered" and "one to whom nothing was sold" respectively, but not "one who did not offer a sacrifice" and "one who did not sell," just as *adatta* is not the same as *adattvā*. Perhaps it would be difficult to explain the accentuation of *ávikrīta* contrary to Pāṇini VI.2.172. But Pāṇini's rule is too restricted as the exceptions listed by Garbe (KZ, XXIII, p. 513, no. 2) show.

78. IF, XLII, AISAK, p. 25.

79. Now I doubt that in another passage which I quoted earlier, IX.50.1, *vāṇásya codayā pavím* is a designation of the Soma stalk, particularly after the remarks of Oldenberg (*Die Hymnen des Ṛgveda* II, p. 162) and Hauer (*Anfänge der Yogapraxis*, p. 47) both of whom think of a musical instrument, the construction of which, however, is not quite clear. Music played an important role in the Soma sacrifice; the very presence of the Udgātṛs suggests this. We are indebted to Hauer (op. cit., p. 42) for further material.

80. Bartholomae, *Altiranisches Wörterbuch* : 1. root, 2. young shoot, branch, 3. stalk, bough.

81. GGA, 1875, p. 595 : "The blossoms of *Sarcostemma intermedium* are white and umbellate, big and fleshy, and appear at the end of completely leafless branches. The upper parts of the branches are soft and are eaten by some animals like goats. Thus *ándhas* obviously means the flowering Soma branch and the plant is general."

82. With *pā* — III.40.1 : *sā pāhi mādhvo ándhasaḥ*; VIII.13.21 : *imásya pāhy ándhasaḥ*; 17.4 : *píbā sú ṣiprinn ándhasaḥ*; 84.2; V.51.5; VII.90. 1; I.135.4. With *mand* — I.82.5 : *mandānó yāhy ándhaso;* 80.6; VI.43.4; VIII.33.7; X.50.1; 167.2 etc. With *máde* — VIII.17.8 : *ándhaso máde*; 32.28; 33.4 etc.

83. V.45.9; IX.68.6; X.144.5 (*mānám ándhasaḥ*, see p. 132 above).

84. IX.61.10, see p. 142 above.

85. VIII.32.28; X.32.1; 50.7.

86. *sutásya somyásyā́ndhaso aṅśóḥ pīyū́ṣam.*

87. In some of these passages it can mean the "drink" also.

88. Cf. IX.8.8; 49.1; 108.10 etc.

89. *andhasī ujjayati.*

90. *grā́vṇā tunnó* IX.67.19.

91. IX.71.2 refers to the god Soma :

prá kṛṣṭihéva śūṣá eti róruvad
asuryàṃ várṇaṃ ní riṇīte asya tám /
jahā́ti vavríṃ pitúr eti niṣkṛtám
upaprútaṃ kṛṇute nirṇíjaṃ tánā //

As far as I know, there is no reliable translation of this verse. Even v. Bradke's translation in *Dyaus Asura*, p. 38 : "he unfolds that variety of the same one" is too insipid. ABr VI.36.14; TBr I.4.7.1; *Tāṇḍya Brāhmaṇa* IX.10.2 show that *asuryà várṇa* is a designation for the Asuran garb or form, and it can be understood only in this sense in our passage also. Like *niriṇānó* in IX.14.4, *riṇīte* is reflexive, and *asya* refers to *drúh rakṣás* in v. 1. Therefore, the passage means "he discards his Asuran garb." We should compare this with similar ideas in IX.66.24 : *pávamānaḥ...śukrám jyótir ajījanat | kṛṣṇā́ támāṅsi janghanat* and IX.41.1 : [*sómaḥ*] *ghnántaḥ kṛṣṇā́m apa tvácam.* We should also keep in mind that on the sacrificial place king Soma is wrapped symbolically in a cloth at first. Therefore, I think that *asuryà várṇa* has the same meaning as *ásiknī tvác.* It is possible that here also, as is often the case, the earthly Soma is compared to the celestial one and that the husk is meant to represent the "Asuran" aspect.

92. See also p. 139 above, *pinvate tvácam.*

93. Thus Ludwig.

94. Geldner, VSt, II, p. 254 : "in a wide orbit."

95. Cf. X.89.5.

96. The dual *gabhástyoḥ* is almost like a formula. Here it stands for the plural as in V.54.11; IX.64.5; (36.4). Oldenberg, *Die Hymnen des Ṛgveda* II, p. 195, treats this differently. He wants to separate this passage from IX.14.4 etc.

97. Thus e.g., Manu VII.147 has *giripṛṣṭha.*

98. Ludwig (330.10) translates this as "with moisture that is meant for his back" and the previous passage as "one who comes from the back (of heaven)." Geldner translates this word in IV.20.4 as "with frothy juice."

99. The word *tripṛṣṭhá,* which is repeatedly used as a designation of the celestial Soma, e.g., in IX.71.7; 75.3, cannot be assessed here. The verses in question will be discussed later.

100. See n. 65 above.

101. TS I.2.7a : *somaṃ te krīṇāmy ūrjasvantaṃ payasvantaṃ vīryavantam abhimātiṣāham.*

102. BKIS, VI, p. 237.

103. *staomi maēγəm ča vārəm ča yā tē kəhrpem vaxšayato barəšnuš paiti gairinąm.*

104. PW and Ludwig, "bearing leaves." Soma does not have leaves; there is no mention of this in any of the reliable passages. Our verse speaks of the god Soma who has taken his seat on the earth and, as it will become evident later, this god is repeatedly styled as a "bird."

105. She is also Indra's mother. In III.48.2 she pours Soma for him in the father's house. In IX.1.6 also the daughter of Sūrya is the season.

106. For detailed information on this, see Part II.

107. For further details, see below.

108. Cf. Oldenberg's different explanation in n. 65 above.

109. *atha yad apām ante krīṇāti raso vā āpaḥ sarasam evaitad krīṇāti | atha yad dhiraṇyaṃ bhavati saśukram evaitad krīṇāti | atha yad vāso bhavati satvacasam evaited krīṇāti | atha yad ajo bhavati satapasam evaitad krīṇāti | atha yad dhenur bhavati sāśiram evaitad krīṇāti | atha yan mithunau bhavataḥ samithunam evaitad krīṇāti.*

110. This fire is represented by the she-goat. The she-goat which brings forth three times a year is described as the symbol of fertility in ŚBr III.3.3.8.

111. V. Henry, *Vedica,* 2e sér., Mémoires de la. Soc. de ling. de Paris, IX, p. 249 : "May Soma rise to your jaw and to the visors of your helmet like on to the side of a mountain."

112. AV III. 20.10 : *yé párvatāḥ sómapṛṣṭhāḥ ā́pa uttānaśīvarīḥ |*
vā́taḥ parjánya ā́d agníḥ

In the sacrificial symbolism this expression is transferred to the press stones also.

ṚV VIII.63.2 : *divó mā́naṃ nót sadan sómapṛṣṭhāso ádrayaḥ |*
ukthā́ bráhma ca śáṅsyā ||

The parallelism that exists between *ádri, ukthá, bráhma* makes it certain that here the stones — and not the mountains — are intended. The same might be the case in IX.46.1.

113. Bartholomae, *Altiranisches Wörterbuch*, p. 1493.

114. *vi-ʒ-paθa*, "everywhere," does not make sense. The old meaning "on the path of the birds" or "on the heights" makes more sense.

115. Bartholomae and Mills translate as "kinds" which makes no sense.

116. Cf. MBr II.4.14 : *agnir iva tejasā vāyur iva prāṇena soma iva gandhena.*

117. Comm. on VS III.61 : *mūjavān nāma kaścit parvato rudrasya vāsasthānam.*

118. BŚS VI.4 (p. 172).

119. *Prayoga*, Munich Manuscript (Codex Sanskrit 86, Haug No. 117, folio 23 b).

120. I have come across this expression once more in the ritual. ĀpŚS XII.5.11, when the Ekadhanā waters are drawn, they are addressed thus : "I take you, the juice, for the Soma from Mūjavat."

121. *tān mūte kṛtvā vṛkṣa āsañcati | rudraiṣa te bhāgaḥ | tenāvasena paro mūjavato 'tīhi pinākahastaḥ kṛttivāsā avatatadhanvā | iti girir vai rudrasya yonir | ato vā eṣo 'nvabhyavacāraṃ prajāḥ śamāyate | svenaivainaṃ bhāgadheyena svaṃ yoniṃ gamayati.* VS III.61; ŚBr II.6.2.17 remarks thus on the mantra : *avasena vā adhvānaṃ yanti tad enaṃ sāvasam evānvavarjati | yatrayatrāsya caraṇaṃ tad anvatra ha vā asya paro mūjavadbhyaś caraṇam.* See the statements in Arbman, *Rudra*, p. 42.

122. AV V.22.5 : *óko asya mū́javantaḥ óko asya mahāvṛṣā́ḥ |*
yā́vajjātás [*takmaṅs*] *tā́vān asi báhlikeṣu nyocaraḥ ||*
7 : *tákman mū́javato gaccha bálhikān vā parastarā́m*
śūdrā́m iccha prapharvyám...
14 : *gandhā́ribhyo mū́javadbhyaḥ |*
áṅgebhyo magádhebhyaḥ
praiṣyáṃ jánam iva śevadhím
takmā́naṃ pari dadmasi ||

123. *Hundert Lieder*, 2nd ed., p. 156. Cf. also Muir, OST, II, p. 352.

124. KŚS VII.8.13 and the comm. on X.9.30; ĀpŚS XII.24.5; Hiraṇyakeśin VIII.7 (vol. III, p. 882 : *na vaiśyarājanyayoḥ somabhakṣaṇaṃ vidyate*; comm. : *yady abrāhmaṇaḥ somaṃ pipāsed nyagrodhastibhinīr āhṛtya tataḥ saṃpiṅṣya dadhany unmṛjya* etc.). *Ficus Indica*, closely related to Aśvattha and often mistaken for it, is called *kṣīravṛkṣa* in the *Śakuntalā* (ed. Pischel, p. 87).

125. TBr I.4.2.4 : *somo vā etasya rājyam ādatte yo rājā san rājyo vā somena yajate.* Even ṚV X.16.6 seems to suggest that the drink is already restricted to brahmins.

126. AV III.6.2. About a silver coin with the moon and a fig tree, see Lassen, IAK, II, 2nd ed., p. 943.

127. III.3.1.1 ff.

128. VII.6.1 ff.

129. Later Kautsas are also mentioned. According to KŚS VII.6.3, 4, a Kautsa or a Śūdra is the Soma seller. The comm. says that a Kautsa is from the same Gotra as Kutsa; others are of the opinion that a Kautsa is one whose behaviour is despicable. BŚS VI. 15 : *kautsād rājānam ādatte.* Even in the later period the Soma seller is considered a thoroughly reprehensible person. Manu III.158; GDS XV.17 etc. For the whole problem see Caland's translation of the ĀpŚS.

130. This water pot is meant to fulfil the injunction of the Brāhmaṇas : *apām ante krīṇāti.* See KŚS VII.6.6 ff.

131. KŚS VII.6.7, 13.

132. The sorting out of Soma is done to remove the grass etc. which might have fallen among the Soma stalks. The comm. on the TS says, I, p. 347 : *vicayo nāma somasya tṛṇāder apanayanam / tasminn oṣadhināṃ rājñi some yat tṛṇādikam āpannaṃ patitaṃ tat tṛṇādikam asya somasya grasitam eva grāsa eva bhavati.* For the more important evidence from the MS, see the next note. ŚBr III.3.2.5; KŚS VII.7.10 ff.

133. MS III.79.7 : *somaṃ vicinvanti pāpavasīyasya vyāvṛttyai.* 8 : *atho devebhya evainaṃ śundhanti / nādhvaryaḥ somaṃ vicinuyāt na yajamāno na yajamānasya puruṣāḥ / nopadraṣṭāro vicīyamānasya syuḥ / yad upadraṣṭāro vicīyamānasya syuḥ kṣudhaṃ prajā nīyur avartir yajamānaṃ gṛhṇīyāt kṣodhuko 'dhvaryuḥ syāt / śundha somaṃ āpannaṃ nirasya iti brūyāt / grasitaṃ vā etat somasya yad āpannam / grasitam ete somasya niṣkhidanti ye somaṃ vicinvanti / tasmāt somavikrayiṇo bahu krīṇanto bahu vindamānāḥ kṣodhukāḥ / grasitaṃ hy ete somasya niṣkhidanti.* TS VI.1.9.

134. KŚS VII.6.16.

135. On this magic circle, see Pischel, *Philologische Abhandlungen zu Hertz' 70. Geburtstage*, p. 73. Also Panzer, *Beitrag* II, pp. 72, 79, 154, 531. On the foot prints of the horse, see ŚBr II.1.4.24; VI.3.3.22; TBr I.1.5.9; Weber, ISt, X, p. 360.

136. Therefore, the pot is also called *paddharaṇī.* ŚBr III.3.1.7; KŚS VII.6.20.

137. KŚS VII.6.25 : *neṣṭā tota ity enāṃ vācayati* (VS IV.22). 26 : *somakrayaṇyā ca samīkṣyamāṇāṃ samākhya iti* (VS IV.23).

All the mantras that are employed here show that the cow with which Soma is bought is seen as a mystic symbol.

138. ŚBr III.3.2.1; KŚS VII.6.27.

139. In TS II.4.8 f. this verse is used in a different way which is probably more original.

140. ŚBr III.6.3.4 ff. differs in some details.

141. TS, comm. I, p. 350 : *pariśrayaḥ śakaṭasyopari gṛhakuḍyavat parito veṣṭanam / chadir uparitanam ācchādanam.*

142. TS, comm. I, p. 349 : *same pradeśe jīvanasādhanaṃ dhānyaṃ ca śakaṭavāhyaṃ tadvat somaḥ / viṣame tu pradeśe śirasā somavāhanaṃ viddhatte...yadā parvate somalatotpattipradeśe somaṃ krīṇāti tadeti śeṣaḥ.*

143. ŚBr III.3.2.9; KŚS VII.7.12.

144. VS IV.25; TS I.2.6b; KŚS VII.7.13.

145. ŚBr III.3.2.13, 14; KŚS VII.7.13 ff.; MS III, p. 80, 2; TS I, p. 350 comm. In the first round with the thumb and the little finger, in the second with the thumb and the ring finger, then with the thumb and the middle finger, and so on.

146. I adhere to the reading *kratūn*. Caland prefers *ṛtūn*.

147. MS III.84.13 : *somaṃ te krīṇāni mahāntaṃ bahvarhaṃ bahu śobhamānaṃ kalayā te krīṇāni* etc. TS I.2.7a; VI.1.10.1 ff; ŚBr III.3.3.1. We have mentioned above that in the ritual of Baudhāyana it is asked whether it is the Soma from the mountain Mūjavat.

148. In somewhat greater detail KŚS VII.8.8; ŚBr III.3.3.1 ff.

149. The gradation in KŚS VII.8.10 is *śapha, pada, ardha, go*.

150. In addition KŚS has the following — VII.8.13 : *krītaḥ somo rājety ante vayāṅsi prabrūhīty āha somavikrayī*, whereupon the Adhvaryu mentions the individual prices. Similarly ŚBr III.3.3.4. Here these individual prices are *candra, vastra, chāgā, dhenu, mithunau, gāvau* and *tisro 'nyāḥ* (*strīgavayaḥ*).

151. ŚBr III.3.3.8; KŚS VII.8.20.

152. Young cow, bull, a pair of calves, and garment.

153. The sequence of the rites is occasionally different in the *White Yajurveda*, but that is irrelevant here. But the following from the KŚS is of interest — VII.8.15 : *śukraṃ tveti hiraṇyam ālambhya vācayati.* 16 : *sagme ta iti* (VS IV.26) *somavikrayiṇaṃ hiraṇyenābhikampayati.* The comm. says that he provokes him with gold in so far as he merley shows the gold to him. 18 : *asme ta iti* (VS IV.26) *yajamānasahitaṃ nidadhāti.* 19 : *somavikrayy etad ādatte*. But later he takes the gold away from him again. 27 : *hiraṇyaṃ sahasācchidya pṛṣatā varatrākāṇḍenāhanti vā*, "having snatched the gold away from him, he may hit him with a variegated strap." (Just like in ĀpŚS). See ŚBr III.3.3.7 and Eggeling on this, SBE, XXVI, pp. 70, 71. Weber, ISt, X, p. 361.

154. Hiraṇyakeśin VII.2.8 : *śuklānām āvikorṇānām amote dve daśāpavitre bhavato daśākam anyatarad udakena kledayitvā kṛṣṇām ūrṇāstukām idam aham upagrathnāmīty upagrathya somavikrayiṇi tama iti tayā somavikrayiṇaṃ rarāṭe vidhyati.* A Prayoga, which I have, states that he should hit him between the eyebrows.

155. TS I.2.7h; ŚBr III.3.3.11; VS IV.27; MS I.2.5; III.7.7 (84.16) : *suvāṅ nabhrāḍ aṅgāre* etc.

156. According to BŚS VI.15, he hands over the head-covering to a Kautsa or a servant.

157. KŚS VII.8.23; ŚBr III.3.3.10.

158. The comm. says *bindumatā*; the comm. on KŚS VII.8.27 explains *pṛṣatā* as *vicitravarṇena*.

159. "Über den Soma" in ZDMG, XXXV, p. 687.

160. SBE, XXVI, p. 71, n. 1.

161. ŚBr III.3.1.16. Likewise MS I.6.4 (92.18). TS VI.1.6.4,5 : *striyā niṣ krīṇāmeti / te vācam striyam ekahāyanīṃ kṛtvā tayā nirakrīṇan*; ABr I.27.

162. Similarly in other texts also, eg., TS VI.1.6.6.

163. TS VI.1.6.1; MS III.7.3 (77.6) etc.

164. "As I said when choosing you at first, we must fight the Asuras for this Soma."

165. *Die Sonnenwendfeste in Alt-Indien*, Erlangen 1890, p. 43.

166. See i.a., Wirth, *Oster- und Passionsspiele*, p. 186; Mone, *Schauspiele des Mittellaters*, II, p. 16; Reuling, *Die komische Figur in den wichtigeren deutschen Dramen*, p. 16.

167. Thus Ludwig. Perhaps more correctly "assembly" or "sacrificial assembly."

168. Ī.3.21 and comm. (ed. Aufrecht, p. 240).

169. *Tāṇḍya Br.* IX.4; MS II.1.7; 2.11; LŚS I.11.12; ŚŚS XIII.5.1 ff.; ĀŚvŚS VI.6.11; KŚS XXV.14.8, 23 ff.; TBr I.4.6.4.

170. III.35.5; 45.1; VIII.15.12 etc. Cf. Ludwig, VI, p. 186 s.v. *saṃsava*.

171. I read with Grassmann *aryā́m* for *aryam*.

172. IV.29.1; X.169.1.

173. Cf. also KŚS XXV.14.14.

174. Ludwig, III, p. 109; V, p. 139.

175. The words *kaṇvavat, atrivat* etc. suggest specific forms.

176. Probably names of musical instruments. (According to Sāyaṇa *gargara*=*vādyaviśeṣa*, *godhā*=*hastaghna*, *piṅgā*=*piṅgavarṇā jyā*). J. W. Hauer, *Anfänge der Yogapraxis*, p. 52. In Iran also musical instruments are employed during the recitation of the Parsi liturgy. See Spiegel, *Eranische Altertumskunde*, III, p. 573.

177. *Die Sonnenwendfeste in Alt-Indien*, p. 40.

178. Some explanations are to be found in the introductory legends in the comm. of Sāyaṇa and in the translation of Ludwig, who refers to TMBr IX.2.14, also in the works of H. Oertel etc., who are mentioned in the introduction to my translation, *Lieder des Ṛgveda*, p. 37. This is based on their statements.

179. I. 28.5 : *yā́ dampatī sámanasā sunutá ā́ ca dhā́vataḥ* /
dévāso nítyayāśíra //

180. We can see the relics of common patriarchal celebrations in the injunctions of ŚBr III.4.2.15; IV.6.8.18 — that, if there are many sacrificers, one of them should represent the master of the house, that further in the case of the Agnīṣomīya paśu the order is given "invoke the comrades of Vrata together," that the sacrificer holds the Adhvaryu, the wife the sacrificer, the sons and brothers the wife, and that he should cover the servants with an unwashed (new) garment (ĀpŚS XI.16.12 ff.) etc.

181. Manu IV.7 comm.; XI.7, 8. Yājñavalkya I.124. Ludwig, IV, p. 73. MBh XII.165.5 : *yasya traivarṣikaṃ bhaktaṃ paryāptam / adhikaṃ cāpi vidyeta sa somaṃ pātum arhati.*

182. *Prolegomena*, I, p. 154.

183. Translated in my *Lieder des Ṛgveda*, p. 134-5, and now by Geldner, who renders v. 1 *ní dhatte* more correctly as "establishes a treasure." Elsewhere (TS II.2.6) we encounter a travelling priest who offers Agni Vaiśvānara for sale thus : "Whosoever aims at profit should make offerings to Agni Vaiśvānara who is the year. At the end of the year he must set Agni Vaiśvānara free, whom he has 'harnessed' for the sake of profit. Otherwise, he would lose his footing (*apratiṣṭhita*)."

184. I note further Turvaśa Yadu VIII.45.27; Saṃvarta, Kṛśa VIII.54.2; Rāthavīti V.61.18; Navagvas and Daśagvas V.29.12; Manu Sāṃvaraṇi, Nīpātithi, Medhyātithi, Puṣṭigu, Sruṣṭigu Vāl. III.1.

185. VIII.52.1 : *yáthā mánau vívasvati sómaṃ śakrā́pibaḥ sutám |*
yáthā trité chánda indra jújoṣasi
āyaú mādayase sácā ||
pṛ́ṣadhre médhye mātaríśvani etc.

186. ĀpŚS XI.20.12.

187. Geldner, "imperishable wealth".

188. Ed. Bhandarkar, p. 11.

189. Further material in Muir, OST, III, p. 224 ff. Ludwig, III, p. 180.

190. Ludwig makes a reference to AV XVIII.3.46 : *yé naḥ pitúḥ pitáro yé pitāmahā́ anūhiré* etc.

191. Max Müller, *A History of Ancient Sanskrit Literature*, p. 386; Weber, ISt, IX, p. 322; Ludwig, III, p. 179. According to ABr II.19.1, Kavaṣa Ailūṣa is chased away as a *dāsyāḥ putraḥ, kitavaḥ, abrāhmaṇaḥ.*

192. TS II.1.5.5 ff. : *aindrāgnaṃ punarutsṛṣṭam ā labheta ya ā tṛtīyāt puruṣāt somaṃ na pibet vicchinno vā etasya somapītho yo brāhmaṇaḥ sann ā tṛtīyāt puruṣāt somaṃ na pibati | indrāgnī eva svena bhāgadheyenopa dhāvati | tāv evāsmai somapīthaṃ pra yacchataḥ | upainaṃ somapītho namati.* MS II.5.5 (53.10) : *aindrāgnam anusṛṣṭam ālabheta yasya pitā pitāmahaḥ somaṃ na pibet | indriyeṇa vā eṣa vīryeṇa vyṛdhyate yasya pitā pitāmahaḥ somaṃ na pibati.* KŚS VII.1.5.

193. GDS XVIII.24 ff.; Manu XI.12 ff.

194. GDS VI.19; Manu II.128.

195. ŚŚS VII.6.11 comm.; MS II.4.1 (38.1 ff.).

196. One comm. explains *saṃkhyāya* as *uccārya.* The other states quite clearly : *somapānāṃ pitāmahādīnāṃ daśagaṇaṃ samūhaṃ saṃkhyāya amukaḥ prathamaḥ somapaḥ asau dvitīyaḥ asau tṛtīyaḥ evaṃ daśamaparyantān somayājino gaṇayitvā sarpaṇaṃ kurvanti.* Quite similarly Hiraṇyakeśin XIII.21 also : *pātrasaṃsādānakāle daśa camasān adhikān prayunakti | unnayanakāle daśa camasān adhikān unnayati | bhakṣaṇakāle ya ā daśamāt puruṣād avicchinnasomapīthaḥ sa bhakṣasya kartā | ā daśamāt puruṣād anvākhyāya śataṃ brāhmaṇāḥ somapāḥ saṃprasarpanti | daśadaśaikaṃ camasaṃ bhakṣayanti.* Patañjali, II, p. 249 under Vārttika 5 : *daśapuruṣānūkaṃ yasya gṛhe śūdrā na vidyeran sa somaṃ pibet.* The Hotṛ in the Daśapeya should be a member of the Bhṛgu Gotra, see TMBr XVIII.9.2; Weber, ISt, X, p. 84.

197. *yeṣām ubhayataḥ śrotriyā daśapuruṣaṃ te yājayeyuḥ.* Comm. : *yeṣāṃ mātṛtaḥ pitṛtaś ca daśadaśa puruṣāḥ śrotriyā bhavanti.*

198. See further ŚBr V.4.5.4 and comm., p. 492; ĀpŚS XIV.32.4; LŚS IX.2.5; ĀśvŚS IX.3.20, 21.

199. *ayáṃ te mā́nuṣe jáne sómaḥ pūrúṣu sūyate | tásyéhi prá dravā píba ||*

200. Aurel Stein, "Some River Names in the Ṛgveda," JRAS, 1917, p. 91 ff.

201. VIII.13.15 : *yác chakrā́si parāváti yád arvāváti vṛtrahan ||*
yád vā samudré ándhaso 'vitéd asi ||

202. Pischel (VSt, II, p. 119) was the first to see that *pastyā̀vat* in VIII.7.29 is a proper name. He presumed that it is identical with Patiala, which seems to be theoretically possible.

203. I give below all the passages where Sāyaṇa explains Suṣomā and Saryaṇāvant.

I.84.14 : *śaryaṇā nāma deśāḥ / teṣām adūrabhavaṃ saraḥ śaryaṇāvat.*

VIII.7.29 : *suṣome śobhanasomayukta ārjīke / ṛjīkā nāma deśaḥ / tatsaṃbandhini śaryaṇāvati / kurukṣetrasya jaghanārdhe śaryaṇāvatsaṃjñe sarasi / pastyāvati / pastyam iti gṛhanāma* etc.

VIII.64.11 : *śaryaṇāvati kurukṣetrasya jaghanārdhabhave śaratṛṇopete sarasi / tat saraḥ kutra vartata ity ucyate / suṣomāyām etannāmikāyāṃ nadyām / sā ca kutra vartate.../ ārjīkīya etannāmake deśe / evamuktaprakāreṇātyantadūradeśe vartate yaḥ somaḥ sa evāyam.*

IX.65.22 : *kurukṣetrasya jaghanārdhe śaryaṇāvatsaṃjñakaṃ madhurasayuktaṃ somavat saro 'sti* etc. 23 : *ārjīkeṣu / ṛjīkānām adūrabhavā ārjīkā deśāḥ / teṣu / tathā kṛtvasu / kṛtvāna iti deśābhidhānam /...kiṃ ca pastyānāṃ sarasvatyādīnāṃ nadīnāṃ madhye....*

IX.113.2 : *ṛjīkānām adūrabhava ārjīko janapadaḥ /...yadvā / ārjīkād ṛjor akuṭilāt pavitrāt...*

X.75.5 : *he vitastayā suṣomayā ca sahita ārjīkeye.*

Thus he seems to regard the three names as one geographical entity. The last passage is explained in *Nirukta* IX.26 also, and according to this work, *suṣomā* is supposed to be the Sindhu, *ārjīkīyā* the Vipāś : *ārjīkīyāṃ vipāḍ ity āhur ṛjūkaprabhavā varjugāminī vā...pūrvam asīd uruñjirā.* Durgasiṃha adds this: *sa kasmād? ṛjīkaprabhavā ṛjīko nāma parvataḥ / tasmāt prabhavati.* Another comm. says (vol. IV, p. 43, note) : *evaṃ ca ārjīkīyeti prathamaṃ nāma / tata uruñjireti / tato vipāḍ iti lokaprasiddhaḥ.*

204. Likewise *suṣóma* is probably the land and *suṣómā* the river.

205. *āvirṛjīko* in IV.38.4 is not clear to me. In the first verse of this hymn Trasadasyu, the Pūru prince, is mentioned.

206. Thus Duncker, *Geschichte des Altertums*, 5th ed., III, p. 306; further Lassen, IAK, 2nd ed., II, p. 154, n. 7.

207. JRAS, 1917, p. 98; note on *Rājataraṅgiṇī* V.217. On the other hand, I cannot dismiss the view of a comm., cited in n. 203, that the Vipāś was called earlier Uruñjirā or Arjikīyā.

208. AIL, p. 32 ff. and earlier.

209. *Der Ṛgveda*, III, p. 199.

210. AV IV.18.1 in feminine.

211. On sorcery among the brahmins of Kashmir, see Bühler, *Detailed Report of a Search of Sanskrit Manuscripts made* (*in* 1875-76) *in Kashmir, Rajputana, and Central India*, Bombay-London 1877, p. 24; L. v. Schroeder, *Maitrāyaṇī Saṃhitā*, p. xxv, n. 3.

212. *Ancient Geography of India*, I, p. 93.

213. See also PW, s. v.

214. Subsequently Pischel has collated the passages from Sāyaṇa more thoroughly in VSt, II, p. 217.

215. A mountain, according to TBr, I, p. 234 comm.(*kaśmiṅś cit parvate*).

216. *Kumārasaṃbhava* , I.16.

217. Lassen, IAK, 2nd ed., I, p. 43.

218. Sāyaṇa on I.84.14 states that the lake is situated in a country called Śaryaṇā. Lassen, IAK, 2nd ed., I, p. 59 mentions Seran in Bissahir.

219. *Der Ṛgveda*. III, p. 201.

220. *Iran und Turan*, pp. 51, 101.

221. I infer from the context that *svàrṇava* also is a proper name.

222. A Kaśyapa is supposed to be the author of IX.113. But this seems to be doubtful since the hymn itself does not contain the name Kaśyapa (it occurs in IX.114.2).

223. How to reconcile this with VIII.7.29 is not certain. The poet, a Kaṇva as is evident from vv. 18, 19, 32, asks : "The Maruts have come down at Suṣoma, Saryaṇāvat, Ārjīka and Pastyāvat. When will they approach here the singer who invokes them ?" Thus it could appear as if the poet did not live at any of these four places, but it is not certain. For he could equally be a priest who offered sacrifices at different places, and thus he could ask : "At such and such a place you (pl.) have heard my call; when will you come this time ?"

224. AIL, p. 102.

225. If IX.113 was really the hymn of a Kaśyapa who lived at the lake Saryaṇāvat and invoked Soma to come to him from Ārjīkā, then this would be one more decisive factor.

226. III.35.9, 10 : "with the tongue of the fire, drink Soma, O Indra." V. 51.2 etc.

227. Cf. VI.47.3.

228. VIII.48.11 cd : *ā́ sómo asmā́ṅ aruhad víhāyā*
áganma yátra pratiránta ā́yuḥ ||
12 ab : *yó ná índuḥ pitaro hṛtsú pītó*
ámartyo mártyān āvivéśa |

229. Kaegi, *Ṛgveda*, 2nd ed., n. 308; Bergaigne, I, pp. 193-4;
IX.113.7 : *yátra jyótir ájasraṃ yásmiṃl loké svàr hitám* |
ásmin mā́ṃ dhehi pavamāna amṛ́te loké ákṣite...

230. E.g., VIII.92.17 and innumerable times.

231. E.g., I.43.7.

232. X.16.6. According to III.62.13-15, he confers nourishing food, prolongs life and protects from ambush.

233. MS IV.8.2 (109.2).

234. Ibid., IV.3.6 (44.4).

235. E.g., GDS XIX.13.

236. Cf. I.91.13; VIII.2.12; X.167.3.

237. MS II.2.13 (26.3) : *somapīthena vā eṣa vyṛdhyate yaḥ somaṃ vamati.*

238. ŚBr V.5.4.9 ff.; XII.7.1.11; TS II.3.2 etc. The ceremony was known by name as early as in AV III.3.2. But I am convinced that it is still older.

239. AIL, p. 275. Cf. also MS II.4.1 (38.14).

SOMA

Part II : King Soma

1. Bergaigne, *Vedic Religion according to the Hymns of the Ṛgveda*, I, p. 183 f.

2. *Les Religions de l'Inde*, p. 29.

3. Op. cit., I, pp. 155, 156 and passim; *Manuel pour étudier le Sanskrit Védique*, p. 150, n. 2, and the Lexicon.

4. *Ormazd et Ahriman*, pp. 44, 99.

5. SBE, XII, p. 176, n. 3 etc.; *Encyclopedia Brittanica*, s. v. Brahmanism; later differently in SBE, XLI, p. xxvii.

6. *Ṛgveda*, pp. 31, 99.

7. IAK, 2nd ed., I, p. 903.

8. *Essays*, 2nd ed., I, p. 166; later differently in his article, "Lunar Myths," in *Chips from a German Workshop*, new ed., London 1895, IV, p. 328 ff.

9. OST, V, pp. 258, 270.

10. PW.

11. AIL, pp. 276, 352.

12. *Indiens Literatur und Kultur*, pp. 70, 71; differently now in his *Arische Religion*, passim, referring to my "Soma" as well as to the views of Max Müller and Eggeling.

13. JAOS, XVI, Proceedings (1894).

14. Op. cit., I, p. 155 ff.

15. Vol. I, passim; see the Index on pp. 186, 187.

16. Bergaigne, I, p. 163.

16a. The Translator is grateful to Dr Bettina Bäumer for rendering this Italian passage into English.

17. Besides the ethnographic parallels, cf. the epithet of the moon in the *Avesta*, *Yašt* VII.5 : *tafnahvaṭ*, "containing white heat."

18. E.g., IX.63.27 : *pávamānā divás pári antárikṣād asṛkṣata |*
pṛthivyā́ ádhi sā́navi ||
66.30 : *yásya te dyumnávat páyaḥ*
pávamānā́bhṛtaṃ diváḥ ||

19. E.g., *diváḥ pīyū́ṣam* IX.51.2; 85.9 etc. Other examples will be cited later.

20. On this cf. v. 5 with its association to the moon :
yū́na ha sántā prathamáṃ ví jajñatuḥ |
gū́hā hitáṃ janima némam údyatam ||
(See Oldenberg, *Die Hymen des Ṛgveda*, II).

21. I have omitted X.99.8 because of Geiger's remark in his *Amešaspentas*, p. 72, n.

22. Pāda *c* : *śatácakraṃ yò 'hyò vartaniḥ* is not clear to me. Does it belong here ? For v. 5 see p. 132 above.

23. Earlier, i.a., A. Kuhn, MSt, I, p. 123 ff. Later Ludwig, *Über Methode bei der Interpretation des Ṛgveda*, p. 66; Pischel, VSt, I, p. 208 ff.; Jarl Charpentier, *Suparṇasage*, p. 139; my review of Geldner's translation of the *Ṛgveda* in IF, XLII, AISAK, p. 25.

24. On *javásā* in IV.27.1 (instrumental, derived adverbially from the adjective) cf. MBh I.33.10 : *utpapāta javenaiva...vīryavān*; 18 : *vavrāja tarasā vegād vāyuṃ spardhan mahājavaḥ.*

25. To *nír adīyat* we should add *nábhaso* or some similar word, and not *puráḥ* : "he arises suddenly," "appears."

26. Only in one passage I see Indra in the company of an eagle.
AV VII.41.1 : *áty apás tatarda śyenó nṛcakṣā avasānadarśáḥ |*
táran víśvāny ávarā rájāṅsī́ndreṇa sákhyā śivá ā́ jagamyāt ||

What is meant here is not the Soma bird, but god Indra himself. This is evident from the use of the optative; this is suggested also by the wording of the next verse : *śyenó divyáḥ sahásrapāt.* Moreover, the assumption that Indra himself is the eagle is ruled out. Of course, Indra plunders Soma; he drinks it in the house of Tvaṣṭṛ. He is compared to an eagle (I.32.14), or called thus (X.99.8); but that he transformed himself into an eagle to plunder Soma is a view not represented in the ṚV, and as such it is very rare. Kuhn (MSt, I, p. 128) cited a passage from the *Kāṭhaka* in support of this view. However, Bergaigne I, p. 176, is quite right when he considers this a "purely accidental identification" as far as it is concerned with the ṚV.

27. Hillebrandt, *Lieder des Ṛgveda,* p. 29, in agreement with Oldenberg, GGA. 1914, p. 447 and Neisser, *Zum Wörterbuch des Ṛgveda.*

28. Johansson (*Solfågeln,* pp. 28, 51 ff.).

29. IX.48.2-4 is a parallel passage to IV.27.1-2. It differs from the latter only in so far as here it is the poet who speaks and not Soma himself. On the eagle Geiger has some comments to make in his *Amešaspentas,* p. 70.

30. While Oldenberg, *Die Hymnen des Ṛgveda,* I, p. 191, wrongly concluded that it is not Soma but the eagle which was imprisoned in the fortress, Sieg translates thus : "While I [Indra !] was still in the mother's womb, I knew all the clans of these gods, (but) hundred brass fortresses and the eagle guarded me; I flew out with the fast one." The eagle, says Sieg, is not the prisoner, but the guard of Indra, who is stated to be still in the womb of his mother by the words *gárbhe nú sán.* That is to say, while Indra was still in the womb of his mother, the Dāsas hold her imprisoned—we have to read this between the lines — in a brass fortress and, to be quite certain that Indra does not run away from them, appoint the fastest flying bird with the sharpest eyes as the guard of the pregnant woman. (*Festschrift für Jacobi,* p. 228 ff.).

Against this we have to say that *púraṃdhi* does not mean "pregnant"; Geldner (Glossar) : 2. adjective, b) *maghavan* IV.26.7; 27.2,3. I do not wish that my discussion in WZKM, IX, pp. 1-21, should be completely ignored. There I have said that *raoraθa,* "with fast chariot," is an adjective of *pārendi,* which does not exactly apply to a pregnant woman. *pārendi* is roughly the same as the designation *raghú* in V.45.9.

Hence, it is not Indra but Soma himself who knows all the clans of the gods, proclaims their names etc. (IX.81.2; 95.2; 97.7, 41; 108.3). Thirdly, there is no mention anywhere of the imprisonment of Indra's mother with the child. Fourthly, the eagle does not guard Indra but brings him Soma as a gesture of friendship. Finally, the "sharpest-eyed one" would be a bad guard if he carried away the mother with the son (the mother must certainly have clung to him secretly). Where does he carry her away ? After overcoming the fortress (which guards the entrance), he flies to heaven. There he would get her really into danger, because there at first he has to fight against the enemies for the sake of Soma. Where do the mother and child remain meanwhile ? There is no trace even of an approximate similarity with the bird Rokhsage as Charpentier describes it.

I understand the passage precisely in the way I have translated it earlier.

I cannot see how Sieg came to compare *indravat* with *himávat* and consider it the designation of a mountain named after (the still unborn) Indra, on which the fortress was situated. *índravat* is a frequent adjective meaning "accompanied by Indra" or something similar. Finally, I do not attach the least importance to the divine genealogies (like "Indra's grandfather from the mother's side") since these are based entirely on fantasy and not on reality (*Vedische Mythologie*, 1st ed., III, p. 409). Bergaigne, III, p. 108 f.; Reichelt, IF, XXXII, p. 44, indulge in futile hypotheses.

31. Birds play a role in the case of Haoma also, as is evident from the passages cited above. On the helmet of the Iranian war god Vərəθraγna there appears a bird, obviously sacred to him since the healing and protecting power of a feather of this bird, worn as an amulet, is the subject of a special comment particularly in *Behram Yašt*. Stein, *Zorastrian Deities*, p. 5; Johansson (*Solfågeln*, p. 31, n. 2). Remotely corresponding sagas are to be found among other peoples also. A. Lang, *Custom and Myth*, p. 54).

32. TS III.5.7.1.; TBr I.1.3.10; 2.1.6; 4.7.5; ŚBr I.8.2.10; XI.7.2.8 etc. Kuhn, MSt, I, p. 131.

33. III.6.2.2 ff. J. Charpentier, *Die Suparṇasage*, p. 289.

34. It is well known that the legend of Kadrū, Suparṇī and the bird that fetches Soma occurs is MBh I.1073 also, as it does in the *Suparṇādhyāya.*

35. There are legends that deviate from this, e.g., in MS III.7.7 (84.16) : *suvāṅ nabhrāḍ aṅgāre bambhārā ity ete vai devānāṃ somarakṣayaḥ / etebhyo vā adhi cchandāṅsi somam āharan;* TMBr VIII.4.1; ABr III.25.2.

36. This remark is nothing but a forced interpretation by the scholiast. On *kuśi* Eggeling has the following remark : "*kuśī* ?=*kośī* 'pod' (or case). Sāyaṇa explains it by '*āyudha*' (? weapon, or vessel, sheath)."

37. E.g., ŚBr XII.7.3.1 ff.

38. Aufrecht, ZDMG, XXXIX, p. 310 (v. 16).

39. Cf. ṚV I.91.3.

40. BI ed., vol. I, p. 425. The text is not always correct.

41. *eṣa vai somo rājā devānām annaṃ yac candramāḥ /*

42. See *Vāyupurāṇa*, BI ed., I, p. 298; VS IX.23.

43. These words recall to mind ṚV IX.84.3 :

á yó góbhiḥ sṛjyáta óṣadhīṣv á

or IX.99.3 : *yáṃ gávo āsábhir dadhúḥ purá nūnáṃ ca sūráyaḥ /*

44. *sa ihāpaś cauṣadhīś ca praviśati / tad enam adbhya oṣadhibhyaḥ saṃbhṛtyāhutibhyo 'dhi janayati sa eṣa āhutibhyo jātaḥ paścād dadṛśe /*

45. Likewise II.4.4.20.

46. II.4.2.13; 6.1.4; AV XVIII.4.72; ŚŚS III.16.4 etc.

47. Also XI.1.3.3; 4.4; 2.5.3.

48. MS II.3.8 (36.10) : *ahaṃ tam asya manasā ghṛtena somaṃ rājānam iha bhakṣayāmi.*

49. Also KBr XII.5. These formulas are in complete contrast to the negative attitude of the poet of ṚV X.85.3 : "He believes to have drunk Soma when they press the plant."

50. ŚŚS III.8.15.

51. ABr I.12.

52. ṚV X.71.10 has the adjective *yaśás* in the place of *yáśas*; I have translated above in conformity with the views of the Brāhmaṇa.

53. MS I.2.6; TS I.2.9; ĀpŚS X.19.1 etc.

54. Soma is wrapped in a cloth. This also has its symbolic significance.

55. ŚBr III.4.1.1. The Soma that has been bought comes to his house as a guest; ABr I.15 : *havir ātithyaṃ nirupyate some rājany āgate.*

56. ĀpŚS X.30.15.

57. The Ātithyeṣṭi is followed by a ceremony which is of great importance from the point of view of cultural history. The microcosm in Indian sacrifice is made up of various elements. From the very beginning the Agniṣṭoma was not the complex sacrifice that it is now. By a close observation it can be analyzed into a number of separate components originating from different walks of Indian life. This fact confers on the vast range of Indian ritual its great significance : that it enveloped the customs of domestic and public life with a religious aura, that it incorporated all of these customs, and thus has become a compendium of ancient customs. Garbe, ZDMG, XXXIV, p. 319, has shown that the Pravargya ceremony can be broken into its separate elements and that originally it was a milk offering. On the significance of the Dīkṣā, see Hillebrandt, "Der freiwillige Feuertod in Indien und die Somaweihe," SBKBAW, 1917, p. 13 ff. At this point I may refer to the Tanūnaptra ceremony, which follows immediately after the guest offering and which can be explained by this association. If it was to represent in the ritual a sort of protective alliance between the sacrificer and the priest, then this sacrificial purpose was attributed to it only later. Its close association with the guest offering confers on it the more general significance of an alliance of hospitality made between the guest and the master of the house at whose hearth the former finds refuge. It is an oath of protection.

The Upasads are also worth mentioning here. According to the myths connected with them, they were sacrifices once common during the attacks and sieges by the enemy. They are distinguished by brevity; Prayājas and Anuyājas are dropped (Eggeling, SBE, XXVI, p. 104 ff.); the Pravara is very short (ĀpŚS XI.3.8). According to an injunction of Baudhāyana (see ĀpŚS XI.3.12), one should perform the Upasads as if one is in a great hurry and need not worry about the things that are omitted. ABr I.23.1 ff. : *jitayo vai nāmaitad yad upasadaḥ*; ŚBr III.4.4.4 : *tad vai devā aspṛṇvata ta etābhir upasadbhir upāsīdaṅs tad yad upāsīdaṅs tasmād upasado nāma te puraḥ prābhindan / imāṅ lokān prājayaṅs tasmād āhur upasadā puraṃ jayantīti;* also ibid., III.4.4.21, 22 etc. The Romans also performed religious ceremonies when they besieged the places of the enemy. Marquardt-Mommsen, *Handbuch*, 1st ed., VI.3, pp. 20, 23. Lubbock, *Origin of Civilization*, 5th ed., p. 249. Keith says that "the siege is a mythical one" (p. 327); so it is, but borrowed from the events in this world.

58. Against this Keith says (pp. 331-2) : "...to suggest, as Hillebrandt does, that the essence of the sacrifice was a piece of magic, the moon's rays being full of nectar and being represented by the shoots of the Soma plant, so that the manipulations of the priests are adequate to supply the gods with the nectar drink which they love, is to misunderstand the nature of the

sacrifice completely..." I can only add that, in such a case, the ceremonies as well as the statements of the ritual texts that are cited would become meaningless just as, according to Keith, many hymns of book IX are meaningless. (The Soma sacrifice is a rain magic only incidentally).

59. Keith refers to — what was after all a late — "native tradition" elsewhere also (*Mythology of all Races*, VI, p. 48). But in this respect, its value, as far as the ancient period is concerned, is more than dubious. Even Yāska is not able to inform us correctly about the Vedic gods any more; how much less Sāyaṇa, who was removed from the former by more than a thousand years and who leaves us in the lurch even about the ordinary exegesis ? By his time the original popular concept that one drinks the moon himself — to be still seen in the ritual — has completely disappeared (see p. 174 above). In ṚV X.85.3 ff. we encounter a heretic who does not believe any more in *candramasaṃ bhakṣayāmi*.

60. Indeed, these two verses show that this concept is not limited only to the last portion of the ninth maṇḍala, but can be seen there throughout.

61. Oldenberg, RdV, 1st ed., p. 182 and p. 178 respectively. U.v. Wilamowitz (*Herakles*, 2nd ed., Vorwort, p. xii) speaks, therefore, of the sublime absurdity of the Soma sacrifice.

62. *Oeuvres* II, p. 109. Elsewhere (ibid., IV, pp. 193, 269), however, he reproaches me for exaggerating. That was true of some views which I have changed here : e.g., when I said that the moon predominates Indian thought instead of the sun, or when I explained Somagopā as the moon.

63. The PW cites I.65.10; 91.1 ff.; 163.3; X.85.1 ff.; 107.2; 116.3.

64. Of course, here Soma does not refer to the sacrificial drink; for this statement is immediately followed by *ukṣā́ bibharti bhúvanāni* in the Bṛhaspati verse IX.83.3, and by *ayáṃ síndhubhyo abhavad u lokakṛ́t* in 86.21, which in the case of the plant or the drink would be quite strange, if not meaningless.

65. See also now H. Weller, *Garbe-Festschrift*, p. 59, on IX.67.28 where he recognizes both the associations "with the plant and the god."

66. v. 6 switches over again from the celestial Soma to the terrestrial one. This change-over, to be seen frequently, is understandable when we assume that it is the moon himself (or his nectar) who goes into the sieve. A parallel to this is the shift from the terrestrial Agni to the celestial counterpart. Quite rightly H. Weller (*Garbe-Festschrift*, p. 58) says "that the imagination of the Vedic brahmins oscillated to and fro between the god and the drink, or to put it more correctly, it could embrace both of them simultaneously."

67. IX.3.7 : *eṣá dívaṃ ví dhāvati tiró rájāṅsi dhā́rayā |*
8 : *eṣá dívaṃ vy ā́sarat tiró rájāṅsy áspṛtaḥ |*
37.3 : *sá...rocanā́ diváḥ...ví dhāvati*
63.8 : *áyukta sū́ra étaśam...antárikṣeṇa yā́tave;* 65.16.
68.4 : *sá mātárā vicáran...*
48.4 : *víśvasmā ít svàr dṛśé sā́dhāraṇaṃ rajastúram*
gopā́m ṛtásya vír bharat ||

68. IX.11.4 : *babhráve...aruṇā́ya divispṛ́śe sómāya*
101.14 : *ā jāmír átke avyata...*

69. IX.22.7; 27.5 :

eṣá sū́ryeṇa hāsate pávamāno ádhi dyávi |
pavítre matsaró mádaḥ ||

37.3; 66.5; 86.30.

70. Not because "he is then pressed and treaded" (Foy); that would be an unusual expression, compatible neither with VI.39.3 nor with X.85.9.

71. IX.66.26 : *rathī́tamaḥ*

63.8 : *áyukta sū́ra étaśaṃ pávamāno manā́v ádhi |*
antárikṣeṇa yā́tave...

65.16; 86.37; 111.3 :

sáṃ raśmíbhir yatate darśató rátho
daívyo darśató ráthaḥ|

72. Immediately thereafter follow the words *ékam ákṣi vāvṛdhúḥ* in v. 4; this eye is, of course, the moon; the sun does not come into the picture here. Cf. v.5 : *yúvānam...índum.*

73. *ná=vṛ́* GGA, 1889, No. 10, p. 414. On this see Delbrück, *Altindische Syntax* 2.540; BKIS, pp. 21,306; Hermann, NGGW, 1919, p. 225 ff. Just as here, so also in VII.87.4 : *padásya gúhyā ná vocat;* for the latter cf. IX.95.2 : *devó devā́nāṃ gúhyāni nā́māviṣkṛṇoti.*

74. Bergaigne, I, p. 182 explains *ubhayátaḥ* as an allusion "to the two worlds." *dhruvásya* is not the Pole Star. Soma himself is called *divó yáḥ skambhó dharuṇáḥ* 74.2; *dhartā́ diváḥ* 76.1 (see under section g).

75. For the content, cf. MBh VII. 184.51 :

utsārayantaḥ prabhayā tamas te candraraśmayaḥ |
paryagacchañ chanaiḥ sarvā diśaḥ khaṃ ca kṣitiṃ tathā ||

His light pervades everywhere, naturally in the house of the sacrificer also.

76. Hence his designation *aruṇá, babhrú, śóṇa, hári,* e.g.,

IX.11.4 : *babhráve nú svátavase aruṇā́ya divispṛ́śe*
sómāya gāthám arcata |

VIII.29.1; IX.78.4; 107.19,20; AV V.7.5.

77. Even otherwise it is said of him that he performs great deeds like Indra, e.g.,

IX.88.4 : *índro ná yó mahā́ kármāṇi cákrir |*
hántā vṛtrā́ṇām asi soma pūrbhít ||

For the martial activity which can be attributed to the moon, I refer to K. Th. Preuss, "Die Naturbeobachtungen in den Religionen des mexikanischen Kulturkreises," *Zeitschrift für Ethnologie,* 1900, p. 800 ("the moon goddesses are particularly martial"); moreover, the statements of the same author in *Zeitschrift für psychologische Forschung,* II, pp. 169 ff., 176, 181; ARW, XXIII, p. 1 ff.

78. Against my view it was said (Hopkins, ERE, s.v. Soma) that Soma was never designated as *mās.* This is not necessary. As little as Sūrya changes places with Mitra, or Vāyu with the Maruts, so is, we should assume, the interchange between Soma and *mās*; for the latter denotes only the "measurer" and not the nectar-containing moon. As long as it occurs alone, *mās* is used mostly in the sense of the month; according to Grassmann in the ratio of 3: 10. The same applies to the query of Oldenberg and

Foy : "Where does the ninth maṇḍala say anything about the Soma who appears in the night, whose companions the stars are and who wanes and waxes ?" It deals only with the festival of the nectar-containing god. See IX.85.10; 89.2 : *apsú drapsó vāvṛdhe*; 97.40 : *vāvṛdhe suvānā́ índuḥ* etc.

79. Ratzel, *Völkerkunde*, 1st ed., II, p. 88; Fritz Schulze, *Psychologie der Naturvölker*, p. 318 ff. and other works (*Vedische Mythologie*, smaller ed., n. 13).

80. See also the passages cited below in section : Soma and the Waters. He is repeatedly called the father of the gods IX.86.10; 87.2; 109.4 etc. Though still in the womb of his mother, he knows their births already IV.27.1; IX.97.41 : *apā́ṃ yád gárbho avṛṇīta devā́n* (see n. 30 above).

81. *Religions of the Primitive Peoples*, p. 173; *Myths of the New World*, 3rd ed., p. 17.

82. *The Golden Bough*, I, p. 102 and II, p. 268 respectively.

83. Even Keith (pp. 258-9) speaks of "the application of the concept sympathetic magic, and this is one of the most obvious and undeniable facts in the whole of the Vedic sacrifice : it is from beginning to end full of magic elements." But the best example escaped his attention.

84. On this, cf. IX.85.10 : *divó nā́ke mádhujihvā asaścáto*
venā́ duhanty ukṣáṇaṃ giriṣṭhā́m |
apsú drapsáṃ vāvṛdhānáṃ samudrá ā́
ūrmā́ mádhumantaṃ pavitra ā́ ||

85. See also IX.73.1.

86. IX.64.11 : *ūrmír yás te pavitra ā́ devāvī́ḥ pary ákṣarat.* II.16.5; III.47.1; VI.41.2; IX.61.5; 78.2; 81.1 etc.

87. *Sāhityadarpaṇa* VII.21 f. A Lettish riddle sees in him "a butter box in the middle of a farm," Mannhardt, *Zeitschrift für Ethnologie*, VII, p. 101.

88. XI.86.40 on p. 206 above.

89. Cf. AV XVIII.4.36 :
sahásradhāraṃ śatádhāram útsam ákṣitam
vyácyamānaṃ salilásya pṛṣṭhé |
ū́rjaṃ dúhānam anapasphúrantam
úpāsate pitáraḥ svadhā́bhiḥ ||

and, above all, ṚV VI.44.24 :
ayáṃ dyā́vāpṛthivī ví ṣkabhāyat...|
ayáṃ góṣu śácyā pakvám antáḥ
sómo dādhāra dáśayantram útsam ||

90. II.16.7; III.26.9 (?); VIII.61.6; IX.96.44.

91. MS I.3.9 (33.9) : *viṣṇos tvorukrame gṛhṇāmi viṣṇa urukramaiṣa te somas taṃ rakṣasva.*

92. I.64.6 : *átyaṃ ná mihé ví nayanti vājínam útsaṃ duhanti stanáyantam ákṣitam* (cf. IX.72.6 : *aṅśúṃ duhanti stanáyantam ákṣitaṃ kavíṃ kaváyaḥ*); I.85.11; V.54.8; VII.57.1. It should be noted that there is always the singular, and not the plural.

92a. *Vedische Mythologie*, 1st ed., III, p. 304; *Asia Major*, II, p. 791.

93. IX.108.11 *vṛṣabháṃ divó.* Thus should be understood also expressions like *pratnáṃ páyaḥ* IX.42.4; *dyumnávat páyaḥ* 66.30; *pīyū́ṣaḥ*

pūṛvyáḥ 110.8 etc.; *sá pūrvyaḥ pavate* 77.2; *pavate pūrvyáḥ kavíḥ* 86.20 This *pūrvyá kaví* cannot be the plant, howsoever one might glorify it, but only the moon.

94. Perhaps VIII.72.10 also :

sincánti námasāvatám uccắcakraṃ párijmānam /
nicīnabāram ákṣitam //

95. Bergaigne, I, p. 166.

96. VIII.41.8 : *sá samudró apīcyàs turó dyā́m iva rohati /*
ní yád āsu yájur dadhé //

The hymn is addressed to Varuṇa.

97. Cf. the designation of the Soma juice as *pratnáṃ páyas* IX.42.4 etc. referred to in n. 93 above.

98. V.41.12 : *śruṇótu na ūrjā́ṃ pátir giraḥ*
sá nábhas tárīyāṅ iṣiráḥ párijmā

"May the lord of nourishments hear our hymns, he who speeds through the atmosphere, the swift wanderer." In so far as the verse refers to Soma, *ūrj* means the same as *pratnáṃ rétas, pratnáṃ páyas*.

99. IX.86.45 : *hárir ghṛtásnuḥ sudṛ́śīko' arṇavó*
jyotírathaḥ pavate rāyá okyàḥ //

100. IX.89.4 : *mádhupṛṣṭhaṃ ghorám ayā́sam áśvam*
ráthe yuñjanty urucakrá ṛṣvám /

101. I.164.30 : *jīvó mṛtásya carati svadhā́bhir*
ámartyo mártyenā sáyoniḥ //

"Living, he moves by the Svadhā offerings (refreshments) to the dead, the immortal one who has the same origin as the mortal."

v. 38 : *ápāṅ prā́ṅ eti svadháyā gṛbhītó*
ámartyo mártyenā sáyoniḥ /
tā́ śáśvantā viṣūcī́nā viyántā
ny ànyaṃ cikyúr ná ní cikyur anyám //

"He goes to the west and to the east, seized by the Svadhā offerings, the immortal one who has the same origin as the mortal. The two (sun and moon) move always in different directions; when men see one, they do not see the other." For its explanation Böhtlingk (BKSGW, 1893, 23.4), with Keith (ZDMG, LXIII, p. 348), has turned to Roth, ZDMG, XLVI, p. 759 ff., according to whom both the verses deal with the body and soul. I do not think that this is true of v. 38. I believe that it is too pedantic to say that *cd* cannot refer to the sun and the moon because occasionally they are seen at the same time. With the exception of a few days, they are *śáśvantā viṣūcī́nā* : one is the light of the day and the other the light of the night. Hence I persist in the view that the verses deal with these two phenomena (see also Pischel, VSt, II, p. 221). The meaning of "soul" is incompatible with pāda *a* since one cannot say *ápāṅ prā́ṅ eti* of the soul. v. 30 is uncertain since pādas *ab* remain unexplained. Do these vv. 30 and 38 belong together at all ?

Sieg, NGGW, 1923, p. 8 refers v. 38 to the sun and translates *svadháyā gṛbhītó* as "led by his divineness"; but *gṛbhītó* does not mean "led" and *mártyenā sáyoniḥ* not "shares his dwelling with the mortal."

102. SBE, XXVI, p. 150, n. 3; see n. 36 above.

103. IX.63.13 : *sómo devó ná sū́ryó 'dribhiḥ pavate sutáḥ |*
dádhānaḥ kaláśe rásam ||
108.9 : *ví kóśaṃ madhyamáṃ yuva*
AV XVIII.4.30 : *kóśaṃ duhanti kaláśaṃ cáturbilam*
íḍāṃ dhenúm...

Cf. the review of Hertel's *Himmelstore* in *Asia Major*, II, p. 791; *Vedische Mythologie*, 1st ed., III, pp. 304-5.

104. AV X.2.31 : *aṣṭácakrā návadvārā devā́nāṃ pū́r ayodhyā́*
tásyāṃ hiraṇyáyaḥ kóśaḥ svargó jyótiṣā́vṛtaḥ ||

105. I.96.5 : *naktoṣā́sā várṇam āmémeyāne*
dhāpáyete śíśum ékaṃ samīcī́ |
dyā́vākṣā́mā rukmó antár antár ví bhāti
devā́ agníṃ dhārayan draviṇodā́m ||

"Night and Dawn, changing their colour, suckle in concert their sole infant. The disc shines between the heaven and earth. The gods protected the Agni Draviṇoḍāḥ."

106. IX.97.2 ; *parīṇasáṃ kṛṇute tigmáśṛṅgo*
dívā hárir dádṛśe náktam ṛjráḥ

"The sharp-horned one brings forth abundance. In the day he appears golden, at night brownish."

107. X.88.6 : *mūrdhā́ bhuvó bhavati náktam agnis*
tátaḥ sū́ryo jāyate prā́tar udyán |

It would make no sense to refer *murdhā́ bhuvó bhavati náktam agníḥ* to the hearth fire or to the altar fire. VI.3.6 : *náktaṃ yá īm aruṣó yó dívā nṝn ámartyo aruṣó yó dívā nṝn*; in any event, it deals with the two great manifestations of Agni. (VS XIII.43 : *ájasram índum aruṣám bhuraṇyúm agním īḍe...sá párvabhir ṛtuśáḥ kálpamānaḥ*). Thus we can easily explain the words of KBr XVIII.9, cited by v. Negelein, *Weltanschauung*, §31, p. 46, as warning against a moon god Varuṇa : *so [yo 'sau tapati] vā eṣo 'paḥ praviśya varuṇo bhavati tasmād vāruṇam ekakapālaṃ puroḍāśaṃ nirvapati* etc. In this connection, we should also refer to AV XIII.3.13 :

sá váruṇaḥ sāyám ágnir bhavati
sá mitró bhavati prātár udyán |

One cannot describe the two facets of Agni more clearly : sun (=Mitra), moon (=Varuṇa).

No value should be attached to the fact that designations of the colour differ; sometimes it is *aruṣá*, sometimes *hári*, at others *śukrá*; these are purely subjective.

108. J. Hertel, IF, XLI, p. 195.

109. VII.55.7 : *sahásraśṛṅgo vṛṣabhó yáḥ samudrā́d udā́carat |*
ténā sahasyènā vayáṃ ní jánān svāpayāmasi ||

Cf. Hopkins, *Epic Mythology*, p. 92; *Rāmāyaṇa* V.5.4 : [*candraḥ*] *sthitaḥ kakudmān iva tīkṣṇaśṛṅgo* etc.

110. VII.19.1.

110a. VI.16.39.

111. VIII.7.9 : *avákolbā udákātmāna óṣadhayaḥ | vyṛṣantu duritáṃ tīkṣṇaśṛṅgyàḥ*. In the ṚV the drink is compared to *vṛṣabhá tigmáśṛṅga* in IX.87.7; X.86.15. See n. 119 below.

112. *prá némasmin dadṛśe sómo antár gopā́ némam āvír asthā́ kṛṇoti |*
sá tigmáśṛṅgaṃ vṛṣabháṃ yúyutsan druhás tasthau bahulé baddhó antáḥ ||

113. Bergaigne, II, p. 469, n. 1, also sees it as accusative plural. Oldenberg's suggestion in *Die Hymnen des Ṛgveda*, II, p. 251 is hardly useful.

114. *kṛśyati candraṃ kṛṣṇapakṣaḥ.*

115. AV XII.3.16: *saptá médhān paśávaḥ paryàgṛhṇan*
yá eṣāṃ jyótiṣmāṅ utá yáś cakárśa |
tráyastriṅśad devátās tā́ṅ sacante
sá naḥ svargám abhí neṣa lokám ||

116. IX.86.43 : *síndhor ucchvāsé patáyantam ukṣáṇam*
hiraṇyapāvā́ḥ paśúm āsu gṛbhṇate |
AV XVIII.3.18.

117. 1.164.4 : *kó dadarśa prathamáṃ jā́yamānam*
asthanvántaṃ yád anasthā́ bíbharti |
anasthā́ is the sun.

118. In the legend of Dadhyañc these bones are employed in a different kind of metaphor. Ludwig, while explaining ṚV X.48.10, has already drawn our attention to I.84.13 (*índro dadhīcó asthábhir vṛtrā́ṇy ápratiṣkutaḥ | jaghā́na*). See also Bergaigne, II, p. 469. In the later mythology it is Dadhīca or Dadhīci out of whose bones the thunderbolt is fashioned. The close connection between Dadhyañc and Soma is suggested by the Vedic saga according to which Soma shows the Aśvins the place of the Madhu. Ludwig's comments on this in *Über die neuesten Arbeiten*, p. 120 ff., are doubtful.

119. On this cf. further IX.70.7, where *śṛ́ṅge háriṇī* are the "yellow horns of the moon." In IX.87.7; X.86.15 the drink is compared to a *vṛṣabhá tigmáśṛṅga.*

120. The same expression is used for Agni in V.2.9; VIII.60.13.

121. W. H. Roscher, *Selene und Verwandtes*, p. 30 ff. discusses the moon in "the shape of a cow or bull" in greater detail.

122. Ed. Stenzler, pp. 44, 22. It should be noted that the position of the moon in India is different from what it is here and there the sickle of the moon is horizontal and not vertical.

123. Ed. Pischel, III.35. I read *sametobhayakoṭir* with the manuscript styled "S" by Pischel.

124. IX.57.2 : *háris tuñjāná ā́yudhā*; IX.89.3; 90.1,6; 96.16.

125. *Śiśupālavadha* IX.25 ff., especially v.31 : "Surrounded by the clusters of stars, he dispersed the hordes of Rākṣasas in the shape of darkness."

126. IX.37.5; 47.2; 48.2; 49.5; 56.1; 61.22, 25, 26; 79.3; 87.2; 88.4; 104.6 110.12. Compare this with AV X.6.10 where Candramas, wearing a Maṇi conquers the fortresses of the Asuras, and AV XIX.27.2 where the moon is explicitly called Vṛtra-killer :

sómas tvā pātv óṣadhībhir nákṣatraiḥ pātu sū́ryaḥ |
mādbhyás tvā candró vṛtrahā́ vā́taḥ prāṇéna rakṣatu ||

127. IX.66.17 : *ugrébhyaś cid ójīyāñ chū́rebhyaś cic chū́rataraḥ.* Occasionally there is a national element involved in these fights. I conclude this from the content of IX.63.14 : *ete dhā́māny ā́ryā śukrā́ ṛtásya dhā́rayā vā́jam...akṣaran.*

128. E.g., IX.59.4; 91.6.

129. *brahmadviṣe tápuṣiṃ hetím asya.*

130. Bergaigne goes beyond what is admissible when he sees the lightning as one of the important forms of Soma in the ṚV. There are very few passages which support this theory, and these few have come down from a different source — from the same source which gave rise to the myth of the bones of Dadhyañc. See n. 118 above.

131. Thus it is said expressly in IX.87.8 :

divó ná vidyút stanáyanty abhraiḥ
sómasya te pavata indra dhā́rā ||

"Like the lightning of the sky that thunders through the clouds, the stream of Soma, O Indra, purifies itself for you."

132. The verse has a different ending in VS XXXIII.90 : *rayíṃ piśáṅgaṃ bahuláṃ puruspṛ́haṃ hárir eti kánikradat |*

133. v. 2 of this hymn is rather obscure. But we should note that vv 3, 4 probably speak of the moon. v. 3 : "May that light yonder, O Gods, never fall from the sky. May we never wander without the friendly light of the moon" (*somyásya śambhúvaḥ śū́ne*). Ludwig, V, p. 443, refers quite rightly *somyá śambhú* to the moon. Likewise v. 4 : "I ask about the next sacrifice. As messenger, he may proclaim it." The proclaimer is probably the moon. (cf. IX.2.10). The hymn itself, or at least its beginning, is a lunar hymn.

134. We can see that the view of the *Chāndogya Upaniṣad* according to which the dead come to the lightning from the moon is not quite incompatible with the real older conceptions.

135. I do not deny that Soma himself is designated as Vajra in isolated verses, nor do I think that this is always meant in a figurative sense. IX.47.3 : *ā́t sóma indriyó ráso vájraḥ sahasrasā́ bhuvat*; 72.7 : *índrasya vájro vṛṣabhó vibhū́vasauḥ | sómo hṛdé pavate;* 77.1 : *eṣá prá kóśe...acikradad índrasya vájro vapuṣo vápuṣṭaraḥ*; 106.3; 111.3. Cf. VIII.100.9. But I think that here a concept which originally developed from the moon in other groups of sagas is transferred to Soma. For this is not otherwise compatible with what the Veda informs us about the god Soma. The other group of sagas is the one which starts from Dadhyañc and his bones. The transference was possible in view of the close connection between Soma and the lightning.

136. Cf. IX.69.3.

137. Bergaigne, I, p. 169 f.

138. The verse is obscure.

139. H. Weller (*Garbe-Festschrift*, p. 55) believes that we should not look for a reference to the god Soma in the form of the moon in IX.70.7. But I think that the number and the frequency of the passages cited do not leave any doubt about this. It is a primitive concept, though unknown among us. By assuming it, we obtain further instances for the double meaning, on which Weller lays stress. There is neither a hyperbole, nor a superlative.

140. In order to make this comprehensive, I have occasionally quoted the same passages completely once again.

141. I translate *vicakṣaṇá* as "all-knowing", but have doubts about its being correct.

142. *vāś*, and not *vaś* "to desire."

143. Also IX.14.6; 30.2, where it is said *iyarti vagnúm* of the self-purifying juice.

144. See p. 10 f. above.

145. IX.26.4; 101.5.

146. I.185.

147. Cf. IX.97.1, 47.

148. IX.67.13 : *vācó jantúḥ kavīnā́m*; 12.6 : *prá vā́cam índur iṣyati samudrásyā́dhi viṣṭápi*; 107.21; 97.34 : *tisró vā́ca īrayati prá váhniḥ*. (Meant here are the voices of the priests, as a comparison with 33.4; 85.7; 95.4, 5 would show). 30.1; 64.9, 25; 72.1; 78.1; 86.33; 106.12; 107.21 etc.

149. *ayáṃ me pītá úd iyarti vā́cam.*

150. Cf. ABr VI.3.3 : *vāg vai subrahmaṇyā / tasyai somo rājā vatsaḥ.*

151. In I.187.9 ff. Soma (Pitu) is called *vātāpi*, i.e., friend of the wind. IX.97.17 : *vicinván bándhūm̐r imā́m̐ ávarām̐ indo vāyū́n*, is obscure.

152. With a slightly different metaphor about the Maruts, the sons of Pṛśni, IX.34.5 : *abhī́m ṛtásya viṣṭápaṃ duhaté pṛ́śnimātaraḥ /*

110.8 : *diváḥ pīyū́ṣaṃ yád ukthyàm*
mahó gāhā́d divá ā́ nír adhukṣata /
índram abhí jā́yamānaṃ sám asvaran //

See also what was said about the well on p. 212 f. above.

153. IX.66.26 : *pávamāno rathī́tamaḥ śubhrébhiḥ śubhráśastamaḥ /*
háriścandro marúdgaṇaḥ //

"Pavamāna, the best of the charioteers, shining brightly through his rays, gleaming golden and accompanied by the host of the Maruts."

154. Geldner, Lindenau : "seer" (ZII, I, p. 34).

155. ZDMG, XXXIX, p. 56 ff. L. v. Schroeder, *Mysterium*, p. 343 : "The friends call me, with their children." But that would be *putravantaḥ*.

156. See e.g., IX.72.6; 102.4; 111.1 etc.

157. Bergaigne, I, pp. 155, 165; II, p. 36 etc.

158. Darmesteter, *Le Zend Avesta*, II, p. 308, deals in great detail with the moon in this association on the basis of the statements of the *Bundahiš*.

159. It cannot be determined in each case whether it is the celestial Soma or the terrestrial one that is meant.

160. As the god is, so is the drink. On the sacrificial place the cows are represented by the milk-drinks and the water that are added to the juice. See Bergaigne, I, p. 206. Here also it is difficult to separate the passages, since the ritual elements and the mythical elements interchange constantly.

161. Foy : "looking through the sacrifice here below." (On this, cf. X.85.4 : *grā́vṇām íc chṛṇván tiṣṭhasi*).

162. The idea of the moon-bull is expressed in many verses of the obscure and mystic hymn AV IX.4.

v. 22 : *piśáṅgarūpo nabhasó vayodhā́*
aindráḥ śúṣmo viśvárūpo na āgan /

On *aindráḥ śúṣmo*, note that in ṚV IX.85.3 Soma is called *ātméndrasya*.

163. Just as the bull roars, so do the cows in return. IX.80.2; 101.8; 107.26 etc. However, the cows are not always the waters or clouds in heaven.

In many passages they are the hymns (of the Maruts) or the voices of the singers.

164. IX.19.5 : *kuvíd vṛṣáṇyántībhyaḥ punānó gárbham ādadhat |*
yā́ḥ śukrám duhaté páyaḥ ||

165. MS I.7.4 (113.5); 10.5 (145.12); II.5.1 (46.1 ff.); III.2.5 (22.12) etc.; ŚBr VI.1.2.4.

166. In connection with the designation of the moon as *retodhā́*, it should be noted that in the *Avesta* he is called gaočiθra, "containing the semen of the bull." *Yašt* VII.1.3 etc. Accordingly, the saga preserved in the *Bundahiš* which narrates that when the bull dies its semen is preserved in the moon and that different types of animals come out of this semen, is based on an old tradition. Spiegel, *Eranische Altertumskunde*, II, p. 70. Darmesteter, *Ormazd et Ahriman*, § 125, 127. SBE, IV, p. 226, n. 4. Gray, *Spiegel Memorial Volume*, 1908, p. 160 ff.

167. Böhtlingk, SBKSGW, 1890, p. 77 of the offprint, translates "paternally inclined." Hertel, *Weisheit der Upanischaden*, p. 159, "from the lord of the world of the fathers, who was procreated anew in fifteen forms."

168. *Kauṣītaki Brāhmaṇa Up.* I.2.

169. Hence, it said of Soma in another image that he opens the cowshed.

IX.86.23 : *sóma gotrám áṅgirobhyo 'vṛṇor ápa |*

102.8 : *krátvā śukrébhir akṣábhir ṛṇor ápa vrajáṃ divá|*

"Through your insight and with your radiant eyes, you opened the shed of heaven." 108.6; 87.3, 8, 9 or IX.90.4 where it is said that he wins the waters.

170. Through Soma's association with the waters we can explain I.23.20 : *apsú me sómo abravīd antár víśvāni bheṣajā́.* (X.9.6).

171. TMBr VI.10.16 : *prāsya dhārā akṣarann iti divo vṛṣṭiṃ cyāvayati vṛṣṇaḥ sutasyaujasa ity antarikṣāt*; cf. also 18. We should compare the concept of the Ṛṣi or bull who was "milked" by the Maruts, a concept which occurs in verses like IX.54.1 (see p. 214 above) and which goes back to the same foundation. Hence, we can explain why in other verses like IX.85.9 the "milk of heaven" is mentioned immediately after the bull of heaven. The moon is called *sahásradhāra* or *śatádhāra* because of the waters which he causes to flow.

172. See Bergaigne, I, p. 165 f.

173. Pischel, VSt, I, p. 87.

174. See pp. 210, 212 above.

175. We can see that *yúvā kavír góṣu, apsú drapsó vāvṛdhānáḥ* and also *ékam ákṣi* (IX.9.4 : *sá...nadyò ajinvad adrúhaḥ | yā́ ékam ákṣi vāvṛdhúḥ*) are mythological synonyms for the young waxing moon. The assumption that Soma can be designated as the son of the waters because he thrives as a plant is not adequate. If that were the case, how could the plant be designated as King, bull of the waters, drop, Kavi !

176. VS VIII.26.

177. Pp. 177-186.

178. *Die altgriechischen Kulte*, I, p. 89.

179. *Gesammelte Abhandlungen*, p. 219.

180. v. Bradke, *Dyaus Asura*, p. 82, thinks that Agni Apāṃ napāt belongs

to the pantheon of the Aryan prehistory,that is to say to the pre-Zarathustran Iranians also.

181. *Essays*, tr. Franke, 2nd ed., II, p. 74.

182. Commentary on II.35.1 (vol. IV, No. 184, p. 181).

183. *Ormazd et Ahriman*, p. 34. Likewise SBE, XXIII, p. 6 n.

184. *Arische Periode*, p. 193. See also Kuhn-Schleicher's *Beiträge*, IV, p. 455.

185. In the *Manuel pour étudier le Sanscrit védique*, it is said more clearly, s. v. Napāt : "a special incarnation of Agni envisaging the son of the waters (lightning born from the cloud)."

186. Gray, ARW, III, p. 18 ff.; H. W. Magoun, JAOS, XIX, p. 137 ff; AJPh, XXI, p. 274 ff. Oldenberg, RdV, 2nd ed., p. 117 ff. : "Because of the increasingly popular speculations about Agni as water-born, and under the influence of a tendency, particularly typical of Agni, what was originally a water-demon became partially merged, as it could hardly be avoided, with Agni, and he preserved his original nature in the other part." This assumption is neither necessary nor correct. From time immemorial it is the moon himself who has a special connection to water. See *Sūryasiddhānta* XII.24 : 'the sun or moon are resp. of the nature of fire and water," and the passages from the Purāṇas cited above.

187. Quite far-fetched explanation in AJPh, XXI, p. 279 : "the unwavering (unmovable ?) god' (cf. the direct fixed course of 'chain lightning' with the crooked paths of other bolts)."

188. See p. 87 above. I add further the following examples. *Kathāsaritsāgara*. ed. NSP, III.5.28, p. 81 : *nisarganiyataṃ yāsāṃ vidyutām iva cāpalam*. The lexicographers style the lightning as *calā*, *cañcalā*, *capalā*, *caṭulā*, Pischel, VSt, I, p. 304. Cf. MBh III.122.10; 124.4 : *lelihan jihvayā raktaṃ vidyuccapalalolayā*.

189. Passages like ṚV VIII.100.9 (see p. 88 above) are, as far as I can see, rare. Oldenberg, ZDMG, XXXIX, p. 57, n. 3 refers to MBh, ed. Calcutta, V.328 ff.

190. On *śukrébhiḥ śíkvabhiḥ*, cf. IX.15.5 : *rukmíbhir īyate | śukrébhir aṅśubhiḥ*.

191. On *dīdā́yānidhmó...apsú*, cf. *vṛ̥thā pā́jāṅsi kṛṇute nadī́ṣv ā́* IX.76.1; 88.5b.

192. On *ghtánirṇij*, cf. *ūrjā́ṃ páti*, *ghṛtásnu*, *svadhā́vat* on p. 215 above.

193. Cf. pāda *ab* with

IX.31.5 : *túbhyaṃ gā́vo ghṛtáṃ páyo...duduhré ákṣitam |*
70.1 : *trír asmai saptá dhenávo duduhre*
satyā́m āśíraṃ pūrvyé vyòmani |

Cf. pāda *c* with the epithets of Soma like *ūrjā́ṃ páti* etc. Cf. pāda *d* with the verses dealing with the light of Soma, p. 207 above.

194. II.35.8 : *vayā́ íd anyā́ bhúvanāny asya*
prá jāyate vīrúdhaś ca prajā́bhiḥ ||

Geldner : "The other beings and the plants with their offspring are born as his branches."

195. Ludwig, V, p.391 remarks that in Apāṃ napāt we can see the *abhimānidevatā* of Soma.

196. VS VIII.24 : *agnér ánīkam apá ā́viveśa*
apā́ṃ nápāt pratirákṣann asuryám |
damédame samídhaṃ yakṣy agne
práti te jihvā́ ghṛtám úccaraṇyat
(KŚS X.8.22).

197. For more precise information see Caland-Henry, *L'Agniṣṭoma*, pp. 120, 121.

198. ABr II.19.1.

199. *Yasna* I.5; VI.4; *Yašt* II.4, 5 etc.

200. *Zoastrische Studien*, p. 181.

201. KZ, XXV, p. 390, n. 4.

202. The metre is not quite correct. Geldner (KZ, XXV, p. 471) drops *yō daršiš. xvarənō* means radiance, and according to *Yašt* XIII. 65 etc. it is *mazdadātəm*; hence we should add *mazda* to it. Moreover, we miss any mention of the waters after *apaṃ napå* and *vāta xvarəno*. The waters must be implied by *awž* (=*āpas*). Perhaps it is better to read with J 10 *aiwiž* (=*adbhis*), "the wind with the waters." Bartholomae, *Grundriss der iranischen Philologie*, I, p. 17 equates *awž* with Sanskrit *ambhas*; Geldner with *avō* (KZ, XXVIII, p. 189). Fritz Wolff : "and the glory resting in water."

203. *xšaθrīm*. The derivation from xšaθri "woman" is started by Windischmann (*Zoroastrische Studien*, p. 178), who did not like the tautology between *xšaētəm* and *xšaθrīm*, if one equates the latter with *xsaθriyəm*. Thus it is understood by others also, eg., Wilhelm who renders it as "with numerous women" ("Contribution *à* l'interpretation...," *Muséon*, 1885, p. 17). Darmesteter, "the lord of females." Also Gray, ARW, III, p. 41. However, Bartholomae's explanation (*Altiranisches Wörterbuch*, p. 548) is dubious.

204. Windischmann, op. cit., p. 180.

205. See n. 166 above.

206. ṚV II.31.6; 35.1; VII.47.2; MS I.11.1 (162.3) etc.

207. AV VII.39 reads *payasám* for *vāyásam*.

208. Ibid., *vṛṣabhám*, which is a better reading. (Thus also TS III.1.11).

209. Ibid., *vṛṣṭyā́*.

210. Ibid., *ā́ no goṣṭhé rayiṣṭhā́ṃ sthāpayāti*.

211. *mádhumatīr apó dāḥ*. Compare these words also with ṚV VII.96.5 :
yé te sarasva ūrmáyo mádhumanto ghṛtaścútaḥ |
tébhir no 'vitā́ bhava ||
and IV.58.5 : *etā́ arṣanti hṛ́dyāt samudrā́t* or v. 11.

212. The manifestation of Sarasvat is not adequately explained by the remark of Oldenberg in his *Die Religion des Ṛgveda*, 2nd ed., p. 243, n. 3.

213. AV IX.4.9 speaks of the bull which is conceived at times as the sun and at others as the moon : *daivī́r viśaḥ páyasvān ā́ tanoṣi tvā́m índraṃ tvā́ṃ sárasvantam āhuḥ*.

214. VII.96.2 : *sā́ no bodhy avitrī́ marútsakhā*. Maruts and Sarasvatī are mentioned together in III.54.13, and Maruts, Sarasvatī and Bṛhaspati in V.43.10-12. MS III.16.2 (184.12) : *sarasvatī saha rudrair na āvīt*. (In V.52.9 the name Paruṣṇī seems to be transferred to her). Bergaigne, I, p. 326. TMBr XXV.10.11 : *sarasvatyā vai devā ādityam astabhnavan | sā*

nāyacchat / sābhyavlīyata / tasmāt sā nyubhjimatīva / taṃ bṛhatyāstabhnuvan etc.

215. The milky way is regarded as a stream or a sea in the sky, Andree, *Ethnographische Parallelen*, p. 110. That would be another explanation of the source of rain.

216. *utkhāya gāḍhatamasaṃ ghanakālam ugram /*
rāmo daśāsyam iva saṃbhṛtabandhujīvaḥ //

217. Stenzler, *Brahmavaivartap.* spec., p. 22, v. 10.

218. Comm. *caramau dehātmānau sthūlasūkṣmadehau yasya so 'khaṇḍaprakāśo yogī yathā.*

219. Ed. Pischel, p. 75 :
pādanyāsaṃ kṣitidharaguror mūrdhni kṛtvā sumeroḥ
krāntaṃ yena kṣayitatamasā madhyamaṃ dhāma viṣṇoḥ /
so 'yaṃ candraḥ patati gaganād alpaśeṣair mayūkhaiḥ...

220. See the legend in TMBr XI.3.9.

221. *nakṣatragrahaviprāṇāṃ vīrudhāṃ cāpyaśeṣataḥ /*
somaṃ rājye 'dadad brahmā yajñānāṃ tapasām api //
Cf. AV XII.3.31 : *oṣadhīr...yāsāṃ somaḥ pari rājyaṃ babhūva.*

222. *candramās tu smṛtaḥ somaḥ tasyātmā hy oṣadhīgaṇaḥ.*
XXXI.38 : *tārābhimānī vijñeyas tṛtīyaḥ parivatsaraḥ /*
somaḥ sarvauṣadhīpatir...

223. For further examples, see PW, s.v. *oṣadhi.*

224. E.g., MS I.10.9 (149.11); II.1.6 (7.13); 5.1 (46.8) etc. ŚBr VIII.4.3.17 etc. Likewise AV II.10.2; VI.15.3; 96.1 etc.

225. For detailed source material on the moon and vegetation, see Frazer, The *Golden Bough*, I, p.318. n.2. Cf. *Avesta*, *Yašt* VII.4; *yaṭ mā̊ŋhəm raoxšne tāpayeiti mišti urvaranąm zairigaonanąm zarmaēm paiti zəmāδa uzuxšyeinti,* "When the moon spreads warmth with his light in spring, all the green plants grow out of the earth."

226. See below the section : Kavi Soma, pp. 246, 248.

227. VII.37.1 : *abhí tripṛṣṭhaíḥ sávaneṣu sómair*
máde suśiprā mahábhiḥ pṛṇadhvam //
I translate as "threefold".

228. ***tŕīn sá mūrdhnó ásuraś cakra ārábhe.***

229. Kaegi, *Ṛgveda*, 2nd ed., n. 308; Negelein, *Weltanschauung*, p. 45 (§31).

230. Tylor, *Anfänge der Kultur*, II, pp. 69, 70; Rhys Davids, Hibbert Lectures, p. 248 ff.; Plutarch, *De Facie in Orbe Lunae*, Cap. 28, p. 943A; 943C; Jamblich (ap. Stob. ecl., ed., Wachsmuth, I.49.39) deals with the Gr. *phukhai peri tēn selēnēn.* I owe the two references to Clemens Baeumker. Cf. also Franz Cumont, *La Théologie Solaire*, p. 18, n. 3.

231. ŚBr II.4.2.12 : *pitṛdevatyo vai somaḥ*; II.6.1.4 : *pitṛmat*; III.2.3.17; IV.4.2.2 etc. MS I.10.3 (158.7), Cf. further MS I.11.3 (163.7) : *ā mā ganta pitaro viśvarūpā ā mā somo amṛtatvena gamyāt;* IV.7.2 (94.15 ff.); IV.2.1 (22.15, 17) : *asau vā ādityo devānāṃ cakṣuḥ...candramā vai pitṝṇāṃ cakṣuḥ;* ŚŚS III.16.2 etc. TBr I.6.8.2 : *saṃvatsaro vai somaḥ pitṛmān.*

232. X.57.3 : *máno nv ā́ huvāmahe nārāśaṅsena sómena /*
pitṝṇā́ṃ ca manmabhiḥ // (see p. 73 above).

233. I.91.6; VIII.48.4, 7; IX.4.6; 91.6.

234. IX.108.3 : *daivyā jánimāni...amṛtatvā́ya ghoṣáyaḥ.*

235. Oldenberg's translation in his *Die Hymnen des Ṛgveda*, II,p. 188 is better: "through whom they...for the sake of the cows...have burnt the mountain." IX.96.11 also belongs here.

236. MS IV.7.2 (95.3) : *sāmadevatyo vai somaḥ.* (TS VI.6.7.1 *saumyaḥ*).

237. Differently Aufrecht, *Ṛgveda*, 2nd ed., II, p. xxxviii; Bloomfield, WZKM, XVII, p. 163.

238. I.91.1 does not belong here :

...tváṃ rájiṣṭham ánu neṣi pánthām
táva práṇītī pitáro na indo /
devéṣu rátnam abhajanta dhī́rāḥ //

"You lead along the most correct path. Under your guidance, O Indu, our wise fathers distributed their treasures among the gods." For this verse refers to the times of sacrifice which the moon taught the Manes to observe, but not to the dwelling of the Manes in the realm of light.

239. L. Scherman, "Die Sterne im indogermanischen Seelenglauben." *Am Urquell*, VI, p. 5 ff., Materialien, p. 29.

240. The texts are fond of representing the stars as living beings. I note the following metaphors.

Stars are the wives of the moon. ŚBr IX.4.1.9 : *candramā gandharvas tasya nakṣatrāṇy apsarasa iti candramā ha gandharvo nakṣatrair apsarobhir mithunena* etc. This conception is popular in the later period also. The constellation Rohiṇī is regarded as the beloved of the moon.

Cows (*gāvaḥ*) ṚV I.154.6 :

tā́ vāṃ vā́stūny uśmasi gámadhyai
yátra gā́vo bhū́riśṛṅgā ayā́saḥ /

Perhaps also VII.36.1 :

prá bráhmaitu sádanād ṛtásya
ví raśmíbhiḥ sasṛje sū́ryo gā́ḥ /

because the parallel passage, III.54.19 :

śṛṇótu naḥ pṛthiví dyaúr utā́paḥ
sū́ryo nákṣatrair urv àntárikṣam //

shows the sun and the stars in a close association.

According to Bergaigne (I, p. 157), VIII.55.2 (Vāl.7.2) belongs here :

śatáṃ śvetā́so ukṣáṇo diví tā́ro ná rocante /

Moreover, I believe that the cows which Bṛhaspati and Indra discover are, in several passages, the stars. II.24.14 : *yó gā́ udā́jat sá divé vi cābhajat*; X.67.4, 6. The name of the annual sacrifice *gavām ayanam* means the "motion of the stars."

Birds — I.105.11 :

suparṇā́ etá āsate mádhya āródhane diváḥ /
té sedhanti pathó vṛ́kaṃ tárantaṃ yahvátīr apáḥ //

"The birds sit there in the middle of the vault of heaven. They drive the wolf, who crosses the swift waters, off the path" (eclipse, or lunar eclipse?).

The two difficult verses, I.164.21 and 22, may find a place here since the Suparṇas mentioned there are not the priests (Ludwig) or metres (Haug), but the stars.

21 : *yátrā suparṇā́ amṛ́tasya bhāgám*
ánimeṣaṃ vidáthābhisváranti |
inó víśvasya bhúvanasya gopā́ḥ
sá mā dhī́raḥ pā́kam atrā́ viveśa ||
22 : *yásmin vṛkṣé madhvádaḥ suparṇā́ḥ*
niviśánte súvate cā́dhi víśve |
tásyéd āhuḥ píppalaṃ svādv ágre
tán nón naśad yaḥ pitáraṃ ná véda ||

"Where the birds hasten ceaselessly towards sacrifices for the share in the nectar, there the strong (moon) is the protector of the entire world. He, the wise one, entered into me, the simpleton" (i.e., I have drunk of him. Cf. *rājānaṃ candramasaṃ bhakṣayāmi*, pp. , 199, 201 above).

"The tree on which the sweetmeat-eating birds fly in and out, upon its top, they say, is the sweet Pippala fruit. One who does not know the father does not attain it." The sweet Pippala fruit is the moon.

vv. 21 and 22 are almost quite parallel. *amṛ́tasya bhāgá* of the first corresponds to the *madhu* in *madhvádaḥ* of the second verse. The *suparṇā́ḥ* (stars, Manes) hasten to the moon (motion of the constellations) in order to obtain their share of nectar there. *amṛ́tasya bhāgám* is governed by *abhisváranti*, and the parallelism between this word and *niviśánte* and *súvate* shows that this word does not have the sense of "to sing in praise," but that of *abhigacchanti*, as given by the commentators often. *ánimeṣam* "ceaselessly" is quite suited to a verb of motion, but "to rush towards" would also be possible. *vidátha* is certainly accusative plural. Pāda *d* of v. 22 is not clear to me. The explanation of Hauer is not acceptable, nor the translation of Geldner, which appears to be too speculative (tree = knowledge).

Stars are designated as guards in I.95.9.

As scouts in I.33.8 (see Bergaigne, I, pp. 158, 160) etc. They run away like thieves at the break of dawn, I.50.2.

As chariots in IX.96.1 :

prá senā́nīḥ śū́ro ágre ráthānāṃ
gavyánn eti hárṣate asya sénā |

"The leader of the host (moon) goes in the forefront of the chariots, longing for victory. His host rejoices."

241. ZDMG, IX. p. 237 ff.

242. OST, V, p. 319.

243. *Ṛgveda*, 2nd ed., p. 216.

244. *Der vedische Mythus des Yama*, p. 92.

245. I, p. 83 f.

246. Oldenberg, RdV, 2nd ed., p. 534.

247. X.85.19 : *prá candrámās tirate dīrghám ā́yuḥ*; X.107.2.

248. *Kumārasaṃbhava* VIII.58 : *nūnam unnamati yajvanāṃ patiḥ śārvarasya tamaso niṣiddhaye.*

249. X.85.19 : *bhāgáṃ devébhyo vi dadhāty āyán.*

250. Similar is the juxtaposition in AV XIX.43. There Agni and medhā, Vāyu and prāṇa, Sūrya and cakṣus, Candra and manas, Soma and payas are grouped together. Cf. also Deussen, *Sechzig Upanischaden*, Index, s.v. Mond, and Jacob, *Concordance of the Upanishads*, s.v. *candramas.*

251. See I.105.4; IX.86.7 : *yajñásya ketúḥ*; 10 : *jyótir yajñásya*; IX.2.10.
252. IX.7.4; 9.1; 92.3; 94.3; 107.6, 28 etc.
253. IV.27.1; IX.81.2; 95.2; 97.7; 108.3.
254. IX.97.34, 36, 37; 95.5.
255. Bergaigne, I, p. 300, n. 2.
256. IX.85.4 : *urúṃ no gātúṃ kṛṇu.*
257. MBh XII.47.39.
258. The case is different in the verse of *Mahāvastu* VI.35.8, cited by Oldenberg, NGGW, 1915, p. 201, while opposing my reference to the above passage.
259. KZ, I, p. 543 ff.
260. *Indogermanische Mythen*, I. Gandharven-Kentauren.
261. *Griechische Götter und Heroen*, p. 69 ff.
262. *Zur Bedeutung von Gandharva*, Breslau 1906 (offprint from the *84. Jahresbericht der Schlesischen Gesellschaft für vaterländische Kultur*). I do not agree completely with Windisch, who has stated his views in the meantime in his *Buddhas Geburt*, p. 14 ff. J. J. Meyer takes up the equation with *garbha* again in his *Rechtsschriften*, p. 375. However, I refer to my work cited above.
263. JPTS, 1885, p. 14.
264. Oldenberg, *Reden des Buddha*, München, p. 297.
265. According to Alexander Wesselofsky (*Beiträge zur Erklärung des russischen Heldenepos*), this word reached Europe and has its counterpart in Slavonic. This I gather from W. Nehring's article on "Die russische Volksepik" (*Mitteilungen der Schlesischen Gesellschaft für Volkskunde*, XV, 1906.)
266. ṚV X.136.6 : *apsarásāṃ gandhárvāṇāṃ mṛgáṇāṃ cárane cáran |*
10.4 : *gandharvó apsv ápyā ca yóṣā*
IX.78.3 : *samudríyā apsaráso manīṣíṇām*
ā́sīnā antár abhí sómaṃ akṣaran |

On X.11.2 : *rápad gandharvī́r*, cf. Pischel, VSt, I, p. 183 ff.

Ludwig, *Über Methode bei* **Interpretation des Ṛgveda, p. 61.**

267. VSt, I, p. 79.
268. On this, cf. also ŚBr VI.3.1.19 : *asau vā ādityo divyo gandharvaḥ*. TMBr XX.15.2 speaks of three Gandharvas : *trayo gandharvās teṣām eṣā bhaktir agneḥ pṛthivī vāyor antarikṣam asāv ādityasya dyauḥ.*
269. The moon and the nakṣatras are often mentioned in this relationship of husband and wives. MS II.2.7 (21.5) : *prajāpatir vai somāya rājñe duhitṝr adadān nakṣatrāṇi*; I.6.9 (100.9).
270. In *Nirukta* VI.28 that water is called *vātāpya.*
271. This mode of expression is not limited to this passage alone. E.g., ŚBr IX.4.1.7 : *agnir ha gandharva oṣadhibhir apsarobhir mithunena sahoccakrāma.* On the other hand it is said again at I.1.1.20 : *yoṣā vā āpo vṛṣāgniḥ.*
272. Cf. IX.9.3 : *sá sūnúr mātárā śúcir...arocayat.*
273. Bergaigne, II, p. 38 ff. refers this hymn to Soma; likewise Ludwig, IV, p. 158. v.2 : *samudrā́d ūrmím úd iyarti véno*, "the moon rise" (see p. 213 above).
274. *Nirukta*, p. 145.

275. *Indogermanische Mythen*, I. Gandharven-Kentauren, p. 155. Quite rightly contested by Bergaigne.

276 : Further AV II.1.2 (VS XXXII.9; TĀr X.1.3):

prá tád voced amṛ́tasya vidvā́n
gandharvó dhā́ma paramáṃ gúhā yát |
tríṇi padā́ni níhitā gúhāsya
yás tā́ni véda sá pitúṣ pitā́sat ||

The Gandharva of this verse is probably not different from the one in AV II.2.1. The three places which belong to him who knows the amṛta and proclaims it remind us of the wording of ṚV VI.44.23: *ayám* [*índuḥ*] *tridhā́tu divi rocanéṣu tritéṣu vindad amṛ́taṃ nígūḍham*...Lindenau (ZII, I, p. 33 ff.) sees Sūrya in the Gandharva of AV II.1.2, which, in principle, would be possible. The Apsarases, with whom Gandharva is united in II.2.3, belong, however, to the moon and not to Sūrya, who, moreover, does not represent the mental element as much as the former does. I would translate AV X.7.11: *yátra tápaḥ parākrámya vratáṃ dhāráyaty úttaram* as "where he, conquering the Tapas, takes upon himself a higher vow." (e.g. as Vrātya. On this cf. J. W. Hauer, *Anfänge der Yogapraxis*, p. 172).

277. *taṃ somam āhriyamāṇaṃ gandharvo viśvāvasuḥ pary amuṣṇāt sa tisro rātrīḥ parimuṣito 'vasat tasmāt tisro rātrīḥ krītaḥ somo vasati.* Therefore, he is mentioned in TS I.2.9.1 next to *pariparin, paripanthin* and the "wicked wolves." Cf. MS III.7.3 (77.14). In this connection it should be noted that at the beginning of the purchase of Soma it is said : "O God Sūrya, we want to buy Soma" (see p. 217 above). See also VS V.39 : *deva savitar eṣa te somas taṃ rakṣasva mā tvā dabhan*; VIII.1 : *viṣṇa urugāyaiṣa te somas taṃ rakṣasva mā tvā dabhan.* Further MS I.3.9 (33.9) : *viṣṇos tvorukrame gṛhṇāmi viṣṇa urukramaiṣa te somas taṃ rakṣasva.* The view of *Tāṇḍya Brāhmaṇa* VI.9.22 is different.

278. X.139.4 : *viśvā́vasuṃ soma gandharvám ā́po*
dadṛśúṣīs tád ṛténā vy ā̀yan |
tád anvávaid índro rárahāṇá āsām
pári sū́ryasya paridhī́ṅr apaśyat ||

279. Presumably *vaṅkū́*. Geldner, VSt II, pp. 164, 258 : "the winged steeds of Vāta, who run along the curves" (following Franke, WZKM, VIII, p. 242, who attributes the same meaning to Vedic *vaṅkū* as the Pāli *vaṅka* "bird" and changes to "the flying winged animals (winged steeds) of Vāta").

If *b* were an independent sentence, then we must expect an independent word on the analogy of *tudát* (*a*) *váhat* (*c*) *tsárad* (*d*). However, *ab* together form a sentence (subordinate clause). It would be strange if two accusatives which are incompatible from the point of view of the meaning are governed by the same word one after the other. Hence, I assume for *vaṅkū* a different meaning other than steed or bird; roughly *todana* or *kaśā* : "As he drove Etaśa with the winged whip of the wind (with the speed of the wind)" etc.

280. Lanman, *Noun Inflection*, p. 580. Collitz, BKIS, VII, p. 182, Brunnhofer, KZ, XXV, p. 367; on the liturgy, see Bergaigne, JA, 1889, p. 177.

281. See also VII.19.2.

282. *Indogermanische Mythen*, I. Gandharven-Kentauren, p. 5.

283. *Vāyu Purāṇa* VIII. 167 assigns *gāndharvaṃ sthānam* to the *śūdrajātīnām praticāreṇa tiṣṭhatām.*

284. ŚBr XI.2.3.7 : ...*tad yajñaṃ tanvānān ṛṣīn gandharvā upaniṣedus te ha sma saṃinidadhatīdaṃ vā atyarīricann idam ūnam akrann iti / sa yadaiṣāṃ yajñaḥ saṃtasthe 'thainān̄s tad darśayāṃ cakrur idaṃ vā atyarīricatedam ūnam akarteti.* In the JBr (Hans Oertel, JAOS, XXVIII, 1907, p. 81 ff.; Caland, AKM, XII.1, 1903, p. 26) a *triśīrṣa gandharvo* helps Uśanas, the leader of the Asuras, to reach the "immortal world of the Gandharvas."

285. XI.5.1.13 : *na vai sa manuṣyeṣv agner yajñīyā tanūr asti yayeṣṭvāsmākam ekaḥ sy ād iti.* Of the other passages, mention may be made of III.9.3.18.

286. Particularly AV IV.37; VIII.6.1 ff. L. v. Schroeder, *Griechische Götter und Heroen,* p. 70, states : "Accordingly, they appear as long-haired shaggy semi-beastly beings with hair all over the body, who become a danger to men in many ways, cause madness and so on, but, above all, they are lecherous monsters who haunt the females, and must be exorcised through effective formulas and herbs (particularly the goat's horn, *ajaśṛṅgī*)." TS III. 4.8.4 : *gandharvāpsaraso vā etam unmādayanti ya unmādayati*; ŚBr XIV.6.3.1 : *patañjalasya kāpyasya...duhitā gandharvagṛhītā*; *Daśakumāracarita,* p. 71 : *vāyugrasta*=mad.

287. Op. cit., pp, 94, 96.

288. Foy, KZ, XXXIV, p. 229, n. 1, objects to the translation "work" but he himself says that they are the protectors and increasers of Soma, which can, after all, be regarded as their work, if one does not want to take v. 7 into account.

289. V.58.7 : *bhárteva gárbhaṃ svám ic chávo dhuḥ.* Of Vā̃yu, ŚBr II.6.3.7 says : *ayaṃ vai vāyur yo 'yaṃ pavata eṣa vā idaṃ sarvaṃ prapyāyayati yad idaṃ kiṃ ca varṣati.* TBr III.9.17.5 : *vāyavyā garbhāḥ.*

290. IX.113.3 : *parjányavṛddhaṃ mahiṣáṃ*
táṃ sū́ryasya duhitā́bharat /
táṃ gandhārvā́ḥ práty agṛbhṇan
táṃ sóme rásam ā́dadhuḥ //

291. In AV IV.4.1 the Gandharva digs out the *óṣadhiṃ śepahárṣiṇīm.*

292. *tvā́m uśíjaḥ prathamā́ agṛbhṇata.*

293. *Meghadūta,* vv. 44, 76. Also the legend about the Vāc being with the Gandharvas at one time suits the wind gods.

294. *Harivaṃśa* 12493, 265 (PW, s.v. vāyu) : *gandhānāṃ caiva sarveṣāṃ bhūtānām aśarīriṇām...vāyur īśaḥ.* MS II.5.2 (49.13) : *vāyur evāsya taṃ gandhaṃ surabhim akaḥ.*

295. AV XII.1.23; ŚBr IX.4.1.4 : *gandharvāpsarobhyo juhoti gandharvāpsaraso hi bhūtvodakrāmann atho gandhena ca vai rūpeṇa ca gandharvāpsaraś caranti.* See also AV VIII.10.27.

296. MS III.10.1 (109.10) : *suvān̄ nabhrāḍ aṅghāre bambhārā ity ete vai devānāṃ somarakṣaya etebhyo vā adhi cchandān̄si somam āharan̄s te somapīthena vyārdhyata / ta etāni dvitīyāni nāmāny adhatta maṅgalecchāyai somapītho nā upanamād iti / tasmād ete dvināmānas te vā anvāyan̄s te na prāpnuvan̄s tasmād ete 'tihāya vasatkriyante.* See also III.7.7 (84.16); 1.2.5 (14.11). In AV IV.34.3 it is said that one who prepares a particular type of food rejoices "*gandharvaiḥ somyebhiḥ.*"

297. ŚBr III.3.3.11 : *atha somakrayaṇān anudiśati svāna bhāja āṅghāre bambhāre hasta suhasta kṛśānav ete vaḥ somakrayaṇās tān rakṣadhvaṃ mā vo dabhann iti dhiṣṇyānāṃ vā ete bhājanenaitāni vai dhiṣṇyānāṃ nāmāni tāny evaibhya etad anvadikṣat;* III.6.2.9, 17; VS V.32; TS VI.1.10.5 : *ete vā amuṣmiṅ loke somam arakṣan / tebhyo 'dhi somam āharan / tam anvāyan* etc. In TS I.2.7 and MS I.2.5 (14.12) the names of the guards of Soma are slightly different. They seem to have been borrowed from different myths and put together by the scholiasts. (cf. p. 164 above, and the previous note).

298. ŚBr III.6.2.19, 20; IV.4.2.7.

299. *samayā.*

300. See Appendix I.

301. See Eggeling, SBE, XXVI, p. 288, n. 1.

302. *yāṃ diśaṃ vāyur eti tāṃ diśaṃ vṛṣṭir anveti;* ṚV I 122.3 : *vāto apā́ṃ vṛ́ṣaṇvān.*

303. The association of the two has become a stereotype, e.g., in AV X.9.9; XI.6.4; 7.27; 9.16, 24 etc. From their connection to the Apsarases and from their character as gods of fertility arises their title to all women. They are called *strī́bhāga* AV VIII.6.19; *yoṣitkāma* ŚBr III.2.4.3; 9.3.20; *strīkāma* MS III.7.3 etc. The young wife remains in the charge of Viśvāvasu until the young husband approaches her and takes his place ṚV X.85.22, 40; 41; AV XIV.2.35.36. In AV XIV.2.9 the Gandharvas and Apsarases are implored for their favours towards the young wife.

304. *vā́to vā máno vā gandharvā́ḥ saptáviṅśatiḥ /*
té agré 'śvam ayuñjaṅs té asmin javám ādadhuḥ //
ŚBr V.1.4.8; TS I.7.7.

305. Among others, see Weber, *Die vedischen Nachrichten von den Naxatra*, II, p. 274 ff.; L. Scherman, "Die Sterne im indogermanischen Seelenglauben," *Am Urquell*, VI, p. 5 ff.

306. Weber, op. cit., p. 269.

307. Stenzler on ĀśvGS I.14.2.

308. In the ṚV the Nakṣatras appear to have been known under different names, although very few passages can be taken into consideration. A study of ṚV IX.66.2 leads me to the conclusion that "lunar mansion" can be one of the meanings of *dhā́man*. IF, XLIV, p. 143 ff. (see p. 208 above).

IX.66.2 : *tā́bhyāṃ víśvasya rājasi yé pávamāna dhā́manī /*
pratīcī́ soma tasthátuḥ //

I translate this differently from my predecessors : "The double constellation which rose, with that, O Soma Pavamāna, you rule over the universe." See also v.3 of this hymn :

pári dhā́mānī yā́ni te tvā́ṃ somāsi viśvátaḥ /
pávamāna ṛtúbhiḥ kave //

where the *dhā́mānī* can be interpreted similarly as constellations, whom Soma visits "according to seasons" (*pari-as*). Oldenberg, *Die Hymnen des Ṛgveda*, II presumes to see the cycle of the Nakaṣtras in *víbhinnaḥ pradhíḥ* in X.138.6 *cd.*

309. *Ormazd et Ahriman*, p. 215, n. 1.

310. On the concept of this *zairipāšan* in the later literature, see Spiegel, *Trad. Lit.*, p. 339; West, *Pahlavi Texts*, II, p. 369 ff.; Darmesteter, SBE, XXIII, p. 63n.

311. E. H. Meyer, *Indogermanische Mythen*, I. Gandharven-Kentauren, p. 12.

312. Ibid., p. 177.

313. ṚV IV.27.3; IX.77.2 (see p. 192 above); ABr III.26 etc.

314. I.155.2.

315. I.112.21.

316. X.64.8. This recalls to mind the hunter *arbuda mṛgaya māyin* in VIII.3.19 etc., whom Indra conquers, and on the other hand, *ərəxša*, the best of the Aryan archers in *Yašt* VIII.6, 37. On these two see, Nöldke, ZDMG, XXXV, p. 445.

317. E. H. Meyer, op. cit., pp. 155, 179.

318. *Avesta, traduit*, 1st ed., II, p. 76; *De l'exégèse et de la correction des textes Avesta*, pp. 108, 159. Spiegel, *Arische Periode*, p. 224.

319. ISt, II, pp. 313, 314.

320. MSt, I, p. 151.

321. *Ormazd et Ahriman*, p. 100; SBE, IV, p. lii, n. 1.

322. Kuhn, op. cit., p. 152.

323. *Bundahiš* 27.4. Darmesteter, *Ormazd et Ahriman*, p. 140.

324. KZ, XXVIII, p. 189.

325. *Yasna* 57.19 : *sraosem...yazamaide yim yazata haomo frāšmiš baēšazyō srīrō xšaθryō zāiridōiθrō barəzište paiti barəzahi...*The next paragraph (20) does not refer any more to Haoma as de Harlez; Geldner, KZ, XXVII, p. 251; Baunack, *Stud.*, I, p. 370, would have it, but probably to Sraoṣa. Otherwise, we would expect the words of § 20, like those of §19, are repeated again in *Yašt* 9.17; 10.88; 17.37.

326. Likewise the words *drājaŋhe mąθrahe* are probably interpolated into the following passage : *aiŋhē ahi aiwyāstō bərəšnuš paiti gairinąm* [*drājaŋhe aiwiδāitiš ča gravas ča mąθrahe*], "with this you are girdled on the heights of the mountains." *drājaŋhe* is, I think, a verb and not dative, a 2nd person singular present middle, which we should expect because of *ča* (as a continuation of *ahi*) and because of the accusative *aiwiδāitiš*; *gravas* is discussed by Geldner, KZ, XXVIII, p. 188; SBKPAW 1903; Bartholomae, *Zum Altiranischen Wörterbuch*, p. 175 f.; Lommel, ZII, III, p. 169. Lommel also regards *drājaŋhe* as a second person singular middle. We have to assume that it was a gloss in order to explain the contradiction between the two halves. How could the knotted girdle, decorated with stars, with which Haoma is girdled on the heights of the mountains, have been the Law of Mazda-Yasna ! This is the fancy of Iranian scholiasts and an interpolation. Lommel translates it thus : "You seize (equip yourself) with coat and staff of the word."

327. *Yašt* 7.2.

328. KZ, XXV, p. 471, n. 44.

SOMA

Part III : Soma and the sun

1. The Soma drops are compared to suns IX.10.5; 101.12.

2. See now Kirfel, *Die Kosmographie der Inder*, p. 31.

3. In Hemādri, *Caturvargacintāmaṇi*, BI ed. III, pt. 2, p. 312.

4. The corresponding section in the *Skanda* and the *Brahmāṇḍa Purāṇas* has the same purport (cited in Hemādri, loc. cit., p. 313) :

amā nāma rave raśmiś candraloke pratiṣṭhitaḥ
tasmāt somo vasaty asyām amāvāsyā tataḥ smṛtā /

The *Bhagavatīpurāṇa* states (loc. cit) :

kalāvaśiṣṭo niṣpītaḥ praviṣṭaḥ sūryamaṇḍalam //
amāyāṃ viśate yasmād amāvāsyā tataḥ smṛtā /
pūrvāhṇe praviśaty arkaṃ madhyāhne ca vanaspatim //
aparāhṇe viśaty apsu svāṃ yoniṃ vārisaṃbhavaḥ /
amāṃ praviṣṭaḥ somas tu śeṣayā kalayaikayā //

5. ŚBr IV.6.7, 12.

6. *ādityo vā attā tasya candramā evāhutayaś candramasaṃ hy āditya ādadhati.*

7. *tayor annāda evānyataro 'bhaved annam anyataro 'nanāda evāgnir abhavad annaṃ somo 'nnādaś ca vā idaṃ sarvam annaṃ ca.*

8. See pp. 251, 256 above.

9. E.g., ABr VIII.28.8 : *candramā vā amāvāsyāyām ādityam anupraviśati.*

10. The Padapāṭha wrongly separates *māsā́-iva* (instead of *māsáḥ iva* or *māsám iva*).

11. Cf. Bergaigne, I, p. 160, who invites attention to X.32.8 :

adyéd u prā́ṇīd...
ém enam ā́pa jarimā́ yúvānam
áheḍan vásuḥ sumánā babhūva //

12. Foy thinks that "other passages, which apparently support this theory, can be explained only when we assume that the hymns are sung at night when the moon actually shines." I have no doubt that many hymns were recited at night during lunar festivals. Here the hymn deals with the festival of the new moon, and we should understand it from this point of view.

Furthermore, IX.10.9 : *sū́raḥ paśyati cákṣasā*, he sees with the eye of the sun. (Thus Varuṇa also sees with the eye of the sun.) IX.63.8, 9 :

áyukta sū́ra étaśaṃ pávamāno manā́v ádhi
antárikṣeṇa yā́tave...

Here *sū́ra* is genitive (J. Bune, *Zur Textkritik...*, p. 37).

IX.2.6. : *sáṃ sū́ryeṇa rocate;* VS XXXVII.14, 15 : *gárbho devā́nāṃ pitā́ matīnā́ṃ...sáṃ devó devéna savitrā́ gata sáṃ sū́ryeṇa rocate.*

13. Ed. Benfey, p. 159.1.

14. See pp. 186f. 224 above.

15. In VS XVIII.40 the moon is called *sū́ryaraśmi*; ŚBr IX.4.1.9 explains that this is a comparison : *sūryasveva hi candramaso raśmayaḥ*; this is possible, but not necessary.

16. *ācāryá upanáyamāno brahmacāríṇaṃ kṛṇute gā́rbham antáḥ* /
táṃ rā́trīs tisrá udáre bibharti táṃ jātáṃ drā́ṣṭum abhisáṃyanti devā́ḥ //

Because of this image, the Brahmacārin can only be the moon, the sun being the Ācārya. This image of the Brahmacārin and Ācārya is transferred to the moon and the sun, but to such an extent that it surpasses reality and becomes an exaggeration. *Lieder des Ṛgveda*, p. 150. In my view, Hauer in his *Anfänge der Yogapraxis*, p. 82, goes too far and says that here we have the expression of the rapture of an ecstatic person, of whom, I am sure, there is no mention in this passage.

17. Cf. the wrapping of Soma in a skin during the sacrifice.

18. Soma has a beard which is shaved. Savitṛ comes with a knife and Vāyu with warm water, AV VI.68. In ṚV I.164.44 also, of the three it is Soma who shaves himself :

tráyaḥ keśína ṛtuhā́ ví cakṣate
saṃvatsaré vapata éka eṣām / (moon).

cf. TBr II.7.17.2.

19. Parjanya is called the father "of the mighty bird" (Soma) in another passage also (see p. 152 above).

20. ṚV V.52.16; 60.5.

21. III.48.2 : *yáj jā́yathās tád áhar asya kā́me*
aṅśóḥ pīyū́ṣam apibo giriṣṭhā́m /
tám te mātā́ pári yóṣā jánitrī
maháḥ pitúr dáma ā́siñcad ágre //

22. I.6.3.23 : *ārdraṃ caiva śuṣkaṃ ca yac chuṣkaṃ tad āgneyaṃ yad ārdraṃ tat saumyam*...24 : *sūrya evāgneyaḥ candramāḥ saumyo 'har evāgneyaṃ rātriḥ saumyā* / *ya evāpūryate 'rdhamāsaḥ sa āgneyo yo 'pakṣīyate sa saumyaḥ*. 25 : *ājyabhāgābhyām eva sūryācandramasāv āpnoty upāṅśuyājenaivāhorātre āpnoti*.

23. XI.1.6.19 : *sa indro 'gnīṣomau bhrātarāv abravīt*...

24. *yad agnīṣomau cakṣuṣī vā 'agnīṣomau*. Likewise ABr I.8.15.

25. II.1.4 (5.9); in TS II.3.3.1 the legend in shorter.

26. ABr I.15.6; II.3.9,12; MS I.5.1 (67.3); 6.8 (99.15); 10.5 (145.12); II.3.5 (32.5); 13.1 (153.1); IV.3.1 (40.5); 12.5 (191.13). TS III.5.1d etc. ŚBr I.5.2.13; 6.3.24, 41; VII.3.1.3 ff. etc. TMBr 14.5.10 : *agnir evainaṃ niṣṭapati pavamānaḥ punāti*.

27. X.19.1; 66.7. The expression *agnīṣomau punarvasū* in the first verse gives the impression as if there it is not the designation of the sun and the moon, but that of a constellation. In the AV *agnīṣomau* are mentioned often : VI.54.2; 61.3; 93.3; VII.114.2; VIII.9.14; XII.4.26. More important are only III.13.5 (=MS II.13.1; TS V.6.1.3) :

ā́po bhadrā́ ghṛtám íd ā́pa āsan
agnī́ṣómau bibhraty ā́pa ít tā́ḥ /

and XVIII.2.53 : *agnī́ṣomau páthikṛtā syonáṃ*
devébhyo rátnaṃ dadhatur ví lokám /
upa préṣyataṃ pūṣáṇaṃ yó váhāti
ajayā́naiḥ pathíbhis tátra gacchatam //

28. VI.44.22.

29. *Die Hymnen des Ṛgveda*, I, p. 267.

30. GGA, 1890, p. 401. Oldenberg, RdV, 2nd ed., p. 95, n. 2, contested this assumption. But the difference in the ritual position between Agni-Soma and the other pairs of gods is too great to be traced back to the mere whim of the Gotamas. "Somewhere," says Oldenberg, (because of ṚV I.93), "perhaps in the family circle of the Gotamas the notion

occurred of fusing those two divine patrons of the sacrifice together. This idea found root" etc. Of course, the custom originated somewhere, in a family of priests or in a clan served by them. But this is not a sign of late origin.

31. Very frequently, e.g., ŚBr V.2.5.9; 3.7 (*etena vā agnīṣomīyeṇa puroḍāśena...indro vṛtram ahan*). It is well known that an Agnīṣomīya Puroḍāśa is offered on the full moon day, when it is most appropriate to make an offering to the sun and to the moon who is illuminated by the former.

32. ŚBr V.3.3.1; MS III.4.6 (52.10); 7.8 (87.12).

33. ŚŚS VI.1.1.

34. It should be noted that Agni-Soma fight against Paṇi and Bṛsaya. The hymn belongs to a Gautama, whose family was close to the Bharadvājas and, like the latter, seems to have been involved in the fight against the Paṇis (see Appendix II).

APPENDIX I

1. Cf. ŚBr III.5.4.1 ff.; ĀpŚS XI.11.1 ff.

2. The resonance holes are small pits. On these are placed the two boards, and upon them the hide. There Soma is pressed. While it is being pressed, these pits, made hollow on the principle of sounding boards, cause a deep humming sound. Hence they are called *uparavas* (commentary). The principle is almost the same as in the case of the *bhūmidundubhis*.

3. The commentary adds that they are circular with a radius of half a span.

4. They are four mantras not considerably different from one another.

5. ŚBr III.5.4.13; ĀpŚS XI.11.5. They are joined below but remain separate from above. HŚS VII.6 : *saṃtṛṇṇā adhastād vidhṛtā upariṣṭāt.*

6. ŚBr III.5.4.22. Quite rightly Eggeling (SBE, XXVI, p. 140, n. 1) speaks of these boards thus : "The pressing boards are a cubit long, and somewhat broader behind than in front. They are placed one south of the other, and so as to lie close together behind (*saṃbaddhānte*, Kāṇva recension), or the space of two inches between them. The space between them is filled with earth." ĀpŚS XI.13.1 : *audambare kārṣmaryamaye pālāśe vā śuṣke taṣṭe pradhimukhe purastāt samāvikarte paścāt.* 6 : *saṃhite purastād dvyaṅgulena paścād asaṃhite bhavataḥ.* According to the same Sūtra (5) two resonance holes are covered with the southern and two with the northern pressing board.

7. The former in the sacrifices that last many days so that they lie firmly. ĀpŚS XI.13.2 : *na samtṛṇatty ekāhe tata ūrdhvam saṃtṛdye.* HŚS VII. 19 : *saṃtṛṇṇe asaṃtṛṇṇe vā.* BŚS VI.28 : *athaine śaṅkubhiḥ pariṇihanti / dvābhyāṃ purastād dvābhyāṃ paścād dvābhyām abhito 'navasarpaṇāya.*

8. With the earth dug out from the holes. ĀpŚS XI.13.7.

9. According to ĀpŚS XII.2.14, the hide for pressing is cut out from the hide used during the measuring of Soma. It is rough (not smoothened), cut all round, has four folds (*puṭa*) in which the stones are placed, and above a drain (*upariṣṭād āsecana*). HŚS VII.6 : *lohitam ānaduham upariṣṭāllomāsecanavad yathābhiṣavāyopāttaṃ bhavati.*

10. Later when the vessels required for the Soma sacrifice are placed on this khara, the Upāṅśusavana stone, i.e., the stone with which the Upāṅśusavana is pressed, should be placed, according to ĀpŚS XII.1.9, between the Upāṅśu vessel and the Antaryāma vessel in such a way that it touches both the vessels and its mukha faces the south.

11. *tasmin [carmaṇi] caturo grāvṇaḥ prādeśamātrān ūrdhvasānūn āhanana-prakārān aśmanaḥ saṃsādayati | uparaṃ pratiṣṭhaṃ madhye pañcamam. aśmanas* is from a commentary. My manuscript of HŚS omits it. *ūrdhvasānu* is probably the side where the stones are held. The hitting surface is *mukha* (Eggeling, SBE, XXVI, p. 227, n. 2, "broad side"). KŚS XII.1.4 states that the Vāyavya vessels are *ūrdhvasānu.* The commentary explains this as *ucchritaśiras.*

A quotation in KŚS I.3.36 speaks thus of the stones : *puṣkarā grāvāṇo hastaparṇamātrāḥ.*

12. BŚS VI.29 : *grāvasu grāvāṇam apyarjati.*

13. *sthavīyāṅsi.*

14. I.89.4 : *tán no vā́to mayobhú vātu bheṣajám*
tán mātā́ pṛthivī́ tát pitā́ dyaús |
tád grā́vāṇaḥ somasúto mayobhúvas
tád aśvinā...

V.31.5 : *vṛ́ṣṇe yát te vṛ́ṣaṇo arkám árcān*
índra grā́vāṇo áditiḥ sájoṣāḥ |

VII.35.3; X.108.11. They are called gods in TBr III.7.9.2 and even surpass the gods, ṚV X.76.5 :

diváś cid ā́ vó 'mavattarebhyo
vibhvánā cid āśvàpastarebhyaḥ |
vāyóś cid ā́ sómarabhastarebhyo
agnéś cid arca pitukṛ́ttarebhyaḥ ||

15. These are the same hymns that are to be recited by the Grāvastut during the pressing. To these can be added some other verses like I.24.3; V.81.1; VIII.1.1; 81.1. Gāṇagāri prescribes some other verses as the Grāvastotra. Some recite only X.76, others X.175. Cf. ĀśvŚS V.12.9 ff. Sabbathier, JA, 8 Serie, 1890, XV, p. 72.

It is worth noting that I.28, about which I shall speak later, does not find a place among these hymns.

16. Cf. also the mantra cited in ĀpŚS XIII.1.11 : *samare rakṣāṅsy avadhiṣuḥ* (TBr III.7.9.2). *apa śvā́naṃ śnathiṣṭana* etc. in ṚV IX.101.1, 13 is obscure : I would suppose that the stones are addressed in these two verses.

17. I.83.6 : *grāvā yatra vadati*; likewise 135.7; 84.3 : *arvācīnaṃ su te mano grāvā kṛṇotu vagnunā*; II.39.1 : *grāvāṇeva tad id arthaṃ jarethe;* IV.3.3 : *grāveva sotā madhuṣud yam īle*; V.31.5 : *yat te arkam arcān indra grāvāṇo*; 12 : *vadan grāvā;* 36.4 : *eṣa grāveva jaritā ta indra iyarti vācam;* 37.2 : *grāvāṇo yasyeṣiraṃ vadanti*; VI.51.14 : *grāvāṇaḥ vāvaśuḥ*; VII.33.14 : *ukthabhṛtaṃ sāmabhṛtaṃ grāvāṇaṃ bibharti*; VIII.34.2 : *ā tvā grāvā vadann iha...somī ghoṣeṇa yacchatu;* X.36.4 : *grāvā vadann apa rakṣāṅsi sedhatu*; 76.6 : *bhurantu...grāvāṇo vācā divitmatā;* 85.4 : *grāvṇām ic chṛṇvan tiṣṭhasi;* 94.1 : *grāvabhyo vadadbhyaḥ;* likewise VII.104. 17 : *grāvāṇo ghnantu... upabdaih.* Furthermore, V.25.8 : *grāvevocyate bṛhad*; X.64.15; 100.8 :

grāvā yatra madhuṣud ucyate bṛhad. Perhaps also X.70.7 : *ūrdhvo grāvā bṛhad.* The word *bṛhat* "loud" is a term that is used repeatedly in connection with the pressing, cf. ĀpŚS XIII.1.10; ṚV X.94.4 : *bṛhad vadanti.*

As against this a verb of speech occurs very rarely with *adri. anūnot* V.45.7; *vivakti* VII.68.4; *śloko adrer* I.118.3; III.53.10; 58.3; X.76.4; 94.1; *śṛṇvantv āpo...babhṛhāṇasyādrer* V.41.12; *śrudhī havam adrer* VII.22.4; *vācam akrata* X.94.4. That is to say, only ten cases against nineteen. In the ṚV, I found *vad* with *adri* in X.94.13 only; I did not look for this in other texts.

On the other hand, I find *su* with *grāvan* only in III.42.2; IX.80.4; X.175.1; in *madhuṣud grāvā* X.100.8, that is, about four times. So much the more frequently *su* occurs with *adri* I.130.2; 135.5; 137.1; II.16.5; III.44.5; IV.45.5; V.40.1; VII.22.1; 68.4; VIII.1.17; 4.13; 22.8; 82.5; IX.11.5; 24.5; 34.3; 63.13; 67.3; 68.9; 71.3; 75.4; 86.23, 34; (101.3); 107.1,10; 109.18; X.28.3.

To this we may add some other verbs synonymous with *su,* which occur not at all or almost not at all with *grāvan,* but always with *adri. krīl (adribhiḥ)* IX.66.29; *duh* I.121.8; 137.3; II.36.1; IX.65.15; 80.5; *adridugdha* I.54.9; *hi* IX.30.5; 32.2; 38.2; 39.6; 50.3; 65.8; 101.3; *pū* V. 86.6; *pū+pari* I.135.2; *mikṣ* X.104.2; *bhas (baps)* IX.79.4; *sic* Vāl. 5.3.

yuj occurs with both.

18. In the later literature, so far as I can see, this distinction is totally lost. There the stones are conceived as "teeth." ŚBr III.5.4.24 : *atha grāvṇa upāvaharati / dantā haivāsya grāvāṇaḥ / tad yad grāvabhir abhiṣuṇvanti yathā dadhiḥ psāyād evaṃ tat tān nidadhāti* etc. Likewise MS III.8.8; IV.5.9; VS XXVI.4 : *vidyadbhir grāvabhiḥ sutam (=khaṇḍayadbhiḥ).*

19. *Studies in Honor of Maurice Bloomfield,* New Haven 1920, p. 325 ff.

20. Practically not much different from what is cited above from Kātyāyana.

21. I do not rule out the possibility that wherever *adrī* in the dual occurs it denotes the stone mortar with stone pestle of the type of *ulūkhala.*

22. In the same meaning *úpara* occurs further in I.79.3 (see below) and AV VI.49.2 : *meṣá iva vaí sáṃ ca ví córvacyase*
yád uttara drā́v úparaś ca khā́dataḥ /
śirṣṇā́ śiró 'psasā́pso ardáyan
aṅśū́n babhasti háritebhir āsábhiḥ //

That this verse refers to the Soma stones is evident from its connection with the verse cited just above. For ṚV X.94.5 is the same as AV VI.49.3. Only the expression *uttaradrā́v* creates difficulties. But it is not necessary to treat this as one word. *uttara* is rather a vocative and is to be separated from *drā́v*; it is at the same time the subject of *acyase.* This second person singular suggests also that we should change *khā́dataḥ* into *khā́dathaḥ.* Hence I translate this verse as follows : "Like a ram you move to and fro, when you, O Uttara (the upper stone with which Soma is crushed), and the Upara consume [Soma] on the wood."

dru is a wooden base, the *adhiṣavaṇaphalaka.* ṚV X.175.3 speaks of several Uparas : *grā́vāṇa úpareṣv ā́ mahīyánte sajóṣasaḥ.*

23. *yuñje ádrim* III.1.1; *yujyā́tām ádrī* VII.42.1; III.30.2; 41.2; 57.4; V.40.8; AV XI.1.9; *grā́vṇām yóge* ṚV X.35.9; *yuktágrāvan* etc. Hence, it is not likely that *prábhṛto me ádriḥ* I.165.4 can be translated as Roth does (*Siebzig Lieder*, "the press is equipped"). *pra-hṛ* is used in KŚS IX.4.13; ŚBr III.9.4.18 in the sense of hitting with stones, but in this Ṛgvedic passage it does not refer to the Soma stone at all.

24. It is doubtful whether one can say with Ludwig that *niktáhasta* IV.45.5 refers to the fact that the priests hold a piece of gold with their fingers.

25. Cf. also II.16.5; V.31.12; VII.90.1. The Adhvaryus are called *suhásta*, "dexterous," for this reason, and also because they have to perform the practical part of the sacrifice. After all, not a single drop should be lost (X.17.13). They have also the duty to prepare admixtures and to make the offerings. Of the individual names, we come across *udagrābhá* (IX.97.15 : *udagrābhásya namáyan vadhasnaiḥ*) and the above-mentioned *grāvagrābhá*.

26. ṚV X.94.7 speaks probably of the straps : *dáśakakṣebhyo dáśayoktrebhyo dáśayojanebhyo dáśābhīśubhyo arcata*. But it is more probable, particularly in view of the word *daśa*, that *yoktra*, *yojana* denote only the fingers. On the other hand, I.109.3 :

mā́ chedma raśmī́m̐r iti nā́dhamānāḥ
pitṝṇā́m śaktī́r anuyácchamānāḥ /

may probably refer to the straps, since these are certainly employed from times long past.

27. ĀpŚS XIV.25.7.

28. Ibid., XII.10.2.

29. In v. 11 of the same hymn they are called *aśrithita*. The commentary explains this as *aśithilīkṛta*.

30. It should also be noted that according to ĀpŚS XIV.25.5 one should take a *palāśadaṇḍa*, i.e. a sort of pestle, when one does not find a lost stone.

31. Plutarch, *de Iside et Os*, Cap. 46. Anquetil Duperron, *Zend-Avesta*, p. 532 : "It is a metal vase meant for receiving the Hom juice. It also serves the purpose of a bell and even of a mortar just as it did at the time of Plutarch. It is in the Hāvan that one piles the twigs of the Hom tree." Haug, *Essays on the Parsis*, 2nd ed., p. 282 : "The Parsi priests use, instead of stones, a metal mortar with a pestle whereby the twigs of the Homa plant, together with one of the pomegranate tree, are bruised, and they then pour water over them to obtain the juice, which is strained through a metal saucer with nine holes." For a more detailed description of the entire process, see ibid., p. 399. See also Spiegel, *Eranische Altertumskunde*, III, p. 571; Darmesteter, SBE, IV, p. 23, n. 1. This mortar is called *hāvana* (with the additional attribute *dāityōkərəta*, "correctly prepared," *Vendidād* XIV.8) and the priest who uses it is *hāvanan* (*Visparad* III.1). On the press in the *Avesta*, see Bartholomae, IF, V, p. 340; Samuel Grant Oliphant, *Studies in Honor of Maurice Bloomfield*, 1920, p. 225 ff.

32. I do not understand why Oldenberg, *Prolegomena*, I, p. 261, n. 3, regards this hymn as "decidedly late."

33. Wilson, *Translation of the Ṛgveda*, note on I.28.4 : "churning staff."

34. Ibid. See also Kuhn, MSt, I, p. 15.
35. That would be *apacyavám* and *upacyavám*.
36. *Bihar Peasant Life*, p. 27 § 144.
37. I hardly need to refer to the myth of the gods and Asuras churning the ocean with Mt. Mandara as the churning staff and the snake as the rope in order to obtain the Amṛta.
38. Oldenberg's view (*Die Hymnen des Ṛgveda*, I, p. 24, n. 2) is slightly different.
39. See also ŚBr I.4.7.10; NVO, p. 29. The pestle also is addressed thus : *bṛhad grāvāsi vānasptyaḥ*.
40. The commentary says in a round-about way : *ulūkhalarūpeṇa pariṇatāḥ pāṣāṇāḥ*.
41. We can see a double meaning also in *apacyavam upacyavaṃ nārī śikṣate*.
42. Some other verses of this hymn (e.g., vv. 6-8) appear to refer to the consecration of the house and of the well.
43. Above all, because of *yónau*, it is improbable that *váhni* could be Soma.
44. Grierson, *Bihar Peasant Life*, p. 207, § 933 (s.v. lever used in raising water) says : "to the west *dhuraī* is a post with two branches at the top." Hence, *dhúrau* could also be a forklike contraption on the mortar.
45. Hence, it is also said that the stones chew Soma (*baps, khād*) e.g., X.94.3, 13 etc.
46. MS III.11.4 (146.11). I uphold my view against Oldenberg's contention (ZDMG, LXII, No. 24, p. 459 ff.) with the following arguments. *i.* v. X.91.15 with the comparisons *sruciva ghṛtam, camvìva sómaḥ*, where *camū́* is clearly a vessel for the offering of Soma, cannot easily be dismissed by Oldenberg's objection (p. 469) : "the Ṛgvedic comparisons being what they are, it is not necessary to assume that a Soma-offering was made with *camū́*; it suffices when Soma was contained in it." The comparison is clear and specific. *ii.* Oldenberg does not take into account that in I.28.9 *camvòr* occurs alternately with *ulū́khala* (Geldner, *Ṛgveda*, also translates it as "press"). *iii.* The procedure as Oldenberg describes it on p. 469 is not in conformity with the frequently used expression *camū́ sutá*. *iv.* Oldenberg ignores the statement of the commentary that the Grahapātras, with which I identify *camū́* to some extent, are *ulūkhalarūpa*. *v.* He underestimates the section ending with IX.67. *vi.* His own evidence to show that here it is to do with the two *kalaśas* seems to be belaboured.
47. Sāyaṇa, *gṛhá=haviṣāṃ grahītā*. This very *yam* is used repeatedly in the sense of the drawing of the Soma juice, IX.24.3; 99.8.
48. According to the deity the cups are deposited on the corresponding places. *áśvaṃ ná tvā vājínaṃ marjáyanto ácchā barhí raśanā́bhir nayanti* IX.87.1; I.16.6; III.42.2; IX.72.4. The expression *vi-nī* is a technical term in the ṚV. Cf. IX.24.3 : *nṛbhír yató ví nīyase;* likewise 15.3; 27.3. In the later ritual (ŚBr IV.3.3.9; KŚS X.3.11) it is employed in a quite different sense, viz., the churning of the Āśir : *agnid ! āśiraṃ vinaya*.
49. ĀpŚS XII.2.8.
50. On I.54.9, see n. 58 below.

51. Even elsewhere Sāyaṇa occasionally equates *camū́* with *graha*, e.g. VIII.82.8, but often he is not consistent. The commentary on VS VIII.58 explains camasa also as *grahapātra*.

52. In one passage it occurs with kośas. VIII.2.8 : *tráyaḥ kóśāsaḥ ścotanti tisráḥ camvàḥ supūrṇāḥ*. As will be shown later, *kóśa* is a big vessel. Here also *camū́* can have its usual meaning.

53. IX.97.21 : *pári srava nábho árṇaś camū́ṣu.*

54. III.48.4 : *sómam apibac camū́ṣu.*

55. IX.93.3 : *mūrdhánaṃ gávaḥ páyasā camuṣv abhí śrīṇanti.*

56. VIII.82.8 : *yó apsú candrámā iva sómaś camū́ṣu dadṛśe.*

56a. VIII.82.7 : *yá indra camaséṣv á sómaś camū́ṣu te sutáḥ* [*asti*].

57. IX.97.46 : *pavate camuúṣu.*

58. Likewise in the sole instance of nominative plural in VIII.2.8 (see n. 52 above). I.54.9 : *túbhyéd eté bahulá ádridugdhāḥ / camūṣádaś camasá indrapánāḥ* is not quite clear. The meaning "situated on the board of the Soma press," given by the smaller edition of the PW, is completely ruled out after what we have stated above, since camū does not denote board. Hence, I translate it thus : "Here are for you many [Somas] lying in the camūs, pressed by the stones and serving as drink to Indra, and the camasas," Accordingly, *camūṣád* is to be separated into *camū́ṣu sád.* I think that here as well as in VIII.82.7 *camū́* and *camasá* are independent of each other, since neither "jars contained in the cups" nor "jars standing on the boards" has any justification.

59. V.51.4 : *ayáṃ sómaś camū́ sutáḥ ámatre pári ṣicyate /*
VIII.4.4 : *āmúṣyā sómam apibaś camū́ sutám*
76.10 : *pītvī...sómam indra camū́ sutám //*
IX.46.3 : *eté sómāsa indavaḥ práyasvantaḥ camū́ sutā́ḥ /*
X.24.1 : *indra sómam imáṃ piba mádhumantaṃ camū́ sutám //*

60. VIII.82.7 is no exception, since in this case *camū́ṣu* occurs beside *camaséṣu* and is not governed by *su.*

61. Delbrück, *Altindische Syntax*, p. 98. The explanation given by ABr VII.17.1 is wrong. It is worth noting that in the *Avesta* also *hāvana* occurs a few times in the dual, e.g., *Visparat* XII.2 : *hāvanayå̊s* *ča haoma hunvaintayå̊*. I do not think that the translation by Mills, "of the two mortars which pour the Haomas out," is correct. Darmesteter leaves untranslated the dual in *Vendidād* XIV.8 (31); *Yašt* X.91. According to S. G. Oliphant, *Studies in Honor of Maurice Bloomfield*, p. 225, it is genitive singular "as a collective designation for the mortar and pestle"; Bartholomae (*Altiranisches Wörterbuch*, s.v. *hāvana-α*) dual, as singular feminine ā-stem (or also genitive dual) "of the mortar."

ṚV I.164.10 is obscure :

uttānáyoś camvòr yònir antár
átrā pitá duhitúr garbham ádhāt //

However, here *camvòr* can only be "thighs."

62. Cf. also the comm. on KŚS IX.6.11; 4.29; the comm. on ĀpŚS XII.1.4; HŚS VIII.1.

63. *á-vācyasva* is not "to gush out of," but "to stream into" as the *pūyamāna* next to it and the preceding examples show. The parallelism

between 97.2 and 108.10 induces me to regard *camvòḥ* in 108.10 not as governed by *sutáh* but by *á vācyasva.*

64. 69.5 and 71.1 are obscure in many points. The explanation by Geldner, VSt, I, p. 134 is not satisfactory.

65. It is difficult to establish positively whether *camvòr* denotes a double Graha, or a single Graha whose external form, in that case, must be such as to justify the dual. Apart from what we have said about the shape of the mortar, it must be noted that there are several Grahas which justify the use of the dual because of their enjoined shape. For example, KŚS IX.2.13 states that the Ṛtupātras are *ubhayatomukhe*, i.e., they have an opening above and below. ŚBr IV.1.15.19; KŚS IX.2.6; ĀpŚS XII.1.11 ff; HŚS VIII.1 give rules for the shape of the Dvidevatyagraha vessels, which are unusual. For instance, the vessel for Mitra-Varuṇa should have marks resembling the teats of a goat, that for the Aśvins should be lip-shaped, or according to others, it should have three mouths (See Haug, *Aitareya Brāhmaṇa*, II, p. 132; Eggeling, SBE, XXVI, p. 272, n. 4). I think that the memories of ancient images of gods are preserved in these shapes of the vessels.

66. Here belongs III.55.20 in which the sky and earth, because of their wealth, are compared to two (full) cups : *mahī́ sám airac camvā̀ samīcī́ ubhé té asya vásunā nyṛṣṭe.* These are called *vásumatī* in III.30.11; *madhudúghe, madhuścútā* in VI.70.1, 5; they confer abundance II.27.15 (*ubhé asmaī pīpayataḥ*) etc.

67. I do not include *camūṣad*, see , n. 58.

68. "Whosoever studies the Pavamānīs, the honey collected by the Ṛṣis, to him flows the Sarasvatī" etc.

69. Hence, we should assume that in VIII.4.4 (*apibaś camū́ sutám*) and 76.10 : *pītvī́...sómam...camū́ sutám, camū́* is governed not by *sutám* but by *apibas* and *pītvī́* respectively (cf. III.48.4 : *apibac camū́ṣu*). Thus all the difficulties in interpretation can be removed.

70. VS VII.26 (and likewise TS) changed the expression *dhiṣáṇāyā upásthāt* which was unintelligible to them to [*grāvacyuto*] *dhiṣaṇayor upasthāt.* Mahīdhara explains it as *adhiṣavaṇaphalakayor utsaṅgāt.*

71. E.g. MS I.1.7 etc.

72. (Another reading *viḍū* in ĀpŚS XII.10.1); the comm. explains it as *dyāvāpṛthivyau.*

73. Very clearly in VI.50.3 :

utá dyā́vāpṛthivī́ kṣatrám urú
bṛhád rodasī śaraṇáṃ suṣumne |
mahás karatho várivo yáthā no
asmé kṣáyāya dhiṣaṇe anehā́ḥ ||

Also 70.3 : *yó vām ṛjáve krámaṇāya rodasī*
márto dadā́śa dhiṣaṇe sá sā́dhati |

I.160.1 : *té hi dyā́vāpṛthivī́ viśvā́śambhuvā...* |
sujánmanī dhiṣáṇe antár īyate devó
devī́ dhármaṇā sū́ryaḥ śúciḥ ||

VI.8.3 : *vy àstābhnād ródasī mitró ádbhuto...*|
ví cármaṇīva dhiṣáṇe avārtayat

Cf. VIII.6.5 : *ubhé yad somávartayat / índraś cármeva ródasī*
X.44.8 : *samīcīné dhiṣáṇe ví ṣkabhāyati... //*

Cf. also VIII.61.2. Hence, in the Nivid formula cited by ŚŚS VIII.19 this word occurs along with *dhanyā* among the designations for the heaven and earth (*pitā ca mātā ca, dhenuś ca ṛṣabhaś ca, dhanyā ca dhiṣaṇā ca* etc.).

74. IV.16.7 : *prā́vat te vájraṃ pṛthiví sácetāḥ* can be regarded as a parallel to this.

75. VII.90.3 : *rāyé nú yáṃ jajñátū ródasīmé*
rāyé deví dhiṣáṇā dhāti devám.

After heaven and earth, once again earth is mentioned specially here. But this is not unusual in the Veda. Cf. X.65.4 : *svàrṇaram antárikṣāṇi rocanā́ dyā́vābhū́mī pṛthivī́ṃ skambhur ójasā.*

76. In III.32.14 *dhiṣáṇā* denotes the *mātā́ pṛthiví* :
vivéṣa yān mā dhiṣáṇā jajā́na
stávai purā́ pā́ryād índram áhnaḥ /

I connect *vivéṣa* with Indra : "He had brought about that the earth gave birth to me. I wish to praise Indra before the decisive day." There is no room here for the meaning "divine spirit."

77. Just as the ŚBr makes a play on *vind* here, so does TS V.1.7.2 with *vid* : *dhiṣaṇās tvety āha / vidyā vai dhiṣaṇā /*

78. *taṃ chandobhir abhitaḥ parigṛhya agniṃ purastāt samādhāya tenārcantaḥ śrāmyantaś ceruḥ / tenemāṃ sarvāṃ pṛthivīṃ samavindanta / tadyad enenemāṃ sarvāṃ samavindanta tasmād vedir nāma / tasmād āhur yāvatī vedis tāvatī pṛthivī* etc. Cf. also III.7.2.1; III.1.1.4; TS II.6.4.1; TBr III.2.9. 12; TMBr XXV.13.3.

79. Another name for this is probably *bhā́rman* VIII.2.8.

80. In I.164.35 it is called *páro ántaḥ pṛthivyā́ḥ*. Probably *vára ā́ pṛthivyā́ḥ* and *nā́bhā pṛthivyā́ḥ* also denote the vedi.

81. III.7.6.4 : *marmṛjyámānā mahaté saúbhagāya*
máhyaṃ dhukṣva yájamānāya kā́mān /
bhū́mir bhūtvā́ mahimā́naṃ pupoṣa
táto deví vardhayate páyāṅsi //

82. The vedi was slightly elevated. Hence, in the later period the vedi is called "stand or pedestal." *dhiṣṇya* is derived from *dhiṣáṇā.*

83. TS I.1.2 : *préyám agād dhiṣáṇā barhír acha mánunā kṛtā́ svadháyā vítaṣṭā*, i.e., the vedi (conceived as a person) came to the barhis, i.e., "it was bestrewed." Thus also Keith on this passage.

84. In this verse earth also could have been meant by *dhiṣáṇā.*

85. *Über die altindische Göttin Dhiṣaṇā und Verwandtes*, Uppsala 1917, p. 103 ff. He thinks that the old Islandic *dis, dísir* and the *Disen* of Nordic mythology are akin to *dhiṣaṇā* linguistically and by their nature.

86. NVO, p. 54, n. 4; Caland, *Āpastamba Śrauta Sūtra*, I, pp. 49, 101. She is called *yuvatiḥ cā́tuśkapardā.*

87. *pávate...hinvānó gór ádhi tvací.*

88. Pischel's remark (VSt, I, p. 109) that the cowhide spread over the stone protects the stalks of the Soma plant from damage is not correct. How else can the juice be obtained if the plant is not crushed ! After all, it is said expressly that the stones "chew" the plant. In V.43.4 the arms are

styled as the slaughterers of Soma. IX.98.9 states : *tám* (*sómam*) *asredhan* (*aghnan*); IX.67.19 : *grā́vṇā tunnó*. Cf. also the passages cited earlier which speak of the remnants of the body (*śárya* etc.). TBr III.7.13.1 : *yat te tvacaṃ bibhidur yac ca yonim*. MS IV.5.6 (72.16) : *ghnanti vā etat somaṃ yad abhiṣuṇvanti*; 7.2 (94.15); III.8.2 (93.14); TS VI.4.4.3; *Tāṇḍya Mahā Brāhmaṇa* XVI.1.12 : *vīrahā vā eṣa devānāṃ yaḥ somam abhiṣuṇoti gāḥ śataṃ vairaṃ tad devān avadayate*.

89. As Pischel rightly notes, III.21.5 does not belong here :

ścótanti te vaso stokā́ ádhi tvací
práti tā́n devaśo vihi ||

Here *tvác* is skin (=the body of Agni like the usual *pṛṣṭhá*, cf. *ghṛtápṛṣṭha*). The drops drip on to the fire.

V.33.7 :...*pāhí gṛṇatáḥ*...*kārū́n* / *utá tvácaṃ dádato vā́jasātau piprihi mádhvaḥ súṣutasya cā́roḥ* is uncertain. Here a distinction is made between *gṛṇat* and *dádat*. That the second word refers to the sacrificers is evident from the Dānastuti which follows after this. Here *tvac* could denote a leather bottle filled with Soma, which is given to the singer of the sacrifice. Apparently Ludwig understands thus.

89a. IF, AISAK, VIII, p. 24.

90. IV.20.6 : *udnéva kóśaṃ vásunā nyṛṣṭam*. X.42.2 : *kóśaṃ ná pūrṇáṃ vásunā nyṝṣṭam*.

91. We have established earlier that *camū́* has the meaning of "cup." In IX.90.20 : *vṝṣeva yūthā́ pári kóśam árṣan kánikradac camvòr ā́ viveśa*, *camvòḥ* occurs almost as a parallel to the *kalaśa* of the present verse. Hence the latter must be also a small vessel.

92. Literally, he poured the kośa into him. Cf. I.130.2 : *kóśena siktám*.

93. IX.76.5; 86.7; (87.1); 103.3; 107.26.

94. VIII.2.8 : *tráyaḥ kóśāsaḥ ścotanti*
tisráś camvàḥ súpūrṇāḥ /
samāné ádhi bhā́rman ||

The preceding verse speaks of *tráya índrasya sómāḥ sutā́saḥ*. It is quite uncertain whether we can understand by these the three larger vessels of the later ritual, viz., Ādhavanīya, Droṇakalaśa and Pūtabhṛt. Bergaigne, I, p. 180 ascribes a mythical significance to this verse.

95. IX.68.9; 84.4; 86.6, 9, 35, 47; 96.23; 97.4; 106.7.

96. X.100.10 does not refer to the Soma drops.

97. IX.96.14 : *sáṃ síndhubhiḥ kaláśe vāvaśānáḥ sám usríyābhiḥ*.

98. VI.69.6 : *índrāviṣṇū*...*samudráḥ sthaḥ kaláśaḥ somadhānáḥ* and v.2 : *yā́ víśvāsāṃ janitā́rā matīnā́m índraviṣṇū kaláśā somadhā́nā*.

99. *ámatra* which occurs in singular and in plural is a vessel of indeterminable size II.14.1; V.51.4; VI.42.2; X.29.7.

100. See the comm. on TS III.2.2.1; ĀpŚS XII.18.16-18; the comm. on KŚS IX.2.23; 5.6; 7.4.

101. ŚŚS XVII.4.8; 17.9.

102. *Somaprayoga*, India Office manuscript 1262, 2nd half, folio 7a.

103. See pp. 280f., 288f. above.

104. In the dual *kaláśa* occurs only in a comparison in VI.69.2, i.e., quite unlike camū.

105. Apart from this, there is another adjective *ádrimātṛ* in IX.86.3, which should be translated as "stony" and be referred to the celestial pail, the stony well of heaven (*Asia Major*, 1924, p. 791).

átyó ná hiyānó abhí vā́jam arṣa
svarvít kóśaṃ divó ádrimātaram |

106. IX.1.2 : *rakṣhā́ viśvácarṣaṇir abhí yónim áyohatam* |
drúṇā sadhástham āsadat ||

The reading of the VS : *ayohate droṇe*, is worse.

IX.71.6 : *śyenó ná yóniṃ sádanaṃ dhiyā́ kṛtám*
hiraṇyáyam āsádaṃ devá éṣati |

64.20 : *ā́ yád yóniṃ hiraṇyáyam āśúr ṛtásya sī́dati* |

80.2 : *yáṃ tvā vājinn aghnyā́ abhy ánūṣata*
áyohataṃ yónim ā róhasi dyumā́n |

Perhaps *hiraṇyayú*, "longing for the golden jar" (?), the epithet of Soma, also refers to this.

107. KŚS XIV.2.9. Cf. the *hiraṇyapātra* of TS V.7.1.3, which is filled with Madhu. TBr I.3.3.7; ŚBr V.1.2.19; 5.28. In TS II.3.11.5 a golden vessel is used for drinking. The *Avesta* also speaks of a golden bowl (*Yasna* X.17).

108. IX.12.6; 23.4; 36.2; 66.11; 103.3; 107.12.

109. VII.101.4 : *tráyaḥ kóśāsa upasécanāso*
mádhvaḥ ścotanty abhíto virapśám ||

I.87.2 : *ścotanti kóśā úpa vo ráthesu...* |

112.11 : *...mádhu kóśo ákṣarat* |

110. I have not discussed again *sadhastha* here since I believe, on reconsideration, that the meaning "seat" suffices everywhere.

111. I.161.1 : *drúṇa íd bhūtím ūdima*; VIII.96.11 : *manīṣā́ṃ drúṇā ná pārám īrayā nadī́nām* (=canoe, boat); V.86.3 : *práti drúṇā gábhastyor gávāṃ vṛtraghná éṣate* (here *vṛtraghna* is a substantive, meaning "fight"); In AV VI.49.2 (see n. 22 above) *dru* is only a wooden base (=*abhiṣavaṇaphalake*). In a fourth passage, X.101.10 : *ā́ tu siñca hárim īṃ drór upásthe*, it is some wooden vessel, probably the mortar. Contra, Oldenberg, *Die Hymnen des Ṛgveda*, II, p. 317.

112. The following three verses are relevant :

IX.1.2 : *abhí yónim áyohataṃ drúṇā sadhástham ā́sadat* |

65.6 : *yád adbhíḥ pariṣicyáse mṛjyámāno gábhastyoḥ* |
drúṇā sadhástham aśnuṣe ||

98.2 : *pári ṣyá suvānó avyáyaṃ ráthe ná vármāvyata* |
índur abhí drúṇā hitó hiyānó dhā́rābhir akṣāḥ ||

113. However, kośa also occurs once in instrumental, but in quite a different sense, viz., *kóśena siktá*.

114. *abhy-arṣ* IX.65.19; *abhi-krand* IX.67.14; *abhi-kṣar* IX.33.2; *pra-gam* VI.37.2; *abhi-dhāv* IX.28.4; 37.6; *nanakṣe* IX.93.1; *mṛj* IX.15.7; *ava-sad* IX.96.13; *abhy-asiṣyadat* IX.30.4; *ā-sthā* VI.44.20.

115. IX.66.9; 78.2.

116. IX.96.23 : *sī́dan váneṣu śakunó ná patvā́*
sómaḥ punānáḥ kaláśeṣu sáttā ||

Likewise IX.107.10 :

jáno ná purí camvòr viśad dháriḥ |

sádo vánesu dadhiṣe ||

when we compare it with IX.86.47 : *yád góbhir indo camvòḥ samajyása á suvānáḥ soma kaláśeṣu sīdasi.* On the other hand, when we compare IX.27.3 with 99.8, we shall see that *vaneṣu* means as much as *camūṣu.* Both meanings are compatible with the fact that Soma flows into the vanas only after he has passed through the strainer. IX.6.5; 45.5; 62.8; 96.23.

117. *púṣkara* occurs in solitary instances (*niṣiktaṃ púṣkare mádhu*) VIII. 72.11.

118. On the drawing of these Vasatīvarīs see further below.

119. IV.5.4. (68.17) : *śvātrāḥ stha vṛtraturā ity eṣa vā apāṃ somapīthaḥ | etaṃ vai viśvāmitro 'pāṃ somapīthaṃ vidāṃ cakāra | tasmai sindhavo dhokṣam anamdnta | apāṃ vā eṣā somapīthah* etc.

120. *āpyāyanaliṅgena mantreṇāvamarśanam evāpyāyanam | adbhiḥ secanam ity anye.* On a later occasion when the jars are refilled, which is also called Āpyāyana, the same scholiast remarks : *somena vardhanam āpyāyanam | tenainam āpyāyayatīti liṅgāt | mantreṇābhimarśanam ity anye | tathābhimṛśerann ity āśvalāyanaḥ | kātyāyanas tv āha, āpyāyasva sametu ta iti dvābhyāṃ camasān ālabhante | somaṃ vāṣiñcatīti | baudhāyanas tu vasatīvarīḥ prakṛtyāha | tābhir āpyāyayet tābhir abhiṣuṇuyād iti* (XII.25.24).

121. The admixture in the pail (*ādhavanīya*) could not have been meant by this since this admixture is added to Soma only after it had passed through the sieve.

122. These serve the purpose of moistening the stalks and are kept in the jar of the Hotṛ. See KŚS IX.3.15 and below. These waters are supposed to have this name because they are to be held against the chest by the sacrificer.

123. I.e., he throws on the stone each time a handful of the Soma brought there. ĀpŚS XII.9.3.

124. Ibid., XII.10.2.

125. Ibid., XII.10.4, 8, 9.

126. According to the rules of Mānava cited in the comm. on the KŚS, while muttering this mantra he washes the pressed stalks in the Hotṛcamasa, squeezes them and throws them back. ĀpŚS XII.10.11 : In the last round he presses the aṅśus kept in the Hotṛcamasa (9.8).

127. ĀpSŚ XII.10.5, 11. According to the comm. on KŚS IX.4.27, the Adhvaryu performs the filling in such a way that the Soma juice, after having been purified through the aṅśus that are held in between, flows into the middle of the Graha vessel. It is not quite clear with which vessel the pouring is done. The same comm. states that the Soma juice is removed from the hide with the Pavitra, the woollen strainer, and this Pavitra is then squeezed with the hands over the aṅśus that are held over the Graha. Accordingly, the Pavitra would serve as a sort of sponge. I do not find it stated in the ritual texts that the juice runs over the hide into a vessel in which it would be collected. It looks as if the stalks are merely crushed and then squeezed in water. ĀpŚS XII.10.6 states this more clearly than the KŚS : *tasminn* [*upāṅśupātre*] *abhiṣutam adhvaryur añjalinā gṛhṇāti.*

This is also the opinion of other Sūtrakāras. Mānava according to a statement in the comm. on KŚS IX.4.28. Likewise the *Kāṭhaka* etc. Yajneśvaraśarman, *Āryavidyāsuddhākara*, p. 84.

128. See the description by Eggeling, SBE, XXVI, p. 256, n. 1.

129. Each one gets a stone and a part of the Soma plants.

130. Not limited as earlier. All the rest is as in the preliminary pressing.

131. *rasapracyutyartham* or *somam ārdrīkartum.*

132. It is called thus because the crushed (*abhisuta*) juicy Soma stalks are collected in it. It is a large vessel made of Varana wood, to be distinguished from the Pariplavā which is used for drawing the Soma from the Droṇakalaśa into the Grahas etc.

133. This is the name of the vessel in which the pressed, but not yet purified, Soma is collected. See the comm. on KŚS IX.5.6 and the comm. on ĀpŚS XII.2.12.

134. 'According to the comm. on KŚS IX.5.6, the sequence of the various acts is as follows : all the four priests fasten a piece of gold to their fingers and take their stones; then pouring the Nigrābhyās, dividing Soma in four parts, and crushing Soma with the stone in an unlimited number of strokes. This is the first round.

After gathering the scattered Soma plants and after some rest, renewed crushing of the Soma. Thus the second round. After once again gathering the scattered plants, the third round. Thereupon he pours water over the plants, places Soma stalks that are lightly pressed out in the Hotṛcamasa, and then the Nigrābha formula is pronounced. Finally, with the Saṃbharaṇī he gathers the stalks that are still juicy, places them in the Ādhavanīya, a container filled with water, and presses them and so on as before.

Yajñeśvaraśarman describes the Mahābhiṣava almost in the same way (*Āryavidyāsudhākara*, p. 85).

135. Comm. : Pouring the Nigrābhyās, dividing Soma and crushing (1); gathering [the scattered Soma] and crushing again (2); gathering again and crushing (3); Āpyāyana, reciting the Nigrābha, placing the stalks in the Ādhavanīya with the Saṃbharaṇī : thus runs the second Abhiṣava. Similarly the third Abhiṣava (which again consists of three rounds). At the end of the Nigrābha formula, the Adhvaryu places his stone in the Hotṛcamasa, causes the formula to be recited for the fourth time, and this is followed by the Saṃbharaṇa.

136. The Droṇakalaśa (comm. *droṇakṛti*) is made of wood, more precisely, of Vikaṅkaṭa wood like the Grahas (ĀpŚS XII.2.11; 1.5).

137. Quite similar are the rules of *Kāṭhaka* and *Mānava* cited in the KŚS.

138. Ādhavanīya and Pūtabhṛt are clay earthen-ware vessels.

139. Unlike the earlier Dhārāgrahas, i.e., the Grahas drawn from the "continuous stream," this one is an Adhārāgraha.

140. Ludwig, III, pp. 376, 384, has discussed much of this already.

141. See pp. 171, 271, 278 above.

142. *gábhastipūtaṃ bharata śrutắya...*

143. *ádribhiḥ sutáḥ pavate gábhastyoḥ..*

144. VS VII.1; TS I.4.2.
145. Cf. e.g., ṚV IX.86.34 : *pávamāna máhy árṇo ví dhāvasi*
sū́ro ná citró ávyayāni pávyayā |
gábhastipūto nṛ́bhir ádribhiḥ sutáḥ...
146. II.36.1; IX.86.11; 91.2. Hence, Soma is called *átyavi* also.
147. IX.8.5 : *sṛjānám áti meṣyàḥ.*
148. IX.16.6. Therefore, the Pavitra is also his garment, 101.15.
149. IX.26.5. Compare this with IX.50.2,3.
150. IX.17.4; 27.2; 42.4. The expression *ā-sṛj* also should be interpreted in the same way; IX.16.3 : *sómaṃ pavítra ā́ sṛja*; 51.1; 62.21 etc. He runs upon the Pavitra : *pari-dhāv* etc.
151. IX.107.22 : *mṛjānó vā́re pávamāno avyáye.* See also IX.36.4; 64.5; 68.7; 86.6; 97.3; 107.11, 17 etc.
152. *mṛj* is connected with *gó* alone also. One of the few instances of this is IX.43.1 : *yó átya iva mṛjyáte góbhir mádāya haryatáḥ*; similarly with *ap*, IX.109.17 : *vājy àkṣāḥ...adbhír mṛjānó góbhiḥ śrīṇānáḥ.*
153. See p. 161 above.
154. *śuddhá āśī́rvān mamattu.*
155. *índraṃ śuddhám, śuddhéna sā́mnā, śuddhair ukthaíḥ...*
156. In all cases, great amounts of water were added as will be shown below.
157. *gávāśiraṃ manthínam indra śukráṃ pibā.*
158. The linguistic usage of VS VIII.57 differs from this. There *śukraḥ* (*kṣīraśrīḥ, manthī saktuśrīḥ*) denotes Soma mixed with milk.
159. II.41.2 : *niyútvān vāyav ā́ gahi ayáṃ śukró ayāmi te |*
I.135.3, 6 : *adhvaryúbhir bháramāṇā ayaṅsata vā́yo śukrā́ ayaṅsata.*
V.43.3 : *prá vāyáve bharata cā́ru śukrám.*

Furthermore, I.134.5; IV.47.1; VII.64.5; 90.2; MS IV.14.2 (216.6) etc. Of course, this is not to deny that like other gods Vāyu also receives Soma mixed with milk. This is expressly stated in I.23.1; VIII.101.10.

160. ŚBr IV.1.3.1 ff. Like other gods, both of them receive mixed Soma also on another occasion. ṚV II.41.3; V.51.7.
161. ŚBr IV.1.5.17, 18.
162. VIII.2.5 : *ná yáṃ śukró ná dúrāśīr ná tṛprā́ uruvyácasam |*
apaspṛṇvaté suhā́rdam

This verse states that neither the unmixed nor the badly mixed Soma repels Indra (*tṛprá* is obscure). In v. 9 (see p. 298 above) Soma is called *dadhnā́ ā́śīrtaḥ* "most intoxicating" (intensification of *śuci*). In the tenth verse of the same hymn it is said : *śukrā́ āśíraṃ yācante*, "the pure [ones] long for an admixture." v.28 : *śrītā́ḥ sómā ā́ yāhi.* See also v. 3. We should probably explain v. 14 of the same hymn similarly by translating *águ* not as "one who has no cows" but as one "who mixes no milk" (*ukthám canā́ śasyámānam ágor arír ā́ ciketa ná gāyatráṃ gīyámānam*). Furthermore, in VIII.31.5 the āśir is described as the "perpetual" one : *yā́ dámpatī...sunutá ā́ ca dhā́vataḥ...nítyayāśírā.* An *ánāśīrdā* is mentioned in X.27.1 (*ánāśīrdām ahám asmi prahantā́*). The PW translates this as "one who does not fulfil the expectation." Would it not be more correct to render it as "one who makes no offering of āśir" ? Quite similarly in MS IV.7.4 (98) the unmixed

Soma is condemned : *prajāpatir vā etam amanyata somaṃ hoṣyan / tam agnir abravīt na mayi tvam etam asuryaṃ somaṃ hoṣyasy aśṛtam advitīyaṃ dvitīyam astv iti / yad dhānābhiḥ śrīṇāti śṛtatvāyātho dvitīyatvāya.*

163. For more information on this subject, see vol. II of this work, s.v. Indra and Kutsa; also Bergaigne, "La forme métrique des hymnes du Ṛg-Veda," JA, VIII. Ser., Tome 13, p. 173 ff.

164. Ludwig, III, pp. 105, 169; Zimmer, AIL, pp. 122, 124; Oldenberg, ZDMG, XLII, p. 218 ff.

165. We have shown on p. 146 above that elsewhere the Soma stalk is considered to be sweet by itself.

166. IX.33.2; 63.4, 6.

167. IX.40.2; 45.3 (*utá tvā́m aruṇáṃ vayáṃ góbhir añjmo mádāya kam*); also *aruṣá* IX.61.21; *śóṇa* IX.97.13.

168. IX.3.9 : *eṣá pratnéna jánmanā devó devébhyaḥ sutáḥ /*
háriḥ pavítre arṣati //

Also 7.6; 65.8, 12, 25; 70.8; 72.1, 5; 86.6 etc. *babhrú* and *hári* together in IX.98.7.

169. TBr III.7.13.2, see p. 149 above.

170. MS IV.5.8 (75.1 ff.).

171. Perhaps the *tráya índrasya sómāḥ sutā́saḥ* ("the three kinds of Soma) in VIII.2.7 also denote the same. Cf. also I.135.8. Contra Bergaigne, I, p. 179.

172. Apart from the verses to be cited later, mention may be made of the designations *rásāśir* III.48.1; *rásavat* VI.47.1. In IX.113.5 *rasín* does not merely denote "juicy"; but it is also as much as *rásavat*=*rásāśir*, i.e., "having admixtures."

173. *ā́...árjune átke avyata...*

174. *góbhiṣ ṭe várṇam abhí vāsayāmasi*; IX.8.5 : *sáṃ góbhir vāsayāmasi*; 86.27 : *pári góbhir ā́vṛta* etc. Probably also 97.15 : *pári várṇaṃ bháramāṇo rúśantam.*

175. In a different way the sheep's wool strainer is the "ornament" IX.70.7. Therefore, it is difficult to say whether IX.99.1 : *śukrā́ṃ vayanty ásurāya nirṇíjam* refers to this or to milk (as *śukrá upastír* 62.28, or *upastáraṇa nabhasmáya* 69.5 does).

176. IX.79.5; 86.27. Neisser, *Zum Wörterbuch des Ṛgveda*, p. 70 : "beautifying"; in 79.5 "well-mixing."

177. Cf. IX.1.9; 11.2.

178. I do not think that Pischel's explanation of *janaśrí*, *adhvaraśrí* etc. (VSt, I, pp. 54, 55) is correct.

179. It follows also from the comparison *rā́jāno na práśastibhiḥ sómāso góbhir añjate* in IX.10.3 that the milk is regarded as "ornament."

180. In one passage (III.43.3) these are specified as *ghṛtáprayas.*

181. Cf. p. 281 above.

182. For detailed rules, see ĀpŚS XI.20.5; ŚBr III.9.2; KŚS VIII.9.

183. See e.g., the comm. on ĀpŚS XI.20.5 : *somopasargārthā āpaḥ.*

184. ŚBr III.9.2.3. See Eggeling's note on this.

185. ŚBr III.9.3.30; 4.14; KŚS IX.3.15; ĀpŚS XII.9.1.

186. KŚS IX.2.23; 3.7 ff.; ĀpŚS XII.5.5.

187. ABr II.20.7 : *āpo vā aspardhanta vayaṃ pūrvaṃ yajñaṃ vakṣyāmo vayam iti yāś cemāḥ pūrvedyur vasatīvaryo gṛhyante yāś ca prātar ekadhanāḥ* |

188. ŚBr III.9.3.34. KŚS IX.2.23; Yajñeśvaraśarman, *Āryavidyāsudhākara*, p. 82.

189. ĀpŚS XII.2.13 : *somavardhanārthāḥ.*

190. Namely, as much as is necessary to prepare the required amount of juice for the morning pressing etc. The comm. : *yāvatībhir vardhitaṃ rasaṃ prātaḥsavanāya paryāptaṃ manyeta tāvatībhiḥ.*

191. So much remains that is necessary to fill the Camasas. KŚS IX.3. 21-22 enjoins that apart from the water in the Maitrāvaruṇacamasa, one third of the Vasatīvarīs and the same amount from the Ekadhanās should be poured into the Ādhavanīya. The statement of Yajñeśvaraśarman is probably based on this injunction.

192. II.36.1; VI.40.2; VIII.33.12; IX.76.5; 107.2, 13, 18, 26; 109.13, 17, 21 etc.

193. E.g., IX.76.1 : *háriḥ sṛjānó átyo ná sátvabhir vṛ́thā pā́jāṅsi kṛṇute nadī́ṣv ā́*; also 88.5.

194. Some examples are given on p. 297 above.

195. Thus, for instance, Sāyaṇa on IX.86.4.

196. IX.20.6; 24.1; 65.26; 96.10. On ĀśvŚS V.12.17 : *mṛjyamāne dvitīyam* the comm. explains : *mārjanaṃ cūrṇam ādāya hastābhyāṃ peṣaṇam (dvitīyam = āpyāyanam = udakasekaḥ).*

197. "Him, who was crushed by the stones, whom the twice five sisters bathe, the beloved friend of Indra" etc. In the *Avesta* there is a priest who takes care of this "bathing," the Āsnātār (see the quotation from the *Nīrangistān* in Geldner, *Avestastudien*, I, p. 49). The custom must be very old. See Bartholomae, *Altiranisches Wörterbuch*.

198. VII.32.6 : *yás te...sunoti ā́ ca dhā́vati;* VIII.31.5 : *sunutá ā́ ca dhā́vataḥ*; AV VI.2.1. *sunotā́ ca dhāvata.*

199. *apsú dhūtásya harivaḥ píbehá nṛ́bhiḥ sutásya jaṭháraṃ pṛṇasva.* IX. 107.5 : *āpṛ́chyaṃ dharúṇaṃ vājy àrṣati nṛ́bhir dhūtó vicakṣaṇáh* is not significant. Besides these instances, *dhūtá* occurs twice in the compound *vṛṣádhūta*, but both times in almost the same expressions (III.36.2 and 43.7 : *piba vṛ́ṣadhūtasya vṛ́ṣṇaḥ*) which do not throw any light.

200. In the *Avesta* also water seems to have been used as an admixture to the Haoma. *ap haomya*, "Haoma water," *Yasna* III.3 etc. See Geiger, *Ostiranische Kultur im Altertum*, p. 230, n. 4; p. 470, n. 4; Spiegel, *Eranische Altertumskunde*, III, p. 572, and above all, Haug, *Essays on the Parsis*, 2nd ed., p. 399 ff. and Anquetil Duperron, *Zend-Avesta*, II, p. 536.

201. TS VI.1.6.4 : *padbhyāṃ dve savane samagṛhṇān mukhenaikam | yan mukhena samagṛhṇāt tad adhayat | tasmād dve savane śukravatī prātaḥsavanaṃ ca mādhyandinaṃ ca | tasmāt tṛtīyasavana ṛjīṣam abhi ṣuṇvanti | dhītam iva hi manyante | āśiram ava nayati saśukratvāya.* See also the comm. on III.2.2.1 (vol. III, p. 88).

MS III.8.10 (110.12); IV.6.9 (92.12). (The position is different in the case of the substitutes, see TBr I.4.7.6-7). The adding of milk in the evening had obviously the purpose of making the juice palatable, which was extracted from the husks. This is true only of the Indragrahas, the custom being different for other cases. For instance, milk is added early in the morning to the Maitrāvaruṇagraha (KŚS IX.6.9; ĀpŚS XII.14.12); in each pressing the Manthin receives an admixture of flour (see p. 307).

202. In the ritual this word has a special meaning which is different from that in the ṚV. In the former it denotes predominantly the curd. The comm. on KŚS X.5.3 : *agnīdhā vinītaṃ mathitaṃ yad dadhi tad āśiram ity ucyate. Pañcaviṃśa Br* XVIII.5.12 : *somamiśrārthaṃ dadhyādikam āśiram ity ucyate.* This āśir is used in the evening pressing.

203. ĀpSS XII.14.12; KSS IX.6.9. On this ŚBr IV.1.4.9 remarks thus : *tad yad evātra payas tan mitrasya soma eva varuṇasya.* MS IV.5.8 (75.14 ff.).

204. ĀpŚS XIV.24.14. Cf. TBr I.4.7.6-7.

205. Great caution is warranted while comparing the Vedic ritual with that of the later period. For not all that is known to the latter should be anticipated in the former and, on the other hand, the differences between the two could also be based on different family traditions.

206. ŚBr I.6.4.7.

207. See pp. 280f.,288f. above. Ludwig, III, pp. 378,379. Also ṚV I.84.11; VIII.69.3; IX.1.9 etc. Furthermore, cf. the expressions *gómat* VIII.3.1; 13.14; *góbhih páriṣkṛta* IX.61.13; *góbhiḥ śrītáḥ* VIII.82.5; *góparīṇas* VIII. 45.24; *payovṛ́dh* IX.84.5; *śukrá upastír* IX.62.28 etc.

208. *Studien zum Avesta,* I, p. 40.

209. Caland, KZ, XXX, p. 459; XXXI, p. 273; de Harlez, BKIS, XV, p. 317; Bartholomae, *Altiranisches Wörterbuch,* s.v. *haomayav.*

I am not convinced that Caland's view is correct. There is one factor which is not insignificant. Usually it is said that milk is added to Soma or Haoma, but never that Haoma is added to the milk. According to Caland's interpretation the reverse would be true. This would make no difference in ordinary practice, but not so in the ritual; for Haoma is the main component. Spiegel, *Arische Periode,* p. 173, does not seem to recognize this mixing with milk.

210. Besides this, the Sāṃnāyya sacrifice also. ŚBr I.6.4.10.

211. ĀpŚS XIII.3.1 ff.

212. I.137.1 : *imé vāṃ mitrāvaruṇā gávāśiraḥ sómāḥ śukrá dadhyāśiraḥ*; v. 2; IX.81.1.

213. ĀpŚS XII.4.5.

214. ĀpŚS XIII.17; Lāṭyāyana II.11.10 etc. See TS VI.5.9.1.

215. I.82.4 : *yáḥ pātraṃ hāriyojanáṃ pūrṇáṃ indra cíketati.*

216. *ayáṃ venáś codayat* etc.

216a. *táṃ pratnáthā* etc.

216b. The sequence of the Grahas differs from text to text. While the Graha for Mitra-Varuṇa precedes these two according to Āpastamba, the ritual of other schools gives precedence to the Āśvinagraha over these two.

216c. See the PW, s.v. Saṇḍa and Marka; MS IV.6.3 (81.1).

217. MS IV.6.3. (81.6) : *tā apanudyāthendrāyājuhavus tasmād etā anyadevatyau gṛhyete athendrāya hūyete.* ĀpŚS XII.23.4; XIII.4.14; 12.2.

218. ŚBr IV.2.1.7. From this we can see how changes took place gradually in the ritual.

219. ĀpŚS XII.15.1 ff.; 22.1ff.

220. MS IV.8.9 (117.10) : *yo brahmavarcasakāmaḥ sa śukrāgrāṅs tejo vai śukro brahmavarcasam / yo 'bhicaret sa manthyagrān [grahān gṛhṇīta] ārtaṃ vā etat pātraṃ yan manthipātram.*

221. Foy objects to the word "extraneous"; he thinks that only popular influences can be taken into account. It is difficult to say what sort of influences these were. In any case, the designation (*marka* for *mṛtyu*) appears unusual and comes from a different linguistic usage.

222. For IX.46.4 this fact is evident from vv. 3 and 6 of this hymn.

223. IV, p. 56.

224. TS I.4.7-9; ŚBr IV.1.5; 2.1; KŚS IX.9.20 ff.; Yajñeśvaraśarman, *Āryavidyāsudhākara*, p. 86.

225. IV.29. MS IV.9.19 (136.1).

226. I read with the MS, *abhyakta* for *avyakta*.

227. ŚBr IV.2.1.1 ff.; MS IV.5.9 (77.11); 9.3 (80.14).

228. VS VII.13, 18; ŚBr IV.2.1.19; TS VI. 4.10.2; VII.2.7. 2, 3; TBr I.1.4, 5; ĀpŚS XII.1.12.

229. IV.2.1.11.

230. The legend is different in MS IV.6.3, since it is connected with Prajāpati and not with Soma. Yava grows out of the left eye of Prajāpati.

231. Sāyaṇa : *yavair āmiśritam.* "The strong-jawed Indra has drunk of the juice, of Indu, of that mixed with barley."

232. "The stalk adorned itself with barley, drawn out by men. He unites himself with the sisters and protects the head (?)"

233. E.g., *Vendidād* XIV.4 : *hamirista aētayå urvatayå yā vaoδē haδānaēpāta.* Bartholomae, *Altiranisches Wörterbuch.*

234. See Haug, *Essays on the Parsis*, 2nd ed., pp. 251, 399; Darmesteter, SBE, IV, p. 94, n. 1; Geiger, *Ostiranische Kultur im Altertum*, pp. 151, 230.

235. See Ludwig, III, p. 379. Not all his examples are relevant here.

236. Perhaps X.65.2.

237. III.10.5 (136.19) : *tasmād anusavanaṃ puroḍāśaḥ prāśyaḥ somapīthasya dhṛtyai.*

238. IV.24.7 : *yá índrāya sunávat sómam adyá*
pácāt paktī́r utá bhṛjjáti dhānā́ḥ /
VI.29.4 : *sá sóma ā́miślatamaḥ sutó bhūd*
yásmin paktíḥ pacyáte sánti dhānā́ḥ /

On the other hand, in VIII.2.11; 31.2 *āśír, puroḍā́ś* and *sóma* occur together. VII.32.8 : *sunótā somapā́vne sómam índrāya...pácatā paktī́r*; II.12.14, 15; V.29.11; 34.1; VIII.31.1 : *yó yájāti yájāta it sunávac ca pácāti ca;* X.116.8.

239. IV.25.6, 7.

240. Perhaps we should understand *riricyāt* as a polemic against the *puroḍāśa.*

241. ĀpŚS XII.20.16; XIII.1.13, 14; ŚŚS VII.1.6; 17.2; VIII.2.2 etc.

242. MS III.10.6 (137.6); ŚBr IV.2.4.22; TBr I.5.11 (slightly different); ĀpŚS XII.4.6 ff. etc. Here the ritual texts differ widely. Among the Taittirīyas a Payasyā is offered in all the three Savanas and among others only in the morning. See KBr XIII.2; the comm. on ŚŚS VII.1.3.

243. ĀpŚS XII.4.13 : *manthaṃ saṃyutaṃ karambha ity ācakṣate.* Comm. : *saktavo manthaḥ / te tv adbhir ājyādinā vā saṃyutāḥ karambha ity ākhyāyante.*

244. Anquetil Duperron, *Usages*, II, pp. 535, 573; Spiegel, *Eranische Altertumskunde*, III, p. 572. To connect them with the offering of the Agnīṣomīya Paśu, as Windischmann wishes to do according to the statement of Stevenson, is wrong. In the ṚV it is often stated that buffaloes are roasted in honour of Indra.

245. VI.43.2 : *yásya tīvrasútaṃ mádam*
mádhyam ántaṃ ca rákṣase /
ayáṃ sá sóma indra te sutáḥ...

246. ŚŚS XIV.20.1 : *ayáṃ tīvrás tīvrasúd indra sómaḥ...*

247. *Meghadūta* 20.

248. Soma as well as the sacrificer can be called *prayasvat*.

249. *abhigataṃ carupuroḍāśādyannaṃ yasya tādṛśasyāsya somasya.*

250. Cf. also VS XX.63 : *tīvráṃ parisrútā sómam índrāya suṣuvur mádam;* AV III.13.5; MS II.13.1 (152.15) : *tīvró rasó madhupṛcām araṃgamáḥ*

251. IV.35.6 : *yó vaḥ sunóty abhipitvé áhnām*
tīvráṃ vājāsaḥ sávanaṃ mádāya /
V.30.13 : *tīvrā́ índram amamanduḥ sutā́so*
aktór vyùṣṭau páritakmyāyāḥ /
14 : *aúchat sā́ rā́trī...*

252. Thus also Sāyaṇa on X.160.1.

253. See also ŚBr I.6.4.6; ĀpŚS XIII.17.9 comm. : [*āpaḥ*] *tīvrīkṛtyeti dūrvārasenāpāṃ ślakṣṇīkaraṇaṃ tīvrīkaraṇam.* Comm. on TBr II.6.12.2 explains it as *tīvragandhopetam.* Comm. on TS VII.2.5.5: *tīvrasomo nāma kaścid ukthyāvāntaraviśeṣaḥ / yasminn āśirārthaṃ gavāṃ śataṃ duhanti.* TMBr XVIII.5.4.

254. Comm. on VS VIII.25 : *gatasāraḥ soma ṛjīṣaḥ* (see p. 315 for Yāska's view). ŚBr IV.4.5.1 : *athaitac charīram / tasmin na raso 'sti / taṃ na parāsyam / tad apo 'bhyavaharanti / raso vā āpas / tad asminn etaṃ rasaṃ dadhāti.* 15, 16 : *eka ṛjīṣasya dvir avadyanti tad u tathā na kuryāt / śarīraṃ vā etad bhavati nālam āhutyai* etc. MS IV.8.5 (113.3) etc. The Sūtras describe in detail the treatment given to the husks in the evening libation, e.g., ĀpŚS XIII.10.5 ff.; 20.8 ff.; KŚS X.3.12 ff.; 9.1 ff. The husks are pressed out in the evening and their juice is mixed with churned curd in the Pūtabhṛt.

255. Cf. VS XIX.72 : *sómo rā́jāmṛ́taṃ sutá ṛjīṣéṇājahān mṛtyúm,* for which MS III.11.6 (148.9), however, reads *oṣadhīnām apām.* In *Nirukta* V.12 occurs the verse (or Praiṣa) :
babdhāṃ te harī dhānā upa ṛjīṣaṃ jighratām.

256. VIII.79.4 : *tváṃ cittī́ táva dákṣair divá ā́ pṛthivyā́ ṛjīṣin* /
yā́vīr aghásya cid dvéṣaḥ //

"By your insight and your skill, O Soma Ṛjīṣin, drive out every wickedness of the sinner."

257. I.32.6 : *ayoddhéva durmáda ā́ hí juhvé*
mahāvīráṃ tuvibādhám ṛjīṣám

Sāyaṇa equates it with *apārjaka.* Ludwig : "he who raised a loud song of praise."

258. III.32.1 in the noon pressing. Neisser, *Zum Wörterbuch des Ṛgveda,* p. 188, rejects a general meaning and supports the meaning "one to whom

the husks are due." He says that *ṛjīṣa* does not change places with *aṅśu*, but the statement of III.32.1 is still valid.

259. The comm. on KŚS XXIV.3.42 : *tiraś ca tad ahaś ceti viśeṣaṇaṃ viśeṣyeṇa bahutvam iti karmadhārayaḥ tiro 'hna iti rūpam / rātryā antarhitaṃ vyavahitam ahar iti tasyārthaḥ / tiro 'hne rātryantarhite 'hani bhavāḥ somās tiro'hnyāḥ / āśvinaśastrakayāgasaṃbandhinaḥ camasasthāḥ somāḥ pūrvadinaniṣpannatvāt tiro'hnyā ity ucyante.*

260. That this addition of the gods is also connected with the later ritual was noticed by Oldenberg, *Prolegomena*, I, P. 227.

261. *Kumārasaṃbhava* VII.72.

262. See the material given by Kuhn, MSt, I, p. 122.

263. Cf. ŚŚS VII.4.4 comm. : *dadhibhakṣaṇaṃ daśarātre / śākhāntaroktaṃ madhvaśanaṃ ghṛtasya vā.*

264. *Mithra*, p. 72; *Zoroastrische Studien*, p. 295.

265. Cf. Roscher, *Ausführliches Lexikon der griechischen und römischen Mythologie*, I, p. 282; Weniger, *Zur Symbolik der Biene*; Kuhn, MSt, I, p. 122. Above all, see Victor Hehn, *Kulturpflanzen und Haustiere*, 4th ed., p. 127 ff.; Schrader, *Reallexikon*, s.v. Bienen, Bienenzucht.

266. *śatáṃ kumbhā́ṅ asiñcatám mádhūnām*; in the parallel passage I.116.7 *mádhūnām* is substituted by *súrāyāḥ*.

267. That *mákṣā* means bee is evident from I.112.21. Bergaigne, *Le Syntax des Compar.*, p. 89, explains *mákṣā* as "the priest who offers his hymn of prayer to them and who arrives like a woman going to her tryst."

268. Cf. also I.119.9; ŚBr IV.1.5.17 ff.; XIV.5.5.16 ff.

269. Cf. also IV.45.4.

270. AV VI.69.2=IX.2.19 :

áśvinā sāraghéṇa mā mádhunāṅktaṃ śubhaspatī
yáthā várcasvatīṃ vā́cam āvádāni jánāṅ ánu /

271. *atha vā etau tarhi devānāṃ bhiṣajā āstām aśvinā asomapau*; TS II. 1.10.2. On this, see Scheftelowitz, ZDMG, LXXIV, pp. 74, 202.

272. Cf. also TS VI.4.9.1 : *apūtau vā imau manuṣyacarau bheṣajau; 2 : apūto hy eṣo 'medhyo yo bhiṣak.* The same legend occurs in MBh III.124. 8 ff.; XIII.156.18 ff.

273. ABr IV.9.5.

274. It is certainly not wrong to use this expression. Brahmanical influence was not powerful enough to eliminate or to modify all the older customs — some of them were even Aryan — which were current before the priestly leadership overpowered all of them. That the influence of the brahmins of a specific priestly clan could only be limited is shown by the state of affairs in the east and by the inferior positions occupied by the Kutsas and the Kaṇvas.

275. ŚBr V.1.1.6 ff; KŚS XIV.2.9; ŚŚS XVI.17.9. I do not find a mention of this custom in the Sūtras of Hiraṇyakeśin and Āpastamba. Cf. also ŚBr V.3.4.17; XIV.2.1.20.

276. Perhaps also IX.11.5 : *mádhāv ā́ dhāvatā mádhu*; I.177.3 : *sutā́ḥ sómaḥ páriṣiktā mádhūni.* Similarly in X.154.1 Soma, Madhu (and Ghṛta) are distinguished from one another.

277. Hence IX.77.1 : *eṣa pra kośe madhumāṅ acikradat.*

278. Zimmer, AIL, p. 280; Bloomfield, *Contributions*, III, p. 54; Oldenberg, NGGW, 1893; Hillebrandt, *Ritualliteratur*, § 82.

279. KZ, XXIII, p. 524. Roth, KZ, XXVI, p. 57, reads *vipipānám* in v. 4 and *indram avathuḥ* in v. 5.

280. *surayā saṃpāditam imaṃ pātrasthaṃ dravyaśeṣam.*

281. Cf. some verses which refer to the mixing, like VS XX.27 (see p. 138 f. above); MS III.11.7 (150.17) : *yas te rasaḥ saṃbhṛtā oṣadhīṣu somasya śuṣamaḥ surāyāṃ sutasya surāsomāḥ*, i.e., the "Surā-Soma," the Soma called Surā (which is not the real Soma).

282. I derive with PW, *abhiṣṇak* from *bhiṣṇojy*. The verse contains a clear allusion to the Sautrāmaṇī ceremony which was performed to cure Indra. Ludwig prefers the derivation from *bhaj*.

283. In X.107.9 Surā is looked upon favourably : *bhojā́ jigyur antaḥ-péyaṃ súrāyāḥ.*

284. ŚBr I.6.3.3 ff. : *sa yat somapānam āsa tataḥ kapiñjalaḥ samabhavat / tasmāt sa babhruka iva / babhrur iva hi somo rājā / atha yat surāpāṇam āsa tataḥ kalaviṅkaḥ samabhavat / tasmāt so 'bhimādyakta iva vadati / abhimādyann iva hi surāṃ pītvā vadati*; V.5.4.2 ff. MS II.4.1 (38.1 ff.).

285. Before and after the race the horses get Madhu to drink or to smell. Mahīdhara explains Madhu as *naivāracarulakṣaṇaṃ madhuraṃ haviḥ*. VS IX.18; KŚS XIV.3.10; 4.12.

286. V.1.1.6 ff.

287. XIV.1.1 ff.; Weber, "Über den Vājapeya," SBKPAW, 1892.

288. The comm. equates it with Surā.

289. According to the comm. : grasses, germinated grains, roasted grains, yeast (*śaṣpatokmalājānagnahusaṃjñānāṃ krayaṇam*). The comm. on VS XIX.13 equates *śaṣpa* with *navaprarūḍhavrīhi, tokma* with *navaprarūḍhayava.* TBr I.7.6.5 : *śaṣpāṇy āśayati / surābalim evainaṃ karoti.*

290. Likewise in the case of the Sautrāmaṇī. See e.g., MS II.4.1 (39.4 ff.).

291. Apparently Parisrut is the same as Surā. The comm. says that usually Surā was prepared from mature shoots (*paripakvadravya*); but that here Parisrut denotes a beverage extracted from young shoots that are not yet ripe.

The comm. on KŚS XIX.1.18 says that some understand *śaṣpa* to mean germinated grains of rice (*vrīhayo virūḍhāḥ*) and that some others, however, take it to mean ordinary grass (*tṛṇa*).

The comm. on the VS explains repeatedly Parisrut as Surā (cf. XIX. 79, 83). This is evident from the discussion above. ŚBr XII.8.1.4. says : *apāṃ ca vā eṣa oṣadhīnāṃ ca raso yat surā.* Thus, the views differ on the best method of extracting Surā. This appears to be a sort of beer to which honey could also be added. VS XX.63 speaks of *tīvraṃ parisrutā somaṃ*, i.e., Soma mixed with Parisrut (=Surā). Probably ṚV IX.68.1 : *parisrútaṃ nirṇijaṃ dhire* also refers to this mixture.

292. Cf. ŚBr V.4.1.2.

293. From this a contrast is developed between the brahmin and the Kṣatriya in ABr VIII.8.6 : *atha yat surā bhavati kṣatrarūpaṃ tad atho annasya rasaḥ: kṣatrarūpam evāsmiṅs tad dadhāty atho annasya rasam* etc.; 20.5; that

is just a whitewashing by the brahmins. I presume that the followers of the Soma cult were opposed to those following the cults of Surā, Madhu and Gharma. We learn that in India people were distinguished by their drinks from a remark in *Kāśikā* III.2.81 : *kaṣāyapāyino gāndhārāḥ, kṣīrapāyina uśīnarāḥ, sauvīrapāyino bāhlīkāḥ.* (Oldenberg, RdV, 2nd ed., p. 94, thinks otherwise).

294. ŚŚS XV.15.1 ff.; (XIV.12.1 ff.); KŚS XIX.1.1 ff.; ŚBr V.5.4.12 ff. etc.

295. This is attested by solitary verses also, e.g., VS XX.27 (see p. 139 above).

296. XV.15.10.

297. For v. 19, see n. 270 above.

298. In the verses used in the Sautrāmaṇī mention is made of *sāraghám mádhu* also. But since only Surā is employed there, it must have contained the honey of the bee. See e.g., VS XIX.95 (MS III.11.9).

299. AV VI.70.1; XIV.1.35; XV.9.1 (Zimmer, AIL, p. 280).

300. ṚV X.131.4; VS X.33; XX.67, 68, 76; ŚBr V.4.1.9; XII.7.1.10; 3.1 ff.

301. On the other hand, Namuci also possesses Soma. VS XX.59. This could be a later interpolation.

302. ZDMG, XXXVII, p. 459; Geiger, *Ostiranische Kultur im Altertum*, p. 233.

303. Cf. *Āfrīngān* I.4.

304. I have the impression that while some schools wish to prohibit the brahmins from the enjoyment of Surā others prohibit all people,. Bühler, SBE, II, p. 186 (note on GDS II.20).

305. *yan na dīkṣayaiva dīkṣate na somāṅśava iva nyupyante 'tha kathaṃ sautrāmaṇī somayajño bhavati* — ŚBr XII.8.2.3.

306. ŚBr XII.8.2.7: *ete khalu vā etasya yajñasya somāṅśava ity āhur yac chaṣpāṇi takmāni lājā iti / prātaḥsavanasyaitad rūpaṃ yac chaṣpāṇi* etc. A similar view in VS XIX.13. Such identifications occur elsewhere also; e.g., ABr II.9.1 where Puroḍāśa and the sacrificial animal are identified in their individual parts.

307. It appears that in this ceremony originally the Aśvins were worshipped in the morning, Sarasvatī in the evening and Indra at noon. VS XIX.26.

308. V.1.2.10; XII.7.3.4.

309. The Prācyas are called *surāpāṇas* in *Kāśikā* VIII.4.9.

310. This is described exactly in HŚS XXIII.1.1 ff.

311. Ed. Jībānanda, p. 609 ff.

312. XI.5.4.18.

313. *havanəm fratarəm* and *uparəm*. In recent times the *havana* is interpreted no more as the act of pressing but as the name of the mortar (trough and pestle) (Bartholomae, *Altiranisches Wörterbuch*; Oliphant, *Studies in Honor of Maurice Bloomfield*, p. 226). I do not think that this is correct. Then, *fratarəm* would need a forced explanation; moreover, *havana* is exactly the same as *savana*. There is no reason to depart from the old interpretation; it explains *dāityō* (*dāityōkərəta*) also quite satisfactorily. However, the case is different with the derivative *hāvana*.

314. E.g. IX.67.10, 12.

315. I.161.8; III.52; IV.33.11; 34.4; 35.4, 6, 7, 9; AV VI.47.3; IX.1.11 ff.

316. ṚV I.161.8 seems to refer to this dispute.

317. This long list of names corresponds very closely to the names of the gods whom the later ritual invites for the evening sacrifice; there the Grahas are called Āditya, Sāvitra, Vaiśvadeva, Pātnīvata, Hāriyojana, Ṣoḍaśa.

318. ṚV III.32.1 : *índra sómaṃ...píba / imáṃ mădhyandinaṃ sávanaṃ căru yát te.* 2 : *gávāśiraṃ manthínam indra śukráṃ píbā sómaṃ rarimă te mádāya / brahmakṛtā mărutenā gaṇéna.* 3 : *...árcantaḥ...marútas ta ójaḥ mădhyandine sávane vajrahasta píbā rudrébhiḥ...*

319. GGA, 1889, No. 10, p. 422.

320. Cf. X.96.13.

321. See the comm. on VS VIII.50.

322. The fact that the Gāyatrī belongs to Agni, the Triṣṭubh to Indra, the Jagatī to the Viśve Devāḥ suggests that this is a very ancient distribution; for these three metres are assigned to the three savanas.

323. Oldenberg, *Die Hymnen des Ṛgveda*, I, p. 235 (on 3.26); RdV, 2nd ed., p. 453; Bergaigne's important work, "Recherches sur l'Histoire de la Liturgie védique," JA, 1889, p. 1 ff. Bergaigne sees an old Āgnimārutaśastra in III.36.

324. Cf. ṚV I.134.1, 6; IV.46.1; 47.1; VIII.100.2 (see Oldenberg, ZDMG. XXXIX, p. 55). In MS IV.5.8 (75.1 ff.); VIII.3.7, Indra is invited *pūrvápītaye*,

325. ĀpSS XI.19.5 ff.; ŚBr IV.3.1.10 (see Eggeling on this); KŚS IX.8; ŚŚS VII.8.1 etc.; Haug, *Aitareya Brāhmaṇa*, II, p. 135.

326. Partly AV XX.2 also.

327. Here Neṣṭṛ takes the place of Tvaṣṭṛ (*gnāvo neṣṭaḥ piba ṛtunā*). The role played by this priest is an unusual one. He is always assigned to women, and performs obscene rites. See, e.g., ĀpŚS XIII.15.8 ff. The Agnīdh sits on the lap of the Neṣṭṛ for a while. ŚBr IV.4.2.18 states : *agnir vā eṣa nidānena yad āgnīdhro yoṣā neṣṭā / vṛṣā vā agnīd yoṣā neṣṭā / mithunam evaitad prajananaṃ kriyate.* The Neṣṭṛ appears to be the priest belonging to the cult of Tvaṣṭṛ, who was admitted into the Brahmanical ritual along with the god. I doubt that he originated in the circle of the Brahmanical Indians. Also the fact that it is this Neṣṭṛ who must draw the Surāgrahas suggests his position outside the group of Indians following the Brahmanical law.

328. In II.36.3 the priest is not mentioned.

329. Through the names of the priests, these hymns — and also occasionally others (like II.1) — attest to the high development of the Vedic ritual. The older name for the Maitrāvaruṇa is Praśāstṛ and moreover, it is almost certain that the Upavaktṛ is also such an older name. In the sacrifices offered by the gods, Mitra is the Upavaktṛ.

330. ŚBr IV.6.6.8.

331. ŚBr III.6.2.12-13; IV.3.1.1 ff. : *ahīyata* [*somasya*] *vā acchāvākaḥ / tam indrāgnī anusamatanutāṃ prajānāṃ prājātyai / tasmād aindrāgnaḥ.* I find no explanation for the role ascribed to the Acchāvāka. TS III.5.2.1 ff.; Weber, ISt, X, p. 34. Perhaps he was only a servant (if we could trust the etymology of his name), or perhaps the reason lies deeper as in the case of the Neṣṭṛ. The explanation given by Hewitt is too bold to be admissible (JRAS, 1890, p. 421) : "The acchāvāka priests are the representatives of the

old priests, who had, under the Gandharvas or Kuśikas, the charge of Soma, the old non-Aryan priests who conducted the moonworship." This theory goes beyond what can be established.

To conclude from MS IV.7.4 (98.8), the Soma drink seems to have been denied originally to the Unnetṛ also, who has the function of drawing out the Soma as his name testifies.

332. In VIII.17.13, "where pitchers are used for drinking." Pāṇini III.1.130 states expressly that this is a sacrifice.

333. X.27.2. King Bhavya performs great Soma pressings, thousand in number (i.e., a year-long sacrifice) on the banks of the Sindhu I.126.1; III.53.7 also speaks of a year-long sacrifice (*sahasrasāva*=1000 pressings).

APPENDIX II

The Paṇis in the Ṛgveda

1. Cf. Hillebrandt, ZDMG, LXX, p. 512 ff.; "Die Heimat des Ṛgveda" in *Aus Alt- und Neu-Indien*, Breslau 1922, p. 1 ff.; "Zur vedischen Mythologie und Völkersiedlung," ZII, III, p. 1 ff. (defence against A. B. Keith, *Cambridge History of India*, I, p. 86 and Sten Konow, *The Aryan Gods of the Mitanni People*, Kristiania 1921). On the subject itself, see also Wackernagel, SBKPAW, 1918, p. 411; H. Jacobson, *Arier und Ugrofinnen*, 1922, p. 155.

2. Similarly Darmesteter, *Ormazd et Ahriman*, p. 100, n. 2, and others.

3. The Bhāradvājas form one branch of the Aṅgiras', the Gautamas the other. (Ludwig, III, p. 128). Of the nine passages in the first maṇḍala in which Paṇi occurs, two (32.11; 33.3) belong (according to the *Anukramaṇikā*) to Hiraṇyastūpa Āṅgirasa, two (83.4; 93.4) to a Gautama; to these we should add two Gautama passages from the fourth maṇḍala. Thus the greatest number of all occurrences of Paṇi seem to belong to a particular family. The Aṅgiras' are mentioned as their opponents in X.108 also.

4. "Miser" is one who does not give any Dakṣiṇā; this is evident from a comparison with VIII.86.2.

5. I.180.7 : *vayáṃ cid dhí vāṃ jaritā́raḥ satyā́ḥ*
vipanyā́mahe ví paṇír hitā́vān |

The translation proposed by Pischel (GGA, 1890, p. 537) : "the miser is praised as benevolent," is not correct because the Paṇi is not praised anywhere and because he is not a mere miser. The verse is somewhat obscure. Geldner was not certain of his translation : "the miser (and) the one who has good friends are different (?)."

6. I. 151.9 *cd* : *ná vāṃ dyā́vó 'habhir nótá síndhavo*
ná devatváṃ paṇáyo nā́naśur maghám ||

In this sentence *dyā́vo, síndhavaḥ paṇáyaḥ* are the subject and *devatváṃ, maghá* the object.

7. VII.19.9 : *yé te hávebhir ví paṇī́ṅ ádāśan*
asmā́n vṛṇīṣva yújyāya tásmai ||

Probably here *paṇi* means a non-believer only.

8. I.104.4 : *vīḍóś cid índro yó ásunvato vadhó...*
76.4 : *ásunvantaṃ samaṃ jahi dūṇā́śam...*

I.110.7; V.34.5-7 (see p. 235 above);

IV.25.6 : *...súṣveḥ paktíṃ kr̥ṇute kévaléndraḥ |*
nā́suṣver āpír ná sákhā ná jāmír
duṣprāvyò 'vahantéd ávācaḥ (cf. IV.24.5).

VI.44.11 : *purvī́ṣ ṭa indra niṣṣídho jáneṣu*
jahy ásuṣvīṇ prá vr̥hā́pr̥ṇataḥ ||

VIII.14.15 : *asunvā́m indra saṃsádaṃ víṣūciṃ vy ànāśayaḥ |*
somapā́ úttaro bhávan ||

VIII.62.12; X.42.4 etc.

9. Geldner's translation "he who does not find any words" is too modern.

10. It is the same as *he 'rayaḥ*, "oh ! the enemies !" See Muir, OST, 2nd ed., II, p. 114; Kuhn, *Beiträge z. P. Gr.*, p. 43; Davidson, ZDMG, XXXVII, p. 23; Eggeling, SBE, XXVI, p. 31, n. 3.

11. X.23.5 : *yó vācā́ vívāco mr̥dhrávācaḥ*
purū́ sahásrā́śivā jaghāna...

"Who with his voice slew many thousand wicked ones having a different tongue, those who spoke the language of the enemy."

12. Ludwig connects *śatair* with *vadhaiḥ*. In Daśoni he sees a priest of the Paṇis (*R̥gveda*, V, p. 107 and III, p. 34). I do not think that he would be described as Kavi.

13. Often what men did is attributed to the gods exclusively. Thus Agni-Soma I.93.4 and Soma IX.22.7 are praised for seizing the cattle from the Paṇis. Here we need not look for a mythical explanation.

14. Roth translates (ZDMG, XLI, p. 674), not very clearly, thus, "he is equal to others only in blood money." Actually it does not make much difference whether we translate *vaira* as "punishment" or as "blood money"; but the main point is that the Paṇi himself must make amends and not the one who kills him. This does not come out clearly in Roth's translation. Oldenberg, *Die Hymnen des R̥gveda*, I, p. 354, proposes the following : "Also the miser (Paṇi) is called a man and he is equal (to others, better men) in blood money. Beyond this, [we must add], the equality stops." It is difficult to believe that one pays blood money for a Paṇi, an enemy, when one kills him.

15. III.58.2 : *járethām asmád ví paṇér manīṣā́m*
yuvór ávaś cakr̥mā́ yātam arvā́k ||

It is not possible to determine if the word *paṇi* had already the general sense of "enemy" in this verse.

16. ZDMG, LXX, p. 512 ff.

17. Pūṣan is conceived thus elsewhere also. In I.42.2-3 a Kaṇva says of him that he drives away the wicked inauspicious wolves from the path.

18. Additional material in my article, "Zur vedischen Mythologie und Völkersiedlung," in ZII, III, p. 1 ff.

19. Zimmer, AIL, p. 431; Ludwig, III, p. 207.

19a. The Translator is indebted to Professor Dr. Wilhelm Rau for translating this passage from the Greek.

20. Gutschmid, *Geschichte Irans*, p. 29. Darmesteter, *Chants Populaires des Afghans*, p. clxxi : In the later period (of the Tīmūi) "the Paṇis refused to provide troops to the imperial army; they looted Mirza

Pīr Muhammed...and retreated into their mountains behind the Helmend..."

21. See my *Vedische Mythologie*, 1st ed., III, p. 268 ff.; *Vedische Mythologie* (smaller ed.,), p. 96 ff.

22. He was the son of Vadhryaśva, who was connected with the fire cult, as is evident from X.69.1 ff. This seems to be the case with Divodāsa also, after whom the fire was called *agni daivodāsi* (Ludwig, III, p. 176).

23. For *avasám*, which makes no sense here, I read *avaśám*. Oldenberg, *op. cit.*, I, p. 405, rejects this emendation. He compares this verse with I.93.4 and connects *ācakhāda* with a double accusative, somewhat like *ā-dar* and says that the goddess bites through the Paṇi and thus crunches the food. The construction, in spite of the reference to Gaedicke's *Sammlungen*, p. 266, looks doubtful to me. The heroic deed of Agni-Soma would become significant only if besides the Paṇi a characteristic of his nature is mentioned, something like "intractable," particularly since the object of the theft is expressed by the word *gā́ḥ* in I.93.4. Geldner construes I.93.4 like Oldenberg.

24. IAK, III, p. 134. The manuscripts read *Parguītai*, *Parguētai* or *Bartietai*. On the basis of a conjecture, Wilberg reads *Parouētai*. Nobbe. has *Parsuētai*. Obviously Lassen's reading is based on the above conjecture It is quite possible, as Brunnhofer thinks, that the *Aparutai* mentioned by Herodotus III.91 along with the Sattagydae, Gandarians and Dadikae are identical with the above-mentioned tribe. Rawlinson, *History of Herodotus*, II, p. 486, n. 6, says that they are unknown otherwise.

25. BKIS, X, p. 263; *Iran und Turan*, p. 99.

26. It is likely that they are identical not with the Paruetae, but with the "*Paroutai in Aseia*" (Ptolemy VI. 17).

27. Kiepert, *Lehrbuch der alten Geographie*, § 61.

28. Hardly the Yaxartes; KZ, XXVIII, p. 215. I doubt if Lommel, ZII, IV, p. 194, was correct in speaking of a stream flowing around the earth.

29. Also the statement of the *Bhāgavatapurāṇa* V.9.16-17 that a Paṇi is the priest of the Śūdras is not quite unfounded if we keep the Gr. *Sudroi* in mind.

30. AIL, p. 5 ff.

31. We should object when Brunnhofer, *Iran und Turan*, p. 127, allows even the possibility that the Sarasvatī is the same as the Oxus; with such transference of names we lose all the firm historical basis.

32. VS XXXIV.11 — a verse whose antiquity was doubted by Zimmer because of the word *deśa* ("five rivers in spate hurry into the Sarasvatī; but the Sarasvatī, divided fivefold, became the stream in the land") — can refer to the Haraxvaitī as well as to the Indus, and also to the later Sarasvatī if need be.

33. Brunnhofer (BKIS, X, p. 261, n. 2) had quite rightly recognized the identity between the Sarasvatī and the Arachotos; but later in his book *Iran und Turan* he departed from it again, explaining the Sarasvatī as the Oxus, as we have noted above.

33a. *Arrian's History of Alexander's Expedition*, tr. by John Rooke, I, pp. 136, 168, 179.

34. The Paṇis are purely mythical also in X.67.6; 92.3; II.24.6 (*nidhiṃ*

paṇinā́ṃ...gúhā hitám); VII.9.2 and probably also I.32.11; VI.44.22. In AV XIX.46.2 they are mentioned along with the Yātudhānas. In solitary instances like AV IV.23.5; V.11.7; ṚV I.182.3; 184.2; VII.19.9; VIII.26.10 it is not possible to make a positive determination. The word *piśāca* also suggests that hostile tribes have been turned into demons.

35. *History of Herodotus*, IV, p. 62, n. 5.

36. Rapson, *Cambridge History of India*, I, p. 564 : "the Sakā Haumavarkā...who have been identified [Thomas, JRAS, 1906, p. 186] with the Śaka settlers in the Persian province of Drangiana, the country of the river Helmand, which was afterwards known as Śakasthāna 'the abode of the Sakas,' the later Persian Sijistān and the modern Seistān." Cf. also J. Marquardt, *Untersuchungen zur Geschichte von Eran*, p. 140.

37. Seven times in book I, four times in book II, twice each in books IV and VII, and not at all in books III, VIII and X.

38. II.14.6; IV.30.14, 15; VI.47.21; VII.99.5.

39. VI.16.5 : *tváṃ imā́ vā́ryā purú divodāsāya sunvaté |*
bharádvājāya dāśúṣe ||
31.4 : *áśikṣo yátra śácyā śacīva dívodāsāya súnvate sutakre |*
bharádvājāya gṛṇaté vásūni ||

40. *yathā bharadvājo bṛbau takṣṇi prastoke ca sārñjaye saniṃ sasāna.*

41. VI.27.7 : *sá sṛ́ñjayāya turváśaṃ párādāt*
vṛcívato daivavātā́ya śík ṣan ||
8 : *dvayā́ṅ agne rathíno viṅśatíṃ gā́ḥ*
vadhū́mato maghávā máhyaṃ samrā́ṭ |
abhyāvartí cāyamānó dadāti
dūṇā́śeyaṃ dákṣiṇā pārthavā́nām ||

"He gave Turvaśa to Sṛñjaya, and, being helpful, gave the Vṛcīvats to Daivavāta. Two chariot-horses, twenty pairs of cattle gave me the noble prince Abhyāvartin Cāyamāna. Not everyone receives such a gift of Pārthavas."

42. By emphasizing this fact, Brunnhofer made a great contribution. Cf. Hillebrandt, NGGW, 1894, p. 648 ff.; *Vedische Mythologie* (smaller ed.), p. 191; ZII, III, p. 21.

43. IV.15.4 : *ayáṃ yáḥ sṛ́ñjaye puró daivavāté samidhyáte |*
dyumā́ṅ amitradámbhanaḥ ||

44. ŚBr II.4.4.4.

45. A purohita of three kingdoms, ŚŚS XVI.29.6. According to TS VI.6.2.2, Vāsiṣṭha Sātahavya was hostile to the Sṛñjayas.

46. Called thus after Avestan *zrayaŋh*, lake, and Old Persian *draya.*

47. Cf. Grierson, JRAS, 1908, pp. 604, 605.

48. Ungnad, *Die ältesten Völkerwanderungen*, 1923, pp. 11-12; Hillebrandt, ZII, III, p. 21 f.; ZDMG, NF, VI, p. 74 ff.

49. By this I did not intend to say anything on the age of the fourth book (see Keith, *Religion and Philosophy of the Veda*, p. 232, n. 5, who misunderstood the problem).

50. Also the way Śambara was mentioned in the second maṇḍala (12.11; 14.6; 19.6) suggests that for the poet of these hymns the wars with Śambara were long past and that posterity regards the conquest over Śambara as

one of the great deeds of Indra himself. The neuter plural *śámbara* (=*vṛtrá*) occurs only among the Gṛtsamadas.

51. See p. 352 below on hymn VII.6. In VII.9.2 Paṇi is to be understood perhaps in the mythical sense. In VII.19.9 — a somewhat obscure verse — already the sense of "unbeliever" is quite appropriate.

52. *Zur Literatur und Geschichte des Veda*, p. 121 ff.

53. Likewise in maṇḍalas VIII and X; only once in II. See also ZII, III, p. 1 ff.

54. Cf. Jarl Charpentier, *Suparṇasage*, p. 94; Macdonell and Keith, *Vedic Index*, II, p. 275.

55. Ludwig, III, p. 185; *Buddha*, 1st ed., p. 413.

56. ZDMG, XLII, p. 207 following Bergaigne, II, p. 373 f.

57. Bloomfield, *Contributions*, V (JAOS, XVI, p. 41), sees in the verse "the account of a battle between the Bharatas (*kṣatriya*) and the Tṛtsu's with Vasiṣṭha (*brahman*), the latter being representatives of brahmanical orthodoxy..."

According to TS VII.4.7, a Vasiṣṭha got into enmity with the descendants of Sudās. It strikes me that the Soma cult does not seem to play the same role in the seventh maṇḍala as it does in other books. Some statistics are remarkable enough to be given here. The seventh maṇḍala contains 104 hymns, that is, more than one tenth of the ṚV; the fourth with its 58 hymns is about an eighteenth part. In the former the word *Soma* occurs 37 times in 25 hymns, in the latter 35 times in 20 hymns; in the former the word *suta* occurs 15 times in 9 hymns, in the latter 15 times in 10 hymns. We should compare this ratio with the fact that ŚBr XII.6.1.41 states that in ancient times the Vasiṣṭhas had to perform the duties of the Brahman priest since they alone knew the Vyāhṛtis. This statement is very strange because the reason lies deeper than what the Brāhmaṇa states. Perhaps, originally the Vasiṣṭhas were not connected with the Indra-Soma cult; for in the light of what we have said above it is no mere accident that most of the Varuṇa hymns belong precisely to these Vasiṣṭhas. (On the other hand, the sixth maṇḍala contains the vocative *varuṇa* only once, and that too in the dual Indrā-Varuṇā).

58. IV. 38.1 : *utó hí vāṃ dātrā́ sánti pū́rvā*
yā́ pūrúbhyas trasádasyur nitośé |
kṣetrāsā́ṃ dadathur urvarāsā́ṃ
ghanáṃ dásyubhyo abhíbhūtim ugrám ||

59. Oldenberg holds the second view, ZDMG, XLII, pp. 204, 205, 219.
I.62.7 : *tváṃ ha tyád indra saptá yúdhyan*
púro vajrin purukútsāya dardaḥ |
barhír ná yát sudā́se vṛ́thā várg
aṅhó rājan várivaḥ pūráve kaḥ ||

Ludwig reads *sudā́sam* for *sudā́se*.

60. This event is described in I.174.2 also.

61. Ludwig, III, p. 168, also considers this hymn to be young. Oldenberg does not attach any special importance to it, ZDMG, XLII, p. 212.

62. In VI.18.3; 25.2 the victory of an Ārya over the Dāsa tribes is glorified. In these two hymns Divodāsa, who certainly would not have called

himself an Ārya, is not mentioned. Perhaps the victor was a Pūru as in VI.20.

63. Ludwig thinks that these two persons are not identical. We have the chronological order as follows : Divodāsa, Sudās, Trasadasyu, Tṛkṣi.

64. Ludwig sought to read an enmity between the Pūrus and Divodāsa in I.130.7; cf. his remarks in III, p. 114. But these are not convincing; enmity cannot be inferred at least from this verse, according to which they could even be allies. It is yet to be explained what the attitude of the author of these hymns, Parucchepa Daivodāsī, was towards Divodāsa. There are very few names mentioned in this group of hymns.

65. I do not attach any value to VII.19.3 where Sudās is mentioned as victorious along with Purukutsi Trasadasyu Pūru. The hymn appears to possess the same character of a chronicle as VII.18 does.

66. Ludwig also, who otherwise follows Roth's interpretation of the Sarasvatī (=Sindhu=Indus), states that here Sindhu cannot come into question (III, p. 175).

67. See also Oldenberg, *Buddha*, 1st ed., pp. 416-7; on geography, see Oldham, JRAS, 1893, p. 94, and Sinclair, ibid., p. 612.

68. See also Hopkins, JAOS, 1896, XVII, p. 23 ff.